FOURTH EDITION

Ethnic Families in America

Patterns and Variations

edited by

Charles H. Mindel
University of Texas at Arlington

Robert W. Habenstein
University of Missouri at Columbia

Roosevelt Wright, Jr.
University of Missouri at St. Louis

PRENTICE HALL
Upper Saddle River, New Jersey 07458

Library of Congress Cataloging-in-Publication Data

Ethnic families in America : patterns and variations / edited by
  Charles H. Mindel, Robert W. Habenstein, Roosevelt Wright, Jr. —
  4th ed.
      p.   cm.
  Includes bibliographical references and index.
  ISBN 0-13-531328-7
    1. Ethnology—United States.   2. Family—United States.
  3. Minorities—United States.   4. United States—Social
  conditions—1980–   I. Mindel, Charles H.   II. Habenstein, Robert
  Wesley.   III. Wright, Roosevelt.
  E184.A1E78   1998   97-24844
  305.8′00973—dc21   CIP

Editorial director: Charlyce Jones Owen
Editor-in-chief: Nancy Roberts
Associate editor: Sharon Chambliss
Project manager: Merrill Peterson
Prepress and manufacturing buyer: Mary Ann Gloriande
Marketing manager: Christopher DeJohn
Copy editor: Victoria Nelson

This book was set in 10/12 Baskerville by DM Cradle Associates
and was printed and bound by Courier Companies, Inc.
The cover was printed by Phoenix Color Corp.

Printed in the United States of America

10   9   8

ISBN 0-13-531328-7

PRENTICE-HALL INTERNATIONAL (UK) LIMITED, LONDON
PRENTICE-HALL OF AUSTRALIA PTY. LIMITED, SYDNEY
PRENTICE-HALL CANADA INC., TORONTO
PRENTICE-HALL HISPANOAMERICANA, S.A., MEXICO
PRENTICE-HALL OF INDIA PRIVATE LIMITED, NEW DELHI
PRENTICE-HALL OF JAPAN, INC., TOKYO
PEARSON EDUCATION ASIA PTE. LTD., SINGAPORE
EDITORA PRENTICE-HALL DO BRASIL, LTDA., RIO DE JANEIRO

Contents

PART FIVE: HISTORICALLY SUBJUGATED ETHNIC MINORITIES

PART SIX: SOCIORELIGIOUS ETHNIC MINORITIES

To Gloria, lover and friend (CM),
to the memory of Jane Habenstein,
and to the most important friend and companion in my life,
my dear wife, Elaine, and to two other very important women,
my granddaughters, Asia and India Wilcox (RW)

Preface

This is the fourth edition of *Ethnic Families in America*. At the time of the publication of the first edition early in the 1970s, the prevailing view of ethnicity seemed to be that the United States was an assemblage of mostly European ethnic groups who had been forged into new amalgam by means of a great "melting pot." Assimilation as a cultural value, the view that immigrants to this land should somehow give up their strange cultural ways, beliefs, and languages and adopt the "American" way, was dominant. The idea that separate ethnic group identification in the United States was valuable in its own right was only beginning to be appreciated. Competing notions of ethnic pride and ethnic self-determination which challenged the value of assimilation were in their infancy.

These changing views were probably the result of a confluence of historical events. The great civil rights struggles of the 1960s had not only mobilized great numbers of the African-American population but also spawned other liberation struggles as well. The war in Vietnam had, among its many consequences, a profound splintering effect on group consensus in the United States. This conflict had strong ethnic and class overtones, centering around a war with Asians fought disproportionately by poor black Americans; this war produced great tears in the American civil fabric that have lasted even to this day.

An equally momentous historical event centered around changes in the immigration laws. The United States had been largely closed to new immigration after 1924, when a discriminatory law effectively barred immigrants from eastern and southern Europe and Asia. Beginning with the Immigration and Nationality Act of 1965, and later with the opening of the immigration doors to Cuban, Vietnamese, Soviet, and Salvadoran refugees, among others, as well as swelling numbers of immigrants who arrived and stayed on illegally, the nature of ethnicity in the United States changed profoundly.

As a result of this transformation and evolution of the role of ethnicity in American life, it was felt that a new edition of *Ethnic Families in America* was appropriate. Original authors were recontacted and asked to revise and update their chapters. When they could not or would not revise their chapter or when they could not be reached, new contributors were sought. In several cases, chapters were updated by the editors. A new chapter on the Asian Indian family was added, another nod to the continuing change in the ethnic makeup of the United States of America.

Currently the mood in the country, as reflected in recent changes in the immigration laws and the reductions in benefits to legal immigrants, is on one of those anti-immigrant downturns that has afflicted this country almost from its inception. We can only say that as the story of ethnicity in America continues, we will be here to record the changes.

We would like to thank all those who contributed to this new addition, including all of the authors who tried to meet the deadlines and requests for changes. We would like to thank Jerry Toops for his assistance in background work for this new edition. Portions of Chapter 2 are taken from the author's previously published "The Ethnic Immigrant Family" in S. Queen, R. Habenstein, and J. Quadagno (1984) *The Family in Various Cultures*, New York, Harper & Row.

Charles H. Mindel
Robert W. Habenstein
Roosevelt Wright, Jr.

Contributors

Melba Sánchez-Ayéndez, Ph.D.
Professor and Coordinator of the Social Sciences Unit at the Graduate School of Public Health, University of Puerto Rico, San Juan, Puerto Rico

Rosina M. Becerra, Ph.D.
Director of the Center for Child and Family Policy Research, UCLA School of Public Policy and Social Research, University of California at Los Angeles, Los Angeles, California

Bruce L. Campbell, Ph.D.
Associate Professor at the Department of Child and Family Studies, California State University at Los Angeles, Los Angeles, California

Eugene E. Campbell, Ph.D.
Deceased, Department of History, Brigham Young University, Provo, Utah

Bernard Farber, Ph.D.
Professor Emeritus of Sociology, Department of Sociology, Arizona State University, Tempe, Arizona

Robert W. Habenstein, Ph.D.
Professor Emeritus, Department of Sociology, University of Missouri at Columbia, Columbia, Missouri

Ellen Somers Horgan, Ph.D.

Gertrude Enders Huntington, Ph.D.

Robert John, Ph.D.
Director, Minority Aging Research Institute, University of North Texas, Denton, Texas

Harry H. L. Kitano, Ph.D.
Professor Emeritus, School of Social Welfare, University of California at Los Angeles, Los Angeles, California

Kerrily J. Kitano, MSW
Ph.D. candidate at the University of California at Berkeley, Berkeley, California

George A. Kourvetaris, Ph.D.
Professor of Sociology, Department of Sociology, Northern Illinois University, Dekalb, Illinois

Bernard L. Lazerwitz, Ph.D.
Professor Emeritus, Department of Sociology, Bar-Ilan University, Ramat Gan, Israel

Helena Znaniecka Lopata, Ph.D.
Professor of Sociology, Department of Sociology, Loyola University of Chicago, Chicago, Illinois

Harriet Pipes McAdoo, Ph.D.
Professor, Department of Child and Family Studies, Michigan State University, E. Lansing, Michigan

Pyong Gap Min, Ph.D.
Professor of Sociology, Department of Sociology, Queens College of the City University of New York, Queens, New York

Charles H. Mindel, Ph.D.
Professor and Director, Center for Research, Evaluation and Technology, School of Social Work, University of Texas at Arlington, Arlington, Texas

Jill S. Quadagno, Ph.D.
Department of Sociology, Florida State University, Tallahassee, Florida

Uma A. Segal, Ph.D.
Department of Social Work, University of Missouri at St. Louis, St. Louis, Missouri

D. Ann Squiers, Ph.D.

Zulema E. Suárez, Ph.D.
Associate Professor of Social Work, School of Social Work, Wayne State University, Detroit, Michigan

Thanh Van Tran, Ph.D.
Associate Professor of Social Work, Graduate School of Social Work, Boston College, Boston, Massachusetts

Morrison G. Wong, Ph.D.
Professor of Sociology, Department of Sociology, Texas Christian University, Fort Worth, Texas

Roosevelt Wright, Jr., Ph.D.
Professor of Social Work, Department of Social Work, University of Missouri at St. Louis, St. Louis, Missouri

1 Diversity Among America's Ethnic Minorities

Charles H. Mindel
Robert W. Habenstein
Roosevelt Wright, Jr.

INTRODUCTION

In this, the fourth edition of *Ethnic Families in America*, the opportunity presents itself to take a brief retrospective view of changes in America's ethnic families and explore the continuing role of ethnicity and the ethnic factor in modern-day American life. In the early 1970s, when the first edition of this work was published, the emerging importance and recognition of ethnic group identification in the United States was only beginning to be appreciated. The now-common notion of "multicultural diversity" had not been conceptualized yet, certainly not in the form it is currently. Ethnic politics took on a much different form then, the black civil rights struggle was not a somewhat forgotten memory, and "affirmative action" was still an emerging idea, its political repercussions not yet apparent. The political machines of big northern cities remained still largely under the control of representatives of European ethnic groups.

The Role of Immigration and Ethnic Diversity

In the introduction to our first edition we stated that "most of the large scale immigration to America has ceased." As we shall see, this statement, like many pronouncements about the future, was shortsighted and woefully misplaced. For one thing, it did not foresee the repercussions of the changes in the Immigration and Nationality Act in 1965, nor did it grasp the impact of the rise in illegal immigration. The world has also witnessed numerous tragic world events, genocide in Cambodia, starvation in Ethiopia, ethnic warfare between the Hutus and the Tutsis, blood feuds between the Bosnians and the Serbs, the breakup of the Soviet Union and the end of the Cold War. One significant result has been the creation of numerous refugee populations and sizable ethnic relocations.

The impact of the post-1965 waves of immigration with their increasing numbers, shifting national origins, and often illegal status has been unsettling for many individuals in older American groups. This sea of new faces is often seen as containing the seeds of new serious social problems for American society or an acceleration of its ongoing breakdown. Talk show commentators and others express fears that the United States has lost control of its borders, its language, its "American" core values, and, increasingly, its ability to afford the cost of caring for new immigrants.

Of course, the current concerns about the effects of immigration on American values, the economy, and the American way of life are not new. The American public has worried about the effects of immigration almost from the beginning of the settlement of this country by Europeans (surely, the Native American peoples also worried about the influx of these foreigners as well). And almost from the beginning of the settlement of this land, the issues concerning immigration most have remained remarkably unchanged. Longer-established immigrants have almost always been bothered by the cultural distinctiveness of the newcomers. Sometimes this distinctiveness manifested itself in language, other times in religion, or skin color, or unfamiliar family practices. Frequently, more "politically correct" concerns have been expressed about the economic impoverishment of the newcomers and what this might do to the wages of native-born workers. These concerns are also voiced as a fear that the newcomers will become a welfare burden placing undue pressures on the state to provide care and assistance. Thus, current concerns about the effects of large-scale immigration have long echoes into America's past.

Protests and outcries about immigrants with different cultural practices, largely language and religious differences, occurred during the initial periods of immigration into the United States (the colonial period through 1860) and were largely directed against German and Irish immigrants. Even then, governments and citizens were not passive in their opposition. Many policies designed to curtail immigration, such as head taxes on ship captains, were enacted by colonies (Jensen, 1989).

The second great wave of immigration, beginning around 1860 until 1920, saw over 28 million people enter the United States. Most were culturally different from the existing population, had darker complexions, were not Protestant but mostly Catholic or Jewish, and came from southern and eastern Europe rather than northern and western Europe. Significant numbers of Asians, largely Chinese and Japanese, came as well. Although these great masses of people were absorbed into the growing industrial machine that demanded ever more numbers of workers, there were great concerns about the ability of the country to deal with the poverty and kinds of people being admitted. Rita Simon (1985:84) quotes comments from *The Yale Review* during this period, which sound not unlike some of the commentary often heard today and illustrate the attitudes often held by individuals from older ethnic groups:

> Ignorant, unskilled, inert, accustomed to the beastliest conditions, with little social aspirations, with none of the desire for air and light and room, for decent

dress and home comfort, which our native people possess and which our earlier immigrants so speedily acquired, the presence of hundreds of thousands of these laborers constitutes a menace to the rate of wages and the American standard of living. . . . Taking whatever they can get in the way of wages, living like swine, crowded into filthy tenement houses, piecing over garbage barrels, the arrival on these shores of such masses of degraded peasantry bring the greatest danger that American labor has ever known.

Comments on the social character of the new immigrants were also often heard in the popular media (as quoted in Simon, 1985:85):

The character of our immigration has also changed—instead of the best class of people, we are now getting the refuse of Europe—outcasts from Italy, brutalized Poles and Hungarians, the offscourings of the world (*Philadelphia Enquirer,* Nov. 29, 1890).

The swelling tide of immigrants from Southern Europe and the Orient who can neither read or write their own language and not even speak ours, who bring with them only money enough to stave off starvation but a few days, is a startling national menace that cannot be disregarded with safety (*New York Herald,* Nov. 10, 1900).

These remarks reflect a deep strain of virulent racism in this country even beyond the horrific racism suffered by African slaves and their descendants. Chinese and Japanese immigrants suffered great indignities and violence. The Chinese Exclusion Act of 1882 effectively halted Chinese immigration, and the Native American population was either slaughtered or settled on reservations during this period. Although the impetus behind these moves was couched in economic terms, the passage of the Immigration and Nationality Acts of 1921 and 1924 were essentially cultural and racial in nature. Grounded in notions of "Nordic" supremacy, they effectively cut off immigration from all but northwestern European countries until 1965 (Jensen, 1989).

The effects of World War II on emigration cannot be underestimated. After the war, there was a stronger move toward changing the rules of immigration. When the Immigration and Nationality Act was ultimately amended in 1965, many of the more egregious biases were eliminated, quotas were now distributed evenly across countries, and first preference was given to persons wishing to be reunited with their families (although this preference was not accorded to Mexicans until 1976). In addition, exceptions were made for refugees from Cuba (over 600,000 between 1960 and 1990), Vietnam and other Southeast Asian countries after the Vietnam War (over 600,000 from 1975 to 1990), and Soviet Jews (approximately 150,000) (U.S. Immigration and Naturalization Service, 1997). There have also been additional 150,000 refugees from such other countries as Poland, Romania, Iran, Afghanistan,

Ethiopia from 1981 through 1990 (U.S. Immigration and Naturalization Service, 1996).

These circumstances led to a major increase in the numbers of immigrants to the United States. Since 1960, almost 20 million people have legally immigrated to the United States and an additional 3–5 million are estimated to be in the country illegally. Experts estimate the rate of illegal immigration to be about 250,000 to 300,000 per year (Simon, 1995). These large increases predictably have brought about a new clamor for restrictions, again largely on economic grounds and fears of welfare dependency. Consequently, the Immigration Reform and Control Act of 1986 added restrictions on immigration while also allowing a one-time amnesty for illegal immigrants. The result has been a steady decline in immigration during the 1990s, from 974,000 in 1992 to 720,000 in 1995 (U.S. Immigration and Naturalization Service, 1996).

The economic impact of immigration has been varied. Julian Simon (1995), reviewing a number of economic studies, found that:

> a spate of respected recent studies, using a variety of methods, agrees that "there is no empirical evidence documenting that the displacement effect [of natives from jobs] is numerically important" (Borjas, 1990, 92). The explanation is that new entrants not only take jobs, they make jobs. The jobs they create with their purchasing power, and with the new businesses which they start, are at least as numerous as the jobs which immigrants fill.

If we had been correct in 1976 in our statement that "most of the large scale immigration to America has ceased" then we might today simply be discussing an interesting chapter in the settlement of the United States, where ethnicity becomes an interesting cultural memory. But this continuing immigration into the United States tells us that, on the contrary, ethnic diversity continues to be important in the way people live their lives and raise their families. New immigrant groups are reinvigorating the notion of ethnicity. They use their ethnic institutions to aid them in their struggle to survive in a difficult global economy, where any advantage they can muster helps. They maintain their traditions as they adjust and cope in a foreign land. At the same time, the more established ethnic groups, more assimilated into the larger American culture, use their ethnicity as something to be recalled and celebrated, at festive occasions such as weddings, confirmations, and *bar mitzvahs,* or at more solemn events like funerals. Ethnicity remains important, still providing a source of identity, values, and unity.

In light of these circumstances, we feel that this edition of *Ethnic Families in America* retains its original purpose and role. We seek to examine a wide variety of American ethnic groups, probing the historical circumstances that impelled them to come to this country and focusing on the structure and functioning of their family life to determine or, at least, raise clues about how and why they have been able or unable to maintain an ethnic identification over the generations. Finally, we look ahead to speculate on what the future has in store for these groups and their constitutive families.

THE CONTINUING IMPORTANCE OF ETHNICITY

What does it mean to be ethnic? Certainly, ethnicity can be divisive and destructive, and ethnic ties can evoke some of the worst in humankind. As Greeley (1974:10) states:

> In fact, the conflicts that have occupied most men over the past two or three decades, those that have led to the most appalling outpourings of blood, have had precious little to do with ideological division. Most of us are unwilling to battle to the death over ideology, but practically all of us, it seems, are ready to kill each other over noticeable differences of color, language, religious faith, height, food habits, and facial configurations.

Greeley further points out that

> Thousands have died in seemingly endless battles between two very Semitic people, the Jews and the Arabs. The English and French glare hostilely at each other in Quebec; Christians and Moslems have renewed their ancient conflicts on the island of Mindanao; Turks and Greeks nervously grip their guns on Cyprus: and Celts and Saxons in Ulster have begun to imprison and kill one another with all the cumulative passion of a thousand years' hostility.

More recently, the Serbs and Bosnians in southern Europe and the Hutus and Tutsis in Rwanda serve as other examples of ethnic conflict. It appears that perhaps the collapse of old colonial empires, the rise of nationalism in the post–World War II period, and more recently the collapse of the Soviet empire have given rise to numerous conflicts at tribal, linguistic, religious, geographical, and cultural levels. The amount of conflict does not appear to be disappearing.

What all these conflicts seem to share is not an ideological character—especially the ideology of modern superpower conflicts, which focus on economic systems and social class—but a concern in some sense with very basic differences among groups of people, particularly cultural differences. There are concerns reflected in these conflicts that apparently are important to people—matters for which they are willing to fight to the death to defend. Clifford Geertz (1963:109) referred to these ties that people are willing to die for as "primordial attachments":

> By a primordial attachment is meant one that stems from the "givens"—or more precisely, as culture is inevitably involved in such matters, the "assured givers"—

of social existence: immediate contiguity and kin connection mainly, but beyond them, the givenness that stems from being born into a particular religious community, speaking a particular language or even a dialect of language, and following particular social patterns, These congruities of blood, speech, custom and so on, are seen to have an ineffable, at times overpowering, coerciveness in and of themselves. One is bound to one's kinsman, one's neighbor, one's fellow believer, *ipso facto*, as a result not merely of one's personal affection, practical necessity, common interest, or incurred obligation, but at least in great part by the virtue of some unaccountable absolute import attributed to the very tie itself. The general strength of such primordial bonds, and the types of them that are important, differ from person to person, from society to society, and from time to time But for virtually every person, in every society, at almost all times, some attachments seem to flow from a sense of natural—some would say spiritual—affinity than from social interaction.

These attachments, these feelings of belonging to a certain group of people for whatever reason, are a basic feature of the human condition. They are called *ethnic ties*, and the group of people that one is tied to is an ethnic group. In this general sense, an *ethnic group* consists of those who share a unique social and cultural heritage that is passed on from generation to generation.

Gordon (1964), in slightly different terms, sees those who share a feeling of "peoplehood" as an ethnic group but believes the sense of peoplehood that characterized most social life in past centuries has become fragmented and shattered. This, he suggests, has occurred for a variety of reasons including, in the last few centuries, massive population increases, the development of large cities, the formation of social classes, and the grouping of peoples into progressively larger political units. However, as many other writers have noted, individuals have shown a continuing need to merge their individual identity with some ancestral group—with "their own kind of people." Gordon proposes that the fragmentation of social life has left competing models for this sense of peoplehood; people are forced to choose among these models or somehow to integrate them completely. In America, the core categories of ethnic identity from which individuals are able to form a sense of peoplehood are race, religion, national origin, or some combination of these categories (Gordon, 1964). It is these categories, emphasizing substantively cultural symbols of consciousness of time, that are used to define the groups included in this book.

Ethnicity in America

Since the 1970s, we have seen a growing interest in the value of cultural diversity, ethnic pluralism, and ethnic differences in the United States. As already indicated, this level of appreciation has not always been the case, and some have argued that the reason that a scholarly examination of ethnic differences was often lacking has much to do with the dominant assimilationist model of American society at the time. According to this model, ethnic differences, though perhaps useful in the past to preserve the familiar or *Gemeinschaft* character of the old country for large numbers of people set adrift in alien America, are not particularly useful today in our more rational and class-oriented society. In addition, the divisive aspects of ethnicity are emphasized and seen as barriers to peaceful coexistence within the American social fabric. The integrative aspects of ethnic ties and culture have been almost entirely neglected. As a result, many individuals with rich ethnic heritages have been encouraged, coerced, and in other ways pushed toward giving up their heritage and becoming "Americanized."

Stereotypes of the negative aspects and consequences of ethnic culture abound: Italians are *mafioso*; Polish are ignorant; Arabs are terrorists, and any number of different ethnic groups are lazy and will not work. These kinds of stereotypes have long been part of the general American culture. The implications of a pure assimilationist approach is that as soon as these people give up their inferior beliefs and ties, as soon as they leave this life—this narrow, dull, provincial life—the better off they will be.

The fact that "Americanization" is now seen by many as overly simplistic or ethnocentric reflects a major shift in attitude, a shift that has not come easily. This shift reflects a renewal of ethnic consciousness—a new awareness of distinctive ethnic culture, partly a consciously remembered one and partly a set of inherited customs and beliefs. Ethnics are now allowed to endorse the theme that they have the right to be different. This new consciousness among ethnic groups reflects the larger changes and upheavals that American society experienced during the 1960s and 1970s, especially the various liberation movements that emerged during this period and most notably the black civil rights movement. These movements in their turn helped renew the ethnic consciousness of the so-called white or "unmeltable" ethnics, as Novak (1973) has referred to them, inspiring renewed interest in cultural diversity and a new sensitivity toward others and their differences. We have seen increases in the personal, conscious self-appropriation of cultural history and a willingness to share in the social and political needs and struggles of one group. The reemergence of ethnic feelings and interests has not necessarily meant a return to Old World culture; it does not, as Novak (1973) points out, represent an attempt to hold back the clock. It represents rather a defense of ties that are important to large numbers of individuals in this country.

The reason these interests are regarded as important to defend and—as we have seen in various locales—sometimes to fight for is that they are not a mere nostalgic defense of some useless cultural artifact but very important to individuals in their daily lives. There are (and were) many reasons for maintaining ethnic communal ties. Some ties are primarily useful at the time when members of ethnic groups are new immigrants to this country; others continue to be important to this day. The utility of ethnic ties and ethnic groups is in large part the reason for their continued existence. As Glazer (1973:169) states:

> The immigrants . . . were as much in favor of the melting pot as native American nationals, indeed more so, because they thought the melting pot, if they really succeeded in dissolving into some American mass, would give them access to every position in society: while native American chauvinists trying to monopolize these positions were not nearly so much in favor of so complete a disappearance of the immigrant groups.

The melting pot, in fact, never fully succeeded, and large numbers of immigrant groups were forced to maintain ethnic communal ties almost as a matter of self-defense. In their work on ethnicity and their analysis of the evolution and persistence of ethnicity, Glazer and Moynihan (1970) argued that "the adoption of a totally new ethnic identity, by dropping whatever one is to become simply American, is inhibited by strong elements in the social structure of the United States." These inhibitions range from brutal discrimination and prejudice to the "unavailability of simple 'American' identity" (Glazer and Moynihan, 1970: xxxiii). Most positively seen, ethnic communities provide individuals with congenial associates, help organize experience by personalizing an increasingly impersonal world, and provide opportunities for social mobility and success within an ethnic context (Greeley, 1969).

Ethnic Family Life

The maintenance of ethnic identification and solidarity ultimately rests on the ability of the family to socialize its members into the ethnic culture and thus to channel and control, perhaps program, future behavior. Consequently, the distinctive family life that developed as a result of historical and contemporary social processes become the focal concern of this work. Contributors were asked to examine the relationships and characteristics distinctive of ethnic family life; to look to the past for an explanation of historical or genetic significance; to describe the key characteristics of the ethnic family today; and to analyze the changes that have occurred in the family and speculate about what lies ahead.

It bears repeating that the historical experience of the ethnic group, both the time when the group arrived on these shores and the conditions under which the members of the group were forced to live, is a vitally important factor in the explanation of the persistence of the ethnic family and the ethnic group in the United States. For this reason, each chapter contains an important discussion of the historical background of the ethnic group under consideration. Besides describing the old country settings, each contributor was requested to summarize the major characteristics of the family as it previously existed or first appeared in America to show subsequent changes and adaptations more clearly.

One of the most significant ways an ethnic culture is expressed is through those events that we identify as family activities. The family historically has been a conservative institution, and those cultural elements concerning family life, if not affected by outside influences, will tend to replace themselves generation after generation (Farber, 1964). Experiences within the family are intense, heavily emotion laden, and apt to evoke pleasurable or painful memories for most individuals. For example, it is no accident that for many of the ethnic groups discussed here, eating—particularly eating ethnic food—remains a significant part of the ethnic identity. These are activities that occur in a family context. If traditional ethnic values are to be found anywhere, they will be found in the family.

In addition to developing historical context, the contributors were asked to discuss four major areas of ethnic family life in which ethnic culture might be generated, sustained, or have an impact. First were demographic characteristics: How is the ethnic culture specifically expressed in fertility, marriage, and divorce rates? How does the group cope with intermarriage? Intermarriage is a cultural matter that can be viewed as an important indicator of assimilation for the ethnic group and ranges in incidence from very low among African Americans and Amish to relatively high among Japanese Americans. Second is the question of family structure, which involves the distribution of status, authority, and responsibility within the nuclear family and the network of kin relationships linking members of the extended family. Most discussions of ethnic family life have focused on this area because many ethnic groups have been characterized as patriarchal, matriarchal, or as having very close-knit extended family relationships. It is in this context that we hear comments about "black matriarchy" or the "Jewish mother." How much is cultural myth or ideology? How much is fact? How much has been the effect of the American experience?

Along with the cultural patterns that define family roles and statuses, rights, and obligations, there are issues of value transmission: attributes of an ethnic culture that are mediated through the family. These are cultural values that concern such issues as achievement, lifestyle, and educational or occupational aspirations. While many historical, economic, and other factors such as discrimination and prejudice have limited the mobility of individuals in many ethnic groups, the possession of a cultural reservoir of motivations and skill has worked to the distinct advantage of many. The cultural tradition of the Jews, for example, with its emphasis on literacy and education, has helped them immeasurably from a socioeconomic standpoint. For others, the lack of such a reservoir has worked to their disadvantage. These cultural distinctions, while existing to some extent outside the family context, are for the most part developed within the family.

Finally, in discussing ethnic family life, it is important to examine the family at different stages of the family life cycle. In this collection of essays, contributors were requested to analyze those aspects of childrearing, adolescence, mate selection, and the place of the elderly in which ethnic culture has had significant influence. The culture of many groups usually specifies what the most desirable end product of the socialization process should be. Whether this product should be a good Mormon or Amishman, the family as the major force of socialization, especially in the critical early years, is the most responsible ethnic institution for making it happen.

Ethnic Diversity as the Criterion of Selection

While many more than the seventeen ethnic groups selected qualify, the ethnic families presented in this book were chosen to represent a rather wide spectrum of distinguishable groups, ranging from the less than 100,000 Amish to the approximately 30 million African Americans, whose ethnicity continues to be expressed through identifiable institutions and, significantly, the family. Nevertheless, large numbers of Americans find it possible to trace descent to foreign nations and cultures such as Germany, Great Britain, and Canada, yet retain little, if any, of an Old World cultural identity. Because their family life is largely indistinguishable from that of others of similar socioeconomic classes (except in certain isolated enclaves here and there), for this reason these groups have been excluded from this work.

We have chosen to group ethnic families into five substantive categories: (1) European ethnic minorities, (2) Hispanic ethnic minorities, (3) Asian ethnic minorities, (4) historically subjugated ethnic minorities, and (5) socioreligious ethnic minorities. These categories help sort out the groups according to several dimensions, but they should in no way be taken as definitive, exclusive, or the only useful classification. The most important criterion in the minds of the editors has been that the categories appear to capture a particularly important contingency or group experience that has a continuing influence on its collective fate. In almost all cases, the chapter on a particular ethnic group is written by a person who identifies him or herself as a member of that group. In the following paragraphs, we briefly discuss the scheme that we have chosen.

1. European Ethnic Minorities

The four ethnic minorities in this category are the Irish, Greek, Italian, and Polish immigrants who arrived in the United States during a period extending roughly from the early 1880s until the outbreak of World War I. In this relatively short period of time, almost 25 million European immigrants entered the United States, an influx that resulted from great upheavals rent by industrialization and war. This is the period we most often think of when we visualize immigrant life and it is from this wave of European immigration that most of today's non-Protestant white ethnics are descended.

2. Hispanic Ethnic Minorities

The three ethnic minorities in this category are the Mexicans, Cubans, and Puerto Ricans. Hispanic ethnic groups have entered the United States in a variety of ways. Although Mexicans have come to this country in the nineteenth and twentieth centuries as voluntary immigrants, they also are by far the source of the largest number of recent immigrants into the United States. Puerto Ricans, too, are a group not clearly part of either voluntary immigration or conquest. Puerto Rico became a territory of the United States in 1898 following the Spanish American War, and in 1917 the inhabitants of the island were granted American citizenship. The greatest influx of Puerto Ricans to the United States was during the 1950s, when nearly 20 percent of the island's population moved to the mainland.

The movement of Cubans to the United States since 1960 has come in a series of waves. Initially impelled mainly by political motives, later waves are increasingly the result of economic reasons as well. The problems that all of these groups have faced include economic integration and social assimilation into American society.

3. Asian Ethnic Minorities

The five ethnic minorities in this category are the Koreans, Vietnamese, Chinese, Japanese, and Indian groups. The Chinese and Japanese American ethnic minorities have been in this country in substantial numbers for 75 to 100 years. The Chinese, Koreans, Indians, and Vietnamese, however, represent a sizable number of recent and continuing immigrants. Important questions for the study of all these groups relate to the effects of time and generation on the cultural heritage but more particularly as they directly affect family life. The extent to which assimilation and acculturation has had an impact on ethnic identity and lifestyle remains one of the key problems these groups of people have encountered. Other problems include adjusting to a modern business cycle and war-plagued industrialized society and to constant infusion of new representatives from their respective countries of origin.

4. Historically Subjugated Ethnic Minorities

The two groups, African American and Native Americans, are placed together because their identity and experience in this country have been the result of, or strongly influenced by, their race. These groups either preceded the arrival of the European Americans or arrived later and were immediately or later placed in some form of bondage. Enslaved to the land, alienated from it, or bound in a latter-day peonage, African Americans and Native Americans have endured the darkest and least savory group life histories from which to build a viable ethnic culture. In both of these groups the role of the family, whether truncated or extended, becomes crucial for ethnic survival.

5. Socioreligious Ethnic Minorities

The three ethnic minorities in this category are the Amish, the Jews, and the Mormons. They are placed together because their identity and experience have largely been a result of or strongly influenced by, their religion. All sought in America a place to live that kind of social existence in which religion could continue to be vitally conjoined with all aspects of their life and livelihood.

REFERENCES

Farber, Bernard. 1964. *Family Organization and Interaction*. San Francisco: Chandler.

Geertz, Clifford, 1963. "The Integrated Revolution," in Clifford Geertz (Ed.), *Old Societies and New Societies*. Glencoe, IL: Free Press.

Glazer, Nathan. 1973. "The Issue of Cultural Pluralism in America Today," in Joseph Ryan (Ed.), *White Ethnics: Their Life in Working-Class America*. Englewood Cliffs, NJ: Prentice-Hall, pp. 168–177.

Glazer, Nathan, and Daniel P. Moynihan. 1970. *Beyond the Melting Pot* (2nd ed.). Cambridge: MIT Press.

Gordon, Milton. 1964. *Assimilation in American Life*. New York: Oxford University Press.

Greeley, Andrew M. 1969. *Why Can't They Be Like Us?* New York: Institute of Human Relations Press.

———. 1974. *Ethnicity in the United States: A Preliminary Reconnaissance*. New York. John Wiley.

Jensen, Leif. 1989. *The New Immigration: Implications for Poverty and Public Assistance Utilization*. New York: Greenwood Press.

Novak, Michael. 1973. "Probing the New Ethnicity," in Joseph Ryan (Ed.), *White Ethnics: Their Life in Working-Class America*. Englewood Cliffs, NJ; Prentice-Hall, pp. 158–167.

Simon, Julian. 1995. *Immigration: The Demographic and Economic Facts*. New York: Cato Institute.

Simon, Rita. 1985. *Public Opinion and the Immigrant: Print Media Coverage, 1880–1980*. Lexington, MA: Lexington Books.

U.S. Immigration and Naturalization Service. 1996. *Immigration to the United States*. Washington, DC: U.S. Government Printing Office.

2 | A "Then and Now" Overview of the Immigrant Family in America

Robert W. Habenstein

Rather than beginning this chapter on immigration in the nineteenth century, as in earlier editions, the author has moved back a century to broaden the sociohistorical context of this analysis and to mention some of the economic, technological, and demographic developments of earlier times. Later in the chapter we will analyze the nineteenth- and early twentieth-century immigrant ethnic family as a transplanted, adaptive, primary social unit engaged in the business of conserving and rebuilding ethnic culture. Finally, we will review the remainder of the twentieth century, with its remarkable influx of immigrants from Third World and established countries after 1965. The focus will be on the impact and consequence of this phenomenon mainly for the immigrants' families, but also, to a lesser extent, on their often strange and unyielding host society.

THE MERCANTILIST SCENARIO

After nearly a thousand years of manorial-centered feudalism—with its slow economic growth and a population held stable mostly by wars, famines, epidemics, and a low level of agricultural technology—a new era in the form of a maritime-centered mercantilism promised a more vibrant and richer society to Western Europeans.

For centuries during the late Middle Ages, the city-states that existed along the Mediterranean coast, around the Iberian peninsula, and north to Scandinavia were known not only for shipping trade but for their banking houses, financiers, and underwriters (known then as "undertakers"). Out of this new financial environment came a range of market instruments and accounting innovations—not the least of which was double-entry bookkeeping (Braudel, 1982). The transition from city- to nation-states, carried upward by a new-found nationalist fever, advanced the mercantilist idea beyond simple control of maritime commerce and the creation of exporting seaports abroad. The expansionist urge led to exploration and colonization as a primary method of increasing wealth for the mother country. At the same time, revenues could be increased by subjecting land trade to duties, customs, and devices for collecting money from itinerant merchants, peddlers, even those exporting from one part of a nation to another (Braudel, 1982). The idea of continuously funneling money into a centralized nation-state took on an extreme character when gold and silver became the preferred plunder or medium of exchange. Nationalism took on a "take-charge" ideology that led to the building of navies, including battleships, to control and protect the nation's ocean commerce.

The Great Transformation

Maritime-centered mercantilism reached its apogee in the eighteenth century. But even in its expanded form mercantilism could not restrain a growing industry-based society. By the beginning of the nineteenth century, mill towns in England and America had sprung up along rivers or near exploitable fossil-fuel deposits. Industrialization soon spread over great segments of Western Europe. By mid-century, engineers supported by civil authorities and men of commerce and capital enterprise advanced a large-scale technology that soon revolutionized not only industry, but also transportation, communication, and agriculture.

The great transformation of the time, then, involved the rapid change of a mercantile-oriented, town-centered, small-scale agriculturally undergirded society into one featuring large-scale capital enterprises, advanced technology, extensive marketing systems, and a large proletarianized labor force. People of the soil—peasants, small landowners, and rural villagers—found their commons enclosed, rents increased, and land increasingly expensive. In the wake of expanded mechanized agricultural production, the small-scale producers and the farm laborers were driven off the lands that they had rented, owned, and/or cultivated for generations. Likewise, artisans organized in guilds lost control of the quality, quantity, and marketing outlets of their goods to merchants, who were themselves organized into leagues and early forms of trade associations.

The ironic result of these developments was that at the very time production of foodstuffs and other agricultural products was increasing along with life expectancy, millions of small farmers, peasants, small producers, and independent artisans were suffering economic dislocation and loss of place in traditional community life (Braudel, 1982; Knapp, 1976). Writes historian Paul Kennedy (1994:4):

> The major cities, swelled by the drift of population, grew fast. On the eve of the French Revolution (1793), Paris had a total of between 600,000 and

700,000 people including up to 100,000 vagrants—combustible material for a social explosion. London's total was even larger, its 570,000 inhabitants of 1750 having become 900,000 by 1801, including a mass of bustling street hawkers, pickpockets, urchins, and felons so well captured in contemporary prints. With more and more "have-nots," was it any wonder that the authorities were fearful and tightened up restrictions on public assemblies, pamphleteering, "combinations" of workers, and other potentially subversive activities?

Throughout the nineteenth century, the great industrial and commercial revolutions, kept dynamic by rapidly changing and improving technology, not only uprooted masses of people, but also reaggregated them in areas where an expanding, vigorous labor force was necessary to keep the mills, factories, mines, and seaports of an expanding capitalism operating at appropriate capacities. Major political and religious institutions, never too stable in Western society, became increasingly incapable of providing protection for, guidance of, and control over the great numbers of people who had come to occupy and identify with particular geographic regions. Likewise, the vagaries of local, national, and international economies (and of nature itself) introduced crises of magnitude often great enough in themselves to effect large-scale social change.

"Push" Factors

The social and historical forces described here have been characterized as *push factors*. Some of these push factors operated in limited geographical contexts—the Irish potato blight of 1847, the religious persecution of Germans in Prussia, the failed German revolution of 1848, and internecine strife among ethnic peoples inside thinly laced-together empires. More widespread disjunctions and large-scale crises might involve regional economic depressions, wars among great nations, crop failures, plagues, and epidemics. But behind all the push factors stood the long-term transformation of land and commercial enterprise in the direction of larger units of production owned and operated by fewer persons. As Europe was shifting from labor-intensive to capital-intensive enterprise, the United States seemed ready to absorb the surplus labor, energies, hopes, and aspirations of Europe's dislocated, migration prone peoples.

"Pull" Factors

America, Lord Acton had proclaimed in an 1866 an address to the Literary and Scientific Institution of Bridgnorth, not far from his Shopshire estate, had become a "distant magnet" whose force had extended across Europe (Taylor, 1971:xi–xii). Perhaps there was a generalized nineteenth-century concept or stereotype of the United States as a land of opportunity where all dreams might be fulfilled. But it is more appropriate to think of the multitudinous Europeans who had to decide whether to move or to stay as constituting an emigration *public*, a loose group of persons who, in the end, made individuals decisions—for many of them the most important decision of their lives. Slaves, of course, had no options and were shipped callously to the Americas in increasing numbers from the early seventeenth into the early eighteenth century. Convicts were exiled from England to Australia, as they were for a brief time to the American colonies. Almost all emigrants, however, went to America out of choice. Dreams were possible, but hope was omnipresent.

The "one big magnet" notion had an important counterpart in the groups, agencies, companies, kin, and native-born Americans already well situated in the United States that exerted their own "magnetic" force in the hope of dislodging and attracting emigrants from their Old World communities. The word was spread across Europe by thousands of publicity agents who worked for passenger ship lines, railways, canal authorities, land developers, towns, and large-scale business enterprises. Their evocative speeches and hortatory literature were reinforced by the rhetoric of journalistic publications, guides, handbooks, pamphlets, and lecturers—all extolling the virtues of and opportunities in America. Many immigrants who had settled into American cities, towns, and farms wrote to European kin as true believers, assuring them that the riches of the new land were available for the taking (Taylor, 1971).

IMMIGRATION WAVES

From the mid-nineteenth century until shortly after World War I, between 30 and 35 million emigrants left Europe for American shores. They came in large waves, from different countries and at different times—first in cargo-carrying sailing ships, then in passenger sailing ships, and finally in steamships, which hauled hundreds of thousands each year in the last three decades of the nineteenth century. And they also hauled great numbers back again, perhaps as many as one-third of the former immigrants, who either had failed to find fortune in the New World or had accumulated enough wealth to ensure a comfortable, enviable life in the community once left behind (Saloutos, 1964).

Historians and scholars refer to the period from 1830 to 1882 as that of the "old" immigration and the period from 1882 to 1930, when federal control replaced that of the states, as that of the "new" immigration. The 10 million immigrants who arrived in the "old" period were predominantly Irish, German, Scandinavian, English, Scottish, and Scots-Irish (Feldstein and Costello, 1974). They came during the preindustrial years, when there were millions of acres to be settled and canals, bridges, and railroads to be built, and when urban work complements were still in their formative years.

There was both dispersion and concentration of the "old" immigrants, by ethnic group and often by religious affiliations. Scots-Irish Protestants arrived early in the century and became some of Pennsylvania's most successful farmers. Irish Catholics—suffering famine, plague, and loss of their small farms in the old country because of absentee landlords' desire for large-scale agriculture units—settled in the larger cities in the Northeast, staying put even though they faced poverty, low wages, and the prejudice of native-born American citizens. The English dispersed almost everywhere, but most shelved their plans for independent living on small farms and ended up in the larger towns and cities. Germans in great numbers went everywhere in the northeastern, Middle Atlantic, and midwestern states; some were content to gather into ethnic communities in cities, while others settled on fertile lands and became successful, often prosperous, farmers. Scandinavians, bridging the "old" and "new" periods, concentrated their settlements mainly in the midwestern states and, like the Germans, became serious and successful farmers but also contributed artisans, professionals, and intellectuals to such rapidly growing cities as Cleveland, Chicago, and Minneapolis.

The "new" immigration followed the great wave of Irish and German immigration of the 1850s. It crested in the 1880s and again, each time higher, in the decades immediately preceding the outbreak of World War I, when immigrants were entering the United States at the rate of 1 million a year (Jones, 1976). Beginning in the early 1880s, the center of gravity of emigration moved steadily southward and eastward. By the end of the century, the bulk of America's immigrants consisted of Slavs, Italians, Greeks, and Eastern European Jews.[1] By 1914, the "new" immigrants constituted over 80 percent of all total immigration. According to Maldwyn Jones (1976), a historian of immigration:

> These "new" immigrants came from the most backward and reactionary regions of Europe. The cultural differences between them and the Americans were infinitely greater than had been the case with the "old" immigration. Hence, the "new" immigrants would be more difficult to assimilate. . . .
>
> In any case, it was becoming apparent that the immediate effect of immigration was to fragment, rather than to unite American society. Although the concept of class was alien to American thinking, a great gulf was developing between the native born and middle classes and the predominantly foreign working class. Under the impact of immigration the United States became in

---

[1]From before the turn of the century until the 1920s, scholars, popular writers, historians of immigration, and social scientists tended to view the mass immigration of millions of southern and eastern Europeans with varying degrees of alarm. The "threat" point of view is somewhat luridly presented by journalist Kenneth L. Roberts (1920); a sympathetic treatment is found in the important sociological novel by Upton Sinclair, *The Jungle* (1905). Written before or after World War I, the arguments presented by Roberts and Sinclair are still alive in the writings of current disputants; see, for example, Sanford J. Ungar (1995), Peter Brimelow (1996), and Roy Beck (1996). A collection of contemporary points of view is found in *Arguing Immigration*, edited by Nicolaus Mills (1994). For an absorbing novel, the first part of a trilogy starting in 1888, see Howard Fast's *The Immigrants*.

effect two nations, differentiated by language and religion, by residence and occupation. The two nations had no more contact with one another than they had when separated by 3000 miles of ocean.

The reaction to the "new" or late-arriving immigration was threefold. In the industrial realm, these migrants, most of whom were between the ages of 15 and 35, were exploited by industrialists and their managers, who sought to pay them low wages, and were resented by established labor as a threat to its hard-earned wage and living standards. In the social realm, there was ostracism and prejudice, not all completely unfounded because many of the "new" immigrants had no intention of staying permanently and worked for little, lived on little, showed little or no interest in the problems of the wider society, and sought to accumulate as much wealth as possible and return to their homelands as soon as possible (Park and Miller, 1921).[2]

Roy Beck (1996:37), a current critic of open-door immigration policy, writes:

> Most of our ancestors who came during the Great Wave (1880–1924) placed an enormous burden on the country. Large numbers didn't learn the language and culture quickly; they were clannish and lived in ethnic enclaves, they remained poor, and their arrival was in numbers that were devastating to many communities. For many of the immigrants themselves, life was a struggle for even a tenuous hold on the American dream.

This perception of immigrants as essentially burdensome to the host society was central to the clamor of anti-immigrationists after World War I, and federal immigration laws were passed in 1921 and 1924 that severely restricted immigration in general and, through a nation-quota system, discriminated against the people of southern and eastern Europe (Jones, 1976).[3]

CHARACTERISTIC FEATURES OF WESTERN EUROPEAN IMMIGRANT FAMILIES

Possessions: The Baggage of Life

Emigrants leaving their homelands faced the difficult and often heartrending problem of which material possessions to take and which to leave. The problem was complicated by marital status and family size. Single

---

[2]Park and Miller developed a sixfold typology of immigrants: settler, colonist, political idealist, allrightnick, *caffone*, and intellectual. In their terms, the *caffone*—the "pure opportunist wanting only to make money and go back"—became the stereotype applied, with only partial justification, to all immigrants who eventually returned to their homelands.

[3]A labor-supported Chinese Exclusion Act was passed in 1882, and in 1885 an Alien Contract Law was passed prohibiting indentured servants' contracts.

persons could travel light more easily; those married and with children had to sacrifice things of symbolic value to practical, basic necessities such as cooking-ware, bedding (nearly always down-filled ticks and pillows), clothing, and tools (important to the immigrant artisan). A few cherished mementos—pictures, Bibles, and missals—could be tucked in the baggage somewhere, but most bulkier household possessions had to be left behind, along with farm equipment, livestock, pets, machinery, and other paraphernalia too large to be transported as passenger luggage. Families whose growth and sense of an immediate, "close" environment had included the accumulation of material objects—some symbolic, others pragmatic, but all incorporated into their lives and work—were subject to the trauma of separation from a significant part of their real world. Memories of this world, romanticized in musing and life review, contributed to a diffuse nostalgia, often tinged with melancholy (Feldstein and Costello, 1974).

Transitory Existence

Immigrants, by definition, are people who purposely move to new geographical settings. Most European immigrants became migratory and moved a number of times, with several transportation breaks between the initial move and arrival at the final destination. Many had a specific goal in mind—Buffalo, St. Louis, or Pittsburgh. They hoped to find a place to settle with or near close relatives in a colony, a settlement, or an area of concentration of their countrypeople (Park and Miller, 1921). Some announced a destination but never got there; others, having reached the proclaimed destination, did not stay—because of disappointment or inability to find an ensured means of survival or because other cities or towns seemed to hold out more promise.

The transitory nature of much immigrant life was, of course, countered by the large numbers who settled down and tenaciously hung on to their dwellings, strongly motivated to acquire land and homes of their own even if it meant living in the basement and renting the top two floors and attic! The tendency to become place centered was reinforced by and to some extent led to the growth of ethnic enclaves into which a person or a family and extended kin might embed themselves, supporting and receiving support from immigrant organizations (Habenstein and Mindel, 1981).

The Family as a Buffer, Filter, and Sorting Mechanism

Insecurity, hopes, fears, misgivings—a panoply of conflicting emotions—heaped themselves on the immigrants' heads. The phrase "ordeal of assimilation" (Feldstein and Costello, 1974) appropriately describes the process by which immigrants as supplicants were required to or at least expected to organize their lives. Even so, there was no guarantee of a full, happy, prosperous life even for the assimilated, who were well aware of the "busts" as well as the "booms" in the American economy. In these periods, ethnic immigrant families operated as buffering, filtering, and sorting social mechanisms. All prescriptions and proscriptions of the host society were carefully judged against traditional standards, and all possible meanings and consequences were pondered at length. The new might or might not be suspect, but it was seldom ignored or left unexamined by members of the immigrant family—often including, close relatives who temporarily or permanently might make up a partially extended family.

Generational Frictions

The large multigeneration family was found less among first-generation and more among second-generation immigrant families. Yet as a social unity, it remained an ideal, even if it often was difficult to achieve. As the aging generations became grandparents and great-grandparents, relationships between rapidly Americanizing children and the elderly and very elderly— whose minds were embedded in the amber of their native language and culture—often became difficult and frustrating. In somewhat varying degrees, depending to a great extent on the language and cultural leap required to become a properly assimilated immigrant or a descendent of such, all immigrant families experienced the anxieties and strains of what has come to be called the "generation gap" (Ross, 1914). When the family and close relatives seemed unable to appreciate and deal properly with children's problems or to give useful advice, alternative sources—schoolteachers, street friends, classmates—were consulted. Some vague sense of family weakness revealed in the family's inability to cope with each member's problems was characteristic of almost all immigrant families.

FAMILY LIFE CYCLE

The Marriage Institution

Marriage has always been a serious and important event among immigrants, both "old" and "new." Its significance lay in the economic impact on ongoing households and in the social, economic, and interpersonal consequences for the married couple. The productive energies of the unmarried family members were an important contribution to the household. Marriage of a son or a daughter usually led to a significant reduction in the income of established households (Tentler, 1981). The gain to society through the addition of legitimately procreating couples was often accomplished at the expense of the economic viability of the newlyweds' parental households. Thus for immigrant families, most of whom were near the poverty line, the marriage of a young adult member was a serious matter. Marriages were not to be entered into lightly. Young people were under heavy social obligation to marry for life and to establish independent households of their own, and mostly by their own efforts.

Marriage had its exactions, but it also had obvious compensations. Whatever the "new freedom" in America might dictate or permit in terms of relations between the sexes, young immigrants still considered marriage to be the overriding legitimating mechanism for a couple to remove the bars to intimacy and companionship. Marriage was not yet equalitarian, but if marriages traditionally had been a family, kin, and community affair, the freedom of a marrying couple to develop an interpersonal unity, even if not always taken advantage of, was at least acknowledged by the traditional groups.

Mate Selection

The choice of a mate was both an important and a difficult matter. *Endogamy*, marriage within a specific group, was preferred in all ethnic groups and prescribed in immigrant families (Habenstein and Mindel, 1981). Given the same ethnic group and religious preference, wives might marry up, becoming the wife of a man of a slightly higher socioeconomic class—a "good catch." Men might look for an attractive younger woman with domestic skills and possibly a small, self-accumulated dowry to help get the marriage off to a good start.

Difficulties arose because of a sex ratio highly favoring males[4] (Duncan, 1933). In some ethnic groups (the Greeks are a good example), opportunities for men to meet and marry eligible women were severely limited because of the scarcity of women. The bachelor ethnic immigrant was a familiar and socially acceptable member of the community. He often lived in a lodging house or perhaps with married friends, unless he returned to his European community. Substantial economic success might, of course, turn the picture around; highly age-discrepant marriages were not uncommon, particularly when the husband-to-be had acquired wealth.

Parental influence on marital choice could be direct and substantial but not necessarily decisive. Daughters increasingly sought to enlarge the scope of their freedom of choice of mates. Parents, relatives, friends, and clergymen nevertheless felt obliged to give friendly, sometimes strong counsel. Arranged marriages through professional matchmakers accounted for a very small percentage of the mate selections made, mostly in Russian and Polish-Jewish ethnic groups. Engagements preceded weddings; marriage ceremonies were important and often elaborate affairs. Civil marriages occasionally took place, but the norm was a church wedding—the larger, the better—with spirited receptions, bands, dancing, presents, speeches, and photographs. The com-

---

[4]Duncan estimates that out of total immigration to about 1930, 65 percent of immigrants were males and 80 percent were between fourteen and forty-five years old.

munity, in effect, laid hands on the principals. Sanctified by the church and sanctioned by the community, the wedding was supposed to take and the marriage to last—as it usually did.

Children and Childhood

Once married, young immigrants immediately set about bringing children into the world. A good—that is, steady—job, an industrious and provident wife, and a large number of children were the cornerstones of immigrant adult existence. Families were expected to grow large (six to eight children were not too many), since children were not only nice to have but also were potential economic assets to the household. Newly married wives might continue to work for a short while, but when they settled down to the long and full-time job of being a mother, they almost never worked outside the home (see, for example, McLaughlin, 1978).[5]

The care of children was primarily the mother's responsibility. Grandmothers who lived with married daughters or sons were helpful and were occasionally used as surrogate mothers if the mother worked away from home. Mothers' sisters who lived near might develop close ties with nieces and nephews. Mothers, grandmothers, and aunts, then, made up one significant sector of the extended or partially extended kinship systems in which the nuclear unit of wife, husband, and children was embedded. Uncles, particularly to male children, and father's best friends, often indistinguishable in the children's minds from "real" relatives, were also important; the latter often became godfathers, who were pledged to take an interest in fictive kin a generation below them (Habenstein and Mindel, 1981).

Childhood was a hit-or-miss proposition. For immigrants, there was little self-conscious domesticity (Ryan, 1982), little concern about the rights of the child, and much concern that the child grow up rapidly to become a sturdy participant in the labor force. Small children were family reared, with parents playing the dominant role in the socialization process but with siblings and close relatives very much involved. Chronic tensions between parents and offspring developed when the children started to attend school. The Old World language, almost always spoken in the first-generation immigrant family, suddenly became extraneous and burdensome to the child in the classroom—where teachers could be unsympathetic to young pupils trying to learn English as a second language—and marked him or her as "Polack," "Mick," "Wop," or "Dago" among other children. What was learned at home might have little meaning compared with or might be at odds with what was learned in the classroom. The embarrassment of poverty and the impoverishment of language brought out resentment not only between children and parents, but also between children and

---

[5]Note, however, that many immigrant wives did cottage industry work at home.

the culture and institutions that gave meaning and direction to the lives of the older generations.

Coming of Age

Children of both sexes were expected to become responsible young adults by the time they were 14 years old, at which age they had completed grade school and were, in most states, eligible for a work permit. Long before this, children had had work experience of some sort—part time, in the summer, after school, in or out of the home. The emphasis on work was matched by an unyielding familism; the goals and needs of the family, nearly always defined by the father, were first and foremost in the minds of all family members. Children spoke of "my family" rather than of "my parents." The dominance of the authoritarian father was buffered and tempered by the mother, who played a mediating and protective role in respect to her children. Thus the mother-child relationship was intensely close and emotional; for children, the most horrible event imaginable would be the loss of the mother.

Formal education was legally required and regarded as a necessity for children, but it was not expected to unduly delay the maturing child from entering the workforce. Boys might reluctantly be permitted to continue attending school past the age of 14 if it seemed that further education might enhance their vocational prospects. For daughters of immigrant parents, opportunities for education beyond the eighth grade were slim. Doubtful parents might accede to some type of business-school training, but girls usually were pitched into the workforce as soon as their parents could get them there, legally or not.

As they came of age and entered the workforce, or perhaps vice versa, immigrants' daughters developed even stronger bonds with their mothers. It was a matter of great pride for the young daughter to give her wages to her mother. Until she was ready for marriage, the working daughter did not pay "board"—a stipulated weekly amount that represented only a portion of her wages (Tentler, 1981). Mothers gave back a relatively small amount of the daughters' wages for carfare, other necessary expenses, and clothing. Sons, however, from the time they began working, were permitted to pay board and were expected to save most of their wage with an eye toward having a reasonable amount of money to get married on.

Marriage of sons or of daughters, we have already noted, led to loss of family income and thus was a family contingency as well as an individual matter. But if the family was large, as it usually was, the departure of the eldest children through marriage was offset by the entry into the workforce of the younger sons and daughters. Perfect synchronization might not be effected, but continual replacement of junior breadwinners could take place in the very large families for fifteen or more years. The blurring between adolescence and manhood or womanhood stemmed directly from the immigrants' universal practice of putting their children to work as early as possible, keeping them in the household as long as possible, and exacting from them as much income as possible. Adolescence in families of this sort could hardly be called a "dalliance" period. What dallying might have occurred was done on Saturday nights, in ethnic-group dance halls, clubs, community centers, and possibly settlement houses.

Adulthood

Adult status for males was achieved by combining efforts to succeed vocationally, taking seriously one's marital responsibilities, and showing concern for parents, relatives, and the "family name." Having sons was somewhat more important—since sons would perpetuate the family name—than was having daughters, although it was generally accepted that the mix of sexes was to be preferred.

As children matured and entered the workforce, the husband accepted the responsibility or challenge for raising the living standard of the family. Having lived for a decade or more in tenements, basement apartments, or occasionally duplexes—sometimes in a household that was much larger than the nuclear family—the family bought or built its own home. Since they had emigrated from countries where social-class division was a crystallized, integral part of social organization, established immigrants in the United States strove to better their lot. The husband was the moving force, making decisions unilaterally if he cared to, but often with the help or encouragement of the wife and other household members. Ownership of one of the nicest houses on the block brought the highest meaning and self-satisfaction to immigrants, for whom such an acquisition would have been impossible in their homelands.

Wifehood for the immigrant generation was a transient and never clearly developed female role. Motherhood, however, in modern parlance, "went on forever." Specifically, being a mother involved nurturing and monitoring children's health and well-being, breast-feeding babies, keeping tabs on children, managing domestic affairs, and at least maintaining household discipline until the father came home from work. Mothers also paid attention to and helped keep alive kinship networks, acting as "kin keeper" for the family and spending what little discretionary time was available in visiting close kin in neighborhood and community.

It is difficult, in describing the immigrant family, to overestimate the importance of the immigrant mother, particularly the energy she expended in carrying out her multidimensional role. Daughters had learned the responsibilities and hazards of motherhood long before they left adolescence. Some rejected the prospect of becoming a working-class wife, burdened with children and with crushing domestic responsibilities, and sought careers. Spinster aunts were no novelty among first-, second-, and third-generation immigrants and descendants. The majority of women had no careers, finding their work tedious and unrewarding. Marriage and motherhood offered a dubious alternative to a life of industrial or shop work, but most women finally chose it.

Sexual Relations

Immigrant men found in America a land where sexual mores were less restrictive and channeled than in the Old World communities. Single men traditionally sought sexual partners among women who were not to be seriously considered as future marriage mates. Once married, men expected their sexual needs to be satisfied by a dutiful and accommodating wife. Ambivalently, the wife might be seen as a replica of the sainted mother or as someone with a suspicious but appealing sexuality. Immigrant husbands found it difficult to assimilate both images, but they did not hesitate to apply a double standard. Wives' sexual needs were considered secondary, at best; in many immigrant communities, they were not considered at all. That part of Victorianism that cautioned that sexual activity was a form of depletion of one's vitality apparently left immigrant men unfazed, except that some believed that it might apply to masturbation (Barker-Benfield, 1976).

Men were not above reproach if it was true or suspected that they might be lacking in manliness. The problem was easily resolved by fathering children, especially sons. If he had no children, the husband had an excuse—his wife obviously was barren!

Old Age

Many immigrant men, particularly the several million who came to the United States between 1880 and 1900, went through all the later stages of the life cycle, starting out in young adulthood and living the next thirty or more years as husbands, fathers, and grandfathers. For women, it was a similar story, although some only later joined husbands who had preceded them to their new country. By 1920, the immigrants of the 1880s were either grandparents, returned emigrants, or dead.

Whatever economic security could be achieved by adults as they aged had to be gained through their own efforts and through the efforts of growing and grown family members. A federally operated Social Security system was several generations away; industrial pensions, when they existed, were woefully small; and investment in stocks and bonds was impossible for the majority of immigrants, who found it difficult to stay above the poverty line.

To achieve an income base sufficient to maintain a comfortable, if scaled-down, old age, adults had to save or invest wisely every possible penny.

In the tradeoff between putting money into children's health and education or into savings, real estate, or other modes of income-earning investments, the children's needs usually came out a bad second. It should be remembered that despite the prevailing ideology of America as a land of opportunity and riches, poverty was omnipresent. Immigrants first had to rise above poverty and start families before beginning to build, albeit slowly, their own type of retirement "package." As already mentioned, the goal of achieving a higher standard of living could best be accomplished by the utilization of each family member's resources and energies to bring money into the household. The standard retirement "package" then consisted primarily of a paid-for house—possibly with rooms rented and rooms full of dated but paid-for furniture—a savings account, and paid-up industrial (burial) insurance. A pension derived from a life of work would complete the package, but it was not always available. Old immigrant workers who had toiled long and hard were less likely to be pensioned off and more likely to be permanently laid off or simply fired.

Older people preferred to live on their own, but many found the desired, often realized retirement "package" impossible to assemble. Living with adult children, however, carried little onus. For most adult children of immigrants, concern and care for aging parents were indubitable signs of maturity, and status was accorded those who were most active in parental and grandparental care. Parents who lived with grown children assumed the usual roles of persons of wisdom and experience who could be helpful, of storytellers and purveyors of cultural heritage, and of performers of practical and necessary small chores about the house. When not too busy with household duties, the elderly had ready access to numerous local immigrant institutions, stores, markets, taverns, clubs, and community centers, and some visited the local library.

Still, the road to old age was rocky and strewn with a variety of obstacles. Most elderly people had exhausted their energies in long hours of shop and mill work. Poor health was endemic among the old, and life expectancy was short (50 years in 1900). Most could not amass the assets necessary to live an independent, comfortable old age, and those who did might not be well enough in their old age to enjoy it.

FAMILY CONTROLS, FUNCTIONS, AND DYSFUNCTIONS

Most, but by no means all, of those Europeans who emigrated to the United States through the nineteenth and into the twentieth century left behind rural societies in which local folkways and mores provided the boundaries for and set the controls over everyday life. External authorities added another dimension of social control, but the villages and towns usually developed local institutions that provided the rules of the everyday game of life for the inhabitants. Folk beliefs—partly mystical and incomprehensible, partly pragmatic and cautionary—gave meaning and instruction to those of a peasant background (Habenstein and Mindel, 1981; Campisi, 1948; Park and Miller, 1921; Ross, 1914). Life was restrictive but more or less predictable. The pace was slow, and change was strongly resisted.

In American society, the immigrants found that external authorities could and did affect their families and their institutions and could modify these social instrumentalities in sometimes alarming ways. School, health and sanitation, police, and taxing authorities are good examples. Against them, the distrustful immigrants could offer noncompliance and avoidance, rejection and indifference. The history of the Great Emigration is not only a history of movement of people from one land to another, it is also a history of efforts, group and individual, to maintain the integrative mechanisms and forces of one kind of society and lifestyle against the influences and controls of a much larger host society.

If the United States were to become a melting pot, the immigrant family, metaphorically speaking, was not to be its cauldron. Rather, it provided in varying degrees a safe haven from quick assimilation, ethnic bashing, and the Americanization for which in the early part of the twentieth century there was such a clamor. The immigrant family did not foster change; it resisted change—especially when its social space and traditional internal roles were threatened. But it did not, by the same token, declare war on change. To a judicious degree, public education was accepted, ambition and social mobility were encouraged, family members were helped to better themselves, and the American culture brought into immigrant families through the mass media was sifted and sometimes accepted. Fashions, fads, large-scale social and political movements, labor unions, child-labor laws, pensions, and medical insurance came to concern and affect immigrant families. The door to progressive thinking was never completely barred, even though the immigrant family was not a change-producing and change-oriented institution.

The test of this openness was in the experiences of immigrants who after some or many years in America, in immigrant families and communities, returned to their homelands and found the often-romanticized folk society to be small scale, "small time," restrictive, dull, and vaguely oppressive. The immigrant family in America might not have been a dynamic institution, but it possessed a protean ongoingness (Habenstein and Mindel, 1981) that must demand the social historian's respect.

THE "GREAT LULL," 1925–1965

Following World War I, in which America was a late but important participant, the country was faced with the pleasant prospect of becoming the world's greatest nation. There was no longer a fear of the German Hun, but

America soon became less concerned about prosperity and more about the conduct of its citizens and the emergence of a threat much larger than that posed by Kaiser Wilhelm and the often-warring Germans.

"Conduct" problems swirled around the refusal of most Americans to take seriously the Volstead Act, prohibiting the sale and drinking of alcoholic beverages, and the turn of the feminist movement, which had succeeded in bringing about women's suffrage, toward a new independence expressed in the appearance of the "flapper," a new free-spirited female who challenged the traditional role of woman as mother, housewife, and dutiful helpmate to a dominant husband.

However deeply these social phenomena were to jolt the expectable placidity of the twenties and beyond, they were of considerably less importance to a populace that had turned conservative than a stereotypical response to the spectre of *bolshevism*, the leaders and followers of the Russian Revolution, who created a huge and threatening socialist nation in 1917.

The blame for this catastrophe, in the minds of most Americans—and certainly most politicians—lay squarely on the Jewish intellectual. Reversing an earlier tolerance, if not exactly welcome, toward Jewish immigrants, this attitude was new and bordered on the hysterical. Writes Ben-Ami Shillony (1993:82) about Jews of the late nineteenth century:

> When integration into European society failed, the only recourse for them was to leave Europe and start a new life elsewhere. Most of the emigrants went to the United States, the land of opportunity, where they could be admitted without restriction, and where they found a democratic society nearly free of anti-Semitism. Between the Russian pogroms in 1881 and the outbreak of World War I in 1914 more than two million Jews, or about one-fifth of the worldwide Jewish population, emigrated to the United States. No other people, except the Irish has transferred such a large part of its population to America.

But even before World War I was over, Americans were being bombarded with anti-Jewish propaganda, that often depicted the "Jew-Bolshevik" as a bewhiskered bomb thrower. Again Shillony (1993:83–84):

> The high percentage of Jews who took part in the Russian revolution and who belonged to European communist parties raised fear that Jewish immigrants from Eastern Europe might introduce the communist "bug" into America. The fear was enhanced by the fact that Jews figured prominently in American trade unions and left-wing organizations of the time. The resulting panic led to the U.S. Immigration Law of 1924, which limited each country's annual immigration quota to 2 percent of the number of its nationals in the United States in 1890. The law, aimed at preserving the Nordic character of American society, gave preference to immigrants from Northern and Western Europe over those from Eastern and Southern Europe. As a result, the annu-

al number of Jewish immigrants dropped from one hundred thousand to only ten thousand.

On the other side of America, immigration from Japan and China was totally cut off by a Congress that, spooked by the spectre of the "yellow peril," did not grant these countries even the 2 percent quota it granted European countries. To put the matter of the reasons for the great clampdown on immigration in 1924 more adequately: Jews were to be kept out for their intelligence and political acumen; Japanese and Chinese for their diligence and ambition; and eastern and southern Europeans for their poverty, ignorance, and clannishness. The argument that the 1924 immigration law and those preceding it back to the early nineteenth century were necessary to keep America from being overrun by the "hard to Americanize" or to safeguard the well-being of Americans in an established labor force being diluted by immigrants of a peasant or coolie mentality does not stand up to a careful examination of historical fact. A last point to remember: it was not immigrants who plunged America into its worst-ever economic depression, but rather an instrument of the well-to-do: the New York Stock Market and the untrammeled greed of its wildly behaving investors.

MOVEMENT AND FAMILIES, 1920–1965

Before World War I was over, several forms of internal migration were discernible. Those who found themselves in cities but were oriented to farming and rural life would push west, finding, in the latter half of the nineteenth century, rail transportation available and comparatively cheap. Much earlier, wagon trains had moved people to and across the Great Plains, but the railroads could do it better and, of course, much faster. The federal government assisted greatly with the Homestead Act of 1862 and with various mining claims arrangements.

For the urban-oriented, all larger cities by the end of World War I would have had grown within them nuclei of ethnic and racial groups containing, importantly for our concerns, three major social institutions: families, neighborhoods, and communities. Immigrants may have had it in their minds that they were coming to a country, but they first found their bearings in all three of these institutions. In many cases, the signal event would be a reunification with other primary relations; often this blood tie would be the basis for being allowed into the country.

Many familiars would be found within the neighborhood of an immigrant's choice, butcher shop, bakery, grocery store, dry goods store, and, of course, the tavern. Other medical/dental, and legal services and service providers, if they were not in the immigrant neighborhood itself, would almost surely be found in the community, which would also likely contain an immigrant-serving bank and, for parties, reunions, marriages and other social gatherings, the community center, often on the second floor of one of the larger buildings in the area.

The localistic life led in ethnic communities suited many occupants, from the newly arrived to those well settled in. But caught up in the ecological metabolism of the larger cities with their shifting, mostly centrifugal population movements, communities would move, one succeeding another, leaving behind a community name and often a few difficult-to-move institutions, banks, and funeral homes. A frequent relic was a small park dotted with statues of war and civic heroes not likely to be known by the new ethnics, racial groups, or (if downtown—and much later) white collar workers caught up in the gentrification movement. Those who moved might find their ethnicity somewhat tattered by the trauma of loss of place in the new country as much as the old.

Working-Class Dormitories

One much overlooked but important pattern of ethnic residential change, well under way by the time of World War I, was the "working-class dormitory" movement that took blue collar workers and their families beyond city limits to open areas and small villages, where the mix of ethnics could be almost random. This type of interior immigration substituted a new and different form of settlement to places "in the sticks"—5, 10, or perhaps as many as 15 miles beyond the limits of the mother city, in which could still be found the old homes and inhabitants left behind in the ethnic nuclei.

Working-class dormitory suburbs could be distinguished physically by rows of low-cost, often jerry-built homes lining the streets that usually began at a 90-degree angle to a main highway, which itself might begin in the nearby city and continue on a straight line toward the state border. Often these major service highways were accompanied by an interurban street car line. With street cars, busses, and private cars, the growing workers suburbs were well served in their transportation needs. Systems of transfers blossomed. The various forms of physical separation between the old and the new are mostly obvious; the difference sociologists notice are changes in place, including workplace commutation, greatly lengthened and time consuming; change of home styles, neighborhood, community; and what has been noted above as "familiars," many of which are subjective, hardly noticed or taken for granted, such as a vine-covered fence marking property ownership. Songs decrying the loss of homesteads are, of course, common in all languages. But new attachments to home, neighborhood, friends, local institutions are eventually rebuilt "in the sticks." The relevant question for sociologists is the extent to which all these changes through the decades have impacted on ethnicity, the repairability of old social bonds, and the construction of new.

A Case of Social and Geographical Mobility

The following case example of ethnic descent, marriage, and occupation is drawn from the history and genealogy of one of the authors. It is meant to exemplify the rapid mixing of ethnicity and occupational mobility in an urban/suburban context.

Gustav and Anne, immigrants, arrived in Cleveland, Ohio in 1880 and moved into the city's major German settlement. Gus was a skilled craftsman, a cooper. His wife was, all her life, a housewife.

The couple had three children. Two sons went through grade school, as did the daughter. All three married Germans from the area. The sons became skilled workers in a steel wire mill. The daughter's husband also worked there, and the daughter became a housewife, as did the marrying-in wives.

The two sons and daughter of Gustav and Anne had a total of three spouses, and later ten children, all of whom were German on both sides of the family. As the second-generation descendants married and started families, two moved to rural suburbs and one farther east from the German settlement, almost to a suburb.

Of the ten children in the third generation, three were female, two of whom became skilled in service and business; the third earned a college degree and became a professional. Three males became skilled workmen and went through high school, and four became professionals. The husbands of the three females became skilled service or businessmen. The wives of the seven males all had work careers, mainly in skilled services or business. Two became professionals.

In the fourth generation, all sixteen descendants and spouses have had advanced careers based mostly on college and graduate school training. Since the third generation, no females became "housewives only": one became a skilled craftsperson, one worked in sales, six were or are in skilled service and business, and the other eight were or are professionals. Gus and Anne would have been proud!

But their pride may have been tempered by the fact that although their sons and daughters married Germans, none of the third generation "marrying in" were Germans. Rather, the spouses from the outside were Polish, Italian, Irish, English-American, and one half-German. Gus and Anne would have been more than satisfied by the fact that all those descendants became professionals and/or skilled service and businesspersons, even if the trade of cooper got lost among the generations.

Eventually the "sticks" became suburbs that are all now incorporated and sit cheek by jowl with no open land in between. Currently a few light rail lines connect some suburbs, bus service is patchy, and most suburbanites, who take their ethnicity lightly, are multiple car owners and build their own environments around lawns and electronic technologies. Much like the "old" and "new" European immigrations, internal movements within the United States, particularly in the period between the two world wars, have also had an "old" and "new" character. Suburbanization in contemporary times has little to do with the "sticks."

ETHNIC IMMIGRATION SINCE 1965

Social scientists writing about periods of change in American immigrant history will likely not use the breakoff period of the year 2000 but instead may well start at 1965, when Congress passed the Hart-Cellar Amendments to the Immigration and Nationality Acts of 1920 and 1924. This radical legislation abolished the national origin system and all restrictions against Asian and Pacific people. An unrealistic quota of 120,000 persons a year from the Western Hemisphere was established and preference was given to those with occupational skills judged to be needed in this country (La Porte 1977; Chilman, 1993). The nation had already experienced a ten-year surge and ordinarily would have been ready for a lull. Not only was the quota immediately breached but the tradition of surges and lulls ended abruptly, and by 1989 the annual figure had climbed to 507,000 (Beck, 1996:40–41). After another seven years—and counting legal immigrants, including students on visas (many overstaying), and a realistic estimate of illegals—the total for 1996 was at least a million![6]

Granting the fact that the rate of immigrant growth, as a percentage of the total population of the United States, remains no worse than during previous surges, some view this gross number with alarm, pointing to specific impact areas such as Miami, Manhattan, Anaheim, San Diego, San Francisco, Minneapolis–St. Paul, and large agricultural areas where extra migratory workers by the thousands can drive down wages and displace established laborers. Organized labor groups have always felt trepidation about what seems to them the hardest of hard-to-organize newcomers. Other interest groups work in the opposite direction, and one critical example might be the relatively recent boost of Irish immigrant quotas, described by Beck (1996:41):

"In February 1997, an estimated 11 million legal immigrants were residing in the United States, most of whom work or are in families where the head of the household works. Most of these want to and are trying to become citizens; they face, however, a five-year residence requirement and an examination in English. Many will remain legal noncitizens. A federal law passed in 1996 makes legal immigrants who are not citizens, including those working and paying taxes, largely ineligible for food stamps, cash welfare, Medicaid, and disability. Of the 11 million legal immigrants (about 4 percent of the country's population), about 1.4 million receive some form of welfare aid. Their ineligibility for federal benefits will shift responsibility for providing aid to the states (*Arizona Daily Star*, February 9, 1997).

According to the first official estimate from the Immigration and Naturalization Service in four years, added to the legal immigrant population are 5 million immigrants living illegally in the United States. About 40 percent live in California, which together with Texas, New York, Florida, Illinois, New Jersey, and Arizona account for 83 percent of the illegal immigrants. More than half are of Mexican origin. El Salvador, Guatemala, Canada, and Haiti were the other major countries of origin (*Arizona Daily Star*, February 8, 1997). These figures double those of 1993, helping to shore up the argument that the problem of undocumented immigrants in America has dangerously worsened.

In 1990, after years of protests from citizens that the immigration numbers were too high, Congress approved what might be called the "Irish-Booster Wave." Congress approved the huge boost incongruously just before the nation sank into an economic recession.

What seems more inglorious than incongruous was the fact that the Irish-American members of Congress seeking legislation to greatly increase Irish admissions found it necessary "to accept all manner of promises that helped other special interest groups, and ballooned the total immigration numbers by 30 to 40 percent" (Beck, 1996:41).

What is most evident here is that the ties between the life chances of the immigrant, the direction of his or her ethnic group, and the ebb and flow of interest group involvement are virtually inextricable. And, as we edge toward the end of the century, the prospects for meaningful and workable change do not seem all that bright. Some are not that concerned. Sanford J. Ungar writes (1995:20):

Since World War II, a much broader range of people have come to live in the United States than ever before. The laws have changed, and the doors have opened wider once more—at least temporarily. But now the people seeking economic or political refuge and human fulfillment has grown dramatically, many of these immigrants look different sound different, and may dress and eat differently from what we have come to regard as typically "American." At first, some immigrant groups may seem far more difficult to assimilate into America's daily routine than most of us think our own ancestors must have been. . . . Despite whatever American customs they begin to observe, once these newcomers reach critical mass, they may try to hold on to and cherish their cultural distinctiveness and separateness as long as possible. They may choose to remain quietly apart from the crowd, to resist being smothered by the materialism and high-tech consumerism they see on television and their children bring home from school. Often this means that they continue to speak the language they brought with them and make a special effort to pass it on to their children and grandchildren.

Yet Ungar goes on to say the dream of economic success and financial independence and of being citizens, living without fear in a democratic country, they soon began to see themselves as Americans, an intangible but self-fulfilling feeling. He continues: "The great ethnic, racial, and linguistic diversity among the new immigrants is probably the main factor causing the old sacred melting-pot image of America finally to give way to something more realistic, like a mosaic or a salad bowl" (1995:20).

Ungar's term to define the ethnic environment of new America is "benign multiculturalism" (1995:21). Obviously, before we can use this concept intelligently, we must have more than a passing awareness of the multiplicity of cultures, particularly the new ones that are contributing to expansion of traditional American society.

Asians, Indians, and Pacific Islanders

Who are the new immigrants, and what in general can be said about them—particularly the cultures embraced, evaluated, and changed in the interminable process of family interaction and fusion of kith and kin? We can think of a dozen Asian countries whose names, if not people, are familiar: Bangladesh, Cambodia, China, India, Japan, Korea, Laos, Pakistan, Philippines, Taiwan, Thailand. Burma, of course, could be added, along with Malaysia, the Hmong people (without a country), and a generous number of Pacific Island countries.

People from these countries are settling, sojourning and studying, in the United States. They include mostly legal immigrants, many political refugees, and not a small number who have paid thousands of dollars to be smuggled into the country. More than half have a good education and would like to improve it. Some find employment hard to come by and will work harder for less, to the dismay of long-settled Americans. They will live several families to a room and eat sparingly to save the money needed to open a small shop. While they have a record of success in climbing the economic ladder, some who come as refugees are in effect supplicants, with as many as one out of seven living at or below the poverty line. Wherever they are, the newcomers are likely to be in groups and among relatives. They will inevitably speak their native language at home (Asian Indians are an exception), and even a third or so will admit to speaking English poorly. With simple eloquence, Harry H. L. Kitano and coauthor show in Chapter 13 the cultural changes found between three generations of Japanese in America. While virtually no first generation would or could speak English as immigrants, the third generation today are almost totally absorbed into, and making exceptional contributions to, the culture and prospects of America.

Readers are urged to use Kitano and Kitano's seminal chapter on the Japanese American family as a model of categories or headings for analyzing any ethnic family change taking place through two or more generations. For convenience, these categories are (1) freedom of choice of spouse, the concept of romantic love, (2) priority placed on conjugal bonds over filial bonds, (3) greater equality of the sexes, (4) more flexibility in sex roles, (5) higher emotional intensity, with emphasis on sexual, romantic attraction and greater instability and verbal communication between spouses. As Kitano and Kitano state, "It is a common process faced by all immigrant groups—the retention of ethnic ways and the attraction of the new culture."

Circular Migration: The Hispanic Example

In his comprehensive *Migrations and Cultures: A World View* (1996) Thomas Sowell brings together economics and social history in describing large-scale, repetitive movements of people who live in one place but migrate to and work in other countries. Some may remain and form settlements, but the majority have a circular work history. They are not refugees, they have almost a certain anchorage when they migrate, and they have a home, a place to which they are almost certain to come back. Understanding migratory worker patterns puts a new face on current immigration as a social problem.

From Asia and the Pacific islands the movements to America took place in the past half-century and were made with the intent to stay. Hispanics in America, some of whose ancestors might have lived here for centuries back, include those who have come to stay, some who cross and recross the border repeatedly, and an interesting and large segment whose peregrinations are routinely circular. This last group lives in their homes in Mexican towns and villages but spend many if not most of the spring, summer, and fall months moving from the rich agricultural valleys along the Rio Grande to states bordering Canada, working in fields and orchards. Writes Mark Potok in *U.S.A. Today* (September 30, 1996, p. 19A):

> The vast majority of Mexicans crossing the border into United States are migrants, not immigrants who intend to stay permanently. Like immigrants, many of the migrants cross the border illegally. But they come here to help harvest crops, and they maintain permanent residences in Mexico and return there when they can.

Migratory workers have a "limbo" status. Without migratory work, which pays Mexican laborers seven to ten times times as much as they make in their home country, the costs of fruit and vegetables would soar in the United States. Thus they are necessary to big business agriculture, but they no longer have "guest worker" status as they had during World War II and, as noted, they have permanent homes in Mexico. All in all, of those crossing the border illegally about 70 percent will return in two years.

In the rest of the country there are many non-Hispanic agricultural laborers who live in labor camps, using these for a base of departure as they move in and out of places of work. They may be lucky just to have a home base; but when they do, most still live in rural poverty. Florida provides a good example of the sheltering of labor camp migratory workers; for circular migrants, Texas, or California. The circular work of Hispanics may or may not be better for families left behind than for those who go along and do harvesting alongside husbands and parents. The latter choice offers more money per family, life together, and a little more independence from work bosses who "look after" the migrants' needs, housing, food, and the rest. For children, however, the constant movement from school district to school district is not a good way to get an education, but at least one way to live in a bilingual world.

CONCLUSION

The concept of America as a Christian, ethnically European nation with certain core cultural values now being threatened by those coming from other cultures, is erroneous, says Francis Fukuyam. "In contrast to other

West European democracies, or Japan, the American national identity has never been linked directly to ethnicity or religion" (1993:154). Rather, there is a common American culture whose elements are visible today, including belief in the Constitution and the individualist-egalitarianism principles underlying it.

The notion that immigrants' family values are discordant and erosive does not stand up to examination. The social pathologies of American center cities and the concurrent collapse of family structure are not a foreign import. As Fukuyama points out, Third World family values have remained relatively strong and remain so wherever immigrant ethnic groups are together. It's not the family values that are collapsing in Third World countries but the local economies that are being swept aside by invasive large-scale, internationally based capitalistic enterprises (Greider: 1997).

Given rising birth rates and internal migration to new foreign-owned or controlled factories, there almost inevitably follows a surplus of labor and the introduction of cost-cutting measures. Employment in Third World countries may, ironically, lead to unemployment, and cost cutting to overproduction. The excess of labor, particularly low skilled labor, is a major cause of migration, uninformed and undirected. (Greider, 1997:44–52). Unskilled migrants are the new *lumpenproletariat.*

But the labor-seeking emigrants do not leave behind family values any more than language and other aspects of their culture. Emigration nearly always involves some separation of kin but it does not mean family ties are ipso facto lost forever. For Asians in particular, work is seen as enterprise, even if to indigenous workers it can only be defined as toil. It would be difficult to define the enterprise of emigrants that has as its goal the growth and rising fortune of an extended family as somehow a dilution of American family values. Rather, networks of communication arise, permitting families and relatives to keep in touch, and great efforts will be expended to bring them together. Informal networks are boosted by formal agencies and federal offices. As the body of immigration law swells, so do the number of immigration lawyers. Things may move slowly, particularly for emigrants seeking refugee status, with hearing officers overwhelmed by applicants. Under these circumstances, it is hard to fault emigrants for their ethnic cohesion, nor family members and extended kin for their solidarity.

When center cities overflow with an incredible number of emigrants, who willy-nilly find themselves displacing each other person by person, ethnic group by ethnic group in hotel service, parking houses, or chicken processing, it is not difficult to understand the rising antagonism among the new groups. It is at this time that both Third World and indigenous groups, particularly the young, begin to question traditional American values.

REFERENCES

Barker-Benfield, G. 1976. *The Horrors of the Half-Known Life.* New York: Harper & Row.

Beck, R. 1996. *The Case Against Immigration: The Moral, Economic, Social, and Environmental Reasons for Reducing U.S. Immigration Back to Traditional Levels.* New York, London: W. W. Norton.

Braudel, F. 1982. *The Wheels of Commerce. Vol. 4, Civilization and Capitalism.* New York: Harper & Row.

Brimelow, P. 1996. *Alien Nation: Common Sense About America's Immigration Disaster.* New York: Harper Perennial.

Campisi, P. 1948. "Ethnic Family Patterns: The Italian Family in the United States." *American Journal of Sociology, 53,* 443–449.

Chilman, C. 1993. "Hispanic Families in the United States." In Harriet Pipes McAdoo (Ed.), *Family Ethnicity: Strength in Diversity.* Newbury Park, CA: Sage.

Duncan, H. 1933. *Immigration and Assimilation.* Lexington, MA: Heath.

Fast, H. 1977. *The Immigrants.* Boston: Houghton Mifflin.

Feldstein, S., and Costello, L. (Eds.) 1974. *The Ordeal of Assimilation.* Garden City, NJ: Doubleday, Anchor Books.

Fukuyama, F. 1994. "Immigrants and Family Values." In Nicholas Mills (Ed.), *Arguing Immigration.* New York: Simon and Schuster.

Gordon, M. (Ed.) 1978. *The American Family in Social-Historical Perspective.* New York: St. Martin's Press.

Greider, W. 1997. *One World: The Manic Logic of Global Capitalism.* New York: Simon and Schuster.

Habenstein, R. W. 1995. *Chicago Light: Selected Sociological Writings of Robert W. Habenstein.* Green Valley, AZ: Robert W. Habenstein.

Habenstein, R. and Mindel, C. 1981. "The American Ethnic Family: Protean and Adaptive." In C. Mindel and R. Habenstein (Eds.), *Ethnic Families in America: Patterns and Variations,* 2nd ed. New York and Oxford: Elsevier.

Hartmann, E. 1948. *The Movement to Americanize the Immigrant.* New York: Columbia University Press.

Jones, M. 1976. *Destination America.* New York: Holt, Rinehart, and Winston.

Kennedy, P. 1994. *Preparing for the Twenty-First Century.* New York: Vantage Books. [See the excellently chosen comprehensive bibliography, including institutional works, government publications, and authored works.]

Kitano, H. L. H. 1980. "Japanese Americans." In S. Thernstrom (Ed.), *Harvard Encyclopedia of American Ethnic Groups.* Cambridge: Harvard University Press.

Knapp, V. 1976. *Europe in the Era of Social Transformation: 1700–Present.* Englewood Cliffs, NJ: Prentice-Hall.

La Porte, B. 1977. "Visibility of the New Immigrants." *Society, 14*(6), 18–22.

McAdoo, H. (Ed.) 1993. *Family Ethnicity: Strength in Diversity.* Newbury Park, CA: Sage.

McLaughlin, V. 1978. "Patterns of Work and Family Organization: Buffalo's Italians." *Journal of Interdisciplinary History, 2,* (1971), 299–314. Reprinted in M. Gordon (Ed.), *The American Family in Social-Historical Perspective.* New York: St. Martin's Press.

Mills, N. (Ed.) 1994. *Arguing Immigration: The Debate over the Face of America.* New York: Simon and Schuster (Touchstone Books).

Mindel, C., Habenstein, R., and Wright, R. (Eds.) 1988. *Ethnic Families in America: Patterns and Variations,* 3rd ed. New York and Oxford: Elsevier.

Mindel, C., and Habenstein, R. (Eds.) 1981. *Ethnic Families in America: Patterns and Variations,* 2nd ed. New York and Oxford: Elsevier.

Moynihan, D. 1996. *Miles to Go: A Personal History of Social Policy.* Cambridge: Harvard University Press.

Park and Miller, H. 1921. *Old World Traits Transplanted.* New York: Harper & Row.

Parrillo, V. 1991. "The Immigrant Family: Securing the American Dream." *Journal of Contemporary Family Studies, 12,* 131–145.

Roberts, K. 1920. *Why Europe Leaves Home: A True Account of the Reasons Which Cause Central Europeans to Overrun America.* New York: Bobbs-Merrill.

Ross, E. 1914. *The Old World and the New.* Englewood Cliffs, NJ: Prentice-Hall.

Ryan, M. 1982. *The Empire of the Mother.* New York: Haworth Press.

Saloutos, T. 1964. "Exodus USA." In O. Ander (Ed.), *In the Trek of the Immigrants: Essays presented to Carl Wittke* (pp. 197–215). Rock Island, IL: Augustana College Library.

Shillony, Ben-Ami. 1991. *The Jews and the Japanese.* Rutland, VT: Charles T. Tuttle.

Sinclair, U. 1905. *The Jungle.* [Reprinted 1960.] New York: New American Library.

Sowell, T. 1996. *Migrations and Culture.* New York: Basic Books.

Taylor, P. 1971. *The Distant Magnet: European Emigration to the USA.* New York: Harper & Row.

Tentler, L. 1981. "The Working-Class Daughter, 1900–1930." In M. Albin and D. Cavallo (Eds.), *Family Life in America, 1600–2000* (pp. 184–202). St. James, NY: Revisionary Press.

Ungar, S. 1995. *Fresh Blood: The New American Immigrants.* New York: Simon and Schuster.

3 The Irish-American Family

Ellen Somers Horgan

INTRODUCTION

This chapter combines historical research, the sociological eye, and detailed memories of growing up in a Massachusetts Irish parish community to chronicle the dynamics of change and development of new meanings among one of the more successful ethnic groups to come to America. An early-arriving group, the Irish immigrants successfully made the shift from life in a disorganized rural setting to an adaptive existence in the turbulence of growing American cities.

In addition to distinctive cultural mannerisms, the Irish brought with them to mid-nineteenth-century America a well-structured variant of the stem family that emphasized familism (a set of beliefs in which the family places its welfare above the idiosyncratic wishes of any one person) matched with a modified, bilateral, extended-kinship system in which consanguineal (blood descent) and sibling relationships were stressed. The role of the church, for most, was central, and parish organization tended to define the limits of the local community. Following World War II, a variety of family lifestyles emerged to make being Irish a complex human condition and to make the specification of the typical American Catholic Irish family difficult indeed.

The assimilation of the Irish to American life has been extensive. As a consequence, writing about their family lifestyles is not easy, especially considering that immigration from Ireland to America took place over a period of at least 200 years—and that the heaviest immigration occurred after the middle and throughout the latter decades of the nineteenth century and, at a somewhat reduced rate, into the twentieth century. Current books and articles on the American Irish, moreover, have concentrated little on the family, and detailed studies of the major cities in which the Irish settled are only now being published. Recent studies indicate that the Irish experience differed depending on the economic opportunity structure, the characteristics of native-born persons in the area, and the nature of the ethnic and racial composition of the urban centers in which the Irish settled (Thernstrom,

1973:220–261). Finally, there are contradictions within the scholarly literature as well as in more popular works.

HISTORICAL BACKGROUND

The history of Ireland is complex. The most significant political fact is that Ireland was ruthlessly subjugated by England, which maintained the country as an agricultural colony for its own interest and that of the minority Protestant citizens of Ireland. Declared under the lordship of Henry II (of England) in 1169, the Irish have a turbulent history of battle, rebellion, intrigue, settlement, suffering, terrorism, and pauperism. Independence was attained in 1922: the current Republic of Ireland is independent of England and populated heavily by Catholics, whereas Northern Ireland is still tied to the English Parliament and dominated by Protestants. This portion of the chapter will focus on only the socioeconomic and familial contexts in which the emigrants made their decisions to come to this country.

The first notable characteristic of American Irish families is that in matters concerning the history of their immigration and early experiences here, Irish families failed to pass on information much beyond the second generation,[1] except in the case of an important relative or a few startling events. Families, most of whose members were illiterate on arrival, also taught little to their children about the history of Ireland. Yet pride in being Irish, and of so identifying oneself, is characteristic of most American Irish.

Socioeconomic Background of Irish Migrations

The reasons for the Irish emigration were many,[2] but the interaction of the patterns of rural Irish society with political, economic, and demographic catastrophes were the most important. Briefly, England kept Ireland as a rural colony, taking steps to destroy the beginnings of industrialization. The population increased from approximately 4.5 million in the last half of the eighteenth century to over 8 million by 1845 (Adams, 1932:3–4; Brody, 1974:49). The excess could not be funneled into a growing industrial economy; in fact, urban growth declined from 1851 to 1891 (Kennedy, 1973: 156–157). Concomitant with this large population increase, subdivision of

---

[1]The numbering system for generations may be confusing. "First generation" refers to the immigrants; "second generation" to the children of the immigrants; "third generation" to the grandchildren of the immigrants, and so on.

[2]For details, see Beckett (1966) for a concise history of Ireland; Adams (1932) for the coalescing of reasons for emigration from 1815 to 1845; and Schrier (1958), Kennedy (1973), and Brody (1974) for short summaries of relevant eighteenth- and nineteenth-century history. Also see Marx and Engels (1970).

the land became prevalent, facilitated by the widespread use of the potato for subsistence.[3]

From 1695 to 1746, Penal Laws were passed that resulted in legal discrimination against the Catholic majority, forging in the minds of the Irish a belief that their national identity and religion were one. During the eighteenth and nineteenth centuries, the peasants tried several times but failed to rid themselves of the oppression of both England and the Irish Protestant minority. In addition, famines caused by the infamous potato blights occurred in 1800, 1807, 1816, 1822, 1839, 1845–1848 (the "Great Famine"), 1863, and 1879 (Kennedy, 1973:27). These famines exacerbated what was already a situation of declining living standards. In the most difficult economic periods, the peasants turned on their landlords and the landlords' agents. These proximate causes for the resulting emigrations were bound up with the ownership and use of land.

Landlordism.   By the eighteenth century, most of the land in Ireland was owned by either the gentry or a landlord class, most of whom were Protestant and many of whom lived in England. Another class was made up of small farmers who held long leases and whose holdings were large enough to make a small profit for themselves. These, too, were primarily Protestant. But about 80 or 90 percent of the population, mostly Catholic, were peasants who leased land and raised grain to pay the landlords' rents.

In the latter half of the eighteenth century, when the cheap, easily raised potato became a staple, peasants began living on smaller amounts of land. Laws favoring landowners encouraged further subdivision of holdings. By the early half of the nineteenth century, subdivision had gone too far, chronic malnourishment was common, and the huts built to house the increased population were inadequate. During the famines, the destruction of the potato crop by disease led to the near starvation of the peasantry, who dared not eat the grain for fear of eviction. By the time landlords and peasants realized that land would have to be consolidated, it was too late to halt overpopulation and economic misery, and the peasants stampeded out of Ireland.

Stem Family Characteristics.   When peasants attempted to raise their standard of living by increasing the size of their farms, their method was a familial one. Under the Penal Laws, at the death of the owner or tenant land had to be subdivided so that *all* sons inherited the land equally. When these laws were no longer in force, farmers reverted to a stem family system of

---

[3]The population increase (aided by a decrease in the age of marriage for men) and the subdivision of land occurred when the use of the potato became widespread, but the cause and effect relationships between these changes are disputed by scholars. See Adams (1932:4) and Brody (1974:49–53) for brief discussions of the problem.

impartible—not to be divided—land holdings, with only one son inheriting the land or, if there were no sons, only one daughter.[4]

Because there was no principle of primogeniture (eldest son inherits) or ultimogeniture (youngest son inherits), fathers were free to designate among their sons the one who would inherit the land and family home. When the parents retired, the heir married and brought his wife to live in the family home, the young couple establishing themselves as household heads. The wife brought a dowry, usually comparable in value to the worth of her father-in-law's farm. The dowry was given to her father-in-law, *not* her husband; the patronymic went with the farm. Other children usually had to move out when the heir married. Their father then used the bride's dowry to make provisions for these children, sometimes arranging a marriage for a daughter with a neighbor's son, using the dowry from his daughter-in-law. If a daughter were the heiress, the groom brought money to the bride's father, usually in excess of the dowries paid by brides. The name of the farm, however, remained that of the bride's father for a generation.

The father and his successor wrote a contract concerning the rights of the retired couple. These often included space for sleeping; the provision of food; land to cultivate; perhaps a cow, depending on the wealth of the farm; and care for the surviving parent when the other died. Fathers understood that the relationship of mother-in-law and daughter-in-law might be strained; the contract specified that if conflict should occur, the parents would be cared for elsewhere.

The two fathers arranged the marriage. The details of the match were often completed within a week. The most important provision was that the fathers should agree on the value of the groom's father's farm, a decision that affected the size of the bride's dowry. The status of the groom changed from that of boy or lad to adult when he married.[5]

Several negative consequences arose for family members from this system. The successor was sometimes 40 or possibly 50 years old when he or she inherited the farm, which resulted in almost-compulsory delayed marriage, with singleness becoming common. Fathers often waited until near retire-

---

[4]Le Play (1871) provided the classic description of the stem family; Zimmerman and Frampton (1935) [reprinted in Farber (1966)] interpret passages from Le Play on types of families. For descriptions of the Irish stem family after it was revived, the reader is referred to Arensberg (1950), Arensberg and Kimball (1968), Messenger (1969), and Brody (1974). For a study of families that migrated from rural Ireland to Dublin, see Humphreys (published in the United States 1966; the fieldwork was done from 1949 to 1951). See Kennedy (1973) for a demographic theory based on the Irish stem family. Glazer and Moynihan (1963: 226–229) point out parallels between Irish rural society and the American Irish political machine of New York City. Stein (1971) uses materials from descriptions of the Irish stem family to interpret stressed behavior of young American Irish males. Scheper-Hughes (1979) updates personal dilemmas of stem family members in Ireland.

[5]Messenger (1969:68) reports that male age grading in Ireland is conceptualized as follows: until age 40, a boy or lad: until age 60, an adult; until age 80, middle aged; and after that, old age.

ment before choosing an inheritor, increasing the probability of rivalry among the sons or, if there were no sons, among the daughters. The wife/mother hoped to have a daughter-in-law (or son-in-law) with whom she would get along, yet her interest in harmony within the household might not coincide with the desires of her husband to receive a large dowry from the heir's bride (or a large sum of money from the son-in-law if his daughter were the inheritor). Unless there were only two children in the family, the system provided no structural way for the other children to obtain an inheritance equal to that of the inheritor. There was, however, a strong norm that the father should make some provision for the other children, however unequal this might be.[6] Additionally, the heir and his wife (or the heiress and her husband) were placed in the difficult situation of living with parents; consequently, their marriage was more regulated than those of their siblings (Mattis, 1975).

The major effect of the system, however, was to disperse the unmarried siblings of the inheritor of the land out of rural Ireland—a pattern of *neolocal* residence. At the time of the Great Famine, when land holdings were small and the stem family was being reinstituted, migration to an industrializing nation became an acceptable alternative to poverty and overpopulation. Two possible solutions were available for the dispersed siblings: moving to an urban area of Ireland (although economic conditions were little better in the cities), or becoming a landless laborer with no economic security (Kennedy, 1973:154–155).

Counterbalancing the problematic aspects of the system was a positive strength—the development of familism. The father accepted responsibility for the economic welfare of members of the family, and children accepted differential treatment in the interest of family loyalty. All members shared the value that the land or leasehold should remain in the family. Sibling solidarity was a natural outgrowth of familism. And, in fact, both the emigration out of Ireland to this country and the continuing economic stability of the farms from which the emigrants came were supported to a large extent by the savings of siblings and relatives in this country who sent money home, even though they were partially destitute themselves (Schrier, 1958:111).

Work, Authority, and the Sexes. The Irish believed that married women should not go out to work, also a view held by their church. This position was reinforced by the belief that a working wife diminishes the status of her husband, that women should stay home and rear children, and that jobs in a marginal economy should go to others. But unmarried daughters were permitted to leave home to go to work. In an economic class with rising material aspi-

---

[6]Mattis (1975) sees the role of the bride as crucial since the other children could not be provided for unless the bride brought the dowry to her father-in-law. She terms the bride the "grand liberator."

rations, some daughters remained single all their lives. Because the maintenance of an acceptable standard of living had become a dominant value in
Ireland, more important than marriage and a family, the numbers of single
people increased over time (Kennedy, 1973:159–160).

This increase in single persons was also a function of the low status of
women in rural Ireland compared that of with urban women in America and
England. Within the family, the father was dominant. He made decisions,
controlled the money, operated the farm, and did no domestic work. The
mother, meanwhile, was in charge of all domestic matters, but she was also in
charge of the ecological area around the hut (the haggard) and of any animals the family owned. She also did heavy farmwork with her husband and
sons when needed. Boys worked with their fathers and did no housework;
they were treated by their mothers in a warm, supportive manner. Daughters
helped their mothers, establishing a no-nonsense quasi-instrumental relationship with them. In the evenings, fathers and sons relaxed, but mothers
and daughters worked. The women were also subservient to the men, caring
for their needs before their own; for example, they served the fathers and
sons first at meals and gave them not only more food but also more nutritious
food (Kennedy, 1973:52).

Male domination had serious consequences for women in Irish society. As early as 1841, men had a higher life expectancy than women in rural
areas (Kennedy, 1973:45). After 1870, life expectancy for women in both
rural and urban Ireland was only slightly higher than that for men and not
as much higher than the same rates for women in America and England
(Kennedy, 1973:55). From 1871 until 1940 moreover, age- and sex-specific
death rates indicate that more Irish females than males died among children between 5 and 19 years of age (Kennedy, 1973:60). Daughters would
have been unaware of these indices, but they were not unaware of their low
status vis-à-vis their brothers and their future low status as wives. Daughters
left rural Ireland for not only jobs, but also for higher status as women and
independence (Kennedy, 1973:7). The uncommonly high number of single women in the Irish immigration may be seen as an early example of
feminism.

Migration Periods

Three distinct periods in the Irish immigration have been identified
(Adams, 1932:68):

Colonial Period to 1815. By 1790, the U.S. Census listed 44,000 Irish
immigrants (Adams, 1932:70), with an estimate of about 150,000 people of
Irish descent (Shannon, 1963:29). After that, the numbers arriving fluctuated (Adams, 1932:69–70), but remained low. Small farmers of an economic
class above the peasantry migrated (Adams, 1932:34–35); they were young,

often single, and mostly Protestants from the north of Ireland, of English and Scottish descent.

1815 to the Great Famine of Ireland in 1845–1848. Although statistics are unreliable for this period,[7] numbers arriving were approximately 50,000 to 60,000 through 1819; approximately 15,000 between 1820 and 1826; approximately 45,000 to 50,000 from 1827 to 1828; and at least 400,000 between 1829 and 1845. The total for the period was probably over one-half million (Adams, 1932).

The types of immigrants in this transition period changed little at first. Most were small farmers, but others were tradesmen, weavers, spinners, deepsea fishermen, shopkeepers, domestic servants, and, by 1818 and 1819, a number of peasants from southern Ireland—the first large exodus of Catholic Celts (Adams, 1932:104–111). By 1835, the latter group had changed the character of the immigration—50 to 60 percent were now Catholics from southern Ireland (Adams, 1932:191–192, 222). Whereas women made up about 35 percent of immigrants in the early 1830s, the proportion rose to 48 percent in 1835. More of the latter were married, because it seems that peasants first came as intact families (Adams, 1932:194–195). Single women continued to migrate, and the numbers of those who spoke only Irish increased (Adams, 1932:223).

Immigration After 1845: The Great Famine Period. About 120,000 Irish immigrants arrived in 1845 and 1846. Then, in only eight years (1847 to 1854), approximately 1.25 million people, mostly Celtic Irish, came (Schrier, 1958:157).

Irish nationals who came during this period were mostly Catholic peasants from southern and western Ireland. From 1850 to 1877, about 66 percent were between the ages of 15 and 35; for the rest of the century, the proportion of those 15 to 35 years of age was never less than 80 percent (Schrier, 1958:4). Except for the early Great Famine years, married immigrants rarely accounted for more than 16 percent (Schrier, 1958:4). After the 1870s, the number of single women increased (Kennedy, 1973:76–85). Twentieth-century immigration seems to have followed much the same pattern, except that more women than men arrived (Ferenczi, 1929:432–443).

To summarize, based on the U.S. Census data: From 1821 to 1850, approximately 1 million Irish entered this country; from 1851 to 1900, about 3 million (Schrier, 1958:159); and from 1901 to 1924, 700,000 (Ferenczi, 1929:432–443). After 1924, the Irish immigration declined.

---

[7]See Adams (1932:410–428) for a discussion of the difficulties of gathering statistics of immigrant arrivals and the kinds of estimate possible from different sources. The figures are taken from Adams. The writer, however, does not endorse Adams's view of the Irish immigration or his biased reporting on the Irish poor.

Social Context of the Lifestyles of the American Catholic Irish

Irish settlement and adjustment in the United States were embedded in a specific social context.

First, the Irish went to cities and stayed in cities. They congregated in Boston, New York, Jersey City, Philadelphia, Pittsburgh, St. Louis, Chicago, and San Francisco (Wittke, 1956:23–24; Schrier, 1958:6–7). The fact that a rural people became urban is not an anomaly, since the migrants entered as neither intact families nor experienced farmers. They did not, for example, have the technology for horse-drawn methods of farming (Kennedy, 1976:358). They were, instead, the young, single, dispersed children of poor, rural Irish.

Second, the Irish established the Catholic church as a powerful institution in this country. Protestant, native-born people feared and hated the church for both rational and irrational reasons. The church absorbed some of the hatred directed toward the Irish and provided the immigrants and their children a clear personal-salvation theology to help them with life-cycle stressors.

Third, the Irish had startling success, as have other ethnic groups, in building parallel institutions to provide services for their mutual benefit (Handlin, 1941:156–183, Kutzik, 1979:32–65). Kutzik points to the following five ways in which the Irish helped each other, including the aged poor: informal aid from kin and neighbors, trade associations (not yet unions), fraternal organizations, creation of their own welfare system through political activities, and homes for the aged, with nuns staffing and priests overseeing (Kutzik, 1979:49–57). These mutual-aid groups and organizations helped the immigrants and protected them from the hurt of exclusion from associations of native-born people, but they also isolated the Irish and impeded rapid acculturation. The Irish, moreover, coopted urban political machines and major influence centers in the Democratic party, the growing labor movement, the police and fire departments. and civil services in several cities.

Fourth, the Irish changed reference groups. Immigrants first compared themselves to their relatives in Ireland and considered themselves fortunate. Later, they compared themselves with other American Irish, congratulating themselves on success—or else resenting failure. Socially mobile Irish used double comparison groups—other American Irish and native-born people— and were vulnerable to an ambivalence thereby engendered, with the less successful Irish putting the more successful down, and native-born people not accepting them.

Fifth, the work experience of the Irish was harsh. On arrival, they did menial, manual labor, as did most of the second generation. They did pick-and-shovel work, building streets and railroads, and were, for instance, the main construction workers on every canal in the north until the Civil War

(Adams, 1932: 151). In the cities, men were, for example, hod carriers, dock workers, stable hands, street cleaners, waiters, bartenders, and porters. Women were servants, cooks, charwomen, laundresses, and aides to the semi-skilled (Wittke, 1956:25). Hours were long, pay was lower than that for native-born people, work was wearying, and employers often unfriendly. The stability of the family was fragile when work was insecure.

Sixth, social class was a factor in the social context of American Catholic Irish lifestyles, as has been often documented (Warner and Srole, 1945; Greeley, 1972; Birmingham, 1973; Rose F. Kennedy, 1974). Matza (1966), Thernstrom (1973), and Esslinger (1975) report, however, the slow rise of American Catholic Irish in the class system. The reasons suggested for the slow rise are the following: the pauperization of the Irish before they migrated (Matza); the low level of skill for work on arrival (Thernstrom); the discrimination against them because of their ethnicity, especially their religion (Thernstrom); values learned and perpetuated within the family, such as the need for security and lack of interest in risk taking (Thernstrom); and the large number of people who were economically mobile downward *(skidding* is the term Thernstrom used). This slow upward mobility is a fact of history that tied the American Catholic Irish to their cultural past. Colloquial terms (some are negative labels) have been used for years to describe American Catholic Irish socioeconomic classes. These include "shanty" Irish, "lace curtain" Irish, "venetian blind" Irish, "oriental rug" Irish, and Birmingham's (1973) contribution, "real lace" Irish, used in the title of his book.

Early Adaptation of the American Irish Family

America was ill prepared for the arrival of the Irish. Squalid living conditions existed in all major cities. The desperate situation in Boston described by Handlin (1941:93–127) were more than matched, for instance, by the miseries in New York, of which McCague wrote (1968:20–27). The immigrants found housing wherever they could: lodging houses; older, larger, subdivided houses; warehouses; shanties (huts); flats; and cellars and attics of old buildings. Sanitation was inadequate or absent, smells deplorable, and the water supply uncertain. Roofs leaked. Walls were damp. Garbage rotted. Privacy was limited. Cleanliness was next to impossible.

Under these conditions, family and community life were often turbulent. Men left for work early and returned late, as did many women; children and young teenagers roamed the streets. In the neighborhoods, pawnbrokers thrived; greengrocers often sold more inexpensive rye whiskey than other items (not exclusively to men); saloons flourished; idle men stood around, hoping for work; fights started easily and spread quickly; prostitution occurred. Handlin (1941:199, 121, 126) reported that after the Irish came, the city of Boston saw infant mortality rates rise, Irish longevity decrease, marriage and fertility rates increase, pauperism rise, and emotional stress increase, as did the rate of illegitimate births. Norms of rural family life and social forms such as drinking, argumentation, and visitation lost much of their meaning in a social context of high-density urban living.

Mattis (1975) found some carryover of structural elements of the Irish family in Buffalo from 1855 to 1875. Delayed marriage remained a salient factor in the Irish immigrant community; when both partners were from Ireland, the average age at marriage for males was 35 and for females, 31. The average age for native-born males was 26; for females, 23. Some Irish, females more so than males, remained single throughout their lives. [For 1950, Heer (1961:236–238) reports that both Irish males and females—immigrants and second-generation people—were more likely to marry late or not at all, compared with twelve other ethnic groups and native-born people. These findings are for the end of the Irish immigration.] These patterns in Buffalo may be seen as consistent with the need for the Irish to establish themselves economically before marriage and with the relatively high number of women who came here seeking increased independence. Mattis's finding of more Irish men marrying non-Irish women rather than the reverse pattern is consistent with her finding that some Irish women did not marry at all. However, by 1920 Irish immigrant men were more likely to have an Ireland-born wife (71 percent) than Ireland-born women were to have Ireland-born husbands (61 percent) (Carpenter, 1927:234–235).

Households Headed by Women. A significant form of adaptation in family organization appeared in the first decades after arrival of the Irish. Mattis (1975) reports that the proportion of households headed by women appeared high—18 percent in 1855, 14 percent in 1865, and 16 percent in 1875. Most of these heads of households were widows, partly a consequence of men marrying women younger than themselves (Mattis, 1975) and partly a consequence of the dangerous occupations of men and their early deaths. As another adaptive aspect, Mattis also notes that *most of the households that expanded to include relatives were headed by women,* a finding noticed in other urbanizing minority groups (Pauw, 1963; Rainwater, 1966; Smith and Biddle, 1975). At the height of the Irish immigration in 1855, families expanded to include parents, siblings, nieces, nephews, and some in-laws. By 1875, the added relatives were mostly grandparents, a finding that might be interpreted as a partial return to the traditional stem family or, more simply, as a reflection of the passage of time during which other relatives found different housing.

Additionally, in both 1855 and 1875, approximately one-fifth or one-fourth of the immigrant households had someone *not* related by blood or marriage living in the house (boarders and *their* relatives). This pattern is one of adaptation to the economic and social exigencies faced by women who headed these households. Women needed the money obtained from rent and assistance with their families. They also provided service for others who had recently immigrated.

THE ESTABLISHED AMERICAN CATHOLIC IRISH FAMILY AND PARISH LIFE: 1920–1950

Over several decades, after the mass immigration and the introduction of further Irish immigrants of a slightly more stable background, the structure, values, and behavior of the Irish stem family combined into an amalgam of the old and new. The immigrant quasi-ghetto neighborhoods in the cities tended to disappear and were replaced by the parish as the unit of community living.[8] Although not a large number were involved, some American Irish families moved as single units into the economically better neighborhoods. The majority, however, remained ethnically and ecologically nucleated, building community and family solidarity around the parish, which was organized by the church. The extensive description in the following sections of family life in one Massachusetts parish represents a form of marshaling ethnographic data through personalized and extended sociological anecdote as recounted by the writer of this chapter, who grew up in the parish described.[9] Apart from the lack of a parochial school, there was little to differentiate this parish from others in Massachusetts. The time period is approximately 1920 to 1950.

No justification need be made for the style of reporting, because there are few sociological sources of information about American Irish family life. Novels, biographies, and works on aspects of the American Irish experience other than the family abound, yet none of these sources provides the kind of sociological information readers may wish to know.

The Parish

The parish was an ecological unit, a community of families and an organized church membership. It was an enclave of American Irish families of the second, third, and sometimes fourth generation living dispersed among native-born people and a few families from other ethnic groups. Church administrators drew boundaries so that families of about the same economic

---

[8]The use of the parish as a neighborhood unit is common when writing of the American Irish, because the coalescence of residence, church, and parochial school (or public elementary school) within a small geographically closed area was a feature of the Catholic parish that the church administrators wisely fostered in the first half of the twentieth century. The parish as a unit has been used most recently by Greeley (1972) when he described the neighborhood of "Beverly." Farrell's *Studs Lonigan* (1938) also took place in a parish and Curran's novel, *The Parish and the Hill* (1948), contrasts a poor Massachusetts Irish parish with a Yankee neighborhood.

[9]Parish people ranged from working class to lower-middle and middle-middle class in the U.S. system.

level were included and built the church near the center. Shops were close to the church and included a drugstore, a laundry, two or three proprietor-run grocery stores, a gasoline station, a variety store, a shoe repair shop, a bakery, a liquor store, and a tavern. Some of the stores had delivery service. Many women shopped daily. Three public schools and a park were found in the parish, not always contiguous to the parish center. The parish served during the week as the unit within which social interaction took place.

Controls

The parish was compact enough that some of the children knew almost everyone and at least half the adults knew one another personally and knew more by sight. People with problems and children with handicaps were enveloped in a relatively closed community. Priests were a familiar sight on the streets, talking with adults and watching the young. Some men would go to the tavern at night, although a few might be there all day. Older teenagers and young adult men would gather at the shops in the evenings and teenage girls in groups would find some reason to shop or to visit the church. There were informal cliques among all age groups and, harking back to Ireland, most of these were age and sex graded. The pace of life was not fast. Small talk passed back and forth. Those in need were visited by the priests. Women individually and voluntarily helped other families at times of crisis. Lest this sound like a mythical village, strains should also be noted. While small talk kept people informed, it also made family happenings public knowledge quickly, worked to induce conformity of behavior, and reaffirmed prevailing attitudes. As a result, new ideas, different values, or changes in custom were slow to occur. Constraints on behavior were as much external as internal.

Families were, however, quite private about family matters; children were usually sent outside while family business was discussed. Adult parishioners kept private within the family how they voted, the size of family income, expenditures planned, gossiped-about sexual behavior, the beliefs of those who left the church, public events on which there might be controversy, job changes, and the futures of children. The conversations to which children might listen involved general discussions about politics and politicians, family events being planned, news about relatives, and comments about those persons whose public behavior was not approved.

Church Membership

The parish was an organized church membership. The priests knew every family. The activities of the family revolved around the church calendar as much as the school schedules of children and the work hours of men (and some women). Most religious activities and rituals took place in the church.

Mothers were responsible for the religious education of children at home. Boys were expected to serve at mass as altar boys. Girls participated in services on Holy Thursday and Good Friday. Children, if they did not attend parochial school, went to religious instructions on weekday afternoons and were separated into groups by school grade and sex. Catechisms were memorized and lessons listened to, with nuns as the usual teachers. Children were expected to go to confession on Saturday afternoon and, after fasting from midnight, to receive communion on Sunday morning. At the children's mass, the same nuns who taught religious classes supervised; again, children were seated by school grade and sex. High school students went to religious instruction on a week night, were taught by priests, and, by custom now, segregated themselves by gender.

Families were urged to attend mass on weekdays and to make short visits to the church when close by, although few did. Attendance at Sunday mass and the special holy days was required, and those who did not attend committed a mortal sin, serious enough to send their souls to hell if they died before confessing. Most parishioners attended these masses. Those who aspired to attend mass as a family, as Protestant families attended their services, were disappointed. Priests insisted that schoolchildren attend their own mass, and parents often went individually to separate masses so that the younger children might be attended by the other, if no kin lived nearby to watch the children.

Church and Family

The most important aspect of the church was the underpinning it gave to the structure of the American Irish family and the clear dogma of personal salvation it gave to members. The de facto theology, the beliefs that the laity thought the church taught (Osborne [969:40] uses this term), was passed from parents to children. The chief points of the doctrine were the following: Each individual has an immortal soul; people are born with original sin, which can only be removed by Catholic baptism; God is three people, the Trinity—God the Father, God the Son, and God the Holy Spirit—but yet only one; Mary, the mother of Jesus was a virgin and, when she died, her body went to heaven; Jesus became a man to provide an opportunity for people to reach heaven and to create a church that would show people the way to live. The Catholic church is the only true church and adherents of other religions, even if they lead exemplary lives, can only go to limbo, a pleasant place but one in which God never appears; all sins committed in one's lifetime have to be suffered for in purgatory before one's soul can go to heaven. The difficulties of life are to be borne as best one can; unequal talents and socioeconomic success or failure are unimportant to God; mortal sins on one's soul at the time of death prevent one from going to purgatory or heaven, so that regular confession is necessary; the list of mortal sins is long but include not only those of murder, lying, and theft but also disobedience of parents and others in authority, sinful thoughts, the use of contraceptives, adultery, fornication, abortion, divorce, marriage in a non-Catholic ceremony, suicide, lack of attendance at mass on Sundays or holy days—and others. A person who is a good Catholic and dies in the grace of God goes eventually to heaven to be with God forever.[10]

The sinfulness of people was stressed, but the way to salvation was clear: Follow the teachings of the church; participate in the sacraments and pray— keep the faith. Children were admonished to obey their parents, believe in their church and show their faith in such ways as not saying the Protestant end of the Lord's Prayer at school, by blessing themselves before batting in a ballgame or going swimming, and by wearing a "miraculous" medal. When children misbehaved, mothers suggested they confess their sins and, if they raised questions about Catholic beliefs, talk to the priest. When children, especially girls, were required to do something they found unpleasant, mothers suggested they offer their difficulties to God as a gift.

Fathers' and Mothers' Positions

The church affected family life by supporting the traditional Irish family's way of doing things. When the man lost the tangible sign of the farm as a basis for family cohesion, he did not forfeit his authority and status as head of the family responsible for the economic welfare of all. Because fathers' work hours were long, mothers were in charge of daily domestic activities within the family and some believed they had effective influence. Even so, husbands made most major decisions alone or perhaps after a brief discussion with their wives. Most important, the husband was in charge of money and provided a set sum to his wife, usually on a weekly basis. Few children had allowances, including those in high school and even some in college.

Men often decided on their children's occupations and educations and, although children's abilities were taken into account, their wishes were sometimes ignored. Fathers were deeply involved in decisions about children's marriages, but mothers' views were often heard that daughters should be socially mobile by making a good marriage and that marriages for both sons and daughters should be delayed as long as possible, certainly until the young people established themselves economically. In fact, both mothers and fathers emphasized good marriages for their children—in economic terms as well as in terms of the character of the future spouse. This was not spoken

[10]The writer wishes to stress that this is the theology as understood by laypeople in the parish circa 1920–1950, to remind readers of the extensive literature created by scholars and philosophers who have astutely interpreted Catholic thought through the centuries, and to note that the Catholic church in the United States has changed extensively since the Second Vatican Council.

about openly.[11] Going steady was discouraged, as was dating a non-Catholic. The father's position was recognized by the expectation that an aspiring groom would ask him for his daughter's hand, not always a ritual matter, for some men were rejected. But, apart from the mother's input concerning marriage, fathers decided when and how the family should move, buy items of furniture, purchase a car, and take a vacation. No matter how quiet, inarticulate, or unassuming the father might have been nor how kindly he exercised his authority, he made the decisions.

There were, of course, some women who *did* make major family decisions. Some of these had mild husbands who allowed them to do so. There were other women who might not have chosen to head the family but whose husbands did not, through default of character, overuse of alcohol, or desperation in the face of an indomitable woman. These were relatively rare. The more usual case was the gentle, friendly, hardworking husband who quietly headed the family and a competent, industrious but mild wife who accepted her husband's authority. It is unfortunate that the family in Ireland and this country has sometimes been portrayed as dominated by women (Greeley, 1972:110–113; McCready, 1974:164-165), since this view hides the real difficulties of energetic and instrumental American Irish women who accepted a subordinate role within the family. One problem was that some men acted at home in an arbitrary or authoritarian manner.[12]

Women were in charge of domestic activity, with some assistance from their husbands, who might take a child for a walk on Sunday, or dry a few dishes, or, more rarely, help prepare a meal. Living in tenements and apartments or rented houses, women no longer were responsible for the haggard, and gardening was not common. Women gained independence in spending the family's money. They also had the responsibility of rearing their sons through the teenage years. They kept up their homes and seldom questioned the family's economic status, over which they worried but had little control.

Marital Matters

As in Ireland, single women were free to work. Despite some stigma, expressed by married women, attached to remaining single, some women chose not to marry, as did some men.[13] Widows, too, went to work but not always full time in a regular job. Some became the itinerant helpers of parish families, helping out when life course events occurred in others' families. Married women usually did not work, either in regular paid jobs or with their husbands, except in small proprietary businesses at busy times of the year.

---

[11]See Humphreys (1966) for a discussion of the openness of Dublin families on this issue.

[12]Studs's father is an example (Farrell, 1938).

[13]Kennedy (1973:152) points out that in Ireland there was little or no stigma attached to remaining single throughout one's life.

The exceptions to this were women who helped establish the family economically and then stopped (as in Buffalo; see Mattis, 1975), or when their husbands were unemployed during the Great Depression or when the country needed workers during World War II (although even then few did). American Irish women behaved very much like their counterparts in Ireland and, out of each cohort of women, some decided to marry and rear a family (having relatively high fertility rates); others delayed marriage or remained single and worked. Widows had little choice. They ran their homes, reared their children, and worked. Widows, although treated deferentially by men, were not usually considered eligible as martial partners. Widowers often married single women, sometimes younger than themselves. Motherhood was considered virtuous; wifehood was rarely mentioned.

Children

Children in American Catholic Irish homes were treated as children, not small adults. Mothers were firm and moralistic but also kind, sentimental, and active. Children learned to be subordinate, obedient, and respectful. Children were also taught to be respectable—to do the right thing and to be polite. A spoiled, whiny, or bold child was unacceptable to mothers and fathers. Punishment for disobedience of children was external and expressed by parents, parishioners, and priests. Shame and ridicule, appeals to the embarrassment caused one's parents (especially one's mother), and mocking were used interchangeably by all. Success of children, however, was underplayed, was assumed to be a part of life, and, when told to others, was understated.

Mothers emphasized physical activity for children and often suggested they go outside and play or exercise rather than stay inside the home and read, hang around, or pursue hobbies. Participation in sports was emphasized, especially for boys. Achievement in school was encouraged. Since success in educational and occupational spheres had not been an experience of mothers, they pointed to people they admired in the parish and encouraged children to make something of themselves.

In one area of parenting, fathers stepped in—they taught sons to fight. Mothers disapproved of boys' fighting and hoped their sons would not become involved in neighborhood arguments. Fathers were ambivalent. They, too, did not want their boys to fight, but even more they did not want their sons to be beaten up or not to stand up for their rights. As a result, many fathers taught their sons to fight; and the boys fought, often over the issue of whether or not they would do so. It was also a part of the youth culture for a boy to be known as a good fighter; girls knew which boys would stand up for their rights and which would not.

Differential treatment by mothers of their sons and daughters continued, as in Ireland. Boys were treated more affectionately than girls. The importance of the boys' work future was stressed while learning how to run a household was emphasized for girls. Children knew from an early age that the resources of the family could not provide for all. If their brothers were older or equally talented, or almost so, daughters knew that the resources of the family would go first to their brothers. In less well-off families, older sons and daughters went to work and younger brothers (and sometimes their sisters) might benefit from the increased status of the family. In the better-off families, the older sons were provided opportunities, the younger waited their turn, and daughters hoped to be helped.

The concept of equal treatment of each child remained subordinate to the concept of providing as best one could for all within the context of limited resources. However different one might consider such familism by today's standards of the enhancement of each individual, there was the advantage that a family in which each looks out for the others has cohesion. Sibling loyalty is not necessary when there are adequate resources but, when they are scarce, some system of allocation *without* rivalry is needed (see Greeley [1972:115–116] on sibling relationships). Families that in the usual course of events had a relatively capable father and a responsible mother who was reasonably warm toward her children were strengthened by the concern of children for one another. When these factors absent, difficulties occurred.[14] In the parish, adult siblings kept in touch, assistance was given to one another when needed. All cared for elderly parents but in different ways, depending on their resources— paying bills, shopping, visiting, and having the parents live in their homes.

Sons may have been confused by being the recipients of both affective and instrumental behavior from their mothers in a way in which daughters were not. As long as sons could look forward to being heads of families catered to by their wives and children, major problems were avoided. If daughters could find a husband who would head the family and achieve economic viability, few difficulties occurred. Change the admixture slightly or lessen the priests' support of the traditional family, and some sons would remain bachelors, some would become priests, some would marry a less demanding woman from another ethnic group, and some might simply drink too much. Likewise, some women would remain single, some would become nuns, some would marry but have no children, some would try to dominate their husbands, and some might marry a man from another ethnic group.

Kinship

Kinship among the American Irish follows that of Ireland. Kin were people related by descent (blood) or marriage to whom one owed mutual assistance and among whom some marriages were tabooed. A modified bilat-

---

[14]See Stein (1971) for a discussion of stress reactions among American Irish *male* adolescents.

eral system prevailed. As an example on the paternal side, in Ireland the kinship bond extended from a husband to his father's father's father (great-grandparent) and all the kin in the descending generations were kin of the husband (ego); thus, kin on the male side of the family were father's father's brother, father's father's brother's son, and the son of the last. But all possible roots were counted, female as well as male, so that the number of consanguineal (blood) kinship *positions* came to thirty-two in ego's generation of first and second cousins. The church but not the people tabooed marriage with third cousins, but dispensations for these marriages were evidently easily obtained. Affinality (kinship by marriage) was limited somewhat, as the spouses of the siblings of one's parents were not considered kin, nor were the spouses of father's and mother's parents' siblings.

The importance of kinship to the Irish cannot be overstated. Although the household in Ireland was both the unit of economic production and of the family (nuclear and husband's parents), farmers needed help from others at times of planting and reaping especially, and families needed assistance or support for some events, such as childbirth, illness, or death. Help was given by consanguineal kin, who by so doing established a "claim" against the household helped and who could expect that when they were in need the household members they had assisted earlier would reciprocate. Household members were ambivalent about giving and seeking help, however, for household self-sufficiency was a matter of great pride. But knowing that the day would come when the household members could not alone solve some problems, families assisted others and stored up "claims" for the future. For minor matters, the immediate families of the spouses helped one another, but for major crises, the wider extended kindred were on hand.

At marriage, both husband and wife acquired the full consanguineal kindred of the new spouse, but only the spouses did so, not their kindred; the wife's parents and the husband's parents, then, did not become kin to one another. After marriage, the immediate families of each spouse were treated by both spouses as if they were consanguineal kin. Members of the immediate family were father-in-law and mother-in-law, brother-in-law and sister-in-law, and son-in-law and daughter-in-law. Again, however, the spouses of one's spouse's siblings (sister-in-law's husband, brother-in-law's wife) were not included as kin although there were often warm relationships among them. The extended kin of one's spouse were less important than the immediate ones, but in times of need mutual help was given, and on ritual occasions kin ties operated more extensively.

In the Massachusetts parish, the immediate families of both husband and wife were the close kin. For the couple, these included the four parents, siblings of both spouses (brothers-in-law and sisters-in-law), and children of the siblings (nephews and nieces). For children of the couple, relatives were grandparents, aunts and uncles, and cousins. And, although from the viewpoint of one's parents, siblings' spouses were ambiguously treated, children used the American system and made no such distinction between aunts and uncles in terminology or gift giving but did know which of these aunts and uncles were relatives by descent and which by marriage. In most matters, kinship relations took place between members of immediate families and more distant relatives attended weddings, wakes, and funerals. When godparents were chosen, one usually came from the father's side of the family and one from the mother's, symbolizing the bilaterality of the kin system.

Rituals and Rites of Passage

Marriages in the parish took place at a mass before noon and usually on a Saturday so that relatives and friends could attend. They ranged from the simple, with only immediate families present, to formal, with several bridesmaids and ushers. Festivities included a meal before which toasts were made, and sometimes dancing after the meal. Because of the expense, the custom arose of sending invitations of two types: one for the church service only and one that also included the reception. Families followed closely the usual American strictures about which family paid for various expenses of the wedding. Those marrying non-Catholics usually had a private service, not always in the parish. The non-Catholic was asked to take instructions in which the tenets of the church were learned and signed a contract with the priest present in which it was agreed that the children of the couple would be reared as Catholics. Almost as often, the non-Catholic was urged to convert to Catholicism. Couples were often engaged for a year or more in order to get to know each other and, equally important, to get to know one another's families. The wait also permitted the young couple to save money to furnish their home. Premarital sex was absolutely forbidden; so serious was the situation of a pregnant bride that the marriage took place in great haste, often outside the parish, and usually without announcement from the altar.

The American Irish wake is somewhat unusual. In the parish the family waked the dead person at home after the body had been prepared at a funeral home. The body was raised up in a casket with the upper half of the body showing, a rosary entwined in the hands. Flowers were banked around the casket. Usually for one or two afternoons and two evenings the family was home to meet friends and relatives. The rosary was said around 10 o'clock. There was sherry or red wine for the women, whiskey for the men, and food for all. The women often stayed in the living room or parlor with the casket, and the men moved to the kitchen. Much of the talk was of happy or humorous events concerning the dead person and the reminiscing helped families to mourn publicly and without embarrassment. Drunkenness and raucous joking were not as common as alleged; the usual case was that a few women had a little too much sherry or a few men had too much rye. Two male relatives often stayed up all night in the room with the body. For the religious services, the funeral home took over and brought the body in a hearse and the family in limousines to the church for the funeral mass. Burial was at a Catholic cemetery. Afterward, all returned to the family home for a luncheon. Very young children did not attend wakes, but by their teen years children in the family were expected to attend. The cars in the funeral procession were assigned by degree of closeness of the kin relationship or of friendship and of children by birth order. Many persons made contributions for masses to the church for the deceased relative or friend. Cremation was taboo. For people who committed suicide or who were apostates, there were no public services and their graves were located in unblessed land in the cemetery.

Baptisms were less ritualized and usually celebrated with a party at the parents' home. The infant was taken to the church by the godparents for baptism by the priest, who usually performed the ceremony on a Sunday afternoon. Children were given one saint's name. But the naming was deemed less important than the sacrament that removed original sin. Guests usually brought small gifts for the baby, sometimes money to start a savings account. Being a godparent carried with it the responsibility to see that the child was not only reared as a Catholic but also remained so until marriage.

The American Catholic Irish family, then, adapted to conditions in this country and succeeded in creating strong, loyal family units. Entering as the least experienced of the immigrant groups that arrived about the same time historically, they moved slowly into solid working-class jobs and the lower levels of bureaucracies, while some became upper middle-class professionals and others successful owners of companies (Birmingham, 1973) or corporation executives. The family of the parish exists in an attenuated degree in enclaves in several of our large cities today. Others who were more successful have made the exodus to the suburbs, bringing with them many of the attitudes of the parish. The children who grew up in the parish are the parents of today's young adults and teenagers. Some of these young people may go on to complete integration in this country without knowing much about their Irish ancestors.

CHANGE AND ADAPTATION

If we allow a thirty-year period for a generation, then young people today of Irish descent are the fifth generation descended from the Great Famine immigrants and the fourth generation descended from those who entered this country in the 1870s. Some immigrants arrived later, of course, and there are some young people today whose grandparents came from Ireland, but these few compared to the total population descended from Irish immigrants. To write about the new generations in general terms is difficult, since there are few data on family lifestyles of American Irish of different generations and differing social classes, with the exception of the now outdated

Warner and Srole work (1945), Thernstrom's study (1973), and Esslinger's book (1975). A few types, however, may be briefly described.[15]

The Enclaved American Catholic Irish Families

Some families remain in enclaves in our large cities or in nearby suburbs and work in blue collar jobs or in the lower echelons of government and business bureaucracies. This group still lives in parishes but now side by side with other ethnic groups. A study of parishes revealed that only half of practicing Catholics believed the parish provided any real sense of community (Gremillion and Castelli, 1987). This is especially true as neighborhoods have changed in their ethnic identity (Alba, 1990; McMahon, 1995)

The family is still highly important to Irish Catholics, as is their religion. The father has a tendency to make decisions for the family, but the participation of wives and children has increased significantly. Intergenerational mobility aspirations are slightly lower than in preceding generations. Married women are more likely to work to maintain the economic viability of the family, and the number of permanently single women has declined. While home ownership remains important, education of children is stressed equally. Some of the children attend parochial schools; some go to Catholic colleges. The views of the Catholic church are heard equally with those of the secular society. The group identifies itself as Irish; usually votes Democratic; and sometimes ignores the beliefs of their church, especially regarding use of contraceptives, although some young people believe contraception introduces an unnatural aspect to sexual behavior. Delayed marriage is a matter of the past, since both spouses work; women often work before the last child enters school. Marriage to non-Catholics is more common. Family schedules are less organized by the church now, while church schedules are more flexible.

Most have become members of working-class America but retain Irish identification. Structural differences in families have disappeared, but many of the characteristics of the group have not. These include the lesser amount of overt affection, the favoritism toward sons, the attitudes of male authority, the preference for action, the use of alcohol to increase sociability, the obligations of families to care for one another, and the gathering of family members for rituals and holidays.

Although this group has not risen high economically, its members form an important part of our industrial society. They also remain a slightly controversial group in our national life. The issue of separation of church and

---

[15]The types described here are not Weberian ideal types and cannot be, because the criteria distinguishing them are too many and the data on which to construct them too few. In fact, the difficulties encountered in trying to present even a few types leads the writer to commend Nancy Scheper-Hughes on her proposed study in Massachusetts of American Catholic Irish families.

state, for example, is seen not as one of civil liberties but as one of unfair taxation, especially in regard to education. Some are resistant to alternate lifestyles for families. They are loyal to this country and patriotic. Convinced that an activity is for the country's good, they are enthusiastic. When they believe that they are being wronged by government action, they will feistily resist. We need only recall the vehemence of opposition from South Boston Irish to bussed racial integration of the school system to underscore the importance of their neighborhoods.

Middle-Class American Catholic Irish Families

Among those who have risen economically, there is a diversity of lifestyles. A few types emerge. First, out of the strength of parish families, in which fathers and mothers stressed economic and educational advancement, and in which the children grew up during the Great Depression and the strains of World War II, have come professional and business men and women whose life-styles vary little from those of other successful urbanites and suburbanites. Many have degrees from private Protestant colleges, from state universities, and from Catholic colleges. They are integrated into American life, live in neighborhoods of professional and business families, understand well the philosophical underpinnings of the country, and have close friends among many groups.

Their orientations are to their organizations, companies, professions, and communities first—their church and neighborhood, second. The new Catholic church does not surprise them. They sometimes complain about the poor quality of parochial schools, which they help maintain but which their children often do not attend. Although not living and interacting with many Irish people on a daily basis, they nevertheless identify themselves as Irish, seem not to accept the pan-Catholic attitudes of the church, and note the ethnic backgrounds of those with whom they work. They are also identified as Irish by others.

This group is mixed in its political party affiliation—perhaps more of the lawyers and teachers remaining Democrats and more of the bankers, physicians, and businessmen and women becoming Republicans. There is little favoritism of sons over daughters. Their children appear less interested in striving for achievement or excellence in professions and business; some are downwardly mobile. Affection within the family is open, especially by mothers. Some of the women work after marriage; others return to work when the last child enters school.

Second, there is a subgroup of successful middle-class American Catholic Irish families begun in the 1950s and early 1960s, in the era of togetherness, have had five, six, seven, or more children *by choice*. Mothers are affectionate, worry little about their matter-of-fact childrearing styles, and identify positively with *traditional* American Catholic Irish families. The men are likely to be preoccupied with their work. They take small part in the rearing of children, expressing most concern when it is time to choose colleges for and with children, although they insist on the best available precollege education for them, and, having succeeded themselves, worry little about an improvement in the economic welfare of their children.

Third is a group among the American Irish middle class who maintain close ties to the Catholic church but in a new way. Many of these people were educated in parochial schools and Catholic colleges. They orient their family life around the church, and they bring the church into their homes, celebrating church holidays with family rituals or days of special significance for the family with religious rituals. As expected, they are active in churches, both with formal councils and groups and with informal groups that join together in members' homes to discuss issues, perhaps adding a semiritualistic aspect by sharing wine and bread. Some are active in the ecumenical movement.

The comfort of this third group of middle-class American Irish as Catholics and their serious concern with religion seem paradoxical when they state that many of the tenets of the Catholic church are not applicable to their lives. Many are in favor of abortion, sterilization, the use of contraceptives, and vasectomy. Others think the celibacy of priests is not necessary. Some think women should be priests. Divorce is considered an alternative to conflict-ridden marriages. They read and interpret the Bible themselves. They participate in communion and in the weekly mass when in a spiritual mood. Many talk of situation ethics regardless of any universal system of morality. McMahon (1995) speaks of this attitude in the light of the changes taking place in the local parish. Following the Second Vatican Council, the parish no longer was a haven from the outside secular world. Instead, Irish Catholics now used the parish as a home base from which to experience their faith. It also inspired and energized them to deal with the wider community and to approach social concerns in the light of Gospel values. Some have little understanding of more traditional Catholics, seem not to know the meaning of heresy, and find it difficult to understand why anyone would be labeled an apostate, now or in the past. At issue, however, is whether they can transmit their religious loyalty to their children.

The family life of this third group of middle-class American Catholic Irish is one of togetherness. There usually are two or three children; women do not work until the children enter school, although some obtain college or professional degrees while rearing their children. Men work hard but are more integrated into family life than other American Catholic Irish men. Children are reared with a mixture of American flexibility overlaid with learning of complex family rules. Some fathers in these families are less successful economically than those in the first and second middleclass groups.

Other American Irish

Many American Catholic Irish do not fit the types described. There are those who are third, fourth, or fifth generation and married to members of other American ethnic groups, some of whom were educated in Catholic colleges, some not—whose pan-Catholicism seems more important than their ethnicity: some live in mixed ethnic enclaves, some in suburbia. There are second-, third-, fourth-, and fifth-generation American Catholic Irish at all class levels who married descendants of native-born people, who have children with no knowledge of their Irish ethnic past. There are those who drifted away from Catholicism and the Irish parish without much concern; their descendants have little knowledge of their ethnic heritage. There are apostates from the Catholic church. Of these, some have joined other religious groups; others, who are not religious, term themselves renegades, apostates, agnostics, or atheists. There remain people of second-, third-, and fourth-generation American Catholic Irish who remained single or who married late and had no children. Many American Catholic Irish in the Midwest and West, and some in the South, were not reared in ethnic parishes, have little identification with the Irish, and are unfamiliar with the ethnic rivalries of their compatriots. Yet others in the Midwest and West, and a few in the South, were reared in Irish enclaves and who share much with their northeastern counterparts. Catholic "communalism" has ended for all practical purposes, being overtaken by American individualism (McMahon, 1995). In the loss of the parish as a cultural entity, a vital aspect of Irish Catholic ethnic heritage has been lost.

Issues of Serious Concern to the American Catholic Irish Family

As an ethnic group, the American Catholic Irish find issues that are problematic for their family life. Particularly difficult are care of the elderly, marital disruption, feminism, and divisiveness within the Catholic church.

The Elderly. Among American Catholic Irish, care of older adults is an issue. As in the colonial United States (Fischer, 1978), older males in Ireland controlled the family and the land, constructing a legacy of ambivalent response and wary distrust among the children. Stivers (1976:51–74) writes that male noninheritors of the farms in Ireland joined with their nephews in an avunculate, often symbolized by joining one another in drinking behavior. In this country, the pattern varied in that the male family head was away working while the woman reared children, including the sons, for a longer time period than in Ireland. Sibling loyalty, familism, and the strength of both parents led to behavior in the United States in which kin cared for older adults. Some older siblings lived with one another.

Today, some middle-aged children prefer expanding families to include older adults, other prefer care within a long-term care residence managed by Catholic orders, and still others prefer use of public or private long-term care settings.

Acceptance of Medicaid funds is difficult for some—not for others. Sons and daughters both share concern for older adults, although their functions sometimes differ, men more often being instrumental and daughters affective. Care for older nuns, brothers, priests, and monks has been resolved by some orders establishing their own long-term care residences. Not quite ready to relinquish the familial system of care and yet not always able to pay the costs of in-home and community-based services and residences, American Catholic Irish remain ambivalent and behave diversely concerning older adults.

Marital Disruption. Problematic issues for Catholic Irish are those of marital status and of parenting after separation, divorce, or desertion. In many urban areas there are groups of single Catholics, largely made up of divorced people but sometimes including widows, widowers, and people single by choice. Of those divorced, separated, or deserted, many seek annulments of their former marriages so that they may rejoin the Catholic church and then they may remarry within their religion. Joint custody of children is sometimes sought by those divorced. Single parenting and stepparenting are common among separated and divorced people and among widows and widowers. Remarriage is relatively common—sometimes within the Catholic church, and sometimes without. Men often marry younger women, thus creating a cohort of women who find a dwindling group of same-aged men to marry. (Norms remain that proscribe women marrying younger men.) Postmarital sexual behavior without the bond of marriage has increased, as has the number of people living together without formalizing the relationship. Problematic for single American Catholic Irish people is the link between their behavior, proscribed by their religion, and maintenance of membership in their church. Celibacy is not welcomed by many, nor are homosexuality, lesbianism, and bisexuality.[16] While some masturbate, this solution is also not a permanent or satisfying one for many.

Feminism. Another issue for the American Catholic Irish is the place of feminism in their lives. Although strong, directed women have always been a part of the group, authority in the family in both Ireland and this country remained with men. With the reemergence of feminism, several

[16]Heterosexual orientation has been the norm among American Catholic Irish. This does not imply, however, that sexual behavior of individuals has usually followed the norm or that there is an absence of bisexual, lesbian, and homosexual behavior among American Catholic Irish.

issues have arisen that have yet to be resolved—the three most controversial being passage of the Equal Rights Amendment (ERA), equality of women with men in decision making within all areas of family life, choice about whether or not to have children, and/or choice about the timing and the number of children.

Catholic Irish women are in many ways prepared to respond to these issues in terms of the history of the group. Yet the close link of the Catholic church with national identity has juxtaposed the issues in a way that makes it difficult for women in the group to ally with one another to gain equality. There would be little controversy over the ERA among the Catholic Irish, for example, were not the issue of choice regarding contraception and abortion a serious concern of the Catholic church. Similarly, egalitarianism within the family would not remain problematic were women socialized within the family and within the Catholic church to take an active stance about control of their bodies. In the present situation, however, where the three issues are intertwined with concepts of sin and with calls to become or remain traditional wives and mothers, it is difficult for women to distinguish among their roles as women, Catholics, workers, wives, mothers, citizens, and simply fallible people.[17] As a result, the defeated Equal Rights Amendment, equality within the family, and choice of family planning remain divisive issues with Catholic Irish families.

Divisiveness Within the Catholic Church. A final issue of concern for the Catholic Irish is the Catholic church itself. Many nuns, priests, brothers, and monks have left their orders with sorrow. Participation in the ecumenical movement is somewhat ambivalent, particularly after the papal visit in 1980 and after the papal notice for withdrawal from political office by those with priestly, sisterly, and brotherly callings. Feminists within the Catholic church and within the orders of sisters find their activities proscribed to more traditional behavior than now expressed, and their hopes for equality within the church may not be met. The tightening of rules about the ritual aspects of religion has led to some dismay. Calls for noncelibacy of priests (on principle and on grounds of assistance in the recruitment of priests) continue, although the same calls have not been made for orders of sisters. At issue for Catholic Irish in this country is the response of those affected by divisiveness within the Catholic community, functionaries and laypeople alike who hold alternate realities to those officially held by the Catholic church. Alienation from one's traditional religion is more than difficult.

---

[17]Mary Daly (1968, reprinted 1973; 1975; 1978), who is distinctively American Catholic Irish, has presented an ideological background or metaethics for radical feminism that illustrates the dilemmas of choice for American Catholic Irish women as well as for women of all groups nationally and internationally.

CONCLUSION

For every family characteristic described, some Catholic Irish person will find his or her experiences at variance with those depicted. Yet there are some cultural and structural tendencies that came from the stem family in Ireland and the established families in the United States that remain.

Despite numerous exceptions, American Irish families are still predominantly Catholic. Fathers remain heads of families, but egalitarian spouseship is rapidly increasing. Mothers continue to work at home and now with full-time paid jobs. Familism is still prevalent; sibling loyalty continues. Extended kinship gatherings still occur. Children receive sensible rearing. Loyalty to the family unit, even with separated and divorced parents, is emphasized. Enthusiasm for feminism has increased.

American Catholic Irish are still very much concerned with the economic welfare of the total family unit. Men and women appear to work for achieved status. Entry to active, rather than contemplative, occupations remains the norm. Many still seek secure jobs. Catholic Irish women appear to maintain resistance to the concept of work as more important than family. Interest in politics is little abated. Higher education is valued. Parents now exercise considerably less authority over the marriages of children. Sexual behavior—premarital, marital, postmarital, and nonmarital—now more closely matches that of other people in this country. Other tendencies have diminished.

American Catholic Irish families retain characteristics that differ from other groups—a striking example of cultural pluralism. It would be facile, then, to predict full structural and cultural integration in the future, particularly in view of the new ethnic assertiveness. If economic conditions turn downward and the gap widens between those who are economically successful and those who are not, ethnic competitiveness might increase. Such an eventuality would be tragic, because the American Catholic Irish have tried to transmit to their descendants a belief in the ability of those with differing backgrounds to live in peace with one another in this country.

REFERENCES

Adams, William Forbes. 1932. *Ireland and Irish Emigration to the New World from 1815 to the Famine.* New Haven: Yale University Press.

Alba, R. D. 1990. *Ethnic Identity: The Transformation of White America.* New Haven, CT: Yale University Press.

Arensberg, Conrad M. 1950. *The Irish Countryman: An Anthropological Study.* New York: Peter Smith.

Arensberg, Conrad M., and Solon T. Kimball. 1968. *Family and Community in Ireland.* Cambridge: Harvard University Press. Original copyright, 1940.

Beckett, I. C. 1966. *The Making of Modern Ireland 1603–1923.* New York: Knopf.

Birmingham, Stephen. 1973. *Real Lace: America's Irish Rich.* New York: Harper & Row.

Brody, Hugh. 1974. *Inishkillane: Change and Decline in the West of Ireland.* New York: Schocken.

Carpenter, Niles. 1927. *Immigrants and Their Children 1920.* Census Monographs 7. Washington, DC: U.S. Government Printing Office.

Curran, Mary Doyle. 1948. *The Parish and the Hill.* Boston: Houghton Mifflin.

Daly, Mary. 1968. *The Church and the Second Sex.* New York: Harper & Row.

———. 1973. *Beyond God the Father: Toward a Philosophy of Women's Liberation.* Boston: Beacon Press.

———. 1975. *The Church and the Second Sex: With a New Feminist Postchristian Introduction by the Author.* New York: Harper & Row.

———. 1978. *Gyn/Ecology: The Metaethics of Radical Feminism.* Boston: Beacon Press.

Esslinger, Dean R. 1975. *Immigrants and the City: Ethnicity and Mobility in a Nineteenth Century Midwestern City.* Port Washington, NY: Kennikat.

Farber, Bernard (ed.). 1966. *Kinship and Family Organization.* New York: John Wiley.

Farrell, James T. 1938. *Studs Lonigan: A Trilogy Containing Young Lonigan. The Young Manhood of Studs Lonigan and Judgment Day.* New York: Random House.

Ferenczi, Imre. 1929. *International Migrations.* Vol. 1. *Statistics.* Compiled on Behalf of the International Labour Office, Geneva. With Introduction and Notes. Edited on Behalf of the National Bureau of Economic Research by Walter E. Willcox. New York: National Bureau of Economic Research, Inc.

Fischer, David Hackett. 1978. *Growing Old in America: The Bland-Lee Lectures Delivered at Clark University, Expanded Edition.* New York: Oxford University Press.

Glazer, Nathan, and Daniel P. Moynihan. 1963. *Beyond the Melting Pot.* Cambridge: MIT Press.

Greeley, Andrew M. 1972. *That Most Distressful Nation: The Taming of the American Irish.* Chicago: Quadrangle.

Gremillion, J. and Castelli, J. C. (1987). *The Emerging Parish: The Notre Dame Study of Catholic Life since Vatican II.* San Francisco: Harper & Row.

Handlin, Oscar. 1941. *Boston's Immigrants 1790–1865: A Study in Acculturation.* Cambridge: Harvard University Press.

Heer, David M. 1961. "The Marital Status of Second-Generation Americans," *American Sociological Review,* 26(2):233–241.

Humphreys, Alexander J. 1966. *New Dubliners: Urbanization and the Irish Family.* New York: Fordham University Press.

Kennedy, Robert F., Jr. 1973. *The Irish: Emigration, Marriage, and Fertility.* Berkeley: University of California Press.

Kennedy, Robert F., Jr. 1976. "Irish Americans: A Successful Case of Pluralism," in Anthony Gary Dworkin and Rosalind J. Dworkin (Eds.), *The Minority Report: An Introduction to Racial, Ethnic, and Gender Relations,* pp. 353–372. New York: Praeger.

Kennedy, Rose Fitzgerald. 1974. *Times to Remember.* Garden City, NY: Doubleday.

Kutzik, Alfred J. 1979. "American Social Provision for the Aged: An Historical Perspective." In Donald E. Gelfand and Alfred I. Kutzik (Eds.), *Ethnicity and Aging: Theory, Research, and Policy,* pp. 32–65. New York: Springer.

Le Play, Frederic. 1871. *L'Organisation de la famille selon le vrai modele signale par l'histoire de toutes les races et de tous les temps.* Paris: Tequi.

Marx, Karl, and Frederick Engels. 1970. *Ireland and the Irish Question: A Collection of Writings by Karl Marx and Frederick Engels.* New York: New World. [This is a relatively recent organization of the writings of Marx and Engels which has been "gleaned from handwritten notes and fragments" (p. 15) taken from the Introduction by L. I. Golman (Moscow).]

Mattis, Mary Catherine. 1975. "The Irish Family in Buffalo, New York, 1855–1875: A Socio-Historical Analysis." Ph.D. dissertation, Washington University.

Matza, David. 1966. "The Disreputable Poor." In Reinhard Bendix and Seymour Martin Lipset (Eds.), *Class, Status and Power: Social Stratification in Comparative Perspective,* 2nd ed., pp. 289–302. New York: Free Press.

McCague, James. 1968. *The Second Rebellion: The Story of the New York City Draft Riots of 1863.* New York: Dial Press.

McCready, William C. 1974. "The Persistence of Ethnic Variation in American Families," in Andrew M. Greeley, *Ethnicity in the United States: A Preliminary Reconnaissance,* pp. 156–176. New York: Wiley.

McMahon, E. M. 1995. *What Parish Are You From? A Chicago Irish Community and Race Relations.* Lexington, KY: University of Kentucky Press.

Messenger, John C.1969. *Inis Beag: Isle of Ireland.* New York: Holt, Rinehart and Winston.

Osborne, William A. 1969. "The Church as a Social Organization: A Sociological Analysis," in Philip Gleason (Ed.), *Contemporary Catholicism in the United States,* pp. 33–50. Notre Dame, IN: University of Notre Dame Press.

Pauw, B. A. 1963. *The Second Generation: A Study of the Family Among Urbanized Bantu in East London.* Cape Town: Oxford University Press.

Rainwater, Lee. 1966. "Crucible of Identity: The Negro Lower-Class Family," *Daedalus: The Negro American*—2, 95(1):172–216.

Scheper-Hughes, Nancy. 1979. *Saints, Scholars, and Schizophrenics: Mental Illness in Rural Ireland.* Berkeley: University of California Press.

Schrier, Arnold. 1958. *Ireland and the American Emigration 1850–1900.* Minneapolis: University of Minnesota Press.

Shannon, William V. 1963. *The American Irish.* New York: Macmillan.

Smith, Hazel M., and Ellen H. Biddle. 1975. *Look Forward, Not Back: Aborigines in Metropolitan Brisbane 1965–1966.* Canberra: Australian National University Press.

Stein, Rita F. 1971. *Disturbed Youth and Ethnic Family Patterns.* Albany: State University of New York Press.

Stivers, Richard. 1976. *A Hair of the Dog: Irish Drinking and American Stereotype.* University Park: Pennsylvania State University Press.

Thernstrom, Stephen. 1973. *The Other Bostonians: Poverty and Progress in the American Metropolis, 1880–1970.* Cambridge: Harvard University Press

Warner, William Lloyd, and Leo Srole. 1945. *The Social Systems of American Ethnic Groups.* New Haven: Yale University Press.

Wittke, Carl. 1956. *The Irish in America.* Baton Rouge: Louisiana State University Press.

Zimmerman, Carle C., and Merle E. Frampton. 1935. *Family and Society.* Princeton: Van Nostrand.

4 The Greek-American Family: A Generational Approach

George Kourvetaris

HISTORICAL BACKGROUND

We can identify three major phases of U.S. immigration. The first phase represents all those immigrants who came prior to the American Civil War, roughly before the 1860s. During this phase only a few Greeks arrived. The second phase of immigration (1865–1920) includes those who came during the later part of the nineteenth and early twentieth centuries. The third phase refers to all those who came after World War II. Most of the Greek immigrants came during the last two phases of immigration. Most early Greek immigrants came to the United States during the second phase of U.S. immigration and industrial capitalism especially at the end of the nineteenth and beginning of the twentieth centuries (1890s to 1910). Late Greek immigrants came after World War II, especially during the 1950s and 1960s up to the mid-1970s. Very few came during the interwar period.

The second phase of immigration to the United States, which was carried out mostly by southern and eastern Europeans, was characterized by intense racism and xenophobia from the earlier European immigrants and their descendants. Most of the early European immigrants came from the countries of northwestern Europe, and immigrants from southeastern Europe and Asian countries were not considered desirable by the old-stock European Americans. The high antiforeign sentiments and the stereotypes held by the early-stock European Americans against the newcomers from southeastern and Asian countries resulted in the passage of restrictive immigration starting in 1917. In 1921, Congress first passed legislation based on nationality quotas. This discriminatory legislation culminated in the Reed-Johnson Act of 1924, in which the number of entering immigrants from southeastern European countries was based on the nationality distribution of the 1890 census. The clear purpose of the 1924 immigration act was to restrict immigrants coming from southern and eastern Europe. The Greek quota was set at only 100 immigrants per year. In 1921, the last year of open immigration, 28,000 Greeks came to the United States. In 1929, the annual

Greek quota was raised to 307, which remained the quota for most of the next three decades. Nonquota immigrants, however—mostly members of immediate family members—averaged about 2,000 yearly between 1924 and 1930 (Moskos, 1990).

Before the 1890s, most external migration of Greek immigrants was limited to eastern Mediterranean and Balkan countries such as Egypt, Romania, southern Russia, and Asia Minor (Turkey). At the beginning of the twentieth century, however, Greek migration shifted to the New World, mainly to North America (the United States and Canada); beginning in the 1950s, the new Greek immigration shifted to North America and Australia. During the first two decades of the twentieth century, about 370,000 Greeks left for overseas and about 352,000 (95 percent) migrated to the United States (Psomas, 1974), but a large number of them also returned to Greece during this period owing to adjustment problems and nostalgia for the old country. Between the 1920s and 1950s, Greek transatlantic immigration subsided. Beginning in the mid-1950s following the Civil War (1946–1949) in Greece, mass exodus from the countryside took place. A large number moved to the cities and a substantial number immigrated in what is known as internal and external migration.

Today the largest Greek presence outside Greece proper is in North America and Australia. Although Greek transatlantic external migration to these continents is more than one hundred years old, we sometimes refer to these immigrants as though they arrived yesterday. While there is no exact count of how many Greeks live in North America and Australia, a rough estimate might be between 3 and 3.5 million, most of them in the United States. However, we still find a smattering of Greek communities in Latin America, Africa, and the Middle East. Approximately half a million Greeks and their decendants live in Australia, making up the third largest immigrant group after the British and the Italians in that country. Although the presence of Greeks in Australia can be traced back to World War I, the majority migrated there after World War II, in the 1950s and 1960s; by the early 1980s and 1990s, external migration to Australia as well as to North America had almost stopped. During the 1950s, 1960s, and the 1970s, an estimated 1,022,000 Greeks left the country, with almost half going to West Germany and the rest to Australia, the United States, and Canada, in that order. A substantial number of these migrants were Greek students and Greek professionals in general. Most Greek immigrants to Germany and other Western European countries were temporary guest workers. In the mid-1970s, the energy crisis, widespread unemployment, and economic recession forced many Greek migrant workers to return to Greece from Germany. Many Greek workers in the former West Germany faced tremendous problems of adjustment and family conflicts, especially those concerning the education of their children.

The overwhelming majority of the early Greek immigrants were working class and came from Peloponnese, the southern region of Greece (especially Arcadia and Laconia provinces). Some also came from other parts of Greece and from the islands. A number of Greeks also came from Asia Minor. Immigration to the United States was looked upon as a vehicle of social and economic mobility, particularly for the farming and lower classes. In the past, immigration has also served as a solution to the unemployment problem of Greece. It has been reported (Fairchild, 1911:3, 35; Xenides, 1922:81; Saloutos, 1964; Kourvetaris, 1971a; Moskos, 1990) that early Greek immigrants, as a rule, were poor, had limited education and skills, came primarily from agricultural communities, and consisted primarily of young males. Included in this group was a small number of Greek school teachers, priests, journalists, and other professionals and semiprofessionals who became the apostles of the ideals and values of Greek society and culture. Like most southern European immigrants, particularly Italians, early Greek immigrants did not come as families because they did not expect to stay in the United States. They intended to better their finances and return to their homeland. Despite their working-class and rural origins, however, the early Greek immigrants had a lower middle-class work ethic. They were industrious, independent, and thrifty. They had what is commonly known as the "Protestant ethic," along with a sense of determination, cultural pride, ethnic consciousness, and community.

The late Greek immigrants were somewhat more educated and did not come exclusively from small agricultural communities. Many came as families, sponsored by friends and relatives who came earlier. Included in this group was a substantial number of students and professionals who came to the United States either to practice their profession or to pursue an education in American institutions of higher learning. By and large, late Greek immigrants followed the same occupational patterns as the early immigrants, becoming restaurant owners, tavern operators, grocers, and some realtors. Early and late Greeks were overrepresented in the service industry. As a rule, Greek restaurants are a phenomenon of the first generation (both early and late) Greek immigrants. Since the migration of Greeks to the United States has stopped,[1] it is only natural that the passing of the first generation will end the restaurant ownership among first-generation Greeks. In most instances, the succession to the Greek restaurateurs will not be the children of Greek immigrants (the second generation) but other ethnic groups such as the Mexicans who at present are employed by the Greek restaurateurs.

Although we find considerable differences between the early and late Greek immigrants and between generations, a number of students of Greek culture (McNeil, 1978; Sanders, 1962; Capanidou Lauquier, 1961; Scourby, 1984) maintain that family and religion seem to be the two social institutions largely responsible for preserving the traditions, values, and ideals of modern

---

[1]The 1990 U.S. census lists about 1 million Greeks and Greek Americans who claimed Greek ancestry.

Greek culture among the Greeks of the diaspora. The importance of religion and family to Greek immigrants sets them and other late immigrant groups apart from the early northwestern European immigrant groups. However, despite the importance of these two institutions to the early Greek immigrants, these very institutions have been challenged by the Greek-American younger generations and, indeed, some of the late Greek immigrants. One can argue that these very institutions have been eroded in American society at large.

Despite a considerable number of Greek Orthodox churches and Greek Orthodox priests in the United States and Canada (according to the 1996 *Yearbook* of the Greek Orthodox Archdiocese of North and South America, there are 667 churches, 631 priests, about a dozen bishops and one archbishop, who is the head of the Greek Orthodox church in the Americas), only a small number of Greek Americans are sustaining dues-paying members. Even fewer are actively involved in church affairs. Furthermore, while Greek communities and churches were established early in the present century, the year 1922 marked the beginning of the organized ecclesiastical life of the Greek Orthodox Archdiocese of the Americas (which includes the United States, Canada, and South America). The average Greek, both in Greece proper and in the United States, does not perceive his/her church and/or faith in institutional/organizational terms. A parish priest was closer to the Greek immigrant than the bishop, archbishop, and patriarch or the hierarchical and administrative leaders of the Greek Orthodox Church. To the Greek immigrant, a Greek church was a personalized extended family system of relationships interwoven with such events of the life cycle as births, baptisms, weddings, deaths, and religious and national holidays.

When the Greek Orthodox church was formally organized, a group of early Greek immigrants met in Atlanta, Georgia in 1922 and established the American Hellenic Educational Progressive Association (AHEPA). Its original purpose was to combat ethnic prejudice and discrimination including the activities of the Ku Klux Klan. Later the scope of AHEPA was broadened to include educational, social, political, cultural, and benevolent activities. It endorsed a policy of "Americanization" and urged all its members to become American citizens. Although AHEPA is a secular organization, it maintains some ties with the Greek Orthodox church in America and has become the formal linkage between the Greek and the larger American communities. Of a proliferation of Greek-American federations and ethnic associations (over 163 in the United States, and this does not include the village and regional fraternal societies known as *topiká somateía*) AHEPA is by far the largest Greek American organization, with an estimated membership of between 20,000 and 25,000 members in America. Other national associations include the United Hellenic American Congress (UHAC), with headquarters in Chicago. This organization is active in cultural, ethnic, and political issues affecting Greece, Cyprus, and the Greeks of the United States. In 1995, the Council of

Greeks Abroad was established in Thessaloniki, the second largest city in Greece after Athens, the capital of Greece. The purpose of the world council (known by its Greek acronym SAE) is to act in an advisory role to the Greek state for all the issues concerning the Greeks of the diaspora.

The American Hellenic Institute and Public Affairs Committee and KRIKOS are two other Greek American organizations. The former is a Washington-based Greek-American political action committee (PAC). During the last twelve years since its inception, the main objective of AHIPAC has been to monitor legislation in the U.S. Congress and activities in the executive branch concerning foreign issues affecting Greece and Cyprus. KRIKOS is a professional and cultural organization whose purpose is to mobilize professional and cultural resources among Greek Americans and friends of Greece to assist Greece in any way possible with its social, economic, and scientific development. KRIKOS also draws from the larger Greek-American professional community and tries to maintain and foster professional ties and exchanges with Greek professionals in Greece. By far the most important academic professional association, however, is the Modern Greek Studies Association (MGSA). Founded by a group of academic professionals in 1968, MGSA's membership varies and includes individuals primarily of academic professionals in social sciences and humanities. It publishes a professional journal and holds a conference every two years. The main purpose of MGSA is to promote modern Greek studies at the university level and disseminate modern Greek studies through its publications.

Greeks established other ethnic institutions, federations, schools, professional societies, and the ethnic mass media that includes over 140 ethnic radio and TV stations. Among these are about eighteen religious radio programs, both in the United States and Canada, forty-one newspapers and magazines, both religious and secular, and the Greek Orthodox parochial school system of about thirty Greek-American daily elementary and high schools and as many afternoon Greek school classes as Greek parishes. Most parishes offer Greek instruction to Greek-American children, usually two to three times a week in the afternoon after public school. There are also a number of private Greek-language schools (Greek Orthodox Archdiocese, 1996). Usually most of these ethnic institutions are managed by first- and second-generation Greek Americans and patronized by those who are active in the church affairs and/or other ethnic organizations. The ethnic press is often the spokesman of the businessmen of the larger Greek-American community and to a lesser extent serves the Greek-American professionals.

Although most Greek churches are bilingual, English is gradually but steadily replacing Greek and the priests are, by and large, American-born, second- and third-generation Americans of Greek ancestry. While most Greek Orthodox priests are American born, the bishops of the Greek Orthodox church are still foreign born including Archbishop Iakovos, who stepped down in July 1996 because of his age and poor health. There are about ten dioceses in the Americas, each administered by a bishop. The archdiocese, the administration of the Greek Orthodox church in the Americas, is located in New York. Chairman of the archdiocese is Archbishop Iakovos and the members of the Synod of Bishops representing the ten dioceses. In addition, there are four bishop assistants to the archbishop (Greek Orthodox Archdiocese, 1996:51). In the last analysis, language has become the differentiating issue between first- and second-generation Greeks. As a rule, the Greek language is valued mostly by the late Greek immigrants, who sent their children to afternoon Greek school, while the second generation tends to value an increasingly Americanized church. This general introduction provides the context and the background for the analysis of three generations of the Greek-American family.

THE MODERN GREEK-AMERICAN FAMILY

The First-Generation Greek Family

In this chapter, three generations of Greek and Greek-American family patterns will be examined. The first-generation Greek family includes both the early (1900–1920s) and late (1950s to date) Greek immigrants. In analyzing the ethnic patterns of the first-generation Greek family, one should keep in mind the sociocultural and economic antecedents in Greece proper and those in the United States at both the time of early and late Greek immigration.[2]

Coming from agricultural communities in which a large and extended kinship family system was more conducive to an agrarian economy, the first-generation family in America had no other choice but to follow patterns similar to those in rural Greece. Even in contemporary Greece, studies (Sanders, 1967; Friedl, 1962; Lambiri, 1965; Safilios-Rothschild, 1967b; Bardis, 1955; McNeil, 1978) have suggested that the Greek family is characterized as traditional, patriarchal, and rural and is one of the most closely knit families in the world. And, despite some changes in the social structure of Greece, the family still maintains its traditional values and character. For example, cultural and societal values such as respect for the elderly; the authority of the husband; morality, honor, shame, and *philotimo* (self-respect) are still maintained. The family as a social unit operates as a constraining influence against any

[2]The Greek embassy estimates the Greek-American population to be 2,000,000, while the Greek Archdiocese estimates it to be about 3,000,000. The 1980 U.S. census of foreign-born Greeks reports that 1.5 percent of the population is mostly concentrated in the northeastern and north central regions, with 2.4 percent, respectively; 1.0 percent is found in the South and 0.5 percent in the western states. Most foreign-born Greeks, estimated at 210,998 persons, live in urban and suburban areas. Insofar as selected ancestry groups of U.S. population, the U.S. census reports Greek ancestry at about 615,882, most of them found in the northeastern and north central regions. Moskos (1982) estimates that there were about 1,250,000 Greek-Americans in 1980 distributed among first, second, third, and fourth generations.

social and moral misconduct of the children and particularly of the daughters. In addition, Sanders (1967) reported that the family unit had to be strong and cohesive in the face of the hostile world in view of the fact that Greece has undergone political, social, and economic turmoil throughout its long history, both from within and without.

Thus, strong and cohesive family orientations and patterns were brought to the United States by the Greeks. For many reasons, however, this did not always work out. First, the socioeconomic conditions of the immigrants and the problems of adjustment and hardships they encountered did not permit them to replicate the Greek village patterns of extended families. Second, the presence of many siblings in the immigrants' family of orientation in Greece forced them to migrate in the first place. Immigrants, therefore, wanted to see their children succeed and projected their own unfulfilled aspirations onto them. The smaller the family unit, the more economic resources that could be used for each child's benefit. Third, the immigrants had many obligations and promises to fulfill in their home communities, such as to provide for their sisters' or nieces' dowries[3] or to pay their fathers' debts. Indeed, many early male Greek immigrants never married for this reason. Fourth, the overwhelming majority of early immigrants were males with no firm decision to settle in the United States. Finally, the immigrants had to support their own families in the United States and having extended families made this more difficult. Despite all this, a number of early and late first-generation Greek immigrants had large families.

As noted previously, early Greeks did not come together as family units: primarily young males migrated. Vlachos (1968) maintains that "very few females crossed the Atlantic Ocean in the early years of Greek immigration and their small percentage increased significantly only after 1923" (quoted in Kardaras, 1977). The scarcity of the first-generation women forced a substantial number of Greek males to marry non-Greek women (Mistaras, 1950). There is some evidence to suggest that those Greek Americans (especially women) who married non-Greek spouses follow the Greek Orthodox faith and Greek traditions. One can observe similar patterns in subsequent gener-

---

[3]The dowry system was an extension of the arranged marriage system whereby the bride's family had to provide their future son-in-law a negotiated amount of cash or property in exchange for marrying their daughter. The dowry system has long been a part of the economic stratification and social status systems in general which views marriage as a vehicle of class mobility or immobility for the parties concerned and favors the higher socioeconomic classes. For example, the higher the socioeconomic class or social status of the groom, the greater the amount of expected dowry. In the past, the dowry system has brought tragedy to many poor families in Greece, particularly to those with large numbers of girls. Since 1975, by law, the institution of the dowry has been abolished. However, in many parts of Greece it is still practiced on a voluntary and informal basis. Although the institutionalized form of dowry as practiced in Greece in the past was discontinued among Greeks in the United States, nevertheless vestiges of this practice continue to exist in informal ways in terms of gifts and elaborate wedding ceremonies provided by the bride's parents. The dowry system was more prevalent in the rural and southern parts of Greece.

ations of Greeks in the United States. These exogamous marriages were neither encouraged nor accepted by the more ethnocentric Greeks. Thus the more tradition bound the Greek male or female was, the more desirable was a mate of the same nationality and religion. Many of the early Greek male immigrants returned to Greece in search of a bride. Some had prospective brides arranged and vouched for by relatives and friends waiting for them in Greece or they simply had arranged a marriage through an exchange of photographs (Saloutos, 1964:85). The arranged marriage should be understood in the context of the Greek kinship system, where mate selection was an affair that went beyond the immediate parties concerned. It was also a matter of economics. Many early Greek male immigrants could not afford to travel to Greece searching for a bride. Furthermore, many of the prospective grooms had known their brides' families prior to coming to the United States.

Attitudes of Greek men toward American women of other nationalities were also based on a great deal of misinformation, superficiality, and poor judgment. There were many reasons for this circumstance. In the first place, early immigrants came to know America from the bottom up. Second, because of the ethnocentric disposition, Greek men perpetuated the widely held belief in Greece that Greek women had a monopoly on virtue, homemaking, and belief in the family (Saloutos, 1964:85). Third, many Greek men as well as other immigrants shared the belief that marriage in America was a "passing convenience," which also meant that American women were more lax in matters of sex and marriage and therefore it was easier to marry exogamously since it was easier to dissolve such a marriage. If a Greek man married endogamously, dissolving the marriage was not as easy.

In the past, the arranged marriage (*proxenió*) was more prevalent in the rural Greek family. At present, it is less often practiced. More and more, mate selection is left to the individual. Sanders (1967:8) distinguished three major types of marital selection in agricultural communities: marriage arranged by parents, marriage with parental consent, and marriage by the future couple themselves. The *proxenió* highlights the importance of marriage and of the family as an enduring, interdependent social institution. Marriage was to be taken seriously. It was not simply the union of two independent individuals but was and still is considered to be a fundamental union of two families. In the early Greek immigrant arranged marriage, romantic love was not a prerequisite in marriage, but among late Greek immigrant marriages romantic love and physical attraction play a more decisive role. The institution of the dowry system also played its part within arranged marriage and mate selection, especially in Greek rural marriages.

In the past, marriage and family ties were viewed as permanent responsibilities. First-generation Greeks would take care of their parents. At present, the situation has changed somewhat, there has been an erosion of family ties. Tensions developed between generations and the young live a divided life between two societies. In many respects, the patterns of the rural Greek family were continued in urban United States, but they had to be adjusted to the existing conditions and could not be replicated exactly. Today's generation rejects the old traditions. Marriage and motherhood are not the only option for women. Mutual attraction and companionship are more important in marriage. In the 1975 Greek Constitution, Article 4, paragraph 2 states: "Greek men and women have the same obligations and rights." No longer is the man the sole head of the household, but rather both husband and wife decide on family matters.

Another important dimension of family organization involves the structural gender role differences and decision-making processes traditionally vested in different family statuses and occupied by different members of the immediate family. Thus, one can speak of father-mother, male-female, husband-wife relationships and gender roles. The majority of fiction and nonfiction writers (Bardis, 1955, 1956; Safilios-Rothschild, 1967b; Vlachos, 1968; Saloutos, 1964; Petrakis, 1966; Chamales, 1959; Stephanides, 1972; Koty, 1958; Lambiri-Dimaki, 1965; Capanidou Lauquier, 1961 Moskos, 1990; Scourby, 1984) have suggested that the early Greek family, both in America and Greece, was a male-dominated, patriarchal, and close-knit social unit. In most of these writings the Greek father is portrayed as an imposing figure whose authority over the rest of the family members, particularly the wife, was absolute. The Greek wife was depicted as a submissive and powerless creature whose major role was homemaking and catering to the rest of the family. Scourby (1984:130) also argues that the "overall image that emerges of Greek women through the eyes of the novelist, the therapist, the ethnographer, and the social scientist is that of good wife, good mother, and good housekeeper whose needs are always subservient to those of her husband and children." This image of the Greek family's authority and gender roles was a carryover from Greece, and it was not unique to the Greeks. However, one can argue that these gender roles were contingent upon the socioeconomic conditions and the prevailing ethos in male-female relationships in the United States and Greece.

That there is an "ideal" and "real" dimension culturally and socially prescribed for every gender role and family member is well documented. However, one finds the tendency among students of the sociology of marriage and the family to describe normative/ideal patterns of gender-role differentiation as real facts. Most studies tend to deemphasize the conflict and pathology of the Greek family. With the exception of some studies[4] conducted by

---

[4]On the contemporary Athenian urban family, for example, see studies by Safilios-Rothschild (1965; 1967a, b; 1969a, b; 1971–1972) whose repertoire of topics is extensive and includes, among others, research on fertility and marital satisfaction; social class and family; deviance and mental illness; morality, courtship, and love in Greek folklore, and sex roles. Also see the study by Vassiliou and Vassiliou (1966) on social attitudes, stereotypes, and mental health in the Greek family.

On the rural and semiurban Greek family, see studies by Lambiri-Dimaki (1965) on dowry and the impact of industrial employment on the position of women in a Greek country town. Also, see studies by Friedl (1962) on dowry, kinship, and the position of women in rural Greece. In addition, Bardis (1955, 1956, 1967), Campbell (1964), and Sanders (1962, 1967) have also written on various aspects of the rural Greek family.

Safilios-Rothschild (1967a, b) and those conducted by Friedl (1967) and Campbell (1964) in Greece proper, as far as I can determine no systematic studies have been conducted on the gender-role differentiation and authority relationships in the Greek family at the level of role performance and conflict in the United States. The Greek woman's role was confined primarily in the private domain—including the home, church, and relatives—not in the public domain.

A more realistic analysis of role differentiation in the Greek family would entail a network of role complementarity rather than strict differentiation on the basis of widely held beliefs of male-dominated (instrumental) versus female-subordinate (expressive) roles. In most instances, a Greek husband-father assumed both expressive and instrumental roles simultaneously whenever the primary group (family) interests were served and family contingencies demanded it. The early Greek immigrant father, as a rule, was older than his wife. Most first-generation Greek men took an active role in the household chores, including shopping, cooking, and so forth. Some of these roles were learned in restaurants owned and managed by Greek immigrant men or arose from the fact that most came alone to the United States and had to improvise to save money. Ideally, the father was the head and authority figure of the family unit, and he expected respect and cooperation from his wife and children. In reality, however, his authority was contingent on his ability to prove himself and be a good provider for his family, a compassionate husband, and an understanding father. Masculinity alone, based on arbitrary exercise of authority without considerations of fairness, family unity, loyalty, trust, and common good, could not sustain the first-generation immigrant family. The Greek father was as compassionate and good-natured as the Greek mother, particularly in times of adversity and life crises. While he was primarily a provider for the entire family and had to work incredibly long hours outside the home, he helped whenever he could in the household chores, in the discipline and socialization of his children. These norms have changed in the contemporary Greek family in Greece proper and even more in the late Greek immigrant family. At present, Greek women work outside the home and men do more chores in the house.

The discrepancy between the "ideal" and "real" aspects of husband-wife and mother-father gender roles is also evident if one examines what Friedl (1967) and Campbell (1964) refer to as the "public" versus "private" domains of behavior in the rural family in Greece. In the public/social sphere, both husbands and wives put up a façade and behave according to the prevailing societal and cultural norms. These norms depict Greek husbands-fathers as if they were the true masters and dominant figures within the family unit. The wives-mothers, however, are expected to behave in a modest and submissive manner, particularly in public places when their husbands are present. However, in a more private family setting, husband-father and wife-mother gender roles change considerably and husbands and wives behave more naturally. What seems to the outsider to be the unequivocal dominance exercised by the husband over the wife is in reality not so in more informal family settings. In some instances, the Greek wife-mother was the most dominant figure in the Greek immigrant family. Her presence and influence was felt not only in the family but in the larger ethnic community affairs. As a rule, early first-generation women did not work outside the home and this gave them more time to run the household.

To an immigrant husband who left his parents at a young age, his wife was more than the sociological sex-role partner. She was the wife, the adviser, the partner, the companion, and the homemaker. She also assisted her husband in business and family decision making. Wives-mothers usually exercised their influence in family decision making indirectly through the process of socialization of the children because the Greek father had to work long hours away from the home. Children were attached to the mother, not the father, particularly in the formative years of immigrant life. Later, it was the wife-mother who had to approve or disapprove of her daughter's marriage, and then she would convince her husband. Furthermore, it has been reported by Tavuchis (1972) that among his "respondents and a large unknown proportion of second-generation Greek Americans, the father emerges as a shadowy, distant figure throughout childhood and adolescence but his sociological presence was always felt." In addition, the relatively higher status and freedom enjoyed by the American women vis-á-vis Greek women in Greece benefited the Greek women more than the Greek men in the United States.

Greek immigrant women have played an important role not only in the family but in the church and the Greek-American community in general. Moskos (1990) argues that the arrival of Greek women contributed greatly to the cohesion of the Greek-American family and indeed the Greek-American community and the church at large. As a rule, early immigrant women—married and unmarried—did not work outside the house. This contrasts sharply with post–World War II Greek immigrant women who, by and large, work outside the house—either in the family restaurant or in some other capacity as seamstresses, beauticians, factory or service workers, or professional women. As a rule, early Greek brides were younger and became widows at a younger age. In addition to being mothers, they assumed other family roles including head of families, father, businessperson, matchmaker, and so forth. The late Greek immigrant brides were not that different in age from their prospective husbands.

Dunkas and Nikelly (1978), in their study of 60 maladjusted first-generation Greek women who had recently immigrated, found that Greek married women were more attached to their mothers than their husbands, which the authors called the "Persephone syndrome." This dependency bond remains between Greek mothers and daughters. According to Scourby (1984:135), as a result of the daughter's dependency on the mother, the daughter is incapable of developing her own self-identity. "The mother keeps her daughter's ego confounded with her own." In Scourby's words, "The ego-boundary weakness compels the daughter to define herself in terms of others, a pattern in keeping with the relational system that has characterized Greek family life." According to her, both the Greek subculture and American culture tend to reinforce these daughter-mother dependency roles. The dependent daughter, when she is married, becomes the dependent wife and then the dependent mother, and the cycle continues. It must be stressed that these two studies are not sufficient to generalize to all the Greek mother-daughter relationships. Another dimension to the Persephone dependency syndrome is known as the Electra complex, or the attachment of Greek daughters to their fathers. This complex contrasts with what Freud called the Oedipus complex, or the attachment of sons to their mothers. Both the Electra and Oedipus complexes are applicable to male-female gender relationships generally as well as to the Greek-American family, of course, and there are no empirical studies to confirm or disconfirm these hypotheses.

As in the American family in general, one of the primary functions of the Greek family is procreation. A family without children was, and still is, thought to be incomplete. It is not by accident that the formal ideology of the Greek Orthodox church (and other religions, for that matter) encourages procreation within marriage. The birth of a child is not only an event for the Greek family but for the church as well. Motherhood is highly esteemed in the Greek Orthodox faith, and those couples who have children are looked upon by the church as fortunate and blessed. Doumanis (1983), in her study of mothering among two dozen rural and Athenian Greek working-class mothers who did not work outside the home, found that motherhood still has been the only means by which a woman can achieve full adult status in Greek society. Mothering, she observed, is a more individual and alienating experience in the modern Greek metropolis than it is in the collectivistic and emotionally supportive village setting. Childless couples (especially the husband) were, and still are, made uncomfortable in the Greek community. Not having children was suspect and reflected adversely on the Greek male's image. In many instances, a childless immigrant family or the old bachelor uncle would support a nephew or niece, but adoption of Greek or non-Greek children was not an accepted practice in the past and it is not widely accepted at present.

It has been reported (Stephanides, 1972; Tavuchis, 1968) that first-generation Greek parents tended to overprotect their children, even to the extent of wanting to find marriage partners for them. This should be interpreted in the context of the traditional ideal norms of a family and kinship system. In most instances, this was part of the arranged marriage practice in Greece that continued in the immigrant family. To some extent, the idea of arranged marriage continues even today in Greece and the United States, especially among more traditional Greek-American families. The idea of arranged marriage as opposed to romantic love has always been more prevalent in non-western societies and cultures; its merits have been obvious in view of the fact that over half of marriages in the United States end up in divorce. Ideally, first-generation Greek parents worked and strived to give their children happiness, love, and material comforts. Parents underwent personal sacrifices for their children and therefore expected their children to continue to meet their high expectations even after they reached maturity. They regulated and guided their children's behavior to a certain point; in return, children were expected to respect their parents, develop a sense of responsibility and self-reliance, and become a credit to their family unit and the larger ethnic and American communities.

Like their immigrant parents, children had a minimum of leisure time. They were exposed to the vicissitudes of life at a tender age and were socialized to postpone their immediate gratification for a future goal. For a majority of the Greek parents, that goal was to see their children happily married, maintain certain ethnic traditions, and move up the social ladder through education, business, and commerce outside the Greek ethnic community.

In general, the Greek immigrant family was adult rather than child centered. The child had to learn to respect his or her parents and the elderly. It has also been reported (Vlachos, 1968; Capanidou-Lauquier, 1961) that there was a differential preference for boys in the immigrant family. One can argue, however, that this preferential treatment was not as pronounced in the United States as it was in Greece because:

1. There was no dowry system in the United States as such, other than the usual gifts from relatives or friends of the couple.
2. Girls maintained Greek traditional norms and ideals more readily than boys.
3. Girls were more attached to their parents, particularly to their mothers.
4. Above all, it was the daughter, not the son, who would look after her elderly parents even after she was married.

Despite many similar experiences between early and late first-generation Greek families, they displayed the following differences, which created many conflicts between them and their progenies:

1. In contrast to the earlier group, the late immigrants arrived when there was a more equal number of males and females in their age groups.
2. In contrast to the earlier group, the later first-generation Greek women (both married and nonmarried), particularly from blue collar and working classes, are gainfully employed outside the household.
3. Late Greek immigrant families more than early Greek families visit Greece via cheap charter flights. This also reflects the affluence of late Greek immigrants. In proportion to their numbers, a large number are restaurant owners.

4. The late Greek immigrants are somewhat less interested in the Greek ethnic (church) community than are the second- and third-generation children of the early arrivals because late Greek immigrants are more ethnically rather than religiously oriented.

5. In contrast to the earlier group, the late Greek immigrant families tend to be more educated, more diverse in social class background, less religious, less conservative, more materially and exogamously oriented, more likely to divorce, less traditional, more business oriented, and more ethnically oriented through Greek language and nationality identification rather than through Orthodox religious identification.

Some of these differences and conflicts stem from generational, age, class, regional, and cultural differences in general. Despite many contrasts between the two groups of first-generation Greek families, both share a work ethic, strong ethnic family ties, the drive to compete for material success, and ethnic pride.

Gender roles are rapidly changing in Greece toward a more egalitarian or shared familial and occupational responsibility among men and women. The position of women has been improved. For the first time, Greek rural women and wives receive some form of social security after sixty years of age. The 1976–1982 family law bill, for example, reflects the gradual liberalization of traditional gender roles that gave men greater power over women. According to the new law, both spouses have equal rights and equal responsibilities. No longer is a woman's role restricted to the domestic domain and the man's to the public domain. Women can pursue their own interests. Schooling is also more coeducational.

These changes in gender roles have been going on in American families and marriages for the last thirty years or so. One would expect that the first-generation late Greek immigrant family is not immune to these changes occurring in Greece and the United States. In a comparative study of the Greek immigrant family in the United States and Canada, Tastsoglou and Stubos (1992) have found that prior to the 1940s immigrant Greeks assumed a more traditional family role characterized by more conservative values of kinship and extended family characteristics of rural life in Greece. Subsequent waves of Greek immigrants after World War II became more Americanized and were characterized by increased distancing from the kinship group, greater emphasis on interfamily and interpersonal relations, equalitarian marital relationships, greater marital autonomy for children, and decreasing interfamily financial obligations.

In general, while many ethnic patterns were replicated in the first-generation Greek-American family, many changes occurred. One such change was the increased interfaith marriages among Greek Orthodox to Roman Catholic and Protestant denominations. The vital statistics of the Greek Orthodox Archdoicese *Yearbook* (1996:87) show that in the period between 1977 and 1994, out of a total of 93,367 marriages they were 58,155 inter-Christian and 35,212 Orthodox marriages. These intermarriages are only those who married within the church and are not an accurate indicator of civil marriages in general. In the same period, divorces have also increased. Out of a total of 13,103 divorces, 6,978 were divorces of marriages between orthodox and 6,125 divorces of inter-Christian marriages (Greek Orthodox Archidocese, 1996:87). These changes reflect the ongoing gender role redefinition and debate both in Greece proper and the United States. Another important demographic change in the first generation is the fact that no more Greek immigrants are coming to the United States. This means that as the first generation ages and dies out, there will be more interethnic and interreligious marriages and an attenuation of Greek ethnicity.

The Second-Generation Greek-American Family

The second-generation Greek family is that social unit in which both parents are American born of Greek extraction or mixed parenthood (one parent Greek from Greece and the other either non-Greek or American-born Greek). As in other ethnic groups, the second-generation Greek family is a transitional family. Children are born and raised in two social worlds or subcultures. One is particularistic, with an ethnic subculture made up of Greek immigrant parents and relatives, immigrant priests, school teachers, Greek religious and national holidays, and Greek peers. These agents of socialization transmitted similar experiences and attempted to socialize the children to traditional norms and values of the Greek subculture. The other is a more universalistic world made up of American public schools, non-Greek peers and friends, and institutional norms and values of the dominant society and culture. The second generation emerges as a product of a Greek subculture on one hand and an American culture and society on the other, a sociocultural hybrid with a dual identity. An identity crisis and/or a generational conflict is a common phenomenon of the second generation.

In many respects, members of the second generation share similar experiences and lifestyles with their immigrant parents throughout their formative and adolescent years. However, pressures from within and outside the family unit make them somewhat ambivalent and marginal. They are torn between two ways of life. The emphasis on family ties, the Greek language, and the Greek Orthodox faith shaped their attitudes and behavior (Saloutos, 1964:311). These early attitudes and behaviors changed, however, as children came of age, went to public schools, began to work, moved away from the original settlement, were married, and started a family. However, it must be pointed out that the influence of the first-generation (immigrant) family on the second generation was not uniform in all Greek-American families throughout the United States. For example, in small towns and communities where fewer Greeks were found, the process of assimilation and convergence (including intermarriage) with the rest of the population was greater than in larger cities with larger numbers of Greek ethnic communities. Furthermore, ethnic identity in the first generation was looked upon as a process and a continuum rather than as a structure. For the second generation, ethnicity was more symbolic and religious. Membership in the Greek Orthodox church, following some of the rituals in the Greek Orthodox faith including elaborate church weddings, baptisms, or the celebration of Greek Independence Day, and going to Greece are some of the symbolic and external aspects of Greek culture (see Gans, 1979; Kourvetaris, 1994). However, not all Greek-American families shared symmetrical ethnic family experiences in the United States.

Three types of family lifestyles seem to be prevalent in second-generation Greek families (Vlachos, 1968:150–151). From a somewhat different perspective, these family lifestyles appear to be understood as phases along a continuum of an assimilation-acculturation process. One type represents a complete abandonment of the traditional Greek way of life. A substantial number in this group Anglicized their names and moved away from the Greek community; some changed their religion and many minimized their interaction with their foreign-born parents and relatives. This group was more concerned with social status and acceptance by their peers and other Americans. They were not interested in maintaining the norms of Greek culture as represented to them by their parents and relatives in the United States, and they wanted to become "assimilated" as soon as possible. In many respects, this type of second-generation family passed for an American family, and it was rather atypical. It was more prevalent in small towns and suburbs with dispersed Greek ethnic populations.

A second type of second-generation Greek family illustrates "cultural atavism," an inward retrogressive orientation and identification with what were perceived, by second-generation Greeks, to be ethnic Greek lifestyles. Ideally, this type of family was economically, culturally, socially, and psychologically tied up with the Greek community and its ethnic institutions. This type was usually working class or blue collar and was found close to Greek immigrant colonies. Many of these families could be described as "stables," or downwardly mobile working-class ethnic families. It is this type of ethnic second generation family that is mostly supportive of the Greek Orthodox church and its institutions, especially the Greek afternoon or parish school.

A third type of second-generation Greek family was marginal at the structural, cultural, and social-psychological levels. Norms and values were of a "hybrid" nature. Social interaction and networks of social relationships were neither genuinely American nor Greek. The family was likely to move out of the original settlement, and its members were less likely to engage in primary-group interaction with other first-generation Greeks outside the immediate intergenerational kinship group. In most instances, this type of family accommodated living between two worlds by taking what it considered the best of each. This family appeared to be more representative of the majority of the second-generation Greeks, a contention supported by the existing literature on second-generation Greek Americans (Moskos, 1990). It is in this group that we find the largest number of Greek American professionals (Kourvetaris, 1977, 1989).

In addition to these three types, we can suggest a fourth type where ethnicity and class intersect, what Gordon referred to as "ethclass." In a study of ethclass (Kourvetaris and Dobratz, 1976), it was found that second- and third-generation Greek Americans follow ethclass rather than ethnicity or class alone in patterns of interpersonal and primary relations, including marriage. Thus, if a second-generation male or female marries within his or her ethnic group or religion, the tendency is that he or she will marry within his or her social class in the Greek-American community. This type of ethclass marriage is also prevalent in the first-generation Greek family. It is more characteristic, however, of the second-generation Greek American family. Research in this type of intraethnic and intraclass marriage is practically nonexistent.

Like other ethnic groups, second-generation Greeks had certain advantages over the first generation. First, they did not have to start from scratch as their parents did. Second, they grew up in a fairly close-knit Greek family in which rudiments of Greek ethnic subculture were transmitted to them, particularly those pertaining to courtship, marriage, language, religion, and respect for mother, father, and the elderly, especially *papoú* (grandfather) and *yiaya* (grandmother). Third, the values of aspiration, hard work, and *philotimo*, or love for honor, were implanted in them by their parents. Achievement and success were a credit not only to their immediate families and kin but also to the entire Greek community. It is within this frame of reference that the organization of the second-generation Greek family emerged in the United States. Although first- and second-generation families actually shared many of these experiences, the first generation family contributed markedly to the mobility of the second generation.

Several writers (Saloutos, 1964; Sanders, 1962, 1967; Friedl, 1962; Vlachos, 1968; Tavuchis, 1968; Scourby, 1984) have reported that Greeks traditionally display a high degree of family cohesion and extended kinship relationships within and across generational lines. It has also been reported (Rosen, 1959; Handlin and Handlin, 1956; Kourvetaris, 1971a, b; Tavuchis, 1972; Chock, 1969; Moskos, 1990) that this intergenerational kinship system is coupled with a strong ideological commitment to social mobility and achievement in the American social structure. Tavuchis (1972), in his study of fifty second-generation male family heads, found an elaborate system of kinship and ethnic ties coupled with strong intergenerational patterns of vertical class mobility.

Unlike other social scientists, particularly family sociologists who have lamented the weakening of kinship bonds and the demise of family as a viable institution, Tavuchis found no evidence of family disintegration among the second-generation Greeks. In fact, Tavuchis argues that the stronger the kinship ties, the more highly mobile its members were found to be: "Differential class mobility was not found to be a detriment to close ties with parents, siblings, and affines." Tavuchis (1972:296–297) mentions five mechanisms that in his judgment prevented potential strains: a strong commitment to kinship values, a close propinquity to relatives, extraclass criteria of ranking, identification with successful kinsmen, and gross status differences neutralizing invidious distinctions. However, in a conference on the Greek-American family organization sponsored by the Greek Orthodox Ladies Philoptochos Society (1985), the participants lamented the erosion of family ties, the rejection of traditions, the increasing divorce rate in the Greek-American family, and the loss of faith among young Greek Americans. To counter these trends, the Greek Orthodox Church has introduced a number of youth and young adult church-affiliated organizations, including: GOYA (Greek Orthodox Youth of America), YAL (Young Adult League), JOY (youth advisors), the Ionian Village (visits to Greece), junior and senior dance troupes, adult Bible classes, and parish retreats for the young Greek orthodox children. Some of these youth-oriented organizations have been active for a long time. Most Greek parishes belong to these youth organizations.

Although Tavuchis' finding is not unique among Greek Americans (Jewish Americans display similar patterns), it is somewhat contrary to the prevailing notion among sociologists who believe that extended kinship relationships are a detriment to intergenerational social mobility. More recently, a somewhat similar finding has been reported by Kardaras (1977), who found no relationship between different types of modernity (marital, sexual, and educational) and structural/psychological assimilation. The second generation was found to be conservative or traditional in one dimension and modern in another. Somewhat surprisingly, the higher the social class among the second generation, the greater the tendency to espouse a more traditional (conservative) view in gender roles.

The structure of authority relations is a source of tension in Greek family life. The assertive or overconfident Greek woman is seen as a threat to the authority of the father. The long absence of the first-generation father from the home made it difficult for the son to identify with him. According to Scourby (1984:128), the father's absence enabled the son to identify not with his individuality and self-reliance but, inaccurately, with his authoritarianism alone. And the son's exposure to the equalitarian model in the United States only magnified the father's authoritarianism and thus created a conflict between dependency and independence. As far as I know, no other studies confirm Scourby's contention of the father's authoritarianism. It is not always true across all first-generation Greek fathers, and this alleged authoritarianism of the Greek immigrant father was perhaps more prevalent in the working-class first-generation Greek family. The attachment of the second-generation son to the mother is more prevalent in the Greek-American family. Thus we have a large number of second-generation single men who either live with elderly mothers or are bachelors. There are no studies or statistics to confirm the extent of this phenomenon. We find the same problem among second- and third-generation Greek-American women who are single, living either with their parents or by themselves. In a study of Greek Orthodox and ethnic identity of an Orthodox singles organization of 300 members in the Chicago area, Kourvetaris (1990) found that the majority of the members were either divorced or never before married. It is safe to suggest a substantial number of Greek-American single men and women in their late 30s, 40s and 50s are either divorced or never married in their lives. Single men and single women feel alienated and uncomfortable in the Greek-American community because the Greek Orthodox Church is a family-oriented institution and singles, especially the divorced, are not integrated into the social structure of the church.

Themes of stress and cultural conflict between the first and second generations are found in a number of novels written by second-generation writers. *Going Naked in the World* is a moving account of the frustrations Tom Chamales encountered as a member of a traditional authoritarian family of the 1940s. Elia Kazan's *The Arrangement* portrays a Greek-American with an unyielding father. In *Lion At My Heart*, Harry Mark Petrakis describes the painful conflict between the patriarchal father and his sons and the subsequent despair and disillusionment experienced by the father (mentioned in Scourby, 1984). Although fictional accounts provide us with insights into human and family relationships, they are not a substitute for a vigorous sociological analysis of intergenerational and family conflicts.

Three trends of authority relations seem to be prevalent in the emerging literature on the second-generation Greek-American family:

1. The "quasipatriarchal" model, or a trend toward lessening the patriarchal orientation in which ultimate authority in decision making no longer is exercised by the father (Tavuchis, 1972).
2. The "equalitarian" model, in which the father shares his status and authority with his wife (Capanidou Lauquier, 1961:225; Kardaras, 1977).
3. The "patriarchal" model (Vlachos, 1969:162), in which the father is still the ultimate authority with final responsibility for providing for his family and for the discipline of his children, partly because that is a father's duty and partly because he is a man and men are economic providers (Chock, 1969:38).

Gender roles of siblings are also viewed in normative terms by most Greek writers, and as a rule they do not describe actual role performances. For example, the traditional Greek cultural norms and ideals of filial piety and respect for one's parents and the elderly persist in the second-generation Greek American family. Unlike the case of the first generation, the father in the second-generation family is not perceived as a fearful and distant person;

rather, the father-son relationship is one of mutual understanding and respect (Tavuchis, 1972; Chock, 1969; Capanidou-Lauquier, 1961; Moskos, 1990). According to Chock, "Greek children are expected to love their parents, to respect them and to assume some care for them if they need it in their old age." Despite the respect between first and second generation, as a rule second-generation Greeks do not live in the same household with their parents and in-laws. More and more immigrant generations (especially widows) live alone or are placed in homes for the aged. The immigrant family, particularly the father, has a sense of pride that does not accept living with one's children, especially not a son-in-law. This is even more true of the second-generation family, especially the father in a mixed marriage.

As in the first generation, both parents in the second generation share in the responsibility for the care, education, and well-being of their children. Second-generation families tend to have fewer children than those of the first generation. However, many second-generation parents tend to spoil their children. Second-generation Greek women are inclined to take a greater interest in the Greek Orthodox church and religion than in Greek language schools. Scourby (1984:131) believes that women more than men identified as "Greek Orthodox" or "Greek American," reaffirming their positive response to the church. They are also less critical of the church. Like the first generation, second-generation families show respect for their parents and the elderly. Grandparents (*papoú* and *yiayia*) are also important figures in the second-generation Greek-American family.

Recently, many gender roles in the second generation have changed. Safilios-Rothschild and her colleagues (1976) and Kardaras (1977) have found that both husbands and wives in the upper-class second-generation families in the Detroit metropolitan area share somewhat similar views on marriage and the family. Thus, both husbands and wives are against a double standard on sexual matters, disapprove of infidelity and extramarital relations, and approve of divorce on grounds of abuse. They also believe that they should have the right both to initiate and refuse sexual activity. Although we do not know the extent to which these findings are uniform among all second-generation Greek-American families, one can suggest that ethclass and generation are more important variables in explaining ethnic family patterns than ethnicity, class, or generation taken singularly.

Greek Americans, regardless of generation, tend to be conservative on civil rights and economic issues. Moskos (1990) contends "the conservatism of the Greek Americans is an attitude of mind rather than a body of ideas— a distaste for confrontation politics and a suspicion of collective action for social improvement." Greek Americans, Moskos argues, "search not for a better world, but for a better life." The conservative ethos of Greek Americans reflects the individualistic orientations of the Greek entrepreneur, the influence of the Greek Orthodox church, emphasis on the cohesiveness of the family, and the rural origins of the early Greek immigrants, the majority of whom came from the southern part of Greece. We can also conclude that second-generation Greek-American families tend more often to be church-goers on Sunday than first-generation families (especially the late Greek immigrants). In short, Greek-American families maintain an ethnic identification through their membership in the Greek Orthodox Church and some ethnically oriented organizations such as AHEPA (American Hellenic Educational Progressive Association), the Hellenic Congress, or various Greek American professional societies.

The Third-Generation Greek-American Family

The third-generation family consists of grandchildren of the first generation or the children of the second-generation Greek family in America. This group also includes the offspring of intermarriages of second-generation couples. By the third generation, there is a significant decrease in Greek ethnic identification (as measured by language and Greek family norms); but some vestiges of ethnic social behavior remain, particularly those pertaining to politics (Humphrey and Brock, 1972), Greek religion, (Scourby, 1984) and Dionysian aspects of modern Greek culture (Kourvetaris, 1994) or what Gans (1979) refers to symbolic ethnicity. For example, the Greek Independence Day of March 25, 1821 is a national holiday for all the Greeks of the diaspora and their descendants.

As a rule, members of the third generation have incorporated the values, attitudes, and norms of the American middle- and upper-middle-class subcultures. Social class and lifestyles are more important to them than ethnicity and religion. Despite the lack of empirical studies, both education and professional achievement seem to be highly valued among members of the third generation. An empirical and comparative study of six ethnic groups (Rosen, 1959:47–60) found that a high level of aspiration and achievement exists among third-generation Greeks. Rosen argued that white Protestants, Jews, and Greeks stand out as being more individualistic, activist, and future oriented than Italian Americans, African Americans, and French Canadians.

Unlike the first and second generations, members of the third generation are not preoccupied with ethnic prejudice and social discrimination. Viewing their world this way, they can afford to be proud of their ancestry. However, they consider themselves primarily American and only symbolically manifest an interest in and liking Greek food, music, and dancing. This Dionysian cultural atavism in things Greek was stimulated by the new influx of Greek immigrants following World War II and the popular movies *Zorba the Greek* and *Never on Sunday*, whose theme songs became worldwide favorites during the 1960s. Furthermore, the marriage of Jacqueline Kennedy to Aristotle Onassis, the election of Spiro Agnew as U.S. Vice President in 1968 and 1972, the Democratic candidacy of Mike Dukakis for President in 1988, the resurgence of ethnic studies and programs, and summer excursions to

Greece have further awakened their interest in modern Greek ethnicity and ethnic culture. In addition, the new influx of post–World War II Greek immigrants has brought a new awareness of Greek ethnic identity. However, one finds little or no interest among members of the third generation in maintaining the ethnic institutional aspects of Greek culture, especially those pertaining to language, family traditions, and endogamous marriage—with the exception of the Americanized form of the Greek Orthodox church.

It has been argued by some Greek-American writers that the new influx of Greeks following World War II would retard the Americanization and assimilation processes of the third generation. However, American-born Greeks (even post–World War II Greeks who have been in America for a longer period of time) do not usually associate with the newcomers. This is primarily because dating within one's own group has a constraining influence. Greek-American women are no different from other American women—especially when they date non-Greeks. When Greek-American women date Greek-American men, they tend to be more serious about marriage, especially if they are members of the same community. There is also a matter of availability of both sexes of the same ethnic group, especially in a college population. In general, the more ethnically oriented the Greek man or woman, the greater the tendency to date someone with similar ethnic background. Furthermore, the more assimilated the Greek, the less likely he or she is to place importance on dating Greek women or men. This is also true of ethnic endogamous patterns of marriage.

If ethnicity (nationality) is the single most important characteristic in the first generation and religion in the second generation, it appears that an awareness of social class characterizes the third generation (Kourvetaris, 1971a, b). Thus, the advent of the third generation brings a concomitant decline in ethnoreligious concerns and an increasing emphasis on the importance of social class as a factor in marriage. However, those who maintain their ethnic (nationality/religiosity) identification tend to date and marry within their class segment of their ethnic group (ethclass). In a study, Safilios-Rothschild, Costantakos, and Kardaras (1976) found ethnic generation and class to be the most differentiating variables between traditional Greek culture and third-generation Greek Americans. Thus, the higher the social class, the more removed is a Greek American woman from her Greek cultural heritage and gender role restrictions. As a rule, the third generation is a college-oriented generation. It is a status- and class-conscious generation rather than an ethnic-conscious generation.

At the same time, while intermarriage in the first and to some extent second generation was not an accepted norm in the Greek-American family, by the third generation it is not only accepted but in some Greek-American communities has become the norm rather than the exception. It has been estimated that one in five Greeks entered a mixed marriage by 1926 (quoted in Moskos, 1990). By the 1960s, intermarriages accounted for three out of ten church marriages, and by the mid-1970s it was about half (Moskos, 1990). In some communities, it is even higher. In the vital statistics kept by the Registry Department of the Greek Orthodox Archdiocese of North and South America (1996:102–103) there is a steady increase of mixed marriages. While up to 1979 there was an equal number of mixed marriages and marriages between Greek Orthodox believers, from 1980 to 1984 there were more mixed marriages than Orthodox marriages. In some areas, mixed marriages reached a ratio of 2 (mixed) to 1 (Greek ethnic). Even the archbishop, in a speech delivered in late 1980s to the Academy of Athens, acknowledged that intermarriage is inevitable, and in some communities has reached 65 percent and higher.

By the same token, we find an increase in the divorce rate among Greek-American families. While divorce was rare in the first generation, the third-generation rate increasingly matches the divorce pattern of the American family at large. A conference of the Greek Orthodox Philoptohos Society (a charitable and benevolent Greek Orthodox institution) on the Greek Orthodox family in 1980 in San Francisco dealt with a number of changing realities and issues (including divorce, abortion, gender roles, cults, and ethnic and religious identity) faced by Greek-American families in the 1980s. They reported an increased number of divorces and mixed marriages.

Scourby (1984) argues that traditional role expectations continue to be the norm across generations, particularly in attitudes toward the institutional Greek Orthodox church, ethnic identity, and views toward gender roles and intermarriage. In her study of seventy-six Greek-born students drawn from three generations of college students from four colleges of the New York metropolitan area, Scourby (1984) found that (1) females of all three generations were more favorable toward traditional adherence to the ethnic church than males; (2) males showed a weaker attachment to their ethnic identity, were more likely to favor exogamy, and displayed a more assimilative attitude for getting ahead in American society; and (3) American-born students perceived the church as the locus of identity in a pluralist society, whereas the first generation identified it as a sign of Greek national identity.

CHANGE AND ADAPTATION

The movement from the lifestyles of early first-generation Greek families to those of the second, third, and subsequent generations is accompanied by an attenuation of the Old World family ideals and norms (as exemplified in the first-generation Greek family) and new values more symmetrical with those of the American middle-class family (as exemplified in the third-generation Greek family). "Greekness" as a form of ethnic identification (nationality) in the first generation gives way to the "orthodoxy" (religion) in the second generation, which in turn gives way to "class" and/or ethclass lifestyles (behavioral identification) by the third generation. The Greek Orthodox church is still part of the Greek ethnic identification but in Americanized form.

A study by Constantinou and Harvey (1985) of a Greek community in Akron, Ohio, found a two-dimensional structure underlying Greek-American ethnicity. One they called *externalities* (that which pulls the Greek American toward the place of origin), and the other *internalities* (that which binds Greek Americans together as a community). While a variation across generations was present, use of the Greek language was found to be on the decrease. They found the first generation to be the most cohesive, tending to identify with the ancestral home especially manifest in preserving the Greek language, while the second generation was found to be the least cohesive of the three because of its transitional nature. This generation had a split identity, one Greek and another American. The third generation was found to be less cohesive than the first but showed signs of ethnic revival. After examining seventeen ethnically related factors including the Greek language, Greek cooking, church membership, family, the Greek press, and endogamy as the most important dimensions of ethnic identity, the authors concluded that no single factor was adequate to define ethnic identity.

This author suggests that by the third generation the "Greekness" of the first generation has been transformed into *philhellenism* (friendship toward Greece). This generational transformation might be genuinely conceptualized as following roughly five processes and/or phases of acculturation, initially suggested in part by Robert Park (1950), one of the early American sociologists and a leading urban sociologist of the University of Chicago school of sociology: *initial contact, conflict, accommodation, assimilation,* and *pluralist* phases. These processes are more applicable to European immigrants or Euroamericans and their decendants rather than those of other ancestry.

The Initial Contact Phase

For both the early and late Greek immigrants, the organization of the Old World family was still fairly intact in the first decades of immigrant life in America. As a result of pressures from within and outside the family structure, the Old World ideal was challenged. Some of the most salient factors were the physical/ecological separation from the parental and kinship system and village subculture in Greece. The urgency of the immigrant's physical survival and social-psychological adjustment to a different sociocultural and urban ecological environment was real. The separation of work and residence and the exposure of the immigrant's children to the lifestyles of the American community and public schools, which in many ways meant ethnic prejudice and social discrimination against those ethnic groups and families, were contributing factors that made the first generation culturally different from the dominant group of northern and western European background. All these made the first-generation Greek immigrant family extremely ethnocentric and highly cohesive, as in the

Old World. In this phase of initial contact, the immigrant family was socially and culturally insulated in the Greek colony and did not seriously feel the pressures of American society. Despite its many problems, the first-generation Greek family was stabilized by its strong desire to return to Greece. It drew social and psychological support from the family unit, the family and kinship system, the Greek Orthodox church, and the Greek community in general. However, this initial phase gave way both to the conflict and accommodation phases with the coming of the second generation.

The Conflict Phase

With the oncoming second generation, the highly ethnocentric, traditional, and folk-oriented outlook of the first-generation subculture was challenged. Although cultural and ethnic conflict between parents and children was not inevitable, in many instances it did take place. Out of this generational conflict, three major subtypes of first-generation Greeks and Greek-American families emerged: the ethnic subculturalist, the social assimilationist, and the convergent types (in some respects ethnic pluralists and in other respects social assimilationist).

The ethnic subculturalists were faced with major difficulties in carrying out their intent to socialize their children in Greek ways of life. These difficulties and their fear of losing control over their children were intensified when the children came into contact with the larger American society. This was evident particularly when they entered public schools, began working and dating, and came of marital age. Greek immigrants' exaggerated fear of losing control over their children was further aggravated by the Greek Orthodox church and the family kinfolk. Furthermore, it stemmed from the inability of the immigrants themselves to adjust more readily to the subtler, nonmaterial aspects of American culture and thus be able to understand their children. This group, usually found in cities with large Greek colonies, proved unyielding. They insisted on preserving their ethnic institutions, particularly those pertaining to religion, language, endogamous marriage, and a close-knit family. They attempted to convince their children of the mystique of Greek ancestry, warned them against the dangers of intermarriage, and made an effort to instill in them a sense of ethnic pride and ethnic consciousness. According to Papajohn and Spiegel, clinical studies of mentally disturbed second-generation Greek American children indicated that these children came from families where an extremely traditionalist Greek form of childrearing was attempted. In fact, those immigrant parents who were more open to American influences were more successful in passing Greek ethnicity than those parents who tried to resist totally all American encroachment (quoted in Moskos, 1990).

The social assimilationists (known also as environmentalists) believed that their children must grow up as Americans but wanted them to retain membership in the Greek Orthodox church, maintain their Greek name, and learn some Greek (Saloutos, 1964:312). This group felt that the assimilation process could not be stopped but only temporarily delayed. The environmentalists were more realistic, experienced less conflict with their children, and were more aware that powerful social and cultural forces operate in the American social structure that exert an unprecedented influence on their children, pulling them toward Anglo conformity and Americanization. This assimilation process has been challenged by the ethnic resurgence of the 1960s and early 1970s, which produced the buzzword of *multiculturalism*, a product of non-European ethnicity. This is especially true among Greek-born, post–World War II Greek immigrants, students, and professionals. The lack of support in American foreign policy for Greek national issues such as Cyprus, the Greek minority in northern Eperus, Albania, the former Yugoslavian Republic of Macedonia (FYROM), the issue of Aegean challenge of sovereignty by Turkey, and other similar issues has alienated many Greeks and Greek Americans. Cyprus became the catalyst for ethnic solidarity and ethnic consciousness, especially for the new first-generation and some second-generation Greek immigrants (especially Greek-American politicians, who expect financial contributions and support from Greek businessmen).

The social assimilationist process began roughly during the second and third decades that the first-generation family lived in America, especially when the first-generation immigrant family abandoned its intent to return to Greece. It was during this period that both the institutional structure of the Greek Orthodox church and by far the largest ethnic association, AHEPA, launched an all-out effort to organize the Greeks in America, to facilitate the transition and Americanization processes, and to maintain the ethnic institutions of church and family, which in many ways became complementary to each other. Nationality was gradually giving way to religion, particularly during the 1920s when Greeks, along with other southern and eastern European immigrants, were targets of prejudice and social discrimination. Second-generation Greeks were discovering that to be of Greek ancestry did not necessarily indicate a particularly high social status. This phase gave way to the new realization that religious identity was preferable to ethnic or national identity, and a new intergenerational relationship emerged. While the first generation perceived both religion and ethnicity as inseparable, many in the second and subsequent generations saw them more and more as separate phenomena.

Many in the first generation, especially the more educated (both early and late), followed a mixed approach; it was a compromise between the two polar opposites. This was compatible with the pluralist ideology of ethnic groups in the United States, which replaced the Americanization and assimilation models. It started in the 1940s but was more evident in the 1950s and 1960s with the influx of new Greek immigrants. Also the general ethnic resurgence of the 1960s gave a new impetus to ethnic consciousness in American society that contributed to the general ethnic cultural pluralism. The defeat of the Italian fascist forces by the Greeks in October 1940 gave a shot in the arm to the second-generation Greeks in America and new ethnic pride and consciousness flourished. This pride, along with the rise of a professional and commercial class of second-generation Greeks and the arrival of post–World War II Greeks, contributed to a new status for Greeks in America. It must be stressed that conflict between the first and second generations was always there, but both groups worked out a *modus vivendum* and followed a pattern of accommodation.

The Accommodation Phase

During the accommodation phase, an effort was made to broaden the base for continued and meaningful interaction between the two generations. On one hand, the first generation realized that they had to modify the Old World family lifestyles for the sake of retaining the affection of their children and maintaining the unity of the family. On the other hand, the second generation came to realize that complete repudiation of their parents' way of life would hurt their parents and leave them isolated. Both generations searched for points of compatibility, mutual levels of tolerance, complementary lifestyles, individuality, and family unity.

This period of accommodation between first- and second-generation family units led to a more stable form of family relationships. The parents came to realize that life in the United States was to be permanent. They also recognized that social and economic status and success could come to their offspring as the latter became more and more socialized into the dominant Anglo-American culture. A parallel effort was made by the second generation to resocialize their parents to their own generational values and lifestyles. The interdependence between parents and children gave way to the dependence of parents on their children as interpreters and informants on the American scene (especially those whose English was not proficient). This dependence led to the conscious and unconscious willingness on the part of the parents to sacrifice certain norms and ideals of the Old World family for the sake of their own happiness and that of their children. Finally, it was a matter of realism and convenience.

As the first generation (both early and late) died out, the conflict and accommodation phases between the first and second generations gave rise to new forms of social and generational change. By the late 1950s and 1960s, the third-generation Greek American was caught between an ongoing process of assimilation and *embourgeoisement*[5] and an ethnic resurgence spearheaded by

[5]For the *embourgeoisement*, success, and struggle of Greeks in America, see Moskos (1990). The book is a second-generation view of Greeks and Greek Americans. It somewhat exaggerates the success and *embourgeoisement* thesis and underemphasizes the failure and problems. Moskos draws primarily from English-language writings and not from Greek sources written by Greek immigrants.

African Americans, later by Mexican Americans, and, during the 1970s and 1980s, by the arrival of the Asians. Added to these ethnic movements was the new Greek immigration of the mid-1960s and early 1970s, which brought a new cultural transfusion and a revitalized ethnicity to Greek Americans. It is my contention that neither the rise of ethnic/racial consciousness in the United States nor the late Greek immigration arrested the Americanization process of the third-generation Greek Americans. By the late 1950s and early 1960s, second- and third-generation and subsequent generations of Greeks had adopted American middle and the upper-middle-class lifestyles. While "ethnicity" had been there all along, it was giving way to class and ethclass lifestyles and patterns of behavior.

Third- and later-generation Greek Americans, hedonistic like most American youth, retained mostly the Dionysian aspects of Greek culture, but with few exceptions had very little knowledge and understanding of the contemporary Apollonian aspects of Greek culture. Greek cuisine, dancing, and music were more appealing to them than the abstract and remote notions of *philotimo* (honor, generosity), *philoxenia* (hospitality), Greekness (ethnicity), nationality, the Greek language, literature, family traditions, history, and the like. Greek-American youth, like American youth in general, were also disenchanted with the institutional forms of religion. During the 1960s, they complained that they could not understand the almost mystical and highly ritualistic practice of Orthodox Christianity. Many turned to more socially minded religions or were converted through intermarriage to other religions. However, during the 1980s and 1990s a new religious spirituality and Orthodox identity emerged. Children of the third generation (the fourth and fifth generations) have shown some interest in Greek culture through participation in the life of the Greek Orthodox church and visiting Greece. But such interest is more symbolic and not substantive. By the third and fourth generations, most Greek Americans do not speak Greek at home but retain the Greek Orthodox faith. The extent to which third- and fourth-generation Greek Americans retain ethnic characteristics other than the Orthodox faith is not known.

Assimilation or Pluralism: Which Way?

By the third and subsequent generations, the Greek-American family's lifestyles become more and more symmetrical with that of the larger American middle-class family. This, however, does not mean that all vestiges of ethnic subcultural lifestyles are lost. The Greek-American family maintains some of its unique ethnic features. For example, Greek names, the Orthodox faith, ethnic food, some holidays, trips to Greece, some intergenerational family ties, and, to some extent, some endogamous marriages remain. Assimilation, a multidimensional process in itself, does not have to be complete. It has been suggested that Greek Americans maintain their ethnic identity through their religion. As subsequent generations of Greek Americans grow remote from the original generation, emphasis on Greek nationality and language is replaced by religion for those who support the organization of the Greek Orthodox church in the United States. The Greek-American family lifestyle is both assimilative and pluralistic. It is a blending, but not necessarily a perfect or equal blending, of two cultures.

We can tentatively suggest that in moving away from the first generation to the second and subsequent generations, there is an increasing rate of intermarriage. This includes interethnic, interreligious, and interclass marriages. The first generation tends to be the most endogamous, the third the least, and the second is in between. By the third generation, intermarriage is more likely to follow class lines. Ethnicity, defined in most cases by nationality, religion, language or a combination of the three, declines as from the first to the second and to subsequent generations (Kourvetaris, 1990; Demos, 1988).

The gradual transformation from the Greek rural traditional (first-generation immigrant) family to the Greek-American urban middle class is somewhat coterminous with those changes brought about by urbanization and internal migration processes in Greece proper. Since the 1920s, and especially the 1940s, these processes have been accelerated. By the third generation, even Greeks in Greece have changed family lifestyles and norms from those found in the traditional rural family to those more symmetrical with the contemporary middle-class urban Athenian family (Safilios-Rothschild, 1967a). The differences lie in linguistic, national, and cultural areas, but the values and norms are similar to Greek-American ones. In short, unless Greek immigration continues, the Greek family in America by the third and subsequent generations will retain mostly the organizational and institutional aspects of Greek-American subculture, particularly the Orthodox faith, some family patterns, and the success work ethic but not the more subtle and cognitive aspects of Greek culture and ethnicity. While the generational family ties will be attenuated, Greeks will not lose respect for those institutions that sustained them throughout their long history—namely, religion and family.

The question then becomes: What is unique about the Greek-American family compared with other ethnic family variations in American society? It seems to me—and it is only a conjecture—that by the next century the Greek-American family will maintain only the more symbolic cultural forms, such as celebrations, some family names, religious identity, food patterns, visits to Greece, and the like. Greek-American families will accelerate their rates of intermarriages among other coethnic and coreligionist Euroamericans. These intermarriages will be mostly inter-Christian, with marriage to Roman Catholics the most dominant. In these inter-Christian marriages, if the wife is Roman Catholic, children are more likely to be raised in the Roman Catholic church. If, on the other hand, the wife is Greek Orthodox and she is strong in her faith, the children of the inter-Christian marriage are more likely to be raised in the Greek Orthodox church.

In conclusion, the Greek-American family is moving away more and more from the ethnic patterns of the Old World and becoming more of a homegrown phenomenon. The divorce rate and pathology of the American family in general have affected the Greek-American family as well. Divorce, unheard of in the first-generation immigrant family, had become a common occurrence by the second and third generations. Parental respect, family traditions, and cooperation among the members of the family unit, all typical of the first generation, have been undermined by the decline of the father's authority. The erosion of family solidarity and the growing individualism within American middle-class families have also affected the Greek-American family. Extrafamily agencies and organizations, including state laws, have taken over many family functions. The American family, including the Greek-American family, feels the pressures and demands of a consumerist psychology that challenges its stability and cohesiveness.

SUMMARY AND CONCLUSION

Using the generational approach, certain aspects of first-, second-, and third-generation Greek and Greek-American family variations were examined. First, the Greek-American family was placed within the sociohistorical context of the second phase of immigration and industrial capitalism (1860s–1920s). Second, three phases of Greek immigration were briefly discussed: those who came prior to the Civil War, those who came during the latter part of the nineteenth and early twentieth centuries, and those who came after World War II. Third, the organizational and ethnic institutional aspects of the Greek-American family were also discussed, including the organization of the Greek Orthodox church and the founding of secular organizations such as the AHEPA. Against this background three generations of Greek and Greek-American patterns were examined.

One can make the following observations on convergences and divergences among the three generations of Greek and Greek-American families.

Convergences. All three generations share certain family traditions, respect for the elderly, religious faith, Greek food patterns, certain Greek national and religious holidays, and the desire to marry within the Greek Orthodox or Christian faith.

Divergences. As the first-generation Greek family dies out, the Greek-American family becomes increasingly a homegrown phenomenon. The first-generation Greek family attempted to replicate Greek rural family patterns in the New World; it was the most ethnic and cohesive of the three generational units. While the second generation shares many experiences with its parental generation, it is a transitional and hyphenated generation caught between two social and cultural worlds: one Greek and one American. It is here that both the assimilative and pluralist forces and processes are more operative. Those members of the second generation closer to Greek ethnic values and traditions tend to resist assimilative influences. They are more ethnocentric, marry within the Greek Orthodox faith, are more likely to learn Greek, and as a whole are more active in the Greek orthodox church. Those of the second generation who are children of mixed marriages are more open to American influences and tend to subscribe to pluralistic model. Both groups, however, experience the assimilative pressures of American society, but the coping mechanisms and responses from these two sub-groups are different. Overall, the second generation is the more problematic, confused, and stressful generation.

By the third generation, Greek Americans show cultural atavism or interest to come back to their Greek roots. However, the interest of third generation in things Greek is symbolic at best. By the third generation, Greek Americans as a rule do not speak Greek, only a few marry coethnic or coreligionists, a large number do not identify with the Greeks. They are American with some historical identification of a Greek or mixed ancestry.

REFERENCES

Bardis, Panos. 1955. "The Changing Family in Modern Greece." *Sociology of Social Research, 40* (October): 19–23.

———. 1956. "Main Features of the Greek Family During the Early Twentieth Century," *Alpha Kappa Delta, 26* (Winter, November): 17–21.

———. 1957. "Influences on the Modern Greek Family," *Social Science, 32* (June): 155–158.

Campbell, J. K. 1964. *Honor, Family, and Patronage*. Oxford: Clarendon Press.

Campisi, J. Paul. 1948. "Ethnic Family Patterns: The Italian Family in the United States." *American Journal of Sociology, 53* (May): 443–449.

Capanidou Lauquier, H. 1961. "Cultural Change Among Three Generations of Greeks." *American Catholic Review* [now *Sociological Analysis*], *22* (Fall): 223–232.

Chamales, Tom T. 1959. *Go Naked in the World*. New York: Scribner.

Chock, P. Phyllis. 1969. "Greek-American Ethnicity." Ph.D. dissertation, University of Chicago.

Constantinou, Stavros T. and Milton E. Harvey. 1985. "Basic Dimensional Structure and Intergenerational Differences in Greek American Ethnicity." *Sociology and Social Research 69*, 2 (January): 241–246.

Cutsumbis, N. Michael. 1970. *A Bibliographic Guide to Materials on Greeks in the United States 1890–1968*. New York: Center for Migration Studies.

Demos, Vasilike. 1988. "Ethnic Mother Tongue Maintenance Among Greek Orthodox Americans." *International Journal of Sociology of Language, 69* 59–71.

Doumanis, Mariella. 1983. *Mothering in Greece: From Collectivism to Individualism*. London: Academic Press.

Dunkas, Nicholas and Arthur G. Nikelly. 1978. "The Persephone Syndrome." *Social Psychiatry 7*: 211–216.

Fairchild, H. P. 1911. *Greek Immigration to the United States*. New Haven: Yale University Press.

Friedl, Ernestine. 1962. *Vasilika: A Village in Modern Greece*. New York: Holt.

———. 1967. "The Position of Women: Appearance and Reality." *Anthropological Quarterly, 40* (July): 97–108.

Gans, Herbert. 1979. "Symbolic Ethnicity: The Future of Ethnic Groups and Cultures in America." In Herbert Gans (Ed.), *On the Making of Americans.* Philadelphia: University of Pennsylvania Press.

Gordon, Milton. 1964. *Assimilation in American Life: The Role of Race, Religion and National Origin.* New York: Oxford University Press.

Greek Orthodox Archdiocese of North and South America. 1996. *Yearbook.* New York.

Handlin, F. Oscar, and Mary F. Handlin.1956. "Ethnic Factors in Social Mobility." *Explorations in Entrepreneurial History, 9* (October): 4–5.

Humphrey, R. Craig, and Helen T. Brock.1972. "Assimilation, Ethnicity, and Voting Behavior Among Greek-Americans in a Metropolitan Area." Paper presented at the 1972 annual meeting of the Southern Sociological Society, April 5–8, New Orleans.

Kardaras, Basil P. 1977. "A Study of the Marital and Familial Options of the Second Generation Greek-Americans in the Detroit Metropolitan Area." Master's thesis, Department of Sociology, Wayne State University.

Kazan, Elia. 1968. *The Arrangement.* New York: Avon Books.

Koty, John. 1958. "Greece," in Arnold M. Rose (Ed.), *The Institutions of Advanced Societies,* pp. 330–383. Minneapolis: University of Minnesota Press.

Kourvetaris, George A. 1971a. *First and Second Generation Greeks in Chicago.* Athens, Greece: National Center of Social Research.

———. 1971b. "First and Second Generation Greeks in Chicago: An Inquiry into Their Stratification and Mobility Patterns," *International Review of Sociology* [now *International Review of Modern Sociology*], *1* (March): 37–47.

———. 1971c. "Patterns of Generational Subculture and Intermarriage of the Greeks in the United States." *International Journal of Sociology of the Family, 1* (May): 34–48.

———. 1973. "Brain Drain and International Migration of Scientists: The Case of Greece." *Epitheoris Koinonikon Erevnon* [*Review of Social Research*], nos. 15–16.

———. 1977. "Greek–American Professionals: 1820s–1970s," *Balkan Studies, 18*:285–323.

———. 1984. "Ethnic Conflicts and Identity Crises Among the Greeks in the Diaspora with Emphasis on the Greeks in the United States: An Exploratory Analysis." Paper presented at the KRIKOS annual conference, Fordham Univ. New York, October 13.

———. 1989. "Greek American Professional and Entrepreneurs," *The Journal of the Hellenic Diaspora.*

———. 1990. "Conflicts and Identity Crises Among Greek Americans and Greeks of the Diaspora." *International Journal of Contemporary Sociology. 27,* 3-4 (July-October): 137–153.

Kourvetaris, George A., and Betty A. Dobratz. 1976. "An Empirical Test of Gordon's Ethclass Hypothesis Among Three Ethnoreligious Groups," *Sociology and Social Research, 61* (October): 39–53.

———. 1989. *A Profile of Modern Greece.* London: Clarendon Press.

———. 1994. "The Dionysian and Apollonian Dimensions of Ethnicity: A Convergence Model." Paper presented at the Illinois Sociological Association meeting, Peoria, IL, October, 19–21.

Kyriazis, Elpis (chairman). 1982. "Focus Greek Orthodox Family." Presented at the Philoptochos Biennial Convention, July 4–9.

Lagos, Mary. 1962. "A Greek Family in American Society." Unpublished transcript, Franklin and Marshall College, Lancaster, PA.

Lambiri-Dimaki, Ioanna. 1965. *Social Change in a Greek Country Town.* Athens: Center of Planning and Economic Research.

McNeill, William. 1978. *The Metamorphosis of Greece Since World War II.* Chicago: University of Chicago Press.

Mistaras, Evangeline. 1950. "A Study of First and Second Generation Greek Outmarriages in Chicago." Master's thesis, University of Chicago.

Moskos, Charles C., Jr. 1982. "Greek American Studies," in Harry J. Psomiades and Alice Scourby. (Eds.), *The Greek American Community in Transition*, pp. 17–19. New York: Pella.

———. 1990. *Greek Americans: Struggle and Success.* New Brunswick, NJ: Transaction.

Papajohn, C. John. "The Relation of Intergenerational Value Orientation Change and Mental Health in An American Ethnic Group." Unpublished ms, Florence Heller Graduate School for Advanced Studies in Social Welfare, Brandeis University.

Papanikolas, Z. Helen. 1970. *Toil and Rage in a New Land: The Greek Immigrants in Utah.* Salt Lake City: Utah State Historical Society.

Park, Robert E. 1950. *Race and Culture.* Glencoe, IL: Free Press.

Petrakis, Harry Mark. 1966. *A Dream of Kings.* New York: McKay.

———. 1959. *Lion at My Heart.* Boston: Little Brown.

Plous, F. K., Jr. 1971. "Chicago's Greeks: Pride, Passion, and the Protestant Ethnic." *Midwest Sunday Magazine of the Chicago Sun Times* (April 25), pp. 22–26.

Rosen, Bernard. 1959. "Race, Ethnicity, and the Achievement Syndrome." *American Sociological Review, 24* (February): 47–60.

Safilios-Rothschild, Constantina. 1965. "Mortality, Courtship, and Love in Greek Folklore." *Southern Folklore Quarterly, 29,* (December): 297–308.

———. 1967a. "Class Position and Success Stereotypes in Greek and American Cultures," *Social Forces. 45* (March): 374–383.

———. 1967b. "A Comparison of Power Structure and Marital Satisfaction in Urban Greek and French Families." *Journal of Marriage and the Family, 29* (May): 345–352.

———. 1969a. "Patterns of Familial Power and Influence." *Sociological Focus, 2* (Spring): 7–19.

———. 1969b. "Family Sociology or Wives' Family Sociology? A Cross-Cultural Examination of Decision-Making," *Journal of Marriage and the Family, 31* (May): 290–301.

———. 1971–1972. "The Options of Greek Men and Women." *Sociological Focus, 5* (Winter): 71–83.

Safilios-Rothschild, Constantina, Chrysie Constantakos, and Basil P. Kardaras. 1976. "The Greek-American Woman." Paper presented at the Greek Experience in America Symposium 1976 at the University of Chicago, October 29–31.

Saloutos, Theodore. 1956. *They Remember America.* Berkeley and Los Angeles: University of California Press.

———. 1964. *The Greeks in the United States.* Cambridge: Harvard University Press.

Sanders, Irwin. 1962. *Rainbow in the Rock: The People of Rural Greece.* Cambridge: Harvard University Press.

———. 1967. "Greek Society in Transition," *Balkan Studies, 8:* 317–332.

Scourby, Alice. 1984. *The Greek-Americans*, pp. 133–151. Boston: Twayne.

Seder, L. Doris. 1966. "The Influence of Cultural Identification on Family Behavior," Ph.D. dissertation, Brandeis University.

Simpson, George, and J. Milton Yinger. 1972. *Racial and Cultural Minorities: An Analysis of Prejudice and Discrimination,* 4th ed. New York: Harper & Row.

Stephanides, C. Marios. 1972. "Educational Background, Personality Characteristics, and Value Attitudes Towards Education and Other Ethnic Groups Among the Greeks in Detroit." Unpublished Ph.D. dissertation, Wayne State University.

Stycos, J. M. 1948. "The Spartan Greeks of Bridgetown." *Common Ground* (Winter, Spring, Summer), pp. 61–70, 24–34, 72–86.

Tastsoglou, Evangelica and George Stubos. 1992. "The Pioneer Greek Immigrant in the United States and Canada (1880s–1920s): Survival Strategies of a Traditional Family." *Ethnic Groups, 93,* 3: 175–189.

———. "The Greek Immigrant Family in the United States and Canada: The Transition from an 'Institutional' to a 'Relational' Form (1945–1970)." *International Migration, 30,* 2 (June): 155–174.

Tavuchis, Nicholas, 1968. "An Exploratory Study of Kinship and Mobility Among Second Generation Greek-Americans." Ph.D. dissertation, Columbia University.

————. 1972. *Family and Mobility Among Greek-Americans.* Athens, Greece: National Centre of Social Research.

Terlexis, Pantazis, 1979. "Metanastefsi Kai Epanapatrismos: 1 Prosklisi to 1980" [Immigration and Repatriation]. *Review of Social Sciences,* July–September.

U.S. Department of Commerce. 1983. *Bureau of the Census. General Social and Economic Characteristics,* vol. 1, part 1 (Dec.). Washington, DC: U.S. Government Printing Office.

Vassiliou, George, and Vasso Vassiliou. 1966. "A Transactional Approach to Mental Health." Contribution to the International Research Conference on Evaluation of Community Mental Health Programs of NIMH.

Vlachos, C. Evangelos. 1968. *The Assimilation of Greeks in the United States.* Athens, Greece: National Center of Social Research.

————. 1969. *Modern Greek Society: Continuity and Change.* Special Monograph Series No. 1, Department of Sociology and Anthropology, Colorado State University.

Xenides, J. P. 1922. *The Greeks in America.* New York: George H. Doran.

5 The Italian-American Family

D. Ann Squiers
Jill S. Quadagno

INTRODUCTION

The central debate among those studying the Italian-American family has focused on the significance of ethnic identity in maintaining family ties. One group of scholars argues that Italian Americans possess unique traits that emphasize the significance of familism and that the pressures of cultural assimilation are unlikely to reduce the importance of this value (Greeley, 1974:22; Kantrowitz, 1973). Another group argues that most of the traits that have been ascribed to Italian Americans are components of working-class culture and that upper mobility will eliminate these supposedly distinguishing characteristics (Gans, 1962; Gordon, 1964; Lopreato, 1970; Alba, 1985; Hraba, 1994). There is no simple way to resolve these issues. This chapter will explore the various dimensions of the impact of ethnic identity on the Italian American family.

HISTORICAL BACKGROUND

Traditional Family Structure

Italian immigrants to the United States brought with them a family structure that was different in many ways not only from American society, but also from other European cultures. The main group of Italian immigrants in the United States came from the Mezzogiorno region in southern Italy. Within Mezzogiorno culture, families, not individuals, held the central place in society as the only truly valued social unit. Nuclear households were prominent but because of strong filial obligations individuals were expected to subordinate their needs to those of the family. Family members included the household, the extended family, and even the extended family of one's spouse (Alba, 1985).

Italian households often contained extended kin rather than solely the conjugal family. This contrasted with the pattern in Western Europe in general, in which the small, conjugal-family household predominated (Wrigley, 1977:78). Particularly among sharecropper families, in which the labor of many people enhanced the entire family's economic situation, married brothers shared a common household with their families. Three-generation households, including aged parents, were likely to be found at the end of the life cycle, when widowed parents moved into the home of their married children and grandchildren (Kertzer, 1978:341).

Family solidarity was the basic code of family life, encompassing the parents, grandparents, aunts, uncles, cousins, and godparents (Covello, 1967:149). The strength of the norm of solidarity meant that the disgrace of one member of the family affected everyone. Thus, a disobedient child was the concern of not only the parents, but also the extended kin. Within the family, a complex system of rules regulated both an individual's relations and responsibilities to the members of his or her family and his or her posture to the outside world.

The concept of obligation was a distinctive aspect of family solidarity. The family council, headed by the *capo di famiglia,* usually the father, made decisions about such diverse matters as the education of a child, a cousin's dowry, or the funeral expenses of an aunt (Covello, 1967:151). A person in need of credit would apply first to family members and only if no help were forthcoming would he or she then turn to *stranieri* ("outsiders").

Although the Italian family has often been perceived as patriarchal, there were many limitations on patriarchal authority. First, because the southern Italian *famiglia* ("family") embraced many marriage units, the decision about who was the head of the extended family was not reached without rivalry among several aspirants. Although authority was usually conferred on the oldest married male family member, this was not always the case. Thus, in a general sense, the oldest Italian male was neither the sole nor absolute authority. The fact that a system of orthodox patriarchy was not adhered to can be seen in the limitations on leadership that prevailed. As long as a man was the main provider, his leadership was not questioned. However, old age or feebleness definitely terminated his role as the representative of family tradition. Similarly, if he became a widower, he retained his leadership only if one of his sons were not married. As soon as a son, preferably the oldest, married, the son assumed the leadership role of his widowed father (Covello, 1967:154). The father retained respect, but there was no longer blind obedience.

A second limitation on male dominance was the power and authority of the Italian mother. An important indicator was the fact that the wife had the right to possess property and dispose of it without her husband's consent (Covello, 1967:206). The dowry was an economic weapon that she retained until her death and, at her death, went either to her children or, if she was childless, back to her own blood relatives. Another source of power for the peasant woman was the fact that she often contributed economically to the family by working part time in the fields. Thus, the husband did not provide the sole support of the family. In addition, cultural tradition granted a prestige to the mother that contradicted her assumed subservience to her husband (Covello, 1967:213). The major kinship ties were with female relatives, and the nurturing of children was performed by the mother and her female relatives. The mother was the center of the family in a society where nonfamilial relationships were secondary. In a world where family status was judged not by the father's occupation but by the signs of family well-being that emanated from the household, the mother played an important role in securing that status.

Traditional Ethnic Culture

The Italian family system formed the basis of the perpetuation of a set of beliefs and values that affected all areas of social life including work, education, and definitions of social status.

The necessity of family ties was of singular importance. One's personal identity was derived from family, and family membership was essential in terms of defining one's place in society. The most shameful condition was to be without a family (Gambino, 1974:31). A man who violated the family code was an outcast from not only his family but also the larger society. He could only become a day laborer, and even in this occupation he was the last hired. For a woman without a family, the only options were to become a beggar or a prostitute. However, loyal kin were rewarded by always having a place within the family. The aged were cared for in the family and "no one went to poorhouses, orphanages, or other institutions of charity in the Mezzogiorno except those few unfortunates without any family intimates" (Gambino, 1974:29).

The strength of familial ties also affected the attitude of the *contadino* ("peasant") toward work: "Work is regarded as moral training for the young. And among adults, it is regarded as a matter of pride. To work is to show evidence that one has become a man or a woman, a full member of the family" (Gambino, 1974:80). Thus work was not defined as abstract but as tangible— something that could be shown to others as a "visible" result of an individual's skills and efforts. The disdain for intangibles was also related to the *contadino's* attitude toward education.

Although the ideal of the *contadino* was to cultivate children who were *ben educato* ("well-educated"), the translation of this phrase is deceptive. Being educated referred not to formal schooling but to education in proper behavior. "*Ben educato* meant raised with the core of one's personality woven of those values and attitudes, habits and skills that perpetuated *l'ordine della famiglia,* and thus one was attuned to the welfare of the family" (Gambino, 1974:225). In this sense, formal schooling was antithetical to proper training for manhood or womanhood, involving the influence of *stranieri* who might interfere with *la via vecchia* ("the old ways"), as well as with keeping young people from the more important lessons they might learn from work.

THE MODERN ITALIAN AMERICAN FAMILY

Demographic and Ecological Factors

Although people tend to associate Italian immigration to the United States with the late nineteenth and early twentieth centuries, the immigration of Italians has actually been a continuing process, beginning much earlier and continuing to the present time. Four different periods of exodus can be identified, each having somewhat distinctive characteristics.

In the eighteenth and nineteenth centuries, small numbers of northern Italians came to the United States. These immigrants were scarcely visible in the population and did not identify themselves with the masses of southern Italians who came later. The 1870s were the starting date of the migratory flow from southern Italy, which increased rapidly during the next fifty years until the outbreak of World War I (Velikonja, 1977:68). In 1860, there were only 9,231 Italians in the United States; by 1904, there were 741,986 (Castiglione, 1974:53). The crest of the immigrant wave was between 1901 and 1914, when the yearly average totaled 616,000 (Gallo, 1974:25).

In this heaviest immigration period, young healthy men were the typical immigrants, with few elderly and even fewer female arrivals. Pushed by economic necessity, many men, both single and married but traveling alone, came to the United States with the idea of going back to Italy as soon as possible. The United States represented a source of work and income for them that would support their families, who during the trying times, by necessity, remained at home. This kind of emigration was not only acceptable but also encouraged in Italy. Although the exact number is unknown, Caroli (1973) has shown that of the millions who left Italy to come to the United States, 1.5 million returned home during the years from 1900 to 1914. Thus, there was substantial return migration. The wandering of these men was permitted by the economic and political leadership of the United States as long as the need for cheap labor outpaced the demands of the ever-growing native xenophobia.

Gradually, migration chains formed as families followed the men to specific sites, assisting each other in the adjustment to the new environment. This second generation of immigrants became more assimilated into American culture and changed the perception of Italian ethnic identity. As Alba (1985:56) explains, "The awareness of a very different set of cultural standards in the surrounding society, of which it was more a part than its parents, weakened its loyalty to Mezzogiorno culture." Thus, ethnic identification extended beyond the village to include people from the same province, sharing a dialect and practicing similar customs. This expansion of ethnic identity included all persons with an Italian surname and heritage. As the boundary of ethnicity grew, new and different social and cultural characteristics became identified as Italian American. This broader scope of ethnicity included many traits of the mainstream culture of the United States (Tricarico, 1985). Until 1925, the number of men remained three times greater than that of women as a result of return migration (Meloni, 1977:7).

In 1926, strict immigration quotas based on national origin were imposed by the U.S. government, and the flow of immigrants decreased to a trickle. The Immigration Act of 1965 substituted the national origin quotas for a new set of preferences, helping new immigrants join close relatives who were already residents of the United States (Velikonja, 1975:191)

Since 1967, an average of 23,000 Italian immigrants have come to the United States annually (Gallo, 1974:45). Recently arrived immigrants are quite different from the peasants who entered the North American continent at the turn of the century. More exposure to the modern world has lessened their isolation in the old country, and they are more likely to be well educated, having been specifically selected for certain occupations and professions that would not replace indigenous workers. Although more familiar with the modern world, these new arrivals also help to strengthen and maintain the traditions and customs of *la via vecchia*.

Residential Mobility and Kinship Ties. In arguing for pluralism or assimilation, a key indicator used by both sides has been residential segregation—that is, to what extent do ethnic groups, regardless of social class, remain ethnically segregated, and how lasting are these patterns of residential segregation?

Several studies have examined residential segregation among Italian Americans. From the very beginning of their immigration, Italians settled in what have been called "Little Italys," and these ethnic communities tended to be concentrated along the eastern seaboard, particularly in New York and the major cities of Rhode Island, Connecticut, Massachusetts, and New Jersey (Lieberson, 1963:79; Lopreato, 1970:41). Americans of Italian descent make up more than one-sixth of the population of New York City (Gallo, 1974:25). To a large extent, these general patterns of residential settlement have been maintained (Abramson, 1973:29; Lopreato, 1970:53). However, some migration between regions is occurring. According to the 1960 census, nearly 70 percent of Italian Americans were concentrated in the northeastern portion of the United States. By the 1990 census, this figure had dropped to 51 percent (U. S. Bureau of the Census, 1993).

Although general patterns of residential segregation have been maintained, a more significant indicator of ethnic pluralism is the maintenance of neighborhoods. There is evidence to suggest that, for Italians, the meaning of "neighborhood" transcends the physical characteristics of housing. Italians imbue neighborhoods with a special significance that creates, in effect, an atmosphere of extended families. In an early study of the Italian North End of Boston, Firey (1947) found that second-generation Italians were more inclined to move to the suburbs than the older, first-generation Italians. He interpreted this to mean that they were seeking identification with American cultural patterns (Firey, 1947:200–209).

Years later, when assimilationist theories were being challenged, Glazer and Moynihan (1963:187) noted that "while the Jewish map of New York City in 1920 bears almost no relation to that in 1961, the Italian districts, though weakened in some cases and strengthened in others, are still in large measure where they were." They also noted two trends among second-and third-generation Italians. One trend was a tendency to refurbish old neighborhoods, so that social mobility did not necessarily mean moving to suburbs. They also noted that when Italians did move, it was often a two-generation process, with both children and parents moving to suburban neighborhoods together. Glazer and Moynihan's findings were confirmed by a detailed analysis of residential segregation by ethnicity in New York City based on 1960 census data (Kantrowitz, 1973). Kantrowitz (1973:7) concludes, "that ethnic segregation . . . has declined little over a generation."

The meaning of the maintenance of ethnic neighborhoods, particularly for Italian Americans, has been investigated in a comprehensive study of ethnicity from the National Opinion Research Center (NORC) (Greeley, 1971). Greeley (1971:77) found that "of all the ethnic groups, Italians most often live in the same neighborhood as their parents and siblings and visit them every week." Further, he notes that, "When the same data are sorted out according to social class and the physical distance that separates the respondents from parents and relatives, Italians are still the most likely to visit both their parents and their siblings." Greeley (1971:78) concludes that among Italians, "ethnic differences seem to persist even when different social classes are examined separately." Similar data were reported by Abramson (1970). Studying ethnic communities in four Connecticut cities, Abramson found that more than 50 percent of Italians and eastern Europeans had friends and relatives in the immediate neighborhood, as compared with 10 to 15 percent for Jews, German Catholics, and other Americans of northern European and British descent.

Extending the analysis to visiting patterns as well as residential propinquity, Gallo (1974:86) found that, although first-generation Italians tended to live in closer proximity to kin than the second and third generation, the younger Italian Americans visited relatives and were in turn visited more frequently. Gallo (1974:86) concluded that "the second and third generation respondents became increasingly active outside the family as they acculturate to urban values, but at the same time retain family contacts. The extended family plays a greater role for the second and third generation respondents than for those of the first." Similar findings were reported by Goering (1971), who found that third-generation Italians were more likely to think of themselves ethnically than first- or second-generation Italians and concluded that ethnic awareness may be increasing.

In contrast to these findings, Lopreato's research on Italians in New Haven, Connecticut, indicates that middle-class Italians visit relatives only slightly more frequently than the general population, whereas working-class Italians visit twice as frequently. Lopreato (1970:51) concludes that "these findings seem to indicate that to a considerable extent the working class still adheres to old world habits and practices. The Italian-American middle-class, on the other hand, is for all practical purposes indistinguishable from the American middle class as a whole."

Drawing data from household surveys in Rhode Island, Kobrin and Goldscheider (1978) compared four Catholic ethnic groups with Protestants and Jews on several issues. On the issue of residential concentration, they found, like Lopreato, that it was affected by social class. Working-class Italians were more likely than middle-class Italian Americans to reside in ethnically cohesive neighborhoods.

Obviously, the relationship between social class and ethnicity is complex, and the final answer has not been provided. It seems unlikely that the upward social mobility of third- and fourth-generation Italians will lead to complete assimilation. Part of the problem stems from the fact that although studies of the relationship between the family system and ethnicity include a comparison by social class, many generalize their findings to the entire population. Thus, it becomes difficult to determine whether behaviors are indeed a function of ethnicity or related to social class. Yancey, Erickson, and Juliani (1985:186) critique this monolithic treatment of ethnic groups, claiming that researchers have not paid enough attention to differences that exist within an ethnic group. Examination of the internal structure of the group would facilitate the identification of conditions that produce ethnicity and ethnically related behavior. Instead, evidence indicates that they will continue to maintain a distinct ethnic identity.

Family Size and Fertility. Although impoverished Italian immigrant women had exceptionally large families, their second-generation daughters completely reversed this pattern. As reported by Rosenwaike (1973:272), the 1910 census showed that women of Italian parentage constituted 4.9 percent of the female population in Boston between the ages of 15 and 44 and accounted for 15.3 percent of the births for that city. Data from New York indicate a similar pattern. First-generation immigrant women generally had more children than other Americans, but those from Italy had exceptionally more. This changed drastically with the second generation. Rosenwaike (1973:275) concludes that "obviously very strong assimilationist pressures had been at work, for not only did the second generation Italian-American women, on the average, have fewer than half the children of the immigrant generation; they curtailed their childbearing to a level below that of Americans of native parentage."

Certainly, assimilationist pressure is one possible explanation for this intergenerational difference in fertility. However, Gambino (1974:163–164) offers an alternative explanation of this same phenomenon:

> Large families were found in the *Mezzogiorno* not because the *contadini* confused womanhood with high fertility. Nor did they have large families to satisfy any religious views. They had large families for two reasons. First, they lacked effective birth control technology. Second, a large number of children was an asset to a family in the economic system of old southern Italy. . . . Italian-American women of the second generation had means of birth control available to them. They were free to exercise only the traditional criterion regarding children— the economic well-being of the family . . . they had children in proportion to their family incomes in America, where economic realities punished families with many children. They and their husbands decided it was better for the family to limit its number of children. And they did so.

Thus, according to Gambino, it was not assimilationist pressures that caused second-generation women to limit their family size, but a continuing tradition of primary concern for family well-being.

The birth rate for third- and fourth-generation Italians still appears to be decreasing. According to the 1990 census, of all Italian-American women aged 35 to 44 years, 22.2 percent had no children, 36.3 percent had two children, and only 1.7 percent reported having five or more. (U. S. Bureau of the Census, 1993). In a study of three generations of Italians in New York City, Russo (1970:207) found definite generational variation in family size, with third-generation Italians reporting the fewest number of children. In response to the question, "How many children do you have?" 42.2 percent of third-generation Italians reported two or less. In contrast, among first-generation Italians, 54.7 percent came from families of five or more children. This trend is apparent despite the fact that most Italians are Catholic. In fact, in a national survey, Ryder and Westoff (1971) reported that Italian Catholics were most likely of all Catholic ethnic groups to use contraception other than the rhythm method. Thus, it would appear that the stereotype of the Italian woman burdened by large numbers of children as a result of religious convictions is certainly not typical of the average second-, third-, or fourth-generation Italian woman.

Endogamy. Rates of intermarriage are useful indicators of social amalgamation and the disposition to lose ethnic identification. Endogamy among Italian Americans has been the subject of several studies, dealing in various ways with each of the immigrant waves.

In one study, Kennedy (1952) investigated intermarriage among seven ethnic groups in New Haven, Connecticut, for the period 1870–1950; she found that, after Jews, Italians had the highest in-group marriage rate of the seven ethnic groups considered. However, the rate of in-group marriage showed a decrease from first-generation to second-generation Italians. In 1900, 97.9 percent of Italian marriages were strictly endogamous, as with most newly arrived ethnic groups. By 1950, this rate had fallen to 76.7, a sizable decrease but still high compared to other ethnic groups.

More recently, Abramson (1973) studied endogamy among nine Catholic ethnic groups using data from the NORC that sampled the entire white Catholic population of the United States between the ages of 23 and 57. He found that Italians were the only ethnic group of those arriving prior to 1920 that still showed relatively high rates of endogamy. Sixty-six percent of Italian Catholics in his sample were endogamous, compared with 50 percent or less for the Polish, Lithuanian, eastern European, German, Irish, and English groups. The only groups with higher rates of in-group marriage were the Spanish-speaking Catholics and the French Canadians. However, these results were tempered by several factors. Among those factors influencing rates of intermarriage was geographic location. Those Italians living in the middle Atlantic states with high concentrations of Italians had very low rates of intermarriage (only 27 percent), but this figure increased to 49 percent in the north central portion of the United States, where Italians are relatively few in number. Even more significant were the different rates of intermarriage when age was used as a control. Whereas only 27 percent of Abramson's sample of Italian Americans between the ages of 40 and 50 married non-Italians, 42 percent of those between 20 and 30 intermarried. He also found level of education to have an effect on endogamy, with those completing high school having much higher rates of intermarriage than those without a high school diploma. This indicates that education is a powerful influence on assimilation and that rates of intermarriage for Italians may continue to increase as they obtain college degrees and are increasingly exposed to individuals of other ethnic backgrounds.

These findings were basically confirmed and further refined by Alba (1976), who used the same data to determine whether there was a generational effect on rates of intermarriage. He found that rates of intermarriage increased in each generation, although they remained lower for Italians than for most other groups. Alba (1976:1039) concluded that "the most obvious finding . . . is the universality of a trend toward increasing social assimilation."

Finally, in the extensive study of ethnic pluralism in American life (previously discussed in regard to residential concentration), Kobrin and Goldschneider (1978) found that Italians of all age groups were more likely than Irish, French Canadians, and Portuguese to have a spouse of the same ethnic origin, although this was less true of younger than older Italians.

Kobrin and Goldscheider's (1978:230) conclusions about the meaning of ethnicity in American life disagree sharply with those of Alba:

> Overall, ethnic homogamy has declined as the most important distinguishing feature of ethnic groups. Ethnicity in America is much less based on marriage within narrowly defined ethnic communities and the role of the intermarried is apparently being redefined in such a way as to allow for the ethnic community identification. . . . These convergences and growing homogeneity among ethnic communities in marriage patterns do not necessarily imply similarities and uniformities. That these marriage differences reflect more than class and cohort variations among ethnic groups suggests that specific ethnic structural and cultural determinants are operating.

Divorce.   Marriage was essential for the southern Italian as a source of social identity, and family stability still seems to be relatively intact. According to the 1990 census report on ethnicity (U.S. Bureau of the Census, 1993), there were 3.1 million families in 1990 whose head was of Italian origin. Most of these families were composed of husband-wife families (83 percent), and only about 12 percent were families with a female head.

The stability of the Italian family is reflected in the low divorce rates for Italian Americans. According to the U.S. Bureau of the Census (1993) only approximately 7 percent of all Italian Americans are divorced, and the divorce rate for younger Italians is not significantly higher than for those over 45 years of age. In a comprehensive study of ethnicity in the United States using data based on seven NORC surveys, Greeley (1974:46) found that Italian-American Catholics had the second-lowest divorce rate (only 2 percent) of all ethnic groups. The only group with a lower divorce rate was Irish-American Catholics (1.8 percent). Similar findings were reported by Kobrin and Goldscheider (1978:40), who found that Italians and Irish were least likely of all Catholic ethnic groups to not only divorce but also to remarry if they did terminate their first marriage. Although the effects of religion cannot be discounted, the relatively weaker ties of the Italians to the Catholic church indicate that family influence is certainly playing some role in maintaining a low divorce rate. This can be illustrated by the fact that other Catholic groups that have stronger ties to the Catholic church have higher divorce rates. For example, Polish, Slavic, and French Catholics all have divorce rates of more than 4 percent, and Spanish-speaking Catholics have a divorce rate of 6.6 percent. Thus, Catholicism cannot be the only explanatory factor for the low divorce rate among Italian Americans. Strong familism is certainly a critical variable.

Social Class.   The Italians came to this country basically illiterate and with few skills to offer except a willingness to work. The significance attached to work and the disdain of the *contadino* for the value of education, as previously described, was carried over into their life in American society by resistance to the educational institutions. This conflict was very conspicuous in the early part of the twentieth century, when Italian children were perceived as "problems" in the school system (Covello, 1967:284). Second-generation Italian children were more likely than other children to be truant, late, and involved in disciplinary infractions (Covello, 1967:285). According to Covello (1967:288- 296), there were many aspects of southern Italian cultural patterns that contributed to resistance to education. First, there was a fear on the part of the parents of the indoctrination of alien concepts that might destroy family unity. This fear was compounded by the belief that all necessary skills could be learned in the home or through apprenticeships. Second, there was an economic aspect to the conflict. The southern Italian peasant was accustomed to economic contributions to the household from children as young as 12 years of age. The idea of adolescents remaining in school throughout their teenage years was perceived by the first generation as enforced idleness of no clear benefit (Covello, 1967:289). Girls, in particular, were actively discouraged from attending school, an attitude that put them in direct conflict with compulsory education laws.

This antagonism toward formal education expressed by first-generation Italians has had long-range repercussions. In terms of level of education, the Italians have ranked behind other ethnic groups that came to the United States at approximately the same time. According to a U.S. census report based on 1972 data, the greatest difference between Italian Americans over the age of 35 and those under 35 was in the percentage of graduations from high school. As shown in Table 1, although only 31.9 percent of those over 35 graduated from high school, 51.1 percent of the younger Italians finished high school—an increase of almost 20 percent. Similarly, whereas only 16.5 percent of those under 35 years of age graduated from college (a relatively low figure), this still represents a marked increase over the 6 percent of college graduates over 35 years of age. According to the 1990 census, these numbers have changed somewhat (Table 2). While the percentages of all Italian Americans completing high school remains relatively high, the rate for persons aged 18-24 years of age

TABLE 1 Years of School Completed By Italian Americans, By Age (1973)

	Elementary			High School		College		Median School Years
Age	0–4 (percent)	5–7 (percent)	8 (percent)	1–3 (percent)	4 (percent)	1–3 (percent)	4 or more	(percent)
25–34	0.9	2.4	3.3	13.0	51.1	12.3	16.5	12.6
35 and over	8.7	10.5	17.0	19.7	31.9	6.1	6.0	11.1

Source: U.S. Bureau of the Census (1973).

TABLE 2   Years Completed By Italian Americans, By Age (1990)

	Elementary	High School		College	
Age	0–8 (percent)	1–3 (percent)	4 (percent)	1–3 (percent)	4 or more (percent)
18–24	4.2	10.1	30.9	43.5	11.3
25 and over	8.9	13.0	32.4	23.8	20.9

Source: U.S. Bureau of the Census (1993).

has fallen to 30.9 percent, while persons age 25 and older graduate high school at a rate of 32.4 percent.

These specific beliefs about the value of formal education are part of a more general orientation toward life. Several studies have attempted to measure these beliefs and assess their impact on social mobility. An early study by Rosen (1959) found that Italian Americans placed relatively low value on independence and achievement training and had relatively low aspirations in terms of expectations for education and occupational choice. In a more recent study of adult males, Featherman (1971) found that Italian and Mexican Catholics expressed a high "materialistic orientation" toward work, regarding work as instrumentally valuable in achieving other goals rather than as intrinsically satisfying. However, Featherman cautions against using adult motivation as an explanatory variable for ethnic group achievement differentials and suggests that motivation to complete school might be the key intervening variable. Finally, in a study of college seniors, Gottlieb and Sibbison (1974) asked students to explain their reasons for attending college. Both male and female Italian-American students rated job training as a more important reason than more abstract reasons such as seeking knowledge.

One visible outcome of these attitudes is that Italians largely went into blue collar work, a pattern that has begun to change only within the third generation. Table 3 compares the employment patterns of first- and second-generation Italian men from the 1950 census and all men from the 1972 and 1990 census. There was very little change between the first and second generations, with men of both generations largely employed in blue collar work as either craftsmen or operatives. As Meloni (1977:10) explains, "As many as two-thirds of the second generation have remained common labourers like their fathers. The gap between the first and second generation is still smaller for Italian-Americans than for any other major European ethnic group in America." By the third generation, a significant shift toward white collar work accompanied by an increase in the ranks of professionals can be seen. However, much of social mobility that has occurred has been in the television industry, newspaper reporting, and sports (Meloni, 1977:10). This can probably be attributed to the lesser role of education in occupational mobility among Italians. Unlike many other ethnic groups,

TABLE 3   Employment Patterns of Four Generations of Italian-American Males

	First-Generation Males (percent) 1950	Second-Generation Males (percent) 1950	All Italian Males (percent)[a] 1972	All Italian Males (percent)[b] 1990
Professional	3	6	13	13
Managerial	13	10	14	17
Clerical and sales	6	17	15	25
Craftsmen	24	22	22	19
Operatives	24	29	16	10
Laborers	14	9	9	5
Service workers	14	6	10	10
Private household workers	0	0	0	0

Sources: Gambino (1974:83); U.S. Bureau of the Census (1973, 1993).
[a]This report did not differentiate by place of birth but by ethnic identification; thus, all three generations are included in this figure.
[b]This report did not differentiate by place of birth but by ethnic identification; thus, all four generations are included in this figure.

upward mobility among Italians has not necessarily been correlated with higher educational levels (Kobrin and Goldscheider, 1978:32). The fourth generation continues to show the move to white collar occupations, particularily in clerical and managerial occupations, with a corresponding drop in craftsmen and laborers.

In analyzing the work history of Italian women, some research has centered on the expected conflict between work and family life. A study of Italian immigrants in Buffalo, New York, in the early part of the twentieth century discovered that although most Italian women were employed, their employment was limited to certain types of work (Yans-McLaughlin, 1977). Specifically, they were likely to work as seasonal laborers for fruit- and vegetable-processing companies. In contrast to Polish immigrants, they rejected domestic labor, which would take them out of the Italian community and into other people's homes. I interpret this pattern of work choice as being compatible with the family orientation of the immigrant, because it allowed the family to continue as the basic productive unit. It was a situation that minimized family strain by permitting mother and child to work together. As Yans-McLaughlin (1977:189) notes: "While 90 percent of the American-born children came to the canneries as independent workers, all the Italian youngsters worked and traveled with their parents. This suggests the foreign parents' willingness to relinquish economic and familial control over their young." In addition, seasonal work was not an assault on male pride, because the women were not working more steadily than their frequently unemployed husbands. Thus, they could contribute to the family income, while minimizing the sex role conflicts. Further, as a community activity,

TABLE 4   Employment Patterns of Three Generations of Italian-American Females

	First-Generation Females (percent) 1950	Second-Generation Females(percent) 1950	All Italian Females (percent) 1972	All Italian Females (percent) 1990
Professional	2	5	12	16
Managerial	4	2	6	13
Clerical and sales	8	40	46	49
Craftsmen	2	2	1	2
Operatives	77	44	18	4
Laborers	0	0	1	1
Service workers	4	4	15	14
Private household workers	1	0	2	1

Sources: Gambino (1974:83); U.S. Bureau of the Census (1973, 1993).

field work permitted more strict familial and sexual control over women than domestic work.

More recently, the work patterns of Italian women have been similar to those of Italian American men. As shown in Table 4, first-generation Italian women were most likely to be operatives. The second generation shifted to clerical work, as did most women during the expansion of this sector of the labor force after World War II. Even so, a relatively high percentage of women remained operatives compared with most other women, who were more likely to be service workers. Further, Italian women are least likely of all ethnic groups except the Spanish to be professionals; although, like the men, they did show a significant increase in this category by 1972. The fourth generation of Italian-American females shows the continued drop in operative occupations with a corresponding increase in white collar jobs, particularly clerical/sales, and managerial fields. Since professional occupations require extensive schooling and a stronger career orientation, which might interfere with family life, the growth in professional employment for Italian women demonstrate changes in the Italian American family life.

Roles in the Nuclear Family

Although the southern Italian family has been termed patriarchal, the limitations of this description have already been discussed. All authority did not reside with the father, largely because of the social and emotional leadership roles of the Italian mother, which gave her considerable power and influence in her family's affairs. However, her power, like the father's, was circumscribed, and there was a distinct separation of roles for men and women. This division of labor was largely maintained by the first-generation immigrant to the United States, and even in the second generation, there are indi-

cations that remnants of fictitious patriarchy remain. As one second-generation mother (and grandmother) describes her marriage, "The most important thing is, that a man wants to be head of the family, so he could be, but in
a roundabout way, I get my own way. So he's the boss, but I get my way if I
know how to work it. . . . But you have to work very hard to make a successful
marriage. You have to be a saint sometimes."

Several writers have explored this theme, comparing attitudes toward
familial roles of first- and second-generation Italians. One study (Ware, 1935)
found quite different beliefs between those over 35 years of age and those
under 35 in regard to the interpretation of familial roles. Ware (1935:193)
found that 64 percent of younger Italians compared with 35 percent of the
older group disagreed with the statement: "The husband's authority should
be supreme." Eighty-six percent of the younger group compared with 58 percent of the older group did not think large families were a blessing. Finally,
54 percent of the younger group compared with 31 percent of the older
group disagreed that a child should sacrifice his personal ambition for the
welfare of the family group.

In a comprehensive study examining changes between the southern
Italian peasant and first- and second-generation Italian Americans, Campisi
(1948) found major changes. He described the southern Italian peasant as
patriarchal, the first generation as fictitiously patriarchal, and the second generation as democratic, with the father sharing high status with the mother
and children. He found little in-group solidarity among second-generation
Italians and a general weakening of Italian culture, which was no longer
transmitted by the family but by the larger society.

Both Ware (1935) and Campisi (1948) performed their studies at a
time when researchers believed that assimilation was inevitable, and thus
both studies concentrated on differences between generations. Other more
recent studies have found more cultural continuity than was originally
believed to exist. In a descriptive study of an urban Italian neighborhood,
Gans (1962) found that although some of the outward manifestations of
Italian culture had disappeared, many traditional patterns remained. One
specific manifestation was what Gans termed the "segregated conjugal pattern," in which husbands and wives had distinctly separate roles, duties, and
obligations and turned to kin of the same sex for advice and companionship
so that the society essentially was sexually segregated. According to Gans
(1962:52):

> The segregated conjugal pattern is closely associated with the extended family,
> for the functions that are not performed by husband and wife for each other
> are handled by other members of the extended family. In a society where male
> and female roles are sharply distinguished, the man quickly learns that, on
> many occasions, his brother is a better source of advice and counsel than his
> wife.

Although Gans's findings have been criticized for being applicable only to second-generation, working-class Italians, not suburban, college-educated Italian Americans (Lopreato, 1970), some more recent empirical studies indicate that even among upwardly mobile individuals, traditional patterns remain. In a survey of graduating college seniors in five schools in Pennsylvania, Gottlieb and Sibbison (1974:49) found that Italian Catholic students were more likely to have a traditional view of sex roles than any other ethnic group, including the Irish, Jews, Poles, and African Americans. They also found that Italian women were less traditional than the men and even more so than women in the other ethnic groups.

Similar findings were reported by Greeley (1974: 157), who attempted to determine "whether ethnic heritage continues to have an influence on the relationships within the contemporary American family despite the process of assimilation and homogenization that was the American context of the immigrant family." In measuring the source of identification for third-generation Italians, Greeley (1974:162) found that the males found their fathers to be their primary source of identification, whereas the females were most likely to identify with their mothers. The identification with the mother was stronger for Italian females than for any other group except African Americans. However, Italian females tended to reject traditional roles for women and not consider domestic skills important. In contrast, Italian men's acceptance of the traditional role for women was particularly high.

Pursuing the issue of generational change in a study of three generations of Italian Americans, Gallo (1974:84) found increasing egalitarianism with each succeeding generation. Although the father still maintained his primary status within the family in the first generation, 80 percent of the second-generation respondents asserted that there was shared decision making among all family members and that discipline was shared between mother and father. This trend was increased among third-generation respondents, who reported democratic decision making within the family and the family performing primarily affectional functions.

Modern Italian-American marriages still appear to be more traditional when compared with the norm of American marriages today. The cultural ideal of the modern American marriage, according to Johnson (1985), is romantic love, companionship, and emotional support. In contrast, Italian-American marriages are more likely to be characterized by sex-role differentiation and an emphasis on instrumental, not emotional, functions. This varies by social class, however, because working-class marriages function with the greatest degree of sex segregation, hierarchy, and lack of emphasis on emotional concerns. The closely bound social network of the working class, including relatives and friends, maintains a greater segregation of sex roles but enables emotional needs to be satisfied by network members other than the spouse.

Socialization of Children

The first generation of Italians who came to the United States and settled in insulated communities were able to resist encroachments of American
culture in their own lives, but the beliefs and customs they valued were more
difficult to instill in their second-generation children. The second-generation
Italians were unable to maintain the same degree of isolation. They were
socialized not only by their parents but also by American institutions, particularly the school system, and what they were taught at home frequently con-
flicted with what they learned at school.

One solution to generational conflict used by many young Italian men
was to identify with peers rather than parents or school, which made friends
an important source of socialization. In Gans's (1962:38) study of Italians in
the West End of Boston, he describes the significance of the peer group:

> Before or soon after they start going to school, boys and girls form cliques or
> gangs. In these cliques, which are sexually segregated, they play together and
> learn the lore of childhood. The clique influence is so strong, in fact, that both
> parents and school officials complain that their values have difficulty competing
> with those being taught in the peer group. The sexually segregated clique main-
> tains its hold on the individual until late adolescence or early adulthood.

Among the concerns of the male adolescent peer groups were self-control,
independence, and a competitive sort of display involving games of skill, verbal bantering, and conspicuous consumption related to clothes or cars (Gans,
1962:38).

In Gans's study, the actual responsibility for childrearing belonged to
the mother, with formal discipline provided by the father (Gans, 1962:59). He
found the West End family to be adult centered in the sense that the household was run to satisfy adult wishes first. Children were expected to act like
adults and not interfere with adult activities. By the age of seven, girls were
expected to assist their mothers, and boys were given more freedom to roam
(Gans, 1962:56). Punishment tended to be physical but intermingled with
verbal and physical signs of affection.

In a recent study, 76 families in which both spouses were Italian
American were interviewed, and their responses were compared with those of
families in nonhomogamous marriages. Distinctive patterns of childrearing
among the Italians were identified. Specifically, the Italian mother was found
to exhibit a high level of nurturing. As Johnson (1978:38) reports:

> Her total devotion to her children in material and emotional support, caresses
> food-giving, and in fact, supportive extension of herself makes her an indis-
> pensable figure in her children's lives. Her love for her children has few con-
> tingencies, and other than diffuse expectations for respect and sociability she
> has few strings attached to it.

A second distinguishing feature was the manner in which discipline as a means of social control was used (Johnson, 1978:38):

> In Italian-American families, discipline is frequently used, and it is physical, swift and directed at the external locus of control (rather than appeals to the child's conscience). . . . Italian parents value love and affection between themselves and their children. Love, enjoyable for its own sake, is also employed to manage and control the behaviors of their children.

According to the author, this use of both punishment and love as mechanisms of social control cements family solidarity while discouraging autonomy and independence.

The Extended Family

Researchers have described the ethos of familism as characteristic of the southern Italian family. The concept of familism refers to the domination of the kinship group over other forms of social organization (Gallo, 1974:87). Because of this domination, interaction with nonfamily members was limited, and in southern Italy few moral sanctions existed outside the immediate family. One indicator of familism is the number of friendships formed outside the immediate family group. In a study of first- and second-generation Italian Americans, Palisi (1966:175) found that first-generation Italians were likely to have fewer friends outside the family and belong to fewer formal organizations than the second generation. However, the extent of participation in family affairs was still stronger for the second-generation Italians. He concluded that "individuals in the second generation are likely to be more assimilated, and more outgoing and have more opportunities to make friends than do first-generation persons. Thus, they make friends fairly easily. But they also retain some of the old world patterns of family participation" (Palisi, 1966:175).

Another indicator of familism is the strength of sibling relationships. One extensive analysis of modern Italian-American families (Johnson, 1982) examined sibling solidarity by ethnicity and social class. Between 1974 and 1977, Johnson interviewed three family subgroups: in-group married Italian Americans, out-group married Italian Americans, and a Protestant, non-Italian control group. The subjects were of comparable ages and stages in the family cycle and geographically stable, which enabled a comparison by ethnicity, religion, and social class of sibling relationships of middle-aged persons in solid marriages.

The availability of relatives often is considered a primary factor affecting kinship interaction. To test this claim, Johnson (1982:160) compared the ethnic subgroups by the number of relatives living within the city. The in-group married Italian Americans were more likely to have siblings living within the city and more relatives in geographic proximity. This finding supports the proposition that Italian Americans establish and maintain households near their closest kin.

Daily or weekly contact of Italian Americans with siblings was found to be quite high. The proportion of in-group married Italians having daily contact with siblings (63 percent) was twice as high as out-group married Italians (32 percent) and was five times greater than the Protestant group (12 percent) (Johnson, 1982:161). The frequency of interaction also varied by sex, with fewer husbands than wives in all three subgroups reporting daily contact with siblings. Still, the in-group married Italian-American men maintained the highest frequency of contact among the males.

When analyzed on the basis of social class, working-class families had the most frequent interactions with siblings. Class differences were large among the out-group married and Protestant families, but the in-group married families showed little social class variation, maintaining higher frequency of sibling contact than the other subgroups. Thus, Johnson's findings support the argument that intermarriage rather than social class accounts for the variation in sibling solidarity.

Johnson attributes the high degree of sibling solidarity among in-group married Italians to the organization of immigrant families. The emphasis on parental respect and authority minimized conflict among children, and the employment of both parents led them to focus their attention on the children as a group rather than on any individual child. Immigrant families were often part of an active, extended family system living near enough to allow frequent contact. This contact enhanced surrogate parenting and diluted strong, emotional relationships between parents and children.

Sibling solidarity served many important functions in Italian American families. Siblings provided physical care, supervision, education, and an amelioration of the family's power structure and parental distraction. The sibling mutuality and interdependence established during the childhood years continued into adulthood as the result of close geographical proximity and the set pattern of "sociability and mutual aid" (Johnson, 1982:164).

The strength of extended family ties also results in exceptional nurturing and support for aged family members. In comparing data on family interaction of Italian-American elderly with a national sample, Johnson (1978:36) found that the Italian elderly were more likely to be integrated into a family system, have a larger number of surviving children, and be in more frequent contact with their children and that the widowed were less likely to live alone. Further, the younger, married Italian families were four times more likely than non-Italians to endorse without reservation the thought of an elderly parent living with them (Johnson, 1978:37). They were also decidedly more likely than non-Italians to reject outright the choice of a nursing home as a last resort for an incapacitated parent. Johnson (1978:39) concluded that because Italian families are more likely to spend leisure time with relatives than friends, they viewed their obligation to aged parents as a natural outcome of the family cycle. Because the family operates as a source of nurturing that fulfills the dependency needs of all its members, the onset of dependency of an elderly member is merely an extension of a lifetime pattern.

Another study (Tricarico, 1984) examined three generations of Italian Americans residing in the southern Greenwich Village. Tricarico (1984) employed an in-depth and extensive collection of historical, census, demographic, geneological, economic, and participant observation data to discover the social and filial characteristics of the elderly Italian Americans residing in Greenwich Village. The elderly in Tricarico's sample had lived in this neighborhood for most, if not all, of their lives. Although characterized by low incomes, the survival skills secured during years of economic hardship left the immigrants and their children with low expectations and a desire for continued independence. The elderly tried to provide their own economic support and live alone rather than with their children or any other family members.

A major determinant of neighborhood status for these elderly was filial obligation to care for an aging parent (Tricarico, 1984:86). Their children usually resided nearby and were available for assistance when advanced age and poor health lessened the parents' ability to maintain total independence and care for themselves. Although family care was clearly a filial obligation, it was often a source of considerable strain on the entire family network. The primary burden of care fell on the child, married or not, who was the last to remain in the neighborhood. This was usually the daughter who lived geographically closest to her parents or in-laws. Children who lived farther away remained in close contact with parents by telephone but did not assist with the physical care.

In the previously cited study of in-group married Italian Americans, out-group married Italian Americans, and Protestant non-Italians, Johnson (1985:10) also analyzed "how variations in values on independence are translated into ongoing relationships between generations in a family: the elderly parents, their middle-aged offspring and the adolescent children." With ethnicity as the independent variable, Johnson (1985:11) asked the question, "Does the family system of this subculture [Italian-American] resolve the dependence-independence dilemma differently from the [dominant] American pattern?"

In this analysis, the three ethnic subgroups were compared in terms of network connections, filial relationships, kinship solidarity, marital relations, and the socialization process. All these categories were expected to vary by ethnic group as well as be significantly influenced by geographical and social mobility, intermarriage, and the transmission of values throughout the developmental cycle of the family. The sample was composed of nuclear households, each maintaining economic independence from the kinship network.

Few had an elderly parent or any other relative residing in the household—only the married couple and their nonadult children. However, elderly parents, siblings, and other relatives often lived in geographical proximity and reported very cohesive bonds throughout the network. Thus Johnson (1985:66) concluded that "although the structure is inclined to be nuclear, the family can readily incorporate members of the extended group into its functions."

Geographic mobility had little effect on the life situation of the 65-years-old and older sample of in-group married Italian Americans, because 97 percent had at least one child living in proximity (Johnson, 1985:146). These elderly reported frequent interaction with their children and a rewarding and satisfying grandparent role. Strong family ties compensated for role losses and helped avoid progressive withdrawal from social interaction.

Social activity and degree of social isolation did not vary by sex, but there was a difference between the "old old" (75 years of age and over) and the "young old" (65–74 years). Many of the young old were born in the United States and had led an active social life involving many contacts outside the family as well as a kinship network that grew larger with each generation. The growing social network also eased the compensation of role losses, including widowhood. Fluency in English was greater with the young old and allowed for an easier integration into family activities and American culture.

This study verified the existence of a strong filial bond between middle-aged children and their elderly parents. The norms of the in-group married Italian Americans' subculture still holds the family in a position of centrality, establishes a familial hierarchy with parents at the top, and prescribes that parents are given respect, gratitude, and love. Johnson found that this subgroup was most likely to include their elderly parents in their social activities and households and would never consider placing them in a nursing home.

CHANGE AND ADAPTATION

Two perspectives characterize present debates regarding the maintenance of ethnic identity. One perspective emphasizes the class-based nature of ethnic traits; the other stresses the uniqueness of Italian ethnicity that will perpetuate a sense of identity among third- and fourth-generation Italian Americans.

According to the class-based view, the problems experienced by Italian Americans and the issues raised about them are expressed in ethnic terms that are produced by the life experiences of the working and lower-middle classes (Tricarico, 1985:80). The focus on the family, which characterizes the lower classes, includes values incompatible with the individualism and consumerism emphasized by the general cultural pattern in the United States.

The family networks of the Italian Americans, dispersed in individual households, have become increasingly mobile. This movement and the resulting transformation of kinship relations is likely to continue as Italian Americans become more integrated with the American middle class. The neolocalism of modern-day Italian American households has changed the family network. Kin are no longer neighbors, and great differences have arisen in income, education, and occupation among members of a family system, causing segregation and isolation of family households (Tricarico, 1984). As Tricarico (1984:89) explains, Italian-American households have "become increasingly neospatial and heterogeneous, having implications for the greater authority of the nuclear unit." This new lifestyle places great pressure on the solidarity of the family network and continues to exist as more married children become absorbed in occupations, homes, and the performance of familial functions as an independent unit.

Similarly, a 1975 study in the Bridgeport, Connecticut metropolitan area of persons of Italian descent found a continuity in close ties among all kin members, with a decline in the closeness of later generations and among those with higher educational and/or occupational levels. Social class had little effect on the closeness of relations within the nuclear family, but higher social class was associated with a diminishment of positive attitudes toward relatives outside the household. The middle-class Italian Americans placed a stronger emphasis on individualism, relying on friends to play the roles once filled by their large family network. From this study, Crispino (1980) concluded that close family ties are likely to continue among nuclear family members, but mobility concerns will exceed the extended family in importance, leaving only infrequent occasions for direct involvement in the family network to strengthen the ties.

The traditional assumption about cultural assimilation is the "straight-line" theory, which assumes a decline in ethnicity with each successive generation of a cultural group as it confronts the focal culture and its standardizing influences. The straight-line theory, confined to an upwardly mobile society, claims that both social and economic mobility have a positive correlation to acculturation and assimilation. In other words, ethnicity is a property of the working class and disappears as second and third generations of immigrants ascend to the middle class.

Tricarico (1985) cites studies that present straight-line assimilation as incompatible with Italian-American ethnicity. The low prestige assigned to immigrants caused them to reject their Italian ethnicity and culture. However, these studies have uncovered new definitions of the relationship to their ethnicity by third- and fourth-generation Italian Americans. The broader social acceptance of cultural diversity has enabled these later generations to have an ethnic identification and expression combined with a mainstream identity and culture.

One problem with recent studies of white ethnicity is that they have only classified persons into ethnic categories and have failed to measure the strength of ethnic commitments. The result has been a lack of empirical data to support the many claims of the resurgence of ethnicity among certain groups of whites in the United States. To fill in this gap, Roche (1984:27) employed the attitudinal ethnicity scale to measure the "degree of attachment to the cultural, national and religious aspects of ethnicity." A large sample of suburban Italian Americans were interviewed to "discover the extent to which individuals in the same ethnic category are committed to the group" (Roche, 1984:28).

The sample was drawn from two suburbs of Providence, Rhode Island, one predominantly Italian American and the other ethnically mixed. Roche employed Sandberg's group cohesiveness scale, comprised of 30 statements, to measure respondents' attitudes toward several aspects of their ethnic groups, including three subscales centered on culture, nationalism, and religion. Roche found a drop in ethnicity on all measures with each consecutive generation. None of his data supported claims of third-generation growth in ethnicity. Instead, measures of the scale supported the straight-line theory that movement away from ethnicity and assimilation into the mainstream accompanies each generation.

Many variables affected the degree of ethnicity. Age was positively related to ethnicity, with stronger levels of commitment found among the elderly and weaker levels among younger people. A strong, negative association was found between education and ethnicity. The highest levels of ethnicity were found among those with the fewest years of schooling, and ethnicity decreased as the number of years in school increased. Occupational status was also negatively related to ethnicity, because it declined in the white-collar portion of the sample.

The concept of symbolic ethnicity was developed by Gans (1985), who argues that ethnicity has become increasingly peripheral to the lives of many upwardly mobile members of ethnic groups. Members of ethnic groups adapt their ethnic identity to their current social position by selecting a few symbolic elements of their cultural heritage that do not affect their social interaction with others of a variety of ethnic backgrounds. This practice is explained in detail by Alba (1985:173):

> Symbolic ethnicity is vastly different from the ethnicity of the past, which was a taken-for-granted part of everyday life, communal and at the same time imposed on the individual by the very fact of being born into the group. The ethnicity that survives in the melting pot is private and voluntary . . . the ethnicity of white Americans has moved from the status of an irrevocable fact of birth to an ingredient of lifestyle.

The mobility of white ethnic groups has enabled them to maintain ethnic sentiments and diversity to an extent beyond that allowed their lower-class counterparts. Still, this ethnicity is American enough, in both behaviors and values, not to be perceived as threatening or divisive of the mainstream culture in the United States today.

As a result of the upward mobility of white ethnic groups, including Italian Americans, the ethnic role played by those reaching the middle classes is no longer ascriptive, but a voluntary role assumed with other social roles. Ethnicity, for these classes, has become an expressive rather than instrumental function in their lives (Gans, 1985). Ethnic identity has lost its focus in culture and organization and, in turn, its relevance to social behavior and family structure and has become a component of social-psychological identity for the individual, not the group.

REFERENCES

Abramson, Harold J. 1970. "Ethnic Pluralism in the Central City." Storrs, CT: University of Connecticut.

————. 1973. *Ethnic Diversity in Catholic America.* New York: John Wiley.

Alba, Richard D. 1976. "Social Assimilation Among American Catholic National Origin Groups." *American Sociological Review, 41* (December): 1030–1046.

————. 1985. *Italian Americans.* Englewood Cliffs, NJ: Prentice-Hall.

Campisi, Paul. 1948. "Ethnic Family Patterns: The Italian Family in the United States." *American Journal of Sociology, 53* (May): 443–449.

Carlyle, Margaret. 1962. *The Awakening of Southern Italy.* London: Oxford University Press.

Caroli, Betty Boyd. 1973. *Italian Repatriation from the United States, 1900–1914.* New York: Center for Migration Studies.

Castiglione, G. E. Di Palma. 1974. "Italian Immigration into the United States, 1901–1904," in F. Cordasco and E. Bucchioni (Eds.), *The Italians: Social Background of an American Group,* pp. 53–73. Clifton, NJ: Augustus M. Kelley.

Chapman, C. G. 1971. *Milocca: A Sicilian Village.* Cambridge, MA: Schenkman.

Child, Irwin L. 1943. *Italian or American? The Second Generation in Conflict.* New Haven: Yale University Press.

Covello, Leonard. 1967. *The Social Background of the Italo-American School Child.* Leiden, The Netherlands: E. J. Brill.

Dore, Grazia. 1968. "Some Social and Historical Aspects of Italian Emigration to America." *Journal of Social History, 2* (Winter): 95–122.

Featherman, David L. 1971. "The Socioeconomic Achievement of White Religo-ethnic Groups." *American Sociological Review, 36* (April): 207–222.

Feldstein, Stanley, and Lawrence Costello. 1974. *The Ordeal of Assimilation.* Garden City, NY: Anchor Books.

Femminella, Francis X. 1961. "The Impact of Italian Migration and American Catholicism." *The American Catholic Sociological Review, 22* (Fall): 233–241.

Firey, Walter. 1947. *Land Use in Central Boston.* Cambridge, MA: Harvard University Press.

Foerster, Robert L. 1919. *The Italian Emigration of Our Times.* Cambridge, MA: Harvard University Press.

Gallo, Patrick J. 1974. *Ethnic Alienation: The Italian Americans.* Rutherford, NJ: Fairleigh Dickinson University Press.

Gambino, Richard. 1974. *Blood of My Blood.* New York: Doubleday.

Gans, Herbert H. 1962. *The Urban Villager.* Glencoe, IL: Free Press.

————. 1985. "Symbolic Ethnicity: The Future of Ethnic Groups and Cultures in America," in N. R. Yetman (Ed.), *Majority and Minority,* 4th ed., pp. 429–442. Boston: Allyn and Bacon.

Glazer, Nathan, and Daniel P. Moynihan. 1963. *Beyond the Melting Pot.* Cambridge, MA: MIT Press.

Goering, John. 1971. "The Emergence of Ethnic Interests: A Case of Serendipity," *Social Forces, 50* (March): 379–384.

Gordon, Milton. 1964. *Assimilation in American Life.* New York: Oxford University Press.

Gottlieb, David, and Virginia Sibbison. 1974. "Ethnicity and Religiosity: Some Selective Explorations Among College Seniors." *International Migration Review,* 8 (Spring): 43–58.

Greeley, Andrew M. 1971. *Why Can't They Be Like Us?* New York: John Wiley.

———. 1974. *Ethnicity in the United States.* New York: John Wiley.

Hansen, Marcus Lee. 1958. "The Third Generation: Search for Continuity," in H. D. Stein and R. A. Cloward (Eds.), *Social Perspectives on Behavior,* pp. 139–144. New York: Free Press.

Hraba, J. (1994). *American Ethnicity,* 2nd ed. Itasca, IL: F. E. Peacock.

Johnson, Colleen Leahy. 1978. "Family Support Systems of Elderly Italian Americans." *Journal of Minority Aging ,* 3–4 (August–June): 34–41.

———. 1982. "Sibling Solidarity: Its Origins and Functioning in Italian-American Families." *Journal of Marriage and the Family,* 44 (1): 155–167.

———. 1985. *Growing Up and Growing Old in Italian-American Families.* New Brunswick, NJ: Rutgers University Press.

Kantrowitz, Nathan. 1973. *Ethnic and Racial Segregation in the New York Metropolis.* New York: Praeger.

Kennedy, Ruby Jo Reeves. 1952. "Single or Triple Melting Pot? Intermarriage in New Haven, 1870–1950." *American Journal of Sociology,* 58 (July): 56–59.

Kertzer, David 1. 1978. "European Peasant Household Structure: Some Implications From a Nineteenth Century Italian Community." *Journal of Family History,* 3: 333–349.

Kluckhohn, Florence R., and Fred L. Strodtbeck. 1961. *Variations in Value Orientations.* Evanston, IL: Row, Peterson and Co.

Kobrin, Frances E., and Calvin Goldscheider. 1978. *The Ethnic Factor in Family Structure and Mobility.* Cambridge, MA: Ballinger.

Lieberson, Stanley. 1963. *Ethnic Patterns in an American City.* New York: Free Press.

Lopreato, Joseph. 1970. *Italian Americans.* New York: Random House.

———. 1976. *Peasants No More.* San Francisco: Chandler.

Meloni, Alberto. 1977. *Italian Americans: A Study Guide and Source Book.* San Francisco: R and R Research Associates.

Palisi, Bartolomeo. 1966. "Patterns of Social Participation in a Two Generation Sample of Italian Americans." *Sociological Quarterly,* 7 (Spring): 167–178.

Roche, John P. 1984. "Social Factors Affecting Cultural, National and Religious Ethnicity: A Study of Suburban Italian-Americans." *Ethnic Groups,* 6: 27–45.

Rosen, Bernard C. 1959. "Race, Ethnicity and the Achievement Syndrome." *American Sociological Review,* 24 (February): 47–60.

Rosenwaike, Ira. 1973. "Two Generations of Italians in America: Their Fertility Experience." *International Migration Review,* 7 (Fall): 271–280.

Russo, Nicholas J. 1970. "Three Generations of Italians in New York City: Their Religious Acculturation," in Sylvano M. Tomasi and Madeline H. Engel (Eds.), *The Italian Experience in the United States,* pp. 195–213. New York: Center for Migration Studies.

Ryder, Norman B., and Charles F. Westoff. 1971. *Reproduction in the United States, 1965.* Princeton: Princeton University Press.

Spiegel, J. 1972. *Transactions: The Interplay Between Individual, Family and Society.* New York: Science House.

Tomasi, Lydio F. 1972. *The Italian American Family: The Southern Italian Family's Process of Adjustment to an Urban America.* New York: Center for Migration Studies.

Tomasi, Sylvano M. 1970. "The Ethnic Church and the Integration of Italian Immigrants in the United States," in Sylvano M. Tomasi and Madeline H. Engel (Eds.), *The Italian Experience in the United States,* pp. 163–193. New York: Center for Migration Studies.

Tricarico, Donald. 1984. *The Italians of Greenwich Village.* New York: Center for Migration Studies.

———. 1985. "The 'New' Italian-American Ethnicity." *Journal of Ethnic Studies,* 12(3):75–93.

U.S. Bureau of the Census. 1973. *Population Characteristics: Characteristics of the Population by Ethnic Origin.* Series P-20, no. 249, April. Washington, DC: U.S. Government Printing Office.

U.S. Bureau of the Census 1993. *1990 Census of the Population: Ancestry of the Population in the United States.* Series CP-3-2, October. Washington, DC: U.S. Government Printing Office.

Vecoli, Rudolph J. 1969. "Prelates and Peasants." *Journal of Social History,* 2(Spring): 217–268.

———. 1974. "The Italian Americans." *The Center Magazine,* 7 (July/August): 31–43.

Velikonja, Joseph. 1970. "Italian Immigrants in the United States in the Sixties," in Sylvano M. Tomasi and Madeline H. Engel (Eds.), *The Italian Experience in the United States,* pp. 23–39. New York: Center for Migration Studies.

———. 1975. "The Identity and Functional Networks of the Italian Immigrant," in Francesco Cordasco (Ed.), *Studies in Italian American Social History,* pp. 182–198. Totowa NJ: Rowman and Littlefield.

———. 1977. "Territorial Spread of the Italians in the U.S.," in S. M. Tomasi (Ed.), *Perspectives in Italian Immigration and Ethnicity,* pp. 67–79. New York: Center for Migration Studies.

Ware, Caroline F. 1935. *Greenwich Village.* New York: Harper & Row.

Wrigley, E. Anthony. 1977. "Reflections on the History of the Family," *Daedalus* (Spring): 71–86.

Yancey, William L., Eugene P. Erickson, and Richard N. Juliani. 1985. "Emergent Ethnicity: A Review and Reformation," in N. R. Yetman (Ed.), *Majority and Minority,* 4th ed., pp. 185–194. Boston: Allyn and Bacon.

Yans-McLaughlin, Virginia. 1977. *Family and Community. Italian Immigrants in Buffalo, 1880–1930.* Ithaca: Cornell University Press.

6 | The Polish-American Family

Helena Znaniecka Lopata

INTRODUCTION

The main thrust of this chapter is the Polish-American family as it exists within the developing and changing Polish ethnic community, called "Polonia" by its residents. This emphasis is different from that of much of the literature on ethnic groups, which is primarily concerned with individualistic assimilation and acculturation and attempts to determine the factors that impede or facilitate the absorption of peoples into a society. This chapter focuses on certain background characteristics of Old World Polish culture, especially in its peasant variations, and on historical trends in Polonia, which have created a unique ethnic community that persists into the 1980s and 1990s. The Polish family must be seen in its relation to the continued existence of the Polish-American community.

The last of the "early" (before the 1920s) immigrants into the United States were the Poles and the Italians. The Poles immigrated in three waves. The largest number came between 1880 and 1924, when entrance into America was cut off by new laws. They are known in the Polish-American community as the *stara emigracja,* "old emigration" (the Poles identify the movement as emigration from Poland rather than immigration to another country). The *nowa emigracja,* "new emigration," followed World War II and consisted of people displaced by the Germans or Soviets. The communists who took over Poland after that war did not allow emigration for many years, and only recently has there been a third wave of immigrants, though smaller in number. There is now also a reputedly large number of Poles in America on visitor visas who are working illegally to earn money to improve the situation of families back home.

HISTORICAL BACKGROUND

Families do not live in a vacuum but within a community and the larger society. Family actions and interactions are patterned by family roles, with obviously idiosyncratic variations growing out of family histories.[1] Family life is embedded in a complex culture, with each member holding beliefs, images, expectations, evaluations, and other ideological patterns relating to themselves, other family members, and the world in which they live. The various immigrant waves consisted of quite different types of people, and the Polish presence in America also included many political emigrés and temporary residents who helped create a very complex community organization. In all, this author (Lopata, 1976a) has estimated that approximately 1 million people identified as Poles or as having been born in Poland came to, and approximately 300,000 left, this country during the years between 1899 and 1972. How many and who came depended not only on the immigration laws of the United States but also on the situation in Poland. The country was occupied by three states—Russia, Austria, and Prussia—from 1795 to 1918. The national cultural society, however, retained its identity despite the absence of a unifying political state (for a discussion of these concepts, see Znaniecki, 1952).

The Polish immigrants to America came from two separate class subcultures, but they shared the Polish language, the Polish version of Catholicism, and many major cultural complexes. The subcultures were in fact variations on the major themes, but these variations basically kept the two groups apart in Poland and in America until recent years. The common themes of the immigrants included belief in a national character and a system of status competition along with the willingness and ability to build a complex ethnic Polonian community with horizontal strata and vertical lines of connection (Lopata, 1976b; Thomas and Znaniecki, 1918–1920). One group consisted of the combined, mutually influencing gentry, or small nobility and intelligentsia, and the other group consisted of various levels of the peasantry (Szczepanski, 1970). Urban bourgeois and working-class lifestyles were not highly developed in Poland during the time of the mass emigration (Jawlowska and Mokrzycki, 1978). In the decades when most old emigration families left Poland, "the social cleavage between peasants and *szlachta* [gentry] was absolute and unbridgeable" (Benet, 1951:33). Each group had its own image of the national character, status arenas, and hierarchies—as well as companionate circles of "ethclass" organization and informal association (Gordon, 1964; Lopata, 1976b).

The Poles in Poland undertook many revolts against the occupying forces, which resulted in the migration of political refugees. In addition, the Poles created governments-in-exile in Europe that needed funds and frequently sent representatives to America's Polonias to develop and nurture nationalism among the immigrants. In the interwar years, few immigrants came here and a fair number of prior settlers in America returned to Poland—although not as many as had originally planned to return once the country was independent, because many had become very comfortable on this side of the ocean.

[1] I am using here Znaniecki's (1965) definition of a social role as a set of patterned, functionally interdependent, social relations between a social person and a social circle, involving duties and rights.

Although the old pre-1920 emigration was heterogeneous, the vast majority belonged to the various subclasses of peasants (Szczepanski, 1970; Thomas and Znaniecki, 1918–1920). At the turn of the century, 34 percent were illiterate. That figure dropped to three percent by 1924. They came from villages and agricultural lifestyles, but most settled in urbanized areas and sought jobs in industry. Their memory of Poland was that of the village and a country under foreign domination. After World War II, the American government allowed a large number of Poles (more than 164,000) to enter the United States as displaced persons outside the quota structure (Lopata, 1976a:13). The new emigration came from a completely different background and much higher level of educational achievement. The country they left had changed considerably over the years since the turn of the twentieth century when the old emigrants left, as documented by many Polish rural sociologists (Jagiello-Lysiowa, 1976; Kowalski, 1967; Turowski and Szwengrub, 1976).[2] The two immigrant waves were so different that they created a great deal of conflict in the community. The new emigration looked down on the old emigration and its descendants, considering their lifestyle to be highly Americanized, their use of Polish archaic, and their subculture peasantlike. The old emigration considered the new emigration "uppity," and the new group's presence pushed the early settlers toward greater assimilation. Over time, the more educated descendants of the old emigration joined groups formed by the new, while the new emigration revitalized established organizations.

Polish-American Families: Common Themes

Despite the differences of emigration waves, social class backgrounds, and generation of residence here, there are certain commonalties among Polish Americans. These common themes include belief in a national character, intense interest in status competition, and the willingness to create and participate in a complex ethnic community. In this last characteristic, the Poles are very different than the Italians, as discussed in this book and by Cohler and Lieberman (1979).

National Character. The socialization of children and the interaction among adults in Poland and Polonia were, and apparently still are, based on a strong belief in a national character—admittedly with regional and even community, age, and sex variations.[3] Each believer in the Polish national character affirms its existence, but careful perusal of the literature, including autobiographies, indicates that the content of this alleged character contains only a few common items when expressed by different people (Super, 1939; Szczepanski, 1970).

[2]There are frequent comments in the Polonian press concerning the vast difference in the way most of the *stara emigracja* and the *nowa emigracja* see Poland. It would be interesting to compare the family life of former peasants who migrated to Polish cities with that of emigrants to American cities from Poland. Bloch (1976) has done that for families remaining in a smaller community in Poland with their relatives in America.

Szczepanski (1970:167) elucidates some of the components of the ideal national character of the upper classes in his *Polish Society:*

> The traditional Polish personality ideal was derived from the culture of the nobility and was composed of such traits as readiness for the defense of the Catholic faith, readiness for the defense of the fatherland, a highly developed sense of personal dignity and honor, a full-blown individualism, an imposing mien, chivalry, intellectual brilliance and dash.

This image includes the moral obligation of members of the Polish national cultural society to develop and perpetuate its culture and to educate potential members into its literary base in an effort to fight denationalization (Lopata, 1976c; Znaniecki, 1952). The obligation to fight the three foreign states that partitioned and ruled the Polish political state for 125 years before World War I resulted in numerous uprisings that failed, adding a tragic-romantic element to the upper-class vision of the national character. The intelligentsia's variation on the major theme added a strong intellectual bent—the members of that class saw themselves as "cultured men" familiar with all aspects of the national Polish culture as well as with the cultures of other nations (Lopata, 1976c; Szczepanski, 1962). This total image was shared by many political emigrés and most of the immigrants to America who had been displaced by World War II. The attempt to nationalize Polish Americans who did not belong to the upper class to gain assistance in the struggle for independence capitalized on this romantic image of the Pole.

Most of the peasants who emigrated prior to World War I did not share the intellectual and nationalistic features in their view of the national character. In fact, they tended to be anti-intellectual, believing that human beings were created for hard physical work. They saw Poles through a mixture of magic-religious prisms—basically as sinful and evil or, at least, weak (Chalasinski, 1946; Finestone, 1964, 1967; Thomas and Znaniecki, 1918–1920). This belief in a basically sinful human nature—the men easily ruled by temper, and both sexes by sexual desire and impulsive, often unwise, action—resulted in relatively harsh methods of socialization of children, different than the patterns evolving in America (Finestone, 1964; Thomas and Znaniecki, 1918–1920).

Despite these major differences between the upper-class and peasant images of the national character, there were many common elements. Super (1939, quoted by Lopata 1976b:114–115), who considered himself an objective observer, listed characteristics all Poles felt were common to them:

[3]Studies of the acculturation of a group of people limited to a few items, such as the use of language and religious celebrations, neglect a very important and more significant aspect of group identity, its feeling and definition of "national character." People who share a belief that they are similar transmit to younger generations this feeling of identity and their whole philosophy of life is incorporated in their child rearing procedures (McCready, 1974). Sandberg (1974) has an extensive set of measures of Polish-American ethnicity, but even he does not deal with beliefs about human nature, "Polishness" and childrearing methods.

A strong emphasis on equality within the two main classes with a strong sense of individualism; tolerance of other groups; religiosity of predominantly Catholic identity; idealism, romanticism; love of the soil; a strong family orientation; hospitality; interest in good food and drink of an international flavor; stress on courtesy, etiquette and manner highly developed and strictly followed.

The anthropologist Benet (1951:216) also pointed to this last characteristic, one that Poles are very conscious of and that is apparent in the letters contained in *The Polish Peasant in Europe and America* (Thomas and Znaniecki, 1918–1920):

> The Polish peasant is probably the most polite and well mannered man in Europe. Rural etiquette prescribes certain expressions and even certain dialogues for everyday life and it is not permissible to improvise substitutes.

One persistent theme passed on from generation to generation that is constantly repeated in the Polish and Polonian mass media and among Poles when they talk of themselves is the emphasis on individualism and competitiveness within one's own stratum (Benet, 1951:33):

> Within each class, however, there is an almost fanatical insistence on the equality of individuals. A Pole would rather bow to a foreigner than give authority to one of his own group.[4]

This belief in a basically competitive rather than solidified national group is a basic component of the fabric out of which Polish and Polish-American men and women weave their life course.

[4]There has developed among social scientists an image of peasants, especially those in countries where serfdom was abolished relatively recently, as passive (Brunner, 1929; Cohler and Lieberman, 1979; Schooler, 1976). This image totally ignores the evidence from such works as Thomas and Znaniecki (1918–1920) or the Nobel Prize–winning *The Peasants* by Reymont (1925), as well as that of the authors quoted earlier. Certainly, the Polish peasant was far from passive within his or her *okolica*. The negative image of the Polish immigrant is contained even in sociological literature.

Janowitz (1966:xxiii–xxv) reports in his introduction to a collection of works by W. I. Thomas and from Thomas and Znaniecki's (1918–1920) *The Polish Peasant in Europe and America* that one of the main reasons Thomas became interested in studying the assimilation of Poles was "Polish murder," so labeled by the Chicago police: "Boys and young men who were law-abiding or at least conforming would suddenly, with little provocation and no forethought, engage in violent and explosive fights, including attacks on police officers." That is hardly a sociological analysis. He further states:

> In the lore about W. I. Thomas that grew up among graduate students at the University of Chicago there was a story of how he came upon the use of letters as a crucial research tool. . . . One morning, while walking down a back alley in the Polish community on the West Side of Chicago, he had to sidestep quickly to avoid some garbage which was being disposed of by the direct means of tossing it out the window. In the garbage which fell at his feet were a number of packets of letters. Since he read Polish he was attracted to their contents, and he started to read a bundle which was arranged serially. In the sequence presented by the letters he saw a rich and rewarding account and in time he was led to pursue the personal document as a research tool.

Status Competition. The belief in individualism and competitiveness has evolved and been institutionalized into an elaborate system of status competition that regulates conflict, adds excitement (even *joie de vivre*), and has contributed to keeping the Polonian community and its families together and internally oriented despite the tendencies toward disorganization and gradual Americanization of the culture (Lopata, 1976b). Concern with and activity on behalf of one's "reputation," or position vis-à-vis other members of the community, underlies much of traditional village and urban life in Poland. The *okolica* (area within which a person's and a family's reputation is contained) can vary from a single village to the entire nation. In Poland, the *okolica* has expanded in size as villages have become less isolated in recent years and villagers enter other occupations (Dziewicka, 1976; Jagiello-Lysiowa, 1976; Jawlowska and Mokrzycki, 1978; Kowalski, 1967; Slomczynski and Wesolowski, 1978; Turowski and Szwengrub, 1976). Both Poland and the United States have provided not only arenas but also entire systems of status sources and hierarchies (Thomas and Znaniecki, 1918–1920:144; Jawlowska and Mokrzycki, 1978).

Traditionally, the major source of status is property, especially land and buildings. Other means of attaining status include less permanent economic goods, such as farm machinery, animals, products grown or hand crafted, and money earned by family members who gain paid employment. Finally, but also significantly, status evolves from a person's reputation derived from physical appearance, accomplishments, actions, and affiliations. The family is a very important source of status, locating the individual in the community at birth and continuing to contribute to status gain or loss throughout the life course. Spouses and children have a moral obligation to assist in the status-building or maintenance process of the family as a unit and of the individual members. Family members must continue to earn their right to the family's position and cooperative action through their own contributions throughout life. Finestone (1964, 1967) found this family system quite different than that of Italian families, whose right to cooperative membership is acquired at birth and never threatened, even in the face of societally disapproved behavior.

Polish immigrants of all classes brought with them to America this interest in status competition within a self-defined *okolica,* and this characteristic may be one of the major reasons why predictions of complete demoralization and disorganization of the family and the immigrant group as a whole were not fulfilled (Thomas and Znaniecki, 1918–1920). Simultaneously, as a major source of involvement in Polonia, this focus on status competition prevented interest in the community's reputation outside of its social boundaries and the use of more popular, external status symbols. Resources for upward mobility within American society as a whole were not used in the internal status competition if they did not have a traditional Polish base. This is especially true of the schooling of youth instead of immediate employment when legal requirements were met.

Polonia as an Organized Community. Although part of their set of five volumes entitled *The Polish Peasant in Europe and America* is devoted to the organizations of Polonia, Thomas and Znaniecki (1918–1920) did not fully stress the importance of the local and larger community in providing an organized, normative base for individual and family life. Immigrants to America, even if they came from small villages to large urban centers, seldom arrived and lived as isolated beings in a sea of foreigners. Most came to friends, former neighbors, or kinfolk who were already partially established among other Poles (Lopata, 1976a). These people built churches and schools, organized parishes and neighborhoods, and formed a multitude of voluntary organizations—pulling new members into the already existing life. The neighborhoods were woven into local communities in large cities, regional circles, and superterritorial complexes (Lopata, 1976b). During the many decades of its growth, Polonia developed multiple webs of companionate circles and services involving daily contact within local areas—at work, church, stores, and clubhouses. It is into this organized community that immigrants came. They involved themselves through various family members in all levels of community life, creating new groups through schisms or new interests while continuing interaction with kin and neighbors. Thus, the image of a totally disorganized slum with increasingly demoralized and isolated former peasants, as depicted by Thomas and Znaniecki (1918–1920), ignores this fabric of social relations within which the Polish-American family carried forth its life course (Suttles, 1968). Undoubtedly, marital and parental conflicts did exist; they were documented in Hamtramck (Wood, 1955), Sunderland (Abel, 1929), and Chicago (Pleck, 1983; Thomas and Znaniecki, 1918–1920), but the families basically survived.

Family Life. Families were needed by members for not only involvement in the status competition and maintenance of a social life within the *okolica* but also in everyday existence. Families worked to create a home and a means of having and raising children. Abel (1929:216) explained that the Polish immigrants who settled in the Connecticut Valley were able to buy up the land at astonishing rates: "The ability of the immigrant to establish himself so quickly and to pay off staggering mortgages in a short time was owing to the cheap labor offered by a numerous family and to the willingness to do hard work, and to his low standard of living." The neighbors of these immigrants were horrified by this standard of living and the level of child care. The death rate of Polish children was much higher than in neighboring families. Yet these immigrants and their children (with whom they fought constantly) not only bought land and homes but also built sturdy and sizable "Polish houses" and parishes.

Life for the immigrants was often very difficult. Parot (1982:165) describes all the problems of families in a Polish-American neighborhood in Chicago:

It was here where young Polish girls were seldom given the opportunity to finish even a grammar-school education; it was here where young Polish girls, out
of cultural background or sheer economic necessity, were hustled into any one
of several dozen sweatshops located in the environs . . . ; it was here where most
Polish women "escaped" the exploitation of the shops by settling into rigidly
endogamous marriages, which, under the best of circumstances, did little to
improve material living standards; it was here, in one of the most degrading tenement districts in all of Chicago, that the Polish working-class female experienced the highest fertility rate of any major ethnic group in the city; it was here
where the mortality rate of children born to Polish women exceeded that of any
other ethnic group—despite the fact that Chicago had witnessed a declining
mortality rate throughout the 1880s and had maintained one of the lowest mortality rates for large cities in the United States in 1900.

The life of the peasant segment of Polonia was described in great detail by
Thomas and Znaniecki (1918–1920) in their famous work, *The Polish
Peasant in Europe and America*. Unfortunately, many readers assumed that
this picture reflected all of Polonia, which it obviously did not or the community would never have developed its institutional and organizational
complexity (Breton, 1964).

Thomas and Znaniecki (1918–1920) were pessimistic about the future
of Polish peasant families in America. They foresaw a loosening of the ties to
the extended families of both the husband and the wife, to the village and the
parish, resulting in "hedonistic" and immoral behavior and individuated
rather than family-based orientation. They witnessed and documented incidents of wives charging husbands in American courts for nonsupport and
parents using the police and the courts in an effort to make their children
obey and contribute to the economic welfare of the family. They distinguished the following problems:

1. Demoralization of adults: (a) economic dependency (on the American welfare
   system—cases from the archives of United Charities); (b) breakdown of conjugal relations (materials chiefly of the Legal Aid Society); murder (criminal court
   and the coroner's office)
2. Demoralization of children (materials from juvenile court): (a) vagrancy and
   dishonesty of boys; (b) sexual demoralization of girls

Their focus on disorganization, arising from their theoretical perspective and
the obvious evidence of conflict in some families recorded by the American
agencies, led to a failure to include other aspects of Polish-American family
life in *The Polish Peasant in Europe and America*.

Several researchers have demonstrated that the predicted dissolution of
Polish-American families did not take place, at least as far as divorce statistics
are concerned. J. L. Thomas (1950), Rooney (1957), Polzin (1973, 1976), and
Chrobot (1982) concluded that the main reason high divorce and desertion

rates are not true of Polish-American families is the strength of their Catholic religion, but there appear to be other binding forces that were not dealt with by Thomas and Znaniecki. I will examine some of these forces and the roles of men and women in Polish-American families throughout the life course as far as data allow.

While all the family commotion was going on, the various Polonian communities were developing, expanding, and building their organizational homes. This is true of Chicago (Ozog, 1942), Hamtramck (Wood, 1955), and Buffalo (Obidinski, 1968). In addition, despite their original idea of working hard and saving all their money to return to Poland to buy land (or more land), these people contributed millions of dollars, clothing, and foodstuffs to the Polish fight for independence, Polish care during wars, and rebuilding of the country following wars. Much of that money went to families and home villages, but a considerable amount was sent to the nation at large.

Polonian families were originally diversified by social class, region, and type of community in Poland, and they became increasingly diversified as the Polonian communities expanded in America (Golab, 1977). The more educated or affluent immigrants organized an entire range of services and businesses needed by newcomers deprived of the established social institutions that existed in Poland. Geographical and social mobility was possible, one step at a time, because the new environment freed individuals and families from restrictions imposed by past family reputations, regulations, and occupations. Lack of language skills and opportunities for training outside a limited number of occupations, however, restricted this mobility for many (Duncan and Duncan, 1968; Hutchinson, 1956; Lieberson, 1963; Miaso, 1971). The insularity of the community prevented the use of American contacts, existing lines of mobility, and status symbols. Thus, the community was built with many layers and companionate circles, becoming relatively self-sufficient and opening opportunities for advancement, although mainly within its own boundaries (Breton, 1964). This community changed over time, modifying traditional family patterns and relations. Unfortunately, we do not know how the tensions and conflicts inevitably produced by migration, problems of settlement, and generational gaps were resolved. The community must have cushioned the effects of migration and change, focusing attention away from home problems, but there is insufficient information available about the scars and the strengths of family life in Polonia.

THE MODERN POLISH-AMERICAN FAMILY

Roles of Women: Growing Up

Polish culture contained, as does any other culture, many assumptions about the nature and proper roles of women in each major stage of their life course. At the time of the mass migrations, particularly among the peasant classes, many of these assumptions centered around women as sexual objects, actually or potentially. Parents were fearful of girls becoming pregnant before marriage or of developing "loose reputations." Thomas and Znaniecki (1918–1920) devoted an entire section of the third part of their work (on the disorganization of the immigrant) to the "sexual immorality of girls," equating it with criminal behavior and the vagabondage of boys.[5] Given the weakness of human character, Polish women were expected to be constantly susceptible to sexual advances, even when married. Strict socialization and control throughout life was their traditional lot.

Peasant families expected girls to continue the work of their mothers—learning to keep house, sew, cook, and take care of younger children (Chalasinski, 1946: chap. 12). Formal education was not considered important for them because the knowledge and skills they needed could be learned only at home. Furthermore, the girls, like their brothers, learned to work early in life, contributing what they could to the economic welfare of the family and carrying out tasks around the home and farm (Thomas and Znaniecki, 1918–1920).

Many observers of the Polish-American scene reported over the years that this attitude toward women's education was carried over by the peasants to this continent and by parents to their children (Abel, 1929; Obidinski, 1968; Wood, 1955). This does not mean that boys were encouraged to get as much education as possible—only that formal schooling was definitely discouraged for girls. If they had to go to school, the parochial rather than public school system was encouraged since parents wanted their girls to be under the close supervision of nuns (Kusielewicz, 1974; Kuznicki, 1978; Miaso, 1971).

The concern for the morality of Polish-American girls extended to their work for pay outside the home. Nonagricultural families faced a dilemma in that they were very interested in having each member bring in earnings and yet wanted to protect their daughters from temptation and even gossip by keeping them close to home or, at least, under close supervision. Domestic service was a preferred occupation for young women because it provided good training for future home roles.

The result of the undervaluation of education for the women of Polish-American families is evident in the types of occupations in which they are and have been found. In 1950, foreign-born Polish women, compared with other foreign-born women, were disproportionately located in such occupations as laborers, factory operatives, and service workers, especially in private service (Hutchinson, 1956:248). Comparatively few Polish women were recorded as clerical workers and professionals. More detailed analyses of job

[5]Actually, this view of the delinquency of girls is not unique to Polonia. Lerman (1973) points out that the American legal system has built its moral code into definitions of delinquent behavior that allow youths to be punished for behavior legally allowed for adults. "The vast majority of the girls in the Home [the State Home for Girls] today, as in past years, were accused of misbehavior that would not be considered crimes if committed by adults."

specialization found them disproportionately among charwomen, janitors, sextons, meat cutters, and self-employed managers of wholesale and retail trade. American-born females of Polish parentage were also disproportionately located among operatives and laborers, with few women in farming, either as farmers or farm laborers, or working in white collar jobs. However, this generation had moved out of service jobs in the private sector. Second-generation Polish-American women displayed an even greater occupational concentration than their first-generation counterparts, and more recent figures document a continuing lag in entrance into white collar occupations, particularly in the professions. Only Spanish and Italian women had lower white collar employment rates in 1970 (U.S. Bureau of the Census, 1971). These statements do not apply to the women of the new emigration, most of whom entered the country with at least a high school education, many going on to school in America and concentrating in white collar jobs. Throughout Polish history, the upper classes have maintained themselves through higher education, often using college as a means of ensuring that their daughters have educated, high-income earning husbands. There is recent evidence that Polish-American boys and girls have discovered higher education as a major means of upward mobility within American society and that their parents have modified their stance on such schooling (U.S. Bureau of the Census, 1993). According to the 1990 census, 30 percent of all Polish Americans aged 18–24 have completed high school, 44 percent have some college, and 11 percent have earned a bachelor's degree or higher (U. S. Bureau of the Census, 1993). One of the reasons Polish parents are becoming increasingly tolerant of the number of years their children, even daughters, spend in school, is that the younger generations appear to have won the struggle for their right to keep the money they earn outside of the home for personal use, so that they no longer contribute to the family economic welfare anyway.

The Role of Wife.[6]   A frequent component of descriptions of Polish and Polish American families is their allegedly total authoritarian and patriarchal nature. Polzin (1976:109) repeats this imagery as late as 1976: "The pattern of male dominance with corresponding unquestioning obedience by the wife and children belonged to the internalized norms on expected family behavior brought to this country." Yet there is much evidence that the status of women in agricultural communities is not that of passive subordinates (Radzialowski, 1977). Their influence in the family is determined by their contribution to its welfare (Sanday, 1974). Farm women make a very visible

---

[6]Of course, not all Polish women married, a relatively large number of them going instead into Catholic religious orders. Radzialowski (1975) studied the largest of the Slavic teaching orders, the Felician Sisters, and there were several Polish orders and Polish American nuns in mixed orders.

and important economic addition to the family's welfare (Thomas and Znaniecki, 1918–1920:82–83):

> In matters of reciprocal response we find among the Polish peasants the sexes equally dependent upon each other . . . under conditions in which the activities of the women can attain an objective importance more or less equal to those of the man, the greatest social efficiency is attained by a systematic collaboration of men and women in external fields rather than by a division of tasks which limits the women to "home and children."

Bloch (1976:5), contrasting the situation of women in Polish villages and American cities, reinforces this point:

> The source of this equality and partnership between husband and wife can be located in the economic nature of the partnership, and particularly in two aspects of village economy. The first of these is the importance of village women to the operation of the house and farm. . . . But even more important than this contribution to subsistence is the strong position of women in terms of the basic wealth of the village—land and buildings.

During times of migration, whether for seasonal work in Europe or America, women on farms or in other economic situations were often left in charge of economic decisions and property maintenance for extended periods of time without their husbands or adult sons (Thomas and Znaniecki, 1918–1920). The pattern of household and family management without the patriarch was not unusual; it had been repeated through centuries of the Crusades, wars, and traveling occupations of men (Origo, 1956).[7] Emigration, however, introduced two major changes in the roles of married women, especially if they moved across the ocean. First, both the husband and wife deprived themselves of rights of inheritable property, if there was any. Parents usually distributed the property they had inherited and, hopefully, contributed to through their work, to the remaining offspring in Poland. The emigrating children were, in fact, expected to contribute to the family's status by sending money earned in America to Poland to be used for increasing property holdings of relatives. Coming to America with few possessions, the emigrants faced a second major change of life circumstances, resulting in changes of roles and relationships. Both the husband and wife, but especially the wife, were freed from the claims on their residence by the older generation whose home or land it had been before retirement. They were also freed from the daily observation and control by the elders of both families.

---

[7]We have a collection of letters exchanged by my great-grandmother and her husband and sons, as well as two years of her diaries during the Franco-Prussian war, which detail her activities in managing the estate. Wars often removed all adult men from their families and businesses, which were then taken over by the women in addition to their usual labor in the home, on the land, and in whatever other enterprises they were engaged.

They were independent of the constant supervision of their behavior found in extended kin village life. At the same time, they were deprived of the support network that exists in stable extended families and neighborhoods (Wrobel, 1979:67–77).

Thomas and Znaniecki (1918–1920:1705) pointed out that "economic ideals, when they exist, contribute, indeed to the maintenance of family life in general, since the immigrant can seldom imagine an economically perfect life without a family." Yet these sociologists worried about what they considered to be an inevitable "Break of the Conjugal Relation" (chap. 3, vol. 2: 1750–1751), mainly because American law "treats him [the husband] and his wife as isolated individuals, not as primary-group members":

> The consciousness that she can have her husband arrested any time she wishes on charges of non-support, disorderly conduct or adultery is for the woman an entirely new experience. Though under the old system she had in fact a part in the management of common affairs almost equal to that of the man, yet in cases of explicit disagreement the man had the formal right of coercing her, whereas she could only work by suggestion and persuasion, or appeal to the large family. Now not only can she refuse to be coerced, since the only actual instruments of coercion which the man has left after the disorganization of the large family— use of physical strength and withholding the means of subsistence—are prohibited by law, but she can actually coerce the man into doing what she wants by using any act of violence, drunkenness or economic negligence of his as pretext for warrant. No wonder that she is tempted to use her newly acquired power whenever she quarrels with her husband, and her women friends and acquaintances, moved by sex solidarity, frequently stimulate her to take legal action.

Pleck (1983:98) also reports child and wife battering by immigrant husbands and fathers and that 60 percent of the complaints by wives were made by Poles.

This image of the Polish peasant family in America neglects some of the forces actually present in social relations when physical coercion or economic dependence are removed. Divorce and desertion were negatively evaluated in Polonia, and strong status handicaps occurred from such behavior. In addition, people needed their spouses, in many ways, even when not fully economically dependent on them.

The economic dependence first of Polish and then Polish-American wives on their husbands varied considerably. Many women were able to earn substantial incomes by providing services or making goods, even in urban settings. Boarding and rooming houses were kept by many women during the height of immigration, mainly serving men who came over without families and would remain for some time until they made enough money to send for relatives back home (Zand, 1956).

In addition to managing boarding homes for income, many Polish-American women cooperated with their husbands in "ma and pa" stores, taverns, or restaurants specializing in Polish food. Each Polonian neighborhood had a number of such businesses requiring work from all family members. Seamstresses, beauticians, piano and English teachers, and writers and readers of letters—all these were needed in Polonia and women of the various classes and skills were able to undertake such roles. Such activities were considered appropriate means of contributing to the family's economic status, and some of the services were a source of prestige.

Of lower community approval was employment by wives and mothers outside the home and its environs, especially among men and, worst of all, among people other than Polish Americans (Wrobel, 1979:76). However, the wish for money was there: initially, to be used to return to Poland and buy land and homes; later, to help people in the homeland; and, always, for material goods for their own use and status and to offset some of the misgivings about the wife's employment away from the home. Interestingly, the employment of the women was seen by the Polonian community and the wider society as an individual choice, and few adjustments were made to help women manage the dual job of working for pay and managing the home and the family.[8]

The Role of Mother. It is possible that the heavy burdens of the job-home combination or of full-time homemaking in a large family have taken their toll in the mother-child relationship. McCready (1974:168–169) uses work by Radzialowski (1974) to support his conclusion, drawn from a National Opinion Research Center sample, that "the mother did not exert a strong influence in the raising of her children because of the dependence on the extended family in the peasant society." McCready found that mothers of Polish-American college graduates of 1961 were not as "salient" as mothers in other ethnic groups, in that they were not mentioned as frequently as were fathers. This was true even of the young women:

> The young Polish women rate themselves high on domestic skills, attractiveness, and sex appeal, indicating that they do espouse the traditional values for women in the society. Their low saliency scores for mother indicate that they have received these values from their fathers rather than emulating their mothers as role models. In other words, they think of themselves as attractive, competent women because their fathers told them they were.

[8]Caroline Bird (1979) details in *The Two-Paycheck Marriage* the difficulties experienced by American women who return to the labor force after having managed the home full time. Their families usually do not distribute the functions of the role of housewife among all members in adjustment to the woman's occupation outside the home. Sokolowska (1964, 1977) lists extensive resources in Poland developed to help working mothers, because that society, unlike America, ideologically wants such members to be in paid employment and because families really need two breadwinners. However, cultural norms of city life, which assigned to the woman the management of the home, still linger, and husbands reputedly are less than egalitarian in sharing work, unless they are of the youngest married generation.

Polish-American Women in the Community.   The first- and second-generation Polish-American women, unlike the Italians, did not limit their involvement to the home and the family. They were active organizers and
participants in voluntary associations and the life of the community. They
founded one of the major insurance and financial companies, the Polish
Women's Alliance, with branches in many neighborhoods, and a feminist
newspaper called *The Voice of Polish Women*, which had "Faith, Enlightenment,
Love of the Native Language, Concord, Perseverance" as its motto, and education as its major function aside from economic activity (Radzialowski,
1975:1977). The newspapers and local meetings taught members to be independent and also taught new ways of cooking, cleaning, child care, health,
and hygiene (Radzialowski, 1977:196):

> It urged on its members the wisdom of saving for the future, avoiding needless
> spending, acquiring training and job skills, shunning gambling and excessive use
> of alcohol and other traits usually subsumed under the misnamed "puritan ethic."

The Polish Women's Alliance had its own doctors, insurance adjusters,
teachers, and business leaders. It encouraged mothers to seek higher education for their children. Other organizations for women, branches of superterritorial associations, and even local groups provided opportunities for
leadership roles, help in the schooling of children in Polish language and culture, social contact, and activities. Again, this extensive activity at each level
of Polonian life negates the image of passive Polish immigrant women (see
also Wojniusz, 1976).

The Later Stages of Life.   In contrast to the situation that appears to have
developed in Poland since World War II, the Polish-American working
woman does not seem to be able to depend on her mother or mother-in-law
to help with the housework or care of the children (Mirowski, 1968;
Lobodzinska, 1970, 1974; Piotrowski, 1963; Sokolowska, 1964). Although
Polish-American widows are more willing to live with a married child, usually
a daughter, than are American women of similar age and marital status situations generally, most elderly women who are able to take care of themselves
choose to live with only their husband or alone if widowed (Lopata, 1977).
They do not undertake household or child care for the younger generations.
In this respect they are quite American, in that Polish mothers often help
extensively with their children's families (Lobodzinska, 1970, 1974).

American society no longer expects the housing of elderly parents with
younger generations, nor the heavy household and child care obligations of
older women to their adult children (Lopata, 1971, 1973). The history of the
society does not provide an ideological base for such action, mainly because of
its disapproval until recent years of the employment of married women who
would then require baby-sitting assistance. In addition, older women are eco-

nomically independent in many cases, albeit often living on very limited incomes and within narrow life spaces (Chevan and Korson, 1972; Lopata, 1973, 1979). Although often residing in the poorer sections of towns no longer inhabited by Polish Americans, as a result of death of older generations and the upward and outward mobility of younger ones, the older women tend to own their homes. Selling these homes could not bring them sufficient monies to afford moving elsewhere, and their roots and unfamiliarity with life outside of the neighborhood preclude such resettlement. These elderly widows are often strongly involved with one of their children but in an "intimacy at a distance" manner typical of that reported by Rosenmayr and Kockeis (1963) for the elderly in Vienna, Austria (see also Bild and Havighurst, 1976 and Siemaszko, 1976).

The social class background of older Polish-American women significantly influences their social life space and support systems; the middle- and upper-class women draw on a much wider set of personal and community resources. However, even the lower-class women retain active involvement in voluntary associations, thereby differing from their counterparts in other ethnic and American communities. The lifelong habit of involvement in the community is broken only if friends and familiar neighbors die or move away, the church loses its Polish-American parishioners, clubs move out of the area, and the family disperses (Lopata, 1977, 1979; Ozog, 1942; Sanders and Morawska, 1975; Wood, 1955). The consequences of the harshness of life for the immigrant and even the second-generation women is reflected in their health problems and the inability to retain contact with siblings and children living at inconvenient distances (Lopata, 1973, 1979).

There is insufficient evidence on the circumstances of the latter stages of the life course for women of the new emigration to determine how they are different from other Polish women in America at the present time. Their background and the situation in which they entered the United States would lead us to assume that few could bring their older parents over (see also Mostwin, 1969, 1971). Many ex-combatants and displaced persons came from places other than Poland during and after World War II, and immigration directly from that country has expanded only in recent years. The new emigration is aging, but we know little about this process, because the group numerically is too small to be located through any means but selective sampling. Mostwin (1969, 1971) reports some intergenerational conflict because the parents did not settle in Polonia, and, as a result, the children have Americanized very rapidly. The parents disapprove of some of the actions of younger generations, especially of the girls.

The Roles of Men

The lives of immigrant men also varied considerably according to the resources with which they entered America. The masses of Polish immigrants entering at the turn of the twentieth century were young men who came from a village background and with relatively little education. They obtained jobs in the mines of Pennsylvania, in the steel mills or meat-packing houses of Chicago, on farms in the Connecticut Valley, or in other locations in which knowledge of English and advanced skills in the industrialized or service sectors of the economy were not needed. Boarding at first in Polish homes in the community, they saved money and sent for their wives and children or siblings. Some of the more affluent returned to Poland to stay or to find a wife. Women of Polish background were scarce in America during the early years of Polish immigration. As late as 1920, there were 131 males per 100 females, but the number of males decreased to 116.1 in 1930, 110.4 in 1940, and 101.8 by 1950 (Hutchinson, 1956:19). Men who married daughters of already established families received help in establishing themselves and tended to develop an egalitarian or, at least, not a strongly patriarchal family demeanor, because they did not have their own families to back them up (Zand, 1956). By 1969, 14.5 percent of Polish men were in professional and technical jobs, 15.2 in managerial positions, and another 15 percent in sales or clerical positions (Lopata, 1985:136). In 1990, 17.3 percent of Polish men were in management, 15 percent in professional jobs, 16 percent in technical and sales, with only 7.1 percent in clerical positions (U.S. Bureau of the Census, 1993).

Husbands and Fathers. Polish male immigrants worked hard, long hours and often were unable to spend much time with their children. The father's function as the main disciplinarian was the only one known to many children, and his European style of relating to them often created strong conflict. The second generation's young men were reputedly involved in street gang behavior (Thrasher, 1927; Fleis-Fava, 1950). Taft (1936:723) felt obliged to point out to American criminologists that the first generation of Polish immigrants had very low criminal records and that the age distribution of the second-generation males pushed up the rate for the entire immigrant group. Polonia contained a disproportionate number of young men in the "criminally significant" ages. Conflict with the father arose from not only the son's delinquent behavior but also his unwillingness to contribute to the family's social status by turning over his earnings for family use (Thomas and Znaniecki, 1918–1920; Wood, 1955). Thomas and Znaniecki (1918–1920) reported frequent and public disagreement between fathers and their children over economic matters. Finestone (1964, 1967) found that family members would completely ignore members who had been sent to prison for criminal activity. They had to reestablish their relations by promising not to disgrace the family again after they were released. This finding adds weight to the thesis of the importance of the status competition to Polish-American families.

Polonia, as an organized community with many mass communication media, also completely ignored problems of juvenile delinquency or criminality. No organization was set up to help the youth or adults in serious trouble and the newspapers did not make mention of it, even in face of American reports. Wood (1955) documents facts of criminal activity never discussed in Polonia except as part of the natural flow of life. Yet whatever gang fights or other juvenile delinquent behavior the second generation of Polonian young men were involved in, it seemed to have worked out by the time they reached adulthood, because their criminal record is not high. The second-generation Polonian men remained organizationally active, although to a lesser extent in ethnic communities than had their parents (Emmons, 1971; Galush, 1975; Obidinski, 1968; Sandberg, 1974). Yet Polish American men did not experience much intergenerational occupational mobility until after the second generation (Duncan and Duncan, 1968; Greeley and Rossi, 1968; U.S. Bureau of the Census, 1971). Hutchinson (1956:248) found the foreign-born Polish males in service, operative, and laborer jobs in metal industries. Their specific occupations disproportionately included tailors, furriers, cleaners, porters, and self-employed managers. The American-born men of foreign-born parents were employed most frequently as operatives and laborers and less frequently than other groups as professional workers, managers, farmers, service employees, or sales workers. They were even more occupationally concentrated than the second generation of most other foreign-stock Americans. Duncan and Duncan (1968) concluded that the Poles "suffer a modest handicap" in achieving upward mobility from the first job to the current one by American standards. The main reason for this is that sons tended to follow their fathers in the type of job they entered among the Polish Americans more than among other ethnic groups currently in the workforce (Duncan and Duncan, 1968:362).

By 1961, Polish-American fathers seem to have developed better relations with their children or, at least, with daughters, than prior researchers indicated. As mentioned before, it was the father, not the mother, who was listed as having more influence on the lives of female college graduates (McCready, 1974). McCready (1974:167) seems to uphold the patriarchal image of the Polish-American father:

> All the members of the post-migration Polish family exhibited a concern for the well-being of the father, who seemed to have suffered most in the move from village to city. The literature on the Polish family in America describes two types of Polish father. One was the man who had been a strong patriarchal figure in Poland, was unable to maintain that role in the new country, and became a dependent person. Warner reviewed literature that indicated that this type of Polish father eventually became a child to his own children. The children were his disciplinarians and protectors. The second type was the man who had been a strong patriarchal figure in Poland and was able to maintain that role in this country.

This is a strongly bifurcated picture of the Polish elderly man in America, seen in isolation from other relations and the community. However,

Lieberman (1978) also reports high incidence of mental illness and withdrawal into passivity vis-à-vis the rest of the family among men who expected to function as patriarchs in relations with their children but did not have the resources to carry off such relations (see also Trela and Sokolovsky, 1979). Wrobel (1979:76) found Detroit men "feeling personally inadequate" because of the kind of work they did and their inability to better their "lot in life."

The men of the new emigration, who entered America with more education and occupational skills and mainly settled away from the established Polonia communities, also may have experienced trouble with their offspring as the latter more rapidly absorbed American values, but the problems do not appear to be as severe as those in former peasant families (Mostwin, 1969, 1971). The recorded violence of temper of Polish peasant and lower-class men, especially explosive when combined with alcohol, may easily have been the consequence of frustration over the lack of resources to lead the type of life and relate to others in the way they had been socialized to do (Thomas and Znaniecki, 1918–1920; Janowitz, 1966). More educated and less culturally insulated men may have had more resources and more tolerance of the changing behaviors of family members. Second-generation men of either emigration may have engaged in less conflict with their children because of the remembered problems with their fathers. At least, the few studies that focused on intergenerational family relations report less attitudinal and value differences than reported for the first-generation immigrants.

CHANGE AND ADAPTATION

There are many people living in the United States who could be called Polish Americans because their parents, grandparents, or great-grandparents came from Poland but who have completely obliterated this identification. These people cannot be identified in any way by census takers or sociologists, especially if they have changed originally Polish-sounding names. Louis Adamic observed the name-changing tendency as early as 1942 in his *What's Your Name?* Several social scientists studied this behavior among "Poles and Polish Americans [who] seem impelled to more changing than any other group" (Kotlarz, 1963:1; see also Borkowski, 1963 and Zagraniczny, 1963). Kotlarz (1963:1–4) estimated that of approximately 300,000 Polish Americans living in the Detroit area, approximately 3,000 modified their names annually. The Polonian press occasionally reports that this process has stopped and that some younger members of Polish-American families are going back to the original name and its spelling. It is almost impossible to determine the extent of either direction of name change.

There is a second layer of Polish-American families whose members have some identification with their ethnic group and belong to some organizations within Polonia, but who otherwise lead ordinary "American" lives. Some studies pick up traces of familial or religious attitudes that harken back to prior generations' culture, but items and complexes vary by family. There are also Poles in America who identify themselves as both Poles and Americans but not as Polish Americans; they tend to have limited involvement in specialized organizations and friendships but otherwise lead middle- or upper middle-class lives (Mostwin, 1969, 1971). Both types of this second layer of involvement in Polonian life are really peripheral to it because the community could not depend on these families to maintain itself. A third layer of Polish-American families is more involved in the ethnic community activities than the other two, although this varies by age, education, generation, and area (Galush, 1975; Obidinski, 1968; Sandberg, 1974). Some Polish Americans still reside in the heart of the remaining neighborhoods, without speaking English and with restricted lives (Hraba,1994). Few families controlled by the middle generation are so located. Others live Polonian lives by being involved in superterritorial organizations in which they have informal contact with other leaders, living their ethnicity almost professionally. The families that have such strong ties are usually controlled by second-generation men or women, with occasional involvement and passing of status and ethnicity to the youth. Some of Polonia's life has been taken over by the families of the new emigration.

CONCLUSION

The heterogeneity of structure, interaction, and cultural base for Polish-American families lies in their original variation when they came to America and in the divergence of paths they followed. The tendency of most social scientists is to focus on the large mass of peasants who migrated before World War I and brought over other family members before the influx was stopped by American legislation. It is they who were studied during their processes of "adjustment" or "disorganization," with frequent reports of interfamilial and intrafamilial conflict. Relations of men and women at all stages of life underwent change, often against the wishes of participants, because such change rarely hits the entire family at the same time. Members who benefited from the village family system had the most to lose when other members refused to follow traditional norms. Yet family members needed each other rather desperately, and the growing community siphoned some of the hurt and conflict by drawing attention to the interfamily status competition. Life in Polonia was very involved and complex, providing many opportunities for individualistic, as well as cooperative, identity and status.

Little is actually known of the processes by which first-generation families worked out the conflicts or, at least, tensions between husband and wife and parent and child. Second-generation children, especially the boys, often expressed their frustrations by moving out into the streets with peers. Most grew up leading "normal" lower- or lower middle-class lives within or outside of Polonian neighborhoods. The women tended to follow the traditional life course of American urbanites, except that some wives had to work outside the home for financial reasons, despite community disapproval, and except that, at all class levels, the women were more organizationally active than is generally true of their non-Polish counterparts. The status competition and community life, as well as their control over their own homes in the absence of a tightly controlling male kin line, gave them more independence and power in the family than is usually attributed to women in traditionally patriarchal cultures. Marital conflict appears to have been strong in some families of the old emigration, particularly of the first and early second generations, but it did not result in high divorce rates for a variety of reasons. The older generations of Polish Americans tend to live independently, although there appears to be a certain segment of the male population that suffers psychological problems from the strain of migration and adjustment to life in America.

Upward mobility within Polonia and out of it has been increasing in recent years, enabling children or grandchildren of peasant families to join the Polish Americans who inherited or had earlier built up higher status. Most third- and fourth-generation Polish-American families are lost to sociological knowledge, especially when they do not identify with this ethnic group in responses to census and other survey questions. The geographical dispersal of this population and the move to higher education have resulted in a great deal of intermarriage, creating new generations that are less likely to identify with the Polish or Polish-American culture or people than is true of people with a single ethnic background. Some of the youth are developing an interest in Poland and its national culture, an interest expressed in a desire to travel to their grandparents' or great-grandparents' homeland and the taking of Polish courses in schools.

REFERENCES

Abel, Theodore. 1929. "Sunderland: A Study of Change in the Group Line of Poles in New England Farming Community," in Edmund De S. Brunner (Ed.), *Immigrant Farmers and Their Children*, pp. 213–243. Garden City, NY: Doubleday.

Adamic, Louis, 1942. *What's Your Name?* New York: Harper and Brothers.

Benet, Sula. 1951. *Song, Dance and Customs of Peasant Poland.* New York: Roy.

Bild, Bernice R., and Robert Havighurst. 1976. "Senior Citizens in Great Cities: The Case of Chicago." Special issue of *The Gerontologist, 16* (1) (February), pt. 2.

Bird, Caroline. 1979. *The Two-Paycheck Marriage.* New York: Rawson Wade.

Bloch, Harriet. 1976. "Changing Domestic Roles Among Polish Immigrant Women." *The Anthropological Quarterly, 49* (1) (January): 3–10.

Borkowsh, Thomas. 1963. "Some Patterns in Polish Surname Changes." *Polish American Studies, 20* (1) (January-June): 14–16.

Breton, Raymond. 1964. "Institutional Completeness of Ethnic Communities and the Personal Relations of Immigrants." *American Journal of Sociology,* 70 (2) (September): 193–205.

Brunner, Edmund De S. (Ed.). 1929. *Immigrant Farmers and their Children.* Garden City, NY: Doubleday.

Chalasinski, Josef. 1946. *Mlode Pokolenie Chlopow.* Rzym: Wydawnicto Polskiej YMCA Przy APW.

Chevan, A., and H. Korson. 1972. "The Widowed Who Live Alone: An Examination of Social and Demographic Factors." *Social Forces,* 51:45-53.

Chrobot, Leonard F. 1982. "The Pilgrimage from *Gemeinschaft* to *Gesellschaft*: Sociological Functions of Religion in the Polish American Community," in Frank Renkiewicz (Ed.), *The Polish Presence in Canada and America,* pp. 81–95. Toronto: Multicultural Society of Ontario.

Cohler, Bertram J., and Morton A. Lieberman. 1979. "Personality Change in the Second Half of Life: Findings From a Study of Irish, Italian and Polish-American Men and Women," in Donald E. Gelfand and Alfred J. Kutzik (Eds.), *Ethnicity and Aging: Theory, Research and Policy,* pp. 227–245. New York: Springer.

Duncan, Beverly, and Otis Dudley Duncan. 1968. "Minorities and the Process of Stratification," *American Sociological Review, 33* (8) (June): 356–364.

Dziewicka, Maria. 1976. "Dual Occupation in Polish Agriculture," in Jan Turowski and Lili Maria Szwengrub (Eds.), *Rural Social Change in Poland,* pp. 251–277. Ossolineum: Polish Academy of Sciences Press.

Emmons, Charles F. 1971. "Economic and Political Leadership in Chicago's Polonia: Some Sources of Ethnic Persistence and Mobility." Ph.D. dissertation, University of Illinois, Circle Campus.

Finestone, Harold. 1964. "A Comparative Study of Reformation and Recidivism Among Italians and Polish Adult Male Criminal Offenders." Ph.D. dissertation, University of Chicago.

———. 1967. "Reformation and Recidivism Among Italian and Polish Criminal Offenders." *American Journal of Sociology,* 72 (6) (May).

Fleis-Fava, S. 1950. "The Relationship of Northwestern University Settlement to the Community." Master's thesis, Department of Sociology, Northwestern University.

Galush, W. T. 1975. "Forming Polonia: A Study of Four Polish-American Communities, 1880–1940." Ph.D. dissertation, Department of History, University of Minnesota.

Golab, Caroline. 1977. *Immigrant Destinations.* Philadelphia: Temple University Press.

Gordon, Milton. 1964. *Assimilation in American Life.* New York: Oxford University Press.

Greeley, Andrew M., and Peter H. Rossi. 1968. *The Education of Catholic Americans.* Garden City, NY: Doubleday, Anchor Books.

Hraba, J. (1994). *American Ethnicity,* 2nd ed. Itasca, IL: F. E. Peacock

Hutchinson, E. P. 1956. *Immigrants and Their Children: 1850–1950.* New York: John Wiley.

Jagiello-Lysiowa, E. 1976. "Transformation of the Way of Life of the Rural Community," in Jan Turowski and Lili Maria Szwengrub (Eds.), *Rural Social Change in Poland,* pp. 123–138. Warszawa, Ossolineum: Polish Academy of Sciences Press.

Janowitz, Morris (Ed.). 1966. *W. I. Thomas: On Social Organization and Social Personality.* Chicago: University of Chicago Press.

Jawlowska, Aldona, and Edmund Mokrzycki. 1978. "Styles of Life in Poland: A Viewpoint on Typology," in Polish Sociological Association, *Social Structure: Polish Sociology 1977,* pp. 93–107. Warszawa, Zaklad Narodowy Imienia Ossolinskich: Wydawnictwo Polskiej Akademii Nauk.

Kotlan, Robert J. 1963. "Writings About the Changing of Polish Names in America." *Polish American Studies,* 20 (1) (January-June):1–4.

Kowalski, Mieczyslaw. 1967. "Basic Directions of Changes in Rural Life System in Poland." Acta Universitatis Lodziensis, *Zeszyty Naukowe Universytetu Lodz-kiego Nauki Ekonomiczne i Socjologiczne,* Seira 3 (10): 5–29.

Kusielewicz, Eugene. 1974. "On the Condition of Polish Culture in the United States." *The Kosciuszko Foundation Monthly Newsletter, 29* (2) (October): 2–6.

Kuznicki, Ellen Marie. 1978. "The Polish American Parochial Schools," in Frank Mocha (Ed.), *Poles in America*. Stevens Point, WI: Worzalla.

Lerman, Paul. 1973. "Child Convicts," in Helena Z. Lopata (Ed.), *Marriages and Families*, pp. 285–294. New York: Van Nostrand.

Lieberman, Morton A. 1978. "Social and Psychological Determinants of Adaptation." *International Journal of Aging and Human Development, 9* (2).

Lieberson, S. 1963. *Ethnic Patterns in American Cities*. New York: Free Press.

Lobodzinska, Barbara. 1970. *Malzenstwo w Miescie*. Warszawa: Panstwowe Wydawnictwo Naukowe.

———. 1974. *Kodzina w Polsce*. Warszawa: Wudawnictwo Interpress.

Lopata, Helena Znaniecki. 1971. "Living Arrangements of Urban Widows and Their Married Children." *Sociological Focus, 5* (1): 41–61.

———. 1973. *Widowhood in an American City*. Cambridge, MA: Schenkman.

———. 1976a. "Polish Immigration to the United States of America: Problems of Estimation and Parameters." *The Polish Review*, 21 (4): 85–108.

———. 1976b. *Polish Americans: Status Competition in an Ethnic Community*. Englewood Cliffs, NJ: Prentice-Hall.

———. 1976c. "Members of the Intelligentsia as Developers and Disseminators of Cosmopolitan Culture," in Aleksander Gella (Ed.), *The Intelligentsia and the Intellectuals*, pp. 59–78. Beverly Hills, CA: Sage.

———. 1977. "Widowhood in Polonia," *Polish American Studies, 34* (2) (Autumn): 5–25.

———. 1979. *Women as Widows: Support Systems*. New York: Elsevier.

———. 1985. "The Polish Immigrants and Their Descendants in the American Labor Force," in Winston A. Van Horne and Thomas V. Tonnesen (Eds.), *Ethnicity and the Work Force*, pp. 124–144. Milwaukee, WI: University of Wisconsin System, American Ethnic Studies Coordinating Committee,

McCready, William. 1974. "The Persistence of Ethnic Variation in American Families," in Andrew Greeley (Ed.), *Ethnicity in the United States*, pp. 156–176. New York: John Wiley.

Miaso, J. 1971. "Z Dziejow Oswiaty Polskiej w Stanach Zjednoczonych." *Problemy Polonei Zadzanichzhej, 4* : 19–49.

Mirowski, Wlodzimierz. 1968. *Migracje do Warszawy*. Warszawa: Zaklad Narodowy im Ossolinskich, Wydawnictwo Polskiej Akademii Nauk.

Mostwin, Danuta. 1969. "Post World War II Polish Immigrants in the United States." *Polish American Studies, 26* (2) (Autumn): 5–14.

———. 1971. *The Transplanted Family, A Study of Social Adjustment of the Polish Immigrant Family to the United States after the Second World War*. Ann Arbor, MI: University Microfilms.

Obidinski, Eugene. 1968. "Ethnic to Status Group: A Study of Polish Americans in Buffalo." Ph.D. dissertation, New York: State University of New York Microfilms.

Origo, Iris. 1956. *The Merchant of Prato, Francesco di Marco Datini: 1355–1410*. New York: Knopf.

Ozog, Julius J. 1942. "A Study in Polish Home Ownership in Chicago." Master's thesis, University of Chicago.

Parot, Joseph John. 1982. "The 'Serdeczna Matko' of the Sweatshops: Marital and Family Crises of Immigrant Working-Class Women in Late Nineteenth-Century Chicago," in Frank Renkiewicz (Ed.), *The Polish Presence in Canada and America*, pp. 155–182. Toronto: Multicultural History Society of Ontario.

Piotrowski, Jerzy. 1963. *Praca Zawodowa Kobiety a Rodzina*. Warszawa: Ksiazka i Wiedza.

Pleck, Elizabeth. 1983. "The Old World, New Rights, and the Limited Rebellion: Challenges to Traditional Authority in Immigrant Families," in H. Z. Lopata and J. H. Pleck (Eds.), *Research in the Interweave of Social Roles: Families and Jobs*, pp. 91–112. Greenwich, CT: Jai Press.

Polzin, Theresita. 1973. *The Polish Americans*. Pulaski, WI: Franciscan Publishers.

———. 1976. "The Polish American Family." *The Polish Review, 21* (3): 103–122.

Radzialowski, Thaddeus. 1974. "The View from a Polish Ghetto." *Ethnicity, 1* (2) (July): 125–150.

———. 1975. "Reflections on the History of the Felicians." *Polish American Studies, 32* (Spring): 19–28.

———. 1977. "Immigrant Nationalism and Feminism: Glos Polek and the Polish Women's Alliance in America, 1898–1917." *Review Journal of Philosophy and Social Science, 2* (2):183–203.

Reymont, Ladislas. 1925. *The Peasants: Fall, Winter, Spring, Summer.* New York: Knopf

Rooney, Elizabeth. 1957. "Polish Americans and Family Disorganization." *The American Catholic Sociological Review, 18* (March): 47–51.

Rosenmayr, Leopold, and E. Kockeis. 1963. "Propositions for a Sociological Theory of Aging and the Family." *International Social Science Journal 15*: 410–426.

Sanday, Peggy R. 1974. "Female Status in the Public Domain," in Z. Rosaldo and L. Lamphere (Eds.), *Women, Culture and Society,* pp. 189–206. Stanford: Stanford University Press.

Sandberg, Neil C. 1974. *Ethnic Identity and Assimilation: The Polish American Community.* New York: Praeger.

Sanders, Irwin, and Eva T. Morawska. 1975. *Polish American Community Life: A Survey of Research.* Boston: Boston University, Community Sociology Training Program.

Schooler, Carmi. 1976. "Serfdom's Legacy: An Ethnic Continuum." *American Journal of Sociology, 81* : 1265–1285.

Siemaszko, Maria. 1976. "Kin Relations of the Aged: Possible Impact on Social Service Planning." Master's thesis, Loyola University of Chicago.

Slomczynski, Kazimierz, and Wlodzimierz Wesolowski. 1978. "Theoretical Orientation in the Study of Class Structure in Poland, 1945–1975," in Polish Sociological Association, *Social Structure, Polish Sociology 1977,* pp. 7–31. Warszawa, Zaklad Narodowy Imienia Ossolinskich: Wydawnictwo Polskiej Akademii Nauk.

Sokolowska, Magdalena. 1964. *Kobieta Pracudaca.* Warsaw: Wiedza Powszechna.

———. 1977. "Poland: Women's Experience Under Socialism," in Janet Zollinger Giele and Audrey Chapman Smock (Eds.), *Women: Roles and Status in Eight Countries,* pp. 347–381. New York: John Wiley.

Super, P. 1939. *The Polish Tradition.* London: Maxlove.

Suttles, Gerald. 1968. *The Social Order of the Slum.* Chicago: University of Chicago Press.

Szczepanski, Jan. 1962. "The Polish Intelligentsia: Past and Present." *World Politics, 16* (3) (April): 406–420.

———. 1970. *Polish Society.* New York: Random House.

Taft, D. 1936. "Nationality and Crime." *American Journal of Sociology* (August): 1–4, 724–736.

Thomas, John L. 1950. "Marriage Prediction in the Polish Peasant." *American Journal of Sociology, 55* (May): 573–583.

Thomas, William I., and Florian W. Znaniecki. 1918–1920. *The Polish Peasant in Europe and America.* Boston: Richard G. Badger. Reprint. New York: Dover, 1958.

Thrasher, F. M. 1927. *The Gang: The Study of 1,313 Gangs in Chicago.* Chicago: University of Chicago Press.

Trela, James E., and Jay H. Sokolovsky. 1979. "Culture, Ethnicity and Policy for the Aged," in Donald E. Gelfand and Alfred J. Kutzik (Eds.), *Ethnicity and Aging. Theory, Research and Policy,* pp. 117–136. New York: Springer.

Turowski, Jan, and Lili Maria Szwengrub (Eds.). 1976. *Rural Social Change in Poland.* Warsaw, Ossolineum: Polish Academy of Sciences Press.

U.S. Bureau of the Census. 1971. *Characteristics of the Population by Ethnic Origin, November 1969,* Current Population Reports, Series P-20. Washington, DC: U.S. Government Printing Office.

U.S. Bureau of the Census. 1993. *Ancestry of the Population of the United States.* U.S. Department of Commerce, Series CP-3-2. Washington, DC: U.S. Government Printing Office.

Wojniusz, Helen K. 1976. "Ethnicity and Other Variables in the Analysis of Polish American Women." *Polish American Studies, 39* (Autumn): 26-37.

Wood, Arthur Evans. 1955. *Hamtramck: Then and Now.* New York: Bookman Associates.

Wrobel, Paul. 1979. *Our Way: Family, Parish and Neighborhood in a Polish-American Community.* Notre Dame, IN: University of Notre Dame Press.

Zagraniczny, Stanley J. 1963. "Some Reasons of Polish Surname Changes." *Polish American Studies, 20* (1) (January-June): 12–14.

Zand, Helen Sankiewicz. 1956. "Polish Family Folkways in the United States." *Polish American Studies, 13* (3–4) (July-December): 77–88.

Znaniecki, Florian W. 1952. *Modern Nationalities.* Urbana, IL: University of Illinois Press.

———. 1965. *Social Relations and Social Roles.* San Francisco: Chandler.

7 The Mexican-American Family

Rosina M. Becerra

HISTORICAL BACKGROUND

The history of the Mexican-American people predates the incorporation of the Southwest into the United States. Native to the Southwest, the Mexican-American people have a history marked by conflict and colonization, first by the Spanish and then by the Anglo Americans. This early history, perhaps because of the proximity of the southwestern states to the Mexican border, has left a legacy of conflict that is present today between Mexican Americans and Anglo Americans. The present position of Mexican Americans as a people, their family life, and the effects of their position on their family life can best be understood through a brief review of their histories as Mexicans and North Americans.

In 1821, Mexico achieved independence from Spain, which had colonized Mexico since the sixteenth century. Because the Spanish *conquistadores* (conquerors) were all men, they intermarried with the Mexicans and indigenous Indians. This mixed heritage of the Spanish, Mexican, and Indian remains predominant among today's Mexican Americans. The Spanish heritage, language, and numerous other contributions have been modified by time and the indigenous cultures of the Indians and Mexicans constitute the foundation of the unique Mexican-American culture. Because the areas that are now the southwestern states were originally settled by the Spanish settlers and their Mexican/Indian children, the Mexican descendants of these Spanish settlers already were native to these territories when they became part of the United States in the late nineteenth century (McWilliams, 1990).

During the nineteenth century, the Mexican government had opened the Texas territory to settlers under the condition that they pledge allegiance to Mexico and agree to become Catholics. The Anglo-American settlers (mostly United States citizens), however, resisted these conditions. At the same time, Mexicans of the territory resisted Anglo-American colonization through various forms of rebellion. Through the political process, Anglo Americans of the territory were able to pass laws favoring their group, and

Mexicans were stripped of what little wealth they had and relegated to the lowest social and economic classes. Often a small group of wealthier Mexicans collaborated with the Anglo Americans to maintain their own positions in the new order (Acuna, 1981).

Between 1821 and 1848, rebellions by the Anglo Americans against the Mexican government occurred throughout the territory of Texas, setting the stage for the conquest of the rest of the Southwest. Until this time, the Southwest had been relatively isolated. The development of the railroad system ended the isolation of this region from the rest of the country and brought larger numbers of Anglo Americans to the region (Acuna, 1981).

In 1832, Stephen Austin went to Mexico City to press for lifting the restrictions on Anglo-American immigration to Texas and for separate statehood. Because of the economic trade that had been established by the territory of Texas and the United States, the Anglo settlers believed that separation from Mexico and statehood in the United States would be to their economic advantage. By 1835, 5,000 Mexicans resided in the Texas territory and the Anglo-American population had risen to 30,000. A full-scale rebellion escalated, and the Anglo Americans in Texas (with some Mexican supporters) declared war on Mexico. To squelch this rebellion, General Santa Ana led an army of approximately 6,000 men from the interior of Mexico. He arrived in San Antonio, Texas, in February 1836, where 187 Texans took refuge in a former mission, the Alamo. Although the Texans lost the battle, a legend grew up from the struggle that continues today. The cry "Remember the Alamo" prompted aid from the United States to assist the Texans, most of whom were U.S. citizens (Acuna, 1981).

Later in 1836, Sam Houston defeated Santa Ana at the battle of San Jacinto. This defeat ended the era of the Texas revolution, or Texas's war for independence. Fear of continued domination by Mexico prompted the annexation of Texas by the United States in December 1845. This act severed U.S. diplomatic relations with Mexico. The Texas victory paved the way for the Mexican-American War.

The Mexican-American War (1846–1848) terminated with the Treaty of Guadalupe Hidalgo, in which Mexico accepted the Rio Grande River as the Texas border and ceded territory in the Southwest to the United States for $15 million. The ceded territory incorporated the present-day states of California, New Mexico, Nevada, and parts of Colorado, Arizona, and Utah. Thus began the occupation of the conquered southwest territory (Acuna, 1981).

Immigration

In 1850, 13,300 persons of Mexican origin resided in the United States, and by 1880, this figure was 68,400. In the intervening thirty years, the Southwest was, for the most part, an isolated, self-contained area that was culturally and economically removed from the rest of the United States. Most of the major movement between Mexico and the United States was concentrated at the borders (Jaffe, Cullen, and Boswell, 1980).

Between 1880 and 1910, the southwestern United States experienced rapid economic development and commercialization of agriculture. Mexican labor was highly sought by United States mining, railroad and agricultural interests. During these three decades, the population of Mexican origin grew threefold as Mexican immigrants gravitated toward the region's growing demands for low-wage labor. In 1910, the U.S. Census recorded 220,000 Mexican-born persons and 162,000 persons of Mexican parentage living in the United States (Jaffe, Cullen, and Boswell, 1980). The railroads played a crucial role in the expanding Mexican immigration because they were a rapid and relatively easy means of transportation from central Mexico and a principal source of employment during the late nineteenth and early twentieth centuries. In 1909, 17 percent of the workforce of the nine largest western railroads were Mexican (Reisler, 1976).

Between 1910 and 1930, the Mexican population in the United States continued to grow rapidly. By 1930, the population of Mexican origin (i.e., those of Mexican birth or parentage) exceeded 1 million persons (Jaffe, Cullen, and Boswell, 1980). Emigration from Mexico continued to be spurred by a strong demand for labor, heightened by the entry of the United States into World War I. The 1910 Mexican Revolution and the Cristero Rebellion (1926–1929) in Mexico also served to heighten Mexican migration to the United States (Massey, 1982).

The 1930s were a period of widespread domestic unemployment, and the demand for unskilled labor decreased. Anti-Mexican feeling swept through the Southwest, resulting in mass repatriations. Between 1929 and 1935, more than 415,000 Mexicans (some of whom were American citizens) were forcibly expelled from the United States. Another 85,000 left "voluntarily." As a result, between 1930 and 1940, the Mexican population dramatically declined and 41 percent of Mexican-born persons actually returned to Mexico (Jaffe, Cullen, and Boswell, 1980).

During World War II, the United States again began to experience labor shortages in the Southwest. Agricultural interests sought and obtained government cooperation in the recruitment and importation of Mexican workers for agricultural labor. In 1942, the *bracero* program was created by an agreement between the United States and Mexico. This agreement arranged for the importation of Mexican workers into the United States for periods not to exceed six months. Although the *bracero* program was originally conceived as a temporary wartime measure, agricultural growers pressured the governments to both extend and expand this program throughout the 1950s. The program ended in 1964, following growing opposition by organized labor. During the twenty-two years of its operation, the *bracero* program recruited over 4 million workers, and at its height over 400,000 workers were entering the United States annually (Reichert and Massey, 1980).

After the *bracero* program was phased out, Mexican workers continued to enter the United States legally and illegally. Between 1940 and 1970, the Mexican population nearly doubled, from 377,000 to 746,000 (Jaffe, Cullen, and Boswell, 1980; Reichert and Massey, 1980).

During the 1970s, Mexican immigration continued because of the years of active recruitment by U.S. businesses. Legal and illegal migration, high fertility rates, and social and economic conditions in Mexico combined to produce a 64 percent increase in the population of Mexican origin between 1970 and 1980. Over the decade of the 1980s, immigration from Mexico continued to grow and the population of Mexican origin increased 84 percent, nearly doubling from 2.2 million in 1980 to 4.3 million in 1990. In 1990, more than 1 in 5, or 4.3 million of the country's foreign-born population, were born in Mexico, the largest foreign-born group (U.S. Census, 1993). In 1994, 28.8 percent of all the foreign-born population were from Mexico. Of the 4.5 million most recent immigrants, over a quarter (1.3 million) came from Mexico (U.S. Bureau of the Census, 1995).

Today 13.4 million persons of Mexican origin or descent inhabit the United States. This figure represents 60 percent of the total Hispanic population of 22.4 million (U.S. Bureau of the Census, 1993). The majority of the Mexican-American population (86 percent) reside in the five southwestern states of Arizona, California, Colorado, New Mexico, and Texas. In 1970, Mexican Americans constituted 2.7 percent of the total population of the United States. In 1986, they were 3.9 percent of the total U.S. population and in 1990 they represent 5.4 percent of the total population, securing their place as one of the fastest-growing ethnic groups in the United States (U.S. Bureau of the Census, 1985, 1993).

Key Components that Shaped the Mexican-American Experience

Mexican Americans are a highly heterogeneous population. Some trace their roots to the Spanish and Mexican settlers who first settled the Southwest before the arrival of the Pilgrims in New England, whereas others are immigrants or children of immigrants who began to arrive in large numbers by the beginning of the twentieth century (Martinez, 1985). Saragoza (1983) points out that this history supports the fundamental cultural variation and social differentiation among Mexican-American families. Crucial factors are variability across region (including Mexico) and changes over time. Mexican-American families in different historical periods have adapted differently to economic and political forces, and family socialization patterns have responded differently to societal pressures (Baca-Zinn, 1991). During most of their time in the Southwest, Mexicans have been the victims of prejudice and discrimination, varying in intensity from time to time and place to place but always present (Grebler, Guzman, and Moore, 1970; Hoffman, 1974; Estrada et al., 1981, McWilliams, 1990).

Because family socialization takes root in the economic and political forces of society, the history of the Mexican-American family must be anchored in the context of the American economy (Saragoza, 1983). The Southwest's geographic proximity to Mexico and its demand for low-wage labor have influenced the high concentration of the Mexican population in the southwestern states—in particular, California and Texas. Mexican-American families, consisting largely of individuals who are descended from or who are themselves unskilled immigrants, came to the United States to work in low-wage sectors of the southwestern economy (Grebler, Moore and Guzman, 1970; McWilliams, 1990). Unlike the members of some other Hispanic groups, very few Mexicans entered the United States as professional people.

What makes the situation of the Mexican American any different than that of other immigrating groups who with the passage of time have been acculturated into mainstream America? Because of their long history of settlement in the United States and continuous emigration from Mexico, Mexican Americans have had more continuous interaction with first-generation immigrants and proximity to their original homeland. They continue to maintain their strong cultural values, although change and, presumably, acculturation are taking place. First-generation community members constantly reinforce traditional values. The rate and direction of acculturative change are thus greatly influenced and cause some cultural values to remain unchanged. The proximity of Mexico to the United States, regardless of the amount of flow back and forth, reinforces the familial ties—and the family values—that span the two countries (Becerra, 1983).

The Civil Rights Movement and the Rise of Chicano Power

During the 1960s, era of the New Frontier and the War on Poverty, the growing ferment of Chicano youth focused on inequities in educational opportunities, the high rate of unemployment and low-wage occupational opportunities, and the general poverty status of the Mexican-American population. This generation of Chicano activists pressed for the rights they had been guaranteed by the U.S. Constitution, as well as for the many rights guaranteed historically by the numerous treaties with Mexico. The mid-1960s gave rise not only to the civil rights movement but also to the Chicano movement. This movement had the effect of generating a new pride in the Spanish, Mexican, and Indian heritage, and it also gave rise to many Mexican-American organizations that continue to press for equal rights in all arenas of society (Acuna, 1981).

Much of the thrust of the 1960s and 1970s came from Cesar Chavez and his farmworkers' Union; Reies Tijerina and the Alianza (a movement focusing on land grant claims in New Mexico); Jose Angel Gutierrez and La Raza Unida Party (a political party uniting Mexican Americans); and Rodolfo "Corky" Gonzales and the Crusade for Justice, a movement of Chicano self-determination. These four leaders formed the foundation of Chicano activism that continues today in a modified form.

With the growth of the Chicano population and the legacy of the Chicano movement, mainstream political power emerged in the late 1970s and early 1980s. Because of their sheer numbers throughout the United States, with major concentrations in both the Southwest and the Midwest, Mexican Americans are becoming a political force. This developing political strength has given Mexican Americans a stronger voice and power base. Since the advent of the Chicano movement, Mexican-American families have increasingly become more involved in the political process. In Los Angeles, the home of the largest concentration of persons of Mexican origin outside of Mexico City, they have increased their political strength by electing the first Mexican-American state senator to the California legislature, the first Mexican-American female assemblywoman, the first Mexican-American city councilman in many years (former California state congressman Ed Roybal was the first), the first Mexican-American member of the Los Angeles County Board of Supervisors, and several other state assemblymen. In 1996, finally, Loretta Sanchez narrowly defeated long-time ultraconservative Congressman Robert K. Dornan in Orange County for a seat in the U.S. House of Representatives. This show of political strength is becoming more apparent throughout the nation.

The Traditional Family Structure

The traditional structure of the Mexican family grew out of the socio-economic needs dictated by the agrarian and craft economies of Mexico. For the traditional Mexican, *familia* ("family") meant an extended, multigenerational group within which specific social roles were ascribed to specific persons. By dividing functions and responsibilities among different generations of family members, the family was able to perform all the economic and social support chores necessary for survival in the relatively spartan life circumstances of the rural Mexican environment. Mutual support, sustenance, and interaction during both work and leisure hours dominated the lives of persons in these traditional Mexican families (Becerra, 1983).

After the conquest of the Southwest, Mexican families who remained in or moved to the United States out of necessity tended to work and live in ethnically homogeneous settings. Minimally influenced by Anglo-American culture, these communities supported the maintenance of Mexican familial structures as they might have been practiced in rural Mexico. The male took the role of authority figure and head of the household, and the female took the role of childbearer and nurturer (Sanchez, 1974). Like all family forms a response to particular economic and political forces, these ideals and values as well as the need for modification under the new economic and political circumstances were carried on in the United States.

Much has been written about the traditional structure of Mexican-American families. Depending on the author, these structures appear rigid, cold, and unstable on one end of the continuum or warm, nurturing, and cohesive on the other end. The three main characteristics of the Mexican-American family these polar views address are the following: (1) male dominance, (2) rigid sex and age grading so that "the older order the younger, and the men the women," and (3) a strong familial orientation (Mirande, 1985:152).

Male Dominance. Of all the popular stereotypes surrounding the Mexican-American family, none has become so much a part of American usage as the concept of *machismo,* often equated with male dominance. Male dominance means the designation of the father as head of the household, major decision maker, and absolute power holder in the Mexican-American family. In his absence, this power position reverts to the oldest son. All members of the household are expected to carry out the orders of the male head.

The concept of machismo has various interpretations. For many, it means excessive aggression, little regard for women, and sexual prowess. The macho man demands complete allegiance, respect, and obedience from his wife and children. In contrast, genuine machismo is characterized by true bravery or valor, courage, generosity, and a respect for others. The machismo role encourages protection of and provision for the family members, use of fair and just authority, and respect for the role of wife and children (Mirande, 1985; Baca Zinn, 1991).

Although *machismo* is a Mexican-American cultural entity as well as a structural component, its counterpart—the self-sacrificing, virtuous, and passive female—is no more true than the selfish, sexually irresponsible, and aggressive male. In fact, since 1848 many men have had to leave the family home for economic reasons, to search for work, leaving the woman behind to head the household. Mexican-American history is full of examples of women who have deviated from the submissive role. The ideals encompassed in the patriarchal tradition, in fact, were often contradicted by the circumstances of day-to-day life. The types of jobs available to Mexican-American men kept them away from their families for long periods of time working as teamsters, wagon drivers, miners, and farmworkers. Over time, more and more women who were heads of households (even temporarily) were forced into the job market, further changing the expected roles of women (Griswold del Castillo, 1984).

Patriarchal values did not disappear under the impact of economic and political changes. Mexican-American men continued to expect women to be submissive, but in this respect the male expectation is similar to that of males in other cultures. Family life became a mixture of the old and new values related to paternal authority and the proper role of women. Increasing poverty and economic insecurity intensified the pressures on Mexican-American nuclear families and led to increased matriarchy and more working single mothers. As a result, the ideology of patriarchy found less confirmation in everyday life. As a system of values and beliefs, however, it continues to thrive (Griswold del Castillo, 1984:39).

Sex and Age Grading.   Complementing the concept of male dominance is the concept of sex and age subordination, which holds females are subordinate to males and the young to the old. In this schema females are viewed as submissive, naive, and somewhat childlike. Males and elders are viewed as wise, knowledgeable, and deserving of respect.

To some degree, these designations were derived from the division of labor. Females as childbearers and childrearers did not perform the more physically difficult jobs, and males took the role of protecting and overseeing the family. In the isolated rural areas where many Mexican-American families traditionally lived, the coordination of role expectations facilitated survival on the frontier. Roles within the familial network were stressed so that the constellation of the minisystem operated to the betterment of the individual and the familial system. Each person behaviorally and institutionally carried out those roles that would ensure family survival. The absolute power of the male was more apparent than real. Respect for the breadwinner and protector rather than dominance was fundamental to the family (Mirande, 1985).

The female child learned the roles and skills of wife and mother early, because she would carry them out both in the absence of the mother and as a future wife and mother. The eldest female child was expected to oversee the younger children so that the mother could carry out her tasks of family upkeep. The eldest male, after puberty, had authority over the younger children as well as his elder sisters because he was expected to take on the responsibility for the family in his father's absence and for his own family as a future father.

Older family members, after they physically could no longer work, assumed the role of assuring family continuity. They were the religious teachers, family historians, nurturers of small children, and transmitters and guardians of accumulated wisdom. Their accumulated wisdom and numerous years of labor for the family was repaid by the respect given to them for their longevity and experience (Becerra, 1983).

Thus, although particular role expectations in the Mexican-American family are based on gender and age and these dictate relationships and interactions, these roles were originally developed in response to a means for family maintenance and survival.

Familistic Orientation. The Mexican-American family form was a result of a style that was brought from Mexico, modified in the United States, and adapted to fit a pattern of survival in the isolated rural areas of the Southwest. Because of this history, some assume that the Mexican family and the Mexican-American family are isomorphic, allowing the Mexican-American family to be evaluated from knowledge of the Mexican family. This assumption is, in fact, fallacious (Montiel, 1970). However, the importance of the familial unit continues as a major characteristic among Mexican Americans to this day.

The familistic orientation continues because the family is viewed as a warm and nurturing institution for most Mexican Americans. It is a stable structure, in which the individual's place is clearly established and secure (Mirande, 1985). The family, as Murrillo (1971:99) indicates, offers "emotional security and sense of belonging to its members," and support throughout the individual's lifetime. The family is a major support system, a unit to which the individual may turn for help when in stress or in other types of need. Fundamental to the family system is the value of sharing and cooperation.

Extended kinship ties assume a prominent place within Mexican-American culture. The extended family may include godparents and/or very close friends. Studies show that Mexican families tend to live near relatives and close friends, have frequent interaction with family members, and exchange a wide range of goods and services that include babysitting, temporary housing, personal advice, nursing during times of illness, and emotional support (Muller et al., 1985:67).

In sum, numerous studies (Ramirez, 1980; Ramirez and Arce, 1981) demonstrate that familial solidarity among Mexican Americans is not just a stereotypical ideal, but a real phenomenon. Although it is expressed differently today because of changing cultural values and socioeconomic pressures, the pattern of a strong familistic orientation continues. It appears that Mexican Americans continue to have more cohesive family support systems than other U.S. ethnic groups (Griswold del Castillo, 1984).

THE MODERN "MEXICAN-AMERICAN" ETHNIC FAMILY

Family Structure and Behavior

Sixty percent of all Hispanics living in the United States are of Mexican origin, and 86 percent of the Hispanic population of the Southwest is of Mexican origin. Despite the stereotype of Mexicans as rural farmworkers, 85 percent of all Mexican Americans reside in major metropolitan areas. In fact, only 7.3 percent of Mexican-American people work as farmworkers (U.S. Bureau of the Census, 1991).

A significant fact about the Mexican-American population is its young median age—23.8 years in 1990, compared with the non-Hispanic population median age of 35.2. The native Mexican population median age is 18.3, while the foreign-born median age is 29.9. Fifty-two percent of Mexican Americans are males compared with a male population of 48.5 percent for the entire U.S. population. Because of geographical proximity, Mexican men may come to the United States to seek work and leave their families behind in Mexico, and this could account for the slightly higher number of Mexican-American males than females (U.S. Bureau of the Census, 1991).

In 1989, Mexican-American families had a median family income of $24,119. Among Hispanic families, Mexican-American families have the lowest median income except for Puerto Rican families, who received $21,941 (U.S. Bureau of the Census, 1991).

Mexican-American families are significantly larger than all other ethnic or racial families in the United States. The mean number of persons in Mexican-American families is 4.01, compared with 3.45 persons in all U.S. Hispanic families and 2.49 persons in white non-Hispanic U.S. families. Almost 20 percent of Mexican-American families compared with 2 percent of white non-Hispanic families have six or more members. This rate is also higher than that for all U.S. Hispanic families, 12 percent (U.S. Bureau of the Census, 1991). Furthermore, 68 percent of all Mexican-American families have children under 18 years of age residing in the home, compared with white non-Hispanic families, who report only 48.9 percent having children under 18 living in the home. Moreover, Mexican-American families are twice as likely to have small children under age 6 (40.3 percent), compared with white non-Hispanic families (20.5 percent). Thus, the larger Mexican-American family must be supported by a family income that is smaller than that of most other groups.

Occupationally, Mexican Americans are far more concentrated in blue collar jobs (46.2 percent) than in white collar jobs (35.2 percent). Compared with other U.S. Hispanics, Mexican Americans are least likely to be found in white collar jobs. The greatest proportion (24.9 percent) are employed as operatives or as clerical and kindred workers (23.6 percent). Except for African Americans and Puerto Ricans, Mexican Americans have the highest unemployment rates (10.7 percent) of any other group in the United States (U.S. Bureau of the Census, 1991).

Mexican Americans also have the lowest median school years completed of any other group in the United States. They are the most likely to have completed less than five years of education (16.9 percent), compared with the next lowest group, Puerto Ricans (9.8 percent). In part, this phenomenon can be explained by the high rate of people who emigrated from Mexico looking for unskilled labor. Because of this factor, compounded by the elevated high school dropout rate among Mexican Americans in the United States, only 45.3 percent of all Mexican Americans, compared with 60.5 percent for Puerto Ricans and 69.6 percent for white non-Hispanics, are high school graduates (U.S. Bureau of the Census, 1991).

Today's Mexican-American population can be characterized as having a disproportionate percentage of members of low socioeconomic status, with many families living in poverty. They make lower incomes that must support larger families. They have lower-paying jobs and higher levels of unemployment, which can partially be explained by low educational attainment and, to some degree, by discrimination. This is not the entire story, however. Like trends for all groups, these socioeconomic trends do not reflect the diversity of the population, especially that portion of the Mexican-American population that fares better than others. If the median family income is $24,119 annually, 50 percent of the population members earn more than that. Any discussion of the sociodemographic trends for the Mexican-American family must be considered within the context of a specific time period by region, overall economic trends, and migration patterns.

Fertility

Of the 6.5 million Hispanic women 15 to 44 years old in 1994, 4 million reported that they were of Mexican ancestry. The fertility rate for Mexican-American women (ages 15–44) in 1994 was 111 births per 1000, a rate about twice as high as for the non-Hispanic population (61 per 1000). Women of Mexican ancestry averaged 1.6 children ever born, about 0.4 children higher than non-Hispanic women (U.S. Bureau of the Census, 1995).

Fertility rates for women of Mexican ancestry were significantly lower for women born in the United States (85 per 1000), compared with those of women born in Mexico (143 per 1000). Women born in Mexico comprised 30 percent of all foreign-born women in the childbearing ages, and they accounted for 48 percent of all the births to foreign-born women (U.S. Bureau of the Census, 1995).

Many researchers have pondered the reasons for the higher fertility and birth rates among Mexican Americans. The question of whether explanations are cultural or structural or both continues to be debated with some evidence on both sides.

Marriage and Divorce

Marriage patterns among Mexican Americans are similar to those of other groups. Among those individuals aged 15 and over, 52.7 percent of Mexican Americans are married, compared with 59.2 percent for the total U.S. population. While the percentage of never-married Mexican Americans is larger than that for persons of non-Hispanic origin (34.3 percent compared with 25.8 percent), this could be accounted for by the large proportion of younger persons in the Mexican-American population (U.S. Bureau of Census, 1991).

Mexican Americans have a divorce rate of 6 percent, the lowest rate of all groups, compared with the non-Hispanic rate of 8.3 percent. However, that divorce rate has increased almost 20 percent over the past decade. Furthermore, if the Mexican-American separation rate is added to the divorce rate, that figure would rise to 9.6 percent (U.S. Bureau of the Census, 1991).

With respect to family stability among Mexican-American families, 81.7 households are nuclear families compared with 77.8 percent of Puerto Rican families, 80.1 percent of all Hispanic families, and 69.6 percent for the non-Hispanic population. Furthermore, only 15.6 percent of Mexican-American families are female-headed households, compared with a high of 33.7 percent for Puerto Rican families and a low of 15.3 percent for Cuban families among the Hispanic population (U.S. Bureau of the Census, 1991).

Assimilation and Intermarriage

Assimilation is a multidimensional process in which ethnic groups begin to blend into a total community. One major dimension in this process is structural integration. Intermarriage is one major measure of integration that reflects the degree of other assimilative processes (Yinger, 1985). Intermarriage in this context usually means marriage between a Mexican American and an Anglo American. Murguia (1982) has compiled one of the most extensive studies on Mexican-American intermarriage. His findings suggest that among the three most populous southwestern states (which have high concentrations of Mexican Americans), the intermarriage rates range from 9 to 27 percent in Texas, from 27 to 39 percent in New Mexico, and from 51 to 55 percent in California. Intermarriage rates are greatly influenced by the forces that influence integration. As educational levels increase, residential segregation decreases, and social class mobility increases with decreases in discrimination, intermarriage should probably increase accordingly. Furthermore, as the Mexican-American socioeconomic profile moves closer to the socioeconomic profile of the population as a whole, the assimilation process should move accordingly.

Religious Affiliation

The majority of Mexican Americans identify themselves as Catholics. The Catholic Church is considered to be a mainstay of Mexican culture although Catholicism has had a turbulent history in the lives of the Mexican people. The Catholic Church's opposition to the 1910 revolution and the

Mexican War of the Reform sparked the anticlericalism in Mexico that still has remnants today. The Catholic beliefs practiced by many Mexican Americans are only loosely tied to the traditional doctrine and formal teachings of the church (Skerry, 1993).

Today, while over 70 percent of Mexican Americans still identify as Catholics, there is a growing Protestant presence. Schick and Schick (1991) found that 72 percent of Hispanic Americans identified as Catholics, 23 percent as Protestants, and 5 percent other.

Hispanics can be said to be religious without necessarily attending church or contributing to the support of the church. While Hispanics may be distanced from the Church, religiosity permeates every aspect of their lives in a focus on ritual and ethical codes, aspects that have become embedded in Hispanic culture. For this reason, for Mexican Americans to identify as Catholics has a different meaning than it might for other ethnic groups because religious values are deeply intertwined with their familial and community structures (Lucas, 1981).

CHANGES AND ADAPTATIONS

Distinctive Features of the Modern Mexican-American Family

What is the modern Mexican-American family? What is the traditional Mexican-American family? There is no easy answer, because the Mexican-American family is a blend of traditional values and the adaptation to new environments and changing times. They are a product of the social, economic, and political milieu in which they live. The ceremonies relating to life cycle rituals—birth, marriage, and death—which have been integral to the Mexican-American culture still survive in greater and lesser degrees. These traditional rituals are sustained by families through ceremonies, often linked to the basic religious beliefs and values of the Mexican-American culture. The extent and elaboration of the ceremonies are often determined by the extent of acculturation and assimilation of the Mexican-American family into the mainstream of American life, yet the perception and recognition of these rituals continues to be part of Mexican-American life (Williams, 1990).

Rituals also highlight the role of the extended family and the conjugal family. Urbanization of the Mexican-American conjugal family has diminished the maintenance of extended family arrangements, and the extended family—la familia—is no longer central to the everyday life of the "modern" Mexican-American family.

In her study of the Mexican-American family, Williams (1990) documents the changes that have accompanied urbanization, bureaucratization, and technological change. From this work it is clear that while extended familial ties still may exist to provide caregiving to the elderly, provide the informal support network, and the transmission of values through generations, these forms of familial relationships are being modified. The necessity for women to enter the workforce has changed the role of women in the family constellation. The roles and responsibilities in the nuclear family have affected traditional male-female relationships. Parenting and what it means to be a husband/father and a wife/mother in the family must be redefined. These factors, in concert with broader economic and social change, have by necessity changed the traditional Mexican-American family (Williams, 1990).

While these changes are occurring, first-generation Mexican families continue to arrive in this country. This constant ebb and flow reinforces the sense of ethnic pride, retention of the Spanish language, ethnic foods, and transmission of values and norms. Thus, as American society impacts the Mexican-American family, so is American society affected by the Mexican culture.

Social Problems

Today's Mexican-American family is a unique culture in American society in that it is fully characterized neither by Mexican culture nor by American culture, but rather maintains elements of both. As an American family form, it also faces the many social problems that all families in America encounter.

Teen Pregnancy. The fertility rate in 1993 of Mexican-American adolescents aged 15–19 (104.7 per 1000) was higher compared to that for other Hispanic teens (96.6 per 1000) and almost three times the rate of that for white non-Hispanic teens (37.7 per 1000). Additionally, the rate for U.S.-born Mexican teens is 84.5 per 1000, compared to Mexico-born teens at 142.7 per 1000, is significantly higher (U.S. Bureau of the Census, 1995).

These higher rates are associated with the differential use of contraceptives among Mexican-American adolescents. The use of contraceptives seems to be linked to levels of acculturation, sex education information, educational levels of the parents, and general peer group networks. These data are not unlike those found by Bean and colleagues (1984) in their study on generational differences among Mexican Americans. Fisher and Marcum (1984) suggest that higher fertility rates seem to be associated with stronger ties, measured by ethnic integration, to the ethnic culture, a measure of acculturation.

Non-Hispanic white teens are more likely than Mexican American teens to terminate pregnancy through abortion. Abortion is not widely used by Mexican American teens, who are more likely to give birth. This fact contributes to the higher birthrates among Mexican American teens. While religion is often cited as a moderating factor in pregnancy termination, cultural values and emphasis on children seems to play the greatest role.

Drugs. It is difficult to determine the actual prevalence of drug use in Hispanic populations. What little is known suggests that there are different patterns and trends of drug use and abuse among Hispanic groups according to type of drugs used, level of use, age, gender, and degree of acculturation (De la Rosa & Maw, 1990). In general, Hispanic men tend to use all types of illegal drugs more frequently than do Hispanic women. However, this trend appears to be changing as Hispanic women become more acculturated.

AIDS. A disproportionately large number of Hispanics have died from AIDS-related conditions (CDC, 1994; DiClemente & Boyer, 1987). The ratio of AIDS cases between Hispanics to non-Hispanic whites is 2.96:1 (CDC, 1994).

As of June 30, 1994, of the total 361,509 reported cases of AIDS among adults and adolescents, 61,337 (17%) were Hispanics (CDC, 1994). Additionally, California and Texas, the two states with the highest concentrations of Mexican Americans, are among the five states with the highest incidence of AIDS. Thus, AIDS is considered to be a major health problem in the Mexican-American community.

Poverty. About one out of four (27.4%) Mexican Americans live in poverty. Although Mexican Americans represent 5.4 percent of the total population, 23 percent of Mexican-American families have household incomes below the poverty level, compared with 9.4 percent of white non-Hispanic families. The highest percentage of Mexican-American families in poverty were two-parent households (54.4 percent) and female-headed households (33.2 percent) (Bureau of the Census, 1991).

Among native-born Mexican Americans, 5.5 percent of those born in the United States receive public assistance, but just 3.1 percent of Mexican immigrants do so. This figure compares to 3 percent of white non-Hispanics and 10.8 percent of African Americans. The mean annual cash grant for a family of three was $4,376 (Pachon, 1996).

Continuing Change in the Family

The Mexican family has been modified by the social and economic pressures of American life, yet the proximity of the Mexican border provides a continual influx of Mexican nationals who serve to maintain familial and emotional ties to Mexico and to reinforce Mexican cultural values.

One key element encouraging change has been the increased movement of families from rural to urban life. Today, 85 percent of all Mexican-American families reside in the urban centers of the southwestern and western United States. This factor has had a profound impact on their family structure. Although a familial orientation remains, Mexican-American families today are less likely to be composed of extended kin in the same household than to be residing nearby, which still facilitates more frequent interaction. The supportive family system is much more characterized by voluntary interaction than by the necessity for economic survival that characterized the rural environment of their forefathers.

Because of the various patterns of immigration, there is much heterogeneity among the Mexican-American population. Mexican-American families span the continuum of acculturation and assimilation, depending on the conditions of their immigration, length of time in the United States, and sense of relatedness to Mexico. Relatedness to language, however, continues. Of all Mexican-American persons 5 years and over, 77 percent speak Spanish and 39 percent are monolingual in Spanish. Additionally, one out four Mexican Americans live in linguistically isolated households (U.S. Bureau of the Census, 1991). However, of the Mexican-American native-born population, 93 percent speak English well, compared with 51.3 percent of immigrant Mexicans. The figure for immigrant Puerto Ricans is 75 percent and for Cubans, 61.1 percent (Pachon, 1996). The proximity to Mexico plays a role in these significant differences.

Although a disproportionate number of Mexican-American families continues to be in the lower socioeconomic levels, there has been increasing social and economic mobility, as characterized by a growing number of Mexican-American students in colleges and universities, an increase in Mexican Americans in professional and managerial positions, and a stronger Mexican voice in all aspects of society. As has been true of all women in society, more Mexican-American women are entering the labor force. Greater numbers of women are entering professions and participating more fully in various walks of life.

These factors come together to keep modifying the Mexican-American family by changing the roles and expectations of all family members. As more opportunities emerge, social forces affect family life, and responses to an economic and political structure occur, the Mexican-American family will continue to change and adapt to the forces around them. However, although the traditional Mexican-American family has changed and will continue to change, the family form among Mexican Americans that fuses the culture of its roots and that of its American homeland will endure.

The Impact of the New Political Climate

The decade of the 1990s has ushered in a renewed conservatism, particularly towards immigrant groups. The growth of immigration from Pacific Rim countries over the last several years, combined with a rapidly changing economy spurred on by technological change, has created a climate of uncertainty and intolerance to difference. The uncertainty of job security for many middle-class Americans has created a climate of fear toward new immigrants, who are viewed as strangers not meriting the same rights as U.S. citizens who have been contributing members of the society.

In general, the largest numbers of immigrants have been Asians and Hispanics, in particular Mexican nationals whose proximity to the U.S. border facilitates both legal and illegal immigration. Unfortunately, many do not distinguish between individuals who are citizens and those who are noncitizens or between those who have arrived legally and those who have not. This movement toward a concept of meritocracy has created a conservatism that is now being realized in the political arena. As a result, public policies are being promulgated that have implications for many classes of people, even for those for whom the policy is not intended.

In recent years, for example, discussions have increased around "English Only" laws. These laws have as their basis that English be designated as the official language of the U.S. government. Several bills supported by English First and U.S. English lobbyist groups have been introduced in Congress. Some implications of such legislation include ending federal support for bilingual education, allowing federal agencies to deliver their services only in English, not allowing federal documents to be translated into other languages, eliminating bilingual balloting, and the like. Several states are seeking implementation of such legislation on the state level. Although these bills have glaring violations of freedom of speech and equal protection rights, in the current political climate there is mounting support for this legislation.

In California, the citizen-backed Proposition 187 was placed on the ballot in 1994 and passed by a wide margin. Proposition 187 denies public education, nonemergency medical care, and social services to undocumented immigrants; it also requires that schools, hospitals and police report suspected undocumented aliens. At this writing, Proposition 187 is being challenged in the courts and has not been implemented, but the sentiments of the citizens of California has been made clear. California hosts about 40 percent of the nation's estimated 3.4 million illegal immigrants, most of whom are of Mexican origin. If such legislation were to be upheld, it would have implications for the whole Mexican population as well as for the nation.

In 1995, the Regents of the University of California voted to eliminate race, ethnicity, and gender from consideration in student admissions decision guidelines. This ruling has been upheld in spite of opposition to it by the chancellors and faculties of the University of California system, and was fully implemented in fall 1997. This departure from affirmative action guidelines reinforces the general mood of the citizenry of California, who also passed, in the fall of 1996, Proposition 209, the California Civil Rights Initiative, a statewide constitutional amendment that reads, in part: "The state shall not discriminate against, or grant preferential treatment to, any individual or group on the basis of race, sex, color, ethnicity, or national origin in the operation of public employment, public education, or public contracting." Discussions are also taking place at the federal level to modify the language of previous affirmative action legislation to reflect the changing times and the gains that have been made. Affirmative action language will clearly be modified, if not eliminated, by the next millennium.

In 1996, the debate on welfare reform in Congress resulted in passage of major changes in the welfare system. At the same time, many states already were implementing requirements for moving people from welfare to work programs. The new federal law includes work incentives to move recipients off the welfare rolls and onto the work rolls, a time limit designating how long a person may receive public assistance, and a family cap (no increases for additional children born while on public assistance). There will be particular sanctions and rewards for teen mothers, who will probably be required to remain at home. These block grants will allow states to develop their own programs to respond to the needs of their residents.

All of these public policies, some yet to be implemented, reflect the mood of the country in the 1990s. Each has significant implications for the Mexican-American population, both directly as citizens as well as a population whose physical characteristics, language, culture, and familial bonds are connected to immigrants toward whom many of these policies are directed. Thus, while the political climate suggests a turbulent future for the Mexican-American family, its history in the United States also suggests a tenacious ability to survive, to overcome adversity, and to adapt to change.

REFERENCES

Acuna, R. 1981. *Occupied America: A History of Chicanos*, 2nd ed. New York: Harper & Row.

Baca-Zinn, M. 1991. "Chicano Men and Masculinity," in L. Kramer (Ed.), *The Sociology of Gender*, pp. 221–232. New York: St. Martin's Press.

Bean, F. D., R. M. Cullen, E. H. Stephen, and C. G. Swicegood. 1984. "Generational Differences in Fertility Among Mexican Americans: Implications for Assessing the Effects of Immigration," *Social Science Quarterly*, 65 (June): 573–582.

Becerra, R. M. 1983. "The Mexican American: Aging in a Changing Culture," in R. L. McNeeley and J. L. Colen (Eds.), *Aging in Minority Groups*, pp. 108–118. Beverly Hills, CA: Sage Publications.

Centers for Disease Control and Prevention (CDC). March, 1994. *Quarterly HIV/AIDS Surveillance Report, Cumulative Cases*. Atlanta: CDC.

de la Rosa, D. and C. E. Maw. 1990. *Hispanic Education: A Statistical Portrait, 1990*. Washington, DC: National Council of La Raza.

di Clemente, R. J. and C. B. Boyer. 1987. "Ethnic and Racial Misconceptions about AIDS." *Focus: A Review on AIDS Research*, 2 (3): 3.

Estrada, L. F., F. C. Garcia, R. F. Macias, and L. Maldonado. 1981. "Chicanos in the United States: A History of Exploitation and Resistance." *Dadeleus*, *110*: 103–131.

Fisher, N. A., and J. P. Marcum. 1984. "Ethnic Integration, Socioeconomic Status and Fertility Among Mexican Americans." *Social Science Quarterly*, 65 (June): 583–593.

Grebler, I., J. W. Moore, and R. C. Guzman. 1970. *The Mexican American People.* New York: Free Press.

Griswold del Castillo, R. 1984. *La Familia—Chicano Families in the Urban Southwest, 1848 to the Present.* Notre Dame: University of Notre Dame Press.

Jaffe, A. J., R. M. Cullen, and T. D. Boswell. 1980. *The Changing Demography of Spanish Americans.* New York: Academic Press.

Lucas, I. 1981. *The Browning of America: The Hispanic Revolution in the American Church.* Chicago: Fides/Clareton Books.

Martinez, M. A. 1985. "Towards a Model of Socialization for Hispanic Identity: The Case of Mexican Americans," in P. San Juan Cafferty and W. C. McCready (Eds.), *Hispanics in the United States—A New Social Agenda,* pp. 63–85. New Brunswick, NJ: Transaction Books.

Massey, D. S. 1981. "Dimensions of the New Immigration to the United States and the Prospects for Assimilation." *Annual Review of Sociology,* 7: 57–85.

McWilliams, C. 1990. *North from Mexico.* Rev. ed. Westport, CT: Greenwood Press.

Mirande, A. 1985. *The Chicano Experience: An Alternative Perspective.* Notre Dame: University of Notre Dame Press.

Montiel, M. 1970. "The Social Science Myth of the Mexican-American Family." *El Grito: A Journal of Contemporary Mexican-American Thought,* 3 (Summer): 56–63.

Muller, T. et al. 1985. *The Fourth Octave—California's Newest Immigrants.* Washington, DC: Urban Institute Press.

Murguia, E. 1982. *Chicano Intermarriage—A Theoretical and Empirical Study.* San Antonio, TX: Trinity University Press.

Murillo, N. 1971. "The Mexican-American Family," in N. N. Wagner and M. J. Haug (Eds.), *Chicanos—Social and Psychological Perspectives,* pp. 97–108. St. Louis: C. V. Mosby.

Pachon, H. et. al. 1996. *Toward a Latino Urban Policy Agenda.* Tomas Rivera Center, Claremont Colleges, Claremont, CA.

Ramirez, O. 1980. "Extended Family Support and Mental Health Status among Mexicans in Detroit," *La Red, 28* (March): 2.

Ramirez, O., and C. Arce. 1981. "The Contemporary Chicano Family: An Empirically Based Review," in A. Baron, Jr. (Ed.), *Explorations in Chicano Psychology,* New York: Praeger.

Reichert, J. S., and D. S. Massey. 1980. "History and Trends in U.S. Bound Migration from a Mexican Town." *International Migration Review, 14*: 479–591.

Reisler, M. 1976. *By the Sweat of Their Brow: Mexican United States, 1900–1940.* New York: Greenwood Press.

Sanchez, P. 1974. "The Spanish Heritage Elderly," in E. P. Stanford (Ed.), *Minority Aging (proceedings of the First Institute on Minority Aging),* San Diego: Campanile Press.

Saragoza, A. M. 1983. "The Conceptualization of the History of the Chicano Family," in A. Valdez, A. Camarillo, and T. Almaguer (Eds.), *The State of Chicano Research on Family, Labor, and Migration.* Stanford, CA: Stanford Center for Chicano Research.

Schick, E. and R. Schick. 1991. *Statistical Handbook on U.S. Hispanics.* Phoenix: Oryx Press.

Skerry, P. 1993. *Mexican Americans: The Ambivalent Minority.* New York: Free Press.

Williams, N. 1990. *The Mexican American Family: Tradition and Change.* New York: General Hall.

U.S. Bureau of the Census, 1985. "Persons of Spanish Origin in the United States: March 1985." *Current Population Reports,* Series P-20, no. 403. Washington, DC: U. S. Government Printing Office.

U.S. Bureau of the Census, 1991. "The Hispanic Population in the U.S.: March 1991." *Current Population Reports,* Series P-20, no. 455. Washington, DC: U.S. Government Printing Office.

U.S. Bureau of the Census, 1993. "Population Profiles of the U.S.: Special Studies." *Current Population Reports,* Series P-23, no. 185. Washington, DC: U.S. Government Printing Office.

U. S. Bureau of the Census. 1995. "The Foreign Born Population, August 1994." *Current Population Reports.* Washington, DC : U.S. Government Printing Office.

Yinger, J. M. 1985. "Assimilation in the United States: The Mexican Americans," in W. Conner (Ed.), *Mexican Americans in Comparative Perspective,* pp. 30–55. Washington, DC: Urban Institute Press.

8 Cuban-American Families

Zulema E. Suárez

INTRODUCTION

After Fidel Castro came to power in 1959, thousands of Cubans left the island to go to the United States. Because it was only ninety miles away, trips to *el norte* were not unusual or difficult. They believed they would go north temporarily until things calmed down and life returned to normal. Almost forty years later, many Cubans have died in this country still cherishing the dream of going home. Although the first generation of exiles spent their youth longing for their country and still cling to the hope of return, the younger generation has by necessity focused its energy on living life in the United States.

The journey to the United States has been short for those who were fortunate enough to exit by airplane, incessantly long for those traveling on makeshift boats and inner tubes braving the perilous sea. But regardless of how they came to these shores, the emotional trajectory of Cubans' journey has been full of pain and hardship. Migration has meant the loss of loved ones, a way of life, and a homeland increasingly idealized with the passage of time. It has meant learning to live with the yearning of return to a paradise lost.

Still, the pain of exile has not deterred the exodus of hundreds of thousands of Cubans. Indeed, about an eighth of the island population has fled the country since 1959 in an effort to preserve their personal, political and economic freedom. And countless others living in Cuba today dream of doing the same.

As a result of a series of waves of migration, Cuban Americans are the third largest group of Latin American descent living in the United States after Mexican Americans and Puerto Ricans. Numbering about 1 million, they are the most prosperous of these three groups. Despite sharing a common language, a Latin American heritage, and Catholic ideology, Cubans are distinct from other Latin Americans in terms of their history of migration, their geographic clustering, and their demographic characteristics. This chapter aims to foster a better understanding of the complex situation and characteristics of the Cuban exile and of a new generation of Cuban-American families.

HISTORICAL BACKGROUND

Cuban migration to the United States dates back to the mid-nineteenth century. In 1870, there were approximately 5,000 Cubans living in this country, most of whom were fleeing the Spanish regime governing the island at the time (Jimenez-Vasquez, 1995). Sizeable Cuban communities developed and thrived first in Key West and later in Tampa, which became the center for the Cubans' cigar industry and workers. New York City attracted business people and professionals who from a distance plotted the fight for Cuba's independence from Spain's colonial rule. New York, however, remained the primary destination for migrants between World War II and the rise of the Castro regime (Grenier and Perez, 1995). Migration to the United States was so sparse that there were only 50,000 Cubans living in the United States prior to the Cuban revolution in 1959.

Castro's rise to power and his declaration in 1961 that his regime would follow Marxist-Leninist ideology stimulated the sudden exodus of thousands of Cubans despite strict governmental restrictions. This exodus, which comprised as much as one-tenth of the island population, occurred in what scholars call "waves." As of the 1990 census, there were approximately 1,042,433 people of Cuban descent living in this country, 73 percent of whom were foreign born (Pedraza, 1996). While Cuban migration to the United States has often been characterized as politically motivated, later migrations are also considered to be economically induced. With the exception of the Mariel wave, which included involuntary migrants who were expelled by the government, Cuban migration to the United States has been voluntary.

The elite were the first to leave the island after the euphoria of the revolution subsided and Castro's communist ideology became evident (Pedraza, 1996). Executives and owners of firms, big merchants, sugar mill owners, manufacturers, cattlemen, representatives of foreign firms, former government, banking and industrial officials, and other members of the well-educated middle and upper middle class initially migrated in limited numbers. With the nationalization of Cuban industry, agrarian reform laws, and the United States' severance of economic ties, this segment of the upper echelon of Cuban society was immediately displaced. The first wave, which occurred between January 1961 and October 1962, the time of the Cuban missile crisis, included more than 150,000 refugees. Anticipating that the United States would help to overthrow the new government, Cubans expected their exile to be temporary. When the United States failed to deliver promised air cover to the freedom fighters who fought against the Cuban army in Playa Girón for the liberation of Cuba, the first phase of migration ended.

Despite strict immigration restrictions after 1961 (when the United States severed diplomatic ties with Cuba), increasing political turmoil caused by the silencing of the Catholic Church, the collapse of the electoral system, and Castro's declaration of his Marxist-Leninist ideology pushed thousands more to flee the island (Pedraza, 1996). The second wave brought an estimated 75,000 Cubans between November 1962 and November 1965. This was still a mostly middle-class cohort consisting of middle merchants and middle management, landlords, middle-level professionals, and a significant number of skilled workers (Pedraza, 1996). Spanning December 1965 to March 1972, the third wave brought an additional 275,000 refugees, with most arriving via Freedom Flights, an airlift initiated by the Johnson administration, that brought 3,000–4,000 passengers a month. Forty-one percent of Cubans migrating to the United States after the revolution came as a result of this airlift (Pedraza, 1996). Unlike the earliest waves, who were primarily upper and middle class and were escaping political persecution, about 40 percent of the airlift group were students, women, and children who were reuniting with their relatives (Bean & Tienda, 1987). During this time, the Cuban government began barring the migration of young men of military age, professionals, and technical and skilled workers because of the disruption their departure would cause for the new order (Pedraza, 1996). Hence, this wave was largely working class and employees, independent craftsmen, small merchants, and skilled and semiskilled workers.

The fourth wave, which spans 1978 to 1980, consisted of approximately 20,000 former political prisoners and their families (Szapocznik & Hernandez, 1990). With each succeeding wave, the exiles became more and more representative of the social class system of the island: The later the migration, the lower the social class of the migrants.

Despite initial enthusiasm from the government and people of the United States toward the early refugees, subsequent migrations have been very controversial. Between April and September 1980, more than 125,000 left Cuba under extremely perilous and chaotic circumstances through a hastily improvised boatlift via the port of Mariel. While thousands fled eagerly to join family members, a significant portion were expelled by the Castro government (Gil, 1983). Gay men and lesbians, people with criminal records (whether they had actually committed crimes or had challenged the government), and other institutionalized were persons overrepresented among those forced into exile (Bach, Bach & Tripplet, 1981; Jimenez-Vásquez, 1995). Unlike the "Golden Exiles" of the earlier waves, who had grown up in a capitalist system, these were the "children of the revolution" (Pedraza, 1996). Known as "social undesirables," this wave was undeserving of that stereotype: although about 16 percent of people exiting through the port of Mariel had been incarcerated in Cuba, this migration represented the source Cuban population more closely than ever before (Bach et al., 1981). That this cohort was approximately 40 percent nonwhite made them even more undesirable in the eyes of some. Another salient characteristic of this group was their youth. Mariel entrants were overwhelmingly working class, with close to 71 percent being blue collar workers (mechanics, heavy equipment operators, carpenters, masons, and bus and taxi drivers.) Many of these entrants were also single males who did not have relatives in the United States (Pedraza, 1996).

The most recent wave consists of *balseros,* people who are so desperate to escape the island that they leave on balsas (rafts, tires or other improvised vessels), fearless of the risks of death from starvation, dehydration, drowning or sharks (Pedraza, 1996). A volunteer rescue team, *Los Hermanos del Rescate* (Brothers to the Rescue), patrols the ocean constantly to rescue potential escapees. Approximately 5,791 *balseros* have survived the trip to the United States between 1985 and 1992 (Pedraza, 1996). In recent years, these numbers have increased as a result of the further deterioration of the already stagnant Cuban economy. With the collapse of communism in eastern Europe and especially in the Soviet Union, Cuba lost trade and economic subsidies that had for decades helped it to subsist. In 1994, an overwhelming 37,000 Cubans were rescued at sea during the months of August and September. Massive protest riots in Havana during this time period led Castro to order the Coast Guard not to stop emigration from Cuba's beaches (Pedraza, 1996). The U.S. government responded by blocking the *balseros'* progress and directing them to Guantanamo Bay Naval Station in Cuba, where over 30,000 aspiring entrants lived in tents until granted permission to enter the United States. Although these *balseros* were finally allowed to come to this country, the United States signed a migration agreement stipulating that future *balseros* found at sea would be returned to the island. The accord, which attempted to discourage other similar incidents, ended a longstanding American policy of granting refugee status to all Cubans rescued at sea (*New York Times,* 1997). It requires the United States to return anyone fleeing Cuba by boat to the island and to grant at least 20,000 immigrant visas to Cubans each year. To date, over 500 Cubans have been expelled back to Cuba since the accord went into effect.

Factors Influencing the Cuban-American Experience in the United States

Several factors have helped to shape the experience of this ethnic group in the United States. These include their wave of migration, their immigration status, and their settlement location. Wave of migration is important because it identifies the contextual and historical aspects of Cubans' migration to this country. For example, the early refugees, who were mostly of European stock and from the upper, middle, and professional sectors of the population, were greeted with open arms and treated like "Golden Exiles" (Bernal, 1984). Their skin color, their education, and the strength of the U.S.

economy at that time contributed to the warmth of that reception. Because the early Cubans also embodied the anticommunist sentiment of the time, they were used as symbols of the dangers of communism. To facilitate the refugees' incorporation to their new country, the U.S. government established a massive Cuban Refugee Program. The program retrained selected groups of skilled and professional workers (i.e., teachers, college professors, doctors, optometrists, and lawyers) and provided resettlement assistance. This effort greatly enhanced this wave's adjustment to their new home (Hernandez, 1974; Pedraza-Bailey, 1980).

Despite the fact that each successive wave brought people of lower socioeconomic, educational and occupational levels than the preceding ones, the second and third waves still benefited from the goodwill toward and the reputation of the earlier waves. Further, having lived under a U.S.-influenced economic system, the earlier Cubans were known for their entrepreneurial talents and activities. Coming from a capitalist order, they shared the ethics of individualism and work cherished in this country (Portes, 1969). The early immigrants proudly recount stories of how "they left Cuba with nothing, arrived . . . without speaking English, without a school transcript and without a diploma" and how they worked two and three often menial jobs, despite their professional and class status in Cuba, in order to transcend the downward mobility inherent in their migration. In the words of a second-generation Cuban American : "I know my parents went from riches there to rags here and I saw them slowly build themselves back up. It would have been very easy for them to quit and watching them succeed has provided me with the initiative to go beyond"(*Miami Herald*, 1988:8a).

Since the Mariel boatlift of 1980, however, Cubans exiting the island have been rejected and treated as "social undesirables," as noted earlier. Those exiting through the port of Mariel found themselves estranged from a host country who saw them as a burden because of a failing economy and from the exile community as well (Fradd, 1983). This estrangement is illustrated in a quote from a Mariel exile: "I have nothing in common with someone my age who has been here for a long time. . . . We have nothing to say to each other" (*Miami Herald*, 1988:8a).

The Refugee Act of 1980 ended the assumption that all Cubans are persecuted in Cuba and should be granted political refugee status (Jimenez-Vasquez, 1995). The Mariel entrants, who arrived one month after the signing of the act, were ineligible for refugee status. Though they were permitted to enter the country, the details of this wave's stay was left pending indefinitely; since that time, Cubans coming to this country have had to provide evidence of political or religious persecution. Their uncertain status limited their access to health and social services and hindered their economic and emotional adjustment to this country (Gil, 1983). Negative media publicity, their "entrant" immigration status, and the state of the economy at the time of their entry jeopardized Mariel entrants' employment opportunities.

The radical difference between the communist society they came from and that of the receiving country has made adjustment more difficult for the Mariel exiles and the *balseros*. Accustomed to living under a socialist government who met their needs, they were forced to fend for themselves with little support in the United States. The earlier Cubans, who were used to taking care of themselves and their families, complained that the Mariel entrants felt entitled and that that they were unmotivated. The Mariel exiles, on the other hand, complained that Cubans who arrived in the 1960s and 1970s "are too busy making money to care about the latest book, the new foreign film, the next concert of classical guitar" (*Miami Herald*, 1988:8a). They feel that the years they spent living under Castro's regime made them less materialistic, although they may have found it hard not to get caught up in the quest for material possessions. For those who had relatives in this country, the adjustment was made easier by the help of family and friends. Those who had no one met with alienation. They missed "the friendliness and spirit of solidarity born of shared hardships during . . . decades of shortages and rationing" (*Miami Herald*, 1988:8a).

Wave of migration is also a reasonable indicator of Cuban Americans' political views. The "older" Cuban community has been characterized by a militant anti-Castro attitude, an attitude so strong that a newly arrived Mariel Cuban was once told by an old family friend that if he ever said anything positive about Cuba, it would be the last time they talked. Still, political views may vary among the second generation and within families. Whereas one sibling may identify as Cuban and hold conservative political views, another sibling may identify as Cuban American and could care less about American policies toward Cuba and politics in general (*Miami Herald*, 1988). The later waves, starting with the Mariel group, see themselves as more politically tolerant. While they may reject Castro's government, they may also be intellectually open to socialist ideas and resent the ultrareactionary attitude of the older waves.

Geographic location has also played a key role in defining Cuban-American identity and their adjustment to this country. Cubans have primarily settled in Miami/Hialeah, Florida (60%), New York/New Jersey (16%), and Los Angeles (6%) (Jimenez-Vazquez, 1995). Whether Cuban Americans settle within an ethnic enclave or in an area of low concentration of Latin Americans will determine their need for acculturation. Residents of ethnic enclaves like Miami and Hialeah who do not have professional employment can easily go through life in the United States without speaking a word of English. They may have Cuban bosses and Latin American coworkers, shop at Cuban stores, and use Cuban health care professionals. During their leisure time they can watch Spanish-language television and attend Cuban social and dance clubs. Children will almost always speak both languages fluently, will go to school with other Cuban Americans, will attend Cuban ballet schools, and will receive musical training from Cuban teachers. The role models that they look up to—mayor, bank president, doctor, and lawyer—may all be Cuban. These Cubans may go through life being unaware of their "minority" status because in their world Cubans are the majority.

Cuban Americans settling in mainstream communities, on the other hand, are hard pressed to learn English if they are to find employment and to generally survive in a monolingual and monocultural environment. In an effort to belong, Cuban children may refuse to speak their parents' native tongue. They may even feel ashamed of their ethnic roots because their environment does not affirm their identity. They may consider themselves different and inferior. To counteract these feelings, they may try to assimilate. In effect, then, Cuban Americans may seem very different depending on when they came to this country and where they grew up.

But regardless of where they settled, the older community and those who have more recently migrated all see themselves as exiles—it may be said that the pain of loss is a part of their identity. For many, no matter how well they do in this country, things are still not the same as they were in Cuba. Both newly arrived exiles and old timers may be heard to lament nostalgically about how aspects of life here are not the same as they were in their homeland. While they may still sympathize with their parents' "24-hour-a-day pain" and all they lost, however, younger Cuban Americans are less preoccupied with the island and more identified with what is happening here in the States (*New York Times*, 1988:9). They see themselves as Cuban Americans. They don't harbor fantasies about going back, except maybe to visit, because they may never have been there. And if they have, they often don't remember.

The Cuban Family as an Ideal Type

Prior to the Cuban Revolution, the Cuban family was a prototype of the traditional Western family system: Father worked while mother stayed home and took care of the children and her husband. Because traditional Cubans value lineality (deference to authority and age), the word of the father, as head of household, was law and grandparents were respected and treated with deference (Queralt, 1984). This meant that children did not rebel against parents and were always respectful of them at any age. An adult child was expected always to defer to an elderly parent.

Although the nuclear unit had been the norm in Cuba since the 1930s, Cuban families generally lived in the proximity of relatives; the family was considered the most important social unit in traditional Cuban society. According to Bernal (1984), "the Cuban family is characterized by a bond of loyalty and unity, which includes nuclear and extended family members, as well as the network of friends, neighbors and community" (p. 193). Blood relatives were also augmented by extensive relationships with fictive kin networks. Of these relationships, one of the most prominent was that of the *compadre* (male coparent) and the *comadre* (female coparent)—the special relationship between the parents and the godparents of a child (Queralt, 1984). Children were central to the family and were included in all family, social, and recreational activities.

The Effect of Migration on Traditional Family Culture

Migration leads to considerable upheaval and to inevitable changes within families. As much as they have wanted to keep things the same as in the old country, Cuban-American families are no exception. Lineality was one of the first things to break down. Intergenerational conflicts between "old world" Cuban parents and their American or Americanized children have been considerable. As with other immigrant groups, problems occurred when second-generation and Cuban-born youth adopted American attitudes and behaviors more rapidly than their traditional or foreign-born parents. The development of marked intergenerational differences in behavioral acculturation within the nuclear family resulted in widespread behavioral disorder and family disruption among Cuban immigrants (Szapocznik et al., 1978). For example, fearful that their children would become Americanized, parents struggled to exert control on their children at levels similar to or greater than they had in Cuba. Young Cubans, on the other hand, wanted to experience the relative freedom of their U.S. counterparts. Feeling more empowered because of child protection laws, Cuban-American children felt less compelled to be obedient. The author, at 5 years old, remembers telling her mother that she couldn't wait to move to the United States because she'd heard that corporal punishment was illegal there. These intergenerational conflicts are less marked now since Cuban parents, now in their forties, were teenagers in this country and are allowing their children more freedom (*New York Times*, 1988).

The transition that the early immigrant women underwent—from nonworking mothers in Cuba to working women in this country—also greatly affected the traditional Cuban family. Although the majority of women were not employed outside the home prior to the revolution, as emigres they were forced to seek employment for economic survival. With increased economic independence, they became less tolerant of their husbands' chauvinist treatment and more outspoken about their views and dissatisfactions (Rodriguez and Vila, 1982). Whereas in Cuba the men tended to make all major decisions, the women now wanted to be considered because of their contribution to the household income. That the Cuban mother was no longer at home to look after the children also contributed to the behavioral problems mentioned.

The centrality of the extended family may have become more or less pronounced with migration and acculturation. Familism, the belief in and valuing of the nuclear and extended family members, is a central value of Cuban culture and of Latin American culture in general. While the retention of the extended family was an economic necessity for Cuban families when they first arrived in the United States, their use of the extended family network primarily occurs during the first three years of migration (Chavira-Prado, 1994; Jimenez-Vazquez, 1995). Initially, families were forced to move to different locations because Miami's economy could not support the influx of refugees with jobs. Resettlement meant that the extended family could not always stay together. Later, more acculturated Cuban Americans who have moved away from the family network by choice tend to be less involved with extended family members and family affairs.

The division between the older immigrant waves and the newer wave has also contributed to the weakening of family ties. For example, Mariel entrants experience tension with their extended families because of value differences. While they are a product of a communist society, their relatives fully embrace capitalism and complain that Mariel exiles feel entitled.

THE MODERN CUBAN-AMERICAN FAMILY

Demographic Characteristics

Fertility. Although Cuba was a predominantly Catholic country prior to the revolution, Cuban-American families in exile have unusually low fertility rates because of "careful family planning." Indeed, they have the lowest fertility rate among all groups of Latin American descent and it is even lower than that of non-Latin American white women (Bean and Tienda, 1987). Unlike other groups of Latin American origin, Cuban Americans tend to delay childbearing. For example, in 1980 fertility rates for Cuban-American women between the ages of 20 and 24 years, a period of heightened childbearing for other Latin American origin subgroups, were equal to those of women between the ages of 25 and 34.

Why Cuban-American women have such low fertility rates is not clear, but one plausible explanation is these women's immigrant status (Bean and Tienda, 1987). Since most Cuban-American women belong to the first generation, their lower fertility rate may reflect the disruptive impact of migration (immigrant women show lower levels of childbirth than their nonimmigrant counterparts). This situation may further be compounded by the fact that most Cuban-American women are also refugees. Yet even though first-generation Cuban-American women show lower fertility rates than their second- and third-generation counterparts, the latter also show lower fertility patterns. This suggests that some factor other than the disruption of migration is contributing to this phenomenon.

Marriage Rates and Characteristics. Marriage continues to be one of the most significant events in the life of the Cuban American family despite rising divorce rates. Young men and especially women are expected to get married and to have children. Among traditional Cuban families, marriage is considered to be a woman's first and foremost career. Almost 62 percent of Cuban Americans aged 15 and over are married (U.S. Bureau of the Census, 1991). In fact, Cuban Americans are more likely to marry these days than they did fifteen years ago; the rate of never-married Cuban Americans declined from 26.4 percent in 1980 to 22.4 percent in 1990. In 1980, males' age of first marriage was 24; women's age was 22 (Bean and Tienda, 1987).

Divorce Rates and Attitudes. While most Cuban Americans live in married families, this group, like others in this society, experienced increased marital instability between 1960 and 1980 as women began to assert themselves at home and in the workplace (Bean and Tienda, 1987; *New York Times*, 1988). The stress of migration and societal change has resulted in a corresponding increase in the rate of divorce. The most recent statistics available show that although only 5.2 percent of Cuban Americans age 15 and older reported being divorced in 1980, 8.3 percent did so in 1990 (U.S. Census Bureau, 1992). It follows that this community has also experienced an increase in the percentage of female-headed families (16.4%) during the last decade. Because of the increase in divorce among Cuban Americans, divorce no longer bears the stigma that it once did.

Cuban marriages and sex roles vary according to social class, level of acculturation, religion and social status in the United States (Bernal, 1984). Cultural elements from their Spanish heritage, such as machismo, female purity and female marital fidelity, may still resonate in contemporary marital relationships.

Intermarriage and Assimilation

Fidel Castro's prohibition of the migration of military-age males to the United States during the 1960s and 1970s forced Cubans to intermarry with white non-Cubans because of the shortage of males in exile (*New York Times*, 1988). Despite a better balance in the ratio of men to women in the second generation, Cuban Americans' rates of outmarriage continue to climb. Forty-six percent of second-generation Cuban-American women had married non-Cuban men by 1980, as compared to 17 percent in 1970. This figure compares with 33 percent and 16 percent for Puerto Rican and Mexican-American women, respectively. Such a high rate of intermarriage may eventually weaken the strength of Cuban cultural traditions.

Household Size and Composition

Despite increasing marital instability, Cuban Americans tend to live in two-parent nuclear family households, the predominant norm in Cuba since the 1930s (Queralt, 1984). The majority of Cuban Americans live in married couple families (76.1%), with 19.4 percent living in female-headed households as compared to 16.4 percent of non-Latin Americans (U.S. Census, 1992:18). Cuban Americans also tend to live in small families, with a mean number of 2.81 persons per household; approximately 65 percent of this group lives in two- and three-person households. This is the case despite the Cuban tradition that children remain living with their parents even after they come of age. Indeed, never-married Cuban Americans between the ages of 18 and 24 are more likely to live with their parents than other Latin American groups and white non-Latin Americans (Bean & Tienda, 1987). According to Bean and Tienda's analysis of the 1980 Census, 79.2 percent of males and almost 82 percent of females in this age group were still living with their families.

Educational and Occupational Attainment

Cubans place a very high value on education. Education is considered an investment *que nadie te puede quitar* (that no one can take from you). For working-class Cubans, education is a way of joining the ranks of the middle and upper middle class; for others, it is a way of recovering the status they lost in Cuba. Younger Cuban Americans are joining the professions so that they don't have to "slave" like their parents did when they first came to this country. Almost 19 percent of Cuban Americans have four or more years of college, while 61 percent have graduated from high school. Thirty-six percent have fewer than twelve years of schooling and 7.7 percent less than five years of school (U.S. Bureau of the Census, 1991).

Cubans take strong pride in a work ethic that has helped many to build themselves back up in their new country. Cubans' occupations, not surprisingly, also vary by waves. Upon first arriving in this country, many built their own retail businesses and worked in the building trades. While over one-third of men and women from the first wave work as managers and professionals and another sizeable group work in white collar jobs in sales, technical and administrative support, this is less true for the Mariel exiles (Pedraza, 1996). The latter are more likely to have occupations as operators, factory workers, and laborers or work in precision, production, craft, and repair work (men), and sales, technical, and administrative support (women). With refined bilingual and bicultural skills, the younger generation in Miami is moving its way up in banking, brokerage houses, and law firms as well as in other social and business institutions (*New York Times*, 1988).

Household Income and Poverty

Of the three largest subgroups of Latin American origin living in the United States, Cuban Americans have the highest household income. In March 1991, the Cuban household income was almost $26,000 as compared to $22,439 for Mexican Americans and $16,169 for Puerto Ricans (U.S.

Census Bureau, 1992). Indeed, Cuban household income was more comparable to that of whites who are not of Latin American descent ($30,513). It should be noted, however, that Cuban Americans' higher family income is a result of their large proportion of dual-income families (Pedraza, 1996).

Despite the relative success of Cubans as an ethnic minority group, significant segments of the population are not exempt from poverty. Although according to the 1990 Census 16.5 percent of Cubans are living below the poverty line, a figure that compares favorably to that of the total U.S. population, one finds significant differences according to race (Pedraza, 1996). While only 14 percent of white Cubans fall below the poverty line, 35 percent of black Cubans and 23 percent of racially mixed Cubans fall below the poverty line. These figures compare to those of African Americans and Puerto Ricans in this country. In marked contrast, only 8 percent of the Cuban elite who migrated during the first wave are living in poverty. Aggregating Cubans without regard to race or social class masks the differences that exist within this population.

Religiosity and Spirituality

Cuban Americans may not always attend church, but they consider themselves to be spiritual. According to Jimenez-Vazquez (1995:1228), "a spiritual orientation is often an ideal and guiding principle in the Cuban culture." The importance of the church (mainly Catholic) and parochial schools has transcended migration. If they can afford it, and sometimes even if they can't, Cuban Americans will opt to send their children to parochial schools. Saints (including a number of females) have played a significant role in Cubans' practice of Catholicism (Jimenez-Vazquez, 1995). The church also plays an important role in the lives of Cuban families in crises and in the lives of the elderly (Bernal, 1982).

Many Cubans are also dualistic in their beliefs. Although the majority are Roman Catholic, they may also believe in spiritism and *santería* (Rogg and Cooney, 1980). The practice of *santería* has especially burgeoned among Cuban emigres from the lower economic strata of society because of their need to have a system that helped them to cope with the problems of migration. *Santería* is an Afro-Cuban religious and folk-healing complex that evolved from the syncretization of Spanish colonialists' Catholic beliefs and of African world-view rituals; it is "the product of an identification between the gods of the slaves and the Catholic saints of their masters" (Sandoval, 1979:137).

Another faith-healing system common in Puerto Rico, *espiritismo*, is also practiced by segments of the Cuban community (Bernal, 1984). This spiritist practice is led by a medium or spiritual counselor who helps clients through the exorcism of spirits who cause illness or mental emotional distress (Bernal, 1984).

Santeros (folk healers) provide Cubans living in ethnic enclaves with advice, spiritual cleansing, and other related services (Jimenez-Vazquez, 1995). The help of *santeros* and *espiritistas* has been successfully elicited at times by mental health practitioners in the provision of mental health services to people of Latin American descent living in this country (Fields, 1976; Garrison, 1977; Sandoval, 1979). Because of mainstream attitudes toward non-Western healing and spiritual practices, Cubans will not readily admit their belief in or their practice of these spiritual systems.

Cultural Patterns

Personalismo, a concern for personal dignity—together with a person-oriented approach to social relations over concepts and ideas and a distaste for impersonal relationships characteristic of some systems (Queralt, 1983; Bernal, 1984)—is considered to be at the root of the Cuban national character. *Personalismo* is the perception "that life is nothing but the flow of interactions with other people (p. 1229), in which case the attainment of trust, respect and warmth in relationships become desirable goals" (Jimenez-Vasquez, 1995: 1229). Not being personable is considered a cultural sin.

Paradoxically, despite Cubans' emphasis on family, they also tend to be highly individualistic; they are not known for their "collective spirit or social consciousness" (Queralt, 1984:118). This cultural value, however, is believed to have helped Cubans adjust to life in the United States. Their individualism is manifested through "a personal pride and self-confidence" that is often misconceived by non-Cubans as arrogance.

Cubans also tend to be oriented to the present, emphasizing present time and problems because the future is seen as unpredictable. Although this attitude does not preclude their having a vision of the future, unlike white non-Latin Americans they are less likely to live in the future and more likely to live in the present. The Cuban Revolution has reinforced this orientation since the Cubans' world and sense of continuity was completely disrupted when Castro came to power. A way of life was completely changed from one moment to the next, leaving them with the heightened awareness that the future is indeed uncertain.

Cuban immigrants have also been found to endorse a "doing" orientation significantly more often than white non-Latin Americans. "Doing"-oriented people judge themselves and others "by what he or she achieves and emphasizes success-oriented activities usually including externally measurable activities" (Szapocznik et al., 1978:962). This value has contributed to Cubans' success in this country since many wanted to either recapture or surpass the status that they had achieved in Cuba after experiencing downward mobility as a result of migration.

Militant anti-Castroism has most characterized the Cuban community in the United States, so much so that it is considered to be part of Cuban exile culture (*New York Times*, 1988). Although not all Cubans are right-wing extremists, right-wing conservatism, anti-communism, and anti-Castroism are so entrenched among the early waves of refugees that it is said that these values are "transmitted to the next generation." This sentiment is so strong that more liberal Cubans who are not vehemently anti-Castro fear retaliation, ostracism, and even the scorn of their family.

Bernal (1984:193), however, cautions that considering Cuban values should be done in light of the migration experience: "Of particular importance are the values and principles transmitted to the children and how these values may have been influenced by migration." Queralt (1984) further warns that "values are not fixed attributes; rather, they are always evolving. The degree of acculturation to this society, for example, determines in part the extent to which Cubans will exhibit purely traditional Cuban-Hispanic values or variations that incorporate aspects of the dominant culture" (Grenier and Perez, 1995:117).

Family Roles

Remnants of *machismo*, a largely misused concept "originally intended to describe the male role as patriarch or autocratic ruler of women and children within the culture" (Bernal, 1982:193) may still be found among Cubans. The male is expected to act as protector and provider for his nuclear family and for his parents and sisters. A male who is unable to find work may not only lose "face, self-esteem and possibly the *respeto* [the respect] of his wife and children, but is likely to develop marital and intergenerational difficulties" (Bernal, 1982:192). The Cuban male can also be expected to save the honor of the family and especially of female members using whatever means necessary. The degree to which *machismo* exists will depend on social class and level of acculturation.

Females should ideally remain pure and chaste until marriage. They are the nurturers of the family and are expected to sacrifice themselves for the well-being of their husbands and children and, if they are single, for their parents. Above all, they are expected to be mothers. Females must also maintain marital fidelity at all times. While adultery by a man may be condoned, an adulterous woman is scandalous. This double standard reflects asymmetrical and oppressive male-female relationships.

Although the image of the *macho* persists, particularly among lower-income Cuban Americans, second-generation Cubans, having been raised in this country, do not necessarily embrace such traditional sex roles (*New York Times*, 1988). Younger couples seem to be moving toward more egalitarian relationships as an increasing number of women in the younger generation are pursuing professional careers (Jimenez-Vasquez, 1995).

Because Cubans value lineality, children are expected to conform and to obey their parents and elders in general. Their primary responsibilities are to behave and to succeed in school. And, as we will see, Cuban-American children are not generally burdened by household chores, nor are they expected to work after school. In fact, part-time work may be discouraged out of fear that it may interfere with their studies.

Women and Work

To survive in this country, Cuban families have needed to become less traditional with regard to work and family relationships. Whereas most women in prerevolutionary Cuba were homemakers and mothers, this situation changed drastically with migration. Upon their arrival, Cuban women were able to find work before their men did and were not as threatened by menial jobs (Boswell & Curtis, 1984). They saw their jobs as an opportunity to help the family and not as an opportunity for self-actualization (Pedraza, 1996). Cuban women's increased labor force participation has persisted throughout the years. In 1991, their rate of labor force participation (55.1%) was similar to that of white non-Latin American women (57.4%) (U.S. Census Bureau, 1992).

Their higher rates of employment outside the home, argues Queralt (1984), "may have been instrumental in Cuban women's achievement of greater equality, more decision-making power, and even some housekeeping assistance from their husbands, particularly in grocery shopping and child care." Male involvement in household chores and in child care will depend on the man's level of acculturation, education and perhaps his own upbringing. Growing up in a home where father cooked, cleaned, shopped and helped out with child care would likely expand his view of the male role to a more cooperative attitude. This outcome would be unlikely, however, if the man had been catered to by females while growing up. The more traditional male who may have "helped" his wife with household chores during her years of work may revert back to a less egalitarian and cooperative marriage once they are both retired.

Extended Family Relationships

The extended family persists as a source of strength and support for its members despite the longstanding Cuban tendency toward the nuclear family and increased familial disruption resulting from migration. Even today, the extended family can be depended for support during difficult times (Gil, 1968; Queralt, 1984).

Parents will rally to help their children emotionally and instrumentally no matter how old they may be. This strong family bond has stimulated parents' hesitant acceptance of their children's emancipation and "American" lifestyles. Although divorce was once frowned upon, a daughter going through a divorce may move back indefinitely into her parents' home.

Geographic distance does not preclude extended family members from aiding family members in need. For example, if a person is ill in Miami, family members living elsewhere may take turns going down to care for the sick relative. Indeed, the concept of the "extended family" is so foreign to Cubans that a comparable word does not exist in Spanish.

Some feel, however, that the value of the extended family in providing support for Latin Americans has been overrated (Rogler et al., 1983; Queralt, 1983). Studies examining the effects of the presence of the extended family on the use of mental health services, for example, have found no significant relationship between the presence of an integrated extended family and contact with a mental health clinic (Keefe, 1978). Although the family can be expected to come together and offer support during times of crises, the extended family seems to be disintegrating and the nuclear tendency in Cuban families becoming more pronounced with migration and acculturation to American society. Although immigrants make extensive use of kin and quasikin relationships in establishing themselves during their early years of residence in the United States, after a while, with the exception of aged parents, an attitude of permanent responsibility and mutual economic obligation diminishes (Grant, 1983). Although this may lead to increased use of formal social services, in the absence of evidence one cannot say that the availability of services is responsible for this change.

Values Transmission

The socialization of Cuban children has not changed much with migration to the United States. Indeed, parents tend to indulge their children by catering to their desires materially and emotionally. However, mothers' need to work outside the home has resulted in increased independence for their children. Nonetheless, children are often pampered, and despite a busy work schedule mothers still cater to their offspring. For example, mothers often cook, clean and wash for their children even though the children are capable of doing these chores for themselves.

Not surprisingly, male and female children are socialized differently (Queralt, 1984). In traditional Cuban families, boys are waited on by their mothers and the other women in their families because of the privilege they hold of being male. As they enter manhood, they are traditionally encouraged to explore and act out their manhood sexually. Although a young man's sexual adventures may be viewed with pride as a sign of his maleness and prowess, females' sexual purity is overprotected (Bernal, 1984). Females may have stricter curfews, may be discouraged from going away to school, and are generally censored from exploring their sexuality outside of marriage. Female purity as an ideal is reinforced from childhood and throughout the life of the Cuban woman, and she is encouraged to emulate the Virgin Mary (Bernal, 1984). Traditional families will "introduce" their daughters into "society" through a great fiesta on her fifteenth birthday called the *quinceañera*. A traditional party may be as extravagant as a formal wedding and is held in a ballroom; it consists of fifteen couples, including the birthday girl, dressed formals. The party begins with a formal choreographed and rehearsed dance performed by fifteen couples, including the girl and her partner. This dance marks her official debut into society. After that, friends and family join in the festivities sharing music, dance, drink, and food.

Length of time in this country has not eroded the expectation that children live in the parental home until the time of marriage. These adult children may choose to contribute to the household, but their contribution is not necessarily expected. This explains why, as noted earlier, more than three-quarters of Cuban American males and females between the ages of 18 and 24 were living with their families, according to the 1990 Census.

The socialization of Cuban children in the United States, however, will ultimately depend on a number of factors. These include parents' level of acculturation and education, social class, and where they live regionally. Cuban children growing up in Miami will have greater exposure to Cuban traditions because of the density of the Cuban community there. Regardless of where they live, however, parents encourage their children to learn Spanish and to be proud of being Cuban, though the latter is becoming increasingly more difficult for those living away from older family members and from the Cuban community. It will be interesting to see what percentage of the second and third generations develop Spanish fluency.

Distinctive Dating and Mate Selection Practices

Traditional sexual mores have loosened with migration and over time. Female virginity still persists as an ideal among Cuban families. Traditionally, young women were never allowed to be alone with a man in public or in private unless she was married. Couples in prerevolutionary Cuba were always accompanied by a chaperone. This practice seems to have disappeared in this country despite efforts to sustain the tradition during the early years of migration. Busy work schedules have hindered family members' ability to supervise couples' courtship, and exposure to the less restrictive dating practices of their American counterparts caused young Cuban Americans to rebel against parents' strict and outdated rules. Still, couples are expected to observe "proper" behavior: no public displays of affection beyond embracing and holding hands and no staying out all night.

Individuals choose their mates, but the family may be very involved in the courtship process if the daughter or son is living at home. Suitors are expected to visit regularly and to interact with the family. A family's level of involvement is determined by their level of acculturation. In a more traditional family, for example, dating is not expected to occur unless it will result in marriage. Church weddings are highly desirable for religious reasons and because they reflect the family's economic well-being.

Sexuality

Males enjoy greater sexual freedom than females, as noted earlier. Females' engagement in premarital sex is still disturbing to Cuban parents. Unlike males, who may become sexually active in their mid to late teens, females are more likely to do so in their late teens to early twenties because of the greater restrictions imposed on them by parents. At the same time, Cuban parents realize that they cannot control and protect their daughters in the way they did in prerevolutionary Cuba. Having become grudgingly resigned to their daughters' premarital sexual activity, parents nonetheless expect the young woman and her partner to be discrete about their sexual relationship. Sex is not discussed with parents, and unmarried couples are generally not allowed to share a room when visiting relatives.

Care of Elderly and Caregiving

Given Cubans' value of lineality and familism, the elderly have traditionally been respected and cared for by extended family members. In Cuba, placing the elderly in nursing homes was unheard of. However, the move to the United States and the accompanying changes in the family structure increased the need for such facilities in this country. With most family members working outside the home, there is no one to care for an elder family member. Elders who do not live in an ethnic enclave may not have access to culturally competent social and recreational activities. Although still rare, nursing homes have been developed by Latin American social service providers to meet the special language, cultural, and dietary needs of this population. Casa Central, a Latin American multiservice agency in Chicago, established a nursing home and apartments for independent living for elderly people of Latin American descent. During the day the elderly can participate in day programs also offered by the agency. While this example is not to suggest that most Cuban elderly are now placed in nursing homes, it does imply that with migration traditional caregiving patterns have begun to change.

CHANGE AND ADAPTATION

Although it is difficult to predict the future of Cuban-American culture in the United States, it is safe to say that for now it is being maintained. Many factors facilitate the retention of Cuban language and culture in the United States.

Cuban ethnicity is both strengthened and maintained by the existence of ethnic enclaves such as Miami. Cuban food and coffee can be found at stands at Miami International Airport and anywhere else in the city. Cuban music can be heard on the radio or in popular nightclubs, while Spanish language television features Cuban anchors or Cristina, the talkshow host also known as the Cuban Oprah. In Miami, homesick Cubans can find "the soft clickety-click of a domino game, the sweet crunchiness of a *granizado*—a Cuban Sno-Cone—the nostalgic talk of boxing heroes" (*Miami Herald*, 1988:22a).

One characteristic considered typically Cuban that has been misunderstood by outsiders "is a sense of specialness that most Cubans have about themselves and their culture" (Bernal, 1984:195). They take so much pride in their heritage that at times outsiders regard Cubans as obnoxious. This specialness, according to Bernal, may stem from the cultural fusion of European, African, and indigenous cultures, which has given rise to, for example, the *son*, a musical genre produced through the syncretization of Yoruban and Spanish lyrics. The *son*, along with other popular rhythms such as the rumba, mambo, charanga, guaguanco, and cha-cha are not only the root of today's *salsa* music, they are also popular ballroom dances. These Latin rhythms are gaining increasing popularity among mainstream audiences as well through the efforts of such Cuban artists as Gloria Estefan and the Miami Sound Machine and Jon Secada, who have managed to cross over to the mainstream music market. The acceptance of Cuban and other Latin music by other audiences reaffirms young Cubans' sense of pride in their cultural heritage.

Because of their pride in themselves, Cubans have not easily succumbed to the negative programming that minority group members are exposed to in this society. They resist the subtle and often blatant messages of inferiority and inadequacy promoted by the mainstream society. Because of these feelings of innate self-confidence and pride, Cubans dismiss the script that society has written for them as "minority" group members.

The family, however, remains at the root of Cuban culture in the United States. Although they may feel "as American as a Burger King Whopper, they prefer speaking English to Spanish" (*New York Times*, 1988:1), young Cuban Americans remain tied to their roots largely through their parents and grandparents. Many of the older exiles, to mitigate the effects of migration, have acted as though it did not happen by attempting to continue to live life exactly as they had in Cuba. Still nurturing the hope of returning to Cuba, they keep the culture alive through stories, memories, and customs. They expect the same behavior patterns from family members, cling to the same values, and maintain the same activities and rituals (Bernal, 1982). According to Bernal (1982:200), "It is as if the culture of origin were frozen in time and recreated continuously in the new environment." The younger generation is not allowed to forget the pain of exile—that would be considered a kind of betrayal of the suffering that their parents underwent when they left Cuba and reestablished themselves in this country.

The influx of new waves of exiles throughout the almost forty years that Cuban Americans have been in this country has also helped Cuban exile culture to evolve. Newcomers have brought the culture of the island to the United States. Some Mariel exiles feel that having lived under a repressive government made them more intellectually inclined and more spiritually contemplative and politically aware (*Miami Herald*, 1988:8a). Despite the ideological and value differences that may exist between the older and the new exiles, living side by side there is bound to be some cultural exchange whereby new and old Cuban values fuse to form a new exile Cuban-American culture.

Given Cuban Americans' emotional and psychological ties to their island, it is expected that this ethnic group will maintain a strong sense of cultural identity. As long as Fidel Castro remains in power, Cuban-American exiles will not be able to let go of the country they left behind and of the pain of exile. In the words of a first-generation exile: "For Cubans there is nothing more important in life than freeing the island. Every time you touch that wound we bleed" (Casuso and Camacho, 1985:20). If and when the doors to Cuba are reopened someday, Cuban Americans will develop even stronger ties with their culture because they will be able to travel effortlessly back and forth because of its close proximity to Florida.

The Effect of the Larger Culture on the Authority of the Family

Mainstream culture's investment in individualism, overwork, and materialism threatens the value of familism, which has traditionally been at the root of Cuban culture. Although Cubans can still be said to have strong family bonds, they are weakening with the passage of time. Whereas in Cuba the individual was expected to sacrifice his or her well-being for the good of the family, the right of the individual prevails in this country. Younger Cubans' pursuit of their educational and professional success is taking them geographically away from family, friends, and the Cuban community. Also, Cuban Americans' drive to recapture what they lost in Cuba, coupled with the materialism of the United States, may preclude making time for family and friends. According to a Mariel exile, "Here the interest to own things absorbs people and it is very difficult to break that cycle. . . . People were always saying, let's get together one day and play a little, but we never did. . . ." And in the words of an early exile, "In Cuba, they say, we worked to live. In Miami, we live to work" (*Miami Herald*, 1988).

The Effect of the Changing Role of Women on the Ethnic Family

The changing role of women in the larger society has had a significant impact on the Cuban family. According to a *New York Times* (1988:9) article, this has been the most debated change within the Cuban community in the decades since migration. For the early migrants, it was unheard of that a female child would move out of her parents' home before marriage. But in subsequent years, Cuban Americans, including the earlier waves, have seen no choice but to accept that their daughters may move out on their own or may go away to college in another city or state. It should be noted, however, that although the role of women in Cuba changed significantly after the revolution, with women enjoying many of the same freedoms as men, most Cuban Americans left the island before those changes occurred. That the emancipation of women was associated in Cubans' minds with the revolution on one hand and with American culture on the other perhaps contributed to the exiles' resistance to embracing the role change. Both were seen as threatening old ways they were desperately trying to salvage in an effort to dull the pain of migration.

The Importance of Social Class on Ethnic Differences

Because Cuban migration was initially politically instead of economically motivated, all social strata of the island are represented in the United States. Unlike other Latin American groups, such as the Mexican Americans and Puerto Ricans, who as economic migrants tend to be lower socioeconomically, class is a significant variable in understanding Cubans Americans. Because the earlier waves were represented by the upper crust of Cuban society while subsequent waves were less prosperous and more rural, whatever social class differences existed in Cuba have been replicated to a certain extent in the United States.

With migration, some of the class differences that existed in Cuba have been eroded because of downward and upward mobility. Still, upper-class Cubans may see themselves as superior relative to lower-class Cubans despite the educational and economic gains the latter may have made with migration. For example, a young Cuban-American woman was once rejected by the mother of the Cuban-American man she was dating because she came from a working-class, rural family in Cuba. The fact that she was a Ph.D. candidate at a world class university was irrelevant since she was still being judged by Cuba's social scale.

Whether class differences supersede ethnic differences may depend on where a Cuban American lives. If he or she is living in an area where there are not many Cubans, then ethnicity will probably be a strong binding force. If, on the other hand, he or she is living in an enclave where all the social classes are represented, then social class will become more salient. Because most Cubans in the United States live within an ethnic enclave, social class remains a prominent source of difference among the exiles. Social class differences add yet another layer of diversity to the Cuban population in the United States.

The Impact of Current Larger Societal Problems on Ethnic Family

Cuban Americans who live in an "ethnic cocoon" are both sheltered from and vulnerable to wider social problems. While problems with drugs have surfaced as a result of the stress of migration and acculturation, other problems that plague mainstream society do not seem to affect this ethnic community.

In the past drug and behavioral problems have been documented in the literature among second generation youth who acculturated faster than their parents (Szapocznik, Scopetta and King, 1978). The development of marked intergenerational differences in behavioral acculturation within traditionally close-knit families was the source of widespread behavior disorders and family disruption in Cuban immigrants. Conflicts between Cuban youth belonging to these families frequently manifested themselves as behavioral disorders and particularly antisocial behavior. Page's (1980) study of Cuban-American adolescents' acculturation and drug use found that rejection of parental heritage was stressful for his subjects because they lacked behavioral models that were consonant with their level of acculturation.

Cuban culture's emphasis on chastity and females' delayed sexual activity may help to explain why teenage pregnancy is not significant problem in the Cuban-American community. If a young woman does become pregnant, it is considered to be very disgraceful and, in a traditional Cuban family, a reflection of the father's inability to exercise his role as *macho*, or protector of his family. To save face, she must marry the baby's father. If for some reason she does not, she will not be turned away by her family despite their shame and pain. This is a reflection of Cubans' strong family ties and devotion to their children.

Abortion has not been an issue in the Cuban community. This seems ironic, given Cubans' predominant Catholicism. Abortion was legal in Cuba. And while it is not taken lightly, it does not seem to be the moral dilemma it is considered to be in this country. As a society, Cuban Americans are also not against the practice of birth control. Openness to family planning is reflected by their low birth rates.

One social problem that Cuban Americans are not sheltered from is that of acquired immunodeficiency syndrome (AIDS). Although Cuban-born persons have a lower incidence of AIDS than Puerto Ricans, it is higher than that of Mexican-born people residing in the United States. Nationally, Florida, where most Cubans reside and comprise 43 percent of the Latin-American population, had the second highest rate of AIDS (57 per 100,000) among Latin Americans (Diaz, Buehler, Castro & Ward, 1993). Miami, the heart of the Cuban exile community, had the second highest overall rate of AIDS (104 per 100,000) among all U.S. metropolitan areas in 1991. The rate of AIDS is reported to be higher among the Mariel exiles; the 1980 migration seems to have contributed to the number of Cuban-born persons with AIDS, inflating the numbers for the overall Cuban population. The predominant mode of transmission is male-male sex. This is not surprising, considering that Castro forced many homosexuals to leave the island during the Mariel crisis.

The New Political Climate and Cuban Americans

The new political climate will affect Cuban Americans differentially— some segments of the population will suffer more than others. The increasing conservatism of the past years has been consonant with the political views of the earlier waves of Cubans. Because of their staunch anticommunist stance and disappointment with the Kennedy administration after the failed Bay of Pigs invasion, noted earlier, older Cubans have strongly sided with Republicans. Many, having picked themselves up by the proverbial bootstraps, are not supportive of public assistance and other government subsidies. Ironically, many of these same Cubans were helped to reestablish themselves in this country by the Cuban Refugee Program, a massive government effort. Younger Cuban Americans, however, are more identified with the issues affecting Latin Americans in the United States and with domestic policies as opposed to the U.S. government's policies towards Cuba and other communist countries.

The poor, who are overrepresented in the later waves, and the elderly are likely to be hard hit by the changing role of government. Many of the elderly are ineligible for social security benefits because they do not have the required period of covered employment in this country (Queralt, 1983). Of those who did work, many had low wages and limited periods of coverage and qualify for minimum benefits only. President Reagan's January 1982 decision to abolish the minimum social security benefit of $122 a month affected many Cuban Americans applying for benefits because it reduced already meager benefits. Because a number of the elderly have either never participated in the U.S. labor force or, if they did, were underemployed within the Spanish language community or had no pension coverage at all, they may be ineligible for retirement income. Those who do not have relatives who can or are willing to support them are forced to rely on increasingly dwindling government assistance. Because the later waves (the Mariel and the *balsero* exiles) have fewer educational and economic resources than the earlier waves and migrated to the United States during times of government fiscal retrenchment, they have probably both required more government assistance than their predecessors and received less.

Ethnic Diversity and the Cuban Family

Cuban Americans' steadfastness in retaining their ethnic culture has had both benefits and negative consequences. The retention of certain Cuban cultural attributes has led to misunderstandings that may contribute to prejudice against this ethnic group. While Cubans' sense of specialness may have contributed to their adaptation and relative success, it has been viewed by others as arrogance and grandiosity (Bernal, 1984). Hence, as noted earlier, because of their love of their culture and their efforts to preserve it, Cubans are often considered to be clannish. In response to this perceived arrogance and superiority, outsiders may react defensively to Cubans.

Cuban humor, *choteo*, may also be misunderstood by outsiders. *Choteo*, a "typical Cuban phenomenon and a type of humor that has been defined as ridiculing and making fun of people, situations and/or things," once "served as defensive function in the social reality of Cubans" (Bernal, 1984). In *choteo*, serious matters are markedly exaggerated and made light of through jokes. People from other ethnic groups and Latin American subgroups may perceive this behavior as inappropriate.

For Cubans, adapting to the United States has meant embracing a culture and lifestyle that is faster, more impersonal and individualistic (Szapocznik et al., 1981). The rapid rate of change has caused dislocations for those who in their eagerness to embrace American culture and to belong have adapted too fast. For example, the young, who are in a greater rush to assimilate, cut themselves off from their roots and cultural heritage. (Szapocznik, Scopetta & Kurtines, 1978). The problem of differential acculturation rates has contributed to the isolation of some Cuban elderly from their children and their grandchildren, causing them to move away (Queralt, 1983). Yet people living in a bicultural environment will have a tendency to become maladjusted if they remain or become monocultural (Santiesban, Szapocznik & Rio, 1981). Becoming bicultural enables Cuban Americans to interact with mainstream society while enjoying the support of the extended family and the other natural helping networks within the Cuban community.

At the same time, although growing up biculturally is advantageous, it can also be a liability (Boswell & Curtis, 1984). For some Cuban Americans who were born on the island but grew up in this country, this has led to an identity crisis—they feel neither completely Cuban nor completely American. While being a part of both worlds, they also feel estranged from both. Value conflicts ensue because of the clash between mainstream culture's thrust toward individualism and Cuban culture's tendency toward familialism, which demands loyalty to the family.

While living biculturally is more adaptive than not, the ability to do so is hindered by monocultural society's persistent discomfort with difference. Cuban Americans' efforts to preserve their ethnic roots are often perceived as clannish, as noted earlier. In Miami, English speakers are resentful of the pervasiveness of the Spanish language in the city since Cuban Americans overwhelmingly (approximately 94%) use Spanish as their household language, according to an analysis of the 1980 Census (Bean & Tienda, 1987). This resentment led to the 1980 repeal of a law passed in 1973 declaring Dade County, Florida a bilingual jurisdiction that made Spanish the second official language in such venues as election ballots, public signs, and local directories (Moore & Pachon, 1985). Actions such as this one would, of course, hinder recent immigrants or those not speaking English from becoming more integrated into American society.

As long as mainstream society insists on conformity to a monocultural Western ideal, the retention of Cuban culture will remain a mixed blessing. Still, research shows that the best possible options for all recent immigrants is to live biculturally since the denial of either world leads to much distress and social dislocation (Szapocznik, Scopetta, & Kurtines, 1978).

Racial Issues Within the Cuban-American Community

Racial issues were a serious problem in Cuba and are likely to also be a problem here in the United States, given the history of racial and social segregation of the island. Before the revolution, Cuba was a multiracial society plagued by the prejudices and discrimination that plagues this country today. Blacks and other nonwhites were systematically excluded from the pinnacle of society (yacht and country clubs, elite vacation resorts and beaches, hotels, and private schools) in prerevolutionary Cuba. Indeed, Castro was able to capitalize on Cuba's racial relations by making these facilities available to all Cuban citizens regardless of color and class, thus enlisting major support from these populations.

Since most of the early immigrants were white (91% of the first wave versus 77% of the Mariel wave), the tensions between the newer and older immigrants are also likely to be racial. That black Cubans are more likely to be poor than white Cubans may be suggestive of ethnic discrimination (in addition to wider societal discrimination), given that many of the emigrés tend to work for other Cubans within the ethnic enclave of Miami. White Cubans' greater tendency to marry non-Cubans (*Miami Herald*, 1988; Bean and Tienda, 1987) than black Cubans may indicate that race is a stronger variable than ethnicity, although this assumption is highly speculative. At the same time, white Cubans are more prejudiced of American blacks than of Cuban blacks. This is probably the only case in which ethnicity supersedes race.

SUMMARY

This chapter traces the historical, psychosocial, and political context of the Cuban-origin family in the United States. While the pain of exile is never forgotten by young and old, Cuban Americans have managed to adapt to life in *el Norte*. Despite painful emotional bruises and wounds of migration and adaptation, Cuban Americans are the most prosperous of the three major groups of Latin-American origin living in this country. Although the chant of *regreso*, return to the island, still resonates in Cuban-American enclaves, for many the United States has become a home away from home.

REFERENCES

Bach, R. L., J. B. Bach, and R. Triplett. 1982. "The flotilla 'entrants'. The latest and most controversial." *Cuban Studies/Estudios Cubanos*, 2: 12.

Bean, F., and M. Tienda. 1987. *The Hispanic Population of the United States in the 1980s.* New York: Russell Sage.

Bernal, G. 1984. "Cuban Families," in M. McGoldrick, J. K. Pearce, and J. Giordano, (Eds.), *Ethnicity and Family Therapy*, pp. 186–207. New York: Guilford Press.

Boswell, T. D., and J. R. Curtis. 1984. *The Cuban American Experience: Culture, Images, Perspectives.* Totowa, NJ: Rowman & Allanheld.

Chavira-Prado, A. 1994. "Latina Experience and Latina Identity," in Thomas Weaver (Ed.), *Handbook of Hispanic Cultures in the United States: Anthropology.* Houston, TX: Arte Publico Press.

David, H. P. 1970. "Involuntary International Migration: Adaptation of Refugees," in E. B. Brody (Ed.), *Behavior in New Environments: Adaptation of Migration Populations.* Beverly Hills, CA: Sage.

Fields, S. 1976. "Storefront Psychotherapy Through Seance. Innovations." *3* (1): 3–11.

Fradd, S. 1983. "Cubans to Americans: Assimilation in the United States." *Migration Today, 11* (4–5): 34–41.

Garrison, V. 1977. "Doctor, Espiritista or Psychiatrist?: Health-Seeking Behavior in a Puerto Rican Neighborhood of New York City." *Medical Anthropology, 1* (2): 165–191.

Gil, R. M. 1968. "The Assimilation and Problems of Adjustment to the American Culture of One Hundred Cuban Adolescents." Master's thesis, Fordham University, Bronx, NY.

Gil, R. M. 1983. "Issues in the Delivery of Mental Health Services to Cuban Entrants." *Migration Today, 11* (4-5): 28–35.

Grant, G. 1983. "The Impact of Immigration on the Family and Children," in M. Frank (Ed.), *Newcomers to the United States*, pp. 26–37. New York: Haworth Press.

Hernandez, A. R. 1974. *The Cuban Minority in the U.S.: Final Report on the Need Identification and Program Evaluation.* Washington, DC: Cuban National Planning Council.

Jimenez-Vazquez, R. 1995. "Hispanics: Cubans." *Encyclopedia of Social Work*, 19th ed. Washington, DC: NASW Press.

Moore, J., and H. Pachon. 1985. *Hispanics in the United States.* Englewood Cliffs, NJ: Prentice-Hall.

Miami Herald. December 27, 1988. "Mariel Generation Feels Separate from Fellow Exiles." *New York Times.* April, 13, 1988. For Cuban-Americans, an era of change.

Pedraza-Bailey, S. 1980. "Political and Economic Migrants in America: Cubans and Mexican Americans." Ph.D. dissertation, University of Chicago.

Portes, A. 1969. "Dilemmas of a Golden Exile: Integration of Cuban Refugee Families in Milwaukee." *American Sociological Review, 34*: 505–518.

Queralt, M. 1983. "The Elderly of Cuban Origin: Characteristics and Problems," in Roger L. McNeely and J. L. Cohen (Eds.), *Aging in Minority Groups.* Beverly Hills, CA: Sage Publications.

Queralt, M. 1984. "Understanding Cuban Immigrants: A Cultural Perspective." *Social Work, 29*: 115–121.

Rodriguez, A., and M. E. Vila. 1982. "Emerging Cuban Women in Florida's Dade County," in R. E. Zambrana (Ed.), *Work, Family, and Health: Latino Women in Transition*, pp. 55–67. Bronx, NY: Fordham University Hispanic Research Center.

Rogg, E. M., and R. M. Cooney. 1980. "Adaption and Adjustment of Cubans: West New York, New Jersey." Bronx, NY: Fordham University Hispanic Research Center.

Rogler, L. H., R. Santana-Cooney, G. Costantino, B. F. Earley, D. T. Gurak, R. Malgady, and O. Rodriguez. 1983. *A Conceptual Framework for Mental Health Research on Hispanic Populations*. Bronx, NY: Fordham University Hispanic Research Center.

Sandoval, M. C. 1979. "Santeria as a Mental Health Care System: An Historical Overview." *Social Science and Medicine, 13b*: 137–151.

Santisteban, D., J. Szapocznik, and A. T. Rio. 1981. "Acculturation/Biculturalism: Implications for a Mental Health Intervention Strategy." Paper presented at the XVIII Interamerican Society of Psychology, Santo Domingo, Dominican Republic, June 21–26.

Schur, C. L., A. B. Bernstein, and M. L. Berk. 1987. "The Importance of Distinguishing Hispanic Subpopulations in the Use of Medical Care." *Medical Care, 25*: 627–641.

Szapocznik, J., M. Scopetta, M. Arnalde, and W. Kurtines. 1978. "Cuban Value Structure: Treatment Implications." *Journal of Consulting and Clinical Psychology, 46* (5): 961–970.

Szapocznik, J., and R. Hernandez. 1988. "The Cuban Family," in C. Mindel and R. W. Habenstein (Eds.), *Ethnic Families in America: Patterns and Variations*, 4th ed. pp. 160–172. New York: Elsevier.

Szapocznik, J. 1980. *A Programmatic Mental Health Approach to Enhancing the Meaning of Life of the Cuban Elderly*. Washington, DC: COSSMHO.

Szapocznik, J., D. Santisteban, O. Hervis, F. Spencer, and W. Kurtines. 1981. "Treatment of Depression Among Cuban American Elders: Some Validation Evidence for a Life Enhancement Counseling Approach." *Journal of Counseling and Clinical Psychology, 49* (5): 752–754.

Szapocznik, J., M. A. Scopetta, and O. E. King. 1978. "Cuban Value Structure: Treatment Implications." *Journal of Counseling Psychology, 1*: 961–70.

Szapocznik, J., M. A. Scopetta, and W. Kurtines. 1978. "Theory and Measurement of Acculturation." *Interamerican Journal of Psychology, 12*: 113–130.

U.S. Bureau of the Census. 1992. "The Hispanic population of the United States: March 1991." *Current Population Reports*. No. 455, Series P-20. Washington, DC: U.S. Government Printing Office.

Wenk, M. G. 1968. "Adjustment and Assimilation: The Cuban Experience." *International Migration Review, 3*: 35, 38–49.

9 The Puerto Rican Family

Melba Sánchez-Ayéndez

HISTORICAL BACKGROUND

Puerto Rican culture has traditionally been understood as developing from the interaction between the Spanish conquerors, Taíno Indians, and black African slaves, with the Hispanic colonial traits predominating. The crystallization of this national culture is assumed to have occurred during the nineteenth century. The United States' domination of this Caribbean island from 1898 to the present has also left its mark on contemporary Puerto Rican social, political, and economic institutions.

In 1898, as a result of the Spanish-American War treaty, Puerto Rico, a Spanish colony, became a possession of the United States. This annexation brought radical changes to the social and economic structure of the island. Through the Foraker Act of 1900, Puerto Rico became integrated into the economic system of the United States by the establishment of free trade between the two nations, the inclusion of Puerto Rican production under the U.S. tariff system and cabotage laws, and the incorporation of the island in the country's monetary system. Under the Jones Act of 1917, Puerto Ricans were granted U.S. citizenship.

The first four decades of domination by the United States were characterized by an emphasis on agricultural production of export crops, especially sugarcane. Coffee production, although growing in value in the world market, suffered a decrease because it was excluded from the U.S. market, which favored sugar exports. This, in conjunction with tight credit restrictions, weakened the position of small- and medium-sized coffee plantation owners, many of whom were forced to sell their lands (History Task Force 1979). It also led to an expansion and concentration of land controlled by absentee U.S. corporations. The development of monopoly capital in the sugar industry brought about an exodus of the unemployed labor force from the mountainous island areas (where coffee production was concentrated) to coastal sugarcane fields and urban tobacco factories (History Task Force 1979). From 1928 and 1940, the Puerto Rican economy suffered the devastating effects of the world depression. The negative consequences of an export economy based on a few products were felt as the world market rapidly contracted and prices dropped during the recession years. After 1935, sugar production declined and the manufacturing sector began to contract.

From 1899 to 1940, the population of the island doubled from a total of 953,243 inhabitants to 1,869,255. At the beginning of the 1940s, a majority of the population lived in rural areas. Almost 45 percent of the labor force was employed in the agricultural sector; more than 50 percent of agricultural workers were involved in sugar cultivation (History Task Force 1979). Manufacturing absorbed 20 percent of the workforce. Male employment in this sector was concentrated in the food industry; female employment was concentrated in the tobacco industry, needlework, and related tasks performed in the house. Women outnumbered men as factory laborers in both rural and urban areas. Between 1941 and 1942, unemployment increased from 99,100 to 237,000 individuals (History Task Force 1979).

As a solution to the serious economic crisis, the government implemented a program of industrialization in the early 1940s and throughout the 1960s that was to transform the economy of the island from agrarian to industrial. The majority of the new firms were branch plants of U.S. companies that exported their finished products to the mainland. During this period, manufacturing, construction, and commerce comprised a rising share of the gross national product. Nonetheless, the number of employed workers during the years from 1945 to 1960 remained almost unaltered (History Task Force, 1979). Agriculture was not rehabilitated during this period. Its growth, compared with other economic sectors, was minimal. The mechanization of agriculture brought a substantial decrease in the proportion of the work force employed in farming.

Since 1968, the pattern of industrialization on the island changed. The manufacturing sector shifted toward petrochemical, chemical, and pharmaceutical industries, relying more heavily on capital investment than labor. The smaller number of available jobs required specialized skills. Manufacturing has remained the most important productive sector, while agriculture has dramatically declined. Today the government is the largest employer on Puerto Rico, followed by the commercial and manufacturing sectors.

The Puerto Rican Migration

The immigration of a large sector of the Puerto Rican working class to the United States is linked to the political-economic relationship between the two countries. These relations served to facilitate the migration of Puerto Ricans, because, as United States citizens, they were able to travel to the mainland without the restriction imposed on other immigrant groups.

In 1920, approximately 12,000 Puerto Ricans were reported to be living in the United States, dispersed throughout the forty-eight states (History Task

Force, 1979). During the Depression years, the migration declined, and between 1930 and 1934 approximately 20 percent of the Puerto Rican population in the United States returned to the island (Vázquez Calzada, 1979). By 1944, the number of those who had left the island increased to 90,000 (López, 1974). After World War II, in the early years of the industrialization period, there was a massive immigration of Puerto Ricans to the United States. A series of factors, including rapid population growth on the 3,435-square-mile island, high rates of unemployment, the prospect of higher wages, and the demand of U.S. corporate interests for cheap labor in the services, agriculture, and garment industry sectors, accounted for the large numbers of immigrants to the mainland.

Efforts were made by the insular and mainland governments to cooperate in the migration of workers to the United States. For the Puerto Rican government, the migration was a way of dealing with a "surplus" unemployed population, particularly rural farm workers; whereas, for the United States, the migration was a source of cheap, unskilled labor (Leavitt, 1974; López, 1974). Reduced air fares, seasonal farm worker contracts between Puerto Rican government agencies and U.S. corporations, and a propaganda campaign about prospective jobs and higher wages resulted. Even Mayor Wagner of New York went to Puerto Rico to inform the people of the availability of jobs in the city (*New York Times*, 1954).

Immigration data show that during the 1940s an average of 18,700 Puerto Ricans immigrated to the United States annually (López, 1974). During the 1950s, the average number of immigrants increased to 41,200 annually and decreased during the 1960s to approximately 14,500 annually. The 1950s were the years of the massive migration; migration during the 1960s was of an erratic nature (Vázquez Calzada, 1978). The 1980s were characterized by a large migration, larger than in the preceding two decades (Conferencia del Gobernador para el Fortalecimiento de la Familia Puertorriqueña, 1987). At the beginning of the 1960s, approximately 900,000 Puerto Ricans were living in the United States (López, 1974). In 1970, the number increased to 1,429,396 (U. S. Bureau of the Census, 1980), despite the fact that during the second half of the 1960s and throughout the 1970s more than a quarter million Puerto Ricans returned to the island (Vázquez Calzada, 1978). The 1980 census counted a total of 2,013,945 Puerto Ricans living throughout the United States (U. S. Bureau of the Census, 1980). The 1990 census reported 2,727,754 Puerto Ricans; an increase of 35 percent from 1980 (U.S. Bureau of the Census, 1991b). The migration of Puerto Ricans from 1940 to 1970 was selective in terms of age—70 percent of those who left were between 15 and 39 years of age—but not in terms of sex (Vázquez Calzada, 1979). The migrants established themselves in urban areas of the United States, particularly in New York, where 95 percent of those who left the island during the 1950s settled (History Task Force, 1979).

Prior to World War II—the period of corporate agriculture in Puerto Rico—the migrants tended to be skilled and semiskilled urban workers (Leavitt, 1974). A great majority of those who migrated after World War II were unskilled rural farm workers who were unable to become incorporated into the labor force during the industrialization period. Abroad, some became employed in unskilled farm labor, and a majority in semiskilled blue collar and service work (Sandis, 1975; U.S. Department of Labor, 1974). For most of those who left the island, migration meant occupational downward mobility despite an increase in earnings (Friedlander, 1965; Sandis, 1975). A migration of young Puerto Ricans professionals has occurred during the last twenty years. Most of them have specialized in medicine, engineering and nursing, and, to a lesser degree, teaching. U.S.-based companies often come to the island, particularly the University of Puerto Rico's Mayaguez campus where most of the engineers are trained, to look for potential workers. Medical graduates go to the United States to pursue areas of specialization and many times are retained by hospitals in the mainland. The low salaries of graduate nurses in Puerto Rico has prompted many nurses to migrate in response to hospitals in cities on the mainland where large nuclei of Puerto Ricans and other Latinos are concentrated. A similar trend among elementary, intermediate, and high school teachers has been observed recently.

An important dynamic of the Puerto Rican migration is the constant ebb and flow of the migrant population between their country of origin and the United States, which is a direct consequence of the political relationship between the two countries. Another trend is return migration. During the second half of the 1960s and throughout the 1970s, more than a quarter million Puerto Ricans returned to the island. The majority of returning migrants in the 1970s were in the age groups 12 to 28 and 55 and over (Vázquez Calzada, 1983). Many of the return migrants of the 1980s and early 1990s are adults 55 and older (Sánchez-Ayéndez, 1991).

CULTURAL DESCRIPTION

The Traditional Family

In speaking of a traditional Puerto Rican family, one must realize that cultural traits are subject to variation by socioeconomic status and other variables. Furthermore, the notion of a traditional family is mostly an idealized version, although one that allows for a starting point from which to make comparisons. Traditionally, and prior to the 1960s, the Puerto Rican family was described as an extended family (Seda Bonilla, 1958; Steward, 1956). Today, a modified extended family pattern predominates on the island, with the primary responsibility for childrearing vested in the nuclear family (Conferencia del Gobernador para el Fortalecimiento de la Familia, 1987;

Mintz, 1966; Safa, 1974). Although husbands have been the traditional source of family authority, most of the decisions concerning childrearing are made by the mothers (Bryce-Laporte, 1970; Landy, 1959; Safa, 1974; Seda Bonilla, 1972; Steward, 1956).

Investigations of the Puerto Rican family indicate that despite rapid social and economic change, the dynamics of familial relations have not been dramatically altered and that the family continues to be central in the lives of its members, greatly influencing individual and group interaction (Conferencia del Gobernador para el Fortalecimiento de la Familia, 1987; Ramos, 1984; Rivera, Serrano and Ramos, 1984; Sánchez-Ayéndez and Carnivali, 1987). Kinship bonds among Puerto Ricans are strong, and inter-action among kin is frequent. The kinship group is a source of strength and support, especially for rural and working-class families (Buitrago, 1973; Bryce-Laporte, 1970; Lewis, 1963; Mizio, 1974; Safa, 1964, 1974; Torres-Zayas, 1983). The family plays the primary supportive role in the lives of its mem-bers and is characterized by strong norms of reciprocity. These norms empha-size interdependence among the various family members, particularly those in the immediate kinship group. The interdependence framework conceptu-alizes individuals as unable to do everything or do everything well and, there-fore, as in need of others for assistance (Bastida, 1979:70–71). Within this value orientation, individualism and self-reliance assume different meanings than those prevailing in the United States.

Puerto Rican grandparents have often helped and continue to help in child-rearing (Alegría, 1985; Martinez, 1985; Sánchez-Ayéndez, 1992, 1994). Adult children are still expected to provide support for their parents in later years, and institutionalization of the elderly is not widely accepted (Rivera Medina, 1978; Sánchez-Ayéndez, 1994). The degree of expected support from adult children when the elderly parent becomes infirm or frail, howev-er, might vary by socioeconomic status. Those in the upper socioeconomic strata have more options to hire formal caregivers and institutionalization[1] than those in the lower socioeconomic strata. Yet the present cohort of the "old old" adhere to the notion of adult children as primary caregivers. The reduction in size of the Puerto Rican family and the incorporation of women into the formal and informal labor force have left their toll on the available number of close relatives that traditionally collaborated in the care of the aged and other infirm family members.

Fictive Kin. Components of the extended kinship system are the ritual form of *compadrazgo* (coparenthood) and the practice of *hijos de crianza* (infor-mal adoption of children). The last one, however, seems not to be as common since the 1970s. Among Puerto Ricans, godparents are selected for different

---

[1]Institutionalization of older adults is not a widespread practice in Puerto Rico. Less than two per cent of the elderly population live in homes (Dávila and Sánchez-Ayéndez, 1995).

occasions but most frequently for the baptism of children (Fitzpatrick, 1971; Mizio 1974). Traditionally, *compadrazgo* has been attributed different social meanings. It is a form of affirming deep friendship and establishing social and economic rights and duties in symmetrical and asymmetrical relations. The important thing, though, is that the coparent is expected to participate in the responsibilities of the extended-kin network.

The cultural practice of informal adoption of children is more common during family crises such as economic hardship and death of parents. Some researchers state that *hijos de crianza* are generally treated by their adoptive parents as though they were their own and that their status within the household is like that of the other children of the parents (Mizio, 1974; Padilla, 1958). Others stress that even though they are considered as part of the family, the awareness of the fact that one is not a biological child always exists (Torres-Zayas, 1984). Even when no legal adoption is involved, *hijos de crianza* know that the family and home of the adoptive parents is their own. The adoptive parents (*padres de crianza*) can be, but are not necessarily, related to real parents by kinship or friendship ties.

Other Dominant Cultural Components

Male and Female Roles. From early childhood, individuals are socialized to a double standard about gender and an interaction pattern of male dominance (Buitrago, 1973; Landy, 1959; Nieves Falcón, 1972; Safa, 1974). The prevailing conceptualization of women derives from the notion of *marianismo*, which uses the Virgin Mary as a role model and stresses that motherhood is a woman's primary role despite her other roles (Stevens, 1973). It is through motherhood that a woman is expected to realize herself and achieve her greatest satisfactions in life. Patience and forbearance are qualities inherent in the value of *marianismo*. However, in real life, patience and forbearance are not synonymous with total passivity and subservience (Sánchez-Ayéndez, 1984).

The woman's world revolves around the household and her children, even when she works outside the home. This involvement has led to a perception of women as having a central role in the household, whereas men are seen as having a marginal role (Leavitt, 1974). In the large majority of the families in Puerto Rico, it is women who perform the household chores (Conferencia del Gobernador para el Fortalecimiento de la Familia, 1987). Women are "of the home" (*de la casa*), whereas men are "of the street" (*de la calle*) and are considered the primary providers.

Men are conceptualized as having authority over women. Often the concept of maleness in the Puerto Rican culture has been defined exclusively as *machismo* and, thus, associated with the need to prove virility by the conquest of women, sexual aggressiveness, dominance over women, and a belligerent attitude when confronted by male peers. The concept of maleness, however, involves more than *machismo* (De la Cancela, 1981; Ramírez, 1993; Seda

Bonilla, 1958; Wells, 1972). It also refers to being the primary provider and protector of the family. In addition, it involves the notion of *respeto* (respect): a man must be brave if necessary, but also respectful of others.

Interpersonal Relations. Traditionally, the basis of all relationships for Puerto Ricans is *respeto* (respect), which involves a recognition of the inherent value of the human being (*dignidad*), not merely his or her accomplishments (Lauria, 1964; Leavitt, 1974; Sánchez-Ayéndez, 1984). Lauria (1964) stresses that *respeto* refers to the notion of "generalized deference" in all social interactions as well as to a variety of deferential acts or rituals relevant to particular kinds of social relations. Even in asymmetrical power relations, those in an inferior position expect a certain ceremonial deference from their superiors. Furthermore, kin relationships, or those characterized by familiarity, do not preclude formality in the form of specific rituals of deference.

Puerto Rican cultural tradition emphasizes personal relations. Face-to-face relationships are considered important. These relationships are dependent on the value of *personalismo*: the notion that what is important is the singularity of each human being. It is believed that this quality can be observed only in a direct interaction, whether it is a political, economic, or social relation. Puerto Ricans traditionally have preferred to deal with others in terms of a network of personal relationships and do not put the same trust in formal organizations. Despite Puerto Ricans' preference for associating with others and their belief in establishing warm interpersonal relationships, as a group they stress individuality more than collectivity and are careful in establishing personal relations with individuals outside their kinship group. Some social scientists (Mintz, 1966; Wells, 1972) stress that the reason for this cautiousness is fear of being used by others. Alternatively, the development of cautiousness may be the result of the familial support network. Because most individual needs are met inside the family, there has been little necessity to establish numerous interpersonal relations with persons other than kin. Nonetheless, this does not imply that cooperativeness is unvalued. Furthermore, once familiarity develops with those other than kin, obligations and patterns of support similar to those existing in the modified extended family become the norm (Sánchez-Ayéndez, 1984).

Language and Religion. The language spoken in Puerto Rico is Spanish, with a few borrowings from the Taíno and African groups. Knowledge of English is more common among the upper and professional classes and in the San Juan metropolitan area. Return migrants who have spent most of their formative years in the United States along with the mainland-born and raised children of Puerto Rican migrants also speak English more frequently. Yet Spanish has great resiliency among most Puerto Ricans, for whom the Spanish language is a major source of ethnic identity (Morris, 1995). The roots of this identification stem from the particular political relationship between the United States and Puerto Rico. Puerto Rico is neither a federal state nor independent. For political purposes, this territorial possession has been called a commonwealth. Steward (1956) has stressed that the Spanish language became a more predominant source of identification for Puerto Ricans when the United States imposed English as the official language in the educational system, a practice that was discontinued some decades ago.

Puerto Rico is a predominantly Catholic society. However, different religious ideologies of the supernatural overlap and interact. This is not perceived as a contradictory situation but as helpful in a better understanding of supernatural forces. Spiritualism attracts many Puerto Ricans, who feel that it does not conflict with more orthodox religious practices. Spiritualism is a set of beliefs found throughout different socioeconomic strata (Saavedra de Roca, 1970). Protestantism, however, is more prevalent among the middle class than the upper and lower classes. Some revivalist sects (Pentecostals and Jehovah's Witnesses) have been attracting a significant number of people in the lower socioeconomic strata during the last twenty-five years.

The Experience During the Early Period of Residence in the United States

The Puerto Rican migrants who came to the United States during the 1950s and 1960s, when the island began to industrialize and agriculture declined, were mostly unemployed rural farmworkers. They had much to gain from the opportunities for unskilled laborers on the mainland that followed the war period. This was not a middle-class migration: their level of education was not high,[2] and their job skills were limited. Given these characteristics, the Puerto Rican migrants were faced by limited job prospects and dealt with problems of underemployment, unemployment, low income, and substandard housing. A majority had never lived in cities or large towns. Because most migrated to New York City, another source of stress derived from becoming accustomed to life in the impersonal metropolis.

Another difficulty faced then and now by Puerto Rican immigrants has been racial discrimination. A conceptualization of this ethnic group as nonwhite has permeated their status as a minority group in the United States. It stems from the wide array of variations in color among Puerto Ricans, the result of intermarriage among Spaniards, Taíno Indians, and black Africans. Although racial discrimination prevails in Puerto Rico (Zenón Cruz, 1974), those in the lower and middle social strata are accustomed to variations in color among family members (Betances, 1972; Seda Bonilla, 1966). Intermarriage on the island is rare among the upper classes, which still adhere to a color criteria to classify individuals socially.

---

[2]Nonetheless, as a group they exhibited higher levels of education than those who stayed on the island (Vázquez-Calzada, 1979).

The racial classification of people in the United States is two sided: white or nonwhite, regardless of appearance. For Puerto Ricans, physical appearance is the basis for racial classification, and they recognized, broadly, three categories—white, black, and intermediate (Leavitt, 1974; Seda Bonilla, 1966). Most nonwhite, mulatto Puerto Ricans place themselves in the intermediate category, which conveys a higher criteria of social stratification than black. In the United States, however, all Puerto Ricans are ascribed a mixed racial ancestry that automatically places them within the lower stratification criteria. The historical experience of the Puerto Ricans in the United States has been that of an ethnic collectivity and a racial minority. Although faced with the additional stigma of speaking Spanish and other distinguishing cultural features that differ from those of "mainstream America," the discrimination they have been subjected to involves not only the notion that they belong to a different cultural tradition from that generally conceived of as North American but also from racial and socioeconomic biases.

What must be kept in mind when trying to understand the process of the adaptation of Puerto Rican immigrants is that while they are willing to migrate to improve their living conditions, they have been a group whose migration was actively enforced by both the Puerto Rican government and U.S. industries. Furthermore, this was a migration of U.S. citizens, not foreigners—a migration of families whose male members have been drafted to participate in all wars or military conflicts in which the United States has been involved since 1918. However, once they arrived in the mainland United States, they were perceived as foreigners and also as nonwhites, and they faced discrimination in such areas as housing and jobs. Likewise, their children faced educational problems that were complicated by language difficulties. Both first- and second-generation Puerto Ricans have confronted the difficulty of integrating into a culturally pluralistic and structurally differentiated urban society besides facing the demands of learning a different language and worldview (Potter, Rogler and Mosciki, 1995).

THE MODERN PUERTO RICAN FAMILY IN THE UNITED STATES

Demographic Characteristics[3]

Geographic and Age Distribution. According to the 1990 census, the 2,727,754 Puerto Ricans living in the United States account for 12.2 percent of the total Hispanic population (U.S. Bureau of the Census, 1991a). This represents a 35 percent increase from the 1980 census count. Puerto Ricans

---

[3]The author wants to express her gratitude to Ms. Lillian Robles, Coordinator of the Census Data Center, Graduate School of Public Health, University of Puerto Rico, for her assistance in providing most of the data presented in this section.

are the largest Hispanic group in the northeastern part of the country; 69 percent of the total population of Puerto Ricans live in the Northeast.

There have been changes in the geographical distribution of the Puerto Rican population during the last three decades. They have shifted from New York, the state with the largest concentration and where 95 percent of those who left the island during the 1950s settled, to other industrial centers in the northeastern and north central areas of the United States (U.S. Bureau of the Census, 1982). The 1990 census reported 1,086,601 Puerto Ricans living in New York, or 40 percent of the total population of Puerto Ricans in the U.S. The next largest concentrations were found in New Jersey (320,133), Florida (247,010), Massachusetts (151,193), Pennsylvania (148,988), Connecticut (146,842), Illinois (146,059), and California (126,417). The Puerto Rican population is concentrated in metropolitan areas, predominantly in the inner-city areas of New York City, Hartford, Chicago, Boston, Philadelphia, and Miami.

The Puerto Rican population in the United States is a relatively young group, with a median age of 24; for 1980, the median age was 22 (U.S. Bureau of the Census, 1991 a, b). It represents a much younger population than its Cuban counterpart (32 years) and a slightly older one than Mexican Americans (23 years). Only 3.6 percent of Puerto Ricans residing in the United States are 65 years of age and older. The percentage of Puerto Ricans 65 years old and over on the island is 9.8 percent (Dávila and Sánchez-Ayéndez, 1995), a fact that stresses the young age composition of this ethnic group in the United States and one that is linked to job availability for a young age group and the ability to return to the homeland.

Economic and Social Characteristics. During 1990, the annual median family income for Puerto Ricans in the United States was $21,941, reflecting lower median incomes than Mexican Americans and Cubans, who earned $24,119 and $32,417, respectively (U.S. Bureau of the Census, 1993). The annual median income for all families in the United States during that year was $35,225. Puerto Rican female householders with no husband present have the lowest annual income of all Hispanic groups, $8,912. This represents a lower median family income than their Dominican counterparts. Puerto Ricans as a group are seriously affected by low income levels. Thirty percent of Puerto Rican families were below the poverty level in 1990 (U.S. Bureau of the Census, 1993). Thirty-five percent of Puerto Rican females, 22 percent of Puerto Rican children under 18 years old, and 30 percent of Puerto Ricans 65 years old and over lived in poverty during 1990.

Latinos as a whole have experienced an increase in educational attainment since 1970 (U.S. Bureau of the Census, 1993). Sixty percent of Puerto Ricans received a high school diploma or higher in 1993. Eight percent of all the population completed four years of college or more. Of all Latino groups, only Cubans fared better than Puerto Ricans.

Forty-five percent of Puerto Rican females 16 years old and over and 71 percent of their male counterparts were in the labor force in 1993 (U.S. Bureau of Labor Statistics, 1994). Fourteen percent of employed Puerto Rican males 16 years old and over and 21 percent of females were in managerial and professional occupations (Riche, 1995). Twenty-two percent of the employed males were technical, sales, and administrative support workers compared with 45 percent of their female counterparts. The underrepresentation of this ethnic group in professional and white collar occupations and the large number of Puerto Rican male blue collar and unskilled workers demonstrate the group's disadvantaged position within the occupational structure of the United States. It is interesting, though, that twice as many Puerto Rican females than males are in the technical, sales, and administrative support occupations, a fact that points to gender differences in this sector of the labor market. What is not clear from the available data is the extent to which gender educational differences are playing a role in this specific job-related trend.

Fertility and Marriage.   The majority of Puerto Rican families live in a household maintained by a married couple (U.S. Bureau of the Census, 1993). Fifty-six percent of Puerto Rican families consisted of married couples. About 37 percent of families were headed by a female with no husband present in contrast to 9 percent of families maintained by a male with no wife present. This proportion is much larger among Puerto Ricans than among Cuban Americans (16%) and Mexican Americans (18%).

Evidence on fertility shows that in 1990 the birthrate for the Puerto Rican population in the United States was 21.9 births per 1,000 women (National Latina Institute, 1996). In 1980, the birthrate was 20.3 children for every 1,000 women. In Puerto Rico, for every 1,000 women there were 37 births in 1990. The total fertility rate for Puerto Rican women residing in the United States was 2.5 children. This places Puerto Ricans in an intermediate position between their Mexican (3.2 children) and Cuban (1.6 children) counterparts in the United States (National Center for Health Statistics, 1994). Twenty-two percent of births among Puerto Rican–American women in 1991 were registered among teenagers (U.S. Bureau of the Census, 1994). Sixty-five percent of Puerto Rican–origin mothers began prenatal care during the first trimester and 10.6 per cent in the third trimester or had no prenatal care at all (U.S. Bureau of the Census, 1994). Nine percent of the births were low weight.[4]

Intermarriage.   Analysis of intermarriage among Puerto Ricans is scant. According to Fitzpatrick (1976, 1979), from 1949 to 1969 there was a significant increase in the rate of out-group marriage among second-generation Puerto Ricans in New York. Data on other geographic areas where Puerto

[4]Births less than 5 lbs., 8 oz.

Ricans have concentrated since the early 1970s are not systematically gathered. The Fitzpatrick study stresses that the increase in the rate of out-group marriage among Puerto Ricans between 1919 and 1959 is similar to that of all immigrants in New York City in the years from 1908 to 1912. It concludes that if intermarriage is accepted as an index of assimilation, Puerto Ricans are moving as rapidly toward assimilation as all immigrant groups during the years 1908 to 1912. The lack of available data on Puerto Ricans outside New York City precludes arriving at the same generalization for the population as a whole.

Family Structure. The diversity of household composition among Puerto Ricans is linked to variations in ecological setting and the need to cope with different economic and social circumstances. For an overall description using a modification of Fitzpatrick's typology (1971), four types of familial household structures can be identified among this ethnic group.

1. Modified extended family. This group includes families with frequent interaction and strong interdependence patterns among two and three generations and other kin members—natural or ritual—outside the direct line of descent. Grandparents, children, and grandchildren may dwell under the same roof or have a separate but relatively nearby household. Frequent visiting (at least once a week) or telephoning are the norm. The familial supportive system is rapidly mobilized during emergencies and crises.
2. The nuclear family. This group includes families comprised of the conjugal unit of father, mother, and children, with weak bonds to the modified extended family. Generally, they do not have close relatives living nearby.
3. Father, mother, their children, and children of another union or unions of husband or wife.
4. Single-parent families. Statistical evidence shows that such groups are more common among low-income females. Safa (1974:39–41) has stressed that female-headed households in urban Puerto Rico tend to occur in middle or late adulthood, when nuclear family structures have been ruptured by the death of the husband, divorce, separation, or desertion. Young female heads of household are more common among the mainland Puerto Ricans (Lowe, 1984). As a whole, more Puerto Rican families on the mainland (36.8%) were maintained by females with no husband present than in their country of origin (23.2%) (Riche, 1995).

The primary problem with describing households according to structural typologies is that patterns of interaction are overlooked and consequently important features of familial lifestyles go unnoticed. For instance, to classify a household as a single-parent family is to overlook that this type of arrangement can very well be part of the modified extended-family pattern. Yet it is important to acknowledge variations in family structure that can lead to variations in adaptation to social and economic circumstances despite culturally shared meanings and styles.

Most of the existing literature on Puerto Rican families in the United States focuses on New York immigrants. Little is known about variations among Puerto Ricans outside New York in such variables as gender, generation, age, income education, age at arrival, length of residence in the United States, and ethnic composition of the neighborhood. No comparable data exist for Puerto Rican communities in other major urban centers as Chicago or those in much smaller urban centers such as Hartford in Connecticut and Holyoke in Massachusetts.

Many Puerto Ricans have a considerable number of relatives and friends within easy social contact, and they can rely on their informal supportive network for confronting economic, social, health and emotional problems (Mattei, 1983; Nazario, 1986; Sánchez-Ayéndez, 1984; Vázquez de Nuttall, 1979). However, this is more common in the inner-city ethnic neighborhoods than in public housing projects. Historically, the immigrants have concentrated in areas of the city or a particular geographical location where members of their family or friends from their hometown are located. This custom has eased adaptation to life in a country different than the country of origin as well as serving as a buffer against a hostile host society. However, the random placement of families in public housing projects tends to separate kin and close friends and undermine prevailing informal networks of support without contributing to the creation of new supportive networks among those living in these projects.

Distinctive Features of the Puerto Rican Family

Some aspects of the Puerto Rican family have already been discussed in relation to the cultural description of the group. In examining certain cultural features and characteristics of contemporary Puerto Rican families on the mainland, it should be noted that although variations based on social class differences exist among Puerto Ricans in the United States, they have not been studied systematically. The young Puerto Rican professionals who have migrated during the last twenty years have not been the focus of research on adaptation and cultural involvement. Like all Puerto Ricans, they are faced with discrimination and misconceptions in their adjustment to life in the United States. However, their higher levels of education, occupational status, knowledge of English, and, in many cases, light skin can make adaptation easier and give them opportunities for different lifestyles. They are likely not to reside in the low-income housing project or ethnic enclave but in more mixed or predominantly Anglo American, middle- and professional-class neighborhoods. They are more likely than their low-income counterparts to interact socially with Anglo Americans. The following section centers on low-income Puerto Ricans because there are no available studies about the adaptation and the lifestyles of professionals with higher socioeconomic position.

Family Values. The modified extended family (Litwak and Szeleny, 1969) continues to be the primary support system for first- and second-generation Puerto Ricans in the United States even in the face of intergenerational differences (Carrasquillo, 1982; Rogler, 1978; Rogler and Cooney, 1984; Rogler and Cortés, 1993; Sánchez-Ayéndez, 1984, 1995). Despite social changes and adaptation to life in a culturally different society, Puerto Ricans families are still characterized by strong norms of reciprocity among the various family members, particularly those in the immediate family.

Family interdependence is conceptualized as positive. Individuals expect and ask for assistance from those in their networks, without any derogatory implications for self-esteem. Interdependence does not conflict with individual self-reliance and independence; it coexists with them and assumes priority in a hierarchy of values. It is not based on mutual giving or reciprocal exchanges relationships. The prevailing reciprocity norms are not predicated on strictly equal exchanges (Carrasquillo, 1982; Sánchez-Ayéndez, 1984, 1995).

Family unity is another theme underlying the conceptualization that Puerto Ricans have of ideal family relations or familism. Family unity refers to the desirability of close and intimate kin ties. Family members should try to get along well and, despite dispersal, keep in touch frequently. Celebration of holidays and special occasions—happy or sad—are seen as opportunities for kin to be together and strengthen family ties. Funerals and weddings draw large numbers of relatives together. Trips to and from Puerto Rico are common at the death of close relatives, even among those with meager resources. It is the norm for adult children to try to please their parents' wishes to be buried in their land of origin.

The value of family unity is also evident in the attitude about the desirability of frequent interaction with kin members. Visits and telephone calls are interpreted by family members as a caring attitude that secure family unity and are more common among women than men. Women, as part of their female role and interrelated with the domestic domain, are seen as responsible for establishing the bases for good relationships among family members. The creation and maintenance of family unity among offspring is considered the mother's responsibility. Good relations with consanguineal and affinal kin are also envisioned to be the wife's concern (Sánchez-Ayéndez, 1984). They are conceptualized as relations between the wife's and other women's domestic units. To fulfill their familial role, many women rely on telephoning and visiting.

There is a continuum of degrees of responsibility in the practice of family unity and the obligation for assistance among those in the kin group (Carrasquillo, 1982; Sánchez-Ayéndez, 1984). More is expected of consanguineal than affinal kin. Among the consanguine, expectation of familial unity and support are greater among those in the inner circle: parents and children, followed by grandchildren. Siblings and their families, as well as those who form part of the fictive kin, follow in this continuum. Such factors as health, gender, personality, compatibility within a specific relationship, and geographical distance also influence the position in this continuum.

Despite the prevalence of family unity and interdependence among Puerto Ricans in the mainland, changes are occurring in traditional attitudes about family relations. In a study of 100 Puerto Rican families in New York City, Colleran (1984) found that first- and second-generation Puerto Ricans realized and regretted the loss of family unity and closeness taking place among their people. They felt that Puerto Ricans residing in the city were less generous and more disrespectful in family relations and were less concerned about family members than those in Puerto Rico. Most believed that the changes occurring were not for the better. Colleran observes that there has been a statistically significant decline in the value of familism among the younger Puerto Ricans in New York and stresses that despite the economic advantages of migration, Puerto Ricans are aware that something valuable is being lost in the adaptation to life in New York. Although this could also be characteristic of other areas where Puerto Ricans have established themselves, it must be kept in mind that adaptation to life in an urban metropolis like New York is not the same to that in a small urban area.

One cultural pattern mediated through the family is *respeto*. Many first-generation Puerto Ricans feel that deferential acts relevant to respect are undergoing change (Colleran, 1984; Sánchez-Ayéndez, 1984) and that the degree of formality necessary in certain personal relations is decreasing. However, despite changes occurring in Puerto Rican families, ritualized acts of deference prevail within the familial networks. They are generally bestowed on elder adults—particularly those in the kinship group—and parents. Respect for aged parents stems from their conceptualization as adults and figures of authority within the household as well as from filial obligation.

Husband and Wife Roles.   Despite changes in the husband and wife roles related to more sharing in decision making and female autonomy (Cooney et al., 1982; Leavitt, 1974; Fitzpatrick, 1971), a strict dichotomy between the sexes is prevalent. Although it is easier for Puerto Rican women than men to get jobs in urban centers and in technical, sales, and administrative support occupations as well as attaining economic independence through work or welfare assistance, women still are primarily conceptualized as responsible for the domestic realm, whereas men are visualized as the main providers. Women are also assigned a status subordinate to men. Although most decisions concerning the household are made by the woman without intervention by her husband, the preeminence of male authority in husband-wife relations is the norm. Once again it must be stressed, however, that preeminence of male authority should not be confused with the image of the totally submissive wife (Sánchez-Ayéndez, 1984).

The high unemployment rate of Puerto Rican men in the United States poses a threat to their undisputed authority. When supplementary income is provided by the wife or welfare assistance or when the man is unable to earn money, male authority within the familial context, based on his role as the primary provider, decreases. In many cases, his reaction results in increased acts of *machismo* as a mechanism for dealing with the loss of status and power (Mizio, 1974), which, in turn, the economically independent female is unwilling to tolerate.

Puerto Rican women brought up in New York are perceived by their male counterparts as demanding a more egalitarian sex role pattern (Leavitt, 1974). They want their husbands to become more involved in household chores and childrearing and believe that husband and wife should share family problems and recreational activities. However, the New York-raised Puerto Rican men often adhere to traditional values about female and male roles despite accepting that their wives work outside the home and contribute economically to the maintenance of the household. A conflict between values and expectations is bound to arise.

Fictive Kin. Fictive kin are part of the modified extended-family group. In a previous section, the cultural practices of *hijos de crianza* and *compadrazgo* were explained. The practice of informal adoption still exists among Puerto Ricans in the United States. However, adaptation to life in a culturally different society and modifications in the legal system are affecting this tradition. Many of those Puerto Ricans who might consider informally adopting a child opt for legal adoption to avoid emotional suffering and legal consequences in the future. Coparenthood is still invested with a symbolic bond and retains some of this reciprocity norm within the family context. Yet family dispersal and the incorporation of women into the labor force are factors affecting the nature of the *compadrazgo* relationship.

A particular group of friends also form part of the kinship networks of Puerto Ricans. The phrase "my friend who is like family" (*como de la familia*) is used on some occasions to distinguish specific friends from others. The obligations to this group of friends and the support expected from them are similar to those in the modified extended family.[5] Relationships with "friends who are like family" are characterized by more familiarity than those with other friends, particularly in the case of the elderly. Within this special group of friends, individuals are assigned priority according to the designated specific relationship among those involved. For example, a person might refer to someone as "my friend who is like my cousin" or "my friend who is like my sister." The interdependence patterns characteristic of the sisterlike relationship involve more assistance and obligations than those arising from the

---

[5]Their functions in the supportive network of migrant Puerto Ricans have been explained by Nazario (1986) and Sánchez-Ayéndez (1984).

cousinlike relationship. The stronger bond on which this particular relationship is based ensue from the evaluation that certain friends are engaging in a particular dynamic of interdependence relevant only to family members. This valorization entails that only a few friends will be considered part of the fictive-kin network.

Childrearing. Childrearing practices among Puerto Rican immigrants tend to perpetuate, although with modifications, the double standard of conduct between the sexes (Leavitt, 1974; Sánchez-Ayéndez, 1984). The modesty training of girls begins during early childhood and continues through adolescence. Overt expressions of affection are more common with girls than boys. Mothers, on the whole, tend to be more warm and playful with children than fathers and interact more frequently with daughters than sons (Weissman, 1966).

Children are rarely consulted on matters that directly affect them or informed of the reasons for a specific action pertaining to them. They are envisioned as passive creatures who are molded entirely by their parents. Good behavior is taken for granted, whereas reasons for punishment are seldom offered. Physical punishment is more frequent among families with the least mobility and status (Leavitt 1974).

Care of the Elderly. Children's marriages do not mean that the middle-aged or elderly couple is left alone. Frequent visits by adult children and the prevalence of family interdependence help prevent the "empty nest" from being a characteristic stage in the life cycle of older Puerto Ricans. This is further reinforced by the eagerly awaited arrival of grandchildren and the active role that grandmothers play in child care. In fact, many older Puerto Rican women have migrated to help their adult children raise their families. Studies of elderly Puerto Ricans demonstrate that adult children are the primary source of assistance to their aged parents and that older Puerto Ricans—particularly women—play functional roles in providing their families with assistance and remain integrated within the familial structure (Cantor, 1979; Carrasquillo, 1983; Sánchez-Ayéndez, 1984, 1986, 1995).

CHANGES AND ADAPTATION

During the past two decades, Puerto Ricans have migrated out of New York City to smaller, urban northeastern communities. The rapid migration to these smaller urban centers is indicative of their search for a better economic situation. However, these urban centers cannot meet the rapidly growing demand of this ethnic group for jobs of low skill level. Unlike other immigrant groups, the proximity to their homeland and the relative ease of return encourage many Puerto Ricans—particularly those in the first and second generations of migrants—to search on the island for the strength and support needed to adapt. This ease of return has given the Puerto Rican migration its distinctive ebb-and-flow characteristic. The fact that a large percentage of return migrants are 55 years old and over could indicate a passive resistance to the adaptation process. However, this is a trend that is possibly related to first-generation Puerto Ricans and not to subsequent ones. On the other hand, young return migrants who have spent their formative years on the mainland often complain about the difficulties of adjusting to life in their homeland. They are perceived as "too Americanized," unfamiliar with island ways, and lacking proficiency in Spanish and are labeled "Niuyoricans" (New York Ricans).

Cultural involvement with the host society is generally described as acculturation in most of the literature on ethnic minorities. Acculturation "refers to the complex process whereby the behaviors and attitudes of the migrant change toward the dominant group as a result of exposure to a cultural system that is significantly different" (Rogler et al., 1987: 567).

Acculturation is not a one-way homogeneous process. It implies gradual change and multiple components. Some aspects of the host culture may be easy to incorporate as part of one's lifestyle and worldview. Others, particularly those that go against the grain of core components and definitions of a group's cultural heritage and orientation, will be confronted with more ambiguity or resistance by first- and second-generation immigrants. It must also be stressed that ethnic loyalty and adherence to one's ethnic group's values is often a coping mechanism for those labeled as minorities in a society where ethnic and racial discrimination prevails. Although cultural heritage from a country of origin can evoke a sense of ethnic identity or "peoplehood," the process by which a group comes to be identified as an ethnic group involves more than cultural traits inherited from the past (Charsley, 1974; Sánchez-Ayéndez, 1984; Yancey, Ericksen and Juliani, 1974).

Ethnicity develops within a sociocultural context in which economic, political, and historical factors play a vital role. It is not a constant but the result of a process that continues to unfold and in which "old" as well as "new" meanings shared by a group of people become relevant to their social relationships. Padilla (1980) has added a new component to the issue by establishing a difference between ethnic loyalty or preference of one's cultural values and worldview over the host society's and cultural awareness or knowledge about features of the society of origin and the host society, such as language, food, music and values.

Among mainland-born second and third generation Puerto Ricans in the United States, ethnicity with its components of ethnic loyalty and preference has continued to develop and differs from that of first generation and that of children who accompanied their parents when they came to the mainland. Intergenerational differences in traditional values from the land of origin has accompanied migration and educational upward mobility (Procidano and Rogler, 1989; Rogler, Cooney and Ortiz, 1980; Cortés, Rogler and

Malgady, 1994). The parents' generation, when compared to their children, adheres more to familism. Children are less likely to speak Spanish with other persons as well as prefer to rely on English-language mass media. The influence of mass media on language preference and acquisition of the host-society values and lifestyles cannot be overlooked. Most of the Puerto Ricans born and/or raised since childhood in the United States rely less on Spanish as the means of communication among peers and siblings than those born and/or raised until adolescence on the island (Colleran, 1984; Cooney et al., 1982; Rogler, Cooney, and Ortiz, 1980). They have greater proficiency in English than Spanish. The younger the person is on arrival, the greater the likelihood of use of English as the principal language. In 1990, about 78 percent of Hispanics reported that they spoke Spanish at home (U.S. Bureau of the Census, 1993). Of the Puerto Ricans who spoke Spanish at home, 59 percent perceived that they spoke English "very well" in contrast to 41 percent who reported that they did not speak English "very well."

The children of Puerto Rican immigrants hold a more activist approach to life and describe themselves as more aggressive and less humble than their parents (Colleran, 1984). Although some parents express their concern about this attitudinal and behavioral change, many agree that it is necessary in order to survive in the United States. However, despite changes related to acculturative involvement in the host society, younger generations cling to their identification as Puerto Ricans. Second- and third-generation Puerto Ricans do not identify themselves as exclusively American (Rogler, Cooney, and Ortiz, 1980), a fact that points out a trend toward biculturalism instead of complete assimilation (Cortés, Rogler and Malgady, 1994). This is even more prevalent in the contemporary low socioeconomic ethnic enclave, because it promotes ethnic cohesiveness and solidarity among its residents. Children living in ethnic neighborhoods are likely to speak and understand Spanish better than those living in housing projects with fewer Puerto Ricans. Other differences among parents and children point to the trend of parents living in neighborhoods with higher concentration of Puerto Ricans and lower educational levels than their children (Rogler, Cooney and Ortiz, 1980; Procidano and Rogler, 1989).

Although data on the impact of social class differences are scant, education has been found to be significantly related to language preference and knowledge of and proficiency in English as well as fertility behavior and sex role values. Differences between the families of Puerto Rican professionals who have migrated and low-skill laborers have not been studied. It could be expected that the opportunities provided by professional status could ease minority status issues to a certain extent and facilitate adaptation to the host culture. Notwithstanding, professional fair-skinned Puerto Ricans in the United States are often faced with the comment that they "do not look Puerto Rican," a fact that underscores the racial overtone of the social situation of Puerto Ricans in the mainland.

During the last two decades, Puerto Ricans as a group have become more politically active. National organizations, such as the Puerto Rican National Coalition, and community-based agencies, such as Inquilinos Boricuas en Acción in Boston and La Casa de Puerto Rico in Hartford, have been defending the rights of Puerto Ricans and promoting grassroots movement among Puerto Ricans communities on the mainland to improve the socioeconomic condition of their people. They are defining their interest as Puerto Ricans, assessing their resource, and stressing the necessity for community-based action. Much remains to be done, but such organizations at the national and local levels have brought forth needed changes related to housing and health problems and improvement of educational and training opportunities to raise the current conditions of the majority of Puerto Ricans families on the mainland. However, cuts in federal programs and changing strategies in affirmative action impose a new challenge to these efforts.

Puerto Ricans have learned to rely on formal health and social services and are claiming the benefits to which they have a right to as American citizens. It cannot be emphasized enough that this ethnic group migration was a migration of U.S. citizens. However, many of formal services providers are not aware of this fact, and many times migration visas are required as part of the documents needed to conduct bureaucratic processes. In other instances, Puerto Rican professionals are asked (much to their dismay and disbelief) by other professionals and agency administrators to present their Puerto Rican passport as part of their credentials.[6] The prevailing lack of knowledge about Puerto Rico and its almost one-hundred-year relationship to the United States as a territorial possession and also of the fact that Puerto Ricans are U.S. citizens by birth and not naturalized citizens exists at all echelons of formal and health services as well as in corporations, foundations and even universities.

The value of family interdependence and social relations within the ethnic neighborhood have eased the adaptation of low-income Puerto Rican families to the United States as well as serving as a buffer against racial discrimination. Strong, supportive familial and community networks are characteristics of economically deprived minorities. In this respect, social class and cultural factors have fostered the development of strong patterns of familial interdependence among low-income Puerto Ricans. There is no doubt that family life is an important source of affirmation and support to mainland Puerto Ricans. Yet it can also be a source of stress among generations. Values and worldviews retained by the first and second generation are not the same as those held by the third generation. Likewise, assertions that the family takes care of its own often overlook the stress that is built into caregiving, a reality that usually is the responsibility of women. Despite demographic, value, and normative changes related to migration, it is women who

[6]Puerto Ricans, as U.S. citizens, carry a U.S. passport.

continue to provide most of the instrumental and emotional support in the family. Another factor to consider is that the pressures for using formal services to complement or substitute for informal ones vary at the different stages of the lifespan and are contingent upon social and economic factors. Poverty and some of the other current larger society social problems will impact the utilization of formal services by Puerto Ricans on the mainland.

To state that changes in familial and community structure that are inherent to adaptation to life in another country have altered the system of meanings of Puerto Rican immigrants is an oversimplification of their situation. Like many immigrant groups, they indisputably have had to undergo modifications in the course of their adaptation to life in the host country. But, unlike other immigrant groups, consciousness of their U.S. citizenship, the proximity to their homeland, the ease of return, and the close contacts maintained with relatives and friends on the island have provided for a continuity of certain shared meanings, particularly family interdependence. This continuity has proven to be their best resource in adapting to their circumstances and dealing with racial discrimination.

REFERENCES

Alegría, Margarita. 1985. "Determinants of Well-Being in Recently Divorced Puerto Rican Women." Paper presented at the annual conference of the American Public Health Association, Washington, DC, November.

Batista, Elena. 1979. "Family Integration and Adjustment to Aging Among Hispanic American Elderly." Ph.D. dissertation, University of Kansas.

Bryce-Laporte, Roy S. 1970. "Urban Relocation and Family Adaptation in Puerto Rico," in William Mangin (Ed.), *Peasants in Cities: Readings in the Anthropology of Urbanization.* Boston: Houghton Mifflin.

Buitrago, Carlos. 1973. *Esperanza: An Ethnographic Study of a Peasant Community in Puerto Rico.* Tucson: University of Arizona Press.

Cantor, Marjorie H. 1979. "The Informal Support System of New York's Inner City Elderly: Is Ethnicity a Factor?" in Donald L. Gelfand and Alfred J. Kutzik (Eds.), *Ethnicity and Aging.* New York: Springer.

Carrasquillo, Héctor A. 1982. "Perceived Social Reciprocity and Self-Esteem Among Elderly Barrio Antillean Hispanics and Their Familial Informal Networks." Ph.D. dissertation, Syracuse University.

Charsley, S. Robert. 1974. "The Formation of Ethnic Groups," in Abner Cohen (Ed.), *Urban Ethnicity.* London: Tavistock.

Conferencia del Gobernador para el Fortalecimiento de la Familia. 1987. "La familia puertorriqueña de hoy." Working paper, April.

Colleran, Kevin. 1984. "Acculturation in Puerto Rican Families in New York City." *Research Bulletin,* Hispanic Research Center, 7: 2–7. New York: Fordham University.

Cooney, Rosemary Santana et al. 1982. "Decision Making in Intergenerational Puerto Rican Families." *Journal of Marriage and the Family* (August): 621–631.

Cortés, Dharma E., Lloyd H. Rogler, and Robert G. Malgady. 1994. "Biculturality Among Puerto Rican Adults in the United States." *American Journal of Community Psychology,* 22(5): 707–721.

Dávila, Ana Luisa and Sánchez-Ayéndez, Melba. 1995. "El envejecimiento de la población en Puerto Rico: repercusiones en los sistemas de apoyo informal." Twentieth Congress of the

Latin American Association of Sociology; Seminar on Population (PROLAP), work group on "Demographic Dynamics and Social Change," round table on "Aging in Latin America and the Caribbean." Mexico City, October.

de la Cancela, Víctor. 1981. "Towards a Critical Psychological Analysis of Machismo: Puerto Ricans and Mental Health." Ph.D. dissertation, City University of New York.

Fitzpatrick, Joseph. 1971. *Puerto Rican Americans*. Englewood Cliffs, NJ: Prentice-Hall.

———. 1976. "The Puerto Rican Family," in Charles H. Mindel and Robert W. Habenstein (Eds.), *Ethnic Families in America*, 1st ed. New York: Elsevier.

Fitzpatrick, J. P. and D. T. Gurak. 1979. *Hispanic Intermarriage in New York City: 1975*. Monograph no. 2, Hispanic Research Center, Fordham University.

Friedlander, Stanley. 1965. *Labor, Migration and Economic Growth*. Cambridge, MA: MIT Press.

History Task Force, Centro de Estudios Puertorriqueños. 1979. *Labor Migration Under Capitalism: The Puerto Rican Experience*. New York: Monthly Press.

Landy, David. 1959. *Tropical Childhood*. Chapel Hill, NC: University of North Carolina Press.

Lauria, Anthony J. 1964. "*Respeto, Relajo* and Interpersonal Relations in Puerto Rico." *Anthropological Quarterly, 37*: 53–67.

Leavitt, Ruby Rohrlich. 1974. *The Puerto Ricans: Cultural Change and Language Deviance*. Tucson: University of Arizona Press.

Lewis, Gordon K. 1963. *Puerto Rico: Freedom and Power in the Caribbean*. New York: Monthly Review Press.

López, Adalberto. 1974. "The Puerto Rican Diaspora," in Adalberto López and James F. Petras (Eds.), *Puerto Rico and Puerto Ricans*. Cambridge, MA: Schenkman.

Lowe, Karen. 1984. "Ven triste cuadro de mujeres boricuas en los Estados Unidos." *El Mundo*, September 19, p. 9A.

Martínez, Ruth. 1984. "Social Support of Recently Divorced Women in Puerto Rico." Paper presented at the Sunbelt Social Network Conference V, Palm Beach, FL, February.

Mattei, María de Lourdes. 1983. "Women's Autonomy and Social Networks in a Puerto Rican Community." Ph.D. dissertation, University of Massachussetts at Amherst.

Mintz, Sidney W. 1966. "Puerto Rico: An Essay in the Definition of a National Culture," in *Selected Background Papers, Prepared for the United States–Puerto Rico Commission on the Status of Puerto Rico*. San Juan, Puerto Rico: Commonwealth of Puerto Rico.

Mizio, Emelicia. 1974. "Impact of External Systems on the Puerto Rican Family." *Social Casework, 55*: 76–83.

Morris, Nancy. 1995. *Puerto Rico: Culture, Politics and Identity*. New York: Praeger.

National Center for Health Statistics. 1994. *Advance Report of Final Natality Statistics*, vol. 44, no. 3 (Supplement).

National Latina Institute for Reproductive Health. 1996. *Status of Latina Health in the United States and Puerto Rico*. January.

Nazario, Teresa. 1986. "Social Support Networks of Migrant Puerto Rican Women." Ph.D. dissertation, Boston University.

New York Times. 1954. "Mayor Wagner in Puerto Rico," June 21, section 1, p. 17.

Nieves Falcón, Luis. 1972. "El niño puertorriqueño: bases empíricas para entender su comportamiento," in Luis Nieves Falcón (Ed.), *Diagnóstico de Puerto Rico*, Río Piedras, Puerto Rico: Editorial Edil.

Padilla, Elena. 1958. *Up from Puerto Rico*. New York: Columbia University Press.

Padilla, A. M. 1980. "The Role of Cultural Awareness and Ethnic Loyalty in Acculturation," in A. M. Padilla (Ed.), *Acculturation: Theory, Models and Some New Findings*. Boulder, CO: Westview.

Potter, L. B., L. H. Rogler, and E. K. Moscicki. 1995. "Depression among Puerto Ricans in New York City: The Hispanic Health and Nutrition Examination Survey." *Soc. Psychiatry Psychiatr. Epidemiol., 30*: 185–193.

Procidano, Mary E. and Lloyd H. Rogler. 1989. "Homogamous Assortative Mating Among Puerto Rican Families: Intergenerational Processes and the Migration Experience." *Behavior Genetics, 19*(3): 343–354.

Ramírez, Rafael. 1993. *Dime capitán: reflexiones sobre la masculinidad.* Río Piedras, Puerto Rico: Ediciones Huracán.

Ramos, Carlos. 1984. "Trasfondo para la discusión del cambio social y la familia puertorriqueña," in Celia E. Cintrón (Ed.), *Conferencia jurídica de 1984: derecho de familia y cambio Social.* Río Piedras, Puerto Rico: Centro de Investigaciones Sociales, Universidad de Puerto Rico.

Riche, Martha Farnsworth. 1995. "The Census—Its Changing Demographics: What the Future Holds." Paper presented at the 66th annual conference of the League of United Latin-American Citizens Federal Training Institute, San Juan, Puerto Rico; June 25–July 2.

Rivera Medina, Eduardo. 1978. "Los escolares y el entendimiento de las personas de mayor edad," in Wencesalao Serra Deliz (Ed.), *La problemática de los envejecientes en Puerto Rico.* Río Piedras, Puerto Rico: Universidad de Puerto Rico.

Rivera Medina, Eduardo J., Irma Serrano, and Antonio Ramos. 1984. "La investigación social de la familia puertorriqueña: Una agenda para el futuro." *Revista Jurídica de la Universidad Interamericana de Puerto Rico, 18*: 409–417.

Rogler, Lloyd H. 1978. "Help Patterns, the Family and Mental Health: Puerto Ricans in the United States." *Internal Migration Review, 12*: 248–259.

Rogler, Lloyd H. and Rosemary S. Cooney. 1984. *Puerto Rican Families in New York City: Intergenerational Processes.* Monograph no. 11, Hispanic Research Center, Fordham University.

Rogler, Lloyd H., Rosemary Santana Cooney, and Vilma Ortiz. 1980. "Intergenerational Change in Ethnic Identity in the Puerto Ricans Family." *International Migration Review, 14*: 193–214.

Rogler, Lloyd and Dharma E. Cortés. 1993. "Help-Seeking Pathways: A Unifying Concept in Mental Health Care." *American Journal of Psychiatry, 150*: 554–561.

Rogler, Lloyd, Robert G. Malgady, Giuseppe Costantino, and Rena Blumenthal. 1987. "What Do Culturally Sensitive Mental Health Services Mean?" *American Psychologist, 42* (6): 565–570.

Saavedra de la Roca, Angelina. 1970. *El espiritismo como religión.* Río Piedras, Puerto Rico: Universidad de Puerto Rico.

Safa, Helen I. 1964. "From Shanty Town to Public Housing: A Comparison of Family Structure in Two Urban Neighborhoods in Puerto Rico." *Caribbean Studies, 4*: 3–12.

———. 1974. *The Urban Poor of Puerto Rico.* New York: Holt, Rinehart, and Winston.

Sánchez-Ayéndez, Melba. 1984. "Puerto Rican Elderly Women: Aging in a Ethnic Minority Group in the United States." Ph.D. dissertation, University of Massachussetts at Amherst.

———. 1986. "Puerto Rican Elderly Woman: Shared Meanings and Informal Supportive Network," in Johnetta B. Cole (Ed.), *All American Women: Lines that Divide, Ties that Bind.* New York: Free Press.

———. 1991. "Puerto Rican Older Adults: Realities and Needs." Symposium "A People in Two Communities." National Puerto Rican Coalition, Puerto Rico Community Foundation, and the Office of Civil Rights of the U.S. Department of Health and Human Services. Washington, DC: U.S. Government Printing Office.

———. 1994. "Puerto Rican Elderly Women," in: Marta Sotomayor (Ed.), *Triple Jeopardy: Aged Hispanic Women: Insights and Experiences.* Washington, DC: National Hispanic Council on Aging.

———. 1995. "Older and Middle-Aged Puerto Rican Women: Cultural Components of Support Networks," in: Dena Shenk (Ed.), *Gender and Race Through Education and Political Activism: The Legacy of Sylvia Helen Forman.* Arlington, VA: American Anthropological Association.

Sánchez-Ayéndez, Melba and Judith Carnivali. 1987. "Reflexiones en torno de la familia puertorriqueña." Contribución de la Universidad de Puerto Rico a la Conferencia del Gobernador para el Fortalecimiento de la Familia. Río Piedras, Puerto Rico: Universidad de Puerto Rico.

Sandis, Eva E. 1975. "Characteristics of Puerto Rican Migrants to and from the United States," in Francesco Cordasco and Eugene Bucchioni (Eds.), *The Puerto Rican Experience.* New York: Littlefield, Adams.

Seda Bonilla, Edwin. 1958. "Normative Patterns of the Puerto Rican Family in Various Situational Contexts," Ph.D. dissertation, Columbia University.

————. 1966. "Social Structure and Race Relations," in S. W. Webster (Ed.), *Knowing the Disadvantaged.* San Francisco: Chandler.

Stevens, Evelyn P. 1973. "Marianismo: The Other Face of Machismo in Latin America," in Ann Pescatello (Ed.), *Female and Male in Latin America.* Pittsburgh: University of Pittsburgh Press.

Torres-Zayas, José A. 1983. "La familia puertorriqueña de hoy: Propuesta para una definición." *Revista Puertorriqueña de Psicología, 1* (1): 5–11.

U.S. Bureau of the Census. 1975. "Persons of Spanish Origin in the United States." *Current Population Reports.* Series P-20, no. 361. Washington, DC: U.S. Government Printing Office.

————. 1982. *U.S. Census of Population: 1980. Persons of Spanish Origin by State,* supplementary report. Washington, DC:. U.S. Government Printing Office.

————. 1991a. *The Hispanic Population in the United States: March 1990.* Series P-20, no. 449. Washington, DC: U.S. Government Printing Office.

————. 1991b. Department of Commerce news release, June 12, CB91-216.

————. 1993. *We, the American Hispanics.* Washington, DC: Population Division, Ethnic and Hispanic Statistics Branch, WE-2. November.

————. 1994. *Statistical Abstract of the United States.* CD-SA-94.

U.S. Bureau of Labor Statistics, Employment and Earnings. 1994. *Bulletin 2307,* January issues.

U.S. Department of Labor. 1974. "The New York Puerto Ricans: Patterns of Work Experience," in Adalberto López and James F. Petras (Eds.), *Puerto Rico and Puerto Ricans.* Cambridge, MA: Schenkman.

Vázquez Calzada, José L. 1978. *La población de Puerto Rico y su trayectoria histórica.* San Juan, Puerto Rico: Universidad de Puerto Rico.

————. 1979. "Demographic Aspects of Migration," in History Task Force, Centro de Estudios Puertorriqueños (Eds.), *Migration Under Capitalism: The Puerto Rican Experience.* New York: Monthly Review Press.

————. 1983. "Estimaciones realizadas sobre migración." Unpublished statistical estimates.

Vázquez de Nuttall, Enna. 1979. "The Support System and Coping Patterns of Female Puerto Rican Single Parents." *Journal of Non-white Concerns, 7:* 128–139.

Weissman, Julius. 1966. "An Exploratory Study of Communication Patterns of Lower-Class Negro and Puerto Ricans Mothers and Pre-School Children." Ph.D. dissertation, Columbia University.

Wells, Henry. 1972. *La modernización de Puerto Rico.* Río Piedras, Puerto Rico: Editorial Universitaria.

Yancey, William L., Eugene P. Ericksen and Richard Juliani. 1974. "Emergent Ethnicity: A Review and Reformulation." *American Sociological Review, 41:* 391–402.

Zenón Cruz, Isabelo. 1974. *Narciso descubre su trasero.* Humacao, Puerto Rico: Ediciones.

10 | The Korean-American Family

Pyong Gap Min

INTRODUCTION

Koreans, along with Asian Indians and Vietnamese, are one of the major Asian immigrant groups whose populations have mushroomed since the enactment of the 1965 Immigration Act. The majority of Korean Americans are immigrants who came to the United States as a consequence of this law. Despite their short immigration history and small group size, Korean immigrants have attracted a great deal of attention, probably more attention than most other Asian ethnic groups, from U.S. media and researchers, mainly because of their concentration in small business and Korean merchants' frequent conflicts with African-American customers.

Korean Americans have gone through critical collective experiences since the publication of the third edition of this book in 1988. The 1992 Los Angeles riots, during which 2,300 Korean-owned stores were destroyed, was a watershed in Korean-American history. Korean immigrants have encountered many other less significant cases of intergroup conflicts because of their middleman economic role bridging between minority customers and white suppliers, a role that has also provided the basis for Korean Americans' ethnic identity and solidarity. Korean Americans have been studied extensively since the publication of the third edition of *Ethnic Families in America*. Many articles that focus on Korean immigrants' family and marital lives have been published over the last several years. This chapter will use these recently published materials to update information about the Korean-American family as well as discussing effects of the Los Angeles riots and other historical events on Korean Americans' ethnic identity and ethnic solidarity.

HISTORICAL BACKGROUND

Immigration and Settlement

The approximately 7,200 Korean laborers who moved to Hawaii between 1903 and 1905 to work on sugar plantations made up the first wave of Korean immigrants in the United States (Patterson, 1987). Although plantation owners in Hawaii needed more Korean workers in the first decade of the twentieth century, in 1905 the Korean government was forced by the Japanese government to stop sending any more laborers to Hawaii. Before the Oriental Exclusion Act of 1924 barred Korean immigration completely, approximately 2,000 additional Koreans moved to Hawaii and the West Coast states. "Picture brides" of the pioneer immigrants in Hawaii and political refugees engaged in the anti-Japanese movement constituted the vast majority of Korean immigrants between 1906 and 1924. Although the earlier Korean labor migrants on the West Coast intended to go back to Korea when they made enough money, most of them and their picture brides remained in the United States permanently. However, the majority of the political refugees went back to their home country when Korea became independent in 1945.

With the outbreak of the Korean War in 1950, the United States maintained close military, political, and economic relations with South Korea. The linkages between the two countries helped to resume the immigration of Koreans to the United States. About 15,000 Koreans immigrated to the United States between 1950 and 1964. Korean orphans adopted by American citizens and Korean women married to U.S. servicemen stationed in South Korea made up the vast majority of Korean immigrants during this period. The immigration of Korean children adopted by American citizens and internationally married Korean women was expanded in the 1970s and 1980s but has moderated since the later 1980s.

Despite nearly one hundred years of immigration history, the U.S. Korean population before 1970 was negligible. The 1970s census enumerated the Korean population as less than 70,000. As previously mentioned, however, Korean immigration has accelerated with the enforcement of the 1965 Immigration Act. As shown in Table 10-1, annual Korean immigrants numbered a few thousands in the late 1960s, but the number rapidly increased in the early 1970s. More than 30,000 Koreans immigrated to the United States every year during the 1980s, the third largest immigrant group in the decade following Mexicans and Filipinos. In the 1990s, Korean immigration has dropped substantially, below the level of 20,000 per year. This reduction of Korean immigration in recent years has been caused by great improvements in economic and political conditions in South Korea and better information there about the difficulties of Korean immigrants' adjustments in the United States.[1]

---

[1]The standard of living in South Korea has risen greatly in recent years, as reflected by the per capita income of over $10,000 in 1994. Moreover, social and political insecurity, which pushed many Koreans to the United States in the 1970s and the early 1980s, has been reduced substantially during recent years. South Korea had a popular presidential election at the end of 1987, ending the sixteen-year-old military dictatorship. While people in South Korea have improved their economic and political conditions significantly, they are well informed of the adjustment difficulties that Korean immigrants encounter in the United States.

TABLE 10-1. Koreans Who Immigrated and Naturalized, 1965–1988

Year	Total U.S. Immigrants	Total Korean Immigrants	Koreans Naturalized
1965	296,697	2,165	1,027
1966	323,040	2,492	1,180
1967	361,972	3,356	1,353
1968	454,448	3,811	1,776
1969	358,579	6,045	1,646
1970	373,326	9,314	1,687
1971	370,478	14,297	2,083
1972	387,685	18,876	2,933
1973	400,063	22,930	3,562
1974	394,861	28,028	4,451
1975	386,194	28,362	6,007
1976	398,613	30,830	6,450
1977	462,315	30,917	10,446
1978	601,442	29,288	12,575
1979	460,348	29,248	13,406
1980	530,639	32,320	14,073
1981	596,600	32,663	13,258
1982	594,131	30,814	13,488
1983	559,763	33,339	12,808
1984	543,903	33,042	14,019
1985	570,009	35,253	16,824
1986	601,708	35,776	18,037
1987	601,516	35,849	14,233
1988	643,025	34,703	13,012
1989	1,090,924	34,222	11,301
1990	1,536,483	32,301	10,500
1991	1,827,167	26,518	12,216
1992	973,977	19,359	8,297
1993	904,292	18,026	9,611

Source: Immigration and Naturalization Service, *Annual Reports*, 1965–1978; *Statistical Yearbook*, 1979–1993.

The influx of Korean immigrants over the last quarter century has led to a radical growth in the Korean-American population. The 1990 census counted approximately 800,000 Koreans in the United States, with the U.S.-born making up 28 percent. Considering a significant underestimation by the 1990 census along with the subsequent increase, the population of Korean ancestry was approximately 1.2 million as of 1996. In 1990, the Korean population accounted for 12 percent of the approximately 7 million Asian Americans. While the immigration flow from other Asian countries has increased greatly in the 1990s, Korean immigration has been substantially curtailed. Thus, the Korean population, like the Japanese, will make up a smaller and smaller fraction of the Asian-American population in the future.

Post-1965 Korean immigrants in the United States are primarily economic immigrants who crossed the Pacific mainly to improve their economic status. Although economic immigrants are largely motivated to come to the United States by a higher standard of living here than their home country, their motives for immigration are still complex. Many Koreans chose to immigrate to the United States to give their children a better opportunity for education, particularly a college education (Kim and Min, 1992; Min, 1995a; Yoon, 1993). This motive may be more important than the purely economic motive for many Korean immigrants in the 1990s, after South Korea has already achieved great economic prosperity.

Individual motives alone, economic or noneconomic, cannot explain the massive immigration of Koreans to the United States before 1990. The military, political, and economic linkages between the United States and South Korea since the Korean War and the consequent U.S. cultural influence in South Korea largely explain why South Korea sent the second largest immigrant group, following the Philippines, among Asian countries in the 1980s (I. Kim, 1987; Light and Bonacich, 1988; Min, 1995a). The U.S. government sent more than half a million servicemen to South Korea during the Korean War and even after the war ended maintained a sizable military forces (approximately 40,000–50,000) in South Korea. Many Korean women married U.S. servicemen stationed in South Korea. More than 3,000 Korean women married to U.S. servicemen immigrated annually to the United States in the 1970s and 1980s, providing the basis for subsequent kin-based immigration. The presence of U.S. forces with their television station (AFKN) in South Korea has also had a strong cultural influence, pushing middle-class Koreans to choose U.S.-bound emigration in the last two decades.

The 1990 census showed that approximately 260,000 Korean Americans resided in California, accounting for 32 percent of all Korean Americans (see Table 10-2). The Korean population in California grew by 150 percent between 1980 and 1990, a higher growth rate than that expressed by the United States as a whole. This trend suggests the tendency of the Korean-American population to cluster in this golden state. Over 180,000 Koreans, 70 percent of the Korean population in the state, live in Los Angeles and Orange Counties, and the San Francisco–Oakland–San Jose area is another metropolitan area in California with a sizeable Korean population.

A unique aspect of the Los Angeles Korean community is the development of a physically segregated location known as "Koreatown." Koreatown, a 25-square-mile rectangle area, is located about three miles west of downtown Los Angeles. Although Koreans in Los Angeles are highly concentrated in Koreatown, they make up only about 15 percent of the residents in the area, with Hispanics constituting the majority. Koreatown is a commercial as well as residential center for Koreans in Los Angeles. Approximately 3,500 Korean-owned businesses with Korean-language signs are located in Koreatown. The vast majority of Korean businesses in Koreatown serve Koreans their native cui-

TABLE 10-2.   Distribution of Koreans in 1980 and 1990, by Region and State

Region	State	1980 N	1980 Percent	1990 N	1990 Percent	Increase Between 1980 and 1990 N	Increase Between 1980 and 1990 Percent
U.S. Total		354,593	100.0	798,849	100.0	444,256	125.3
Northeast	Total	68,151	19.2	182,061	22.8	113,910	167.1
	New York	34,157	9.6	95,648	12.0	61,491	180.0
	New Jersey	12,845	3.6	38,540	4.8	25,695	200.0
	Pennsylvania	12,502	3.5	26,787	3.4	14,285	114.3
Midwest	Total	62,214	17.5	109,087	13.7	46,873	75.3
	Illinois	23,989	6.8	41,506	5.2	17,517	73.0
	Michigan	8,714	2.5	16,316	2.0	7,602	87.2
	Ohio	7,257	2.0	11,237	1.4	3,980	54.8
South	Total	70,381	19.9	153,163	19.2	82,782	117.6
	Maryland	15,089	4.3	30,320	3.8	15,231	100.9
	Virginia	12,550	3.5	29,697	3.7	17,147	136.6
	Texas	13,997	3.9	31,775	4.0	17,778	127.0
	Georgia	5,968	1.7	13,275	1.7	7,307	122.4
West	Total	153,847	43.4	354,538	44.4	200,691	130.4
	Washington	13,083	3.7	29,697	3.7	16,614	127.0
	California	103,845	29.3	259,941	32.5	156,096	150.3
	Hawaii	17,962	5.1	24,454	3.1	6,492	36.1

Sources: U.S. Bureau of the Census, 1983, table 63; 1993a, table 276.

sine, groceries, books/magazines, and sundries and provide services for other distinctively Korean cultural tastes (Min 1993a; Yu 1985).

In 1990, 12 percent of all Korean Americans were settled in New York State, a substantial increase from 9.6 percent in 1980. About 100,000 Koreans currently reside in New York City, 70 percent in the borough of Queens. Koreans in Queens are heavily concentrated in Flushing, which has gone through a radical ethnic change in the last two decades, from a predominantly white area to a multiethnic community. Korean immigrants have developed another overseas Seoul along Union Street in a downtown Flushing area where several hundred Korean stores with Korean-language signs are lined up. According to the 1990 census, another 5 percent of Korean Americans were settled in New Jersey, which marked a 200 percent growth rate in the Korean population between 1980 and 1990, higher than any other state. The New York–New Jersey metropolitan area, the home to approximately 150,000 Korean Americans, is the major Korean population center in the Northeast.

Cultural, Religious, and Economic Bases of Korean Ethnicity

Members of an ethnic group share cultural, historical, and/or even economic experiences unique to the group, which become the bases for ethnic identity and group ties. Korean immigrants maintain distinctive characteristics in all three areas—culture, religion, and economic adjustment. Their unique experiences in these areas have enhanced their own and even second-generation Koreans' ethnic identity and group solidarity (Min, 1991a). Let us examine Koreans' unique experiences in each area in some detail.

Korean immigrants are a highly homogeneous group in culture and historical experiences, more homogeneous than any other Asian group with the exception of the Japanese. This group homogeneity and lack of diversity provide the cultural basis for Korean ethnic identity and group solidarity. Language is probably the most significant element of ethnicity, and Korean immigrants have a single language. This monolingual background gives Korean immigrants a big advantage over other multilingual Asian immigrant groups, such as Indians and Filipinos, for maintaining their ethnic ties. For example, Korean immigrants, almost all of whom can speak, read, and write the Korean language fluently, depend mainly on Korean-language ethnic dailies and Korean-language television and radio programs for news, information, and leisure activities. Their almost exclusive dependence on ethnic media has in turn strengthened their ties to the ethnic community and the home country, although it has hindered their assimilation into American society.

The vast majority of Korean immigrants are affiliated with Korean Christian churches, which is also their defining characteristic. Although only 25 percent of the population in South Korea is Christian (Protestant or Catholic) (Park and Cho, 1994), approximately 75 percent of Korean immigrants in the United States are affiliated with Korean immigrant churches (Hurh and Kim, 1990; Min, 1992a).[2] Koreans' involvement in ethnic churches provides the religious basis for Korean ethnic ties. Korean churches have positive effects on Korean immigrants' ethnic attachment partly by providing them with fellowship and ethnic networks. Korean immigrants usually do not live in physically separate ethnic communities, but they can make friends with coethnic members and maintain ethnic networks mainly through participation in ethnic church services and activities. Also, Korean churches contribute to Korean immigrants' and even their children's ethnic attachment and ethnic identity by helping to maintain Korean cultural traditions. Korean churches provide Korean language and other cultural programs for children, teach traditional Korean values, and celebrate important Korean holidays with a variety of Korean food. In their efforts to sustain Korean subculture and identity through Christian churches, Korean immigrants have "Koreanized" Christianity significantly (Min, 1992a).

[2]The concentration of the Korean Christian population in large cities from which Korean immigrants are largely drawn, the selective migration of more Korean Christians to the United States, and the participation of many non-Christian Koreans in Korean immigrant churches explain the affiliation of the vast majority of Korean immigrants with Korean churches.

In addition, Korean immigrants have developed a unique mode of economic adaptation that has also contributed to their ethnic ties and ethnic solidarity: they are heavily concentrated in a limited range of small businesses. Korean immigrants in the late 1960s and the early 1970s expected to obtain white collar and professional positions in fields that they were originally trained for. However, because of language barriers and other disadvantages for employment,[3] most of these immigrants had to switch to low-level, blue collar occupations (Min, 1988). Reluctantly they turned to small business as an alternative to undesirable blue collar occupations, and it took a long time to accumulate starting capital, acquire business information, and train themselves on how to start a business.

Recent Korean immigrants are better prepared to start their own businesses than those who came in the 1970s, since they are informed in Korea that self-employment in small business is the only alternative for most Korean immigrants. Recent Korean immigrants can therefore start their own businesses much more quickly than the Korean immigrants of the 1970s. Accordingly, the self-employment of Korean immigrants has gradually increased over the years. Survey studies conducted recently suggest that nearly half of Korean immigrant workers are self-employed and that about 30 percent work for Korean stores (Min, 1989a, 1996a; Hurh and Kim, 1984). Thus, the vast majority of Korean workers are segregated in the Korean subeconomy either as business owners or employees of co-ethnic businesses.

The segregation of Korean immigrants at the workplace facilitates their preservation of Korean cultural traditions and their social interactions with coethnics (Min, 1991a). The vast majority of Korean immigrants work with family members and fellow Koreans, speaking the Korean language and practicing Korean customs during work hours. Although most Korean-owned businesses serve non-Korean customers, they do so with limited language skills. Koreans, who are segregated at the workplace also have little opportunity to make friends with non-Korean residents. Thus, even during off-duty hours they extend social interactions mainly with coethnics. In contrast, Filipino and Asian Indian immigrants, most of whom work in the general economy, speak English and practice American customers at the workplace and have more opportunity to make friends with Americans.

Korean immigrants' concentration in small business has strengthened not only their ethnic ties but also their ethnic solidarity. Korean immigrants specialize in several business specialties such as grocery, produce, liquor and dry cleaning services, and retail sales of Asian-imported manufactured goods. Korean merchants engaged in the same business have a strong sense of soli-

---

[3]Korean immigrants have more serious language barriers and are less familiar with American customers than other Asian immigrants. For example, Filipino and Indian immigrants spoke English prior to immigration and thus speak English more fluently than Korean immigrants. Also, Filipino, Indian, and even Taiwanese school systems are more Americanized and Westernized than the Korean school system.

darity because their class and ethnic interests overlap. Korean merchants in each Korean community have established various trade associations to protect their business interests against white suppliers, white landlords, and government agencies that restrict small business activities. Through their associations, they have taken a number of collective measures against white suppliers, including boycotts, demonstrations, group purchase, and price bargaining (Min, 1996a, chap. 8). They have also lobbied administrators and politicians extensively to moderate various regulations. In their efforts to negotiate with suppliers and government agencies to protect their business interests, Korean merchants have also learned important political skills.

Korean small businesses are overrepresented in low-income minority neighborhoods (I. Kim, 1981; Kim and Hurh, 1985; Min, 1988, 1996a). Korean immigrants dominate grocery, liquor, produce, and a few other businesses in many black neighborhoods in Los Angles, New York, and other cities. As middleman merchants bridging white corporations and minority residents, Korean merchants in black neighborhoods have encountered boycotts, arson, and other forms of rejection and hostility by customers, a circumstance that has, in turn, strengthened Korean ethnic solidarity (Abelmann and Lie, 1995; Min, 1995b, 1996a). Korean immigrants' business-related conflicts with black residents climaxed in the 1992 Los Angeles riots, during which approximately 2,300 Korean stores in South Central Los Angeles and Koreatown were burned and/or destroyed. Since then, large numbers of these businesses have not rebuilt or reopened.

The victimization of many innocent Korean merchants during the riots was the most significant event in Korean-American history, strengthening pan-Korean solidarity and awakening Koreans' political consciousness more than any other historical event. More significantly, the victimization of many Korean merchants during the riots also heightened younger-generation Koreans' sense of ethnic identity and ethnic solidarity. It was the first major historical event that provided second-generation Koreans with an opportunity to think about their common fate as Korean Americans. Younger-generation Koreans suspected that the police did not care about protecting Koreatown mainly because Korean Americans were a powerless minority group. Thus, many young Koreans responded to the victimization of Korean merchants by writing articles in English dailies, attacking the media bias against Koreans and police inactivity in protecting Koreatown during the riots.

Korean History, Culture, and Family System

Korea is a peninsula extending northwest to Manchuria and southeast nearly to the southern islands of Japan. Historically, the Chinese cultural influence spread southward to Korea and then to Japan. Thus, Chinese culture came to have a greater influence on Korea than on Japan, although

Japan was under the strong cultural influence of China. In fact, until very recently, the one dominating feature of Korean culture was the impact of Chinese culture, especially through Confucianism. Under the influence of the old Chinese culture, Chinese characters are still used in newspapers and magazines in Korea.

At the turn of the twentieth century, three Asian superpowers—Japan, China, and Russia—struggled for political control over Korea. When Japan won its war against Russia in 1905, it established hegemony on the Korean peninsula. Korea remained under Japanese colonial rule for thirty-six years until the end of World War II. During the colonial period, the Japanese government tried to "Japanize" Korean society by repressing ruthlessly Korean culture and appropriating private and public lands. Because of this historical background, there is still strong anti-Japanese sentiment in Korea, although South Korea normalized diplomatic relations with Japan in 1965.

Since the end of World War II, Korea has been politically divided into two halves: South Korea under the influence of the United States and North Korea under the influence of the former Soviet Union and China. The United States, however, exerted cultural influence on Korea through Protestant missionaries even before the Korean War; it was American Presbyterian and Methodist missionaries who first established modern schools and hospitals in Korea at the beginning of the twentieth century. Koreans fought a civil war between 1950 and 1953, and the Korean War was also the first major confrontation between communists and anticommunists in the Cold War period. Although the Korean War ended in 1953, military tensions in the Korean peninsula have continued until today. However, the end of the Cold War period along with the great economic improvements and diplomatic success achieved by South Korea in the 1990s has increased the possibility of a peaceful unification of the Korean peninsula in the near future. The close political, economic, and military connections between South Korea and the United States in the years after the Korean War have accelerated American cultural influence in South Korea.

The Chinese Confucian cultural tradition had such a deep influence on Korean society that it is almost impossible to understand Korean traditional culture in general and its family system in particular without understanding the influence of Chinese Confucianism. Concerned mainly with life in this world, Confucius provided several important principles that he advised individuals to follow for harmonious social relations. Five categories of interpersonal relations form the basis of his teachings on the duties and obligations of each individual. These are the relations between parents and children, king and people, husband and wife, older (brother) and younger (brother), and friends. The significance of Confucianism for the Korean family system is clear because three of these five cardinal relations involve the family.

Confucius taught that parents and children should maintain a mutual attitude of benevolence. However, Confucianism, as applied to the Korean family system and social life, demanded children's one-sided obedience to and respect for parents and other adult members. Children were required not only to pay the highest respect to their parents throughout their lives but also to fulfill important obligations to them. The first son was supposed to live with his parents after marriage, providing them with financial support and care. Moreover, filial piety was extended after the death of a parent in the form of ancestor worship. Sons observed ritual mourning for three years after a parent died, and younger generations of sons showed worshipful veneration to their ancestors. Filial piety is still considered one of the central norms in contemporary Korean society and ancestor worship is widely practiced. Confucianism also emphasized a clear role differentiation between the husband and the wife, and this principle helped to establish an extreme form of patriarchy in Korea. In traditional Korean society the husband was considered the primary breadwinner and decision maker in the family and exercised authority over his wife and children. The wife was expected to obey her husband, devotedly serving him and his family members, and to perpetuate her husband's family lineage by producing children. The wife was eliminated from decision making in all important family affairs, including children's education.

In traditional Korean society based on patriarchy and patrilineage, sons were considered more valuable and given more power than daughters. The first son very often attended important family meetings from which his mother was excluded. Interpersonal relations between brothers or between sisters were regulated by Confucian ideology, which put an emphasis on age: older brothers or sisters were allowed to exercise a moderate level of authority over younger brothers or sisters. Because of this emphasis on age, sibling rivalry was not frequent in the traditional Korean family. Age was important not only for sibling relations but also for interpersonal relations in general. People were expected to be polite and respectful to people with whom they interacted if they were younger than the others by even a few years.

Another major effect of Confucianism on Korean society was the adoption of the civil service examination, originally devised in China, in the tenth century. The system, which was intended to bring men of intelligence and ability into government regardless of social position, annually gave examinations based on Chinese literature and Confucian classics. Those who passed the examination were offered high government positions that gave great power and economic rewards. Thus Koreans have traditionally put great emphasis on education because historically the civil service examination provided the only efficient outlet for upward social mobility.

Under the impact of this Confucian cultural tradition, people in South Korea still put great emphasis on their children's education. Parents, particularly mothers, evaluate their success largely by what college their children get into. Since South Korean colleges and universities can accept only a small fraction of high school candidates each year, competition in the college entrance examination is excessively strong. Despite their hard work, many students fail in the entrance examination, which is given only once a year. They try it again and again under considerable pressure, even in the third year after graduation from high school. Parents spend large amounts of money to give children extracurricular studies after school. While the zeal for children's education and the rigid college entrance examination system push high school students to work hard, they are also the root causes of many social problems, including parents' heavy financial burdens, children's excessive mental pressure, and the test-oriented high school education. Because of these social problems, the South Korean government plans to make sweeping changes in the college admission system, adopting much of the U.S. system beginning in 1997.[4]

KOREAN-AMERICAN FAMILIES

The 1990 census revealed that native-born Koreans made up 28 percent of Korean Americans and that their median age was 8.8 (U.S. Bureau of the Census, 1993c: table 1). This figure suggests that the vast majority of American-born Koreans were children who lived in their families of orientation or young adults who were not married. In fact, the 1990 census showed that only 4 percent of Korean-American families were headed by native-born Koreans (U.S. Bureau of the Census, 1993c, table 2). For this reason, I will use Korean-American and Korean immigrant families interchangeably.

Using an ideal type construct, we can make a distinction between the traditional and the modern family. The traditional family has more members (more children and more nonnuclear family members), a higher level of family stability (a lower divorce rate and a lower proportion of female-headed families), and a stricter gender division of labor (a lower rate of married women's labor force participation) than the modern family. Overall, families in South Korea are more traditional than U.S. families because of the Confucian cultural tradition. Korean immigrant families are likely to stand between Korean and U.S. families in the traditional–modern continuum. Korean immigrant families are likely to be more modern than Korean families in Korea because of Korean immigrants' assimilation into more modern American family lifestyles. Yet Korean immigrants have achieved a low level of assimilation, and thus their families are more traditional than U.S. families. However, not only Koreans' cultural changes, but also their high socioeconomic status—higher than that of the U.S. population as a whole—and their

[4]To normalize high school education on one hand and to relieve students' and parents' pressures arising from the entrance examination on the other, the government has proposed a new plan for college admissions according to which colleges and universities should put more weight on the high school GPA and extracurricular activities than on results of the entrance examination and SAT scores for college admissions.

immigrant status have an effect on their family patterns. Therefore, it is possible that Korean immigrant families are more modern than even U.S. families in some characteristics.

Family Size and Composition

The first five rows in Table 10-3 provide data on family size and composition for three populations: (1) the non-Hispanic white, (2) the Korean-American, and (3) the Korean population in Korea, based on the 1990 U.S. and Korean census reports. As expected, Korean Americans, on average, have larger households and larger families than white Americans but smaller ones than Koreans in Korea. Although the Korean population has a larger family than the white population, it has a smaller family than other Asian groups. For example, the average number of family members is 4.36 for the Vietnamese group, 4.02 for the Filipino, and 3.83 for the Asian Indian, compared to 3.60 for the Korean (U.S. Bureau of the Census, 1993a, table 48).

TABLE 10-3.   Family Characteristics of White, Korean-American, and Korean Populations

	Non-Hispanic White	Korean-American	Korean in Korea
Number of persons per household	2.5	3.2	3.7
Number of persons per family	3.0	3.6	4.0
Percent of single-person households	25.5	15.2	9.0
Number of children per family	1.1	1.9	—
Number of nonnuclear family members per family	0.1	0.4	—
Number of divorced persons per 1,000 persons 15 years old and over	74 (male) 95 (female)	23 (male) 54 (female)	7 (male) 9 (female)
Percent of married couple families	83.5	83.4	—
Percent of female-headed families	12.3	11.6	—
Percent of persons under 18 in married-couple families	78.7	86.6	—
Percent of women (16 years old and over) in the labor force	56.4	55.5	44.2[a]
Percent of married women in the labor force	57.9	59.8	25.3[a]
Number of children ever born per 1,000 women 25–34 years old	1,233	1,067	1,873
Number of children ever born per 1,000 women 35–44 years old	1,849	1,776	3,100

[a]The nonfarm population.
Sources: U.S. Bureau of the Census, 1993a; tables 40, 48; 1993b; tables 41, 44, 105, 108, and 109; Korean Bureau of Statistics, 1993; tables 2-1, 2-2; Korean Women's Development Institute, 1994; tables 2-1-2, 2-2-1, 2-2-2, 4-1-1, 4-1-2.

The Korean-American population has a smaller proportion of single-person households (15%) than the white population (26%), which partly contributes to its larger household size. Korean-American unmarried adults, unmarried women in particular, usually live with their parents unless they go to college at another city, whereas their white American counterparts often live away from their parents. This difference in unmarried adults' living arrangements seem to contribute partly to the differential in the proportion of single-person households between Korean and white Americans. As will be discussed later, Korean-American widows and widowers tend to live with their adult children more frequently than their white counterparts, which also contributes partly to the differential in the proportion of single-person households. Although Korean-American women have a slightly lower fertility rate than white American women (see the bottom two rows), Korean Americans, on average, have more children per family than white Americans. This is so mainly because of Korean unmarried adults' tendency to cohabit with their parents. Korean-American families include not only more adult children but also more nonnuclear family members, including elderly parents. These two factors are mainly responsible for Korean Americans' larger family size compared with that of white Americans.

Marital Stability

Table 10-3 also provides data reflecting marital stability for the three comparison groups. The United States has the highest divorce rate in the world and a much higher divorce rate than South Korea. Using the number of divorced persons for 1,000 persons 15 years old and over as an indicator, the United States has a divorce rate approximately twenty times higher than that of South Korea for men and twelve times higher for women. A much higher divorce rate for women than for men in South Korea is mainly the result of the difficulty of divorced women there to remarry because of a strong double standard. As expected, Korean Americans have higher divorce rates than the Korean population in South Korea but lower divorce rates than white Americans. It is, however, surprising that the Korean-American population, which consists mainly of recent immigrants, is closer in its divorce rate to the white-American population than to the population in Korea. This suggests that Koreans have experienced a radical increase in the divorce rate since their immigration to the United States. The following three factors seem to largely explain this remarkable increase.

First, a high divorce rate of first-generation Koreans who immigrated to this country at an early age inflated the divorce rate of Korean immigrants. As will be noted later, native-born Koreans have a much higher divorce rate than foreign-born Koreans, and first-generation Koreans (who make up a significant proportion of foreign-born Koreans) are likely to have a high divorce rate close to that of native-born Koreans. Second, residence in this country has led to a change in Korean immigrants' attitudes toward divorce. In South Korea, many people continue to maintain unhappy marital relations because custom discourages divorce. In this country, however, divorce is not considered deviant behavior, and thus exposure to this liberal cultural milieu has led many Korean immigrants to make a decision to divorce more easily than they would have in Korea.

Third, an exceptionally high divorce rate of Korean brides married to U.S. servicemen has also contributed to the marital instability of the Korean-American population in general. Korean-American women have a divorce rate higher than Korean-American men by about 2.5 times. The 1980 and 1990 census reports showed that for females the Korean group had the highest divorce rate among all Asian ethnic groups but that for males it had a lower divorce rate than Japanese or Filipino Americans (Min, 1989b; U.S. Bureau of the Census, 1993b, table 48). Since the Korean War, many American servicemen stationed in South Korea have brought home Korean wives, and a high percentage of these interracial marriages have terminated in divorce (see the section on intermarriage).

Korean-American and white American families have similar proportions of female-headed families. However, despite similar figures in this indicator of family instability, Korean-American families are more stable than white American families, as already shown by the lower divorce rate of the Korean-American population. This similar proportion of female-headed families results mainly from the fact that Korean widows and female divorcees have a greater tendency to live with unmarried adult children without getting remarried. Korean-American families with children under age 18 include a higher proportion of intact families than white American families. As shown in Table 10-3, a higher proportion of Korean children under 18 (87%) than white American children (78%) live with two parents. As shown in other chapters, much higher proportions of African-American and Hispanic-American children live in female-headed families than white American children. This statistic suggests that Korean and other Asian groups have an advantage for furthering their children's education over other minority groups and even white Americans because of family stability.

Conjugal Role Differentiation

Although a high level of urbanization and industrialization has led to great changes in the traditional family system in South Korea during recent years, the Confucian ideology of conjugal role differentiation has not been modified significantly. The wife is still expected to stay home as a full-time homemaker, while the husband's role is limited to earning a living. Both role expectations and employment discrimination discourage married women from participating in the labor market. Table 10-3 shows that only 25 percent of married women in urban areas in South Korea participate in the labor force.[5] Many women work outside the home before they get married. But after marriage, they quit their jobs—very often involuntarily—to focus on housework, child care, and services to their husbands.

The immigration of Koreans to the United States has brought about many changes in the traditional Korean family system, but the most noteworthy is probably a radical increase in the labor-force participation rate of married women. The 1990 census shows that approximately 60 percent of Korean-American married women participate in the workforce, in comparison to 58 percent of white married women (see Table 10-3). Nearly 40 percent of Korean immigrant working wives work for the family business, and another 30 percent are employed in coethnic businesses (Min, 1997). Many of these Korean women in the ethnic subeconomy are unlikely to report their work either to the Internal Revenue Service or to the census survey.

Thus, the 1990 census seems to have underestimated the workforce participation rate of Korean married women. A survey in New York City shows that 70 percent of Korean immigrant married women worked outside the home and that 54 percent worked full-time (Min, 1992b). Although 42 percent of the New York City respondents had had job experience in Korea, many of them engaged in paid work there before they got married. This figure indicates that the immigration of Koreans to the United States has led to a radical change in the economic role of Korean women. Korean immigrant women not only participate in the workforce in great proportions but also work extremely long hours. The New York City survey shows that Korean married women spent 51 hours per work in their jobs (Min, 1992b), working longer hours than other American working women. A study conducted in 1987 showed that other American married women who participated in the workforce spent an average of 37 hours per week for paid work (Shelton, 1992: 39). Most Korean immigrant women participate in the workforce out of practical necessity rather than career aspirations. Almost all respondents in my New York City survey endorsed the statement: "In a normal family the wife should stay at home as a full-time housewife while the husband should be the main breadwinner." Most women in Korean immigrant families are forced into undertaking the economic role because of their special immigrant situation even though they generally hold the traditional gender role orientation. Korean immigrant families need extra workers for economic survival particularly because most have their own businesses. To survive in a family business, not only the husband but also his wife needs to work long hours. The New York City survey revealed that self-employed Korean women worked longer hours than those employed and that Korean married women

---

[5]Of course, the majority of married women in rural areas in South Korea, like married women in other agrarian societies, undertake the economic role.

employed by Korean-owned businesses worked longer hours than those employed by non-Korean firms (Min, 1997). Korean immigrant women's active economic role without a significant change in their own and their husband's gender role attitudes has important implications for their marital relations, which will be discussed later.

How much has the radical increase in the Korean wife's economic role in this country reduced her homemaker's role and increased her husband's share of household tasks? Several survey studies conducted in major Korean communities reveal that the Korean immigrant wife's employment or self-employment has not reduced her homemaker's role significantly. For example, Kim and Hurh (1988) showed that Korean married women in Los Angeles, regardless of their employment status, performed traditional household tasks predominantly. My survey in New York City yielded similar findings (Min, 1992b). Korean working wives shouldered most major household tasks except garbage disposal and some of them were able to reduce their share of housework mainly because other family members (usually elderly mothers and/or daughters) helped them at home. As a result, Korean working women spent 12 more hours per week on their job and housework than their overworked husbands spent. This suggests that most Korean immigrant women suffer from overwork, stress, and role strain. Another study of Korean immigrant married women in New York City (Choi, 1995: 72) showed that Korean women's employment level, hours of housework, and role strain have significant effects on their stress levels.

Women's Power and Status

Another important issue is to the extent to which the increased economic role of Korean immigrant women has increased their power and status in the family and the Korean community in general. The wife's employment usually increases her marital power because it provides her with economic and other resources to bring to the marriage (Blood and Wolf, 1960). However, how much employment increases her marital power depends on a particular cultural context that prescribes marital relations (Rodman, 1967). We previously noted that both Korean immigrants' concentration in small business and their affiliation with ethnic churches have positive effects on their ethnic attachment. Yet the same factors also hinder Korean immigrant women from increasing their marital power and status in proportion to their contribution to family economy.

The concentration of Koreans in small business makes Korean immigrant working women disadvantaged in increasing their power and status in two different ways (Min, 1997). First, their occupational segregation hinders them—both husbands and wives—from altering the traditional patriarchal ideology brought from Korea. Thus, the employment or self-employment of Korean immigrant women in the conservative cultural milieu will discourage them from bargaining actively to improve their power and status. Second, a significant proportion of Korean immigrant working women work for the family business as unpaid family workers, and the nature of their work is not helpful to increasing their power and influence. Employed women increase their bargaining power mainly because they have an independent source of income. Korean women who assist their husbands in the family store do not seem to enjoy the economic and psychological independence that most U.S. employed wives do. Also, the participation of most Korean immigrants in a Korean Christian church perpetuates the patriarchal ideology and thus diminishes the positive effects of Korean women's economic role on their power and status (A. Kim, 1995; Min, 1992a). It reinforces the Confucian patriarchal ideology in two ways. First, the hierarchical structure of Korean immigrant churches, like Christian churches in South Korea, usually does not allow women to serve as head pastors or to hold important positions. Women in a Korean immigrant church are usually involved in such activities as fundraising, prayer meetings, visiting the sick, sending money to poor churches in Korea, and sponsoring children's scholarships, all of which cover women's traditional roles as nurturers and caretakers (A. Kim, 1995: 76). In contrast, men hold important positions that involve decision making on organizational and financial affairs. Second, Korean immigrant churches teach women their subordinate position in the family and society. Many Korean women experience conflicts between the sexist and hierarchical Korean culture and the more egalitarian American culture, but they try to resolve their inner conflicts by legitimating Korean culture and women's subordinate status with their "Christian" religious beliefs (A. Kim, 1995: 118).

Fertility

The bottom two rows in Table 10-3 provide data on fertility for two age groups: 25–24 years and 35–44 years. For both age groups, Korean-American women have a much lower fertility rate than women in South Korea and a slightly lower fertility rate than even white American women. Korean-American women who have passed the peak childbearing age (35 and 44 years old) have, on average, less than two children whereas their counterparts in South Korea have approximately three children. Since the vast majority of Korean-American women 35 and 44 years old are Korean immigrant women, the low fertility rate of Korean-American women in the bottom row in the table indicates the low fertility rate of Korean immigrant women. That Korean immigrant women have a lower fertility rate than women in South Korea is to be expected, but the fact that the Korean immigrant population shows a slightly lower fertility rate than the white American population is surprising.

Two major factors seem to explain the low fertility rate of Korean immigrants. First, it is largely the result of selective immigration. Korean immigrants, particularly those who came to this country in the 1970s, represent the well-educated middle class segment of the Korean population. Middle class couples, whether in South Korea or in the United States, have a lower fertility rate than lower class couples. Korean immigrants are also a selective group in terms of their motives for economic success and social mobility. All immigrants are self-selected in that more progressive, economically aggressive, and achievement-oriented people choose to leave their native country for life in an alien environment (Chiswick, 1982). Korean immigrants as a group have a higher level of aspiration for economic success and social mobility than the middle class in Korea, and this mobility orientation seems to have a negative influence on their childbearing behavior.

Second, a high workforce participation rate of Korean married women serves as a restrictive force to fertility. A small proportion of married women work outside the home in South Korea, although many of them can depend on a cohabiting mother-in-law or a housemaid for child care. In contrast, most Korean immigrant women need to work long hours outside the home for economic survival, but they usually do not live with an elderly mother or a mother-in-law who can help them with babysitting. Thus, Korean immigrant women have difficulty in raising children while holding their paid work. This suggests that many Korean immigrant women have to delay pregnancy while undertaking their economic role. Women's economic role and fertility mutually influence each other. But for immigrant women, economic role seems to influence fertility behavior more than the other way around.

Child Socialization

Confucianism has had the most significant effect on child socialization practices in Korea. As previously noted, filial piety is one of the major elements of this religion. As a consequence of the strong Confucian cultural tradition, child socialization in South Korea still places a great emphasis on children's obedience to and respect for parents and adults. Korean immigrant parents, the vast majority of whom completed their formal education in South Korea, are more authoritarian than white American parents, although there are significant class differences in Korean immigrants' child socialization practices. The authoritarian child socialization practice of Korean immigrant parents was well documented in a survey in which Korean children and mothers in the New York area were asked to report their common complaints about their parents or children. The child respondents cited "restricting my freedom too much" and "too strict" as two of the most common complaints about their parents while many mother respondents complained about their children "not respecting parents" and "talking back" (Min, 1995c). Naturally, Americanized Korean children want to escape parental control and authority, leading to a high level of intergenerational conflicts.

Another core element of Confucianism is its emphasis on children's education and social mobility through education. We noted in the previous section that parents in South Korea do everything possible to send their children to good colleges. Many Korean immigrants have chosen U.S.-bound emigration as a way of giving their children a better opportunity for an education (B. Kim, 1978: 189). Thus, Korean immigrant parents are likely to put more emphasis on children's education than white American parents. Many scholars have indicated that emphasis on children's education is what differentiates Jewish Americans from other ethnic groups (Heilman, 1982; Sklare, 1971). However, a survey study of Korean immigrant and Jewish mothers' child socialization (Rose and Min, 1992) showed that Korean immigrant parents may put more stress on children's success in school than even Jewish-American parents. The majority of the secondary-school children of the Korean mothers included in the study were found to attend private institutes specializing in mathematics and English or to receive tutoring in those subjects in the previous summer, whereas only 6 percent of Jewish children attended such programs.[6] Korean immigrants have brought with them the Korean practice of giving children after-school lessons. Thirty percent of the Korean children were found to be participating in extracurricular study programs at the time of the interview, in comparison to 11 percent of the Jewish children. The same comparative study (Rose and Min, 1992) also found that Korean mothers pressured their children to study longer hours after school and to get better grades than Jewish mothers.

Gender socialization is another area in which Korean immigrant parents differ significantly from white American parents. We already noted that under the impact of Confucianism people in South Korea maintain a more traditional gender role differentiation than here. Closely related to a strict gender role differentiation, Korean parents practice a conservative gender socialization, treating boys and girls differently. This rigid gender socialization, though somewhat moderated, still persists in the Korean immigrant community today. My personal observations strongly suggest that Korean immigrant parents treat boys and girls differently and assign different chores to them. Results of a survey of Korean and Jewish mothers also support these observations (Rose and Min, 1992): Korean-American mothers were found to agree to the statements reflecting traditional gender stereotypes to a far greater extent than Jewish-American mothers. Also, Korean mothers were found to be more traditional than Jewish mothers in assigning housework chores to boys and girls. For example, 63 percent of Korean mothers felt that "setting the table" should be done only by girls while all Jewish respondents said it should be done by both boys and girls.

[6]It was found that Jewish parents usually sent children to camps during the summer.

Living Arrangements and Care of the Elderly

In South Korea, elderly parents usually reside with their first married son. They receive financial support and health care entirely from children, particularly from the cohabiting first son, as government programs for support and care of elderly persons are almost nonexistent. According to the 1990 Korean census, 80 percent of elderly persons in South Korea reside with their children—66 percent residing with their married children—(Eu, 1992: 206). The immigration of Koreans to the United States has modified living arrangements of elderly persons significantly. As shown in Table 10-4, only 32 percent of Korean-American elderly persons live in their own children's family. Assuming that some of those in the first category (family householder or spouse) live with unmarried children, still less than 45 percent of Korean-American elderly persons seem to live with their children, a phenomenal decrease from 80 percent in South Korea. However, compared to the white elderly population (less than 3%), a large proportion of Korean-American elderly do cohabit with their children. Those elderly Koreans who were invited to this country as parents are more likely to reside with children than those old timers who immigrated here in their forties and fifties and have reached retirement age. The latter group will share a greater proportion of the Korean-American elderly population in the future, and thus the proportion of Korean-American elderly persons who cohabit with their children will continue to decrease.

Korean elderly persons in small Korean communities in the United States have difficulties making successful adjustments because of their lack of peer networks, ethnic media, and ethnic-language social services. Thus, most of them reside with their adult children and depend on them for health care and support. However, elderly Korean persons in large Korean

TABLE 10-4. Living Arrangements of White and Korean-American Elderly Persons, 1990

	White	Korean
All elderly persons	27,050,819	35,247
	(percent)	(percent)
Living as a family householder or his/her spouse	57.7	37.5
Living in his/her own child's family	2.9	32.3
Living in a family of a relative other than his/her own child	2.6	10.4
Living in a family of a nonrelative	1.2	2.0
Living in a nonfamily household	29.7	16.2
(living alone)	(28.6)	(15.5)
Living in a group quarter	5.9	1.5

Sources: U.S. Bureau of the Census, 1993a: tables 42, 48.

communities such as Los Angeles and New York are actively involved in peer and other ethnic networks and have access to the Korean-language media and services provided by coethnic social workers. For example, the New York Korean community has four ethnic dailies, two 20-hour TV stations, and a 24-hour radio station. Since the Korean language is used for all these ethnic media, the elderly Koreans in New York have access to news and information about their home country, the Korean community, and the larger society in the Korean language. In fact, they have access to news edited by the Korean Broadcasting Station in Seoul and sent through a satellite station at nine every evening.

Thus, improvements in media technologies have made it easier for elderly immigrants to live in the United States without losing their ties to the home country. Many Korean elderly persons in the Flushing area of New York City, in which Korean immigrants are residentially concentrated, live in several apartment complexes in order to maintain social networks among themselves. During the daytime, they get together at two Korean senior centers for free lunch and recreational activities. Because of these conveniences, many Korean elderly parents choose to live in the Flushing area independently when their adult children move to the Long Island and New Jersey suburban areas for better schools for their children.

Intergroup Marriage

To present Korean intergroup marriage effectively, three groups are analyzed separately: Korean Americans in Hawaii, Korean war brides, and contemporary Korean immigrants.

Intermarriage in Hawaii. The oldest Korean community in the United States was established in Hawaii when approximately 7,200 Koreans came to the islands between 1903 and 1905. The pioneer immigrants and their descendants in Hawaii were isolated from the rest of the Korean population because no significant group of Koreans migrated there before the liberalization of the U.S. immigration law in 1965. The absence of chain migrations, a small group size, and Korean immigrants' high assimilation contributed to a high intermarriage rate of Korean descendants in Hawaii. Harvey and Chung (1980) reported that during the period between 1960 and 1968, 80 percent of Korean brides and grooms in Hawaii married out-group members. They indicated that the intermarrying Korean females tended to prefer white grooms, whereas the intermarrying Korean males chose more Japanese than white brides. This pattern is primarily the result of the difference between Korean men and women in accepting traditional conjugal relations. American-born Korean women want to maintain more egalitarian conjugal relations and thus consider white men preferable to Asian-American men as spouses. Intermarrying Korean men, however, feel more comfortable with traditional conjugal relations than with those practiced by the majority of white Americans and thus prefer Asian to white brides.

Korean War Brides. The United States has maintained a sizable military forces (40,000 to 50,000 servicemen) in South Korea since the Korea War. As previously noted, many of the American servicemen stationed there have brought home Korean wives. According to *Annual Reports* by the Immigration and Naturalization Service, approximately 42,000 Korean women immigrated to the United States as wives of U.S. citizens in the 1970s (Shin, 1987); a similar number of Korean women were admitted in the 1980s (Lee, 1991). The vast majority of these women are considered wives of U.S. servicemen. A study based on the 1980s census showed that 27 percent of married Korean women in California, compared to only 6 percent of their male counterparts, had spouses with non-Korean ethnic backgrounds (Jioubu, 1988: 161). The immigration of Korean women married to U.S. servicemen partly explains this gender differential in the intermarriage rate.

Korean women married to U.S. servicemen generally have a low socioeconomic status, although there are many exceptions (B. Kim, 1972; Lee, 1991; Ratliff, Moon, and Bonacci, 1978). Many were born and raised in rural villages and migrated to Seoul and other large cities in search of urban employment. Their language barrier and lack of assimilation make their adjustments to American society and to intermarriages very difficult (Jeong and Schumm, 1990). Moreover, many interracially married U.S. servicemen neglect and even abuse their Korean wives, feeling that the women who provided them with companionship in Korea are no longer valuable to them in this country. For these reasons, an unusually high proportion of the intermarriages between Korean women and U.S. servicemen are known to have ended with divorce, although no hard data are available. As already discussed, using the number of persons divorced per 1,000 persons 15 years old and over as an indicator, Korean-American women have a higher divorce rate than their male counterparts by two and a half times (see Table 10-3). As noted, this great sex differential in divorce seems to be mainly the result of the high divorce rate of Korean women married to American servicemen. Those Korean women who fail in this type of intermarriage usually have a severe language barrier and do not have useful job skills. Thus they face great economic and adjustment difficulties.

Intermarriage Patterns Among Korean Americans. The immigration of many Korean nurses and Korean women married to American servicemen, along with the adoption of more Korean girls than boys by American citizens, have contributed to a sex imbalance in favor of women for the Korean-American population. In 1980, females outnumbered males by 58 to 42 for Korean Americans (U.S. Bureau of the Census, 1983a: table 47). The sex imbalance was much greater for those at marital ages (20 to 29 years old), with females constituting 68 percent of the Korean-American population in that age category. Although the sex imbalance has been moderated recently, Korean-American women still have a disadvantage in finding suitable Korean partners in the Korean community because of the sex imbalance. The 1990 census showed that Korean-American women 20 to 29 years old outnumbered their male counterparts by 54 to 46 (U.S. Bureau of the Census, 1993a: table 23). Moreover, more Korean-American men than women tend to bring their marital partners from Korea. A 1986 survey of Korean immigrants in Los Angeles and Orange Counties showed that 37 percent of the Korean men who married in the past five years brought their partners from Korea in comparison to 31 percent of women (Min, 1993b). The tendency of more Korean men than women to bring their marital partners from Korea gives Korean-American women a further disadvantage in finding Korean partners in the Korean-American community.

These two factors force more Korean-American women than men to look for their marital partners outside the Korean community. In addition, more Korean-American women than men are attracted to white American partners because they expect to maintain more egalitarian conjugal relations with white partners than with Korean ones. For these reasons, we expect Korean-American women to marry non-Korean partners far more frequently than Korean-American men. This expectation is supported by empirical data. For example, in their study based on marriage license records in Los Angeles County, Kitano and Chai (1982) reported that about 21 percent of Koreans who got married in 1975, 1977, and 1979 married non-Korean partners and that more than 70 percent of those intermarried were women. Another study based on a survey of Korean immigrants in Los Angeles and Orange Counties (Min, 1993b) revealed that 14 percent of the Korean women who got married in the five years before the survey married non-Korean partners, in comparison to only 2.5 percent of the male counterparts. Intermarried Korean Americans usually select white partners. Yet they—intermarried Korean men in particular—also prefer Japanese and Chinese partners (Kitano and Chai, 1982). Because of similarities in physical and cultural characteristics, younger-generation Chinese, Japanese, and Korean Americans maintain high levels of social interaction and intermarriage.

CHANGES AND ADAPTATIONS

We noted previously that three factors—Koreans' group homogeneity, high affiliation with Korean immigrant churches, and concentration in small business—have helped them to maintain a high level of ethnic attachment. These three factors have contributed to preserving particularly Korean traditional family values, such as filial piety, emphasis on children's education, the patriarchal ideology, and customs related to them. However, their adaptation to American society have also resulted in modifications of their traditional family lives.

Major Changes in Korean Immigrant Families

We already noted that a phenomenal increase in women's workforce participation is the radical change that has occurred to Korean immigrant families. Most Korean immigrant working women are self-employed in their own family businesses or work for Korean-owned stores as employees. Additionally, it was noted that the occupational concentration of Korean immigrants in the Korean ethnic economy helps them to maintain Korean cultural traditions, including traditional family values. However, it is important to understand that the economic coordination between the husband and the wife in the family store also represents a major change in Koreans' marital relations with immigration. No clear demarcation between work and family life characterized the "small producer family," a term used to describe a Chinese small business family in the United States in the early twentieth century (Glenn, 1983). Many Korean immigrant families are small business families where the distinction between family and work life is blurred. In South Korea, where the gender role division is still rigid, many women complain that they have little time to talk with their husbands. In sharp contrast, many Korean immigrant women complain that they spend too much time—all day—with their husbands to the extent that they have frequent arguments in the family store.

Korean immigrant women's long hours of work and increased economic role have far-reaching effects on their marital relations and family lives. Although married women in South Korea usually do not work outside the home, they can depend on a housemaid or a mother-in-law for child care and housework. Middle-class women who have professional careers in South Korea usually have a housemaid. In contrast, few Korean immigrant families have the luxury of a housemaid or a mother-in-law who can help them with housework and child care, although most Korean immigrant married women work outside the home for long hours.[7] Thus, Korean immigrant women lead far more hectic lives than their counterparts in South Korea. Also, Korean immigrant women spend much less time with children than women in Korea. In a survey of Korean junior and senior high school students in New York, 64 percent reported that neither parent stays at home after school, and 46 percent said that no one stays at home after school (Min, 1991b).

The immigration of Koreans to the United States has also brought about a significant change in the degree to which elderly persons depend on their children for support and care. As already discussed, less than half of elderly persons live with their children in the Korean immigrant community, while a predominant majority of them maintain the same type of living

---

[7]According to my survey of Korean married women in New York City (Min, 1992b), only 4.3 percent of the homes represented by the sample were found to have a housemaid working part time or full time.

arrangements in South Korea. The Social Security support for elderly persons encourages Korean-American elderly persons to live independently. Whether they reside with children or independently, Korean elderly persons depend mainly on their spouses and children for health care. In a survey of Korean elderly persons in the New York area (Min, 1996b), 42 percent reported that they depended on their spouses for health care. Another 33 percent said they depended on their children, whereas only 2.7 percent said they depended on Korean social workers for health care. However, the availability of government and other formal service programs has helped Korean elderly persons to maintain some level of independence from their children not only for financial support but also for other services. In the same New York survey, 36 percent of the respondents reported that they depended on social workers for paperwork (Min, 1996b).

Class Differences in Family System

Korean immigrant families can be classified into three groups that have differences in occupations and family characteristics: professional families, small business families, and working-class families. A small proportion of Korean immigrants are professionals employed by U.S. firms and U.S. governments. They include public school teachers, college professors, accountants, attorneys, and medical professionals. Also, some Korean professionals hold jobs in the Korean community. They include self-employed lawyers, accountants, and medical professionals who serve mainly a Korean clientele, social workers employed by various Korean social service agencies, and clerical professionals employed by many Korean churches. Korean immigrant professionals have been in this country for a longer period of time than other Korean immigrants. Most received professional education in this country, whereas the vast majority of other Korean immigrants completed their education in Korea. Wives of Korean professionals usually do not work outside the home, focusing instead on children's education.

Partners of professionals, partners of female professionals in particular, are often self-employed in small business. Thus, Korean professional families with partners in small businesses enjoy economic security and usually live in suburban white neighborhoods. Because of their class advantages in child socialization (resources, time, and familiarity with the U.S. educational system), Korean professional families are successful in sending children to prestigious universities.

Korean small business owners cover a wide range of the socioeconomic spectrum from highly educated, successful store owners to marginal peddlers. But most Korean small business families share common characteristics: the wife working outside the home, usually in the family store; both partners' hectic work schedules; and wives' unrewarded overwork, previously discussed. Successful Korean business families, like professional families, usually live in suburban white neighborhoods, whereas most Korean small business families are in Korean ethnic enclaves. Although some well established Korean business families have advantages in children's education in terms of time and resources, most others have difficulty in taking care of their children because of both partners' intense work schedules. Self-employed fathers in particular have little time for their children. Successful Korean businessmen take a leadership role in the Korean community, often spending much time and providing donations for community activities. Korean business families, including marginal business families, are actively involved in ethnic networks and maintain Korean customs and traditions faithfully.

Working-class Koreans consist of recent immigrants who are employed either in blue collar or low-level white collar occupations. Most of these Koreans work for Korean-owned businesses either as cashiers, skilled workers, or even manual laborers. They work for Korean-owned stores partly to gain business experience to start their own businesses in the near future. Compared to many Chinese immigrants who are trapped in Chinese-owned businesses more or less permanently, most Korean employees of coethnic stores start their own businesses quickly (Min, 1996a, chap. 11). Korean working-class families are heavily concentrated in Korean ethnic enclaves. Because of their residential and occupational segregation, they have the least contact with American citizens and therefore have achieved the lowest level of assimilation among the three occupational groups (Min, 1989a: 167–168). Thus, most Korean working-class families maintain Korean lifestyles, including traditional Korean family lifestyles, almost perfectly. Like working-class families in Chinatown (Glenn, 1983; Kwong, 1987), Korean working-class families have an exceptionally high female workforce participation rate. In terms of economic resources, availability of parents at home, and facility with the English language, this group is most disadvantaged in children's education among the three occupational groups.

Younger-Generation Koreans' Coming of Age and Changes in the Family System

About one generation (twenty-five years) has passed since the contemporary mass migration of Koreans to the United States started. This means that many second- and first-generation Koreans have already completed their formal education and established their own families. As Korean immigration has continued to decline since the late 1980s and will continue to decline in the future, these younger-generation Koreans will constitute an increasingly larger proportion of the adult population in the Korean community in the future. The increase in the proportion of younger-generation Koreans, in turn, is likely to lead to significant changes in the structure of the Korean community and family system.

We previously noted that Korean immigrants have three major advantages—group homogeneity, economic segregation, and affiliation with Korean immigrant churches—over other Asian immigrant groups for maintaining strong ethnic ties. Younger-generation Koreans may still have a slight advantage in preserving their language and subculture over other Asian groups because of their cultural homogeneity. However, they will not have the other two major advantages. The majority of second-generation Korean children regularly attend Korean churches accompanied by their parents, yet their ethnic church participation rate is likely to decline to an insignificant proportion when they move away from their parents.[8] Moreover, few second-generation Koreans would be interested in opening up their own businesses involving long hours of work. Instead, they will move into the general labor market, breaking up the economic segregation of their parents. The 1990 census showed that only 11 percent of native-born Koreans in the Los Angeles metropolitan area were self-employed, a rate lower than even that of native-born white Americans (13%) and much lower than that of Korean immigrants (35%) (Min, 1996a, Chapter 5). The high occupational assimilation of second-generation Koreans is likely to facilitate their cultural and social assimilation further, whereas it will diminish ethnic attachment and ethnic solidarity to a great extent.

The high cultural, social, and occupational assimilation of second-generation Koreans will lead to significant changes in their family lifestyles, making their families very similar to white American families. As previously noted, Korean immigrants have a much higher divorce rate than that of the population in South Korea. The assimilation of second-generation Korean Americans into American lifestyles is likely to increase their divorce rate sharply to the level of that of the white American population. The 1990 U.S. census (U.S. Bureau of the Census, 1993c, table 1) revealed that the ratio of married to divorced for the foreign-born Korean male population (15 years old and over) was 30.1 to 1, but the ratio for the native-born Korean male population dropped to 6.9 to 1, even lower than the ratio for the white male population (8.0 to 1) (U.S. Bureau of the Census, 1993a, table 34). The divorce rate of native-born Koreans was inflated because native-born Koreans consisted mainly of young adults who tended to have a higher divorce rate than middle-aged or elderly people. Nevertheless, the radical intergenerational increase in the divorce rate is unquestionable. Moreover, younger-

[8]There are several reasons that the participation of Koreans in an ethnic church will drop in the second generation. First, second-generation Koreans are likely to lose their religious faith more than their parents as they become more secularized with assimilation. Second, participation in church services is less meaningful to native-born Koreans, who do not have the adjustment difficulties that Korean immigrants encounter. Many Korean immigrants attend the church to endure their hardship deriving from their adjustments to an alien environment. Third, many Korean immigrants attend a Korean church to get involved in Korean networks, but most native-born Koreans many not need to find social networks in a Korean church because they have already established networks, ethnic and nonethnic.

generation Koreans, who are generally very critical of their parents' marital relations based on the patriarchal tradition, are likely to maintain more egalitarian marital relations. In addition, second-generation Koreans, who do not embrace the Confucian value of emphasizing education as the main avenue for social mobility, are likely to differ significantly from their parents in child socialization.

SUMMARY AND CONCLUSION

Korean-American adults with their own families of procreation consist mainly of recent immigrants. Characteristics of Korean-American families therefore largely reflect those of Korean immigrant families. Korean immigrants' group homogeneity, occupational concentration in small business, and high level of affiliation with Korean immigrant churches have helped them maintain strong ethnic ties, stronger than those of other Asian immigrant groups. The same factors also have helped them preserve the traditional Korean family system based on Confucian ideology. Their concentration in small business and affiliation with Korean churches in particular have perpetuated more patriarchal marital relations and achievement-oriented socialization practices brought from Korea, isolating them from the larger society. The structure of work at the family store and the nature of the Christian religious ideology themselves have also reinforced Confucian patriarchal ideology.

While Korean immigrants have preserved some traditional Korean family values and practices without much alteration, they have experienced significant changes in other aspects of family life. The radical increase in the workforce participation of Korean immigrant women probably is the most significant change that has occurred to Korean immigrant families. The increase in Korean immigrant women's economic role without significant changes in their or their husbands' gender role attitudes has resulted in Korean women's overwork, stress, and role strain. The Korean immigrant population has a lower divorce rate than that of the white American population but a much higher divorce rate than that of the population in Korea. The radical increase in divorces is another major change that Koreans have experienced since immigration to this country. While 80 percent of elderly persons in South Korea live with their children, most elderly people in the Korean immigrant community live independently. The change in the living arrangements of Korean elderly immigrants involves changes in the other aspects of their lives. The greater independence of elderly Korean Americans from their children in living arrangements and other aspects of their lives can be considered another major change that has occurred to Korean immigrant families.

One generation has already passed since the contemporary mass migration of Koreans to the United States. As more and more second-generation

Korean Americans reach adulthood in the future, younger-generation Koreans are likely to make up an increasingly larger proportion of the Korean-American population in the future, as Korean immigration has been substantially reduced recently. Younger-generation Koreans' movement in the general labor market away from self-employment in small business and their noninvolvement in Korean churches, characteristics that reflect their assimilation into American society, are likely to facilitate their social assimilation further and radically diminish their integration in the Korean ethnic community. Thus, younger-generation Koreans will significantly modify the structure of the Korean family inherited from their parents. An exceptionally high divorce rate of native-born Korean Americans, comparable to that of the white American population, is a good indication of the kinds of changes second-generation Koreans will experience in their family lives.

REFERENCES

Ablemann, Nancy and John Lie. 1995. *Blue Dreams: Korean Americans and the Los Angeles Riots.* Cambridge: Harvard University Press.

Blood, R. O. and D. M. Wolfe. 1960. *Husbands and Wives: The Dynamics of Married Living.* New York: Free Press.

Chiswick, Barry. 1982. "The Economic Progress of Immigrants: Some Universal Patterns," in Barry Chiswick (Ed.), *The Gateway: U.S. Immigration Issues and Policies,* pp. 119–158. Washington, DC: American Enterprise Institute for Public Policy Research.

Choi, Helen. 1995. *The Korean American Experience: A Detailed Analysis of How Well Korean-Americans Adjust to Life in the United States.* New York: Vintage Press.

Eu, Hongsook. 1992. "Health Status and Social and Demographic Determinants of Living Arrangements among the Korean Elderly." *Korea Journal of Population and Development,* 21: 197–224.

Glenn, Evelyn Nakano. 1983. "Split Household, Small Producer, and Dual Wage Earners: An Analysis of Chinese American Family Strategies." *Journal of Marriage and the Family, 45*: 35–46.

Harvey, Young Sook, and Soon-Hyung Chung. 1980. "The Koreans," in John McDermott et al. (Eds.), *People and Cultures of Hawaii,* pp. 135–154. Honolulu: University of Hawaii Press.

Heilman, Samuel. 1982. "The Sociology of American Jewry: The Last 10 Years." *Annual Review of Sociology, 8*: 135–160.

Hurh, Won Moo and Kwang Chung Kim. 1984. *Korean Immigrants in America: A Structural Analysis of Ethnic Confinement and Adhesive Adaptation.* Madison, NJ: Fairleigh Dickinson University Press.

———. 1990. "Religious Participation of Korean Immigrants in the United States." *Journal of the Scientific Study of Religion, 29*: 19–34.

Jeong, Gyung Ja and Walter Schumm. 1990. "Family Satisfaction in Korean/American Marriages: An Exploratory Study of the Perceptions of Korean Wives." *Journal of Comparative Family Studies, 21*: 325–335.

Jioubu, Robert. 1988. *Ethnicity and Assimilation: Blacks, Chinese, Filipinos, Japanese, Koreans, Mexicans, Vietnamese, and Whites.* Albany, NY: State University of New York Press.

Kim, Ai Ra. 1995. *Women Struggling for a New Life: The Role of Religion in the Cultural Passage from Korea to America.* Albany, NY: State University of New York Press.

Kim, Bok-Lim. 1972. "Casework Work Japanese and Korean Wives of Americans." *Social Casework, 53*: 273–279.

———. 1978. *The Asian Americans: Changing Patterns, Changing Needs.* New York: Association of Korean Christian Scholars in North America.

Kim, Hyun Suk and Pyong Gap Min. 1992. "Post-1965 Korean Immigrants: Characteristics and and Settlement Patterns." *Korea Journal of Population and Development, 21*: 121–143.

Kim, Illsoo. 1981. *New Urban Immigrants: The Korean Community in New York.* Princeton: University of Princeton Press.

———. 1987. "Korea and East Asian: Remigration Factors and U.S. Immigration Policy," in James Fawcett and Benjamin Carino (Eds.), *Pacific Bridges: The New Immigration from Asian and the Pacific Islands*, pp. 327–346. Staten Island: Center for Migration Studies.

Kim, Kwang Chung and Won Moo Hurh. 1985. "Ethnic Resources Utilization of Korean Small Businessmen in the United States." *International Migration Review, 19*: 82–111.

———. 1988. "The Burden of Double Roles." *Ethnic and Racial Studies, 11*: 151–167.

Kitano, Harry and Lynn Kyung Chai. 1982. "Korean Interracial Marriage." *Marriage and Family Review, 5*: 35–48.

Korean Bureau of Statistics. 1993. *A Comprehensive Analysis of The 1990 Korean Population and Housing Census (4–3): Korean Household and Family Types.* Seoul: Korean Bureau of Statistics.

Korean Women's Development Institute. 1994. *1994 Statistical Yearbook on Women.* Seoul: Korean Women's Development Institute.

Kwong, Peter. 1987. *The New Chinatown.* New York: Free Press.

Lee, Daniel. 1991. "Contributions and Adjustment Problems of Enterocele Married Korean Women," in Pyong Gap Min (Ed.), *Koreans in the United States* [in Korean]. Seoul: Yurim.

Light, Ivan and Edna Bonacich. 1988. *Immigrant Entrepreneurs: Koreans in Los Angeles, 1965–1982.* Berkeley: The University of California Press.

Min, Pyong Gap. 1984. "From White-Collar Occupations to Small Business: Korean Immigrants' Occupational Adjustment." *Sociological Quarterly, 25*: 333–352.

———. 1988. *Ethnic Business Enterprise: Korean Small Business in Atlanta.* Staten Island: Center for Migration Studies.

———. 1989a. "Some Positive Functions of Ethnic Business for an Immigrants: Koreans in Los Angeles." Final report submitted to National Science Foundation, Queens College of CUNY.

———. 1989b. "The Social Costs of Immigrant Entrepreneurship: A Response to Edna Bonacich." *Amerasia Journal, 15*: 187–194.

———. 1990. "Problems of Korean Immigrant Entrepreneurship." *International Migration Review, 24*: 436–455.

———. 1991a. "Cultural and Economic Boundaries of Korean Ethnicity: A Comparative Analysis." *Ethnic and Racial Studies, 14*: 225–241.

———. 1991b. "Children's Education and Problems in the Korean Immigrant Community," in Pyong Gap Min (Ed.), *Koreans in the United States* [in Korean], pp. 217–248. Seoul: Yurim Publishing Company.

———. 1992a. "The Structure and Social Functions of Korean Immigrant Churches in the United States." *International Migration Review, 26*: 1370–1394.

———. 1992b. "Korean Immigrant Wives's Overwork." *Korea Journal of Population and Development, 21*: 121–143.

———. 1993a. "Korean Immigrants in Los Angeles," in Ivan Light and Parminder Bhachu (eds.), *Immigration and Entrepreneurship*, pp.185–204. New York: Transaction.

———. 1993b. "Korean Immigrants' Marital Patterns and Marital Adjustment," in Harriett McAdoo (ed.), *Family Ethnicity: Strengths in Diversity*, pp. 287–299. Newbury Park, CA: Sage.

———. 1995a. "Korean Americans," in Pyong Gap Min (Ed.), *Asian Americans: Contemporary Trends and Issues*, pp. 199–231. Newbury Park, CA: Sage.

———. 1995b. "The Entrepreneurial Adaptation of Korean Immigrants," in Silvia Pedraza and Ruben Rumbaut (Eds.), *Origins and Destinies: Race, Immigration, and Ethnicity in America*, pp. 303–314. Belmont, CA: Wadsworth.

————. 1995c. "The Relationship Between Korean Immigrant Parents and Children." [in Korean]. *The Academy Review of Korean Studies, 18*: 119–136.

————. 1995d. "Technological Advances and Korean Immigrants' Integration to the Home Country." Paper presented at the annual meeting of the American Sociological Association, Washington, DC.

————. 1996a. *Caught in the Middle: Korean Merchants in America's Multiethnic Cities.* Berkeley: University of California Press.

————. 1996b. "Ethnic Networks and Korean Elderly Persons' Adjustments in the United States." Unpublished manuscript, Department of Sociology, Queens College of CUNY.

————. 1997. "Korean Immigrant Wives' Labor-Force Participation, Marital Power, and Status," in Elizabeth Higginbotham and Mary Romero (Eds.), *Women and Work: Race, Ethnicity, and Class.* Newbury Park, CA: Sage.

Park, In-Sook Han and Lee-Jay Cho. 1995. "Confucianism and the Korean Family." *Journal of Comparative Family Studies, 26*: 117–135.

Patterson, Wayne. 1988. *The Korean Frontier in America: Immigration to Hawaii, 1986–1910.* Honolulu: University of Hawaii Press.

Ratliff, Bascom, Hariett Faye Moon, and Gwendolyn Bonacci. 1978. "Intercultural Marriage: The Korean American Experience." *Social Casework, 59*: 221–226.

Rodman, Hyman. 1967. "Marital Power in France, Greece, Yugoslavia, and the United States: A Cross-National Discussion." *International Migration Review, 20*: 4–20.

Rose, Jushua and Pyong Gap Min. 1992. "A Comparison of Jewish-American and Korean Immigrant Families in Child Socialization." Paper presented at the annual meeting of the American Sociological Association, Pittsburgh.

Shelton, Beth Ann. 1992. *Women, Men and Time.* New York: Greenwood Press.

Shin, Eui-Hang. 1987. "Interracially Married Korean Women in the United States: An Analysis Based on Hypergamy-Exchange Theory," in Eui-Young Yu and Earl Phillips (Eds.), *Korean Women in Transition: At Home and Abroad*, pp. 249–276. Los Angeles: Center for Korean and Korean-American Studies, California State University.

Sklare, Marshall. 1971. *America's Jews.* New York: Random House.

U.S. Bureau of the Census. 1983. *1980 Census of Population, General Population Characteristics, United States Summary* (PC80-1-B1). Washington, DC: U.S. Government Printing Office.

————. 1993a. *1990 Census of Population, General Population Characteristics, United States* (CP-1-1). Washington, DC: U.S. Government Printing Office.

————. 1993b. *1990 Census of Population, Social and Economic Characteristics, United States* (CP-2-1). Washington, DC: U.S. Government Printing Office.

————. 1993c. *1990 Census of Population, Asian and Pacific Islanders in the United States* (CP-3-5). Washington, DC: U.S. Government Printing Office.

Yoon, In-Jin. 1993. "The Social Origin of Korean Immigration to the United States, 1965–Present." Honolulu: East-West Population Institute.

Yu, Eui-Young. 1985. "Koreatown, Los Angeles: Emergence of a New Inner-City Ethnic Community." *Bulletin of Population and Development Studies, 14*: 29–44.

11 | The Vietnamese-American Family

Thanh Van Tran

INTRODUCTION

The Vietnamese population in the United States has grown rapidly in the past two decades: from 261,729 in 1980 to 614,547 in 1990. The percent of population change between 1980 and 1990 was 134.8. This is the highest rate of change among all Asian-American populations (Gardner, Robey, and Smith, 1985; Barringer, Gardner, and Levin, 1993). Demographers have projected that by the year of 2000, the Vietnamese American population will reach 1,574,385 making up 16 percent of all Asian American populations and becoming the third largest Asian-American group after the Filipino and Chinese (Barringer, Gardner, and Levin, 1993). Most Vietnamese Americans are urban residents (95.4%) and have concentrated in major cities, with 9.8 percent in the Northeast, 8.5 percent in the Midwest, 27.4 percent in the South, and 54.3 percent in the West (Barringer, Gardner, and Levin, 1993).

The family is a fundamental social institution in every human society. It follows, then, that to understand the culture of a group or a society, one needs to understand the structure, the evolution, and functions of the family in such a group or society. With this in mind, this chapter will attempt to provide a comprehensive review of the Vietnamese family in American society. It will focus on the following areas:

1. The historical background of Vietnamese society
2. The traditional Vietnamese family in the context of history and culture
3. The history of immigration and resettlement
4. The present-day Vietnamese family in the United States
5. The processes of adaptation of the Vietnamese family in America

HISTORICAL BACKGROUND

A well-known national legend has it that the Vietnamese people are children of the dragons and grandchildren of the fairies. According to this ancient legend, the son of the first Vietnamese king of the Xich Qui kingdom, Lac Long Quan, whose mother was a daughter of the dragons, married Au Co, who was a daughter of the fairies. Au Co gave birth to 100 eggs that became 100 sons. Then Lac Long Quan decided to separate from Au Co, telling her they could not live together as a family because he came from the dragons and she came from the fairies. They agreed to split their family; he took fifty sons and moved to the seashore, and she took fifty sons and moved to the mountains. Lac Long Quan later made his first son the king of Van Lang, and he became the ancestor of the Vietnamese people (Dao, 1961; Do, 1962). This legend might be interpreted as a symbol of the first Vietnamese family conflict.

There are, in fact, different scholarly theories about the origin of the Vietnamese people. Some believe that the Vietnamese came from China; others that the Vietnamese have Melanesian and Indonesian origins (Pham, 1960; Nguyen, 1967). Hinton (1985:91) suggests that "from their physical appearance, the Vietnamese appear to have a common ancestry with the Malays, Indonesians and Polynesians of Southern Asia, but there is a definite Mongolian element also present."

No matter what their origin, the Vietnamese developed their own culture and national identity over thousands of years (Nguyen, 1967:2). They have their own language and social institutions, including family, religion, education, economy, and political systems. Historically, the Vietnamese people have been continuously subjected to the domination, colonization, and invasion from outside forces, including a thousand years of Chinese domination and a hundred years of French colonization. In addition, they have been torn apart by political conflict within the nation itself (Nguyen, 1967; Marr, 1981). At the end of the French colonization, Vietnamese started fighting each other and the country was divided into North and South Vietnam. The civil war between the North and South ended in 1975. In 1978, Vietnam invaded Cambodia and another war began (Hinton, 1985). More than 1 million Vietnamese have fled their country seeking asylum in the West since 1975.

In 1994, Vietnam had an estimated population of 74 million, with an annual rate of population growth of 2.4 percent. The country had an infant mortality rate of 36 per 1,000, and life expectancy was 67 years for women and 63 years for men. Currently, Vietnam is one of the poorest countries on earth, with a per capita income of about $220 (U.S. Department of Commerce, 1995; Swearer, 1984; Hinton, 1985). Several ethnic groups that make up the total population of Vietnam: the Vietnamese (85–90%), the Chinese, the Muong, the Thai, the Meo, the Khmer, the Man, the Cham, and mountain tribes (U.S. Department of State, 1995; Hinton, 1985). Ethnic minority groups in Vietnam have their own languages and cultures (Kunstadter, 1967; Hickey, 1982). In religion, Vietnam has traditionally been a tolerant society. Religions practiced in this country include Confucianism, Buddhism, Taoism, Christianity (Roman Catholicism and Protestantism), Hoa Hao, Cao Dai, animism, and Islam there is no one national religion. There have been times when Confucianism and Buddhism were considered the main national religions, but people were not forced to belong to any religion. Buddhism has the largest number of adherents because many Vietnamese tend to claim they are Buddhist if they do not belong to any particular religion.

In prehistoric times, Vietnamese society was a matriarchal tribal society in which the mother was the head of the family. Later, Vietnam developed a simple feudal society in which the king was the head of the country. Under the king were chiefs of tribes, and each tribe had different family clans, with a clan head called the Truong Toc. In the feudal period, Vietnamese society was dominated by the male, who was also the head of the family.

During a thousand years of Chinese domination of Vietnam, the Chinese significantly influenced Vietnamese culture. However, most Vietnamese and Western historians agree that Vietnamese culture, while containing many similarities to Chinese culture, has managed to preserve its own unique national characteristics and identity (Dao, 1961; Do, 1962). The ability to preserve their unique identity under different external influences was determined by their will to fight against the invaders. Taylor (1983:xviii) explains that "no theme is more consistent in Vietnam history than the theme of resistance to foreign aggression." With such a long history, Vietnamese society accumulated many traditions that have been passed down from generation to generation.

Traditional Vietnamese Society

Although it is hard to describe traditional Vietnamese society exactly, Pham (1960) and other historians agree that following the prehistoric period it was similar in many ways to traditional Chinese society. The king occupied the highest social position. He was considered the "Thien Tu" ("son of God") and had absolute power. In the family, the head of a family also had absolute power. There were two main social classes, the rulers and the ruled. The rulers were kings and their significant others. Among the ruled, there were four traditional occupations: scholar, farmer, artisan, and trader. Scholars held the most respected occupation in society. Because this social group had access to governmental positions, they could potentially help their entire family and their village. Not all scholars were appointed to serve the king; many remained in their villages as teachers or medicine men. Their sons had continued the scholarly tradition of learning, preparing for exams, and waiting for the chance to become mandarins. Most of the population were farmers, including landless farmers, and landowner farmers; a small number were artisans or traders. An old Vietnamese proverb says: "The scholar ranks first, and then the peasant; but when the rice fails and men run wildly about, then the peasant comes first, and the scholar second" (Do, 1962:138).

In traditional Vietnamese society, the village was considered next in importance to one's family. Nguyen (1967:16) describes a traditional Vietnamese village as "a group of patriarchal families whose members shared the same family name." More than that, the village was the place in the past where most Vietnamese were born, grew up, got married, built their houses, and died. A typical traditional village is a combination of several extended families. In those villages, the larger the family, the more influential and powerful tends to be. Traditional villages have their own cultures, deity, traditions, and laws.

Recent studies offer new revelations about the traditional Vietnamese village. It could be a single extended family–based type, with all village members belonging to an extended family system. Such single extended family–based villages often bear the names of their founders. Outsiders are excluded from these family-based villages. In some villages, outside people could only migrate to a village if they changed their family names and adapted the village family name. Other villages require that an outsider can live in the village if that person is adopted by the village. Many traditional villages are founded on public land where villagers farm the public-owned land and pay taxes to the government for use of the land.

The Traditional Vietnamese Family

Toan Anh (1969), a well-known scholar of Vietnamese tradition and culture, notes that a Vietnamese person usually cares about his or her family more than himself or herself. In traditional Vietnamese society, the family is the center of an individual's life and activities. The word "family" in Vietnamese means a social entity that consists of all an individual's relatives, not just father, mother, and siblings. Some authors have argued that the traditional Vietnamese family was modeled after the traditional Chinese family in terms of its ethical and moral structure (Pham, 1960: Toan Anh, 1969: Vuong, 1980; Che, 1979). Others have stressed that the traditional family in Vietnamese culture is a dynamic concept that is not really capable of definition (Tran, 1991). Though Chinese culture has had a deep influences on Vietnamese culture, the Vietnamese family has its own unique structure and culture.

The teachings of Confucius clearly define the power, position, and relationship of each member of a family. There are certain fundamental characteristics of the traditional family, such as domination by sex hierarchy (father-son relationship), by age hierarchy (the elderly have more power), the center of loyalty, and the cult of ancestor worship. An individual is expected to be loyal to his or her family and obey and respect elders. Parents are required to raise and educate their children. Children are required to take care of their parents when they become old or sick and to worship their parents when they die.

Tran (1991) discusses two typical traditional Vietnamese families: the scholar family and the peasant family. These two types of traditional family differ in economic and social factors. Scholar families enjoy high social status and respect from society and depend on the achievement of the male head of the family. If he is a success, that is, he passes exams and is appointed to serve the king, his family will receive salaries and be given public land. For traditional scholar families, family life and activities are centered around the men's studies and taking exams. The main goal of traditional scholar families is to support the husbands or sons in their studies and wait for their educational success to secure the family's economic well-being. Scholars who do not pass exams or are not called to serve the king often stay in their villages as teachers or medicine men. Women are the key providers in scholar families. In classic Vietnamese literature, several scholars praised their wives for their economic support. A renowned classic Vietnamese scholar, Tran Te Xuong (1870–1907), who failed his exams and never had adequate means to support himself and his family wrote several famous poems praising his wife as the key breadwinner of his family. Tran Te Xuong's poems about his wife reflected the role of women in traditional scholar family, especially those who did not pass exams or were not appointed to serve the king.

The majority of traditional Vietnamese families are peasant families organized around agricultural seasons and activities. In a typical traditional village, most peasants do not own land. They work on public land or for more wealthy peasant families. Landless peasant families have to earn their living by doing different things beside farming. Wealthy peasant families are self-sufficient in every aspects. Family activities in the traditional Vietnamese family are agricultural and related farming structures.

Vietnamese Kinship System

The Vietnamese kinship system is a patrilineal, or male-oriented, kinship system (Hickey, 1964; Luong, 1984). The term for the kinship system in the Vietnamese language, *Ho*, describes an extended family system that includes both living and the dead members. The *Ho* consists of a combination of small families (*Nha*) of different generations. There are two types of *Ho*: *Ho Noi* and *Ho Ngoai*. The *Ho Noi* consists of all relatives on the father's side, and the *Ho Ngoai* consists of all relatives on the mother's side. Members of the *Ho Noi* are prohibited from marrying each other. Members of the third generation of the *Ho Ngoai* are allowed to marry each other. Spencer (1945:286) in his classic study describes the Vietnamese kinship system as "bifurcate collateral in that it distinguishes paternal and maternal aunts and uncles from one another as well as from the parents."

Very little has been written about the Vietnamese kinship system. The available anthropological studies examine only the structural pattern of the kinship system (Spencer, 1945; Benedict, 1947; Luong, 1984), and there are few studies on the evolution, relationship, and function of the kinship system in terms of individual Vietnamese life situations. To better understand the traditional Vietnamese family, we must to study the role and function of each member within the family unit.

The Head of the Family and the Father

In a traditional Vietnamese extended family, the head of the family is called the *Truong Toc*. The *Truong Toc* is the oldest male, and he is responsible for maintaining the patrimonial land, ancestral graves, and the worship of the common ancestors. He makes decisions about matters related to the lives of the extended family.

The heads of the traditional Vietnamese nuclear family (*Gia Truong*) are the grandparents, if they are alive. On the death of the grandparents, the father becomes the head of the family, and the eldest son will take over this position at the death of the father. Traditionally, the head of the family has absolute power over the members of his family. Toan Anh (1969) notes that the role of the head of the family is similar to the role of the king. Nguyen (1967:15) explains this further: "At the top of each family, the paterfamilias or *gia-truong* exercised an absolute authority over his wife and children. He had full power to act and command. He was invested with rights prevailing over those of the other members of the family."

The head of the family is responsible not only for the living members of the family but also for those who are deceased. His obligations are to take care of the living and to worship the spirits of the dead. Under traditional law, the head of the family also bears the legal responsibility for all members of the family. The law punishes a father for failing to prevent his children or other members of the family from committing crimes (Whitfield, 1976).

The Mother and the Wife

In traditional society Vietnamese women, like Chinese women (Toan Anh, 1969; Che, 1979) have no power and fewer privileges than Vietnamese men. A Vietnamese woman is expected to obey her father when she is single and her husband after she gets married and to live with her eldest son when she becomes a widow. Morally, she is not expected to marry again after her husband dies. After her marriage, a Vietnamese woman is expected to live with her husband's parents until her husband is ready to have his own house, to obey them absolutely, and to serve and care for them. Her husband has the right to punish her if he thinks that she has done something wrong. She can be divorced by her husband under seven conditions: (1) if she disobeys her husband's parents, (2) if she cannot have children, (3) if she commits adultery, (4) if she is overly jealous, (5) if she has an incurable disease, (6) if she is garrulous, and (7) if she is a thief (Toan Anh, 1969). There are three conditions under which a husband is not permitted to divorce his wife: (1) if she has been in mourning for her husbands' relatives for three years, (2) if she and her husband become rich after the marriage (they were both poor before their marriage), and (3) if no one will be available to take care of her if her husband divorces her (Phan, 1975). A woman cannot leave or separate from her husband; this act is viewed as a crime. The only area in which a husband and wife have equal rights are properties and debts.

In many traditional villages, polygamy was common before the 1959 Family Bill was passed by the National Assembly of the South Vietnamese government, making both polygamy and concubinage illegal (Hickey, 1964). At the same time, the North Vietnamese government also abolished polygamy in its national constitution (Nguyen, 1993). Under polygamy, the first wife in a family had more power than her followers. The first wife could decide to find another wife for her husband if she felt that he needed one. There were some common features in the practice of polygamy: It often occurred among the rich; in families in which the first wife could not have children, especially sons; and in families that needed more people to work on the farm.

As a woman and a wife, a Vietnamese woman has very limited rights. She has to accept control by the men in her life: father, husband, and son. Vietnamese women in traditional society begin to gain some power when they become mothers. A mother holds the second rank in power in a family after the father. She can expect her children to obey and respect her and she manages her family in the absence of her husband. Many Vietnamese mothers raised and managed their families while their husbands were engaged in war(s). Vietnam has experienced so many wars and revolutions in its history that as a result Vietnamese women had no choice but to assume the role of head of the family.

Children

The teachings of Confucius require children to obey and respect their parents. Children's piety for their parents is regarded as the most important moral obligation of children while their parents are alive and after they die (Phan, 1975). Vietnamese children must live with their parents until they are married and have their own house (Toan Anh, 1969); they are expected to contribute to the family economy, but they own nothing. When they are old enough, they are required to work and bring home their wages and salaries. The parents are obligated to provide for all of the children's needs.

Socialization

The socialization process of Vietnamese children take place in everyday life situations. The teachings of Confucius give the father the most responsibility in socializing children. One of the traditional principles of the role of the father is that of *Duong bat giao, phu chi qua*, which means that failing to raise a child appropriately is the mistake of the father. However, society tends to blame the mother for the child's misconduct or deviant behavior. An old Vietnamese saying, *con hu tai me*, means that a child is spoiled by the mother (Toan Anh, 1969). Mothers tend to take their children with them to visit neighbors and attend religious or social ceremonies, to teach them how to deal with different people, and how to behave in different social situations. A boy's socialization is dependent on the father when the boy reaches 6 or 7 years old. The mother continues to socialize her daughter as long as the daughter is single. In general, children learn social conduct by participating in the family's everyday activities and by observing the parents' and older siblings' behaviors in different social situations. Parents and the older siblings are expected to set good examples for their children and younger siblings. Life experiences are passed down from grandparents to parents, from parents to older siblings, and from older to younger siblings.

Sibling

In the traditional Vietnamese family hierarchy, older people have more power than younger people. The eldest son in the family (*Anh Ca* or *Anh Hai*) is expected to assume more responsibility in taking care of the family after the death of his father. A Vietnamese proverb states, "The older brother has the same power as the father in the absence of the father." The older sister also has more power than her younger brothers and sisters. Siblings of the same parents are called *Dong Bao*; siblings of the same father but different mothers are called *Di Bao*. Siblings are expected to express mutual affection and protection for each other. When one is in trouble, the others are obligated to help. Vietnamese siblings are expected to share everything they have with each other while they live under the same roof. However, Vietnamese parents often think about their son's education before that of their daughters. In traditional Vietnamese society, only boys are educated; females are excluded. Traditional scholars are all males because only male scholars take exams and are called to serve the king. Although there are female heads of the country, no females had been appointed as mandarins throughout the ancient history of Vietnam.

The Elderly

As in many traditional societies (Keith, 1990), old age is respected and valued in traditional Vietnamese society (Toan-Anh, 1965). The hierarchy of social status differs between government and village. In government, the hierarchy is defined by position, whereas age determines social status in a village. The older a person is, the higher his social status. For example, Le (1992) noted that in traditional village festivals the most important ceremony (*Dai*

Tè) was performed by seventeen or twenty-one men who were the elders or people with highest education in the village. It should be noted that although both elderly men and women are equally respected, the attendant social status is for men more than for women.

Old people are respected because of their experience, skills, and knowledge. They are also respected because of their longevity. In Vietnamese culture longevity is one of the three conditions of happiness after esteem (social status) and numerous children. When a person reaches 50, 60, or 70 years of age, his children must give him a reception at the village's communal hall to honor and celebrate his longevity. The older the person is, the bigger the reception. The children have to prepare special food as thanks-giving-gifts to the gods for their parent's longevity. The longevity reception is also a way for children to show appreciation to their parents and their willingness to take care of them in their old age. However, because Vietnam is a traditionally patriarchal society, old men have more power than their women counterparts. In many regions in Vietnam, if both elderly parents are alive, children often celebrate their father's longevity, not their mother's. The mother's longevity is celebrated if the father is dead.

The traditional civil code requires children to take care of their elderly parents. Those who mistreated their elderly parents are subjected to caning, with the maximum punishment eighty lashes. However, the punishment is executed only if the elderly parent files a formal complaint against his or her children (Dao, 1961). It is unusual, however, for parents to bring their children to court for abuse and/or neglect. Because of close social control and fear of losing face with neighbors and relatives. Contemporary Vietnamese family codes require that all children share equal responsibility in taking care of their parents when they are unable to take care of themselves. Grandchildren are responsible for their grandparents' economic well-being when they don't have the means or sources of support (Nguyen, 1993). A study of an ancient village in North Vietnam found a written village code of social conduct that specifically required all villagers to assist the elderly. The village law stated that "anyone who met an elderly on a street carrying heavy things must assist that elderly person. Those who ignored such an elderly, person were subjected to punishment" (Phan, 1992).

Marriage

The ultimate goal of marriage in traditional Vietnamese society is to bear children (Toan Anh, 1965). According to the teachings of Confucius, marriage is a ceremony that allows a man to continue his family clan by having new children (Dao, 1961). Parents chose the marriage partner for their children. There is an old Vietnamese saying that "one needs to know the origin of the man or woman whom one would marry." It is also assumed that only parents have the proper knowledge to choose a wife or a husband for their children. Boys and girls are not allowed to date or choose their own mate. In traditional Vietnamese society, boys are allowed to marry at 16 years of age and girls at 13. However, in traditional scholar families, parents look for a wife for a student after his graduation.

Marriage is one of the most important events in a Vietnamese person's life. Traditionally, the marriage ceremony is complicated and colorful, encompassing five different traditional ceremonial events in the celebration (Toan Anh, 1965). The first ceremony, *Le Ban Tin*, is held after the parents and the son find the right girl in the village. The parents ask the *Ba Mai* ("matchmaker woman") who knows the young woman's family to deliver a message about their desire to marry her to their son. The *Ba Mai* also observes the reaction of the young woman's family to the proposal and reports it to the young man's parents. The second ceremony, *Le Cham Ngo*, is held after the young woman's parents accept the proposal of the young man's parents and allows the young man and his parents to take a good look at the young woman and her family. In the third ceremony, *Le An Giam*, the young man's parents send someone with gifts to the girl's family to ask for her birth certificate. The fourth ceremony, *Le An Hoi*, requires both families to officially announce the engagement of their children. Between *Le An Hoi* and the wedding ceremony, the young man must practice *Sieu*, which means that he has to bring gifts to the girl's parents in March, May, August, and October, with each of these months representing a season. These gifts are often local agricultural products. Besides the *Sieu*, the man is required to bring gifts to the young woman's house for special religious or social ceremonies such as the *Tet* (New Year's day). In many traditional villages, the young man has to work for the woman's family for a certain period of time and do anything that the girl's family wants. Last comes the wedding ceremony, *Le Than Nghinh* or *Le Hon Nhan*, in which the man's family brings the new daughter-in-law home. This is the most important ceremony, and it is complicated and costly. Often the entire village, including relatives and guests from the bride's family, is invited to the ceremony, and all expenses are paid by the groom's family.

These wedding traditions vary from village to village or among geographical regions. Today marriage ceremonies have become simpler. People often practice only three ceremonies: the first meeting between the man's family and the woman's family, the engagement ceremony, and the wedding ceremony. In general, after the marriage ceremony, the young couple live with the husband's family. The new daughter-in-law has to completely adjust and adapt to her husband's parents. She is expected to obey her husband's parents and to do everything to please them. The couple will live with the husband's parents until they are able to build their own house or can afford to live independently.

Marriage to Foreigners

Vietnam was under the domination of China for a thousand years, followed by a hundred-year period of French colonization and twenty years of U.S. and Soviet influence during the period of the Vietnam War. Though Vietnam has a long history of exposure to foreigners and foreign cultures, marriages with foreigners have been considered taboo. Traditionally, Vietnamese women were expected to marry men in the same village. An old Vietnamese saying states, "A woman is better off marrying the poorest man in her own village than the richest man in another village." This traditional attitude has had significant influence on the Vietnamese attitude toward women who marry foreigners. Toan Anh (1969) notes that there is more concern about women who marry foreigners than about men who do so. Although noblewomen such as women from the royal family married foreigners, general public opinion has been negative toward women who marry foreigners, especially Western foreigners.

Immigration History and Resettlement

The terms "Indochinese refugee" or "Southeast Asian refugee" have been used to refer to refugees who have arrived in the United States since 1975 from the three nations of Indochina: Cambodia (Kampuchea), Laos, and Vietnam. Although Indochinese refugees share some cultural, historical, and religious similarities, differences remain to make each of them a unique group of people with their own language, nationality, ethnic identity, history and culture (see Strand and Jones, 1985; Gordon, 1987). Since they share a similar history of immigration to the United States, it is important to include all three nations in this discussion of immigration history and community development.

Unlike other Asian-American groups with a long history of immigration in the United States, Indochinese refugees are the most recent immigrant group, arriving in large numbers since 1975. Statistics show that before 1975 there were very few Indochinese immigrants in the United States. Indeed, in the 1950s there were only 179 Indochinese immigrants; this population increased to 3,503 in the 1960s, and 18,558 in 1974 (Gordon, 1987). The Vietnamese make up the largest subgroup of the Indochinese population in the United States.

On April 30, 1975, when the South Vietnamese government collapsed, more than 100,000 Vietnamese escaped from South Vietnam to avoid persecution by the North Vietnamese communists. South Vietnamese soldiers, government officials, businessmen, religious leaders, students, fishermen, and people from every social class in South Vietnam risked their lives for a new, unknown homeland. The American government quickly responded to the Vietnamese refugee crisis by ordering its navy in the Pacific to rescue

Vietnamese refugees (Montero, 1979). Refugee centers were established to receive and process the first group of Vietnamese refugees arriving in America even though more than half of the American people believed that Vietnamese refugees should not be allowed to enter or remain in the United States (Newsweek, 1975). Schaefer (1979:122) describes the American perception of Vietnamese refugees in 1975:

> In almost all segments of the population—the college educated, the rich, the poor, Blacks, Protestants, and Catholics—only the minority favored permitting the South Vietnamese to live in the country. Only the young, those under thirty, seemed to favor settlement but even a third of that group rejected the idea. Rejection was greatest among the working class, where almost two-thirds opposed accepting South Vietnamese.

Despite this strong rejection by the American public against the settlement of Vietnamese refugees, the U.S. government felt a moral obligation to receive Vietnamese refugees. (The United States was not the only nation that gave political asylum to Vietnamese refugees; more than a dozen nations in the world responded kindly to the problem.) The influx of Vietnamese refugees has continued from 1975 to the present, and Vietnamese refugees have concentrated and built their communities in specific areas of the country. Thus, despite the U.S. government's initial resettlement policy (that attempted to disperse Indochinese refugees throughout the country), another migration occurred within the Vietnamese refugee population soon after their arrival in the United States. After their initial settlement, many Vietnamese started moving to California, Texas, and other areas with a high concentration of Vietnamese.

The first wave of Vietnamese refugees who arrived in the United States in 1975 were well educated and have successfully adapted to American society. More recent Vietnamese refugees, however, have come from a lower socioeconomic level in Vietnam and tend to experience more socioeconomic problems than their first-wave counterparts (Strand and Jones, 1985). Nguyen (1985) identifies four types of Vietnamese refugees in the United States:

1. The first-wave refugees, who left South Vietnam at the end of the war in 1975 and tend to be more educated than the later refugees or immigrants.
2. The second-wave refugees, also called the "boat people," who left Vietnam during the 1978/1979 period, when the Vietnamese communist government tried to eliminate the Chinese business community and forced them to leave the country. Thousands of ethnic Chinese Vietnamese along with Vietnamese who falsified their ethnic identification as Chinese left Vietnam.
3. The escapees, who either organized their trips by way of boats to Thailand, Malaysia, Singapore, and Japan or by walking across the borders of Laos and Cambodia to Thailand.

4. The orderly departees, who emigrated since 1979 after the Vietnamese communist government agreed with the United Nations High Commissioner for Refugees to allow Vietnamese to join their immediate relatives such as parents, spouses, children, and siblings abroad. In addition, the U.S. government also accepted its former employees from Vietnam.

Since then there are also two special groups arriving in the U.S.: Amerasians and former political detainees and their families. The former political detainees are people who were imprisoned in Vietnam because of their links with the former South Vietnamese governments or with the U.S. government. The majority of these people are men in their late forties or mid-fifties. They often arrived with their immediate families. These unique groups of Vietnamese immigrants, who came with different backgrounds and expectations, have brought a new life to Vietnamese-American communities.

Since 1980, many Vietnamese communities have been developed and established throughout the United States. These communities offer newcomers all kinds of supports and services that the earlier Vietnamese refugees did not have. In addition, many recent immigrants were more prepared because they knew their destination while their predecessors did not, nor did they had time to prepare for their journey. For example, a well-educated former political detainee recalls his story:

> Once I knew I was permitted to come to America, I did everything I could to prepare myself and my family for the journey. I forced my children to learn English as much as they could. I myself got a job as a tourist guide for a travel agency so I could practice my English with English speaking tourists. I also worked as a waiter in restaurants which catered to foreigners to practice my English.

A middle-aged woman who came to join her husband from a rural village in Vietnam recalls:

> I knew I had to prepare myself to get a job in America. He [my husband] warned me that everybody needs a job here and it's not like working in a rice or coffee farm in my village. So I went to town to learn to sew and to operate sewing machines. Unfortunately there are no sewing jobs around here. And even if there were sewing jobs, I could not do it because things are different here. I need to learn English first. I wished I could learn English in Vietnam, but there were no English classes in my Village.

From 1975 to the end of 1993, more than 1 million Indochinese refugees arrived in the United States. Among them are 632,713 Vietnamese, who accounted for 59 percent of all Indochinese people (U.S. Office of Refugee Resettlement, 1993). The 1990 census data show that Vietnamese Americans are concentrated in fourteen U.S. metropolitan areas (see Table

TABLE 11-1. Distribution of Large Vietnamese-American Communities in Fourteen U.S. Metropolitan Areas

Metropolitan Areas	Number
Anaheim–Santa Ana, CA	71,822
Los Angeles–Long Beach, CA	62,594
San Jose, CA	54,212
Houston, TX	33,035
Washington, DC–MD–VA	23,408
San Diego, CA	21,118
Oakland, CA	16,732
Seattle, WA	12,617
San Francisco, CA	12,451
Dallas, TX	11,522
New Orleans, LA	11,419
Riverside–San Bernardino, CA	10,454
Sacramento, CA	10,454
Philadelphia, PA	10,418

Source: Gale Research Inc., Statistical Record of Asian Americans, 1995.

11-1): eight in California, one in Philadelphia, two in Texas, one in Washington, one in Louisiana, and one in Washington, D.C. and surrounding areas (Gall and Gall, 1995).

THE VIETNAMESE FAMILY IN AMERICA

Background

There is no doubt that the present-day Vietnamese family in the United States is the product of the traditional family in Vietnamese society. One of the significant values of the traditional Vietnamese family is the mutual caring or concern among its members; the old saying "One drop of blood is much more precious than a pond full of water" means that one should always value one's relatives no matter who they are. As Bell (1985:30) notes: "All the various explanations of the Asian Americans' success tend to fall into one category: self-sufficiency. The first element of this self-sufficiency is family." Although traditional family values continue to influence contemporary Vietnamese families, one should realize that changes in economic, social-cultural, and technological environments have modified the family structure, traditions and values of overseas Vietnamese families. Vuong (1976:21–22) describes the Vietnamese family prior to arrival in the United States:

It is a mini-commune where its members live and share together, a maternity center where children are born, a funeral home where funeral rituals are performed, a religious place where the family altar is set up to revere ancestors or observe rituals, a welfare center where assistance and social security services are rendered, a nursing home where the elderly are taken good care of, an educational institution where family and formal education is provided, a bank where money is available, and a place where all members share the joys, the sadness, the enjoyments, the suffering of life.

Vuong's description of the Vietnamese family is an ideal one which is no longer true of many contemporary Vietnamese families, especially the Vietnamese-American family. In the midst of a changing world, traditional values seem to be losing ground. However, a Vietnamese person can always depend on family or relatives in time of need, and it is a moral obligation to support one's family and relatives. The responsibilities of an individual Vietnamese person to his or her family are the same no matter how far this person may live from his or her family. Haines, Rutherford, and Thomas (1981), who have studied the Vietnamese refugee family and community structure in the United States, note that the Vietnamese family has no geographical boundary; its members are bound together by traditional values and moral obligations.

The following case is an example of a Vietnamese person's responsibilities toward his family though he has been separated from them since his early teens.

Phan is a Vietnamese graduate student in his late twenties who arrived in the United States with his relatives some fifteen years ago when he was still a young boy. His parents and siblings are still in Vietnam. Phan carries great responsibilities because he is the only son who has opportunities to provide economic support to his family. Since he is able to support himself, he has managed to send home at least $2,000 a year in the last couple of years. This source of income has tremendously improved the quality of life of his parents and siblings in Vietnam. However, he has concerns about whether he will be able to send home money forever, especially, when he marries and raises his own family.

Phan's story is not an exception in the Vietnamese-American community and other overseas Vietnamese communities. Numerous Vietnamese persons of all ages and gender groups have continued to support their immediate and extended families even though they live far apart. However, not all Vietnamese persons feel the same sense of responsibility toward the well-being of other family members. The following case is an example of Vietnamese persons who place their own well-being before their family.

The Nguyen A family is a well-to-do family who arrived in the United States in 1975. Mr. and Mrs. Nguyen A have three children, and all of them are college graduates with decent jobs. Mr. and Mrs. Nguyen have been constantly in conflict because they cannot agree on whether they should send money to help their siblings in Vietnam. Mrs. Nguyen's philosophy is that she has to work very hard to maintain her family living standard; therefore, she is responsible only for her children. Mr. Nguyen has complained that his wife is extravagant in many respects. For example, he argues that she could use the money she spent on her jewelry to help his and her siblings in Vietnam. Mrs. Nguyen's rationale is that she bought expensive jewelry as an investment for her children. She will give them all of it when she dies. Mr. Nguyen has not been able to influence her in helping relatives and has been very resentful toward her.

In other families, conflicts often occur either because the wife or the husband has sent too much money to help relatives in Vietnam. Long-distance family responsibilities are a source of family stress and conflict in many Vietnamese-American families.

Characteristics of the Vietnamese-American Family

The structure of the Vietnamese American family has changed significantly during the past two decades. Table 11-2 shows several of these interesting alterations. The overall number of families has increased threefold between 1980 and 1990, there is a slight decrease in the percent of married-couple families. This last change reflects the divorce problem in the Vietnamese-American family. Although there has been a lack of accurate information on the Vietnamese-American divorce rate, divorce has increased in all overseas Vietnamese communities. Changes in social structural, attitudes toward the family, economic conditions, and gender roles are thought to be contributing factors to the divorce phenomena within the Vietnamese American population. There were also changes in the percent of single head-

TABLE 11-2.   Demographic Characteristics of the Vietnamese-American Family

Characteristics	1980 Census	1990 Census
Number of families	42,261	119,466
Married-couple families	72.8%	70.6%
Female householder	14.8%	16.2%
Male householder	12.4%	13.2%
Persons per family	5.15	4.36
Median family income	$12,840	$30,550
Median household income	$12,549	$29,772
Per capita income	$3,382	$9,032
Families in poverty	14,834	8,332
Percent of families in poverty	35.1%	15.6%
Percent of workers in families		
No workers	21.4%	13.6%
1 worker	27.5%	25.1%
2 workers	35.9%	40.0%
3 or more	15.2%	21.3%

Source: U.S. Bureau of the Census, 1983, 1993.

of-household families between 1980 and 1990, a figure that further corroborates the reduction in married-couple families. The average size of the family appears to be smaller in 1990 than 1980, indicating some structural changes. This could mean that family members, such as older children, married or moved out to live independently.

In terms of economic conditions, several positive changes have occurred in the past two decades. The family income increased twofold between 1980 and 1990, per capita income increased threefold, and the percent of families in poverty also decreased drastically. Economic achievement seems to be influenced by the increase in the number of workers in the Vietnamese family. In short, the data in Table 11-2 reveal significant changes in the Vietnamese-American family structure and its economic adaptation in the past two decades. From an economic perspective, the Vietnamese-American family has adjusted and adapted well to the mainstream American way. Changes in median family income and percent of families in poverty between 1980 and 1990 have demonstrated the economic success of the Vietnamese American family.

The following case illustrates some family factors that contribute to the economic adaptation and success of the Vietnamese family in America.

> The Nguyen B family arrived in the United States in 1975. This extended family has seven small families with thirty-seven persons. The families first resettled in Iowa through the refugee sponsor program of the United States Catholic Conference (USCC). Because no sponsor could take the whole extended family in one community, they decided to settle in close proximity as adult members of the families found jobs in various local mink farms and food processing factories. This extended family stayed in Iowa for about two years. The head of the extended family, a strong and wise man, decided that the family had to move to an area with a larger Vietnamese population because some of the children in the families were ready to marry and there were not enough Vietnamese in Iowa for them to court. Accordingly, they moved to Southern California, with the largest Vietnamese community in the United States. They stayed in California for two years, during which time some older children were able to marry. Mr. Nguyen learned a trade, which later became the main source of economic stability for the whole extended family, by becoming an upholsterer through a public job training program.
>
> Because California was too expensive for the family to own a decent house, they decided to move to Texas in 1978 and have lived in the Dallas–Fort Worth metropolitan area ever since. Few Vietnamese Americans have done as exceptionally well as the Nguyen B family. All children who arrived in the United States in their early twenties and younger have college degrees in engineering, business, and medicine. There are four medical doctors in the immediate family of Mr. Nguyen, three with masters degrees. Children from other branches of this extended family also have done exceptionally well, and many graduated from colleges with advanced professional degrees in engineering, law and medicine. Education attainment was the family's goal, and all activities of

the family centered around the children's education, putting great pressure on all children to achieve. Mr. Nguyen demands great respect from his own children and members of his extended family. At the same time, he gave them a sense of direction and goals. Family ties and respect for education are the key for economic and educational success of the Nguyen family.

Although Mr. Nguyen B's family appears to be an exception, many Vietnamese-American families have done well because they were able to preserve their traditional family values. There are also a number of Vietnamese-American families whose children are not as successful as those in the Nguyen B's family. The two following cases illustrate the lack of traditional family values and its impact on the children and family members.

Mr. Phan was a middle-aged man who arrived in the United States in 1980 with a 15-year-old son and left his wife and three other children in Vietnam. The whole family was reunited in the United States seven years later. Mr. Phan was busy earning money to support the family in Vietnam and paid very little attention to his son while they shared an apartment with three other single men to save money. There was no sense of a family relationship in the household and Mr. Phan never gave his son any encouragement or was able to help him with schoolwork. The boy got a part-time job and spent his own money as he wished. Eventually he dropped out of school and moved away without his father's permission. He did not even contact his family after his mother and other siblings arrived in the United States.

The second case involves the family of a single mother whose husband was in Vietnam when she and four children came to the United States.

Ms. Hai came to the United States with four young children in 1975. As a single mother in her late thirties with little education and skills, she worked in a factory and moonlighted by sewing for a Vietnamese man who had a work contract with a local garment factory. Basically, she worked at least 15 hours a day seven days a week to support the family. The children were doing fine until their adolescence, when the oldest boy dropped out of high school, held several odd jobs, and became an alcoholic. Two girls finished high school and got married early as a means of getting out of the house. The youngest boy was involved in drugs and had problems with the law. Economically, Mrs. Hai has been a successful woman. After several years of hard work, she now owns three houses, but she has never been happy because of her children's failure in education.

In contrast to the Nguyen B family, the families of Mr. Phan and Mrs. Hai did not have a head of household who could provide guidance and moral support for the children. Unfortunately, family relationships in many Vietnamese-American families have deteriorated because of economic pressures and lack of knowledge about the host society.

Family Values

Many of the traditional values of the Vietnamese family are still held by the majority of Vietnamese now in America. However, the American economic system tends to force some changes. For example, Vietnamese children are becoming more economically independent, and many young Vietnamese are now able to work and bring home wages and salaries. Traditionally, the majority of this group would be nonproductive members of their families. If they were students, they would have to depend on their parents for financial support. In addition, many Vietnamese parents are aware of the fact that their children know more about America and Americans than they do; therefore, young Vietnamese are now allowed more freedom. Parents also no longer require their children to live with them until they get married, as they did in Vietnam. Many young Vietnamese, because of their job and career situations, now have to move away from home to work in another city or state. With communication and transportation technology available, the young Vietnamese are changing their attitudes toward dating and marriage. Boys and girls are allowed to go to parties at night without parental supervision.

Family members are still expected to help each other. However, there are some changes in the roles of family members as a result of external influences from the new sociocultural environment. Table 11-3 presents data on a small nonrandom sample from a Vietnamese community on the East Coast that reveal some differing attitudes about families values between children ($N = 52$) under 18 years old and their parents ($N = 56$). Data in Table 11-3 show that children often have different attitudes toward family values than their parents. Although the majority of Vietnamese parents agree with the four selected family values listed in Table 11-3, not all parents surveyed agree with this particular set of values.

The Vietnamese-American Father

Many Vietnamese refugee fathers spent their lives as soldiers in Vietnam. Their entire professional careers involved military service with perhaps one or two weeks annual vacation with their family. A majority never played the role of full-time father or head of the family. They depended on their wives to take care of the family and raise the children. As a result, the Vietnamese father in America has had to learn how to adjust to American society and also to being a full-time father and husband. He has further had to learn to accept the fact that he has no absolute power over his family. His wife, likewise, is now able to get a job and bring home money. His children are living in a different culture; they think and act differently, and he finds that his use of the types of punishment that he could have used in Vietnam to correct or discipline his children is not always acceptable. The following

TABLE 11-3. Agreement in Family Values Between Vietnamese-American Children and Parents

Values	Children (N = 52) Percent	Parents (N = 56) Percent
A person should talk over important life decisions with family members before taking action		
Agree	62.7	90.4
Disagree	37.3	9.6
Family members should give more weight to each other's opinions than to the opinions of outsiders		
Agree	61.5	72.2
Disagree	38.5	27.8
If a person finds that the lifestyle he/she has chosen runs so against his/her family's values that conflicts develops, he/she should change		
Agree	57.7	76.4
Disagree	42.3	23.6
If possible, married children should live close to their parents		
Agree	34.4	63.0
Disagree	64.6	37.0

case illustrates a situation that many Vietnamese-American fathers have experienced.

> Mr. Do, an ex-official in the South Vietnamese Army, spent seven years in prison after the war like many other Vietnamese persons who were involved in the war one way or another. His wife and three children managed to escape Vietnam and were resettled in the United States in early 1980. The children were between the ages of 5 and 10 when they left. Mr. Do never spent more than a month with his children because he was a soldier during the war and a prisoner after the war. Mrs. Do decided to leave Vietnam when she saw no future for her children and herself after her husband was imprisoned without hope of release. She was told that he could be home after a short time in a reeducation camp, but years passed and she lost track of his locations because he had been transferred from place to place, and the family had no means to visit or support him. Mr. Do was finally released in 1987 and reunited with his family in 1992. When he arrived in the United States, his oldest son was 22 years old and the youngest one was 17. The children had grown up without their father and had very little connection with him emotionally. Unfortunately, the children also forgot the Vietnamese language and could no longer communicate with their father. Mr. Do was very upset and depressed, but he soon realized the fact and has learned to accept it bitterly. He blamed his wife for not knowing how to raise their children and letting them becoming too Americanized. He learned

English but never feels comfortable speaking to his children. The family situation and environment are constantly tense.

Many Vietnamese fathers have had a rough time adjusting to the new life and to their own family life in the United States. Changes in parenting styles and authority have created stressful consequences for many Vietnamese parents.

The Vietnamese-American Woman

Vietnamese women in the United States have a significantly higher fertility rate than all major groups of Asian-American women, including Chinese, Japanese, Filipino, Korean, and Asian Indian women. Vietnamese women's fertility rate is similar to that of Hispanic and African-American women. There have been 1,785 Vietnamese children born per 1,000 Vietnamese women aged 15–44. It is interesting to note that educational levels have a significant influence on fertility in that Vietnamese women with higher levels of education tend to have fewer children. This inverse correlation is also true among the general U.S. population and other major ethnic groups.

Vietnamese women in America are in a process of transition. They are being forced, out of economic necessity, to enter the job market. As a result, they are gaining increased status and power in the family because of the contributions they make to the family income. The U.S. Bureau of the Census (1993) reported that among Vietnamese people age 25 years and older, 53.3 percent of the women had high school education or higher compared to 61.2 percent of the men. Women also made up a lower percent (12.2%) of persons with a bachelor's degree than men (17.4%). Overall, 55.5 percent of Vietnamese women age 16 and over were in the workforce and 8.9 percent were unemployed.

Even when they work outside the home, Vietnamese women are still expected to be good wives and mothers and take care of their children, husbands, and homes. In many Vietnamese-American families, even though both husband and wife work full time, the wife is expected to cook, clean the house, and take care of the children; the husband remains the dominant authority figure. For example, in the Nguyen C family, Mrs. Nguyen C is employed by a local sewing factory, where she works 40 hours per week and often works overtime. Her husband, Mr. Nguyen C, is a machinist employed by a local factory, who also works 40 hours per week. The couple have four children, all of school age. Every morning, Mrs. Nguyen C gets up early to cook breakfast (her husband only eats Vietnamese food) and prepares lunches for the children, her husband, and herself. In the evening, Mrs. Nguyen C hurries home to cook dinner. When she has to work overtime, her oldest daughter, a 16-year-old, prepares dinner for the family. Mr. Nguyen C never knows what is going on in the kitchen, but he would become angry if dinner were not ready at 7:00 p.m. Mrs. Nguyen C takes care of all domestic affairs, including controlling and planning the family budget. During the weekend, Mr. Nguyen C spends most of his time working with the Vietnamese Catholic community (attending meetings or other social activities) while his wife stays home and cleans the house or works in the garden.

Gradually, however, domestic labor has become more equally divided among younger Vietnamese couples than it is among older couples. Data in Table 11-4 show some attitudes of adults age 18 and over about sex roles between men and women in Vietnamese-American families. The data reveal that both men and women tend to agree on shared responsibilities between husband and wife. It is expected that sex roles within the Vietnamese American family will change and will be similar to those in the mainstream and dominant society.

Marriage

Vietnamese parents in America no longer make all decisions about their children's marriages. The relocation from Vietnam to America destroyed many traditional ceremonies that were part of the marriage celebration. Moreover, Vietnamese young people are more economically independent from their parents and more self-sufficient; they have more freedom to make decisions on all matters relating to their marriage. Parents and older members of the family still exercise important influence over their children's marriages, but their influence is not absolute. Most Vietnamese parents still expect their children to marry other Vietnamese rather than people of another race, and interracial marriage is still an uncommon practice among Vietnamese Americans.

In regard to the traditional goal of marriage, many young Vietnamese in America, unlike their parents, do not see bearing children as the ultimate goal of marriage. Birth control methods are becoming more widely used by many young Vietnamese, and this practice is affecting family size. However, young Catholic Vietnamese are still influenced by the teachings of their

TABLE 11-4. Attitudes Toward Sex Roles (*N* = 176)

Sex Roles	Female (N = 90) Percent	Male (N = 112) Percent
Men should share the work around the house with women, such as doing dishes, cleaning, and so forth		
Agree	58.0	63.0
Disagree	42.0	37.0
Important family decisions should be made jointly by a husband and wife		
Agree	85.9	83.0
Disagree	14.1	17.0

church on birth control as well as other issues. In Vietnam, before and during the civil war, a Catholic priest was the most powerful person in a Catholic village or town. However, more and more young Vietnamese are venturing into a new era of sexual freedom, and premarital sexual activities are increasingly common among young people. The size of families among young couples also tends to be smaller. In fact, many young couples are realizing that it is costly to have children in America and that their new standard of living does not allow them to have as many children as they might like to have. In this way the new economic environment has changed traditional values and practices pertaining to marriage among the younger generation of Vietnamese Americans.

Table 11-5 presents some information on marriage in the Vietnamese-American family. The majority of Vietnamese women in the study tended to think that premarital sexual relationships are not acceptable. Men were more ambivalent about this issue than women. Birth control also appears to be a sensitive issue among Vietnamese Americans. Again, women were more likely to oppose the idea of making information about birth control available to teenagers than men. The majority of respondents were still ambivalent or against marital divorce.

TABLE 11-5.   Attitudes Toward Marriage Issues (N = 176)

Sex Roles	Female (N = 90) Percent	Male (N = 112) Percent
Do you think it is all right for a man and woman to have sexual relations before marriage?		
Yes	14.1	27.4
No	60.0	33.0
No ideas	25.9	39.6
Do you think birth control information should be made available to Vietnamese teenagers?		
Yes	15.7	34.9
No	61.4	37.6
No ideas	22.9	27.5
Do you think birth control information should be made available to Vietnamese adults?		
Yes	45.8	53.6
No	21.7	17.0
No ideas	32.5	29.5
Should Vietnamese couples divorce when they think they can no longer live together?		
Yes	23.6	27.2
No	25.8	34.2
No ideas	50.6	38.6

Socialization of Young Vietnamese Americans

Young Vietnamese Americans have less opportunity to interact with other young Vietnamese than do young white Americans. In a state or city with a high concentration of Vietnamese, the opportunity to interact with other Vietnamese is naturally greater. However, many Vietnamese children quickly learn about America and Americans through a daily diet of television, and many Vietnamese parents are too busy working and have little time to teach their children the Vietnamese language and culture. Vietnamese children are learning to become Americans on their own. In some Vietnamese families, children communicate with each other in English and with their parents in Vietnamese. Their parents, in most situations, do not have enough knowledge about American culture to help their children. As a result, many young Vietnamese Americans tend to experience conflict between their parents' culture and the culture they learn from school and television. Also, the communication gap between parents and children in the Vietnamese family is becoming wider. Vietnamese children also experience conflict between their Vietnamese and American identities. Stonequist (1961) explains this phenomenon via the concept of the "marginal man." A "marginal person" stands on the edges of two cultures, torn between their differences. A marginal person cannot make up his or her mind to choose what culture is right for him or her: his or her parent's culture or the culture of the host society. Even so, a marginal person who attempts to assimilate to the host culture may experience rejection from members of the dominant group.

Old Age in America

Elderly Vietnamese are isolated from not only American society but also their own family members. Most elderly Vietnamese in this country are unable to speak English and cannot drive; they spend most of their lives at home alone. Although they live with their children, there is rarely an opportunity to talk to them because of the amount of time spent working outside the home in America. Their grandchildren prefer to speak English rather than Vietnamese, and when they are at home, they spend most of their time in front of the television. Elderly Vietnamese have lost the respect they would have had in Vietnam, where their age status allowed them to pass down their knowledge to the younger generation. In America, their knowledge becomes useless. There is no doubt that elderly Vietnamese experience loneliness and homesickness in the United States. In most Vietnamese communities in the United States, churches and Buddhist temples are the only places for elderly Vietnamese to socialize. In small communities, elderly Vietnamese are completely cut off from the outside world.

CHANGE AND ADAPTATION

The Vietnamese-American family has gone through several stages of change and has been transformed into a different entity as Vietnamese Americans themselves change and adapt to their new identity and culture. In many Vietnamese families, traditional values still have some influence on the members. However, lack of communication between parents and children in many families makes it hard to preserve and maintain many traditional familial values, norms and processes.

Communication Gap

Many Vietnamese parents are similar to first-generation Japanese American parents (Issei) in believing that if their children learn English and adopt Western customs, they will become respected American citizens. Unfortunately, in extreme cases, some young Vietnamese tend to favor English over Vietnamese and quietly rebel against their parent's culture, just as many Nisei (second-generation Japanese American) did (Knoll, 1982). In some Vietnamese families, children prefer to speak English rather than Vietnamese and prefer to eat hamburgers or hot dogs rather than traditional Vietnamese food. The communication gap between the elders and the youngsters in a family has become wider and wider. The older Vietnamese try to hang onto their traditional culture and values, whereas the youngsters are quickly learning the new dominant culture and absorbing new values— American values. Many Vietnamese parents cannot understand the new culture and the values that their children are absorbing at school and at home through television. As a result, Vietnamese parents appear to be losing their authority in educating their children. They cannot understand their children and do not know how to communicate with them. Their children have become Americanized too quickly and too soon. In the long run, Americanization of Vietnamese children may have negative effects. As Gardner, Robey, and Smith (1985:39) suggest:

> In the past, Americanization has involved the absorption of values relating to schooling and work which encourage both individual success and national productivity. But the Americanization of Asian immigrants may have the opposite effect—reducing their exceptionally high level of dedication to learn and work.

Marital Conflicts

Vietnamese husbands and wives most likely will experience more role conflict and role ambiguity in their marital relationship. In many traditional Vietnamese families, as mentioned previously, the husband rarely stayed home because he was a soldier. Now he plays the role of a husband and father and assumes more responsibilities in everyday family life. At the same time, he must deal with his wife, who now is a competitor with him in the outside world—the job market. He realizes that he is not the only breadwinner in the family. As a result, the divorce rate probably will increase because many Vietnamese women are now free from their traditional social obligations.

The data presented in Table 11-6, taken from interviews conducted among 116 adults age 18 and over illustrate marital roles within the Vietnamese-American family. The data indicate that responsibilities that require social involvement, including health and education of the children, are expected to be shared by both men and women. However, domestic affairs are not evenly divided between husbands and wives. Most Vietnamese Americans still expect wives to do most of the domestic work.

CONCLUSION

In 1995, overseas Vietnamese communities and the Vietnamese community in the United States commemorated their twenty years of resettlement in the host societies. When they first arrived in this country, many could not imagine what would happen in the ensuing years. Few people believed that they would return to visit their country of origin or be reunited with their spouses

TABLE 11-6.   Marital Responsibilities (N = 116)

Responsibilities	Percent
Care for sick children	
Husband	5.0
Wife	3.3
Both	91.7
Educate children	
Husband	1.7
Wife	1.7
Both	96.6
Manage family finance	
Husband	3.2
Wife	27.4
Both	69.4
Prepare dinner	
Husband	3.2
Wife	44.4
Both	52.4
Wash dishes	
Husband	1.6
Wife	35.5
Both	62.9

and loved ones. Between 1980 and 1990, several anticommunist groups have been formed in overseas Vietnamese communities with a common hope of overthrowing the Vietnamese communist government of Vietnam. Many anti-communist diehards had a false hope that the U.S. government would eventually support their cause to fight for the freedom of Vietnam, and few Vietnamese Americans believed that the United States would normalize its diplomatic relation with Vietnam. Twenty years later, hundreds of ex-Vietnamese refugees have returned to their homeland as visitors with a new identity as Vietnamese Americans and the United States and Vietnam finally normalized their diplomatic relations.

One cannot talk about changes in the Vietnamese-American family without talking about changes in the Vietnamese-American community. Obviously, these two social institutions are intertwined. Most major Vietnamese communities started to form after the first five years of resettlement (i.e., around 1980). Though no systematic study has investigated the factors that contributed to the development of Vietnamese communities in the United States, there is no doubt that religious beliefs have played a major role. The Catholics and Protestants formed their communities around their local American churches, but the Buddhists had a tougher time in forming their communities because of the lack of Buddhists temples in their communities.

The second major factor is social and economic. Vietnamese people tend to gather in a few concentrated geographical areas because of their social and economic needs. The symbols of their communities are ethnic Vietnamese restaurants, social services agencies, ethnic groceries, and other services. The largest Vietnamese community in southern California, Little Saigon, has earned its name on the official map and stands out as a major commercial and tourist center. Vietnamese communities such as Little Saigon offer all types of services from ethnic food to health, legal, and travel services.

Communication and media technology has also facilitated the development of Vietnamese-American communities. Several Vietnamese-language newspapers, magazines, and books circulate in Vietnamese communities. The development of Vietnamese word-processing software in the late 1980s has tremendously helped Vietnamese communities link their people throughout the United States and other continents. The Vietnamese media and computers have linked Vietnamese Americans together to form a new type of community that is the informational or cyberspace community.

Overall, Vietnamese Americans have adjusted and adapted relatively well to their host societies. Many have done exceptionally well. Vietnamese Americans have gradually entered many fields, including politics, education, business, health, military, and others. As mentioned earlier, between 1980 and 1990 Vietnamese Americans improved their economic conditions tremendously and showed significant gains in educational achievement. Among the four major Indochinese groups that have arrived in the United

States since 1975, the Vietnamese have done much better than their Cambodian, Laotian and Hmong counterparts. For example, the 1990 census data show that 17.6 percent of the Vietnamese population holds managerial and professional occupations compared to 9.8 percent of the Cambodians, 5.0 percent of the Laotians, and 12.8 percent of the Hmongs. The percent of the Vietnamese population that lives below the 1989 poverty level is 25.7 percent, much smaller than the 42.6 percent of Cambodians, the 34.7 percent of Laos, and the 63.6 percent of Hmong.

Inevitably, the Vietnamese family will have to continue its changes in order to survive. The critical issue is the direction in which the Vietnamese family will change and the degree to which it will adapt to American culture. Although with recent attacks on public bilingual education, many Vietnamese community leaders and parents seem to agree that preservation of the Vietnamese language is one of the major factors that will help to foster the development and maintenance of the Vietnamese-American community. Efforts have been made in many Vietnamese communities to teach the Vietnamese language to children in hopes that in this way the younger Vietnamese will preserve traditional Vietnamese values and their ethnic identity. An ideal Vietnamese-American family will be one that adopts to American culture in order to survive but still preserves its traditional Vietnamese values and ethnic identity.

REFERENCES

Barringer, H. R., R. W., Gardner, and M. J. Levin. 1993. *Asian and Pacific Islanders in the United States.* New York: Russell Sage Foundation.

Bell, D. A. 1985. "The Triumph of Asian-Americans." *The New Republic* (July 15 and 22): 30.

Benjamin, R., T. V. Tran, and M. Benjamin. 1983. "Alienation Among Vietnamese Students in American Society." *Free Inquiry in Creative Sociology,* 5: 32–34.

Benedict, P. K. 1947. "An Analysis of Annamese Kinship Terms." *Southwestern Journal of Anthropology, 3*: 371–392.

Caplan, N., J. K. Whitmore, and Q. L. Bui. 1985. *Southeast Asian Refugee Self-Sufficiency Study.* Ann Arbor, MI: Institute for Social Research.

Che, W. 1979. *The Modern Chinese Family.* Palo Alto, CA: R & E Research Associates.

Dao, D. A. 1961. *Vietnam van-hoa so cuong* [History of Vietnamese Culture]. Saigon, Vietnam: Nha Xuat Ban Bon Phuong.

Do, M. V. 1962. *Vietnam: Where East and West Meet.* Rome, Italy: Edizioni.

Gall, S. B., and T. L. Gall. (Eds). 1995. *Statistical Record of Asian Americans.* Detroit, MI: Gale Research.

Gardner, R. W., B. Robey, and P. C. Smith. 1985. "Asian Americans: Growth, Change, and Diversity." *Population Bulletin, 40*: 1–44.

Haines, D., D. Rutherford, and P. Thomas. 1981. "Family and Community Among Vietnamese Refugees." *International Migration Review, 15*: 310–319.

Hickey, G. C. 1964. *Village in Vietnam.* New Haven: Yale University Press.

Hickey, G. C. 1982. *Free in the Forest: Ethnohistory of the Vietnamese Central Highlands 1954–1976.* New Haven: Yale University Press.

Hinton, H. C. 1985. *East Asia and the Western Pacific 1985.* Washington, DC: Skye-Post.

Keith J. 1982. *Old People as People: Social and Cultural Influences on Aging and Old Age.* Boston, MA: Little, Brown and Company.

Knoll, T. 1982. *Becoming Americans.* Portland: Coast to Coast Books.

Kunstadter, P. (Ed.). 1967. *Southeast Asian Tribes, Minorities, and Nation,* vol. 2. Princeton: Princeton University Press.

Le, T. V. 1992. *Le hoi co Truyen* [Traditional Folk Festivals]. Ha Noi: Nha Xuat Ban Khoa Hoc Xa Hoi.

Luong, H. V. 1984. "'Brother' and 'Uncle': An Analysis of Rules, Structures, Contradictions, and Meaning in Vietnamese Kinship." *American Anthropologist, 86*: 290–315.

Marr, D. G. 1981. *Vietnamese Tradition on Trial, 1920–1945.* Berkeley: University of California Press.

Montero, D. 1979. *Vietnamese Americans: Patterns of Resettlement and Socioeconomic Adaptation in the United States.* Boulder, CO: Westview Press.

Newsweek. 1975. "The New Americans." May 12, pp. 132–141.

Nguyen, H. M. 1985. "Vietnamese," in D. W. Haines (Ed.), *Refugees in the United States: A Reference Handbook.* Westport, CT: Greenwood.

Nguyen, K. K. 1967. *An Introduction to Vietnamese Culture.* Tokyo, Japan: Centre for East Asian Cultural Studies.

Nguyen, T. D. (1991). *A Vietnamese Family Chronicle: Twelve Generations on the Banks of the Hat River.* Jefferson, NC: McFarland.

Nguyen, T. G. 1993. *Luat hon nhan va gia dinh* [Marriage and Family Law]. Ha Noi: Nha Xuat Ban Chinh Tri Quoc Gia.

Pham, S. V. 1960. *Diet so toan the: To throng co den hien Dai* [Vietnamese history: From ancient times to the present day]. Saigon, Vietnam: Thu Lam An Quan.

Phan, D. D. 1992. *Lang Vietnam: Mot so van de kinh te xa hoi* [The Vietnamese village: Some social and economic issues]. Ha Noi: Nha Xuat Ban Khoa Hic Xa Hoi.

Phan, B. K. 1975. *Viet-Nam phong tuc* [Vietnamese Traditions]. Paris: Ecole Française D'Extreme-Orient.

Schaefer, R. T. 1979. *Racial and Ethnic Groups.* Boston: Little, Brown.

Spencer, R. F. 1945. "The Annamese Kinship System." *Southwestern Journal of Anthropology, 1*: 284–310.

Starr, P. D. 1981. "Troubled Waters: Vietnamese Fisherfolk on America's Gulf Coast." *International Migration Review, 15*: 226–238.

Stonequist, E. B. 1961. *The Marginal Man.* New York: Russet & Russell.

Strand, P. J., and W. Jones, Jr. 1985. *Indochinese Refugees in America: Problems of Adaptation and Assimilation.* Durham, NC: Duke University Press.

Swearer, D. K. 1984. *Southeast Asia.* Guilford, CT: Dushkin.

Taylor, K. W. 1983. *The Birth of Vietnam.* Berkeley, CA: University of California Press.

Toan Anh. 1965. *Nep cu: con nguoi Vietnam* [The old way: The Vietnamese people]. Saigon, Vietnam: Dai Nam.

Toan Anh. 1969. *Phong Tuc Viet-Nam: To ban than den gia dinh* [Vietnamese customs, from individual to family]. Saigon, Vietnam: Dai Nam.

Tran, D. H. 1991. "Ve gia dinh truyen thong Vietnam voi and huong Nho Giao" [The traditional Vietnamese family and the influences of Confucianism]. In R. Liljestrom, and Tuong Lai, *Nhung nghien cuu xa hoi hoc ve gia dinh Vietnam* [Sociological Studies of the Vietnamese Family]. Ha Noi: Nha Xuat Ban Khoa Hoc Xa Hoi.

U.S. Department of Health and Human Services. 1985. *Refugees Resettlement Program, Report to the Congress.* Washington, DC: U.S. Government Printing Office.

U.S. Department of State. 1995. *Vietnam: Background Notes.* Washington, DC: U.S. Government Printing Office.

U.S. Department of Commerce. 1988. *We, the Asian and Pacific Islander Americans.* Washington, DC: U.S. Government Printing Office.

U.S. Department of Commerce. 1993. *We, the American Asians.* Washington, DC: U.S. Government Printing Office.

Vuong, G. T. 1976. *Getting to Know Vietnamese and Their Culture.* New York: Ungar.

Whitfield, D. J. 1976. *Historical and Cultural Dictionary of Vietnam.* Metuchen, NJ: Scarecrow Press.

12 | The Chinese-American Family

Morrison G. Wong

INTRODUCTION

The Chinese have been present in the United States in significant numbers for almost a hundred and fifty years. In 1990, there were 1,648,696 Chinese residing in the United States—a 103 percent increase from the 1980 population (U.S. Census, 1983, 1993). Barring any major immigration reform, this number is expected to continue to increase (Gardner, Robey, and Smith, 1985). Although they comprise less than half of 1 percent of the total U.S. population, the Chinese are the largest of the various Asian-American groups. Despite their lengthy residence and their numbers, a review of the literature on the Chinese-American family suggests that theories on their family life are almost nonexistent and empirical studies are few and sparse. With the exception of a few early studies (Hayner and Reynolds, 1937; Lee, 1956; Schwartz, 1951), only the last two decades have seen major contributions to the literature on the Chinese-American family (Glenn, 1983; Huang, 1981; Lyman, 1968), their marriage and intermarriage rate (Barnett, 1963; Beaudry, 1971; Burma, 1963; Chin, 1994; Ferguson, 1995; Kitano and Yeung, 1982; Lee and Yamanka, 1990; Sung, 1987, 1990; Wong, 1989; Yuan, 1980), or their childrearing practices and sexual behavior patterns (Cheng and Yang, 1986; Huang and Uba, 1992; Sollenberger, 1968). The delay in research on the Chinese-American family may have been a consequence of their small numbers and geographical concentration in major cities on the West and East Coasts, their underrepresentation among social scientists to develop theories and carry out research on the Chinese family and lifestyle, and/or the perception that the Chinese-American family is not a "problem" in American society but instead bears a close resemblance to the white middle-class model—a hardworking, conforming, cohesive family that is the carrier of a traditional culture (Staples and Mirande, 1980; Sue and Kitano, 1973).

For the most part, past and present research on the Chinese-American family has focused on traditional Chinese cultural values and how they are manifested and modified in the Chinese family in America (Glenn, 1983). The portrayal of the Chinese-American family includes such favorable characteristics as: (1) a stable family unit, as indicated by low rates of divorce and illegitimacy (Huang, 1981); (2) close ties between generations, as shown by low rates of juvenile delinquency (Sollenberger, 1968); (3) economic self-sufficiency, as demonstrated by the avoidance of welfare dependency (Light, 1972); and (4) conservatism, as expressed by the retention of the Chinese language and customs (Braun and Chao, 1978) and sexual behavior (Huang and Uba, 1992). This chapter will review, evaluate, extend, and synthesize the literature on the Chinese family in the United States.

Before beginning the discussion, several issues need to be addressed. First, there is no typical Chinese family, just as there is no typical American family. Family variations within the culture are as wide as they are between cultures. It would be a gross simplification and inaccuracy to single out one Chinese family form as representative of all Chinese-American families. Instead, a greater understanding of the formation, development, and modification of the Chinese-American family necessitates looking at the different types of Chinese families that have existed and currently exist in the United States, realizing that even these are ideal types.

Second, although cultural factors have been emphasized in past research, the Chinese-American family is a product of the complex interaction between structural factors (i.e., social, legal, political, and economic) and cultural factors. For example, although the cultural values of filial piety and respect for elders have been proposed as the major reason for the low juvenile delinquency rate among the Chinese during the first half of the twentieth century, a convincing argument can also be made that the Chinese custom of leaving the wife at home when the husband went to work, even to distant countries (cultural values), and the racist and exclusionist immigration laws that prevented Chinese females from entering the United States (structural factors), prevented the development of a significant Chinese-American population, which may account for their low juvenile delinquency rate. The Chinese rate was low because there were very few juveniles.

Third, because both structural and cultural factors are constantly undergoing change, the Chinese-American family is best viewed not as a static entity, but as one also undergoing constant changes and adaptations. Knowledge and awareness of these various structural and cultural influences on the Chinese family will result in a greater understanding of the changes and adaptations the Chinese-American family has undergone and will continue to undergo. It is within this framework that the Chinese family in the United States will be analyzed.

The discussion of the formation and evolution of the Chinese-American family in the United States will be presented within the context of five historical periods, with the understanding that there is considerable overlap between historical periods and family types. They are: (1) the traditional

Chinese family before their arrival in the United States; (2) the "mutilated" or "split household" Chinese family between 1850 and l920; (3) the small producer Chinese family between 1920 and 1943; (4) normalization of the Chinese family between 1943 and 1965; and (5) the Chinatown and the uptown Chinese family from 1965 to the present. Speculations on future changes and adaptations of the modern Chinese family in the United States will be offered.

THE TRADITIONAL CHINESE FAMILY

The Chinese-American family, both past and present, has its foundation in the traditional family structure of China. Remaining unchanged for many centuries and encompassing a much broader connotation than the Western nuclear ideal of the conjugal unit of father, mother, and children, the traditional Chinese family also included the extended kinship groups and clan members (Sung, 1967:152).

The traditional family in China was patriarchal. Roles were clearly defined, with males, particularly the father and eldest son, having the most dominant roles (Hsu, 1971a). Authority passed from the father to the eldest son, whose authority and decisions were absolute. Females, relegated to a subordinate position, were expected to please and obey their fathers and, if married, were subordinate to not only their husbands but also their husbands' parents (De Vos, 1984; Hsu, 1967; Kitano, 1985:223-224).

The traditional Chinese family was patrilocal; that is, the married couple lived with the husband's parents. According to this ideal, the grandparents, their unmarried children, their married sons, together with their wives and children, all lived in one household. Because of patrilocal residence, daughters were considered less valuable and important than sons in the Chinese family. Parents felt that daughters were being reared at their expense for the benefit of another family or clan (Sung, 1967:152). In some cases, particularly if the family was extremely poor, infanticide of the female child was practiced. The traditional family in China was an extended family in which many generations and their offspring lived under one roof. Ideally, the more generations living under the same roof, the more prestigious the family. The Chinese extended family structure provided another important function. In an agriculturally based economy, there was an urgent need for many workers to cultivate and till the land and harvest the crops. A nuclear family would be at a disadvantage in this economy. The extended family system was a much more suitable arrangement, providing the family with much-needed additional laborers as well as giving members of the extended family some degree of economic security.

According to the Chinese system of patrilineal descent, the household property and land were to be divided equally among the sons, either at the father's death or the marriage of the youngest son. However, in exchange for the property and land, the sons were expected to reciprocate by sharing equally in the responsibility for the care and support of their parents in their old age (Fei, 1939; Hsu, 1971b; Ikels, 1985; Nee and Wong, 1985). Ancestor worship was greatly emphasized. It was believed that a Chinese male could achieve some sense of immortality only if his family line were continued (i.e., if he bore sons). In fact, one of the greatest sins that a man could commit was to die without having any sons to carry on the family line and perform the ancestor worship ritual of burning incense at his grave. As a consequence, an intense desire to have sons, and as many sons as possible, existed among the Chinese. Ancestor worship reflected the strength and importance of lineage solidarity, providing a link between the past and present (Hsu, 1971b).

Filial piety was a highly cherished value in the traditional Chinese family. This was a set of moral principles, taught at a very young age and reinforced throughout life, of mutual respect to those of equal status and reverence toward the dominant leader and elders. Duty, obligation, importance of the family name, service, and self-sacrifice to the elders, all essential elements of filial piety, characterized Chinese family relations (Hsu, 1971a, 1989; Kung, 1962:206).

As in many other agrarian-based societies, marriage was a family concern, not a private matter between a couple in love. Love was not a prerequisite for marriage and was highly discouraged. Because his bride lived with the husband's parents, the parents felt that they should have an important voice in the decision about who would live with them. The arranged marriage, another characteristic of the traditional Chinese family, is a classic case of not leaving important decisions to the impetuous young. In many cases, the son did not know who his bride was until after the wedding ceremony, when the bride unveiled her face (Fong, 1968).

In sum, because of the strong traditional bonds of the family, Chinese peasants during this period may be characterized as "familist": lacking any sense of a developed national identity and valuing the family first and foremost (Fei, 1939; Johnson, 1962). The Chinese family entailed much more than a family in the Western sense. It was a link to a much larger chain of extended kinship and clan members, bringing large numbers of people together with a common bond, whether real or imagined, and promoting a sense of solidarity, security, and belonging (Liu, 1959; Yang, 1959).

The "Mutilated," or "Split Household" Chinese Family (1850–1920)

Although Chinese resided in the United States as early as 1785, the discovery of gold in California and the political and economic instability of China provided the major impetus to the immigration of a significant number of Chinese to the United States in the early 1850s (Chinn, Lai, and Choy,

1969:7; Hirschman and Wong, 1981; Lai and Choy, 1971:22). The Chinese practice and custom of expecting emigrating men to leave their wives and children behind in China had three major consequences. First, it guaranteed that the emigrating sons would continue to send back remittance to their parents to support them in old age (Glick, 1980). Second, it instilled in the emigrating Chinese a sojourner rather than immigrant orientation. The single male or the husband who left his wife in China looked on his stay in the United States as temporary and evaluated American society primarily in terms of its economic opportunities. They sought to make and accumulate as much money as possible as quickly as possible to pay off debts and hoped to rejoin their family in China with a much higher status (Barth, 1964:157; Lyman, 1968; Siu, 1952). Third, it ensured a continual bond to the family and the village on the part of the emigrating men (Nee and Wong, 1985).

From their arrival in the 1850s until the 1920s, the overwhelming majority of the early Chinese immigrants were men. More than half of the arriving men were single, and those who were not often were separated from their wives and condemned to live a good portion of their lives as "bachelors" in Chinese communities scattered throughout the United States (Coolidge, 1909; Kingston, 1981; Lyman, 1968, 1977; Nee and Nee, 1973; Siu, 1952; Weiss, 1974). As a consequence, the majority of the early Chinese immigrants did not lead normal family lives. In fact, one can hardly speak of Chinese family life during this period because there were so few Chinese women (Glenn, 1983; Lyman, 1968; Nee and Nee, 1973; Sung, 1967).

Table 12-1 presents the sex ratio of the Chinese in the United States from 1860 to 1990. A glance at the table shows the tremendous imbalance in the sex ratio among the Chinese. From 1860 to 1890, the sex ratio fluctuated from 1,284 to 2,679 Chinese men per 100 Chinese women. After 1900, the imbalance among the Chinese began to decline. However, in 1920 and 1930, when an American-born Chinese population began to emerge, the sex ratio was still highly unbalanced. Without a significant number of Chinese women, the formation of Chinese families was greatly hindered. The view of emigration solely as a temporary economic proposition, coupled with the Chinese practice of leaving the wife and children in China, resulted in a bizarre family structure among these early Chinese immigrants. In these "mutilated" families (Sung, 1967), or "split household" families (Glenn, 1983), the married Chinese male in the United States was physically separated from his wife and children in China. The economic or production function of the family was carried out by the Chinese male living in the United States, whereas other family functions, such as socialization of the young, were carried out by the wife and other relatives in the home village in China. In essence, many Chinese men in the United States were family men without the presence of a wife or family members. Obviously, this family form was not preferred but was tolerated because many Chinese males looked on their stay in the United States as temporary.

TABLE 12-1. Chinese Population in the United States by Sex, Sex Ratio, Percentage Foreign Born, and Percentage Under 14 Years of Age: 1860–1990

Year	Total	Male	Female	Sex Ratio	Foreign Born (percent)	Under 14 Years of Age (percent)
1860	34,933	33,149	1,784	1,858	—	
1870	64,199	58,633	4,566	1,284	99.8	
1880	105,465	100,686	4,779	2,106	99.0	
1890	107,475	103,607	3,.868	2,679	99.3	
1900	89,863	85,341	4,522	1,887	90.7	3.4
1910	71,531	66,856	4,675	1,430	79.3	
1920	61,639	53,891	7,748	696	69.9	12.0
1930	74,954	59,802	15,152	395	58.8	20.4
1940	77,504	57,389	20,115	286	48.1	21.1
1950	117,140	76,725	40,415	190	47.0	23.3
1960	236,084	134,430	100,654	135	39.5	33.0
1970	431,583	226,733	204,850	111	46.9	26.6
1980	812,178	410,936	401,246	102	63.3	21.1
1990	1,079,700	821,542	827,154	99	69.3	19.3

Sources: Gardner et al. (1985); Glenn (1983: 38); Lyman (1970a: 79); U.S. Bureau of the Census (1993b).

Racial and ethnic antagonism, coupled with white xenophobia against the early Chinese immigrants, culminated in the passage of the Chinese Exclusion Act of 1882. This act, the first national act that excluded a specific nationality group from immigrating, barred Chinese laborers and their relatives from entering the United States. However, Chinese officials, students, tourists, merchants, and relatives of merchants and citizens were exempt from this exclusion. Although Chinese custom prevented most women from joining their husbands, the Chinese Exclusion Act erected an official barrier to their coming. Because a Chinese wife was accorded the status of her husband, Chinese merchants were allowed to bring their wives from China with them. However, wives of Chinese laborers were denied entry into the United States by the same law that excluded their husbands (Kung 1962:101; Lyman 1974:87).

The shortage of women among the Chinese immigrants in the United States might have been mitigated if the Chinese had had the opportunity to intermarry with the white population. However, the mutual peculiarities of dress, language, customs, and diet; the physical and racial distinctiveness; the mutually exclusive associations; prejudice and discrimination; and the enforcement of antimiscegenation laws restricted the amount of intimate contact and interaction between the two groups, precluding any possibility of romantic involvement. As a consequence, Chinese laborers, faced with an unfavorable sex ratio, forbidden as noncitizens from bringing their wives, and prevented by laws in most western states from marrying whites, had three options regarding their marital status: return permanently to China; if single, stay in the United States as bachelors; or, if married, remain separated from families except for occasional visits (Glenn, 1983). Thus, for many Chinese immigrants, the establishment of a family in America was a near impossibility.

The 1888 Scott Act further exacerbated the plight of many Chinese laborers, stipulating that they would be barred reentry into the United States if they left. Those Chinese laborers who wished to stay in the United States could look toward a future of only loneliness and isolation (Kung, 1962:101). Table 12-2 shows the number of Chinese immigrants to the United States by time period and the dramatic impact these two acts had on Chinese immigration. There was a continual and dramatic increase in Chinese immigration, reaching its peak of 123,201 Chinese immigrants during the decade of the 1870s. However, after the passage of the 1882 Chinese Exclusion Act, Chinese immigration declined precipitously. Only 10,242 Chinese immigrated to the United States in the 1880s and 14,799 Chinese in the 1890s. With the restrictions placed on Chinese entering the United States and without the

TABLE 12-2.   Chinese Immigrants[a] to the United States: 1820–1992

Years	Number of Immigrants
1820–1850	43
1851–1860	41,397
1861–1870	64,301
1871–1880	123,201
1881–1890	61,711[b]
1891–1900	14,799
1901–1910	20,605
1911–1920	21,278
1921–1930	29,907[c]
1931–1940	4,928
1941–1950	16,709[d]
1951–1960	9,657[e]
1961–1970	34,764[f]
1971–1980	120,271
1981–1990	456,702

[a]Beginning in 1957, includes Taiwan.
[b]In 1881 and 1882, before the Chinese Exclusion Act, 51,469 Chinese immigrated the United States.
[c]Before the Immigration Act of 1924, from 1921 to 1924, 20,393 Chinese entered the United States.
[d]After various immigration and refugee policies were passed, about 15,341 Chinese immigrants entered the United States (1946–1950).
[e]The McCarran-Walter Immigration Act was passed in 1952.
[f]The 1965 Immigration Act was passed.
Sources: U.S. Department of Commerce (1975), U.S. Department of Justice (1981, 1992).

establishment of families in America, there was little incentive for these early Chinese immigrants to invest in acquiring the social and cultural skills necessary to integrate or blend into American society (Siu, 1952).

Although immigration laws excluded the majority of Chinese from entering the United States, it did allow entry of relatives of U.S. citizens of Chinese ancestry. The 1906 San Francisco earthquake and fire destroyed not only most of Chinatown and much of San Francisco but also most of the municipal records (including Chinese immigration and citizenship records). This provided a loophole by which the Chinese could immigrate to the United States, and the "slot racket" or "paper son" form of immigration soon developed. Chinese residents would claim American birth, and the authorities were powerless to disprove their contention. These American-born Chinese, whether actual or claimed, would then visit China, report the birth of a son, and thereby create an entry slot. Years later, the slot could be used by a relative or the birth papers could be sold to someone wanting to immigrate. The purchaser, called a "paper son," simply assumed the name and identity of the alleged son. Under the terms of this type of immigration, the Chinese in America developed a long-term pattern of sojourning (Glenn, 1983; Kung, 1962; Lyman, 1974; Sung, 1967).

A limited number of Chinese women immigrated to the United States in the latter part of the nineteenth century (see Table 12-1). Those women who immigrated between 1850 and 1882 were either prostitutes or wives of the small group of Chinese merchants (Lyman, 1977:69; Nee and Wong, 1985). Chinese prostitution was an important element in the maintenance of the "split household" family, helping men avoid long-term relationships with women in the United States and ensuring that the bulk of their meager earnings would continue to support the family in China (Hirata, 1979). From 1882 to 1924, a period of restricted immigration, the few Chinese women who immigrated to America were usually married to merchants (Lyman, 1968).

For those few Chinese men who were fortunate enough to have resident wives in the United States, the old patriarchal Chinese family system continued. Values of the old country were stressed. The husband was expected to be obeyed by the wife. She was kept in seclusion by her husband, seldom ventured forth alone in the Chinese community, and almost never ventured beyond the community into white America. Obedience and filial piety to the patriarch were prime virtues and were often exhibited by children long after maturity. Parental control even extended to matters of courtship and mate selection. Marriages were always arranged, either by relatives living in China or between or with relatives in other Chinatowns in the United States (Hsu, 1971a; Kung, 1962; Lee, 1960; Lyman, 1968; Weiss, 1970, 1974:32–33). Men were expected to accept jobs under the direction or sponsorship of their father or male relatives to provide economic support of the parental household (either in China or the United States) and to take care of their parents in their old age (Ikels, 1985).

In sum, Chinese custom and tradition, the sojourner orientation of the Chinese immigrants, and the unbalanced sex ratio all had profound consequences for the personal, social, and family life of the early Chinese in the United States. One consequence was the formation of the "mutilated" or "split household" family structure and the subsequent perpetuation of this Chinese family type by various racist and exclusionist immigration laws. Another consequence was that only a small number of Chinese immigrant families were established in America during this early period. The emergence and maturation of a substantial second-generation Chinese-American population was delayed for almost seventy to eighty years after the initial arrival of the Chinese immigrants.

The Small Producer Chinese Family (1920–1943)

Despite the numerous obstacles to family formation, by the 1920s and 1930s a sizable second-generation Chinese population became increasingly evident in the major Chinatowns in the United States. These early Chinese families consisted primarily of small entrepreneurs or former laborers who were able to accumulate enough capital to start their own business, either alone or with partners. They were involved in such enterprises as laundries, restaurants, mom and pop grocery stores, and other small shops. The change in immigration status from laborer to merchant was of no small consequence for the Chinese. It allowed the new merchants to return to China and bring over their wives and children (Glenn, 1983; Nee and Wong, 1985). This is evident in the slight increase in Chinese immigration after 1900 (see Table 12-2). From 1920 to 1950, the percentage of Chinese born in the United States grew from 30 percent to a little over 50 percent of the total Chinese population in the United States. However, the sex ratio still remained highly unbalance (see Table 12-1).

Two types of Chinese families tended to predominate during this period. The first type, already discussed, was the "mutilated" or "split household" family. Chinese tradition was certainly one barrier keeping Chinese families separated. Another barrier was the discriminatory features of the Immigration Act of 1924, which made it impossible for American citizens of Chinese ancestry to send for their wives and families. Even Chinese merchants, who were previously able to bring their wives to the United States, were denied this privilege. This law was later changed in 1930 to allow wives of Chinese merchants, as well as those married to American citizens before 1924, to immigrate to the United States (Chinn, Lai, and Choy, 1969:24). The "mutilated" family remained one of the predominant forms of family life among the Chinese in the United States until the end of World War II, when more liberal immigration legislation was passed (Sung, 1967:156).

Another type of Chinese family, the small producer family, emerged during this period. This family type consisted of the immigrant and first-generation American-born family functioning as a productive unit (Glenn, 1983). All family members, including the children, worked in the small family business, usually within the ethnic economy. The business was profitable only because it was labor intensive and family members put in extremely long hours (Mark and Chih, 1982: 66).

The small producer family had four distinctive characteristics. First, there was no clear demarcation between work and family life. Second, the family was a self-contained unit in terms of production and consumption. Third, although all family members participated in the family enterprise, there was a division of labor according to age and gender with gradations of responsibility according to capacity and experience. Fourth, there was an emphasis on the collectivity over the individual (Glenn, 1983).

Children undertook a great deal of responsibility and gained considerable status at a very early age in the small producer family. Children played a crucial role in carrying out the daily business and domestic affairs of the family because their knowledge of English was superior to that of their immigrant parents. They acted as mediators between their immigrant parents and the outside society, performing such tasks as reading and translating documents and business contracts, filling out bank slips, and negotiating with customers (Kingston, 1976; Lowe, 1943; Nee and Nee, 1973; Wong, 1950).

Wives in the small producer Chinese family had much higher status compared to their traditional counterparts. As a result of limited immigration, the small producer family tended to be nuclear, consisting of husband, wife, and children. Consequently, wives did not have to contend with in-laws. Moreover, being more or less equal producers in the family business enabled Chinese wives to improve their position in the family and attain considerable autonomy and equality. Although the women did not have much economic power, they were considered the emotional centers of the household—the guardians of Chinese traditions and customs (Glenn, 1994).

The traditional Chinese family system lived in the minds of the older Chinese during this period. The Chinese-American family was patriarchal, with the oldest living male theoretically the master of the household. In actual practice, however, the opinion of the mother of the oldest living male carried considerable weight in major family decisions. In relations between parents and children, the father occupied the seat of authority and expected to be obeyed. The practice of deferring to the wishes of the elders was strengthened by the difficulty the children encountered in finding employment outside Chinatown, making them economically dependent on the older members of the family and clan. Patrilocal residence was still practiced among the Chinese in America during this period. The Chinese family conformed to traditional sex roles. A good husband was expected to be a good provider who earned the money but also spent it. A good, traditional Chinese wife in America was expected to spend very little money and rear as many children as possible—preferably sons (Hayner and Reynolds, 1937).

However, there was considerable variation in this pattern. If the wife was born and educated in this country, her position in the family approximated the American pattern. Likewise, American-born Chinese children who were educated in American schools developed attitudes very similar to those of native-born children of European immigrant parents and other native-born Americans.

In sum, the shortage of Chinese women and various racist immigration policies resulted in the "mutilated" or "split household" family continuing to be a predominant family form among the Chinese in America from the 1920s to the 1940s, with the small producer family running second. A distinguishing characteristic of this sizable second-generation Chinese-American family was that the Chinese children divided their time between growing up as active participants in the small family enterprise serving the ethnic community and trying to get ahead in school. Despite the emergence of this new Chinese family form, the cultural link between the Chinese family in the United States and the traditional family in China was maintained, though there were signs of gradual weakening as the family members became more acculturated into American society.

The Normalization of the Chinese Family (1943–1965)

The racist and exclusionist immigration policies during the early tenure of the Chinese in America played a major role in the resultant shortage of Chinese women in the United States and in the delay in the emergence of a second-generation Chinese population in the United States. Ironically, the liberalization and reforms of immigration policies during and after World War II were instrumental in partially rectifying past discrimination against the Chinese, which slowly led to the development and normalization of family life among the Chinese in the United States. In 1943, the Chinese Exclusion Act of 1882 was repealed, making Chinese immigrants, many of whom had been living in the United States for decades, eligible for citizenship. In recognition of China's position as an ally of the United States in World War II, a token quota of 105 persons per year was set for Chinese immigration. Although small, the quota did open the door to further immigration and had an impact on the future formation of Chinese families in the United States.

In 1945, the War Brides Act was passed, allowing approximately 6,000 Chinese women to enter the United States as brides of men in the United States military. In 1946, an amendment to this law put Chinese wives and children of United States citizens on a nonquota basis. The Displaced Persons Act of 1948 gave permanent resident status to 3,465 Chinese visitors, seamen, and students who were stranded here because of the Chinese civil war. This same year saw the California antimiscegenation law declared unconstitutional. In 1952, the McCarran-Walter Act was passed eliminating race as a bar to immigration and giving preferences to relatives (Chen, 1980: 211–213; Lee, 1956; Li, 1977a). The Refugee Relief Act of 1953 allowed 2,777 Chinese into the United States as refugees of the Chinese civil war. A presidential directive issued in 1962 permitted refugees from mainland China to enter the United States as parolees from Hong Kong. By 1966, approximately 15,000 refugees had entered under this provision. During the period from 1943 to the repeal of the quota law in 1965, Chinese immigration was overwhelmingly female, approximately nine females for every one male. Most of these women were alien wives of citizens admitted as nonquota immigrants (Simpson and Yinger, 1968: 350–351; Sung, 1977; Yuan, 1966).

Although many of the Chinese male immigrants remained bachelors or separated from their wives during most of their lives in the United States, the liberalization of immigration policies after World War II enabled many "mutilated" or "split household" families to be reunited. Reform in immigration policies also encouraged Chinese men to return to Hong Kong in droves to find wives. The quest for a bride generally conformed to the age-old pattern of getting their family elders to find a mate for them through a go-between or matchmaker (Sung, 1967: 156–157). The courtship was usually instantaneous and complete strangers often married after knowing each other for as little as one week. These trans-Pacific marriages were characterized by a wide disparity in age—men in their thirties and forties marrying women between 18 and 22 years old—and level of education.

Tremendous differences also existed in the cultural upbringing between the partners, with older, traditional men marrying younger, more modern women (Kitano, 1985: 225; Sung, 1967: 162). After their wedding, these newlyweds returned to the United States to ghetto conditions and a life of hardship in the urban Chinatowns of the West Coast. Despite the stress, strain, and cultural shock, these Chinese families usually remained intact. However, the relatively low divorce rate among the Chinese may be a result of the practice of turning marital discord and unhappiness inward on the self, resulting in a high suicide rate. For example, the suicide rate among the Chinese in San Francisco was four times higher than for the city as a whole, predominantly women committed suicide (Sung, 1967: 162).

For those Chinese families in which both spouses were native-born Americans, the family pattern approximated the American form, consisting of the husband, wife, and children and, occasionally, elderly parents. The parent-child relationship may be characterized as situated somewhere between the strict formality of the traditional Chinese family and the high degree of permissiveness of the American (white) family (Sung, 1967: 162, 176). The stranded Chinese who were displaced by the Chinese civil war in 1948 had family backgrounds strikingly different from the other Chinese in the United States. They were well-educated, having attended teacher-training institutions and colleges in China and having received postgraduate education in the United States. Selection of a spouse was based more on individual preferences and love rather than the traditional reliance on or the decision of elders or matchmakers. These former students settled in the suburbs near the universities and research facilities where they ultimately found employment (Ikels, 1985).

The size of Chinese families in the United States during this period was much larger than that of the general American population. One study found that Chinese families in New York's Chinatown had an average of 4.4 children compared with 2.9 children for white families (Liu, 1950). This difference may be the result of the Chinese value that a man's stature rose in direct proportion to the number of sons he sired and that women gained status by producing sons. It may also result partly from generational differences. Kwoh (1947) observed that if both parents were born in China, the median number of children in the family was 6.2; if both were American born, the median number was 3.2 children. Taken together, the average Chinese family had 5.5 children. As the Chinese became more Americanized and acculturated, the number of children in the Chinese family declined.

There are several general characteristics of the Chinese family during this period that hold regardless of the nativity or generational status. First, filial piety or loyal devotion to one's parents was still highly stressed, although in varying degrees. No matter how old a son was or how exalted his social position, his first obligation was to his parents. Second, Chinese children were taught the concept of "face" at a very early age. If the children did something wrong, it was not just a personal matter between themselves and their conscience, they also brought dishonor and shame to their family, family name, and loved ones. Related to the concept of "face" was the fact that the Chinese went to great lengths to keep their "dirty linen" within the family walls. This may account for their infrequent use of social agencies and the common perception or misconception that the Chinese take care of their own or that the Chinese family is relatively problem free.

In sum, the liberalization of immigration policies after World War II slowly led to the normalization and formation of Chinese families in the United States. As Chinese families became more acculturated to American society, their family patterns began to closely resemble those of their American counterparts.

The Chinatown and the Uptown Chinese Family (1965 to the Present)

The Immigration Act of 1965 has had a profound influence on the family life of Chinese in America. Emphasizing family reunification, this act abolished the national-origins quota system of 1952 and granted each country a quota of 20,000 immigrants per year. Since 1968, when the law went into effect, approximately 22,000 Chinese have immigrated to the United States through Hong Kong each year (Wong, 1985, 1986; Wong and Hirschman,

1983) (see Table 12-2). Unlike the pre-1965 immigrants, who came over as individuals, most of the new Chinese immigrants are coming over as family groups—typically husband, wife, and unmarried children (Hong, 1976); a family chain pattern of migration has developed (Li, 1977b; Sung, 1977; Wong and Hirschman, 1983). Initially, many of these new immigrants usually settled in or near Chinatown so that they could trade in Chinese-speaking stores, use bilingual services, and find employment (Glenn, 1983).

Before discussing the characteristics of the various types of modern Chinese families, it may be informative to first briefly discuss some of the general social, demographic, economic, and family characteristics of the Chinese in the United States. A glance at Table 12-3 shows that 1990 marked the first time since their arrival a hundred and fifty years ago that there was a slightly greater proportion of Chinese females to males; the Chinese sex ratio has become much more balanced than in previous decades. The Chinese are more urban and younger than the white population. As a consequence of renewed immigration, over two-thirds of the Chinese population is foreign born and this proportion is increasing.

Both Chinese males and females in the new immigration were more likely to be never married and less likely to be married or separated, divorced, or widowed compared to their white counterparts. This may explain the significantly lower fertility rate for Chinese women for every age category compared to that of their white counterparts. However, the average number of persons in Chinese households was higher than for white families. This apparent contradiction may be partially explained by the tendency of many adult sons and daughters of Chinese ancestry to live with their parents until they marry and/or the presence of extended family members, such as elderly grandparents. It may also be partially explained by a slightly greater proportion of Chinese families consisting of married couples with children living with them than white families.

There was basically no difference between the Chinese and white population in workforce participation rates, although Chinese males had a slightly lower and Chinese females a slightly higher labor force participation rate than their white counterparts. There was no difference between the Chinese and white population in class of worker, with 78 percent of each population involved as private workers. Over one-third of the Chinese were involved in managerial and professional occupations—the modal occupational category. Approximately 31–32 percent of the Chinese and white population was involved in technical occupations; the Chinese were slightly overrepresented in low-skilled service occupations. It seems that the Chinese no longer exhibit a bimodal occupational distribution of a high concentration in high-status professional jobs and low-status service jobs.

With the exceptions of the overrepresentation of the white population in agriculture, mining, and construction and the much greater overrepresentation of Chinese in retail trade, the industrial distributions of

TABLE 12-3. Demographic, Social, Economic and Family Characteristics of the Chinese and White Population in the United States: 1990

Characteristics	Chinese (percent)	White (percent)
Sex		
Male	49	49
Female	51	51
Sex ratio (males/females)	99.3	95.3
Residence		
Urban	98	72
Rural	2	28
Age		
0–14	19	20
15–34	36	31
35–64	36	35
65+	8	14
Median	32	34
Nativity Status		
U.S. born	31	95
Foreign-born	69	5
Marital Status		
Male		
Never married	36	24
Married	60	66
Separate, divorced, widowed	4	10
Female		
Never married	28	17
Married	60	62
Separate, divorced, widowed	12	21
Fertility		
Women 15–24 years per 1,000	51	254
Women 25–34 years per 1,000	690	1257
Women 35–44 years per 1,000	1703	1878
Household Size[a]		
1–2 persons	42	42
3 persons	19	23
4 persons	20	21
5 persons	11	9
6 persons	5	3
7 persons	4	2
Family Type, by Presence of Children		
Total families		
with natural children under 18 years of age	54	46
Married couples (percentage of total)	89	83
with natural children under 18 years of age	58	45
Female heads of household (percentage of total)	9	12
with natural children under 18 years old	38	53
Persons under 18 years old living with two parents	88	79
Workforce Status		
In the workforce (16 or more years old)	66	65
Male	72	75
Female	59	56

TABLE 12-3. *(continued)*

Characteristics	*Chinese* *(percent)*	*White* *(percent)*
Class of Worker		
Private	78	78
Government	14	14
Self-employed	8	8
Workers in Family		
Total families		
0	8	13
1	26	27
2	48	47
3 or more	19	13
Occupation		
Managerial and professional	36	28
Technical, sales, and administrative support	31	32
Service	16	12
Farm	0	2
Crafts	6	12
Operatives and laborers	11	14
Industry		
Agriculture, mining, and construction	3	10
Manufacturing	19	18
Transportation and communication	6	7
Wholesale trade	5	5
Retail trade	24	17
Banking and insurance	8	7
Business and repair and service	4	5
Entertainment and personal service	5	4
Professional	23	23
Public administration	3	5
Workers in Family		
0	8	13
1	26	27
2	48	47
3 or more	19	13
Family Income		
Median	$41,316	$37,152
Mean	$51,931	$46,330
Poverty Status of Family		
Below poverty level	11	7
Native born	3	
Foreign born	12	
Ability to Speak English		
Linguistically isolated	35	2
Do not speak very well	50	4
Speak another language	84	10

ªThe statistic for household size for the white population actually represents the total population.
Sources: U.S. Bureau of the Census (1993a, 1993b).

these two groups were roughly the same. A greater proportion of Chinese than white families had multiple workers, which may partly explain their higher family income, approximately $4,000–$5000 higher than that of white families. However, at the other end of the income continuum, Chinese families were more likely to have family incomes below the poverty level. Approximately 11 percent of all Chinese families lived in poverty compared to 7 percent of white families. About 3 percent of the native-born and 12 percent of the foreign-born Chinese families had incomes below the poverty level, suggesting that many Chinese families barely make ends meet. For many of these families, even if members work, they are involved in the secondary labor market or enclave economy, barely making enough to survive.

The present-day Chinese-American family can be divided into two major types. The first type is the "ghetto" or "Chinatown Chinese" (Huang, 1981) or "dual worker family" (Glenn, 1983). This family type consists of the new immigrant Chinese family living in or near Chinatowns in the major metropolitan areas of this country. Both husband and wife are usually employed in the secondary labor market or enclave economy, in the labor-intensive, low-capital service and small manufacturing sectors, such as tourist shops, restaurants, and garment sweatshops (Light and Wong, 1975; Wong, 1980a, 1983; Wong and Hirschman, 1983). Husbands and wives are more or less coequal breadwinners in the family. However, unlike the small producer family, there tends to be a complete segregation of work and family life. Parents and children are separated for most of the day. Moreover, it is not uncommon for parents to spend very little time with each other because of different jobs and job schedules—one parent having a regular shift (i.e., sweatshop) and the other parent having the swing shift (i.e., restaurant)—or with their children. The parents' fatigue, the long hours of separation, and the lack of common experience can undermine communication between parents and their children. Chen (1980: 227–228) vividly describes the lifestyle of these new immigrants:

> Penetrate, if you can, into the crowded tenements, and you will find families of four, five, and six living, working, playing, and sleeping in a single room. Pots, pans, and food must be taken to a community kitchen shared with other families. Privacy is a sometime thing. These facts speak for themselves: for all its gaiety, good humor, and indomitable spirit this area suffers from widespread poverty, high unemployment, substandard and overcrowded housing, inferior public services and facilities, and resulting grave health problems.

The latest influx of new Chinese immigrants has helped preserve some of the old traditional ways. Parental authority, especially the father's, is more absolute, and the extended family, if present, plays a much more significant role than typically found in middle class Chinese or white families (Schaffer, 1984: 350).

A variant of the "ghetto" or "Chinatown" family are the "out-of-town" or "trans-Pacific" families. Many new and old Chinese immigrants still return to China to marry. As a result, the number of trans-Pacific marriages involving U.S. citizens and brides from China, Hong Kong, and Taiwan has increased in the late 1970s and early 1980s—about 5,000 Chinese brides arrived in the United States annually in the late 1980s (U.S. Department of Justice, 1988, 1989). Like the brides of the reunited "mutilated families," shock and a sense of betrayal are probably the initial reactions of these new brides upon their arrival to the United States. They are shocked to learn that their husbands must wash other people's clothes, shocked at the heavy load of work their husbands must bear, and shocked at the heavy load of work they themselves must bear. Many feel a sense of betrayal on the part of their husbands for mis-informing or misleading them about their future lifestyles. These factors exacerbate the problems these brides already face in accommodating and adjusting to their husbands and to American society (Chin, 1994).

The second type of Chinese family is the middle class, white collar, or professional Chinese-American family that moved away from Chinatown into the surrounding urban areas and suburbs. These "uptown" immigrant or American-born Chinese are more modern and cosmopolitan in orientation and view themselves as more American than Chinese (Huang, 1981; Kitano, 1985:224; Weiss, 1970, 1977). Highly educated, the parents, one if not both, probably have college degrees and are involved in professional or white collar occupations. Their relatively high socioeconomic status and degree of acculturation to American society allow these Chinese to live fairly comfortable lives in the better parts of the city or in the suburbs (Kuo, 1970; Yuan, 1963, 1966). These Chinese tend to reestablish a Chinese community in the suburbs (Lyman, 1974:149; Fong, 1994; Horton, 1995), a situation that may be structurally termed "semiextended." Although grandparents may prefer to establish their own household, many prefer to live in the same building, block, or neighborhood as their children (Huang 1981:123).

The modern Chinese family, whether Chinatown or uptown, has a lower fertility rate, fewer out-of-wedlock births, and more conservative or traditional attitudes toward the role of women than the white population (Braun and Chao, 1978; Monahan, 1977). Divorce is a rarity among the Chinese (Huang, 1981:122; Schaffer, 1984:351). It is not uncommon for unhappy Chinese couples to remain together out of fear of public opinion, social disgrace, and social ostracism. However, among the younger generation, brought up to believe in the American ideal of romantic love and personal happiness in marriage, the incidence of divorce has increased. The economic position of the husband and wife as cobreadwinners and/or their high socioeconomic position lends itself to a mutual sharing of responsibility and authority in decision making on most aspects of family life (Sollenberger, 1968), although the wife usually assumes the role of helper rather than equal partner (Huang, 1981).

In childrearing, the father maintains his authority and respect in the Chinese family by means of a certain amount of emotional distance. The mother does not interact with the children but commands and decides what is best for them and the children are expected to obey (Huang, 1981; Sollenberger, 1968; Sung, 1967: 165, 168–169). Although Chinese parents may be more indulgent with their young children than parents of the white American culture, discipline is much more strict than that the typical American child receives (Petersen, 1978). Punishment is immediate and generally involves withdrawal from the social life of the family or the deprivation of special privileges or objects rather than physical punishment. As the child grows older, overt expressions of physical and emotional affection exhibited among family members, whether between the husband and wife or between the parents and children, are withdrawn. Many Chinese children have never seen their parents kiss or hug each other, nor are they expected to kiss or hug their parents (Huang, 1981:126). Moreover, public display of affection is considered in poor taste by many Chinese. Independence and maturity are stressed at a very young age and the child is expected to behave as an adult. Aggressive behavior and sibling rivalry are not tolerated and are highly discouraged (Sollenberger, 1968). Older children are expected to be directly or indirectly involved in the socialization of their younger siblings—serving as role models of adult behavior. Huang (1981: 124–125) notes that Chinese children are brought up in the midst of adults, not only their parents but also members of the extended family. As a consequence, they learn at a very early age socially approved patterns of behavior and also what others think of them. Instead of individual guilt governing their behavior (as is true of their white counterparts), the sense of face, or shame, to themselves and to their family acts as a major form of social control.

Studies on Chinese students suggest that they are more sexually conservative than their white counterparts. A lower proportion of Chinese have engaged in premarital intercourse and put off physical intimacy longer than their white counterparts (Bauman and Wilson, 1974; Huang and Uba, 1992; Murstein and Holden, 1979). Possible explanations for this difference are: (1) the need to feel more certain of an emotional commitment; (2) the less positive body image of some Asian Americans, which may cause them to be more sexually modest; (3) lack of social acculturation; (4) the stereotype of Asian men as "nerdy" and socially inept, hence making them undesirable dating partners; and (5) a reflection of traditional Chinese culture's emphasis on modesty (Chen and Yang, 1986; Hsu, 1970; Huang and Uba, 1992).

Education is highly valued in the Chinese family and Chinese parents will undergo extreme financial sacrifice and hardship so that their children can receive as much education as possible. This value on education may stem from numerous factors: the parents' traditional Confucian respect for learning; the realization that education is an avenue by which their children will gain security and lead to a better life than they have; the social status that the parents receive in the Chinese community if they have a college-educated or professional child; and the demographic and high socioeconomic characteristics of the Chinese (Hirschman and Wong, 1986; Wong, 1980b). Education does not stop with the typical American school curriculum. Fearing a loss of Chinese heritage, many Chinese parents feel that their children should be instilled with knowledge about Chinese culture, traditions, customs, history, and language. As a consequence, in areas with a significant Chinese population, many native-born and foreign-born Chinese children attend Chinese language school after American school or during the weekends (Fong, 1968).

A common stereotype of the Chinese family is that because of their adherence to the Confucian ethic of filial piety, Chinese children will take care of their elderly parents and will show greater concern and devotion toward their elders than average American (white) children. The exact strength of this concern compared with other ethnic groups, and the validity of this stereotype of the Chinese family, is an empirical question for which limited data are available. However, studies do suggest that family members are the primary source of assistance for elderly Chinese and that assistance from social service agencies and professional persons is almost nonexistent. Hirata (1975) found that approximately 90 percent of both native-and foreign-born Chinese youths and their parents indicated that they believed children should support their aged parents. Chinese children felt a strong sense of guilt and shame over what they considered inappropriate care for elderly parents, such as the placement of their elderly parents in nursing homes (Kalish and Moriwaki, 1973). Part of this reaction may be because of their sense of filial responsibility or their knowledge that their parents' lack of familiarity with the English language may result in problems of adjustment, mistreatment, inadequate care, and a sense of isolation and alienation in nursing homes (Wong, 1984).

In sum, the modern Chinese family can be categorized into two types. As a result of the Immigration Act of 1965 and its emphasis on family reunification and subsequent immigration policies, many new Chinese immigrants are arriving at the shores of the United States and settling in Chinatowns scattered throughout the United States. This form of Chinese family life has been called the "ghetto" or "Chinatown Chinese," or the "dual worker family." Another form of the modern Chinese family is the uptown, white collar or professional Chinese family, which, because of its higher socioeconomic status and degree of acculturation, has moved to the suburbs and is gradually integrating into the American mainstream.

CHANGE AND ADAPTATION

The Chinese family in the United States has undergone tremendous changes and adaptations during its one hundred and fifty years in the United States—from the "mutilated" or "split household" family to the small producer family to the trans-Pacific marriage pattern to the present-day Chinese-American family structure, consisting of the "ghetto or Chinatown Chinese" or "dual worker family" and the uptown professional immigrant or Chinese-American family. Many of these changes and adaptations were the result of complex interactions between cultural and structural factors. During the latter half of the 1990s and into the next millennium, the Chinese family will probably continue to change, modify, adapt, and reorganize according to the ebb and flow of societal forces and the constraints on and expansion of opportunities in American society.

The Chinese family is intensely involved in the process of urban socio-cultural changes and acculturation. One indicator of this process is the geographic dispersion of the Chinese away from the Chinatown areas and into the metropolitan areas and the suburbs (Fong, 1994; Horton, 1995). As Chinese children attend American schools and develop friendships with white American children, as they become more competent in English than in Chinese—in essence, as they become more acculturated—they will probably view themselves as more American than Chinese. With their high degree of acculturation, the younger Chinese Americans will probably face a clash of generations and identity conflicts between themselves as primarily "American" and their appearance to others as "Chinese" or "Asian" (Chen, 1972, 1981; Chen and Yang, 1986; Fong, 1965, 1968). A number of Chinese-American personality types, ranging from the "banana" (yellow on the outside but white on the inside), who rejects or denies all aspects of being Chinese in order to try to appear completely American or white, to the "radical" Chinese, who may espouse a new Asian consciousness while rejecting the values of traditional Chinese and American culture, are already emerging. (Sue and Sue, 1971; Chen, 1981).

Another indicator of the acculturation of the Chinese family is the recent dramatic increase in the incidence of interracial marriages, particularly with whites, among the younger generation (Barnett, 1963; Burma, 1963; Lee and Yamanaka, 1990; Simpson and Yinger, 1965; Staples and Mirande, 1980; Sung, 1990; Weiss, 1970; Wong, 1989). Approximately 33 percent of all marriages among the Chinese are intermarriages. Other trends in intermarriage include a strong inverse relationship between age and the proportion of those who intermarry (Yuan, 1980), more Chinese women than Chinese men intermarrying (Barnett, 1963; Hsu, 1971a; Wong, 1989; Yuan, 1980), and a strong positive relationship between generational status and incidence of intermarriage (Kitano and Yeung, 1982). Numerous explanations for these trends have been suggested: (1) dissatisfaction with the more traditional Chinese male's limited attitudes toward women by more acculturated Chinese women (Braun and Chao, 1978); (2) the inability of Chinese-American males to relate positively to Chinese-white social/sexual situations (Huang and Uba, 1992; Weiss, 1970); (3) occupational, housing, social mobility, and acculturation of the Chinese, especially by generation (Hirschman and Wong, 1984; Kitano and Yeung, 1982); (4) changes in the attitudes of the Chinese as well as of the dominant group (Kitano and Yeung, 1982; Wong, 1989); and (5) the social class position of the Chinese and the increasing dispersal of Chinese away from the Chinatown ghetto (Huang, 1981; Labov and Jacob, 1986; Parkman and Sawyer, 1967; Wong, 1989).

Whatever the reason, there is no question that the incidence of intermarriage among the Chinese has dramatically increased in recent years. One ramification that this increase in interracial marriages will have for the Chinese family is the further acculturation of the Chinese into American society and, hopefully, their greater acceptance by the dominant group. However, intermarriage is not without its costs. A loss of ethnic tradition, heritage, and a distinct sense of Chinese identity resulting in "symbolic ethnicity" (Gans, 1979) along with intergenerational strain and conflict between the Chinese parents and their interracially married children are but some of the costs. Sung (1990: 350) sums it up best when she states:

> There is no question that the children will experience problems of identity physically as well as culturally. The children will not look wholly like the mother or the father. . . . The children will be teased and taunted and possibly excluded for no other reason except that they look different. They are quickly labeled half-breed, half-caste, or mixed bloods, all disparaging terms. In some homes, if one of the ethnic cultures is suppressed as if it should be covered up, the child is left wondering if one half of him/her is something to be ashamed of. In other homes, the parents cannot agree on how the children are to brought up, so the offspring are baffled and confused.

Although the 150-year history of settlement of the Chinese in the United States suggests high intermarriage rates, the continued dramatic influx of Chinese immigrants of diverse socioeconomic backgrounds and national origins may slow down or even reverse this trend. This effect is suggested by the much higher intermarriage rate among the native-born Chinese than the foreign-born Chinese (Lee and Yamanaka, 1990; Wong, 1989).

Acculturation is also affected by immigration rates. Language or proficiency in English is a key to assimilation. People who speak English are more assimilated, not just because they can communicate with members of the dominant group, but also because they can be more effectively socialized by the dominant culture (Jiobu, 1988; Ferguson, 1995). About 84 present of the Chinese in the United States speak another language other than English. While one can make the argument that many Chinese are bilingual, it should also be noted that about 50 percent Chinese in the United States do not speak English very well. Moreover, about 35 percent of Chinese households considered themselves linguistically isolated (U.S. Bureau of the Census, 1993b). With the continued tremendous immigration of the Chinese to the United States, we should expect an increase in the proportion of their foreign-born population, in those not being able to speak English very well, and in those who live in linguistically isolated households. In essence, we should see the Chinese, as a group, become less acculturated.

Change and adaptation were important elements in the formation and development of the Chinese family in the United States, and it is probably safe to say that they will continue to play important roles in the future. Although some people may regard the Chinese family as breaking down or undergoing social disorganization, as evidenced by the increase in accultura-tion, interracial marriages, and juvenile delinquency rates (Fong, 1968; Sung, 1967: 185–186), one can view the recent changes and adaptations in the Chinese family as essential elements of the greater process of modification and reorganization that has been occurring for the past hundred and fifty years and will continue to occur in the future. The present-day Chinese fam-ily in the United States is much different from Chinese-American families of the past. With the continued influx in Chinese immigration to the United States and the further acculturation of the Chinese population to American society, the Chinese-American family of the future will probably continue to successfully evolve, develop, and adapt from its present-day form.

REFERENCES

Barnett, Larry D. 1963. "Interracial Marriage in California." *Marriage and Family Living, 25*(4): 425–427.

Barth, Gunther. 1964. *Bitter Strength: A History of the Chinese in the United States, 1850–1870.* Cambridge: Harvard University Press.

Beaudry, James A. 1971. "Some Observations on Chinese Intermarriage in the United States." *International Journal of Sociology and the Family, 1* (May): 59–68.

Braun, J. and H. Chao. 1978. "Attitudes Toward Women: A Comparison of Asian-Born Chinese and American Caucasians." *Psychology of Women Quarterly, 2* (Spring): 195–201.

Burma, John H. 1952. "Research Note on the Measurement of Interracial Marriage." *American Journal of Sociology, 57*: 587–589.

———. 1963. "Interethnic Marriages in Los Angeles, 1948–59." *Social Forces, 42* (December): 156–165.

Chen, Clarence L. 1972. "Experiences as an American in Disguise." *Newsletter of the Midwest Chinese Student and Alumni Services, 14*, 4 (Summer): 4–8.

———. 1981. "An Asian American Approach to Confronting Racism." *East West: The Chinese American Journal, 15*: 27 (July 8): 2, 5.

Chen, Clarence L. and Dorothy C. Y. Yang. 1986. "The Self Image of Chinese American Adolescents: A Cross Cultural Comparison." *International Journal of Social Psychiatry, 32*(4): 19–26.

Chen, Jack. 1980. *The Chinese of America.* San Francisco: Harper & Row.

Cheng, Eva. 1978. *The Elder Chinese.* San Diego, CA: Campanile Press.

Chin, Ko Lin. 1994. "Out of Town Brides: International Marriage and Wife Abuse among Chinese Immigrants." *Journal of Comparative Family Studies 55*(1): 53–69.

Chinn, Thomas, H. Mark Lai, and Philip Choy. 1969. *A History of the Chinese in California: A Syllabus.* San Francisco: Chinese Historical Society of America.

Coolidge, Mary. 1909. *Chinese Immigration.* New York: Henry Holt.

Fei, H. T. 1939. *Peasant Life in China: A Field Study of Country Life in the Yangtze Valley.* London: Routledge and Kegan Paul.

Ferguson, Susan J. "Marriage Timing of Chinese American and Japanese American Women." *Journal of Family Issues 16*(3): 314–343.

Fong, Stanley L. M. 1965. "Assimilation of Chinese in America: Changes in Orientation and Social Perception." *American Journal of Sociology, 71*(3): 265–273.

Fong, Timothy P. 1994. *The First Suburban Chinatown: The Remaking of Monterey Park, California.* Philadelphia: Temple University Press.

———. 1968. "Identity Conflict of Chinese Adolescents in San Francisco," in Eugene B. Brody (Ed.), *Minority Group Adolescents in the United States*, pp. 111–132. Baltimore, MD: Williams and Wilkins.

Gardner, Robert W., Bryant Robey, and Peter C. Smith. 1985. "Asian Americans: Growth, Change, and Diversity." *Population Bulletin*, vol. 4, no. 14. Washington, DC: Population Reference Bureau.

Gans, Herbert J. 1979. "Symbolic Ethnicity: The Future of Ethnic Groups and Cultures in America." *Ethnic and Racial Studies, 2*(1): 1–20.

Glenn, Evelyn Nakano. 1983. "Split Household, Small Producer and Dual Wage Earner: An Analysis of Chinese-American Family Strategies." *Journal of Marriage and the Family, 45*(1): 35–46.

Glenn, Evelyn Nakano and Stacey G. H. Yap. "Chinese American Families," in Ronald L. Taylor (Ed.), *Minority Families in the United States: A Multicultural Perspective*, pp. 115–145. Englewood Cliffs, NJ: Prentice Hall.

Glick, Clarence E. 1980. *Sojourners and Settlers: Chinese Migrants in Hawaii.* Honolulu: University of Hawaii Press.

Hayner, Norman S. and Charles N. Reynolds. 1937. "Chinese Family Life in America." *American Sociological Review, 22*(5): 630–637.

Hirata, Lucie Cheng. 1975. "Youth, Parents, and Teachers in Chinatown: A Triadic Framework of Minority Socialization." *Urban Education, 10*(3): 279–296.

———. 1979. "Free, Indentured, Enslaved: Chinese Prostitutes in Nineteenth-Century America." *Signs, 5* (Autumn): 3–29.

Hirschman, Charles and Morrison G. Wong. 1981. "Trends in Socioeconomic Achievement among Immigrant and Native-Born Asian-Americans, 1960–1976." *Sociological Quarterly, 22*: 495–513.

———. 1986. "The Extraordinary Educational Attainment of Asian-Americans: A Search for Historical Evidence and Explanations." *Social Forces, 65*: 1–27.

Hong, Lawrence K. 1976. "Recent Immigrants in the Chinese-American Community: Issues of Adaptations and Impacts." *International Migration Review, 10*: 509–514.

Horton, John. 1995. *The Politics of Diversity: Immigration, Resistance, and Change in Monterey Park, California.* Philadelphia: Temple University Press.

Hsu, Francis L. K. 1970. *Americans and Chinese.* Garden City, NY: Doubleday Natural History Press.

———. 1971a. *The Challenge of the American Dream: The Chinese in the United States.* Belmont, CA: Wadsworth.

———. 1971b. *Under the Ancestors' Shadow: Chinese Culture and Personality.* Stanford, CA: Stanford University Press.

Huang, Lucy Jen. 1981. "The Chinese American Family," in Charles Mindel and Robert Habenstein (Eds.), *Ethnic Families in America*, 2nd ed. New York: Elsevier, pp. 115–141.

Huang, Karen and Laura Uba. 1992. "Premarital Sexual Behavior Among Chinese College Students in the United States." *Archives of Sexual Behavior 21*(3): 227–240.

Ikels, Charlotte. 1985. "Parental Perspectives on the Significance of Marriage." *Journal of Marriage and the Family, 47*(2): 253–264.

Johnson, C. 1962. *Peasant Nationalism and Communist Power: The Emergence of Revolutionary China.* Stanford, CA: Stanford University Press.

Kalish, Richard A. and Sharon Moriwaki. 1973, "The World of the Elderly Asian American." *Journal of Social Issues, 29*(2): 187–209.

Kingston, Maxine Hong. 1976. *Woman Warrior*. New York: Knopf.

———. 1981. *China Men*. New York: Ballantine.

Kitano, Harry H. L. 1985. *Race Relations*. Englewood Cliffs, NJ: Prentice-Hall.

Kitano, Harry H. L. and Wai-Tsang Yeung. 1982. "Chinese Interracial Marriage." *Marriage and Family Review*, 5(1): 35–48.

Kung, S. W. 1962. *Chinese in American Life: Some Aspects of Their History, Status, Problems, and Contributions*. Seattle: University of Washington Press.

Kuo, Chia-Ling. 1970. "The Chinese on Long Island—A Pilot Study." *Phylon*, 31(3): 280–289.

Kwoh, Beullah Ong. 1947. "The Occupational Status of American-Born Chinese Male College Graduates." *American Journal of Sociology*, 53: 192–200.

Lai, H. Mark and Philip P. Choy. 1971. *Outline History of the Chinese in America*. San Francisco: Chinese-American Studies Planning Group.

Lee, Rose Hum. 1952. "Delinquent, Neglected, and Dependent Chinese Boys and Girls of the San Francisco Bay Region." *Journal of Social Psychology*, 26 (August): 15–34.

———. 1956. "The Recent Immigrant Chinese Families of the San Francisco-Oakland Area." *Marriage and Family Living*, 18 (February): 14–24.

———. 1960. *The Chinese in the United States*. Hong Kong, China: Hong Kong University Press.

Lee, Sharon and Keiko Yamanako. 1990. "Patterns of Asian American Intermarriage and Marital Assimilation." *Journal of Comparative Family Studies* 51(2): 287–305.

Li, Peter S. 1977a. "Fictive Kinship, Conjugal Tie, and Kinship Chain Among Chinese Immigrants in the United States." *Journal of Comparative Family Studies*, 8: 1 (Spring): 47–63.

———. 1977b. "Occupational Achievement and Kinship Assistance Among Chinese Immigrants in Chicago." *Sociological Quarterly*, 18(4): 478–489.

Light, Ivan H. 1972. *Ethnic Enterprise in America*. Berkeley, CA: University of California Press.

Light, Ivan H. and Charles Choy Wong. 1975. "Protest or Work: Dilemmas of the Tourist Industry in American Chinatowns." *American Journal of Sociology*, 80: 1342–1368.

Liu, Ching Ho. 1950. "The Influence of Cultural Background on the Moral Judgment of Children." Ph.D. dissertation, Columbia University.

Liu, Hui-chen Wang. 1959. *The Traditional Chinese Clan Rules*. Locust Valley, NY: J. J. Augustin.

Lowe, Pardee. 1943. *Father and Glorious Descent*. Boston: Little, Brown.

Lyman, Stanford M. 1968. "Marriage and the Family Among Chinese Immigrants to America, 1850–1960." *Phylon*, 29(4): 321–330.

———. 1970a. "Social Demography of the Chinese and Japanese in the U.S. of America," in Stanford M. Lyman (Ed.), *The Asian in the West*, pp. 65–80. Las Vegas: Western Studies Center.

———. 1970b. "Red Guard on Grant Avenue: The Rise of Youthful Rebellion in Chinatown," in Stanford M. Lyman (Ed.), *The Asian in the West*, pp. 99–118. Las Vegas: Western Studies Center.

———. 1974. *Chinese Americans*. New York: Random House.

———. 1977. *The Asian in North America*. Santa Barbara, CA: Clio Press.

Mark, Diane Mei Lin and Ginger Chih. 1982. *A Place Called Chinese America*. Washington, DC: Organization of Chinese Americans.

Monahan, T. 1977. "Illegitimacy by Race and Mixture of Race." *International Journal of Sociology and the Family*, 7 (January-June): 45–54.

Nee, Victor and Brett Nee. 1973. *Longtime Californ': A Study of an American Chinatown*. New York: Pantheon.

Nee, Victor and Herbert Y. Wong. 1985. "Asian American Socioeconomic Achievement: The Strength of the Family Bond." *Sociological Perspectives*, 28(3): 281–306.

Petersen, William. 1978. "Chinese Americans and Japanese Americans," in Thomas Sowell (Ed.), *Essays and Data on American Ethnic Groups*, pp. 65–106. Washington, DC: Urban Institute Press.

Schaffer, Richard T. 1984. *Racial and Ethnic Groups.* Boston: Little, Brown.

Schwartz, Shepard. 1951. "Mate Selection Among New York City's Chinese Males, 1931–1938." *American Journal of Sociology, 56*: 562–568.

Simpson, George E. and J. Milton Yinger. 1965. *Racial and Cultural Minorities.* New York: Harper & Row.

Siu, Paul. 1952. "The Sojourner." *American Journal of Sociology, 58*: 34–44.

Sollenberger, Richard T. 1968. "Chinese-American Child-Rearing Practices and Juvenile Delinquency." *Journal of Social Psychology, 74* (February): 13–23.

Staples, Robert and Alfredo Mirande. 1980. "Racial and Cultural Variations among American Families: A Decennial Review of the Literature on Minority Families." *Journal of Marriage and the Family, 42*(4): 887–903.

Sue, Stanley and Harry Kitano. 1973. "Asian American Stereotypes." *Journal of Social Issues, 29* (Spring): 83–98.

Sue, Stanley and Derald W. Sue. 1971. "Chinese American Personality and Mental Health," in Amy Tachiki et al. (Eds.), *Roots: An Asian-American Reader,* pp. 72–81. Los Angeles: Continental Graphics.

Sung, Betty Lee. 1967. *Mountain of Gold.* New York: Macmillan.

———. 1977. "Changing Chinese." *Society, 14*(6): 44–99.

———. 1987. "Intermarriage Among the Chinese in New York City," in *Chinese America: History and Perspectives 1987,* pp. 101–118. San Francisco: Chinese Historical Society of America.

———. 1990. "Chinese American Intermarriage." *Journal of Comparative Family Studies 21*(3): 337–356.

U. S. Bureau of the Census. 1995. *Statistical Abstract of the United States: 1995.* Washington, DC: U.S. Government Printing Office

———. 1993a. *1990 Census of Population. Social and Economic Characteristics. United States.* CP-2-1. Washington, DC: U.S. Government Printing Office.

———. 1993b. *1990 Census of Population. Social and Economic Characteristics of the Asian American Population.* Washington, DC: U.S. Government Printing Office.

U. S. Department of Commerce. 1975. *Bureau of the Census. Historical Statistics of the United States.* Washington, DC: U.S. Government Printing Office.

U. S. Department of Justice. 1992. *1991 Statistical Yearbook of the Immigration and Naturalization Service.* Washington, DC: U.S. Government Printing Office.

———. 1981. *1980 Statistical Yearbook of the Immigration and Naturalization Service.* Washington, D.C: U. S. Government Printing Office.

———. 1988. *Statistical Yearbook of the Immigration and Naturalization Service.* Washington, DC: U.S. Government Printing Office.

———. 1989. *Statistical Yearbook of the Immigration and Naturalization Service.* Washington, DC: U.S. Government Printing Office.

Weiss, Melford S. 1970. "Selective Acculturation and the Dating Process: The Patterning of Chinese-Caucasian Interracial Dating." *Journal of Marriage and the Family, 32* (May): 273–278.

———. 1974. *Valley City: A Chinese Community in America.* Cambridge, MA: Schenkman.

———. 1977. "The Research Experience in a Chinese American Community." *Journal of Social Issues, 33*(4): 120–132.

Willmott, W. E. 1964. "Chinese Clan Associations in Vancouver." *Man, 49*: 33–36.

Wong, Jade Snow. 1950. *Fifth Chinese Daughter.* New York: Harper and Brothers.

Wong, Morrison G. 1980a. "Changes in Socioeconomic Achievement of the Chinese Male Population in the United States from 1960 to 1970." *International Migration Review,* 14: 511–524.

———. 1980b. "Model Students? Teachers' Perceptions and Expectations of their Asian and White Students." *Sociology of Education, 53*: 236–246.

———. 1983. "Chinese Sweatshops in the United States: A Look at the Garment Industry," in Ida H. Simpson and Richard L. Simpson (Eds.), *Research in the Sociology of Work,* vol. 11, pp. 3, 7–79. Greenwich, CT: JAI Press.

————. 1984. "Economic Survival: The Case of Asian-American Elderly." *Sociological Perspective,* 27(2): 197–217.

————. 1985. "Post-1965 Immigrants: Demographic and Socioeconomic Profile," in Lionel A. Maldonado and Joan W. Moore (Eds.), *Urban Ethnicity: New Immigrants and Old Minorities. Urban Affairs Annual Review,* vol. 29, pp. 51–71. Beverly Hills, CA: Sage.

————. 1986. "Post-1965 Asian Immigrants: Where Do They Come From, Where Are They Now, and Where Are They Going," in Rita J. Simon (Ed.), *The Annals of the American Academy of Political and Social Science,* vol. 487, pp. 150–168. Beverly Hills, CA: Sage.

————. 1989. "A Look at Intermarriage Among the Chinese in the United States in 1980." *Sociological Perspectives* 32(1): 87–108.

Wong, Morrison G. and Charles Hirschman. 1983. "The New Asian Immigrants," in William McCready (Ed.), *Culture, Ethnicity and Identity: Current Issues in Research,* pp. 381–403. New York: Academic Press.

Yang, C. K. 1959. *The Chinese Family in the Communist Revolution.* Cambridge: Technology Press.

Yuan, L. Y. 1963. "Voluntary Segregation: A Study of New Chinatown." *Phylon, 24* (3): 255–265.

————. 1966. "Chinatown and Beyond: The Chinese Population in Metropolitan New York." *Phylon,* 27(4): 321–332.

————. 1980. "Significant Demographic Characteristics of Chinese Who Intermarry in the United States." *California Sociologist,* 3(2): 184–197.

13 | The Japanese-American Family

Kerrily J. Kitano
Harry H. L. Kitano

INTRODUCTION

Given the history of the Japanese Americans in the United States, it is surprising that they have survived and have even gained a degree of mobility and recognition that would have been deemed impossible several decades ago. For they were sent en masse to "internment centers" during World War II, a euphemism for living behind barbed wire enclosures and under armed guard, then encouraged to return to Japan. It did not matter that most were American-born citizens—the hostility towards them was such that the Constitution and the Bill of Rights were scraps of paper, not guarantors of rights.

In 1988, however, came the passage of a Civil Rights Act benefiting Japanese Americans. And in October 1990, Harry Kitano received the following letter:

> A monetary sum and words alone cannot restore lost years or erase painful memories; neither can they fully convey our Nation's resolve to rectify injustice and to uphold the rights of individuals. We can never fully right the wrongs of the past. But we can take a clear stand for justice and recognize that serious injustices were done to Japanese Americans during World War II. In enacting a law calling for restitution and offering a sincere apology, your fellow Americans have, in a very real sense, renewed their traditional commitment to the ideals of freedom, equality and justice. You and your family have our best wishes for the future.

The document was signed by George Bush, President of the United States. In addition there was a check for $20,000. Since part of the ability of Japanese Americans to survive these major events has been credited to their families and the ethnic community, the purpose of this chapter is to provide a picture of the Japanese-American family—the influence of both the ancestral and the American cultures; how it has dealt with crises; and the importance of generational changes and the current family.

HISTORICAL BACKGROUND

Japan was an isolated island until 1853, when American ships under the command of Admiral Matthew Perry came seeking trading agreements on behalf of the United States. The Emperor Meiji, restored to the throne in 1868, reversed the earlier imperial policy of isolation and in order to increase Japan's trade and to consolidate his dynasty's political power encouraged greater contacts with the Western world (Kitano, 1980).

By 1890, 12,000 Japanese had settled in Hawaii and 3,000 on the continent, most of them in California. A much greater emigration soon followed— by 1930, the U.S. Census recorded 138,834 Japanese, with 97,456 in California. How this small population, always less than 1 percent of the nation's total, could be viewed as a danger to "White America," indicates the strength of paranoia reinforced by the image of the "Yellow Peril."

The first-generation immigrant, called the Issei, was primarily young and male, and although many had a sojourner's orientation—to make money, then return to Japan was a common goal—others opted to establish permanent roots in the new country. One established route for starting a family was through the custom of picture brides, where an exchange of pictures with the prospective bride's family in Japan was the primary source of contact. However, marriage by proxy was legal under Japanese law, and the background of each young person was often investigated.

Harry Kitano's mother was a picture bride who came from the same "ken" or province of her husband and was considered by the matchmakers in Japan to be an ideal choice to be sent to America because she was judged to be a little more independent and scholarly than her peers. It is difficult to provide an objective analysis of her marriage; perhaps it is enough to say that she and her husband raised seven children and were grandparents to scores of others. They remained together for most of their lives, except for a two-year separation when Mr. Kitano was sent to a World War II concentration camp in Montana, while Mrs. Kitano was sent to the "civilian" concentration camp in Topaz, Utah.

There was seldom any demonstration of affection between husband and wife or to their children. But they provided the functions of a solid family— family meals, family outings, gettogethers with other Japanese families, and an emphasis on the importance of the family name. Shame was one means of social control: Don't do things that will bring shame on the Kitano family and the Japanese community. There was a strong emphasis on obedience, especially to the Caucasian teachers, to study hard, to keep quiet, and not to complain (*monku*). Mr. Kitano lived past 90 years of age, while Mrs. Kitano lived to the ripe old age of 103.

The Issei were exposed to the values and lifestyles of the Meiji Period of Japan (1868–1912). It was a period where Japan was being influenced by the Western world and "modernization." However, there were certain traditional ways of looking at the family, such as a hierarchical family structure with male dominance, prescribed role behavior dependent on age, sex, and the importance of duty and obligation. Loyalty to larger units than the individual was important—the family, the village and the nation. Arranged marriages were common and deference to parental priorities was important. Love was not a high priority in marriages, and individual choice was rare. The Issei came from a culture that placed high value on a group and family orientation in which prescribed roles for males and females were clearly drawn and individualistic attitudes and behavior at variance with stated role prescriptions were discouraged.

Central to the family system was the *ie* (family, household, house), the primary unit of social organization. This was a legal and political organization based on Confucian political principals, which emphasized that stable families ensured a stable society. The *ie* structure endured over time and was of greater importance than the individuals constituting the unit; individual interest and goals were secondary to the larger unit. It was a composite of the concrete and abstract, the material and spiritual, and included such elements as family name, occupation, property, tradition, family altar, graveyard, and codes of expected behavior (Wagatsuma, 1977).

Because the continuation of the *ie* was of utmost importance to the family's future, marriage and the selection of prospective mates was a serious matter and involved the entire family. The social, psychological, and physical background of prospective mates and their families was carefully scrutinized before final arrangements were made. Marriages were made for the purpose of producing heirs and the continuation of the *ie*; marriage for love was considered immoral because it placed individual interest above that of the *ie*. The continuation of the unit was considered to be of such importance that adoption of a daughter, husband, or husband and wife was practiced when there was no offspring.

The moral and legal duty of continuing the *ie* was vested in the household head (*kacho*) who, as eldest son and heir to the property rights, had the obligation of securing a stable environment for its members and providing arrangements for marriage, occupation, food, and living comforts. The jurisdiction of his authority encompassed final decisions in matters concerning marriage, choice of occupation, place of residency, and expulsion from the family for each member of the *ie*.

Dedicating one's life to the advancement and good reputation of the *ie* was an obligation. Respect, obedience, and filial piety to parents and ancestors were highly emphasized, along with observance of rank order within the family structure. Generally, respect was required from person of lower to higher rank, from children to parents, and from wife to husband (Wagatsuma, 1977).

Given this structure, the importance of shame as a means of social control was important. To bring shame to the *ie* and to the family were major transgressions; current discussions of the effectiveness of shame in the American culture can be best understood in the context of the structural arrangements of the society. Shame in a society based primarily on individualism may not be as effective as in one with a strong group orientation.

It is clear that not all, or even most Issei behaved according to these role prescriptions, but most were exposed to them.

Community Organizations

The Issei quickly realized that complaints about their unfair treatment as individuals and families could be easily ignored. As a result, they developed their own organizations, the most prominent being the local Japanese Associations. The leadership was primarily male; the associations raised funds, sponsored picnics, provided interpreters, participated in American parades, cared for cemeteries (Japanese were forced to develop their own because of discrimination), and supplied a variety of social welfare services. The associations were especially concerned with upholding the reputation of Japanese as good and loyal citizens and functioned as the source of information for the community.

Other important Issei organizations were the *ken* (prefectural) groups so that immigrants from, for example, Hiroshima *ken* could get together for social and occupational opportunities. There were the churches, both Buddhist and Christian, and the all-Japanese congregations developed religious youth clubs, and women's auxiliaries. The Issei also established Japanese-language schools for their children and formed study and hobby groups to foster such activities as flower arranging, cooking, and martial arts. Fishing, both individually and in groups, was a popular activity. But for most Issei, making a living was the highest priority and took up the majority of time.

Feelings Against the Japanese

The attitudes of some groups, such as the Asiatic Exclusion League, illustrated the barriers faced by the Issei. In a copy of their 1910 proceedings (Daniels, 1962: 28), the exclusion of Japanese from the United States was based on the following assumptions:

1. We cannot assimilate them without injury to ourselves.
2. No large community of foreigners, so cocky, with distinct racial, social and religious prejudices, can abide long in this country without serious friction.
3. We cannot compete with a people having a low standard of civilization, living and wages.
4. It should be against public policy to permit our women to intermarry with Asiatics . . .

5. We cannot extend citizenship to Asiatics . . .
6. If we permit the Jap to come in, what will . . . become of our Exclusion with [sic]
   Chinese.

Organized labor, often identified with liberal causes, was much more racist in pre–New Deal days. Along with the conservative right wing groups, Socialists also advocated for a "white man's" country. One spokesperson wanted to restrict immigration from all "backward races," while another insisted that the United States and Canada be kept for the "White Man." Jack London, the famous novelist, declared that, "I am first of all a white man and only then a Socialist" (Daniels, 1962: 30).

In summary, the Issei faced a large number of barriers in adjusting to life in the new country. Most damaging were the discriminatory laws—they could not become citizens; they could not intermarry; they were segregated and were limited in terms of occupation. But they did start family life so that expectations were placed on their American-born children, the Nisei.

The Nisei

The Nisei possessed one advantage denied their parents: They were U.S. citizens by birth and not "aliens ineligible for citizenship." Therefore, Issei parents often placed an undue burden on their children—after all, weren't they citizens, familiar with the language and culture? But there was also the worry they the Nisei might become "Americanized" too fast and forget about the ancestral heritage.

The Nisei were brought up to work hard, conform to community standards, do their best, study diligently, and respect authority. They were good students; some went to college and to graduate school. But they remained targets of prejudice and discrimination. Civil service positions were closed as well as teaching posts in the public schools. Professionals were often confined to their own community; farming, gardening, small businesses, and mom and pop stores were important ways of making a living. Concern for the limited employment opportunities for the Nisei was such that the Carnegie Foundation funded a study in 1929 that focused on the second-generation Japanese American problem. Interviews with selected Nisei respondents showed a constant picture of despair, of questioning the value of education and hard work since there was little chance of obtaining decent jobs (Strong, 1934).

Richard Nishimoto, coauthor with Dorothy Thomas of *The Spoilage* (1946), graduated from Stanford in 1929 in engineering. Every one of his white classmates was interviewed by corporations for jobs except for Nishimoto. When he asked the reason, he was reportedly told: "Look at your face. It's Oriental. No one will hire you." Despite his strong scholastic record, he never applied for employment as an engineer again (Nishimoto; 1995).

The Nisei were born into bilingual homes, and though most Issei continued to use Japanese among themselves, Nisei took part in both cultures. One Nisei (Daniels, 1962: 14) remembers:

> [I] sat down to American breakfasts and Japanese lunches. My palate developed a fondness for rice along with corned beef and cabbage. I became equally adept with knife and fork and chopsticks. I said grace at meal times in Japanese and recited the Lord's Prayer at night in English. I hung my stocking over the fireplace at Christmas and toasted "mochi" at Japanese New Year.

Prior to World War II, the Nisei struggled for a degree of independence and autonomous living, but most were economically dependent on the Issei. Discrimination and prejudice from the mainstream community strengthened the influence of the Issei family and community on their children.

World War II and the Wartime Incarceration

The Japanese attack on Pearl Harbor on December 7, 1941 set into motion an event that will always be remembered by Japanese Americans. The long history of anti-Japanese prejudice had conditioned the public to believe that this tiny minority was an actual threat to the United States. Although the vast majority were loyal to the United States, members of Congress, the mass media, farmer's associations, and the administration were able to pass legislation that led to the evacuation of 110,000 Japanese Americans from the Pacific Coast and incarceration behind barbed wire. They were not the death camps of Nazi Germany, but they were America's concentration camps (Daniels, 1971).

A large number of studies cover this period, including Weglyn (1976) and Daniels, Taylor, and Kitano (1991). The following is a brief summary of this period in U.S. history.

On February 19, 1942, President Franklin D. Roosevelt signed Executive Order 9066, which designated restricted military areas and authorized the building of "relocation" camps. The ten camps were scattered over California, Arizona, Idaho, Wyoming, Colorado, Utah, and Arkansas. In March 1942, the forced evacuation of West Coast Japanese, most of them American citizens, began; by November, more than 110,000 were behind barbed wire. It was a rapid, smooth evacuation, aided by the cooperation of the Japanese people themselves. They responded to posted notices to register and to assemble voluntarily at designated points, and then they marched off to the trains and buses that took them to the camps.

Beneath this accommodating face lay the disruption of years of suffering and effort. Homes and possessions were abandoned or stolen; personal treasures were sold for a fraction of their value; farms and gardens were ruined; and families disintegrated.

Harry Kitano remembers:

> My father was taken away soon after Pearl Harbor, so my mother was nominally in charge. She was unable to function—she thought that we were going to be taken away and shot. It meant that the burden of family responsibility was taken over by my older sister—to register, to assemble, to store belongings, and to pack for an unknown future—they were done in the context of panic and anxiety.

Camp life also encouraged peer group over family interaction. Meals were served in community mess halls so that peer groups ate together; barracks were small and overcrowded so that family gatherings were difficult, if not impossible. Family discipline was difficult to enforce; the concept of shame was stretched. Kitano remembers that going for second helpings at the mess hall was sanctioned for adolescent males, but if one went for a third helping, one might hear that one had "no shame." As with most norms that might prove functional in camp settings, very few made much sense upon release.

The camps were closed in 1946, and there was some difficulty in getting some people to leave. Having grown accustomed to living behind barbed wire, they feared their reception by an anti-Japanese populace. For many, there was no place to go. Nevertheless, the postwar years saw the need to reintegrate their lives to the "free" world; to look for jobs and housing and start family life anew. Although there was an initial scattering to the Midwest and East Coast, the great majority eventually returned to California, where they were able to take advantage of the booming economy. They also found a diminution of anti-Japanese prejudice as new targets were the influx of blacks from the South and immigrants from south of the border (Daniels and Kitano, 1970).

Effects of the camp experience varied widely among Japanese Americans, dependent on such variables as age, marital and family status, American identity, and expectations. A common reaction was an attempt to forget about the period, at least in terms of sharing this experience in public. Many of the younger generation indicate that they only heard about the evacuation when they took a college class about the topic; as one consequence, open discussion was silent for many decades.

The Issei Family

The family has been central to the Japanese-American experience. It has undergone change, especially by generation, so that a summary of each generation's experience will be presented. Only remnants of the Issei family survive. Survivors of the early immigrants are well past 90 years old; most arrived prior to 1924, when immigration was totally denied.

Issei marriages were built on the social models of Meiji Japan, and Yanagisako (1985) summarizes some of their characteristics:

1. Absence of choice in the selection of spouse (arranged marriage)
2. Interaction based on obligation
3. Strong involvement in other family relationships
4. Priority of filial bond over conjugal bond
5. Male dominance
6. Rigid division of labor by sex
7. Emotional restraint, with emphasis on compassion, respect, and consideration
8. Stability
9. Little verbal communication

There were clear role prescriptions—males were to handle external matters while females were assigned tasks within the home. Education was valued, especially for male children, and family and community gatherings were important. Many American celebrations were incorporated with ethnic ones: Christmas, July 4th, with the New Year and the Emperor's birthday celebrated Japanese style. Harry Kitano, who grew up as a Nisei under an Issei family, remembers:

> Father was strict and foreboding, especially when we were growing up. Mother was always busy—cooking, washing and trying to keep us all busy. This was in the 1930s where times were hard—how she made ends meet, how she was able to put hearty food on the table every day with limited income, is a source of wonderment. Their lives were hard; there seemed to be little to enjoy. One thing that I remember—when they showed Japanese movies at Kimmon Gakuen, we went with mother. She would give us a summary of the plot—then we would ride home in a taxi. I don't remember father going with us, but it was a special treat

Wartime evacuation broke up the family. After World War II, the Issei tried to reestablish their families even though by then most of the children were married and out of the home. However, many Issei still remained central to their families; there would be family gatherings and a comparison of the progress of their Nisei children and the growing number of Sansei, or third-generation grandchildren. It appeared that as the Issei grow older, they somehow seemed to mellow and, especially if successful, become quite generous and giving. The interview continues:

> I was amazed how different father had become as he aged. He was gentle, soft spoken and much warmer than when we were growing up. Perhaps life had become easier for him, or we had changed, possibly both. Mother was also gentler and caring, although she seemed to still prepare food for large families and for hard times.

It is our observation that Issei families were especially able to deal with hard times—the depression of the 1930s, the wartime evacuation—while feeling somewhat uncomfortable with the relative affluence of the 1960s and 1970s. The idea of saving for a rainy day and preparing for hard times seemed imprinted in their minds; when Kitano's mother, at the age of over 100, received her $20,000 redress check, one of her first utterances was, "I should put some money in the bank for the future." Low expectations can serve to cushion some of the blows of a hostile society.

The Nisei Family

Not all Issei families subscribed to the norms of the Issei society, just as not all Nisei followed the norms of the American society. Yanagisako (1985) provides some of the contrasts between Issei and Nisei views of marriage. Exposure to American models meant that for the Nisei there was much more freedom of choice of spouse, the concept of romantic love, relative freedom from other family relationships, priority placed on conjugal bonds over filial bonds, greater equality of the sexes, more flexibility in sex roles, higher emotional intensity, with emphasis on sexual, romantic attractions, and greater instability and verbal communication between spouses. It is a common process faced by all immigrant groups—the retention of ethnic ways and the attraction of the new culture. Generally, youngsters prefer the more "American way," which is often equated as becoming more modern than remaining "old fashioned."

The Nisei developed their own organizations, such as the Japanese American Citizen's League (JACL), patterned on American models in contrast to the Japanese Associations of the Issei. The transition of the group from its early days can be gathered from the sites of their national conventions: Initially meetings were held at modest ethnic sites; currently they are held at first-class hotels in major cities. The early organization was male dominated; recently women have begun to play a more prominent role. The JACL has also seen the retirement of the older Nisei, and one of its primary missions has been to attract the newer generations.

One effect of the World War II years was the scattering of the Japanese Americans from their West Coast enclaves. There was a program to grant release from the concentration camps—Nisei were able to go to college and to relocate to the Midwest and the East. Others volunteered for the U.S. Army so that at the end of the war many Nisei had seen and experienced a world that was different from their West Coast experience. This exposure meant that many were not content to return to their prewar status as second-class citizens. Nisei took advantage of the G.I. Bill, resulting in a highly trained and educated cadre of Japanese Americans who were able to achieve upward mobility in the expanding economy of the postwar period.

The Nisei are now in their retirement years; most are past 60 years of age. They face questions that the elderly of all cultures face: health, income, retirement, and dependence. What are the roles of the ethnic family and community? What is the role of the public sector? In areas of concentration such as Los Angeles and San Francisco, they have developed their own senior citizen facilities; other Nisei have relied on the family. There appears to be a special bonding among the Nisei, primarily among those who went through the World War II concentration camp period. Camp reunions are popular, and the question of "What camp were you in?" remains an opening line that is sure to gain a positive response.

Older Nisei are more likely to be closer to Issei models, while younger ones are more familiar with postwar America. The Nisei have been a high achieving group; many are college educated and have been occupationally mobile. They were fortunate in purchasing land and homes in California before the tremendous leap in real estate prices so that the majority are in comfortable surroundings. One of the problems for their children, the Sansei, is the specter of downward mobility.

The Sansei

The Sansei and subsequent generations of Japanese born in the United States demonstrate the waning influence of the ancestral culture and the almost total acquisition of American culture. Yet, the stereotype of "traditional Japan" remains very strong so that those unfamiliar with the ethnic group expect the Sansei, as well as all Japanese Americans, to be familiar with Japan. But most of the newer generations do not know the Japanese language and are unfamiliar with its history and culture. Some can't even answer the standard question, "Where are the best Japanese restaurants in Los Angeles?" primarily because their favorite restaurants may be French, Italian, or Chinese. The extent of their integration varies with area of residence, expectations, ethnic identity, and the socialization practices of their families.

For example, a Sansei growing up in New York will be different from one growing up in Chicago, who in turn will be different from one growing up in Los Angeles or Honolulu; each will reflect the "local" flavor. The one common factor will be that of visibility, a variable that has not changed significantly over time. A common experience faced by all generations are questions of their "real" nationality—aren't they really from Japan?

Sansei follow the model of love as the primary reason for marriage and, depending on the social class status of their parents, participate in activities that were not a central part of the Issei and Nisei culture. Trips to Europe and Asia, skiing vacations, enrollment at prestigious and expensive private schools and universities, and purchase of expensive cars are not that uncommon. But living off the generosity of Nisei parents may not be a permanent reality. It appears that many Nisei have compensated for the deprivation of their early years by lavishing money on their children and grandchildren.

Compared to previous generations, there is much more of an openness about sex, about the role of males and females and the division of labor in marriage, among the Sansei. Many families include working wives, and priority is given to the husband-wife relationship over kinship ties, although it is interesting to note that there is a resurgence of extended family ties among families. For example, the Sansei in Kitano's family have planned a family reunion for 1996 at the Asilomar in Monterey, California with an expected attendance of over seventy relatives. Generational differences can be seen— the Issei family reunions were at the parents' home with home-cooked meals; the Nisei family gatherings would have been a picnic or a potluck.

Certain expectations have characterized all Japanese-American families. Good grades, discipline, concern about what others think and not standing out in any deviant fashion remain a strong part of the ethnic group culture. Although there remain "safe" choices of college majors—education, medicine, pharmacy, and engineering—Sansei can also be seen majoring in English, theater, and television.

A survey of Asian Americans in fraternities and sororities (very few Nisei belonged to such organizations in their college careers) revealed the following picture. The vast majority had close relationships with their parents, positive feelings about their grandparents, and did not feel competitive with their siblings. They worked hard for their grades, and most of them held part-time and summer jobs while attending school. They were active in high school activities, but less active in college. The majority did not participate in the drug and alcohol culture and felt more comfortable with Asian than Caucasian friends. They were financially dependent on their parents; a high percentage received assistance from their parents in purchasing a car. They were comfortable with their ethnic background and had few problems with their ethnic identity (Takahashi, 1985).

A current impression is that the picture remains somewhat similar, but an interview with an older Nisei female (K. Kitano, 1996a) indicates the following:

> Things have really changed. In the JACL National Convention held in Salt Lake City in 1995, they even passed a resolution supporting same sex marriages. Women have become more independent and outspoken and have taken over leadership in some of the local chapters. But there also appears to be a rising interest in Japanese cultural activities—a school that opened in her neighborhood teaching about the traditional Japanese culture was oversubscribed. Many of the enrolled were products of interracial marriage.

A male Sansei working in the community answered the question of the future of Japanese Americans by responding, "What Japanese Americans?" With low immigration and Japanese Americans marrying out of the group, the answer was an accurate reflection of the changing identity of Japanese Americans (K. Kitano, 1996b).

Ethnic Identity

Ethnic identity in the context of these changes remains an important variable. Most of our acquaintances identify as Japanese Americans, although the meaning of this identity has undergone changes by generation. The Issei were Japanese—language, culture, and history were intimately related to Japan. Food, newspapers and recreational activities were also more Japanese than American, and most Issei were more conversant about what went on in the home country than in the United States.

The Nisei had exposure to and identification with both the Japanese and the American cultures, making a Japanese-American identity appropriate. The Sansei identity may be closer to what Gans (1979) terms a "symbolic ethnicity." Sansei identity may include such diverse activities as attending ethnic festivals, eating ethnic foods, and seeing a Japanese movie, but it would not necessarily include studying and learning about Japan, its language and its culture, or becoming deeply involved in ethnic group activities and giving high priority to ethnic group concerns.

Although their experience is similar to many other immigrant groups, changing by generation from an ethnic to an American perspective, it is important to realize that Japanese Americans have been singled out by their race. Restrictions on immigration and citizenship were based on race, and imprisonment during World War II was because of membership in an "enemy race." Even third- and fourth-generation Japanese, thoroughly Americanized, hear such comments as, "My, you speak English well;" "You people make such wonderful cars," and "Where are you really from?" As Omi and Winant (1994) indicate, race remains a powerful variable in modern American society.

The Japanese-American Family in Comparison with Other Asian American Groups

A picture of Japanese Americans in relation to other Asian-American groups is drawn from the U.S. Bureau of the Census (1993), based on the 1990 census. Their population of 847,562 placed them third behind the Chinese and Filipinos (see Figure 13-1). The majority lived in two states: California with 312,989 and Hawaii with 247,486. The Japanese have the smallest portion of foreign born among the Asian groups. Less than 33 percent were foreign born, compared to over 65 percent of the total Asian American population.

Before 1975

1975 to 1979

1980 to 1990

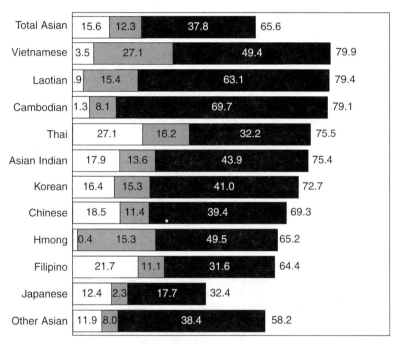

FIGURE 13-1   Foreign Born by Year of Entry: 1990 (Percent)

Source: U.S. Bureau of the Census (1993: 3).

A somewhat surprising finding is the 42.8 percent of the group who speak Japanese at home; the 57.7 percent who do not speak English very well and 33 percent who are linguistically isolated (see Table 13-1). In our surveys of Japanese Americans we have found that well over 90 percent prefer to speak English and do not need a Japanese translation.

The Japanese are the oldest of all Asian groups, with a median age of 36.3 years, compared to the total Asian median age of 30.1 years. The Southeast Asian groups are quite young (see Figure 13-2).

The Japanese male, with 89.9 percent, and the female, with 85.6 percent, have the highest completion rate of high school among all Asian-American groups. In terms of bachelor's degree or higher, both the Japanese male and female rank lower than several other Asian groups but are higher than the total Asian population (see Table 13-2).

The size of the Japanese family, 3.1 members, is the lowest among all Asian-American groups. It probably reflects the more acculturated and older Japanese population (see Figure 13-3).

TABLE 13-1. Percentage of Persons Who Speak Other Language at Home and Ability to Speak English: 1990 (Percent)

	Speak Asian or Pacific Islander Language at Home	Do Not Speak English "Very Well"	Linguistically Isolated[a]
Total Asian	65.2	56.0	34.9
Chinese	82.9	60.4	40.3
Filipino	66.0	35.6	13.0
Japanese	42.8	57.7	33.0
Asian Indian	14.5	31.0	17.2
Korean	80.8	63.5	41.4
Vietnamese	92.5	65.0	43.9
Cambodian	95.0	73.2	56.1
Hmong	96.9	78.1	60.5
Laotian	95.6	70.2	52.4
Thai	79.1	58.0	31.8
Other Asian	21.0	49.9	30.2

[a]Linguistic isolation refers to persons in households in which no one 14 years old or over speaks only English and no one who speaks a language other than English speaks English "very well." *Source:* U.S. Bureau of the Census (1993: 5).

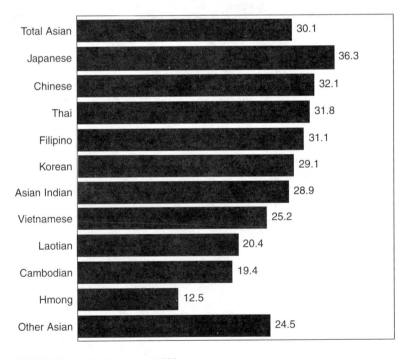

FIGURE 13-2   Median Age: 1990

Source: U.S. Bureau of the Census (1993: 3).

TABLE 13-2. Educational Attainment by Sex: 1990 (Percent 25 years old and over)

	High School Graduate or Higher		Bachelor's Degree or Higher	
	Male	*Female*	*Male*	*Female*
Total population	75.7	74.8	23.3	17.6
Total Asian	81.7	73.9	43.2	32.7
Chinese	77.2	70.2	46.7	35.0
Filipino	84.2	81.4	36.2	41.6
Japanese	89.9	85.6	42.6	28.2
Asian Indian	89.4	79.0	65.7	48.7
Korean	89.1	74.1	46.9	25.9
Vietnamese	68.5	53.3	22.3	12.2
Cambodian	46.2	25.3	8.6	3.2
Hmong	44.1	19.0	7.0	3.0
Laotian	49.4	29.8	7.0	3.5
Thai	88.6	66.2	47.7	24.9
Other Asian	85.9	78.7	47.5	34.2

Source: U.S. Bureau of the Census (1993: 4).

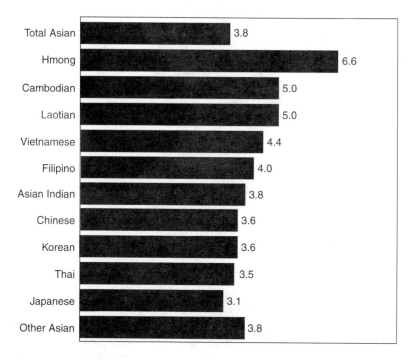

FIGURE 13-3   Family Size: 1990

Source: U.S. Bureau of the Census (1993: 4).

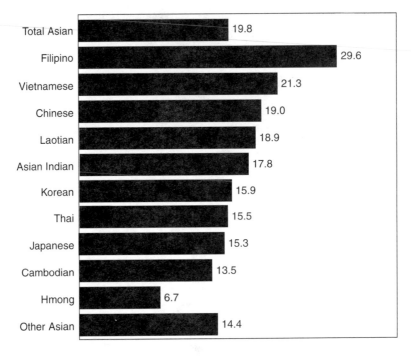

FIGURE 13-4   Families with Three or More Workers: 1990 (Percent)

Source: U.S. Bureau of the Census (1993: 6).

There were 15.3 percent of Japanese families with three or more workers, compared to 19.8 percent among all Asian American families (see Figure 13-4). The relatively small size of the Japanese-American family is one factor in the lesser number of family workers.

The Japanese workforce participation rate of 64.5 percent is similar to the 67.4 labor participation rate of all Asian Americans (see Figure 13-5). It places them at the middle of comparative groups and may be a reflection of the number of elderly retirees in the community.

The Japanese per capita income of $19,373 is the highest of all Asian groups, where the average Asian per capita income was $13,806 (see Figure 13-6).

The Japanese poverty rate of 7.0 percent is among the lowest; the total Asian poverty rate was 14.0 percent. The rates of poverty among the Southeast Asian Refugee groups remains very high (see Figure 13-7).

Outmarriage, defined as marriages where one partner is not of the same ethnic group, is shown in Table 13-3. The Japanese outmarriage rates are the highest, with over 50 percent marrying out of the group. Females in all of the Asian groups outmarry more than males. The most significant factor for the Japanese is generation; while outmarriages of most of the other Asian groups are of the first generation, Japanese-American outmarriages

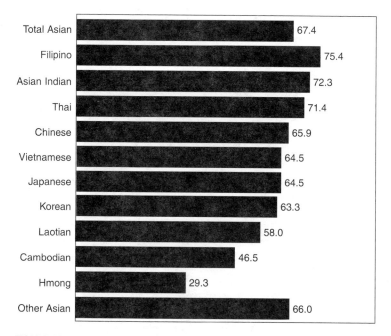

FIGURE 13-5   Labor Workforce Participation Rates: 1990 (Percent 16 years old and over)

Source: U.S. Bureau of the Census (1993: 5).

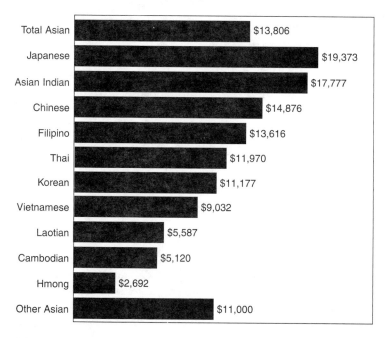

FIGURE 13-6   Per Capita Income: 1990 (In 1989 dollars)

Source: U.S. Bureau of the Census (1993: 7).

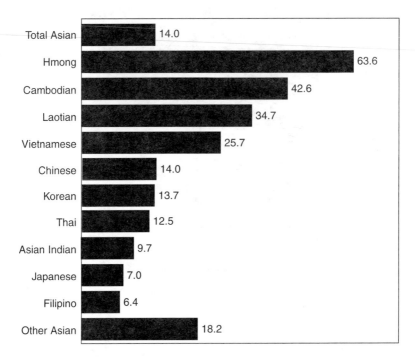

FIGURE 13-7   Poverty Rates for Asian Persons: 1989 (Percent)

Source: U.S. Bureau of the Census (1993: 7).

are primarily of the third generation. The trend is very strong; the first generation marries within their own group, and there are higher rates of outmarriage in succeeding generations. It should also be recalled that antimiscegenation laws were in effect until the 1950s.

The following generalizations are appropriate when discussing the Japanese-American family.

1. Visibility remains the thread that ties the various generations together. However, with the rise of interracial marriages, mixed-race children provide another category.
2. Some cultural styles of the Issei generation remain. These include hesitation and modesty, family ties, ethnic foods, and high educational expectations. Retention and change vary by families in terms of size, socialization, area of residence, ethnic identity, and contact with the dominant community.
3. The most visible change is that of outmarriage. Hypothesized reasons for the high rates include integrated housing, loss of family control over marital choices, changes in the law, a more open dominant society, and generation.
4. Most contemporary Japanese-American families are similar to their dominant community counterparts, sharing the same problems and concerns.

TABLE 13-3. Outmarriage Rates of Chinese, Filipino, Japanese, Korean and Vietnamese, Total and By Gender for 1975, 1977, 1979, 1984, and 1989, Los Angeles County

Ethnicity	Year	Marriages	Number	Percent	Percent of Outmarriages by Gender	
					Women	Men
Chinese	1989	1.836	622	33.9	63.0	37.0
	1984	1.881	564	30.0	56.6	43.4
	1979	716	295	41.2	56.3	43.7
	1977	650	323	49.7	56.3	43.7
	1975	596	250	44.0	62.2	37.8
Filipino[a]	1979	1.384	565	40.8	74.2	25.8
Japanese	1989	1.134	588	51.9	58.3	41.7
	1984	1.404	719	51.2	60.2	39.8
	1979	764	463	60.6	52.7	47.3
	1977	756	477	63.1	60.6	39.4
	1975	664	364	54.8	53.6	46.4
Korean	1989	1.372	151	11.0	74.8	25.2
	1984	543	47	8.7	78.6	21.4
	1979	334	92	27.6	79.6	20.4
	1977	232	79	34.1	73.4	26.6
	1975	250	65	26.0	63.1	36.9
Vietnamese[b]	1989	555	147	26.5	54.4	45.6
	1984	560	34	6.0	74.7	25.3

[a]Data for Filipinos is limited to 1989.
[b]Data for Vietnamese is limited to 1984 and 1989.
Source: H. Kitano, D. Fujino, and J. Takahashi (in press)

5. Compared to the past, Japanese Americans are doing well. However, the tendency of Americans to equate the policies of the Japanese nation with Japanese Americans may still cause problems. In the past, hostility towards Japan has affected the treatment of Japanese Americans, and similar events may occur in the future.

A middle-aged Sansei (Kitano, 1996c) who grew up in a Nisei family, interacted closely with her Issei grandparents, and is herself the mother of teenaged Yonsei (fourth-generation) children sums it up:

I think that the Issei family was close, they spoke Japanese and their friends were other Issei. My parents were close to the Issei, especially as they grew older. There were a lot of family gatherings, and they kept in touch with other Nisei, especially those from the same World War II camps. I grew up as a Sansei and feel quite American—I don't know Japanese and my friends are not exclusively other Japanese Americans. But I know that I am a Japanese American, but my kids have almost no ethnic identity.

REFERENCES

Daniels, Roger. 1962. *The Politics of Prejudice.* Berkeley and Los Angeles: University of California Press.

Daniels, Roger. 1972. *Concentration Camps, USA: Japanese Americans and World War II.* New York: Holt, Rinehart and Winston.

Daniels, Roger and Kitano, Harry H. L. 1970. *American Racism.* Englewood Cliffs, NJ: Prentice-Hall.

Daniels, Roger, Sandra Taylor, and Harry H. L. Kitano. 1991. *Japanese Americans: From Relocation to Redress.* Rev. ed. Seattle: University of Washington Press.

Gans, Herbert J. 1979. "Symbolic Ethnicity: The Future of Ethnic Groups and Cultures in America." *Ethnic And Racial Studies, 2* (January): 1–20.

Kitano, Harry H. L. 1980. "Japanese Americans," in S. Thernstorn (Ed.), *Harvard Encyclopedia of American Ethnic Groups,* pp. 561–571. Cambridge, MA.: Harvard University Press.

Kitano, Kerrily. 1996a. Interview with C. Iiyama, El Cerrito, CA. March.

———. 1996b. Interview with B. Aoki, San Francisco, CA. March.

———. 1996c. Interview with S. Shiromoto, El Cerrito, CA. March.

Kitano, H., Fujino, D., and Takahashi, L. (in press) "Interracial Marriages: Where are the Asian Americans & Where are they going," in N. Zane and L. Lee (Eds.), *Handbook of Asian American Psychology.* Newbury Park, CA: Sage Publications.

Nishimoto, Richard. 1995. *Inside an American Concentration Camp.* [Lane Hirabayashi, Ed.] Tucson: University of Arizona Press.

Omi, Michael, Winant, Howard. 1994. *Racial Formulation in the United States.* New York: Routledge.

String, Edward K. Jr. 1934. *The Second Generation Japanese American Problem.* Stanford, CA.: Stanford University Press.

Takahashi, Linda. 1985. "What Gardena Means to Me." Unpublished manuscript, University of California, Los Angeles.

Thoams, Dorothy, Nishimoto, Ricard. 1946. *The Spoilage.* Berkeley and Los Angeles: University of California Press.

U.S. Bureau of the Census. 1993. *We the American Asians.* U.S. Department of Commerce, Economics and Statistics Administration. September.

Wagatsuma, Hiroshi. 1977. "Some Aspects of the Contemporary Japanese Family: Once Confucian, Now Fatherless." *Daedalus, 106* (2): 181–210.

Weglyn, Michi. 1976. *Years of Infamy.* New York: Morrow.

Yanagisako, Sylvia J. 1985. *Transforming the Past.* Stanford: Stanford University Press.

14 | The Asian Indian–American Family

Uma A. Segal

INTRODUCTION

The economic, political, and social opportunities promised by life in the United States have drawn immigrants from numerous countries. Although the term "Asian/Pacific Islander" (Asian American) has been officially established by the Immigration and Naturalization Service (INS) to include all Asians and Southeast Asians, it actually overlooks major national and racial differences as well as the cultural variations that exist within and among nations and races from Asia. The general public's overwhelming perception of Asian-American immigrants is that they constitute a "model minority," are professionally successful, and, according to their own cultural notions of health, are well adjusted both emotionally and mentally. Despite this stereotype, it is increasingly apparent that people who migrate carry with them culturally ingrained values, roles, and behaviors (Fong and Peskin, 1973), often making acculturation a difficult and painful process. This chapter isolates one national group—Asian Indians—from among the many within the Asian/Pacific Islander category and explores its immigrant experience in the United States.

HISTORICAL BACKGROUND

Immigration Patterns

Although doumentation of the presence of Asian Indians dates back to 1790 in Massachusetts, it was essentially in the latter part of the nineteenth century that Indians began migrating to North America in significant numbers. These were voluntary emigrants, primarily agricultural laborers from the northwestern part of India, who settled in California between 1899 and 1920 and numbered about 7,300 (Balgopal, 1995; Chandrasekhar, 1982). Perhaps because of cultural and/or economic reasons, which were reinforced by restrictive immigration laws, only men from China (Lyman, 1973), Japan (Ogawa, 1973), and India (Balgopal, 1995) entered the United States. During the years 1928–1946, Indians were denied citizenship and further immigration was prohibited. Isolated from their families because of punitive immigration policies, 3,000 Asian Indians returned to India between 1920 and 1940. After the passage of the Immigration Act of 1946, Asian Indians were once again able to immigrate legally to the United States, but only at the rate of 100 per year. Between 1958 and 1965, only a few more Indians came to the United States and on the whole these were a small transient community of students, Indian government officials and businessmen, although there was a small number (4,756) of new immigrants (Leonhard-Spark and Saran, 1980).

While immigrants from India continue to enter the United States, an exceptionally large influx of Indians occurred in the mid-1960s with the liberalization of immigration policies and passage of the Immigration and Naturalization Act of 1965, which abolished national quotas and allowed in immigrants based on profession and skills. Many Asian Indians (henceforth referred to as Indians) came to the United States in the mid-1960s as students, most with intentions of returning to India, yet the majority remained and established themselves on the East and West Coasts as well as in several metropolitan areas around the country (Table 14-1).

The 1990 census (U.S. Bureau of Census, 1992) indicates that Indians are the fourth largest Asian-American group (815,447), but more recent data developed by the Census Bureau (sphs@fyvie.cs.wisc.edu, 1994) indicates that there are currently over 1 million Asian Indians in America and that between 1980 and 1990 the community grew 125.6 percent from 361,531. This figure has surpassed projections that the number would be close to 1 million by the year 2000 and 2 million by 2050 (Bouvier and Agresta, 1985).

As is evident from population data, Indians compose one of the fastest-growing immigrant groups, resulting not only from the arrival of new immigrants, but also from the birth of the second generation. A 1988

TABLE 14-1. Population Density of Indians in Select Urban-Metropolitan Areas

Geographic Area	Population Size
Boston-Lawrence-Salem, MA	16,549
Chicago-Gary-Lake Country, IL	59,046
Dallas-Fort Worth, TX	17,831
Detroit-Ann Arbor, MI	18,509
Houston-Galveston-Brazoria, TX	26,559
Los Angeles-Anaheim-Riverside, CA	68,887
New York-Northern New Jersey-Long Island, NY	199,010
Philadelphia, PA-Wilmington, DL-Trenton, NJ	26,120

Source: Adapted from sphs@fyvie.cs.wisc.edu. (1994, October 4): Indians in the United States: A success story.

Bureau of Census sample revealed that whereas 22.3 percent of the Indians in the United States 14–24 years of age were foreign born in 1979, only 12.6 percent of this group was born outside the United States in 1988 (Dutt, 1989). Thus, increasing numbers of Indian children are second-generation, U.S.-born citizens.

Defining Characteristics of Indians in the United States

The migration of Indians is not a new phenomenon because they have long tended to move to different parts of the world to settle whenever the opportunity was ripe (Saran, 1985). However, the large wave that immigrated to the United States between the years 1965 and 1987 was distinctly different from the populations that emigrated to other countries, and is also different from other groups that have come to the United States, in being highly educated and professional. Those who came to the United States from India during those years did not represent a cross-section of the Indian subcontinent; as a result of personal reasons for emigrating and restrictions on immigrants from Asia, most belonged to a very select group that was seeking professional or advanced (graduate level) educational opportunities. Because India has an educational system with a distinct British orientation, most Indians who came to the United States prior to 1985 were fluent in English and had some exposure to Western values and beliefs, facilitating their entry into American society (Leonhard-Spark and Saran, 1980). Because of their facility in English, their high levels of education, and their professional skills, most were soon able to establish themselves successfully in the United States, and because they tended to select residences based on convenience and locality rather than proximity to other Indians, few Indian ghettos exist in the United States.

Under the family reunification provision of the Immigration and Naturalization Act of 1965 (PL 89-236), U.S. citizens and permanent residents of Asian Indian origin can sponsor their immediate family members for immigration. Many of the immigrants of the 1960s, 1970s, and 1980s are now citizens and/or permanent residents of the United States, are well established economically, and are in positions to sponsor relatives. Many of these new immigrants are not as skilled as their sponsoring relatives, and consequently the median income of Indians who immigrated between 1987 and 1990 is one-fifth of those who arrived before 1980 (Balgopal, 1995; Melwani, 1994). Despite this fact, the mean family income is $59,777, the highest of any Asian group in the United States. The per capita income is 25 percent higher than the national average and second only to that of Japanese Americans among all ethnic groups (sphs@fyvie.cs.wisc.edu, 1994).

Overall, the educational level of Indians is also high. The 1990 census data show that 87.5 percent of Indians have completed high school, 62 percent have some college education, and over 58 percent have at least a bachelor's degree. Professionally, 14 percent are engaged in careers related to science, medicine, engineering and technology, and 19.3 percent are in managerial, administrative, sales, and teaching positions. Over 5,000 Indians are faculty members at universities in the United States.

The influx of newcomers into a new country often strains the host country's cultural homogeneity and may be perceived as a threat to societal norms (Mayadas and Elliott, 1992; Mayadas and Segal, 1989). Although Asian Indians have generally been highly successful in their professional and business endeavors and are recognized as productive contributors to the United States' economy, because of sociocultural differences between the Indian and American societies a marked distance exists between long-established Americans and this group of naturalized citizens. The difference is further highlighted as intergenerational conflicts emerge between these immigrant professionals of the 1960s, 1970s, and 1980s, and their American-born offspring (Segal, 1991).

Regardless of reasons for emigrating, all immigrants to a new country find adjustment to foreign values, expectations, and environment baffling. However, although European immigrants and their descendants faced cultural conflicts, because their features are Caucasian and the color of their skin is white their assimilation into the American mainstream was largely dependent on their individual decisions to adopt the American culture (Portes and Zhou, 1993), unlike the more recent immigrants from Africa, South America, and Asia, who are always distinguishable because of their physical characteristics. While the different experiences of the immigrant groups from Asia varies in the extent to which they have experienced overt discrimination, injustice and oppression, their experience of acculturation in terms of value adjustment and orientation of family life tends to be similar. Immigrants often experience an identity crisis and feel isolated and alienated from both their culture of origin and the American culture (Sue, 1973). Such stress results in one of three reactions: The individual (1) adheres closely to the values of the culture of origin, (2) becomes overly Westernized and rejects Asian ways, or (3) attempts to integrate aspects of both cultures that he or she perceives as most amenable to the development of self-esteem and identity (Sue, 1973). Portes and Zhou (1993) propose a fourth reaction, selective assimilation, through which a group engages in rapid economic advancement with the deliberate preservation of the immigrant community's values and tight solidarity. In their study of relationships between acculturation-related demographics and cultural attitudes of a group of 105 Indians living in the United States, Sodowsky and Carey (1988) found that 65 percent defined themselves as mostly Indian, 21 percent preferred an equal mix of Indian and American lifestyles, and 7 percent chose not to identify themselves as being Indian.

Indian Demography and the Family

Located in South Asia, India's southern half is bordered by the Bay of Bengal and the Arabian Sea and its northern portions border on Pakistan, China, Nepal and Bangladesh. The country is 1,269,340 square miles (3,287,590 sq km), slightly more than one-third the size of the United States, with an estimated population in 1995 of 936,545,814. Thirty-five percent of the population is below 14 years of age, 61 percent is between the ages of 15 and 64, and only 4 percent is 65 and over (Netscape, 1996). The population is ethnically diverse in religion (Hindus 80%, Muslims 14%, Christians 2.4%, Sikhs 2%, Buddhists 0.7%, Jains 0.4%, others 0.4%), language (although English has an associate status, it is the most used language for national, political, and commercial communications; Hindi, the official language, is spoken by about 30% of the population, with at least twenty-four other languages, each spoken by a million or more persons and numerous other languages and dialects), and culture (many regional groups have their own forms of art, music, literature, style of clothing, and food). Politically, India is a federal republic and the world's largest democracy and received its independence from the British on August 15, 1947. It is composed of twenty-five states and seven union territories, with a government consisting of executive, legislative, and judicial branches and a universal suffrage age of 18 years.

The Traditional Indian Family

Most Indians base their family lifestyles on the following traditional values, beliefs, and expectations that appear to be common to most Asian cultures.

1. Asians are allocentric (group oriented), not idiocentric (self oriented), and the individual is expected to make sacrifices for the good of the group—more specifically, the family (Hofstede, 1980; Segal, Segal and Niemczycki, 1993; Segal, 1988, 1993; Triandis, Bontempo, Villareal, Asai and Lucca, 1988).
2. Males are valued more than females. The society is clearly patriarchal, and men act as head of the household, primary wage earners, decision makers, and disciplinarians. Women are subordinate and serve as caretakers; as children, they are groomed to move into and contribute to the well-being of the husband's family (Dhruvarajan, 1993; Ho, 1988; Mullatti, 1995; Segal, 1993; Sue, 1981).
3. Children are docile and obedient. Their role is to bring honor to their families by exhibiting good behavior, high achievement, and contributing to the well-being of the family. Mates are selected for children by their parents; the selection is based on various factors unrelated to the emotional expectations of the child. Choice of career is heavily influenced, if not dictated, by the family (Dhruvarajan, 1993; Dutt, 1989; Saran, 1985; Segal, 1995a; Sinha, 1984).
4. High levels of dependency are fostered in the family. The female is expected to be dependent throughout her life—first on her father, then on her husband, and finally on her eldest son. Children are dependent emotionally, and often

socially, on their parents throughout the parents' lives. Authority and respect for elders are paramount, and the family unit controls members in all areas of their lives. Traditionally, difficulties are handled within the family, whether these difficulties are familial, emotional, professional, financial, or health related (Ho, 1988; Segal, 1995b, Sinha, 1984).

5. Two major concepts tend to permeate all significant relationships: obligation and shame. One is expected to be selfless and obligated to significant others—especially to parents and husbands—within the family. Furthermore, one's behavior should never bring shame upon oneself or one's family (Chatrathi, 1985; Ho, 1988; Segal, 1995a, 1995b; Sue, 1981).

Consistent with these patterns, the traditional Indian family system is that of the joint family, in which the family is strictly hierarchical, patriarchal, and patrilineal. Three or more generations may live together, with age, gender, and generational status of individuals serving as the primary determinants of behavior and role relationships. Two or more family groupings of the same generation may be found in the joint family system as sons bring their spouses to the parental home. A high premium is placed on conformity. Interdependence is fostered, self-identity is inhibited (Sinha, 1984), and a conservative orientation, resistant to change, is rewarded. Despite the many changes and adaptations to a pseudo-Western culture and a tentative move toward the nuclear family among the middle class, this system is preferred (Mullatti, 1995) and continues to prevail in modern India.

In the joint family, each child has multiple role models and the supervision and training of children is shared by all family members. Whereas infants are generally overindulged, young children are reared in an authoritarian atmosphere in which autonomy is not tolerated (Mullatti, 1995). As children enter their teen and young adult years, guilt, shame and a sense of moral obligation are used as the primary mechanisms of control (Sue, 1981). This control model has a positive aspect in providing a structure that maintains family integrity through a deep-seated belief in societal norms and an obligation to duty (Table 14-2).

TABLE 14-2. Traditional Joint Family vs. the Modern Nuclear Family: Some Changing Characteristics

Joint Family Structure	*Nuclear Family Structure*
Highly hierarchical	Minimally hierarchical
Multiple adult models	Few adult models
High infant indulgence	Low infant indulgence
Authoritarian and severe childrearing	More permissive and less punitive child rearing
Emphasis on conformity	Greater freedom of choice
Deemphasis on autonomy	Greater emphasis on individual development
Father's limited and mother's dominant role in childrearing	Shared roles in child rearing

Source: Adapted from D. Sinha (1984).

Belief in the integrity of the group provides the family with a group identity and strengthens family stability, albeit at the cost of individual autonomy (Triandis et al., 1988). Western authors often overlook this aspect of Indian culture, which serves to bind the intergenerational family together (Segal, 1991).

Indian Adolescents

Biological puberty is considered the onset of adolescence; the end is marked by the integration of one's psychological identity and the establishment of a goal-directed life (Seltzer, 1982). In an individualistic society, adolescence extends over a long period and involves tasks that require considerable trial and error. Surmounting these difficulties and emerging as a well-functioning individual with a discrete self-identity can create high levels of stress, especially if adolescents' struggles to establish their identities are not understood or supported by significant adults.

The phenomenon of adolescence, as conceptualized in the West, is relatively absent for the Eastern teenager. Among Indians, the transitional period of adolescence is generally not recognized. Children continue to remain submissive to parents even after they get married, become employed, and leave the parental home (Sue, 1981). Because youth must always defer to age, the autocratic parent-child relationship tends to persist. Although each subcommunity may have a rite of passage with the onset of biological puberty to mark adulthood, there is no concurrent change in role, status, responsibility (Arrendondo, 1984), or autonomy in decision making, and children accept parental authority throughout the latter's lifetime. The traditional family structure and norms do not reward competitiveness, achievement orientation, or self-orientation within the family. The welfare and integrity of the family supersedes individual self-identity (Chinese Culture Connection, 1987; Sinha, 1984; Triandis, 1988).

THE MODERN "INDIAN-AMERICAN" ETHNIC FAMILY

Mayadas and Elliott (1992) argue that key issues in the adjustment and integration of immigrants are the dimensions of economic advantage/disadvantage and cultural identity. They suggest that the immigrant group's socioeconomic status (including class, education, age and gender) and cultural identity (language, religion, rituals, values, dress, food, art, music and political affiliation) greatly impact acceptance by the host country, which, in turn, has implications for the adjustment, resocialization, and modification of values and beliefs of that immigrant group. Regardless of where Indians have migrated over the years (to the United States, England, Africa, the Caribbean, or the Far East), they have tended to move for economic reasons and not because they have been politically or socially oppressed in India. They have always maintained strong social, emotional, and cultural ties with their homeland, often return to visit India, and usually provide financial support to members of their families who remain in that country (Leonhard-Sparks and Saran, 1980). Even those who left several generations ago, like those in the United Kingdom, South Africa and the Caribbean, maintain a strong cultural Indian identity, and marital patterns have tended to remain endogenous.

This pattern is consistent with the experience of the more recent Indian immigrants to the United States and of Portes and Zhou's (1993) framework, which indicates segmented assimilation into the country. As a group, they have advanced rapidly economically but have deliberately preserved their values and maintained tight community solidarity. This tendency has had significant implications not only for their own integration into the Western society, but also for the socialization of the second generation and the conflicts associated with balancing North American and Eastern values, beliefs and lifestyles.

Family Structure, Family Behavior, and Ethnic Culture

Because the Indian immigrant group is a relatively new one, with members of the majority of the first generation now in their mid-life years and with strong connections with their homeland, several family patterns have remained consistent with traditional ones. In fact, in an attempt to protect tradition, family patterns may not have experienced normal cultural evolution. Many immigrants arrived in the United States as married couples or family groups or, in the late 1960s and early 1970s, returned to India to follow prescribed rules of arranged marriage. It is only now, when large numbers of second-generation Indians are reaching adolescence and adulthood, that traditional cultural values and practices are being questioned, presenting conflicts of a nature the first generation had not envisioned. Furthermore, concerns about aging parents, many of whom still remain in India, and about their own retirement in a country into which they have not truly assimilated are added issues that were not prevalent in Indians' early immigration experience.

To understand the Indian family in the United States, it is advisable to look at current role relationships within the family, demographic characteristics of the family, extended family relationships, and processes for the maintenance and transmission of the culture.

Family Roles

Most Indians who grew up and lived in a joint family system in India, found themselves living in a nuclear family after immigration to the United States because immigration policies permitted only spouses and children to accompany the young professional/student population. What did accompany these immigrants was the Indian patriarchal, paternalistic system, in which adult male members of the family continue to be the primary wage earners, decision makers, and protectors of the young, women, and the elderly. While a large proportion of immigrant Indian women are highly educated professional women who work outside the home, a fact that might suggest their emancipation from traditional role behaviors, this assumption warrants discussion.

Regardless of the religious and cultural backgrounds of Indian families, perceptions of the role of women in the Indian family have been inculcated into the society through classical literature and throughout Indian civilization, and three pervasive models are prevalent: (1) Sita, the heroine of the *Ramayana*, who provides the feminine ideal of the chaste, self-sacrificing wife (Lebra and Paulson, 1984); (2) the powerful archetype—the Mother—who can be gentle or aggressive, but ultimately is the supreme nurturer (Lebra and Paulson, 1984; Thomas, 1984); and (3) the dependent—first on her father, then on her husband and, finally, on her son (Ho, 1988; Sinha, 1984).

India, with its diverse cultures, has always been a country of apparent dichotomies—one of the most obvious contradictions being its highly patriarchal structure that nevertheless allowed the election of a female prime minister, Indira Gandhi, who was repeatedly reelected to the position. Perhaps the contradiction can be understood through the alternative perception of women's emancipation embodied in Mahatma Gandhi's belief that women have stronger moral principles and Indira Gandhi's belief that women's problems are associated with poverty, illiteracy, and lack of economic opportunities (Bumiller, 1990). Evident by its absence in the principles of these two prominent and influential political figures in recent Indian history is the mention of gender inequality (Bumiller, 1990), especially in the home. Despite the Western belief that women's movements and higher social class increase gender equality (Dhruvarajan, 1993; Goode, 1982; Scanzoni, 1979), this equalization has not occurred in the Indian tradition. Thus, although women may become powerful in the political structure, they are still responsible for upholding the images of Sita/the pure, the Mother/the revered, and the dependent/fragile within the boundaries of the family.

These role models for women and the relationship between the genders persist both in modern-day India and in the United States today. Although many Indian immigrant women are encouraged into higher education by their families, it is often more to increase their attractiveness to successful eligible bachelors than to ensure their personal independence. Even though an educated wife increases the social status of professional man, however, she is always aware that even if she should work, her professional responsibilities will always be subordinate to those to her family. In a study examining the relationship between occupation and sex-role attitudes, findings indicated that there were no differences between homemakers and working women in their views of sex-role expectations, even among those who were aware of the inequities in the traditional role behaviors (Dasgupta, 1986). In a recent qualitative, in-depth study of Indian immigrant families, Dasgupta (1992) found a rigid division of roles, with women being primarily responsible for housekeeping, including cooking, cleaning, and child care, and men fulfilling the role of the primary breadwinner. Eighty percent of the women reported that their most important activities were to care for their husbands and children by cooking for them and "keeping the house," while the majority of the men felt their responsibility was to protect and provide for their families and make major family decisions in areas such as the children's education, home/car purchase, and family vacations.

Traditionally, especially among the middle classes, finances related to the maintenance of the home and the family have generally been handled by the women. Nevertheless, contrary to the belief that "money is power," Indian women are not the decision makers on major issues within the family. They may have input into decisions but generally defer to the will of the man. Interestingly, however, in the absence of a strong extended family network and domestic help, both of which are the norm for this socioeconomic group in India, Indian men in the United States are likely to help with the care of the children and with some of the household chores (Dasgupta, 1992). Nevertheless, as the term "help" implies, these are still clearly women's areas of responsibility. Across the board, both male and female respondents in Dasgupta's (1992: 476) study concurred that

> the "ideal husband" . . . is friendly, understanding, affectionate, humorous, smart, educated, cooperative, a good companion, unselfish, a good provider and mild natured. . . . [the] 'ideal wife' . . . is a good mother, understanding, supportive, a good homemaker, friendly and self-sacrificing. She . . . can share her husband's work, can take care of everybody and look after the well-being of the family.

Although the allocentric value orientation is clearly evident in role expectations for both men and women, it is worth noting that the term used by both genders to describe the ideal behavior for men is "unselfish," while for women it is "self-sacrificing."

While traditional male-female patterns persist in the immigrant generation, the patriarchy is experiencing considerable turmoil as the second generation reaches adolescence and adulthood. Whereas teenagers in India mature in a protected, unidirectional environment, their Indian counterparts in the United States grow up in a dual culture. Indian youth in the United States are faced with a critical need to establish their identities—not only in terms of moving into adulthood, but also in determining their identity within the Indian and American cultures. Many of these children, and their parents, experience a turbulent adolescence as a result of these conflicts (Segal, 1991).

Depending on the degree to which immigrant parents are willing or able to assimilate Western values, the second generation faces considerable value conflict, role conflict, and role discrepancies, often resulting in role partialization (Merton, 1957) during the adolescent and young adulthood phases of development. Especially because the parent generation retains traditional values and attitudes and is unaware of the conflict their children experience, it continues to exert pressure toward conformity (Saran, 1985).

Literature suggests that adolescents generally conform to their peer culture in lieu of parental norms (Blos, 1979; Segal, 1991; Seltzer, 1982). In a given society, the cumulative effect of parental/peer cultures provides continuity and impetus to the cultural evolution of society. However, when parents and peer group originate from different cultures, this continuity is often dramatically disrupted, giving rise to major intrafamilial conflict. Segal (1991) reports that at least five issues are identified by both parents and children as causing emotional difficulty within the family: control, communication, marriage, prejudice, and expectations of excellence.

1. *Control.* Many immigrant Indian parents do not recognize the ability of their children to make sound judgments and view their children's desire for independent decision making as cultural contamination that will eventually result in deviant behavior. To the children, this conflict represents a power struggle to which many respond with rebelliousness, verbal retaliation or passive-aggressive behavior. Many exercise their freedom away from home, reinforcing their parents' fears of the adverse effects of independence.

2. *Communication.* Communication is often poor between the first and second generations. It tends to be unidirectional, flowing from parent to child, with the expectation that the latter will listen, attend and agree. Children usually do not share personal concerns as they believe that parents will not listen, understand or help. Both parents and children are cognizant of the poor communication between them.

3. *Marriage.* The major area of conflict appears to center on the relationship between young men and women. For the majority of Indian immigrant parents, marriages were arranged by their respective families. Although there are now some changes in India, dating then was not allowed, and immigrant parents have brought with them the Indian norms of the 1960s and 1970s. Furthermore, then and now, sexuality is not recognized, sex education (both at home and in school) is not available and premarital sex is abhorrent. When Indian children in the United States seek permission to date, many parents fear dating will lead to sexual involvement. Thus, children who date—with the parents' knowledge—are the exception.

   Parents' greatest fear is that the children will marry non-Indian Americans and thus lose their cultural identity, heritage, values, and mores. In India, people marry only within their own subculture and subcaste; therefore, the idea of marriage to a non-Indian is especially disturbing. The parents' fears are compounded by the perception that most American marriages end in divorce.

   Children's concerns about not being allowed to date, on the other hand, culminate in their fear of having a marriage arranged with someone unknown.

Because most parents want their children to marry Indians and the availability of partners in the Indian community in most cities in the United States is limited, arranged marriages are encouraged. However, to children reared in a country where individuals select their own spouses, the concept of an arranged marriage is alien and distressing.

4. *Prejudice.* Most first-generation Indians socialize only with other Indians. While they are well integrated with the dominant American society professionally, they tend to have few non-Indian friends. Consequently, prejudicial notions about the American culture have had little opportunity for rectification. This lack of integration (Table 14-3) into the American society suggests segmented assimilation (Portes and Zhou, 1993) and raises some important issues: Are Indians responding to underlying discrimination? Is the American culture so alien that distance is necessary to avoid contamination? Does retention of the Indian culture supersede other factors? Whatever the parental reasons, children often view their parents as narrow minded and may respond by developing negative attitudes toward the Indian culture.

Prejudicial attitudes of both parents and children create additional barriers to effective communication, making cross-cultural adjustment more difficult. In rural areas, because the Indian community is small, Indians must interact more with their American counterparts allowing for the removal of some intercultural barriers.

5. *Expectations of excellence.* As a result of the high selectivity in immigration criteria, a large majority of Indians in the United States are professionals and high achievers. This "model minority" image is upheld as a standard for Indian youth. Success is expected because the behavioral norm is that "all Indians do well." However, unlike their parents, Indian children are not necessarily

TABLE 13-3.   Areas of Nonintegration

	Parental Preference	*Family's Coping Strategy*
Food	Indian, vegetarian	Two menus: Indian for parents, American for children
Clothing	Sari, *salwar kameez*	Parental garb: professional—Western; social—Indian. Children's garb: contemporary Indian
Religion	Primarily Hinduism, some Islam	Organization of Hindu religion and practice in temples (normally, not an organized religion)
Language	Hindi or one of the 24 or more Indian languages	Poor mastery of Indian language by children; English primary in home
Friendship	Indian, preferably with those from the same region in India	Parents—minimal social contact with Americans; children—significantly more friendships with Americans
Entertainment	Movies, eating out, dinner parties	Few Indian movies, restaurants available; primary entertainment is large dinner parties with Indians. Children often excuse themselves.

Source: U. A. Segal (1991).

achievement driven. Although some may be outstanding in their performance, most will be average and a few will fail. Since perfection and excellence are expected, many average achievers perceive themselves as failures and experience low self-esteem. Moreover, these children may not receive intervention because seeking professional help is considered a sign of weakness and disgrace.

Despite these intrafamilial conflicts, inherent strengths within the family often support Indian children during critical periods. Most adolescents feel that despite the control exercised by their parents and the lack of communication, because of the training and guidance of parents they are firmly grounded in basic human values. Many have an unshakable confidence that their ties with the family are stable and permanent (Segal, 1991).

Demographic Characteristics of the Family

Data of the U.S. Bureau of Census (1992) support the contention that the Indian lifestyle and philosophy is highly centered around the integrity of the family. Only 4.5 percent of Indian families in the United States have no husband present, and only 1.3 percent of Indian households consist of unmarried, or cohabiting, couples. Fertility rates in the United States appear to differ from those in India. While the majority of lower-class families in India may have large families of four or more children (Segal and Ashtekar, 1994) and the upper and middle classes may be limiting the number of their children to one or two (Segal, 1995c), the norm of the Indian family in the United States appears to be two or three children. Perhaps this trend is an offshoot of family planning efforts in India in the 1970s and 1980s, when many of the first generation came to the United States, that had as their slogan "*Do, ya theen bachchen, bus*" ("Two or three children are enough"). Younger generations of new immigrants seem to be having no more (but no less) than two children. Once again, concerns about family relationships may guide this decision. In India, relationships between first cousins are often as close as those of siblings. In the United States, where the support of extended families may not be readily accessible, most Indian families feel it important to ensure that their children have siblings to whom they can turn when they are adults and the parents are no longer living.

There appear to be no large-scale studies of the Indian population in the United States or representative data on the rates of marriage and/or divorce, yet observation suggests that marriage continues to be the preferred choice of lifestyle among Indians, and parents encourage their children (especially women) to marry while they are in their twenties. Most first-generation Indians, regardless of when they come, bring their spouses and children with them or return to India to marry according to family tradition. Therefore, changes in marriage patterns become most evident among the second generation of Indians. In India, partner preference is for someone from the same subgroup as oneself (culture, religion, region, caste). Ideally, parents in the United States would also select such Indian partners for their children, but because of limited choices, they are likely to accept a partner from any Indian subgroup.

The actual choice of marriage partner is significantly affected by the process of mate selection permitted by parents. Oommen (1991) suggests that it is imperative not only to examine the family from without as a part of a cultural tradition governed by society's norms, but also from within to understand its internal dynamics based on individuals' experiences and their psychosocial characteristics. Thus, while arranged marriages may be the norm, based on their own experiences and the extent to which they have accepted alternative options families may, or may not, opt to engage in the process of arranging marriages for their children.

If, consistent with tradition, an arranged marriage is expected by the first generation for its children, the family may follow a few established routes to the identification of a potential partner. The marriage partner may be sought either in the United States or in India, and parents inform their friends and family members that they are seeking a spouse for their child. They specify characteristics that may be important to them. In addition to looking for someone of the same subgroup, they may specify age, profession, food preference, interests, height, and even complexion of skin. In addition, parents may advertise in the matrimonial sections of any of the several Indian newspapers in the United States such as *India Abroad,* which has the widest circulation. The traditional arranged marriage occurred sight unseen between the couple; in the modern arranged marriage, however, both in India and the United States, appropriate potential partners are encouraged to meet and get to know each other. "Getting to know each other" is left to the discretion of the family, and the length of time, the frequency of contacts, and other details are based on the personal preferences of the particular family. Regardless of parental hopes, the man and woman can usually now decide whether they are suited for marriage.

The alternative is a "love" marriage, in which the couple meets, is attracted, and decides to get married after having established a relationship and engaging in an American-style courtship. Marriage partners are selected by the children themselves, and increasing numbers of parents are beginning to accept that if they choose to live in this country, such "love" marriages may be inevitable. Despite parental partiality toward an Indian spouse for the child, there is evidence of a rise in the number of intermarriages between Indians and Americans. This should not be surprising because second-generation children are in constant contact with non-Indians and, though they do have Indian peers, the choice of partners is relatively limited.

Observation over the last thirty years has revealed two interesting patterns: (1) Often second-generation Indian men will date American women, yet will marry Indians—either those they have met and courted in the United States or those with whom their marriages have been arranged either in the United States or in India; and (2) frequently, second-generation Indian women will date American men and then marry them. It remains to be determined whether the men are as more susceptible to the expectations of their parents or whether they perceive marriage to an Indian more consistent with familiar patterns and necessary to maintain traditional role relationships within the family.

Further observations on intermarriage suggest that, in general, men who marry American women either assimilate into Western society or, alternatively, integrate their wives into the Indian ethnic group. Indian women, on the other hand, tend to balance the unique qualities of both cultures. Perhaps this is a function of the differing family relationships and norms. In Indian culture women are expected to leave their families of origin and become a part of the husband's family (Mullatti, 1995), whereas in American culture the woman's family maintains a strong presence even after the marriage. For Indian men, tradition may indirectly dictate that he integrate his wife into his family; if he is unable to fulfill this expectation, he might find it necessary to separate himself from his family. The Indian woman, however, who is socialized to compromise while taking care of her husband, may find the differing cultural expectations a surprisingly pleasant compromise as she participates in her husband's family but also has the option of including him in her own. The few studies that have addressed tradition and role relationships among Indians in the United States have focused on the immigrant generation. The time is ripe to study the experience of the second generation and the extent to which it has adopted, adapted and/or rejected tradition.

One of the major concerns of Indian parents about intermarriages is an outgrowth of the fact that half of all marriages in the United States end in divorce within the first two years. In India, there is a general acceptance that divorce should be legally available (Desai, 1991); it is also believed to be objectionable (Chouhan, 1986; Singh, 1988), and a divorced individual, especially a woman, is highly stigmatized regardless of whether or not the divorce is based on mutual consent (Amato, 1994). Further, because a woman is expected to be self-sacrificing and devote herself entirely to her husband, people are inclined to blame the termination of the marriage on the wife (Kumari, 1989). Although both men and women receive emotional support from their respective families following marital separation, women are usually likely to receive less support than men from other sources (Amato, 1994). Divorced men are able to overcome the stigmatization and it is often possible for them to remarry, while a divorced woman is often isolated and rarely remarries.

Given the perceptions of divorce and the future of the divorcee in India, the concerns that Indian parents voice about divorce rates in America are understandable. However, there are no indicators that intermarriages in the United States between second-generation Indians and Americans are ending in divorce any more frequently than marriages between Indians. Perhaps, therefore, the worries of parents may be unfounded. It is possible that those individuals who intermarry are more cognizant of potential problems and difficulties arising out of conflicting cultural expectations and consequently invest more effort in compromise and adjustment.

Extended Family Relationships

The extended/joint family system is the norm in India, but the familial structure favored by Indians in the United States is that of the nuclear family living in separate households. With changes in immigration laws and the naturalization of many Indians has come the sponsorship of family members, many of whom have been unmarried siblings or aging parents. While unmarried siblings initially reside with the sponsoring family, they soon establish themselves in separate households, either living alone or with other individuals. Even if they do remain with the family during their single years, they move as soon as they marry (Saran, 1985). Thus, it is rare to find two or more families living within the same dwelling. However, many make their residences in the same city or geographical area to maintain proximity to the family. There appear to be no studies that examine the size of the Indian population with extended family in the United States, although Dasgupta's (1992) study suggests that it is probably relatively small. However, this group may not be as limited as Dasgupta suggests in view of the fact that it is rare to find an Indian in the United States who does not have at least one relative who has settled in the country.

Aging parents, often widows or widowers, compose another group that has come to join its children in the United States. These parents live with the immigrant generation, often making their home with the family of the eldest son, but travel between the residences of their children and spend extended periods of several months in the home of each. If both parents are alive, they may visit their children in the United States for four to six months at a time every few years, but most choose not to uproot themselves because there is little to occupy them in the United States. Furthermore, most find they are too dependent on their children financially for their entertainment and for their transportation. Nevertheless, once they are widowed, and if most of their children are in the United States, they frequently emigrate from India. While they become an integral part of the family, their position of dependence and their lack of knowledge about Western society often obliges them to renounce their authority. Thus, although they retain their status and are told of decisions, they are only perfunctorily consulted. If the immigrant wives are working outside the home, most elderly parents—especially women—assume many of the household responsibilities. They provide child care, prepare the dinner before the family returns in the evening, and assume some of the lighter housekeeping duties. On the whole, however, since they lack a peer group, lack transportation, and do not understand the culture, they are often isolated, alienated, and depressed.

Ties with other relatives, such as aunts, uncles, first cousins, and more distant cousins, are nurtured by Indian immigrants in order to maintain continuity and a sense of the family community. Families may travel to meet for festivals, important celebrations, rites of passage, and vacations; despite distances, traditional, extended family role relationships between family members are generally maintained. In addition to defining role relationships, the extended family provides financial, emotional and social support to its members. Younger siblings, their spouses, and their children continue to consult older siblings, and younger generations are expected to evidence respect toward older generations through actions and words. Although it is understood that the immigrant family will support the parental generation, first-generation immigrants have fewer expectations that their own children will care for them as they age, and many are beginning to plan retirements without dependence on their children.

Although Indians have a strong sense of community and unite to maintain and transmit culture and values (Dhruvarajan, 1993), the ties with the community are limited to intense social contacts and are not associated with affective ties or long-term help (Dasgupta, 1992), which are an integral part of the relationship with the extended family. Thus, although the Indian community provides social interaction for its members as well as short-term mutual help in times of emergencies, death, and childbirth, there is little provision for long-term help. Consequently, when possible, Indian immigrants nurture relationships with extended family members, because despite their dispersion throughout the United States the latter continue to provide the necessary emotional support and important affective ties.

Maintenance and Transmission of Culture

Although India is a multicultural country, there appear to be certain patterns that underlie all its cultures. The transmission of culture and values is inextricably interwoven with religious affiliation, and Indians define themselves simultaneously as Indian, as affiliated with a particular religion, and as belonging to a specific region of India. Religion prescribes not only the form of worship but also guides daily behavior, while the region usually identifies the language one speaks; the literature, art, and music one enjoys; the food one eats; and the clothing one wears. In the United States, if the community of Indians is small, it is united by its Indian heritage. As the community grows, it subdivides socially along regional (there are fifteen or more groups in India) and religious (Table 14-4) lines and also develops its own subgroup organizations for the maintenance and transmission of culture.

Indian culture is transmitted in various ways: (1) within the home, through the family, that often maintains strong Indian practices in role rela-

Table 14-4. Religions of India

Religion	N Percent	Origination	Text	Fundamental Principle	Philosophy	Some Important Occasions
Hinduism	80	1500 B.C.	Vedas	A philosophy of life, guided by Karma and Dharma.	Cyclical nature of life, time Good deeds result in a better rebirth, eventual release from rebirth and reunion with God	Holi, festival of spring; Diwali, festival of lights honoring King Rama; Deshera, worship of Devi, goddess of pantheon.
Islam	14	A.D. 570–632	Koran	Surrender to the will of God. God's functions: creation, sustenance, guidance, judgment.	Reforming the earth to benefit humanity, not self. Duties of profession of faith, prayer, alms giving, fasting, pilgrimage.	Muharram, day of mourning; Bakr Id, commemorates Abraham's obedience to God; Ramzan Id, feast following a month of daylight fasting.
Christianity	2.4	A.D. 3–30	Bible	Love of God and man	Call to discipleship and service. Ultimate reunification with God.	Christmas, birth of Christ; Good Friday and Easter, Christ's martyrdom and resurrection.
Sikhism	2	1469–1539	Adi Granth	Fuses elements of Hinduism and Islam—unity, truth, creativity of God and surrender to his will.	Advocates active service. Belief in transmigration and karma, union with God through meditation.	Holi; Diwali; Baisakh, date of foundation of Khalsa—militant religious order; Gurupurab birth of first and last Gurus.
Buddhism	0.7	563 B.C.	Tripitaka	The understanding and management of suffering.	Management of human existence—material body, feelings, perceptions, predisposition and consciousness.	Buddha Jayanthi, Buddha's birth (only holiday recognized by Government of India).
Jainism	0.4	599–527 B.C.	oral	Actions of mind, speech and body result in bondage and violence.	Eschew violence, free the soul. Better suffer injury than cause it.	Diwali; Mahavir Jayanthi, birth of Mahavir; Paryushana, end of rains and request for forgiveness.
Others (Judaism, Zoroastoism, tribal religions)	0.5					

tionships, eating patterns, preferred music, and language; (2) through religious organizations or groups that meet in places of worship such as temples, mosques, churches, gurdhwaras, or individuals' homes; and (3) through formal classroom instruction on the history of the country and the religion, on language, and on literature and mythology. Female children are often enrolled early in dance classes because Indian girls traditionally have been expected to be trained in the dance, music, and song of the country. Boys, on the other hand, are generally exempt from initiation into this aspect of the culture.

Major Indian artists, usually musicians and actors, often tour cities in the United States with large enough numbers of Indians to sponsor them. In addition, Indian movies often are shown in theatres around the country, and most cities with an Indian population usually have grocery and retail stores that serve Indian consumers. These stores also carry a very wide range of Indian movies and plays on videotape and music on audiotapes and compact discs. Second-generation children frequently accompany their parents to Indian social and cultural events and are usually exposed to video movies in the home—all of which contribute to the transmission of the culture.

Indians are also involved in ongoing community events that might be secular or non-secular in nature. The secular celebrations take place on India's Independence Day, August 15, and on Republic Day, January 26, when the country was formally established as an independent republic. These celebrations are often accompanied by music, dances, songs, plays, food, and fairs in which children either participate or assist. Since the large majority of Indians are Hindus, not only in India but in the United States, Indian community organizations tend to celebrate Hindu festivals such as Holi (a festival of spring) and Diwali (the festival of lights), while Indians of other religions (Muslims, Christians, and Jews) celebrate their nonsecular festivals with non-Indians of similar religions.

Transmission of Values

In addition to concerns about the transmission of culture, Indian immigrants are anxious to ensure that the second generation internalizes Indian values, many of which are allocentric and have been discussed earlier. The transmission of these values is also embodied in childrearing patterns, reactions to dating, recognition of sexuality, acceptance of cross-cultural friendships, and emphasis on education.

Childrearing is primarily the responsibility of the mother, although discipline is often enforced by the father (Segal and Ashtekar, 1994). Infants and young children are usually overindulged, and they are pampered, coddled, and allowed to wander freely and do as they wish. As they reach middle childhood, they are expected to "be seen and not heard," and must be a source of pride to their families through their appearance and their actions. Corporal punishment is perceived as an acceptable means of discipline and, since it is still generally sanctioned in the United States, is quite likely to be used by Indian parents in the United States.

Children are an integral part of the Indian family unit in the United States; it is rare for social activities to exclude children. Almost all Indian gatherings and private parties are family occasions (Dasgupta, 1992); in the few instances when children are not invited, a significant number of families arrive with their offspring anyway. Furthermore, not until the children are old enough to be away with their own friends do the parental couple go out on their own. It is unclear whether this practice arose because the family feels it is important to include children to socialize them or whether it is through a sense of protectiveness. This pattern is very inconsistent with the norm in India where children are often left at home with extended family members or domestic help while their parents pursue their social activities. It is less common to find an Indian family in the United States hiring a babysitter to care for its young children, unless it is because of work-related activities.

In addition to ensuring that Indian children are exposed to as much as possible of Indian culture, parents are also anxious to have children avail themselves of as many American extracurricular opportunities as possible, perhaps because these were not available to them when they were children growing up in India. Consequently, most Indian children participate on sports teams, learn musical instruments, and enroll in additional enrichment programs. In high school, many are encouraged to participate on forensics and debate teams, assume leadership roles in the school's student council, and become a part of the larger community.

Despite the fact that most Indian immigrants have few American friends and encourage friendships between their children and other Indian children, they still feel it is important that their children receive status and respect in their school environments. As a result, they are becoming increasingly open to their children's friendships with Americans. With these friendships, however, comes the possibility of cultural contamination in the form of parties and dating and the threat of substance abuse and sexual activities.

Although most second-generation children are willing to accept most of the traditions and values of their parents, the most difficult rule for them to accommodate is prohibition of dating. While many American children are dating when they are 14 and 15 years old, Indian children are generally not permitted to date. Furthermore, parents often differentiate between boys and girls inasmuch as they may be willing to reconsider their position for boys but rarely do so for girls. The consequence of this practice is that children often date without their parents' knowledge; when there are difficulties, however, they are unable to turn to the parents for support or guidance. Even if children do not date while they are living at home, they do begin to date when they leave home to attend college. At that time they have a handicap—they are unfamiliar with the rules of the game with which their cohort has become fairly adept and thus may be more vulnerable to use and abuse by their more experienced partners. This fact should be a cause for alarm for Indian parents, especially with the increasing information about the frequency of acquaintance rape and date rape among teenagers and college students (Holmes, 1996).

Indians are generally inhibited when it comes to talking about sex and sexuality, especially with children. Sex education in India is unheard of, and in general even the professional group of immigrant Indians finds it difficult to overcome stereotypical responses and discomfort in discussing the subject with its children. Often, given the sex education children receive in the schools, they may be more knowledgeable on the subject than some of their parents. The overriding concern of parents is that they must protect their children, especially their female children, from becoming sexually active, because this taints their purity. In this day of the rapid spread of sexually transmitted diseases, and with the terrifying knowledge that victims of the HIV/AIDS virus are growing rapidly in number among the teenage and young adult populations, precautions are warranted. Nevertheless, in many cases, parents do not recognize their children's developing sexuality and the importance of keeping channels of communication open so that children do not find themselves grappling alone with difficult situations.

Since most Indian immigrants to the United States are professional people, a high premium is placed on secular education. In addition to the transmission of culture, this group of Indians stresses the necessity of a college degree, at the minimum. Many independent secondary (private-secular) schools report a disproportionate number of Indian students. Second-generation children are encouraged to study for professions in the medical field, in the sciences, or in business. There is less support for interest in the fine arts, humanities, and social sciences because these are not associated with success. Most Indians came to the United States to improve their quality of life, and this goal now encompasses their children; since professions in the fine arts, humanities, and social sciences are not financially rewarding, these fields are discouraged. Because of the control mechanisms in place in the Indian family and the power of the parent-child relationship, children very often strive to fulfill parental expectations, even in choice of profession.

Thus, consistent with patterns for all immigrant populations (Parrillo, 1991), values are transmitted across generations through the family and through social and cultural organizations. They are modeled by parents as they socialize, discipline, and guide their children. High premiums are placed on the Indian culture, religion, allocentrism, and education. In this context, children are encouraged to be achievement oriented. In essence, segmented assimilation (Portes and Zhou, 1993) is endorsed.

CHANGES AND ADAPTATIONS

Maintenance of Culture

The Indian family, whether nuclear or extended, continues as a strong, viable unit that is cohesive and provides social, emotional, and financial support to its members. It is instrumental in transmitting Indian cultural norms and values to its children. With its increasing numbers, the community is able to consolidate its resources and provide organized vehicles for the transmission of norms and values to the second generation. Furthermore, despite the absence of Indian ethnic enclaves, close ongoing social contacts with other Indian families ensures that children develop friendships with other second-generation Indians. Because of the shared experience of growing up in a multicultural environment, these friendships persist and complement friendships with children from other ethnic-cultural groups in American society.

Children of immigrants identify three themes in their expressions of cultural identity (Sue, 1979): (1) their sense of belonging versus estrangement (an increased sense of belonging in American culture results in increased self-esteem), (2) their identification with the new country's cultural values (the accommodation of their culture-of-origin values within the framework of American values provides stability and guidance and enhances the integrative process), and (3) their family and peer relations (to the extent that these are congruent, a synthesized identity emerges).

In urban metropolitan areas, the numbers of second-generation Indians are significant. Now, more so than in earlier decades, these adolescents and young adults have the option of meeting other Indians of like interests since the pool of potential friends is significantly larger. As they aim to establish their identities distinct from those of their immigrant parents and distinct from that of young immigrants of their own age, they have coined an acronym for themselves—the ABCDs—American-Born Confused *Desi* (*Desi* is the Hindi vernacular for an Indian national), clearly indicating the struggle many encounter. A large number weave their way through the process of adolescence by becoming "more American than the Americans" and gradually attempt to balance what they perceive to be the best of both cultures—that is, those elements most amenable to the development of self-esteem and self-identity (Sue, 1973). This attitude is dramatically different from the segmented assimilation perspective (Portes and Zhou, 1993) of the immigrant generation, which is protectionist about its culture while advancing economically.

Contemporary humanists in the dominant American society seek to understand ethnic diversity and multiculturalism and recognize the vast differences in the ethnocultural composition of the country. With the increasing realization that it is impossible for people of color to truly integrate into the society, the country has evolved in its prescriptions for inclusion. The last few decades have seen the move from a belief in the melting pot theory (in which everyone blends into one indiscernible whole), through the salad bowl theory (in which separate groups maintain their differences but mix well with each other), to an understanding of the society as a mosaic (in which groups may be different, at times enmeshed with the dominant society, at other times maintaining a separation from it, preferring to remain with members of their own culture).

With more respect and acceptance accorded to differences, second-generation immigrants may not feel as great a need to reject their cultural heritage. This is apparent in the number of Indian high school students who are beginning to join Indian youth groups in several urban metropolitan areas of the country. In addition to providing social support for each other, these youth often assume responsibility for increasing awareness about the Indian culture among the non-Indian populations in their schools and communities. Much of the Hindu philosophy revolves around fulfilling duties toward family and occupations; on the whole, there is little emphasis on service to the less fortunate. Nevertheless, many Indian youth groups around the country have also assumed community service activities, suggesting the incorporation of a very positive aspect of the American value system.

Numerous indicators suggest that second-generation Indian Americans continue to be, on the average, relatively high achievers, and most appear to be much more comfortable socially with their American counterparts than are their parents. Thus, they may serve as bridges between American culture and Indian culture. With the acceptance of human diversity—and because they can often compete successfully academically, professionally, *and* socially in the dominant culture—increasing numbers are able to truly develop in a dual culture and integrate the superior qualities of both societies.

Race, Ethnicity, and Prejudice

Much of the future of the Indian ethnic group lies in the hands of the dominant culture. Although their numbers are large and they have been in the United States for three decades, Indians remain peripheral to discussions of American culture, experience, or history (Balgopal, 1995). Ironically, the restrictive legislation that permitted immigration of only professional Indians into the United States in the 1960s and 1970s had a beneficial effect for the Indian community: Those Indians who emigrated very rapidly became contributing members of society. Because most were influenced by the British through the Indian educational system, were fluent in English, and had some exposure to Western culture, pseudoadjustments in the United States were relatively easy. Moreover, since over the last three decades they have generally not established Indian enclaves, have not been socially and politically visible, and converse in English with other Indians at their place of work, they have not been perceived as a threat to the status quo of American society. Indians have truly constituted a silent minority.

Because little has been understood about their culture, Indians have escaped the overt discrimination that other Asian groups have experienced in the United States and that Indians have experienced in other countries such as the United Kingdom and Canada. They have made unique contributions to several fields in the United States, and they continue to project a positive image in the United States (Balgopal, 1995). Among their ranks, they can identify two Nobel laureates—Har Gobind Khorana for medicine in 1968 and Subrahmanyan Chandrase Khar for physics in 1983—and a music maestro, Zubin Mehta, the former conductor of the New York Philharmonic (Abraham, 1990).

With increases in their numbers, decreases in the professional and educational levels of relative-sponsored (versus business-sponsored) new immigrants, and rises in the number of Indian-owned businesses, this population is becoming more visible and separate. It is estimated that about 25 percent of all small hotels and motels are owned by Indians (sphs@fyvie.cs.wisc.edu, 1994), and Indians are now significant players in the world of computer software (Balgopal, 1995).

In recent years, with the growth of the Indian community, Indians are beginning to feel a need to participate in the political process. The Association of Indians in America, a national organization focusing on the mainstreaming needs of Indians, was instrumental in the establishment of a separate category for Asian Indians for the 1990 U.S. census. Additionally, not only have increasing numbers of Indians been elected to political offices at the city and state levels (Abraham, 1990), with some cities and towns, including Teaneck, New Jersey, Hollywood Park, Texas, and Burien, Washington, having elected people of Indian descent as mayors (sphs@fyvie.cs.wisc.edu, 1994), but the Clinton Administration has appointed Indians to federal posts in Washington. The director of the National Institute of Standards and Technology in the Department of Commerce, an administrator in the Department of Transportation, and a counselor in the Office of the White House Counsel are Indian Americans (sphs@fyvie.cs.wisc.edu, 1994).

Because of their greater visibility and activism in the political arena, recent years have seen dramatic increases in anti-Indian sentiment, especially in areas such as New York and New Jersey, which have the largest Indian populations (Table 14-1). Groups have emerged that call themselves the "Dot Busters" (in reference to the red *bindi* worn by many Indian women on their foreheads) and engage in hate crimes (acts of violence perpetuated on people because of their race, religion, national origin, or sexual orientation) against Indians, attacking them in their homes and places of business. On a more subtle level, Indians have always experienced discrimination as they encounter the "glass ceiling"; they have not had access to the top group's levels of organizations in the corporate sector (Balgopal, 1995).

Thus, much of the fate of the Indian population and the transmission of its culture may be controlled by the group's level of acceptance by the dominant American society. Indians have proven their ability to cooperate and contribute to the functioning of the United States, yet they have tried to maintain their cultural heritage. Increases in overt discrimination will have significant impact on the behavior of second and subsequent generations of Indians. On the whole, the second-generation is beginning to forge a new identity that allows it to integrate the best of both cultures and to function satisfactorily in both the Indian and American environments. Prejudice and fear of violence will threaten the synthesis of a healthy identity and successive generations may reject one or the other culture.

Social Problems, Services, and Informal Support Systems

The high level of success of Indians in the United States, their image as part of the "model minority," and most of the foregoing discussion of this chapter obscure the social problems of isolation of the elderly, conjugal violence, intergenerational turbulence (Khinduka, 1992), and poverty (Balgopal, 1995) that are, of course, experienced by significant numbers of Indians.

As the elderly population of Indians, the retired and widowed parents of immigrants, arrive in the United States to be supported by the children as dictated by tradition, they find themselves increasingly isolated. Without access to financial resources, separated from their peer group and support systems in India, with little understanding of the American culture, with no familiar activities to occupy them, they remain at home while their children and grandchildren pursue their respective occupations. American senior centers are alien to them, and since Indians do not live in ethnic enclaves, access to other elderly Indians is practically nonexistent. Even if access were possible, many elderly may be from different regions and cultures of India, may not speak the language of other Indian elders, and may have little in common with each other.

The isolation of the elderly has received little attention, but the prevalence of conjugal violence among Indians in the United States is becoming increasingly apparent as shelters for battered Indian women are being established around the country. Although the highly educated and sophisticated population of Indian immigrants in the United States chooses not to acknowledge it, the first formal organization to provide protection and assistance to women experiencing conjugal violence, Manavi, was established in New Jersey in 1985. Since then, other agencies have been formed to offer similar services to Indian women in New York (Sakhi), Chicago (Apna Ghar), Philadelphia (SEWAA), and Washington, D.C. (ASHA), among others. In Indian culture, as in many others, women and children have been perceived of as the property of males, and power has often been operationalized through violence in the process of subjugation. It is surprising that spousal violence is evident in this professional population of Indians, but is consistent with literature that suggests that family violence is not culture or class specific and is often evidenced in patriarchies (Dobash and Dobash, 1992).

Since the number of elderly Indians in the United States is still relatively low, since violence against women (and children) is hidden from public view, and since Indians have been most concerned about the enculturation of their children, the major areas of foci within the Indian family have been the behavior of the children and parent-child relationships. Even within these areas, issues that have been addressed are those of autonomy, mate selection, and career choice. There appears to be no information about teen pregnancies, abortion, or sexually transmitted diseases (including AIDS). There is little knowledge of the extent of drug usage or substance abuse, although these are significant problems in India, and while there may be a sizable gay and lesbian Indian population in the United States, as is evident in advertisements of publications in *India Abroad*, the group is not visible.

Indians traditionally have depended on their family networks to provide social, emotional, and financial support. In the absence of these supports, and because seeking help from mainstream or external resources is considered shameful, Indians often struggle in silence. For example, the unemployment rate for new Indian immigrants is more than twice that of immigrants who arrived before 1980 (Melwani, 1994). Limited income has placed additional burdens and increased the isolation of many such Indian families, who often are not aware of external sources of support and emergency assistance. Balgopal (1988) suggests that since most Indians migrated to improve their economic condition, failure to do so often results in depression, alcohol abuse, psychosomatic problems, marital conflict and even suicide.

Most Indians are loathe to utilize the services of formal human service agencies. Mental health problems often manifest themselves as psychosomatic ailments such as chronic headaches, backaches, dizziness, and weaknesses. These physical ailments are more understood by the family, and the services of a health care professional are much more acceptable than are the services of mental health care professionals. Increasingly, however, through the referrals of schools and physicians, social services and other human service agencies are contacting families experiencing distress (Balgopal, 1995). Most effective, however, is the provision of services that mobilize the family's own resource network in addition to the formal networks of the heath care and social service delivery systems.

Clearly, since the Indian population has projected the image of the model minority, has apparently acclimated itself to its new environment, and has been silent about its needs, the issues and problems it has been facing have been marginalized. Because Indians, like other Asians, prefer to keep concerns within the boundary of the family, they have not sought formal human services even in the absence of traditional informal support systems, including a viable and proximate extended family network. Since they have not come to the attention of mainstream human service agencies, the myth of the model minority is perpetuated, and few researchers in the social and behavioral sciences have seen a need to focus on their experiences, reinforcing the "squeaky wheel" phenomenon. Just as politicians are beginning to recognize that the Indian population is worth courting because of its size and overall economic power, the human service organizations will need to become cognizant of the growing problems and issues facing this population, which, unattended, will also in time impact the larger society.

SUMMARY

This chapter has traced the experiences of one of the United States' newer immigrant groups, the Asian Indian, over the last three decades. Perceived as part of the "model minority," this group numbers over 1 million, is generally highly educated and professional, and has a strong commitment to family and the Indian culture. Major issues this group is currently struggling with are the transmission of culture to the second generation; support of its aging parents, most of whom remain in India; and planning for its own retirement. Indicative of its ties with its homeland, the immigrant generation is contemplating returning to India to retire, especially since it has not truly integrated itself socially into mainstream America. The major barrier to completing the circle of exodus and return to the native land is the realization that its dual-culture second-generation children are more at home in the United States than they would be in India; to maintain contact with them and with their grandchildren (or future grandchildren), the immigrant group will have to remain in the United States. It waits to be seen whether, as a group, this generation of immigrant Indians will find that the benefits of returning to India outweigh the benefits of retiring in the United States, the land that drew them with its promise of economic and professional opportunities.

REFERENCES

Abraham, T. 1990. "Indian American Community—A Perspective," in *Handbook for Indian Immigrants*, pp. 57–61. Pittsburgh: Spindle.

Amato, P. R. 1994. "The Impact of Divorce on Men and Women in India and the United States." *Journal of Comparative Family Studies*, 25 (2): 207–222.

Arrendondo, P. M. 1984. "Identity Themes for Immigrant Young Adults." *Adolescence*, 19: 977–993.

Balgopal, P. R. 1988. "Social Networks and Asian Indian Families," in C. Jacobs and D. D. Bowles (Eds.), *Ethnicity and Race: Critical Concepts in Social Work*, pp. 18–33. Silver Springs, MD: National Association of Social Workers.

———. 1995. "Asian Indians," in R.L. Edwards (Ed.), *Encyclopedia of Social Work*, 19th ed., pp. 256–260. Washington, DC: NASW Press.

Blos, P. 1979. *The Adolescent Passage.* New York: International Universities Press.

Bouvier, L. F. and A. J. Agresta. 1985, May. "The Fastest Growing Minority." *American Demographics,* 31–33: 46.

Bumiller, E. 1990. *May You Be the Mother of a Hundred Sons: A Journey Among the Women of India.* New York: Faucet Columbine.

Chandrasekhar, S. 1982. "A History of United States Legislation with Respect to Immigration from India," in S. Chandrasekhar (Ed.), *From India to America,* pp. 11–28. La Jolla, CA: Population Review Publications.

Chatrathi, S. 1985, September 13. "Growing Up in the U.S.—An Identity Crisis." *India Abroad, 15:* 2.

Chinese Culture Connection. 1987. "Chinese Values and the Search for Culture-Free Dimensions of Culture. *Journal of Cross-Cultural Psychology, 18:* 143–164.

Chouhan, I. 1986. *From Purdah to Profession: A Study of Working Women in Madhya Pradesh.* Delhi: B. R. Publishing.

Dasgupta, S. D. 1986. "Marching to a Different Drummer? Sex Roles of Asian Indian Women in the United States." *Women and Therapy, 5* (2/3): 297–311.

————. 1992. "Conjugal Roles and Social Network in Indian Immigrant Families: Bott Revisited." *Journal of Comparative Family Studies, 23* (3): 465–480.

Desai, M. 1991. "Research on Families with Marital Problems: Review and Implications," in TISS Unit for Family Studies (Ed.), *Research on Families with Problems in India,* vol. 2, pp. 337–373. Bombay: Tata Institute of Social Sciences.

Dhruvarajan, V. 1993. "Ethnic Cultural Retention and Transmission Among First Generation Hindu Asian Indians in a Canadian Prairie City." *Journal of Comparative Studies, 24* (1): 63–79.

Dobash, R. E. and R. P. Dobash. 1992. *Women, Violence and Social Change.* New York: Routledge.

Durvasula, R. S. and G. A. Mylvaganam. 1994. "Mental Health of Asian Indians: Relevant Issues and Community Implications," *Journal of Community Psychology, 22* (2): 97–108.

Dutt, E. 1989, October. "Becoming a 2nd Generation." *India Abroad, 20* (2): 16.

Fong, S. L. M. and H. Peskin. 1973. "Sex Role Strain and Personality Adjustment of China-born Students in America: A Pilot Study," in S. Sue and N. Wagner (Eds.), *Asian-Americans: Psychological Perspectives,* pp. 79–85. Ben Lomond, CA: Science and Behavior Books.

Goode, W. J. 1982. "Why Men Resist," in B. Thorne (Ed.), *Rethinking the Family: Some Feminist Questions.* New York: Longman Canada.

Ho, M.K. 1988. *Family Therapy with Ethnic Minorities.* Beverly Hills, CA: Sage.

Hofstede, G. 1980. *Culture's Consequences.* Beverly Hills, CA: Sage.

Holmes, C. 1996. March 13. "Rape: Still a Source of Shame and Blame." *St. Louis Post-Dispatch,* pp. E1, 6.

Khinduka, S. K. 1992. Foreward, in S. M. Furuto, R. Biswas, D. K. Chung, K. Murase, and F. Ross-Sheriff (Eds.), *Social Work Practice with Asian Americans,* vii–ix. Newbury Park, CA: Sage.

Kumari, R. 1989. *Women-Headed Households in Rural India.* New Delhi: Radiant Publishing.

Leonhard-Spark, P. J. and P. Saran. 1980. "The Indian Immigrant in America: A Demographic Profile," in E. Eames and P. Saran (Eds.), *The New Ethnics,* pp. 136–162. New York: Praeger.

Lebra, J., and J. Paulson. 1984. Introduction, in J. Lebra, J. Paulson, and J. Everett (Eds.), *Work and Women: Continuity and Change,* pp. 1–24. New Delhi: Promilla.

Lyman, S. 1973. "Red Guard on Grant Avenue: The Rise of Youth Rebellion in Chinatown," in S. Sue and N. Wagner (Eds.), *Asian Americans: Psychology Perspectives,* pp. 22–44. Ben Lomond, CA: Science and Behavior Books.

Marger, M. 1989. "Business Strategies Among East Indian Enterpreneurs in Toronto: The Role of Group Resources and Opportunity Structure." *Ethnic and Racial Studies, 12* (4): 539–563.

Mayadas, N. S. and D. Elliott. 1992. "Integration and Xenophobia: An Inherent Conflict in International Migration," in A. S. Ryan (Ed.), *Social Work with Immigrants and Refugees,* pp. 47–62. New York: Haworth Press.

Mayadas, N. S. and U. A. Segal. 1989. "Asian Refugees in the U.S.: Issues in Resettlement." Unpublished manuscript, University of Texas—Arlington, Arlington, TX.

Melwani, L. 1994, January 31. "Dark Side of the Moon." *India Today*, pp. 60c–60f.

Merton, R. K. 1957. "The Role-Set: Problems in Sociological Theory." *British Journal of Sociology*, 8: 106–120.

Mullatti, L. 1995. "Families in India: Beliefs and Realities." *Journal of Comparative Family Studies*, 26 (1): 11–26.

Netscape. 1996. Nations of the Commonwealth Home Page: India.

Oommen, T. K. 1991. "Family Research in India: Issues and Priorities," in TISS Unit for Family Studies (Ed.), *Research on Families with Problems in India: Issues and Implications*, vol. 1, pp. 19–30. Bombay: Tata Institute of Social Sciences.

Ogawa, D. 1973. "The Jap Image," in S. Sue and N. Wagner (Eds.), *Asian Americans: Psychological Perspectives*, pp. 3–12. Ben Lomond, CA: Science and Behavior Books.

Parrillo, V. N. 1991. "The Immigrant Family: Securing the American Dream." *Journal of Comparative Family Studies*, 22 (2): 131–145.

Portes, A. and M. Zhou. 1993. "The New Generation: Segmented Assimilation and its Variants." AAPSS, *Annals*, 530: 74–96.

Ramisetty-Mikler, S. 1993. "Asian Indian Immigrants in America and Sociocultural Issues in Counseling." *Journal of Multicultural Counseling and Development*, 21 (1): 36–49.

Scanzoni, J. 1979. "Social Processes and Power in Families," in W. R. Burr, R. Hill, F. I. Nye and I. L. Reiss (Eds.), *Contemporary Theories about the Family*, vol. 1. New York: The Free Press.

Saran, P. 1985. *The Asian Indian Experience in the United States*. New Delhi: Vikas Publishing House, PVT. Ltd.

Segal, M. N., U. A. Segal, and M. A. P. Niemcyzcki. 1993. "Value Network for Cross-National Marketing Management: A Framework for Analysis and Application." *Journal of Business Research*, 27: 65–84.

Segal, U. A. 1988. "Career Choice Correlates: An Indian Perspective." *Indian Journal of Social Work*, 69: 338–348.

———. 1991. "Cultural Variables in Asian Indian Families." *Families in Society*, 74 (4): 233–242.

———. 1993. "Cross-Cultural Values, Social Work Students and Personality." *International Social Work*, 36: 61–73.

———. 1995a. "Children of Southeast Asian Refugees." Paper presented at the 1995 National Symposium on Child Victimization, Washington, DC, November 9–12.

———. 1995b. "Group Work with Southeast Asian Refugees." Paper presented at the 17th Symposium of the Association for the Advancement of Social Work with Groups, San Diego, CA (October 25–29).

———. 1995c. "Child Abuse by the Middle Class? A Study of Professionals in India." *Child Abuse and Neglect*, 19 (2): 213–227.

Segal, U. A., and A. Ashtekar. 1994. "Detection of Intrafamilial Child Abuse: Children at Intake at a Children's Observation Home in India." *Child Abuse and Neglect*, 18 (11): 957–967.

Seltzer, V. C. 1982. *Adolescent Social Development: Dynamic Functional Interaction*. Lexington, MA: D.C. Heath.

Singh, K. B. K. 1988. *Marriage and Family System of Rajputs*. Delhi: Wisdom.

Sinha, D. 1984. "Some Recent Changes in the Indian Family and Their Implications for Socialization." *The Indian Journal of Social Work*, 65: 271–286.

Sodowsky, G. R., and J. C. Carey. 1988. "Relationships Between Acculturation-Related Demographics and Cultural Attitudes of an Asian-Indian Immigrant Group." *Journal of Multicultural Counseling and Development*, 16 (3): 117–136.

Sue, D. W. 1973. "Ethnic Identity: The Impact of Two Cultures on the Psychological Development of Asians in America," in S. Sue and N. Wagner, (Eds.), *Asian-Americans: Psychological Perspectives*, pp. 140–149. Ben Lomond, CA: Science and Behavior Books.

———. 1979. "Eliminating Cultural Oppression in Counseling." *Journal of Counseling Psychology*, 23: 419–428.

————. 1981. *Counseling the Culturally Different.* New York: John Wiley.

sphs@fyvie.cs.wisc.edu. 1994, October 31. "Indians in the USA: A Success Story."

Thomas, P. 1984. *Festivals and Holidays of India.* Bombay: D.B. Taraporevala & Sons.

Triandis, H. C., R. Bontempo, M. J. Villareal, M. Asai, and N. Lucca. 1988. "Individualism and Collectivism: Cross-Cultural Perspectives on Self-ingroup Relationships." *Journal of Personality and Social Psychology, 19*: 323–338.

U.S. Bureau of the Census. 1992. *1990 Census of the Population—General Population Characteristics.* Washington, DC: U.S. Government Printing Office.

15 | African-American Families

Harriet Pipes McAdoo

To understand the realities of family life of African Americans, it is essential to realize that diversity is an overriding fact. African-American families represent a range of differing groups who have had diverse experiences. Given the many patterns of family life and socioeconomic levels in which African Americans have lived in North America, it is impossible to use median data to describe the situation today, yet authors almost consistently do so. Never has it been more obvious that the African American experience is not one reality. Some families have made major gains and are prospering; others are barely holding onto their gains; still others are sliding backward into economic distress. This socioeconomic diversity is increasing every day. Despite attempts by the media and academia to present African Americans as one social, and usually lower, class, it is important to understand that being of African descent does not in itself determine what the life pattern of an individual will be (McAdoo, 1995a). It has simply become more difficult for African Americans to excel in the present environment.

This chapter is an overview of the history, culture, and diverse family life experiences of African Americans. An ecological approach will attempt to balance the tragedies of history, achievements, and the problems that remain. The focus will not be only on the problems or the strengths of African-American families. Many are resilient and have overcome numerous life-threatening and often overwhelming barriers that exist. Many are in trouble. Many are coping with difficult situations while rearing their children to be competent adults. The complexities of family life will be covered, including the challenges and joys of being African American in today's society.

In the past, it has been suggested that African Americans could be divided into two groups, survivors and nonsurvivors, but this characterization was and continues to be overly simplistic. We also no longer can accurately describe the United States as two nations, one black and unequal and one white and equal. African-American families, in the main, do not fare as well as families from groups who are not of color, but to explain African-American families only in relation to nonblack families would be a fallacy, for we would miss the essence and dynamics of African-American family life today. Both the terms "African American" and "black" will be used interchangeably in this chapter, for this is the prevailing mixed use in this period of transition of self-identification. It has been found that both terms are acceptable to the majority of blacks (Hill, 1981).

HISTORICAL BACKGROUND

Migration to the United States for Africans has occurred on many levels. Some Africans came to the Americas as explorers and were as free as the next man. Others came as indentured servants who also worked off their indebtedness and went on to lead a normal life. Some were freemen who were never enslaved and who developed skills and a trade that enabled them to accumulate a certain level of wealth. Others entered enslaved but earned or were given freedom for themselves and their families, became members of the community, and in some cases grew wealthy.

The historical past of many African-American families is uniquely different from all of the other immigrant groups that have come to the United States. The African experience has resulted in many of the strengths that have helped families to cope with adversities (Dodson, 1997; Sudarkasa, 1993, 1997). Among the cultural legacies that are African derived and have been transmitted and altered in the United States have been oral traditions, reliance on extended families, spirituality, rhythmic-movements expression, and communalism (Boykin, 1997; Jones, 1991; Dodson and Townsend-Gilkes, 1996). The importance of coresidential extended families and their support systems has been cited as one of the major survival systems (Billingsley, 1968; Hill, 1968; McAdoo, 1992a; Hatchell and Jackson, 1993).

A large number of Africans were brought enslaved to the Caribbean and North America. Enslavement also took on many forms, different in the North than in the South. Northern farms tended to be smaller because of the terrain, and owners and the enslaved worked in the fields together. The families of both groups were often intact. After the invention of the cotton gin, the southern plantations began to have large populations of enslaved persons who worked the field under overseers and owners. Black families were composed primarily of mothers and children, with black males put into a secondary position behind white males. Most black males did not gain their freedom until Emancipation, and during the period before and immediately afterward they faced poverty and dislocation. Some gradually resumed an enslavementlike relationship with their former owners as sharecroppers, often on the same land as before. Almost as tragic as physical enslavement was the marginalization of African males under the plantation and small farm system. Black men, for the most part, were totally unable to protect their women, who had been victimized for 250 years (Wilkinson, 1993).

Other black men found work and, since marriages could be legal, established families. Southern African Americans established cohesive communities under the segregated housing systems that reinforced religious and family values. Most were working poor, a few became wealthy, yet all were living together in a self-contained system. Others were unconnected to communities and drifted around from town to town, but a century later, in the devastating economic recessions of the 1970s, a large number of these families were again crippled (Marable, 1993). They became part of an intergenerational transfer of impoverishment that has had devastating effects on families.

There are many family similarities among African, Brazilian, West Indian, and American families (Herskovitz, 1938). Caribbean families of African descent have continually gone back and forth between the American mainland and the islands. Those who came to the United States in search of a better life often maintained close relationships with family members in the islands, which gave them an advantage over many mainland blacks (Billingsley, 1992). While enslavement was experienced in both sites, the Caribbean family was more intact and had an emotional security that helped it withstand the antiblack codes and hostile attitudes found in mainland America (Blackwell, 1975; Kerns, 1989). The strong sense of family, self-respect, and pride meant that they could avoid some of the extreme negative self-conceptions of their northern brethren (Reid, 1939). The pride handed down through generations has had a positive effect in those families. While the first wave of Caribbean immigrants did not intermarry, intermarriage occurred between islanders and mainland residents for later immigrants. Intermarriage also occurred between different Native American groups and former Africans, especially in the southern states. Although the ties with the native peoples often were lost, there are descendants who maintained contact or, through research, reestablished it (McAdoo, 1997). All these experiences with different origins and family systems resulted in a mixture among African Americans that was overlooked in earlier examinations of black family life. The combination of African, European, and Native American genes has resulted in the rich color palette in the diaspora that distinguishes North American blacks from Africans around the world.

The Devaluation of African-American Families

African-American families have always been faced with the devaluation of their institutions, persons, values, and artifacts that are related to their cultures. This devaluation is based upon the historically ingrained concept of white superiority. The concept of white superiority was transplanted from Europe to the Americas and has resulted in attitudes and institutions that indeed have put people of African descent in inferior positions. Although this is an irrational concept, it has been the predominant cultural belief that has been handed down for generations in the European context and has been continued into the Americas. The implementation of this concept has placed persons of African descent into situations and institutions that are indeed inferior. As a consequence, African-American people (as well as other people of color) have often found themselves isolated from many of the educational and economic institutions of American life. These are socioeconomic elements that allow individuals and families access into the mainstream of American life. The devaluation of their cultural attributes had to have profound impact on the development of African Americans.

A subtle form of devaluation occurs with the present "color caste" that continues in many forms to this day. During the slavery period, the wider society as a whole tended to be more accepting of those whose African blood was mixed with that of nonblacks. These individuals were offered advantages during enslavement and afterwards. White male slave owners in reality were in a polygamous patriarchical family system that included both women who were legal wives and women of color. African women were sexually exploited by white enslavers and were forced to bear children of mixed heritages. These children, although they were part of the owner's families, were enslaved, as were all of the other African descent children born during that time. A few women were given increased status and were able to keep their miscegenated family units together (McAdoo, 1997).

This apartheid system led to the differential status within enslavement (e.g., the "house nigger" and the "field nigger"). Those of lighter skin color were often selected to be slaves within the household, while others (of darker skin color) were given the harder manual field work. The ability to observe and adapt mainline habits and attitudes led to even greater diversity within the enslaved populations (McAdoo, 1997). Those persons who were the product of miscegenation and interracial unions were sometimes given help to gain education in white schools or in historically black institutions, which were sometimes founded as a refuge for these children. These individuals were able to accumulate wealth that allowed intergenerational transfer of accumulated resources.

Many of these advantages exist even to this day. The preference for lighter-color skin pigmentation was unfortunately internalized by the former enslaved Africans. Though the black consciousness movement relaxed this negative ideal, some remnants of it are still evident today. Skin color, hair type, and facial features have played an important role in the experiences that almost all African Americans have had. The preference for certain physical traits and characteristics that exists among some African Americans reflects an internalization of those preferences of the wider society (Boykin and Toms, 1985), and the importance of these physical characteristics is often unknown outside this racial group. There were attempts to mute these preferences during the heyday of the civil rights period of the 1960s–1970s.

African-American preschool children have consistently shown a preference for whiteness over blackness (Cross, 1985). The preference for whiteness over blackness has caused many problems with the development of the racial attitudes and preferences of African-American children and adults (McDonald, 1970; Cohen, 1972), and it has been found to result in mental distress (Guthrie, 1976; Fulmore, Taylor, Ham and Lyles, 1994). While originally it was believed that this preference was a rejection of their own selves, research has shown that children are able to discriminate between their racial preference (white oriented) and their self-esteem (black oriented). Thus their racial attitudes can be modified (J. McAdoo, 1985).

Researchers and scholars of African-American families have had considerable problems in presenting accurate interpretations and meanings of data on these families. For example, most family researchers tend not to disaggregate family data for analysis. I would argue, on one hand, that it is necessary for researchers to separate out African-American families from their general samples of families if they want to capture and present a more realistic analysis and view of these families. On the other hand, it is often impossible to disaggregate the experiences of families of different backgrounds, and this may cover the real diversity that exists in families. There are several distinct groups within the African-American community, yet when we are able to relate only to mean or median statistics, the wide diversity of family experiences becomes buried.

Demographic Characteristics

Based on U.S. census projections, it has been predicted that by the year 2050 families of color will become the majority in North America (Marable, 1993). During the period between 1980 and 1990, there have been very rapid changes in the diversity of race in the United States. Families of color are younger than the mainstream and larger; their size is the result of cultural patterns and, often, religious orientation. From 1980 to 1990, the number of African Americans increased by 26 percent and will grow even more in the near future (Frey 1993). African Americans have increased by 13 percent, an increase of 3.5 million by 1990. By 1990, African Americans constituted 12.1 percent of the total population or over 30 million individuals.

African Americans are one-eighth of the American population, and will be one in seven within twenty years (O'Hare and Frey, 1992). While 62 percent of blacks have incomes less than $25,000, 12 percent have incomes of $50,000 or more; there is a growing disparity of income within the African-American community. About 47 percent of the black population are male and 53 percent are female; over one-third of the black population is now under 18 years of age (U.S. Census, 1993). The median age is 28 years; males have a lower median age than females. Life expectancy is 69 years of age. As in all races, women have a longer life expectancy than men: The life expectancy for black women is 74 years and 64 years for men (U.S. Census, 1993). More African Americans are living longer, with 2.5 million elderly in 1990 and 9 million expected in 2050 (U.S. Census, 1992). Education of African Americans has improved. High school diplomas or higher were earned by 63.1 percent of blacks, and 11.4 percent had a bachelor's or higher degree (U.S. Census, 1993).

Home ownership is an important goal of African Americans. Of the nation's 10 million black householders, 43 percent own their homes compared to 64 percent of all Americans. Of the fifty metropolitan areas with the most African-American households, New York has the largest number, over 750,000. Blacks account for the largest share (37%) of households in Jacksonville, Florida (Russell, 1996).

Geographical Distribution of African Americans. There have been many changes in the geographical distribution of African Americans in the United States. At one time, the majority of African Americans were found in the South in the former areas of enslavement. These areas became known as the "Bible Belt" or "Black Belt," so called because there were so many African Americans and their religious institutions (Pipes, 1992). As the South became increasingly racially hostile to African Americans with the demise of the cotton and farm industries, many African Americans moved North to seek a better life to take advantage of the industrialization in the northern states. During the 1890s over 90 percent of the African-American population resided in the South, but by the 1990s a majority of the population had scattered into urban centers in the South, the North, and the West (Billingsley, 1992).

The massive Northern Migration was one of the most vivid movements of our time (Lehman, 1986). While living in the South, most African Americans lived in large extended families composed of kin and fictive kin (Stack, 1974; McAdoo, 1992b; Staples, 1994). The move to urban centers in the North and South fragmented extended family systems and made their informal network of social support more difficult to maintain and sustain. Sixteen states had African-American populations of 1 million or more and three states had over 2 million (U.S. Census, 1993a). African Americans tend to live in the four most populous states: California, New York, Texas, and Florida. Some urban-metropolitan areas are disproportionately African American in population, but the areas of greatest national growth now are the outer-ring suburbs of central cities (*Black American*, 1991).

The highest proportion of African Americans still live in the "Black Belt" or "Bible Belt." Although the share of blacks in the South fell steadily during most of the twentieth century, this trend has now shifted, and more have moved into that region than have moved out. The children of the migrants to the North have begun to return to the South. In the 1980s, the South's African-American population rose for the first time since the turn of the century. Today about 53 percent of the African-American population lives in the

South, while their population in the Midwest is steadily decreasing (Robinson, 1992). According to one source, African-American in-migrants to the South tend to be young, well educated, and the parents of young children (*American Demographics*, 1992). For the most part, these new in-migrants are not moving into the rural areas but rather the urban-metropolitan centers of the South.

Many decades of South-to-North migration changed with the demise and movement offshore of the "smokestack industries" of the northern states. The midwestern and northeast regions of the country, including the cities of Chicago, Detroit, and New York, were the major sources of out-movements. Over a quarter million jobs were lost during the 1985–1990 period (Frey, 1994). The pattern of African-American migration took a sharp turn to the Southeast and West as African Americans left the North in large numbers. For example, there were significant increases in African-American migration to the western cities of Los Angeles and San Francisco–Oakland as well as to the southern cities of New Orleans and Shreveport. Employment opportunities expanded significantly in California, Texas, and in other areas of the so-called Sun Belt.

The 1990 Census shows that the "return migration" from the North to the South has continued. But instead of California, the state of choice now appears to be Georgia. Frey (1994) states that the next four states likely to experience substantial (positive) growth in their African-American populations are Maryland, Florida, Virginia, and North Carolina. All of these states have the "new" Old South metropolitan communities, including such urban cities as Atlanta, Georgia, Norfolk, Virginia, and Raleigh-Durham, North Carolina. Attraction to and movement into these states is, in part, related to employment opportunities—the existence of new jobs. Perhaps more important is the lure of those extended families, fictive kin, and family kinship networks still remaining in these regions.

Economic Differences in Migratory Movements

African-American and white migration patterns were comparable, and the groups also tended to move in similar patterns. When 1990 census data were used to categorize African-American families into college educated and impoverished and to examine their migration patterns, there were clear differences in the areas of the country to which they tended to move. The two African-American subgroups tended to migrate in different ways and went for the most part in separate directions. As a result, the groups became ever more separated and economically polarized (Frey, 1994).

The lack of a monolithic view of the African-American family is reinforced when the movements of the past twenty years are examined (McAdoo, 1997). African Americans splintered and went into different states and urban-metropolitan areas. College-educated professionals sought jobs and rising incomes in university towns and in growing manufacturing communities. Frey (1994) found that college graduates were more likely to be drawn to larger cosmopolitan areas inside the South (Washington, DC, Dallas–Fort Worth, Miami, and Baltimore) and out of the South (Los Angeles, San Francisco–Oakland, and Philadelphia) as well as to the recreational center of Orlando, Florida. Middle class, college-educated African Americans were responding to the economic pulls of certain geographical areas.

Impoverished African Americans, on the other hand, went wherever lower-paying or blue collar jobs dominated and where the cost of living was lower. Poor African Americans retraced the traditional and historic roots of their southern origins. They were attracted to smaller southern metropolitan areas (Norfolk, Tallahassee, Richmond, and Greensboro). The extended kinship networks that are located in small, nonmetropolitan areas of North Carolina, for example, hold the potential to attract larger number of "return" poverty migrants than other South Atlantic states (Frey, 1994). The 2000 census data will offer valuable information on the continued migrations of African Americans as they seek better lives and will probably show even greater economic separation among distinct subgroups.

AFRICAN-AMERICAN FAMILIES

The Extended Family

The major distinction that can be made between families of African and European descent lies in the domestic arrangement of family units. African-American families tend to be more multigenerational and to include differing combinations of roles within the units. These patterns seem to derive from West Africa, where traditionally there have been many forms (both patriarchal and matriarchal). All have been built around a traditional unit of stable adult relatives that extend over time and across generations (Sudarkasa, 1980; 1988). The African commitment to "blood" kin has been the basis of established relationships for a significant number of household and family types, formed around the core of several adult consanguineal relatives (Sudarkasa, 1993). This core may consist of husband and wife; mother and another adult relative; women and children alone; grandparents; and a grandmother alone or with another adult relative. The consanguineal bond is often stronger than the marriage relationship. Marriages may end, but blood ties last forever.

This African perspective was brought to the Americas, where the matrilocal pattern was reinforced by the inhumane treatment of enslaved families. Parents did not control their own lives or those of their children. Young children lived with their mother but at a certain age could be sold away and the father could be sold away from the mother. Marriage was illegal during slavery. After Emancipation, more than 75 percent of previous unions were formalized by the couples, who went to county courthouses and recorded their relationship. Many former slaves relocated across the South to rejoin those who had been sold away (Franklin, 1996). Families ordinarily were formed around married unions and relatives. The one-parent units that formed usually resulted from the father's death; since the mother and child could not survive alone, they attached themselves to a larger family unit (McAdoo, 1991b; Glick, 1988). These extended families, composed of relatives and nonrelatives, continued the collective pattern of African and Caribbean family forms (Aschenbrenner, 1975).

As part of extended family living arrangements, extensive helping arrangements have been typical in many families, cutting across families and households (Stack, 1974; McAdoo, 1996; Fortes, 1949). Such help becomes difficult, however, when family resources are very limited. The 75 percent level of marital union prevailed until the 1970s, when a series of economic crises accelerated the decline in marriage. Many young people today are growing up without the wider family network that has long provided its resiliency in the African-American community.

These coping mechanisms cut across religious beliefs and origins, being similar for example, among Caribbean as well as American persons of African descent. Very similar mechanisms are found in other groups of color as well, such as among Native Americans, Mexican Americans, and Asian Americans. For example, the concept "extended family" has much the same meaning in all three groups, although this commonality is rarely discussed or compared (see relevant chapters in this book for an in-depth discussion of these groups). All these groups have evolved culturally in unique ways that reflect their origin and geographic location, yet they share many similarities in their family patterns (McAdoo, 1993).

Marital and Family Stability

Marital stability and family stability are not the same thing. This confusion is common in writings about African-American families. Stability as well as instability can be found in two-parent as well as in one-parent or grandparent homes. The important fact is not the marital relation of the children's parents, but the stability, love, and adequate resources that are available within the family home. African-American families are often built around the "blood-based" or consanguineal-based household that includes a woman, her children, perhaps a sister or another adult, or grandparent. This core of adult relatives is often a stable unit that remains together over time (Sudarkasa, 1993). They can provide a stable unit for bringing up children that can be as supportive an environment as that provided by a two-parent family.

Hackett and Jackson (1993), in the first probability sampling of over 2,000 of African Americans within the United States, found that more than 90 percent of these Americans felt that they were close to their families, though in a variety of structural arrangements. They interacted frequently with their kin, and those who felt close to their kin frequently reported that they received aid from their kin.

The economic reality of gender discrimination and pay inequity does cause mothers who are alone with their children (single-parent families) not to have the resources that are found in two-parent families (Wilkinson, 1993; 1997). If the resources are augmented by those within the extended or fictive kin circle, the child may have a stable family. The changes that have occurred in family structures are the result of many strongly interacting forces. However, in recent times the economic situations have become difficult and former family arrangements may not be as effective as they have been in the past.

Marital Structures of Families

Marriage over the long term is no longer a model lifestyle for African Americans. A larger proportion of African Americans are postponing marriage or not marrying at all (McAdoo, 1991b; 1993). African Americans are frequently delaying marriage until their late twenties, and the marriage rate itself is declining. This decline among African Americans is greater than the decline experienced by the population as a whole.

Only 44 percent of African American adults were married in 1991 compared with 64 percent in 1970, according to the Census Bureau (U.S. Census, 1993). Of the men, 44.4 percent have never married, 38.5 percent were married, 8.3 percent were divorced, 5.5 percent have separated, and 3.3 percent were widowed. For the women, 38.3 percent have never married, 30.9 percent are married, 11.9 percent are widowed, 11.4 percent were divorced, and 7.5 percent were separated (Sudarkasa, 1993).

There were many reasons for the decline in marriages, but simple causal explanations have not been found to be supported by hard data. The changes in family structures are the result of many factors. Economic factors alone cannot explain the changes in African-American family structures (Ellwood and Crane, 1990b); marriage rates have fallen for employed as well as unemployed men. It has been contended that the number of unemployed men was the cause of marriage decline (Wilson, 1987; Ellwood, 1990a), but studies have shown that marriage rates fell more for the employed than the unemployed between 1970 and 1988 (Ellwood and Crane, 1990). Overall, the wages of men and the weaker employment of men can explain at the most only 10 to 20 percent of the decline in marriage. Welfare has also been questioned as a reason for the decline and has also been rejected by empirical studies (Wilson, 1987).

The sex-ratio imbalance explains some of the decline in marriages. Among blacks there is an inadequate supply of males for females; there are simply many more women of marriageable age than men. This fact has been noted since DuBois's work in 1908 and has consistently been addressed over the years by other writers (Cox, 1940; Jackson, 1971; Tucker and Mitchell-Kernan, 1985;

1991; Tucker and Myers, 1991; Hatchett, Cockran, and Jackson, 1991). Darity and Myers (1991) have estimated that there are approximately 32 men for every 100 women in the marriage pool. This imbalance is caused by the high death rate in the teen years experienced by African-American boys, the high incarceration rate, poor health conditions, and the insecurities of the labor market. The imbalance of the male-to-female ratio prevents young marriage unions from forming. These facts are reflected regardless of how the sex ratio is viewed. Darity and Meyers (1991) have stated there are four distinct sex ratios within African-American communities: (1) the ratio of unmarried males to unmarried females; (2) the ratio of men to women who are of marriageable age; (3) the ratio of employed males to females; and (4) the ratio of unmarried males who are in the labor market, or in schools, to unmarried females. All four sex ratios indicate low ratios of male to females (Darity and Meyers, 1991).

Clearly, the level of divorce for African-American women is high and there are difficulties in remaining married (Hatchell, 1991). The divorce level for African-American women is twice as high as for white women. Although researchers and policymakers tend to assume that African-American single mothers are only the result of adolescent pregnancies, the Children's Defense Fund data show that in reality the majority of the children who are born to unmarried African Americans are born to women who are over 20 years of age (Edelman, 1987; McAdoo, 1995a). These numbers include women who have never been married and women who have been previously married and have since divorced as well as a few women of middle class status who have been unable to find a husband and have decided that they are in a position of raising a child(ren) without husbands.

The death of eligible African-American males is overlooked by those who are in positions of formulating national policies and programs. Even if all available men in the African-American community were married, many African-American women would still be left without marriage partners. So the problem of African-American children growing up without fathers cannot be solved only by getting unmarried men married off; the marginalization of males contributes to the stresses that could lead to the high level of divorce in these families. The parenting roles that black women had in Africa, during enslavement, and now in contemporary times show a continuation of dependence upon extended, consanguineal relationships of the mothers, not the conjugal relationships found within European and American families. This pattern points to a major difference between African-American families and other mainstream American families.

Parents and Children

Bumpass (1993) has estimated that African-American children have only a 1-in-5 chance of growing up with two parents until the age of 16. The number of children who are born without marriage are the result of many factors: the heavy economic and psychological isolation of the African-American male, growing tensions between African-American men and women in relation to sex-role expectations; and vestiges of the African-derived family organizations that depend upon relatives rather than marriage partners. But most important is the growing disparity between African American and white incomes that is, in the main, a latent consequence of systemic economic restructuring, discrimination, and impoverishment (Hatchett, 1991; McAdoo, 1997). Poverty in the African-American community is present for 65 percent of single mother–child(ren) units as compared to only 18 percent of married couples–child(ren) units (Ingrassia, 1993).

But having children without the benefit of marriage occurs across all economic levels. Among well-to-do African-American women with incomes of $75,000, 22 percent have children out of wedlock (Ingrassia, 1993). This is, sad to say, almost ten times the white out-of-wedlock rate. Those African-American women who are not so well to do (poor), have more children without benefit of wedlock, 65 percent; a figure almost double that found among not so well-to-do (poor) white women.

One major problem that the African-American family faces is related to the fact that too many children must grow up without the resources and love that are often found within two-parent families. Because of the distinctive African-American family structures, African-American children in one-parent families are acutely aware of the fact that the resources available for them are not the same as those that are available in families with two parents. One family scholar has suggested that children need unconditional love from one or two persons who are dedicated to the child (Bronfenbrenner 1979). These persons can be parents, grandparents, or other significant relatives. African Americans have traditionally formed families that have included many persons in the parenting role. Today, however, for a growing number of families, economic situations and conditions are so problematic that these arrangements are not as effective as they have been in the past (McAdoo, 1997).

Many factors have contributed to the substantial increase in the number of children who are growing up in one-parent (generally mother-only) families with limited access to resources. The high divorce rate and the delay of marriages, even after the birth of children, have resulted in more families being composed of stepparents and many types of blended families.

Most children of all races in 1990 did not live in a "traditional" home in which the father is the main breadwinner and the mother is a homemaker (Whitmire, 1996). Only 5 percent of African-American families and 20 percent of white families fit this model. The proportion of African-American children who lived with two parents was 37 percent; with mothers only, 49.3 percent; with fathers only, 5.4 percent; and 8.3 percent with no parents. The children who lived with their parent(s) and a grandparent numbered 16.2

percent, and those with one parent were more likely to have a grandparent in the home. Moreover, many grandparents have become primary parents for young children because of the high incarceration rate of parents, the AIDS epidemic, unemployment, and drug use. While they are a source of resiliency for the children, it is often at the expense of their own health and financial needs.

In African-American families with a father in the home, 52 percent worked full time, 32.7 percent worked part time, and 8.8 percent did not work. Almost 30 percent of the mothers with children worked full time, 40.9 percent of them worked part time, and 29.4 percent did not work. African-American women, along with Asian and Pacific Islanders, have the highest labor force participation rate—a rate of over 60 percent (U.S. Bureau of Census, 1993a).

The incomes of African-American families with children are relatively high for 8.9 percent, 25.0 percent are comfortable or prosperous, 15.8 percent have enough to get by, but 50.3 percent are of low income (U.S. Bureau of Census, 1993a). For the most part, family incomes appear to be associated with structural characteristics and the parental configurations of families; those families with two parents in the home (and both working), for example, are far more prosperous (e.g., have substantially higher incomes) than those families with fathers only or mothers only. African-American children live in 46.6 percent of those families that are relatively comfortable, prosperous, or high income and have two parents present (aptly called "well-to-do families"); children live in 35.7 percent of those prosperous ("well-to-do") families with a father only; and children live in 18.0 percent of those prosperous ("well-to-do") families with a mother only. Of those families that live in poverty (aptly called "not-so-well-to do families") and only have a mother present in the home, almost 53 percent have children; of those families that live in poverty and have only a father present in the home, 32.7 percent have children; and of those families that live in poverty ("not-so-well-to-do") and have both parents present in the home, 14.9 percent have children (U.S. Bureau of the Census, 1993a).

CHANGES AND ADAPTATIONS

Families and Poverty

There are many challenges to African-American family resilience. Our future will be determined by our abilities to improve the situations of African-American children, and poverty is the paramount concern of persons who are serious about the welfare of all children. There will be a majority of persons of color in the United States soon and all of our futures are dependent upon the well-being of these families and their children. Even more now than in the past, African Americans will have to draw on more than the sources of support that have traditionally provided resiliency for their families.

The Carnegie Corporation of New York recently released a summary of the plight of all of America's children (Chira, 1994). The report stated that young children with certain characteristics—those who are born to unmarried mothers (28%); who live with only one parent (27%); and, when they are under 6, have a mother in the labor force—were at risk to suffer neurological effects that can be irreversible. They may never be able to reach their full potential. It is a very serious concern for African-American families because black children are at an untenable level on each of these dimensions.

The rate of poverty among African-American children has decreased from 75 percent in 1949 to 29 percent in 1991 (Danziger, 1993). However, the fact remains that the rate of poverty for African-American children is more than double the rate for all American children. Since the early 1990s, economic conditions have deteriorated and, for a number of reasons that will be discussed in this section, African-American children have fallen into ever-greater despair. Children now are at great risk because of their reliance on parents who are now in even more tenuous situations. They do not receive adequate health care, their homes have a tendency to be deteriorated, and their schools tend to be inferior.

The Children's Defense Fund has stated there is a crisis in the health care of African-American babies and young children. The lack of progress in maternal and child health is especially pronounced for black infants, who are more likely to have low birth weights and have a greater likelihood of dying before their first birthday than other children. In 1991, almost 13.6 percent of African-American babies were born at low birth weight, a rate double that of white infants and one that has not changed in twenty years. In 1991, the African-American infant mortality rate was 17.6 deaths per 1,000 live births. Black babies die at a rate that is twice as high as that for white babies, or at a rate that whites had twenty years ago (Children's Defense Fund, 1994). The lack of health care is shown most starkly in the lack of immunization that children receive. In 1991, only 5.55 percent of all 2 year olds in the United States received the immunizations that they needed. Only half as many African-American 2 year olds had the shots that they needed in comparison with white children.

Births to young girls are a predictor of poverty. Young girls who have children are the most destitute and vulnerable group of mothers; they have the lowest education and the highest levels of poverty for their entire lives. The birth rate of young African-American girls 15 to 19 years old is twice the rate of other groups, although the rate for teenage childbearing between 1986 and 1991 rose at a faster rate among whites (19%) than among African Americans (Usdansky, 1994). The nonmarital rate for African-American teens has varied. In 1970, the level was 97 births per 1,000; in 1980, 86 per 1,000; and rising to 110 in 1990 (National Center for Health Statistics, 1993).

The teen birth rates varied by ethnicity and race for girls 15–19 years, with 116.2 for every 1,000 births of black girls (Moore et al., 1993). These pregnancies appear to be unplanned, and they are not the result of a need to "have someone to love," as the media often relates as the reason that teens get pregnant (Usdansky, 1994).

Transmission of Values

There is no one value system for African Americans, since once again the level of acculturation determines the level of European-oriented values and some of those, no doubt, are based on African spiritual values. The debate about the absence or presence of cultural values has been a long-existing debate that has gone on in the black and in the white academic communities. There are writers who feel that African values were lost as a result of the enslavement experience and that the only values are those that have developed during enslavement and because of poverty (Frazier, 1932; 1939). On the other hand, some values are universal and others are unique to African Americans. However, there are writers who feel that the values that are embraced by African Americans have a common thread running through them that ultimately is linked to Western African culture (DuBois, 1903; Park, 1919; Herskovitz 1930; Franklin, 1947).

Parents of young children have been found to value self-sufficiency, a strong work orientation, positive racial attitudes, perseverance, and respect for the mother's role in the family (McAdoo and Crawford, 1991). These values have been found to be highly regarded by single mothers (McAdoo, 1991a). There is often a strong blend of the spirit of volunteerism and service to others who may be less fortunate. Family-oriented values and values that reinforce African-American culture have been found in the history and oral traditions of many grandparents, and, most important, these histories and traditions are passed down from one generation to another.

The Role of the Church

The African American/black church was often the only organization under African-American control, and this is where many leadership skills were developed. The African American/black church has been one of the special strengths of families (Hill, 1978). Churches were places where, in addition to religious reinforcement, members were able to obtain solace, relief, and support. Church communities were important providers of employment, financial assistance, and informal adoptions of children. This assistance allowed members to cope with the realities of a devalued life found within their everyday situations. Churches provide spiritual sustenance and a refuge, on temporary basis, from the discrimination and racism that is found in the broader society and often serve as the organizational hub of community life (Taylor and Chatters, 1991). Additionally, churches of all sizes engage in social service outreach programs, with memberships that range from 250 to 10,000 members.

There is a conservative traditional element of values that cuts across all phases of African-American life. Churches have been strong, powerful, and responsible sources of family support. It is no accident that in the past the civil rights leaders have come from within the churches. As families have moved into the present, ongoing mixtures of American and African backgrounds are found within their religious practices (Pipes, 1992).

African Americans have subsequently joined Protestant, Catholic and Moslem religions. In Christian denominations, the largest number are Baptists. Taylor and Chatters (1991) found in their sample that half were Baptist (50%), followed by Methodist (11.7%), and Roman Catholics (6.3%), while 10 percent had no religious affiliation. Islam, a religion with adherents in the pre-enslavement period, is also growing in African-American communities (Bernstein, 1993). It has been estimated that approximately one-third of Africans were Muslim when they first were brought to this country. Islam resurfaced in the mid-1940s in the Nation of Islam, and since then in the late 1970s has realigned itself more with traditional Islam (Rule, 1992; Terry, 1993; *New York Times*, 1993; Winkler, 1994). Today about one in four American Moslems is African American (American Demographer, 1994). In addition, an ever-growing number of African Americans belong to other "nontraditional" religious organizations.

CONCLUSION

The diversity of histories and the pluralism of experiences within the African-American community has resulted in a multitude of distinct individuals and subgroups and a quite heterogenous population. Despite some obvious and not so obvious differences among individuals and subgroups, they have all had to, and still must to this day, face racism, discrimination, and oppression within our society. No matter how little or how great the amount of African-descent blood that persons have, they are considered inferior persons of color by most people in the wider and dominant Anglo society. African Americans are still not given (and have never been given) equal access to the social, political, and economic resources and rewards of the society. It seems clear that for African Americans as a social collective, more not less racism and systematic oppression are on the horizon and political agenda of this society. This is becoming evident by the current national move to dismantle affirmative action policies and programs in both the private and public sectors, the withdrawal, demise, and/or serious fiscal reductions in financial aid programs for people of color, the information hiring restrictions, the social and political exclusions, and an increasing tolerance among non-African

Americans for racial and ethnic violence (especially against African Americans) in society.

Social, religious, economic, political, and cultural differences have prevented a common or singular view of events within our society. There is a need to avoid the usual (common) view of examining life from the despair of poverty, single parenthood, underemployment and unemployment, and the lack of access to opportunities and resources. The essence of African-American life, while it is in part a product of the context and milieu of the dominant society, is found within the diversities of social and individual life experiences. These experiences are manifested in the interactions of family members and friends, in music, in the religions of the churches, in the blues and jazz that grew from these experiences, and in the writings that record the stories of African Americans. Only when these experiences are perceived and understood in their cultural context, then, and only then will we be able to discern, ascertain and, most important, appreciate the reality of African-American family life.

REFERENCES

Ahlburg, D., and C. DeVita. 1992. "New Realities of the American Family." *Population Bulletin, 47* (2): 18–19.

Allen, W. 1993. Black Families: Protectors of the Realm. *Morehouse Research Institute Bulletin, 93* (3): 1–3.

American Demographic. 1992. "Marriage, Homeownership, and Other Recent Census Releases. September, p. 16.

Aschenbrenner, J. 1975. *Lifelines: Black Families in Chicago.* New York: Holt, Rinehart and Winston.

Bernstein, R. 1993. "A Growing Islamic Presence: Balancing Scared and Secular." *New York Times,* May 2, A1, 14–14.

Billingsley, A. 1968. *Black Families in White America.* Englewood Cliffs, NJ: Prentice-Hall.

———. 1992. *Climbing Jacob's Ladder: The Enduring Legacy of African American Families.* New York: Simon & Schuster.

Black American. 1991. *American Demographic Desk Reference, 1:* 8–10.

Blackwell, J. 1975. *The Black Community: Diversity and Unity.* New York: Harper & Row.

Boyd-Franklin, N. 1989. *Black Families in Therapy.* New York: Guilford Press.

Boykin, A. 1997. "Communalism: Conceptualization and Measurement of an Afro-cultural Social Orientation." *Journal of Black Studies, 27* (3): 409–418.

Boykin, A. and F. Toms. 1985. "Black Child Socialization: A Conceptual Framework," in *Black Children: Social, Education, and Parental Environments,* pp. 35–51. Newbury Park, CA: Sage.

Bronfenbrenner, U. 1979. *The Ecology of Human Development: Experiments by Nature and Design.* Cambridge, MA: Harvard University Press.

Bryce-LaPorte, R. 1979. "New York and the New Caribbean Immigrants." *International Migration Review, 12:* 212–19.

Bumpass, L. Quoted by Ingrassia, M. "A World Without Fathers. The Struggle to Save the Black Family." Special report. *Newsweek.* August 30, pp. 16–29.

Children's Defense Fund. 1994. *State of America's Children Yearbook.* Washington, DC: Children's Defense Fund.

Chira, S. 1994. "Study Confirms Worst Fears on U.S. Children." [Review of *Starting points: Meeting the needs of our youngest children*. Carnegie Corporation of New York.] *New York Times*, April 12, pp. A1, A11.

Clark, K. 1955. *Prejudice and Your Child*. Boston: Beacon Press.

Clark, M. 1992. "Racial Group Concept and Self-Esteem in Black Children," in Burlew, Banks, McAdoo, and Azibo (Eds.), *African American Psychology: Theory, Research, and Practice*, pp. 159–172. Newbury Park, CA: Sage.

Cohen, R. 1972. *The Color of Man*. New York: Bantam.

Cox, O. 1940. "Sex Ratio and Marital Status Among Negroes." *American Sociological Review*, 5: 937–947.

Danziger, S. 1993. Lecture on family poverty presented at the Institute for Children, Youth, and Families, Michigan State University, July 17.

Darity, W., and S. Myers. 1991. "Sex Ratios, Marriageability, and the Marginalization of Black Males." Paper presented at the biennial meeting of the Society for Research in Child Development, May. Seattle, WA.

DeParle, J. 1994. "Clinton Target: Teenage Pregnancy." *New York Times*, March 22, A10.

Dodson, J. 1997. "Conceptualizations of African American Families," in H. McAdoo (Ed.), *Black Families*, 3rd ed., pp. 67–82. Thousand Oaks, CA: Sage.

Dodson, J., and J. Townsend-Gilkes. 1989. "There Is Nothing like Church Food: The US and Afro-Christian Traditional Community and Feeding." *Journal of American Academy of Religion, 57*: 519–538.

DuBois, W. E. B. 1899. *The Philadelphia Negro*. NY: Schocken.

———. 1903. *Souls of Black Folks*. Chicago: McClurg.

Durant, T., and K. Sparrow. 1997. "Race and Class Consciousness Among Lower- and Middle-Class Blacks." *Journal of Black Studies, 27* (3): 334–351.

Edelman, M. 1987. *Families in Peril*. Cambridge, MA: Harvard University Press.

———. 1988. "An Advocacy Agenda for Black Families and Children," in H. McAdoo, *Black Families*, 2nd ed. Newbury Park, CA: Sage.

———. 1997. "An Advocacy Agenda for Black Families and Children," in H. McAdoo (Ed.), *Black Families*, 3rd ed., pp. 323–332. Thousand Oaks, CA: Sage.

Ellwood, D. 1990. "Men and Marriage in the Black Community." *Research Bulletin: Malcolm Wiener Center for Social Policy*, pp. 1–2, 5. John F. Kennedy School of Government. Cambridge, MA: Harvard University.

Ellwood, D., and J. Crane. 1990. *Journal of Economic Perspectives, 4* (4): Fall.

Feagin, J. 1989. *Racial and Ethnic Relations*. Englewood Cliffs, NJ: Prentice-Hall.

Fortes, M. 1949. *The Web of Kinship*. London: Oxford University Press.

Franklin, J. 1994. *From Slavery to Freedom*. NY: Alfred Knopf.

———. 1997. "African American Families: An Historical Note on Black Families," in H. McAdoo (Ed.), *Black Families*, 3rd ed., pp. 5–8. Thousand Oaks, CA: Sage.

Frazier, E. 1932. *The Free Negro Family*. Nashville: Fisk University Press.

———. 1939. *The Negro Family in the United States*. Chicago: University of Chicago Press.

Frey, W. 1993. "University of Michigan Researcher Sees Patterns in Census Data." Quoted by J. Tilove and J. Hallinan, "A Nation Divided: A Melting Pot We're Not." *Ann Arbor News*, November.

———. 1994. *College Grad, Poverty Blacks Take Different Migration Paths*. Research Report No. 94-303, Population Studies Center, University of Michigan, February.

Fulmore, C., T. Taylor, D. Ham, and B. Lyles. 1994. "Psychological Consequences of Internalized Racism." *Psych Discourse, 24* (10): 12–15.

Galen, M., and T. Palmer. 1987. *Workforce 2000: Work and Workers for the 21st Century*. Indianapolis, IN: Hoover Institute.

Galen, M., and T. Palmer. 1994. "White, Male, and Worried." *Business Week*, January 31, pp. 50–55.

Garcia-Coll, C., B. Lambert, R. Jenkins, H. McAdoo, K. Crnic, B. Wasik, and H. Garcia. 1997. "An Integrative Model for the Study of Developmental Competencies in Minority Children." *Child Development, 67* (5): 1891–1914.

Glick, P. 1988. "Demographic Pictures of Black Families," in H. McAdoo (Ed.), *Black Families*, pp. 107–132. Newbury Park, CA: Sage.

Guthrie, R. 1976. *Even the Rat Was White.* New York: Harper & Row.

Hatchett, S. 1991. "Women and Men," in J. Jackson (Ed.), *Life in Black America*, pp. 84–104. Newbury Park, CA: Sage.

Hatchett, S., D. Cochran, and J. Jackson. 1991. "Family Life," in J. Jackson (Ed.), *Life in Black America*, pp. 46–83. Newbury Park, CA: Sage.

Hatchett, S., and J. Jackson. 1993. "African American Extended Kin Systems," in H. McAdoo, *Family Ethnicity: Strength in Diversity*, pp. 90–108. Newbury Park, CA: Sage.

Herskovitz, M. 1930. "The Negro in the New World." *American Anthropologist, 32*, November.

———. 1941. *The Myth of the Negro Past.* New York: Harper & Row.

Hill, R. 1978. *The Strengths of Black Families.* New York: Emerson-Hall.

———. 1981. "Multiple Public Benefits and Poor Black Families," in H. McAdoo, *Black Families*, 1st ed. Beverly Hills, CA: Sage.

Ingrassia, M. 1993. "A World Without Fathers: The Struggle to Save the Black Family." Special Report. *Newsweek*, August 30, pp. 16–29.

"Islam in New York: Growing Presence of Diverse Peoples United by Faith." 1993. *New York Times*, May 8, p. A12.

Jackson, J. 1971. "But Where Are All the Men?" *Black Scholar, 3* (4): 34–41.

Jones, J. 1991. "Racism: A Cultural Analysis of the Problem," in R. L. Jones (Ed.), *Black Psychology*, 3rd ed., pp. 609–635. Berkeley, CA: Cobb & Henry.

Kerns, V. 1989. *Black Carib: Kinship and Ritual: Women and the Ancestors.* University of Illinois Press.

Lehman, N. 1986. "Origin of the Black Underclass." *Atlantic Monthly*, July.

Marable, M. 1993. "Racism and Multicultural Democracy." *Poverty and Race, 2* (5): 4, 12–13. Poverty & Race Research Action Council.

McAdoo, H. 1991a. "Family Values and Outcomes for Children." *Journal of Negro Education, 60* (3): 361–365.

———. 1991b. "A Portrait of African American Families in the United States: A Status Report," in S. Rix (Ed.), *The American Woman 1990–1991: A status report*, pp. 71–93. New York: W. W. Norton.

———. 1992a. "Reaffirming African American Families and Our Identities." *Psych Discourse, 23* (3): 6–7.

———. 1992b. "Upward Mobility and Parenting in Middle-Income Black Families," in A. Burlew, W. Banks, H. McAdoo, and D. Azibo (Eds.), *African American Psychology: Theory, Research, and Practice*, pp. 63–86. Newbury Park, CA: Sage.

———. 1993. "Family Equality and Ethnic Diversity," in K. Altergott (Ed.), *One World, Many Families*, pp. 52–55. Minneapolis, MN: National Council on Family Relations.

———. 1995a. "African American Families: Strength and Realities," in H. McCubbin, E. Thompson, A. Thompson, and J. Futrell. *Resiliency in Ethnic Minority Families: African American Families*, pp. 17–30. Madison, WI: University of Wisconsin System Press, Center for Excellence in Family Studies.

———. 1995b. "Stress Levels, Family Help Patterns, and Religiosity in Middle- and Working-Class African American Single Mothers." *Journal of Black Psychology, 21* (4): 424–449.

———. 1997. *Black Families*, 3rd ed. Newbury Park, CA: Sage.

McAdoo, H. and V. Crawford. 1991. "The Black Church and Family Support Programs." *Families as nurturing systems: Support across the life span*, pp. 193–222. New York: Haworth Press.

McAdoo, H. and L. McWright. 1994. "The Roles of Grandparents: The Use of Proverbs in Value Transmission," in V. Jackson (Ed.), *Aging Families and Use of Proverbs for Values Enrichment*, pp. 27–38. New York: Haworth Press.

McAdoo, J. 1985. "Modifications of Racial Attitudes and Preferences in Young Black Children," in H. McAdoo and J. McAdoo (Eds.), *Black Children: Social, Educational, and Parental Environments*, pp. 243–256. Beverly Hills, CA: Sage.

McDonald, M. 1970. *Not By the Color of Their Skin.* New York: International Universities Press.

"Monthly Vital Statistics Report." 1993. *Advance Report of Final Natality Statistics, 1990, 41*(9): tables 11 and 12. National Center for Health Statistics, Public Health Service.

Moore, K., A. Snyder, and C. Halla. 1993. "Facts at a Glance." Unpublished Data from the National Center for Health Statistics, Department of Health and Human Services; forthcoming in *Vital Statistics of the United States, 1990,* vol. 1, *Natality,* pp. 1–6.

Myrdal, G. 1964. *An American Dilemma.* New York: McGraw-Hill.

O'Hare, W., and W. Frey. 1992. "Booming, Surburban and Black." *American Demographics,* (Sept.): 38–44.

Park, R. 1919. "The Conflict and Fusion of Cultures with Special Reference to the Negro." *Journal of Negro History, 4* (2), April.

Pipes, W. 1992. *Say Amen, brother!* Detroit: Wayne State University Press.

Prince, K. 1997. "Black Family and Black Liberation." *Psych Discourse, 28* (1): 4–7.

Progress and Peril: Black Children in America, A Fact Book and Action Primer. 1993. Black Community Crusade for Children, coordinated by the Children's Defense Fund. Washington, DC.

Reid, I. 1939. *The Negro Immigrant: His Background, Characteristics, and Social Adjustment, 1899–1937.* New York: Columbia University Press.

Robinson, I. 1992. "Blacks Move Back to the South." *Black Americans.* Ithaca, NY: American Demographics (10–12). [Reprint package #318–A.]

Rule, S. 1993. "Malcolm X: The Facts, the Fictions, the Film." *New York Times,* November 15, pp. A1, A8.

Russell, C. 1996. *The Official Guide to Racial and Ethnic Diversity.* New York: New Strategist.

Stack, C. 1974. *All Our Kin: Strategies for Survival in a Black Community.* New York: Harper & Row.

———. 1996. *African Americans Reclaim the Rural South.* New York: Basic Books.

Staples, R. 1994. "Changes in Black Family Structure: The Conflict Between Family Ideology and Structural Conditions," in R. Staples (Ed.), *The Black Family: Essays and Studies.* Belmont, CA: Wadsworth.

Sudarkasa, N. 1980. "African and Afro-American Family Structure: A Comparison." *Black Scholar, 22*: 37–60.

———. 1988. Interpreting the African Heritage in Afro-American Family Organization," in H. McAdoo (Ed.), *Black families,* 2nd ed. pp. 27–43. Newbury Park, CA: Sage.

———. 1993. "Female-Headed African American Households," in H. McAdoo (Ed.), *Family Ethnicity: Strength in Diversity,* pp. 81–89. Newbury Park, CA: Sage.

———. 1997. "African American Families and Family Values," in H. McAdoo (Ed.), *Black Families,* 3rd ed., pp. 9–40. Thousand Oaks, CA: Sage.

Taylor, R., and L. Chatters. 1991. "Religious Life," in J. Jackson (Ed.), *Life in Black America,* pp. 105–123. Newbury Park, CA: Sage.

Terry, D. 1993. "Black Muslims Enter Islamic Mainstream." *New York Times,* May 3, pp. A1, A9.

Tucker, B., and C. Mitchell-Kernan. (Eds.) 1991. *The Decline of Marriage Among African-Americans: Causes, Consequences, and Policy Implications.* New York: Russell Sage.

———. 1985. "Sex Ratio Imbalance Among Afro-Americans: Conceptual and Methodological Issues," in R. Jones (Ed.), *Advances in Black Psychology,* vol. 1. Berkeley, CA: Cobb & Henry.

Tucker, B. and S. Myers. 1991. "Sex Ratios, Marriageability, and the Marginalization of Black Males." Paper presented at the Biennial meeting of the Society for Research in Child Development. Seattle, WA: May.

"Understanding Islam in America." 1994. *American Demographer* (January): 10–11.

U.S. Bureau of the Census. 1992. *We the American Elderly.* U.S. Department of Commerce, Economic and Statistics Administration, pp. 4–5. Washington, DC: U.S. Government Printing Office.

———. 1993. *We the American Blacks.* U.S. Department of Commerce, Economic and Statistics Administration, pp. 1–8. Washington, DC: U.S. Government Printing Office.

———. 1993. *We the American Women.* U.S. Department of Commerce, Economic and Statistics Administration, pp. 1–8. Washington, DC: U.S. Government Printing Office.

————. 1993. *We the Americans: Our Education.* U.S. Department of Commerce, Economic and Statistics Administration, p. 6. Washington, DC: U.S. Government Printing Office.

————. 1993. *We the American Children.* U.S. Department of Commerce, Economic and Statistics Administration, pp. 1–17. Washington, DC: U.S. Government Printing Office.

Usdansky, M. 1994. "One in Three Born Out of Wedlock." *USA Today* [Source: U.S. Census Bureau (1993)], February, pp. 22, 2A.

Wilkinson, D. 1993. "Family Ethnicity in America," in H. McAdoo (Ed.), *Family Ethnicity: Strength in Diversity,* pp. 15–59. Newbury Park, CA: Sage.

————. 1997. "American Families of African Descent," in M. DeGenova (Ed.), *Families in Cultural Context: Strengths and Challenges in Diversity,* pp. 335–360. London: Mayfield.

Wilson, W. 1987. *The Truly Disadvantaged: The Inner City, the Underclass, and Public Policy.* Chicago, IL: University of Chicago Press.

Winkler, K. 1994. "Islam and Democracy." *The Chronicle of Higher Education,* October 1, p. A10.

Whitmire, R. 1994. "Just Half of the Kids in Traditional Homes." *Lansing State Journal,* August 30, p. 5A. [Quoted S. Furukawa (1994). Source: U.S. Census Bureau.]

16 Native American Families

Robert John

HISTORICAL BACKGROUND

As the indigenous people of the western hemisphere, Native Americans[1] have a long and rich historical past. Depending on the source consulted, it has been estimated that at the period of contact with European cultures there were anywhere from 1 million (Kroeber, 1939) to 7 million (Thornton, 1987) to as many as 18 million (Dobyns, 1983) Native Americans living north of what is now Mexico. The diversity of this population is an overriding characteristic, reflected by a high degree of linguistic and cultural variation. At the time of contact with European cultures there were around 300 languages spoken. Few scholars, however, have attempted to estimate the number of separate groupings or "tribes" that existed, and no accurate estimate is possible.

Because the number of groups was large, for most of the last century anthropologists have attempted to summarize the cultural practices and reduce the cultural complexity to a few cultural types. Toward this end, modern anthropologists have divided North America into ten to twelve different culture areas. However, this division is based largely on material artifacts and modes of subsistence in a given geographical area rather than on social organization or a people's way of life, including their family relationships.

The task of reducing Native American societies to relatively few cultural types has been made more difficult because diverse family practices existed not only within each culture area but within each group, so that a wide variety of family practices were common and accepted. Indeed, according to Driver (1969:222), "almost all of the principal variants" of marriage and family practices can be found among American Indian groups. Those practices found

---

[1]I use the terms *Native American, Indian,* and *American Indian* interchangeably throughout this chapter to denote all aboriginal people, whether American Indian, Eskimo, or Aleut. According to 1990 census figures (U.S. Department of Commerce, 1993) American Indians comprise 96 percent of the Native American population, 3 percent are Inuit, and 1 percent are Aleut.

among American Indians include bride price, bride wealth, bride service, and dowry; arranged marriage and bethrothal; interfamilial exchange marriage and adoptive marriage; bride abduction and elopement; cross-cousin and parallel-cousin marriage; patrilocal, matrilocal, neolocal, avunculocal, and bilocal residence patterns; patrilineal, matrilineal, bilateral inheritance and descent; infanticide; primogeniture; monogamy, polygyny and temporary polyandry; premarital and extramarital sexual relations; divorce; temporary marriage; trial marriage; wife lending; spouse exchange; sororate and levirate marriage; couvade; adoption; patriarchy; and matriarchy.

Obviously, the degree of diversity within Native American populations has been greatly reduced since first contact, largely because of the extermination of many groups through the introduction of European pathogens including smallpox, measles, chickenpox, influenza, scarlet fever, malaria, typhus, typhoid fever, diphtheria and other diseases. An indication of the degree of impact can be recognized by the fact that nearly half of the aboriginal languages are now extinct, and within the United States there are now only around 300 federally recognized American Indian groups. It has been estimated (Porter, 1983) that there are another hundred "nonrecognized" tribes, mainly in the eastern states and California, from which the federal government withholds benefits. Although many of these tribes are in the arduous and complex legal process of petitioning to be recognized by the federal government, the inescapable fact is the dramatic reduction of Native American population and peoples since the time of Columbus when sustained contact with European cultures began.

Within the last century, attempts to force acculturation to Anglo-European practices has resulted in the further reduction of the range and diversity of American Indian family practices. The influences with the greatest impact on Native American family practices that have played a major role in bringing about change include the intrusive nature of formal education, missionary activities, federal policies to force individual landholding, expropriation of their landbase, economic exigencies on reservations, intermarriage, and federal government inducements to relocate to urban areas. More recently, the overweening influence of American popular culture on Native American youth has also contributed to a convergence of Native American values and practices with the Anglo-European mainstream. However, despite nearly five hundred years of destructive contact with Anglo-European cultures, important differences in family practices persist among Native Americans.

MODERN NATIVE AMERICAN FAMILIES

Academic research on the status and needs of Native American families continues to lag far behind research on other minority families, and scholarship remains erratic, idiosyncratic, and meager. Moreover, much of the research on crucial topics is becoming dated. One need only contrast the amount of information available about other minority groups, much less middle class whites, to realize the relative paucity of information on Native American families. Indeed, the difference is easily seen when one looks at the model of family life believed to describe whites and American Indians and the theoretical concepts used to explain current Native American family practices.

Coming out of the "isolated nuclear family" debate that dominated family studies during the immediate post–World War II era, the "modified extended" family model has been established as characteristic of white family life since 1965 (Brody, 1995). However, studies of Native American family life have not achieved a similar level of understanding. If any model of Native American family life is offered at all, it is the "extended family" model, a family form that has never been universally practiced by American Indians (Driver, 1969). This model is largely the legacy of anthropological studies that have shaped our conceptualizations of Native American family life until now.

Indeed, if one looks at works on family life published during the post–World War II period, one must conclude that Native Americans were studied exclusively by anthropologists. Based upon this anthropological perspective, in comparison to the family structure of white Americans the opposite presumption was thought to characterize the family life of Native Americans. As examples of cultures that were not fully modernized, family life was presumed to approximate forms typical of "primitive" societies (see Queen and Adams, 1952).[2] It is true that the existence of extended family structures among many Native American groups was well documented in the anthropological literature, but very little of that literature was of recent origin, having been written during the prolific era of ethnographic studies that ended with the Great Depression. This situation of viewing Native Americans as living in an unchanging "ethnographic present" began to alter during the late 1960s, when researchers began to study Native Americans from other perspectives and with other research questions in mind.

During the 1960s, the rapid pace of change within American society that had taken place since World War II was apparent among Native American cultures, too, and scholars adopted a generalized version of acculturation theory in order to explain changes that were evident in Native American family practices. The two characterizations of Native American family life derived from anthropological studies—that extended families are the norm and that families can be classified according to degree of

---

[2]An interesting reflection, and perhaps a sign of academic irrelevance in shaping social policy during the 1950s, is the divergence between how academics and politicians viewed Native Americans. While academics continued to treat Native Americans as examples of "primitive" societies, the federal government was busy terminating Indian groups because of a belief that many groups were already, and all groups should and would be, assimilated into the American cultural mainstream.

acculturation—persist today as the twin themes of Native American family studies.

Although studies of various aspects of Native American family life have appeared during the last twenty-five years, these studies do little to clarify precisely what is occurring within Native American families as a whole. This fundamental problem is illustrated by a dual tendency to characterize Native American family life as based upon the existence of extended families that integrate all generations into a cohesive Native American family, along with a general acknowledgment of the importance of culture change in modifying family practices. For example, Schweitzer (1983:173) has acknowledged the tension between continuity and change in Native American family life:

> The most important social structure which operates within the Indian community remains that of the family. It is the family which provides the framework in which the elderly Indian occupies roles which constitute the most important area of power and prestige for old people. . . . If prestige accrues in any context just for the sake of being old it is in the family.[3]

In one of the few studies to challenge the prevailing consensus, Manson and Pambrun (1979:92) have questioned whether the common view of elders' position in Native American family and community life may be a stereotype.

> The popular image of Indian elders places them in their children's homes, caring for young, respected in turn, and totally dependent upon these circumstances for a sense of self-worth and fulfillment. Communities presumably provide social and psychological support by seeking their counsel and apprenticing members to them to preserve rare skills and valued knowledge. The relevant literature is dated, limited theoretically as well as substantively, and provides no insight into this image.

As these authors recognized, we have no definitive research to give a measure of certainty to our knowledge of the current status of Native American families or how Native American families are changing.

Native American Family Typologies

Based on fieldwork conducted on a reservation band of coastal Salish in the mid-1950s, Lewis (1970:87ff.) advanced a tripartite model of family life. Lewis categorized Salish families as following the "old Indian ways," "between

---

[3]It is important to recognize that the family life of Native Americans may be the residual institution of their societies that has been most resistant to change. Other native institutions, notably their political, economic, educational, even their religious institutions, were decimated long ago, having been changed through violent or legal force.

old and new," or following "new ways" based on an assessment of the degree of acculturation derived from family lifestyles and values. The characteristics that distinguished the group following the "old Indian ways" included extended family households, use of Indian language, participation in tribal religious practices, low educational attainment and little value placed on education, a communal family economy with minimal participation in wage labor, low and tolerant supervision of children, and the importance of grandparents in childrearing. At the other extreme, families following "new ways" were characterized by nuclear family households, higher educational attainment and value on education, more material possessions, steady employment in wage labor, Christian religion, more contact with whites, strict supervision of children, and intermarriage outside of tribal boundaries. Despite these differences, Lewis does make clear that this more acculturated group has not severed all participation in traditional Native American cultural practices, and she rejects the influence of intermarriage as a special determinant of style of family life, largely because a great deal of "admixture" with whites had occurred before tribal rolls were created.

Wagner (1976), however, has claimed that rather than being a cause of assimilation, intermarriage reflects the degree of assimilation that has already taken place. Based on a sample of seventeen urban Indian women Wagner constructed a typology that, like others, is divided into three categories based on degree of acculturation. Wagner (1976:219) has identified these as:

> Tradition-oriented (those who adhere to traditional values, including a de-emphasis of material possessions, and seek to preserve or revitalize their culture); . . . Transitional (those who identify with their ancestral group but evidence more of the values of the dominant culture . . .); and . . . American middle-class (those whose cultural identification is with the dominant society but who identify themselves as Indians.

All those among the traditional group had married other Indians; had strong ties to their families, reservation, and tribes; adhered to values that were distinctly Indian; and had social lives centered around other Indians. Degree of Indian blood, however, was not found to be a factor in acculturation or intermarriage. The factors that were most significant in acculturation were the presence of a white father or grandfather, "an Indian parent who deliberately chose to abandon his cultural heritage" (Wagner, 1976:227) as well as white school teachers, schoolmates, and clergy. Having a white husband represented another "potent maximizing agent."

Miller and Moore (1979), on the basis of a longitudinal study of 120 American Indian families in the San Francisco Bay area, constructed a four-category typology of Native American "modes of adaptation" based on the degree to which the families she studied exhibited Indian or white values and behaviors. Miller and Moore (1979:479) identified the four groups as:

Traditional, in which the person clings to Indian values and behaviors; Transitional, where the individual adapts to white means and ends . . . ; Bicultural, in which the person is able to hold onto Indian values and means and is also able to adapt to white ends without considering them the primary value structure; and Marginal, whose individuals are anomic in both worlds.

The most recent effort to create an American Indian family typology (Red Horse, 1988) has suggested a six-category continuum of family types[4] based on preferred language (native or colonial), religious beliefs (native, pan-Indian, Christian), attitudes about land (sacred or utilitarian), family structure (extended, fictive, nuclear), and health beliefs and behaviors (native health practices versus Anglo-European). According to Red Horse, the Traditional Indian family speaks Indian, has an extended family system, a sacred view of the land, practices the native religion, and retains native health beliefs and practices. The Neotraditional family has many of the same characteristics as the traditional family type but has converted or integrated elements of a new religion into their native spiritual beliefs and rituals, including new healing rituals, remedies, or spiritual healers to deal with health problems. The Transitional family is described as having suffered a geographic dislocation (i.e., moving to an urban environment) that has disrupted the transmission of the native language to younger generations, extended family ties, and native religious practices. Although daily life generally is based on non-Indian family practices and forms, this family type attempts to maintain cultural connection with the extended family, native spiritual practices, the native homeland, and health beliefs and practices through frequent trips to the cultural community. Within the Bicultural family, most native elements have been replaced in daily practice by Anglo-American forms (English, nuclear family structure, non-Indian religion, view of nature, and health care practices) although people in this family type maintain a generic Indian identity. The Acculturated family type is indistinguishable from Anglo-Americans in beliefs and practices and has severed all ties to native culture. The Panrenaissance family type has passed through the loss of native culture and is engaged in an attempt to renew Indian beliefs and practices although in pan-Indian or hybrid form.

With this latest formulation, Red Horse has moved away from his claim (Red Horse et al., 1978:69) that "extended family networks represent a universal pattern among American Indian nations." While this statement may have been *generally* true of most Native American groups in the past, it is not true of the present. Promotion of the continued existence of extended fami-

---

[4]In a previous conceptualization, Red Horse and colleagues (1978:69) has offered a typology of "three distinct family patterns" among urban Chippewas ("traditional," "bicultural," and "pantraditional").

lies may serve to reinforce an important generic Native American cultural value, albeit increasingly in an ideological manner.

Despite weaknesses in existing data, there is little doubt that extended families are most important on recognized Indian lands, and that historical evidence, case studies, and population statistics suggest that Native American extended family structures, regardless of how they are defined, continue to weaken, particularly among the growing urban Indian population. Of the family types identified by Red Horse (1988), only three (Traditional, Neotraditional, and Transitional) continue to exhibit extended family values and behaviors although with less fidelity to the Native American ideal as one moves along the continuum. The remaining three Native American family types reveal values and behaviors closer to those of Anglo-Americans or, at best, other American ethnic groups, who are also experiencing the harsh pressures borne by a mass, commodified, acquisitive, technological, competitive, invasive, hegemonic American culture.

Given this inconsistent evidence, one is tempted to conclude with Staples and Mirande (1980:168) that there "is no such institution as a Native American family. There are only tribes, and family structure and values will differ from tribe to tribe." Although this has always been true, as the recent feminist reconceptualization of family studies has shown, there is no such institution as "the family" among other groups in the United States, either.

The error of comparing Native American families with a nonexistent isolated nuclear family believed to be typical of whites makes it easy to identify an important between-group difference that distinguishes Native American families. However, the actual differences in family values and behaviors are more extensive and subtle. As Red Horse (1980a) has suggested, many Native American families are more firmly based upon *interdependence* than Anglo families. Indeed, there is a good deal of evidence to support this somewhat more modest conclusion. For instance, Tefft (1967:148) found that Shoshone and Arapaho youth "place many more job restrictions on themselves than whites by refusing to seek jobs for which they are qualified very far from the reservation." Lewis (1970) also found a similar self-imposed limitation among the Salish in the mid-1950s. In addition, Witherspoon (1975) provided ample detail of the interdependence of "traditional" Navajo family economic activities and kinship expectations (see also Lamphere, 1977). Interdependence also extends to childrearing activities. Ryan (1981:28) has characterized childrearing in traditional American Indian families as a "total family process" in which a number of relatives, rather than just the parents, provide guidance and instruction although he states that it is being less utilized today.

Red Horse provided further support for this conclusion in revealing a difference between Indian and Anglo intergenerational family relations. Red Horse (1980a:464) contends that "eventual retirement, with self-responsibility apart from the mainstream of family, serves as a life goal in a nuclear model. Ego identity in extended family models, however, is satisfied through interdependent roles enacted in a family context."[5] Hennessy and John (1995:222–223) also found interdependence to be an important feature of caregiving situations in Pueblo families.

In American Indian families, total dependence is no more valued than total independence. With a highly dependent elder sometimes family harmony can be reestablished through encouraging greater personal autonomy and ability to contribute to the group that are the central features of family interdependence.

If we are to refine our model of Native American family life, then studies of Native American family networks are essential to advance our understanding of contemporary Native American families. Although now somewhat dated, Guillemin (1975) has written the best account of family networks among a group of Native Americans. Her qualitative research on the Micmac of the Canadian maritime provinces and Boston provides the most complete portrait of the operation of what Red Horse (1980b) characterized as "interstate extended families." She describes the network processes she witnessed that link Micmac family members and their friends within a highly mobile but tribally based "community" grounded in the ethic of sharing resources, which extends over much of New England.

Despite this very rich portrait of Micmac extended family operation, Guillemin (1975:246ff.) does describe a group of Micmac, which she characterized as few in number, that lives outside or, at best, on the margins of Micmac community life. These urban "spin-offs" include people who have married outside the tribe, elders, people with tuberculosis, heart disease, or drinking problems, and vagrants, as well as another group of families who live in neighborhoods where few Indians reside and restrict their extended family and peer group contacts more in line with family patterns of the cultural mainstream.

A more recent study of Native American family support networks (John, 1991b) investigated the availability and proximity of kin and the frequency of nine common family activities with each child and sibling among Prairie Band Potawatomi elders living on a rural reservation in the midwest. This study attempted to understand each elder's total matrix of interaction with their children and siblings, how gender and marital status affected contact, and the equity of their relationships. Although a majority of Prairie Band Potawatomi elders had frequent contact with their children and siblings, John (1991b) found that 11 percent of these elders did not have a living child or sibling and 32 percent did not have a child or sibling living on or near the reservation. This suggests that key members of the extended family do not exist or live too

---

[5]For example, see Troll (1978); Ward (1978); Cantor (1980); Powers, Keith, and Goudy (1981); or Mercier and Powers (1984) on the normative value Anglos place on independence. In fact, McKinlay, Crawford, and Tennstedt (1995) found that disabled elders in need of assistance acknowledged using formal services in order to maintain independence rather than asking family for help and feeling dependent. Few American Indian elders would feel the same way.

far away to provide much assistance for a significant proportion of Prairie Band Potawatomi elders. John (1991b) concluded that ritualistic contact may be the most important type of interaction when a conjugal pair exists. However, children and siblings do appear to mobilize resources in the event of greater need, but until a need exists they serve a largely symbolic purpose.

Native American Family Change

Currently, the American Indian population is, and should continue for some time to be, one of the fastest growing and youngest subpopulations in the United States. According to the 1990 census (U.S. Department of Commerce, 1993), between 1980 and 1990 the American Indian population increased by 42 percent, from 1.4 million to 2 million. However, the accuracy of census data has been an area of debate among demographers for some time (Harris, 1994; Passel, 1976; Passel and Berman, 1986; Snipp, 1989). Passel (1996) investigated the 255 percent growth in the American Indian population that has occurred since 1960 and concluded that the increase is demographically impossible without substantial immigration, which cannot be the case for American Indians. In large part, this enormous growth has occurred because of a change in census enumeration procedures beginning in 1960 through use of self-identification to classify the race of the respondent. Passel (1996) has estimated that one-third of the total Indian population in 1990 have adopted a new self-identification as an American Indian between 1960 and 1990. Plausible reasons for the change in ethnic identity are discussed in Nagel (1995). However, natural increase and greater efforts to accurately count the Native American population are also responsible for the population increase. In addition to the 2 million people who are considered Native Americans in this chapter, another 6.8 million people claimed to be of partial Native American ancestry (Passel, 1996), a figure that is virtually the same as it was in 1980 (U.S. Congress, 1986; cf. Eschbach, 1993).

Rapid population growth occurred between 1960 and 1990 in tandem with urbanization and a geographic redistribution of the Indian population to states that had few Indians in 1960 (Eschbach, 1993; Passel, 1996). Both demographic shifts have been greatly influenced by changing ethnic identification. As Eschbach (1993) has shown, almost all of the redistribution of the Native American population (particularly to California and the eastern states) is attributable to new self-identification as a Native American rather than migration. Based on his findings, Eschbach dismissed the reservation-to-city migration model as only a minor factor in understanding Native American demographic change.

Despite the growth and redistribution of the Indian population, census data reveal that Native Americans continue to be the most rural of any ethnic group in the United States. Almost one-half (48.6%) of all Native Americans reside in non-metropolitan areas, another 23 percent live in central cities, and the remaining 28 percent live in metropolitan areas outside central cities (Snipp, 1996; U.S. Department of Commerce, 1993).

The 1990 census changed the way it classifies Indian lands and the Indian population living in Indian areas. Slightly more than one-third of the Indian population live in what are now labeled American Indian jurisdictional or statistical areas. In 1990 (U.S. Department of Commerce, 1993) approximately 22 percent of the Indian population lived on American Indian reservations or trust land, 10 percent lived in tribal areas of Oklahoma, approximately 3 percent lived in areas (not in Oklahoma) that are inhabited by a federally or state-recognized tribe that does not have a land base, and 2 percent lived in an Alaska Native Village Statistical Area. Seventy-five percent of all American Indians live west of the Mississippi River. Four states (Oklahoma, California, Arizona and New Mexico) have over 100,000 Native Americans each, together accounting for 43 percent of the total population.

Fertility. The median age of the American Indian population is substantially lower than the general population (U.S. Department of Commerce, 1993). The median age of American Indian females (27.9) is more than eight years less than the median age of the non-Hispanic white population (36.2), and the median age of American Indian females residing in rural areas is even lower. The significance of this difference is that a substantially higher proportion of American Indian females are in their prime childbearing years.

Findings for the period 1980 to 1982 (U.S. Congress, 1986) for thirty-two Reservation States revealed that fertility was highest among Native American women between 20 to 24 years old, followed by the 25–29 age group, with the 15–19 age group having the next highest fertility rate (although roughly half that of 20–24 year olds), followed by 30–34 year olds. Despite somewhat lower fertility rates among teenage Native American females compared to Native American women in their twenties, this evidence documents that a substantial proportion of American Indian fertility is attributable to adolescent childbearing (U.S. Congress, 1986). Data for 1990 to 1992 (Indian Health Service, 1995) reveal that the pattern of fertility has changed little during the last decade.

American Indian women are far less likely to delay childbearing than white women. Compared to whites, very few American Indian women wait until age 30 to have their first child. From 1990 to 1992, only slightly less than 6.6 percent of first births among American Indian women residing in Indian Health Service service areas were to women 30 years of age and older, compared to nearly 20 percent among white women (Indian Health Service, 1995). These data also reveal that far fewer Indian women wait until age 25 to have their first child. Only 20 percent of first births among American Indian women were to women aged 25 and over compared to nearly half of first births among white women (48%).

During the twentieth century, fertility among American Indians has declined although American Indian fertility is still higher than it is in the general population. According to the Indian Health Service (1995), the Native American birth rate for 1990 to 1992 (27.3 per 1,000 population) was almost double the rate among whites (15.4). In a study of children ever born (parity) to married women aged 15–44, Thornton, Sandefur, and Snipp (1991) have shown that fertility patterns between 1940 and 1980 were similar to the United States pattern, although Native American fertility was somewhat higher during each decade than among whites. As with the white population, American Indian fertility increased during the postwar baby boom years but has shown an overall decline between 1940 and 1980.

Table 16-1 documents the number of children ever born to American Indian and non-Hispanic white women aged 35 to 44 by urban and rural residence. This table provides an indication of desired family size and fertility among women who are nearing completion of the childbearing years. Although urban Indian women were more likely than rural Indian women to be childless and fewer of them have had five or more children, their fertility pattern is quite similar to that of rural non-Hispanic white women until the two highest categories. In contrast, urban non-Hispanic white women have sharply lower fertility than the other groups.

Thornton and colleagues (1991) have shown that ethnic identity and intermarriage affect fertility. Since 1940, fertility has been higher among American Indians married to another American Indian, compared to Indians who have married someone from another race. Using 1980 census data, Thornton and colleagues (1991) also documented higher fertility among females who identify themselves as American Indian compared to fertility among women who claim some degree of Indian ancestry, while the fertility of women who identify themselves as Indian but who claim multiple ancestry was in between. For these authors, each of these categories represents degrees of assimilation. Using 1990 census data, Eschbach (1995) found a strong relationship between racial endogamy and mean number of children ever born. Indian couples averaged 3.41 children ever born compared to 2.36 children ever born to an Indian wife

TABLE 16-1. Percentage of Children Ever Born to Women Aged 35 to 44 by Place of Residence :1990

Number of Children	American Indians Urban	Rural	Non-Hispanic Whites Urban	Rural
No Children	14.9	10.4	22.0	13.3
1 Child	16.6	12.5	17.4	15.5
2 Children	27.9	26.7	35.5	38.6
3 Children	20.7	22.1	17.3	21.4
4 Children	10.6	14.4	5.5	7.6
5 or More Children	9.2	13.9	2.4	3.5

Source: U.S. Department of Commerce (1993: tables 54, 56).

and non-Indian husband, and 2.21 children to a non-Indian wife and Indian husband.

Out-of-Wedlock Childbearing.   In many cases, births are to unwed mothers. The historical trend and full extent of out-of-wedlock childbearing among American Indians is not known. The evidence suggests that out-of-wedlock childbearing has increased, and it is relatively common since in most tribes little or no stigma is attached to having a child whether a woman is married or not. Bock (1964:144) characterized the attitude toward illegitimacy among reservation Micmac in Canada as "matter-of-fact and tolerant," although he stressed that legitimacy is still considered the norm by the community as it had been prior to contact with European cultures. His study of illegitimacy from 1860 to 1960 on this Micmac reservation found a 20 percent incidence of illegitimacy throughout the period.

More recent research has indicated that the prevalence of out-of-wedlock childbearing among Native Americans is now more than twice as high as Bock's estimate. According to a study by the National Center for Health Statistics (1995), 55.8 percent of American Indian births in 1993 were to unmarried women, nearly three times the rate among non-Hispanic whites (19.5%). Previous evidence from New Mexico and South Dakota (U.S. Congress, 1986) has shown that there is some regional, and probably tribal, variation in out-of-wedlock births. Census data (U.S. Department of Commerce, 1993) suggest that out-of wedlock birth is higher among rural Indian women than among urban Indian women, especially among women aged 15–24.

Guillemin (1975:219) found that a "pattern of pregnancy and the birth of the eldest child out of wedlock followed by a marriage to a man who was not necessarily the father of that first child" had been prevalent among the Micmac for some time. This explanation fits the cross-sectional fertility data that shows a "marriage lag" (i.e., a number of women have children first and get married later). Since birth can and frequently does precede marriage and the likelihood of ever getting married is quite high regardless of previous childbearing, the fertility figures (U.S. Department of Commerce, 1993) show that marriage catches up with fertility.

Guillemin (1975:226) has identified cultural reasons for this pattern by noting that among the Micmac "a woman's ability to have children is a mark of her strength and value and there is really no one to shame her for having had a child out of wedlock." An Ojibway woman (Katz, 1995:259) characterized the importance of childbirth at the same time that she reinforced the normative value placed on marriage.

> Giving birth was considered a woman's sacred role. She attained dignity in the process of giving birth, no matter who she was. Even if a girl was known to be irresponsible, if she married someone more respected than she and then gave birth, she'd redeem herself.

Clearly, the sacredness of the mother role easily outweighs the secular preference that marriage precede childbearing. The interdependent nature of Native American families makes it possible to absorb an event like this without travail.

Contraception and Birth Control. Very little systematic research has been conducted on contraception and birth control among American Indians. There is some evidence to suggest that there is less use and less knowledge of contraception among American Indians, especially youth, than among other Americans. For example, Haynes (1977) found that unwed teenaged Arapahoe and Shoshone girls between 15 and 19 years old comprised 37 percent of the females who did not practice contraception on the Wind River Reservation. A study by Davis and Harris (1982) of 288 rural New Mexico youths between the ages of 11 and 18 showed that Native American adolescents incorrectly answered significantly more questions about sex, pregnancy, and contraception than did Anglo or Hispanic youth. Davis and Harris (1982:490) reported that the Native American youth were "the least informed, both in test scores and self-reported knowledge of the sexual vocabulary terms presented."

Liberty and colleagues (1976) explored Seminole and Omaha attitudes toward abortion. Although approval of abortion was generally higher among the urban residents of both tribes and fewer urban women were undecided on their attitude toward abortion given a particular situation in which an abortion may be contemplated, women in both reservation and urban environments held similar opinions with few exceptions. Both urban and reservation women disapproved of abortion simply because the couple could not afford another child, or did not want another child, or because the woman was not married. A majority of Omaha women in both reservation and urban environments and urban Seminole women approved of abortion if the pregnancy seriously endangered the health of the mother, if there were good reasons to believe the child would be deformed, or if the woman had been raped. Reservation Seminole women also approved of abortion if the mother's health was seriously endangered but were less certain that fetal deformity or rape were adequate justifications, although opinion on these last two issues was equally divided, with a large proportion of women who were undecided.

This study of attitudes toward abortion is complemented by a study of the use of surgical procedures to avoid childbearing among the Navajo and Hopi. Consistent with the attitudes expressed in the two studies just discussed, Kunitz and Slocumb (1976) found that the incidence of induced abortions among Navajo and Hopi women was lower than it was for the general population of Arizona and New Mexico. Overall, there was almost no difference between the two tribes in the rate of induced abortions. However, induced abortions varied greatly by age group. Navajo women made relatively uniform use of induced abortion regardless of their age, whereas induced abortions among the Hopi increased with the woman's age. Hopi women between the ages of 40 and 49 had the highest rate of induced abortions (approximately 5.5 times the overall rate among Navajo and Hopi women in general).

Overall, the current incidence of sterilization among Native American women is not known. Kunitz and Slocumb (1976:19) acknowledge the controversy that has arisen over the use of sterilization procedures on American Indian females, stating that there "has been considerable feeling on the part of some individuals that the Indian Health Service has engaged in unethical practices in some areas by performing sterilization procedures without informed consent or after exerting undue pressure on patients." Indeed, these authors report that over 90 percent of bilateral tubal ligations are performed on postpartum patients, and that females are far less likely to undergo the operation at other times. This leads to the possible conclusion that females may be more willing to agree to sterilization while the painful experience of childbirth is fresh in their memory and make a decision that they will later regret. Haynes (1977) found that the controversy over sterilizaton was associated with a reluctance to use contraceptives among Arapaho and Shoshone females.

In comparison to use of sterilization procedures among females, Kunitz and Slocumb (1976:9) found that "vasectomies are virtually never done on Hopi and Navajo men." Warren and colleagues (1990) also found no male sterilization among the sexual partners of a sample of reservation and urban Indian women in Montana (and only 4% of each sample of women reported use of a condom as a contraceptive device). Whether or not males share concern about contraception, pregnancy, and childbearing, this evidence strongly suggests that Native American females bear the brunt of the responsibility to avoid pregnancy and childbearing.

Martial Status.   Data support the idea that American Indian females tend to marry at a younger age than American Indian males, who tend to delay marriage for a variety of reasons. Marital disruption—whether through separation, widowhood or divorce—is more common among American Indian females for all age groups.

Intermarriage.   Although intermarriage has taken place since first contact with European cultures, intermarriage has also changed contemporary Native American family life. Although less than 1 percent of marriages in the United States in 1970 were between individuals from different racial groups, American Indians were the least likely of six races studied (Clayton, 1978) to practice racial endogamy. This relatively high prevalence of intermarriage is reflected in the fact that overall, American Indians were involved in 27 percent of all interracial marriages in 1970, most commonly between an

American Indian and white person. In comparison to intermarriage with whites, black/American Indian intermarriage is far less common, which is consistent with some suggestive findings by Feagin and Anderson (1973) at an all-Indian high school that prejudice against blacks was expressed by a majority of these students despite extremely limited contacts with them.

Figures available from the decennial Census for subsequent years (Eschbach, 1995; Sandefur and Liebler, 1996; U.S. Congress, 1986) reveal that intermarriage has increased substantially since 1970 so that in 1990 around 60 percent of currently married Native Americans were married to someone from another race. Using 1990 census data, Eschbach (1995) has documented a pronounced age difference in intermarriage among four cohorts of American Indians. Among currently married American Indians, 65 percent under the age of 25, 61 percent aged 25–44, 57 percent aged 45–64, and 52 percent aged 65 and over were married to a non-Indian.

Sandefur and McKinnell (1986) have suggested that some portion of the increase in intermarriage is the result of a change in self-identification between 1970 and 1980, a process that has also been shown to affect the inter-generational transmission of an American Indian ethnic identity (Eschbach, 1995). However, there are significant differences in intermarriage between urban Indians and Indians living in rural areas, and important regional differences in intermarriage (Eschbach, 1995; Snipp, 1989). Racial endogamy is much lower among urban Native Americans and among Native Americans who live in regions that have experienced the largest increases in the Indian population because of a change in self-identification than it is among Native Americans residing on identified reservations (Eschbach, 1995; John, 1988; U.S. Department of Commerce, 1986). Eschbach (1995) documented that approximately three-quarters of currently married American Indians who live in twenty-three states were married to someone from another race. Within each "marriage market" there are only minor differences in the marital practices of Indian males and females (John, 1988; Sandefur and McKinnell, 1986; Sandefur and Liebler, 1996). According to Eschbach (1995:94), except for a limited number of states in which American Indians tend to live in enclave communities, "in the remainder of the United States the Indian population is amalgamating rapidly." As Yellowbird and Snipp (1994:188) have pointed out "the data on marriage patterns raise the prospect that Indians, through their spousal choices, may accomplish what disease, western civilization, and decades of Federal Indian policy failed to achieve."

Female-Headed Households. A major change in Native American family life is documented in census data. The U.S. census reports a steady increase in the prevalence of American Indian families maintained by women between 1970 and 1990 from 18.4 percent to 26.2 percent of all American Indian families (U.S. Department of Commerce, 1973, 1993). However, female-headed families with no husband present are more common in urban areas.

According to census data (U.S. Department of Commerce, 1992), 29.4 percent of urban families are female headed with no husband present compared to 24.7 percent of rural Indian families.

An increase in female-headed families has occurred in the general population as well, but the proportion among Native Americans is more than double the proportion for the non-Hispanic white population (12.4%). This appears to be a new adaptation to American society. Although a number of authors, past and present, have commented that marriage and divorce among Native American groups has always been more casual (Christopherson, 1981; Guillemin, 1975) and not fraught with guilt, recriminations, trauma, or adverse effects on extended family life including affinal relations (Heinrich, 1972), this elevated rate of female-headed families does not appear to be a continuation or legacy of traditional cultural practices since remarriage, except by elders, was common for both men and women in the past.

Naturally, this increase in female-headed families has been at the expense of other family forms. Between 1980 and 1990, the percentage of married couple families among American Indians decreased from 71.8 percent to 65.8 percent of families (U.S. Department of Commerce, 1983, 1993). Sandefur and Liebler (1996) have documented the decrease in the percentage of Indian children under 18 years of age who reside with two parents that has occurred between 1970 and 1990. In 1970, more than two-thirds (68.6%) of Indian children under 18 resided with two parents compared to slightly more than half (54.4%) in 1990. In contrast, 70 percent of children in the general population were residing with two parents in 1990. Sandefur and Liebler (1996) also show that fewer children on Indian reservations live with two parents (48.8%) and that there is considerable tribal variation in this family characteristic on the ten largest Indian reservations (ranging from a low of 35.2% on the Pine Ridge Reservation to 57.2% on the Navajo Reservation).

Sandefur and Liebler (1996) articulated a number of reasons for concern about the increase in female-headed families among American Indians since family structure affects the ability of the family to accomplish central functions and has a detrimental effect on the life chances of the children. According to Sandefur and Liebler (1996), female-headed families have fewer economic resources, have lower access to parental resources, experience an unavoidable alteration of the parent-child relationship, and have lower access to community resources because of less residential stability. Although they suggest that cultural influences also play a role, Sandefur and Liebler (1996) associated the increase in female-headed families to increases in the proportion of women who have never married (primarily because of a delay in age at first marriage) and an increase in divorce.

Income and Poverty. Median family income of American Indian families ($21,750 in 1989) was nearly $16,000 a year less than the median family income of the non-Hispanic white population (U.S. Department of

Commerce, 1993), and per capita income among American Indians was approximately half the amount among non-Hispanic whites. Households headed by an American Indian female are particularly disadvantaged financially compared to American Indian married couple families and non-Hispanic whites. In 1989, the median family income of American Indian female householders with no husband present ($10,742) was approximately one-third the median income of American Indian married couple families ($28,287) and approximately half that of non-Hispanic white female householders with no husband present ($20,807).

Sadly, poverty among the American Indian population increased during the 1980s, and poverty is relatively common (Gregory, Abello, and Johnson, 1996; John and Baldridge, 1996; Trosper, 1996). Nearly 31 percent of all individual American Indians lived below poverty level in 1989 (U.S. Department of Commerce, 1993). American Indian families also experience poverty. In 1979, there were 81,078 American Indian families (24%) with income below poverty level. By 1989, there were 125,432 American Indian families (27%) living below poverty, making Indian families nearly four times as likely to be impoverished as families in the general population. Several authors (Guillemin, 1975; Miller and Moore, 1979) explain that the accumulation of wealth is difficult for Native Americans, in part because of the nature of their work experience, but also because of the ethic of sharing with others within the family network.

An even more somber picture emerges if we look at just those Native Americans living in rural environments including identified reservations. Poverty, even according to official figures, is pervasive. According to the United States Department of Commerce (1993:95), 32.5 percent of rural Native American families were living in poverty in 1989. The poverty rate in rural areas for unrelated individuals, an indication of poverty among people who live alone, was 50.9 percent compared to 36.5 percent among unrelated American Indian individuals living in urban environments.

As income figures suggest, unemployment among Native Americans is another pervasive problem with a direct impact on family life. The 1990 census reported that unemployment among American Indians was 14.4 percent compared to 5 percent among non-Hispanic whites (U.S. Department of Commerce, 1993). Unfortunately, the standard Labor Department definition only counts people who are not employed but are actively seeking work. Undoubtedly, this figure, like the ones for poverty rates for the Indian population, is an underrepresentation of the extent of this social problem because a disproportionate number of American Indians would not be counted as unemployed since there is little point in actively seeking work in environments like Indian reservations where few employment opportunities exist. The Labor Department labels these individuals as "discouraged workers."

The effects of employment or unemployment on Native American family life have not been adequately studied. Bock (1964) found that periods of unemployment were associated with high rates of premarital pregnancy among the Micmac between 1860 and 1960. Oakland and Kane (1973) studied the relationship between working mothers and child neglect among the Navajo. They were interested in whether the growth in women's participation in wage labor was linked to child neglect as was maintained by popular opinion at a local Indian Health Service Unit. Oakland and Kane (1973:849) concluded that "child neglect was not . . . closely related to the mother's age, education, [or] employment, but the significant factors appeared to be marital status and size of family." Oakland and Kane (1973:852) concluded from their research that "close and extended family ties remained intact" even when mothers secured wage labor although extended family supports were not universally available.

Witherspoon corroborates the impact of wage labor on Navajo subsistence residential units in one area of the large Navajo reserve. Witherspoon documents that neolocal residence patterns are now typical among the under-forty generation and that there was little neolocal residence before wage labor became an option. Change has occurred, but like Henderson, Witherspoon emphasizes the Navajo-like character of these adaptations. According to Witherspoon (1975:78):

> the traditional subsistence residential units are continuing to function much the way they have for a long time. At least half of the younger people, however, are not living in these units but are supporting themselves in other ways. . . . Thus, the new economic and residence patterns are not destroying the old patterns; they are just supplementing them.

Witherspoon also illustrates the important difference between household composition and residential proximity as measures of Native American family life. Witherspoon found that 64 percent of the subsistence residential units were composed of three or more generations, but household composition was overwhelmingly nuclear. Seventy-eight percent of the households were two-generation households, 13 percent were three-generation households, and 9 percent contained one generation.

Life Course

Childhood.   Research on the Native American life course has tended to focus on childhood. A good deal of attention (Blanchard and Barsh, 1980; Blanchard and Unger, 1977; Brieland, 1973; Byler, 1977; Edwards, 1978; Edwards and Egbert-Edwards, 1989; Fanshel, 1972; Fischler, 1980; Garcia, 1973; Goodluck, 1993; Ishisaka, 1978; Red Horse, 1982a; Red Horse et al., 1978; Slaughter, 1976; Unger, 1977) was devoted to the subject of the state's intervention into Native American family life through the routine placement or adoption of Indian children into non-Indian families.

Claiming that this policy contributed to the further destruction of Native American cultures by disrupting the socialization process whereby children learned tribal values and customs, this debate and attendant political efforts were particularly intense in the mid-1970s and led to the enactment of the Indian Child Welfare Act of 1978 (PL 95-608). This legislation limited the right of the states to intervene in Native American family life by giving tribes the right to protect the welfare of Indian children as an aspect of tribal sovereignty and self-determination.

Under the authorization provided by this legislation (Pipestem, 1981), many tribes have established tribal agencies and judicial procedures to oversee the placement of Indian children within the tribe (preferably with a family member). As a consequence, the child's tribe now has legal jurisdiction in these cases. Pipestem (1981:60) has stated that the preponderance of cases in which the Indian Child Welfare Act has protected children are in circumstances of "neglect, what we call dependent and neglected cases, where there is a substantial amount of chemical abuse by the parents." Edwards and Egbert-Edwards (1989) noted that while progress has been made in the areas of adoption and tribal jurisdiction as a result of the Indian Child Welfare Act, implementation and compliance with all of the act's stipulations have been uneven. Based on a nation-wide survey conducted in January 1986, Edwards and Egbert-Edwards (1989) reported that the number of American Indian children in substitute care represented more than three times their relative percentage in the total child population. More important, while the number of children in substitute care from other races decreased, the number of American Indian children in substitute care *increased* 25 percent between 1980 to 1986. Just under half of the 9,005 children in subsititute care lived in homes where one or both parents were Native American.

Another line of research on childhood has focused on the socialization process in Native American cultures (Boggs, 1956; Brendtro, Brokenleg, and Van Bockern, 1991; Downs, 1964; Guillemin, 1975; Lefley, 1974, 1976; Lewis, 1981; Miller and Moore, 1979; Ryan, 1981; Schlegel, 1973; Tefft, 1968; Underhill, 1942; Williams, 1958). According to Downs (1964:69) the socialization process among the Navajo operates on the principle of "the inviolability of the individual," a system that operates by "light discipline, by persuasion, ridicule, or shaming in opposition to corporal punishment or coercion." I would interject that to some interpreters this would appear to mean "permissive." Lewis (1981:104) has stated that the lack of corporal punishment is attributable to the respect that is "at the very center of a person's relationship with all others starting with the child's relationship to the family." Brendtro and colleagues (1991:8) pointed out that "adults will respect children enough to allow them to work things out in their own manner." Supernatural sanctions (Lefley, 1976; Ryan, 1981; Williams, 1958) are also used to control behavior.

Underhill (1942), Boggs, (1956), Williams (1958), Guillemin (1975), and Miller and Moore (1979) have stressed that much of the socialization process among Native Americans is non-verbal, with communication by stern looks, or simply ignoring inappropriate behavior. In addition, children are supposed to learn by observing others (by example), to share with others, to not make unreasonable or selfish demands, to show deference to everyone older than themselves, to take responsibility for themselves and others in the family, and contribute to the group from an early age.

Tefft (1968) investigated changes in the socialization practices and values of the Wind River Shoshone and found what amounts to a generation gap between people over fifty years old and younger people. According to Tefft, the values of older Shoshone were more "Indian-oriented" than the values of their adult children. Tefft (1968:331) found that among people over fifty years old "Collateral, Past, Subjugation-to-Nature, and Being Orientations predominated . . . while Individual, Future, Over-Nature, and Doing Orientations predominated" among their children. He attributed this difference to a shift in the agents of socialization that have had the greatest influence on the formation of values of each of these generations. Respondents in the oldest generation identified their parents and grandparents as most influential in their lives, while their children mentioned representatives of white institutions (white school mates, teachers, church leaders, or neighbors).

Tefft concluded that socialization practices have changed from "cohesive and structured" households characterized by high dominance–high support parent-child relations in which the older generation grew up to "loosely structured" households with low dominance-low support parent-child relations of the younger generations. My own research (John, 1985:305 ff.) among Prairie Band Potawatomi elders confirms, at least, the perception of similar changes in childrearing practices as well as values and behaviors of younger generations. A composite portrait of these changes can be summarized as follows. Back when these elders were growing up, the family was much closer, was more organized and protective, combined discipline with permissiveness better than today, and had the advantage of having parents (particularly the mother) around the home.

Lefley (1974, 1976) studied the effects of the socialization process on self-esteem among the Seminole and Miccosukee tribes of Florida. These two tribes were chosen because they are closely related and represent more and less acculturated groups respectively. She posited that members of the less acculturated Miccosukee tribe would have higher self-esteem because greater cultural integrity would provide a higher level of social integration that would be more conducive to the development of psychological health. Results confirmed her hypothesis. In fact, both mothers and children in the less acculturated Miccosukee tribe had significantly higher self-esteem. Rotenberg and Cranwell's (1989) research on cross-cultural differences in self-concept, however, questions the appropriateness of conventional measures of self-esteem for Indian children. They point out that, although there are definite differences between white and Indian children, the attributes measured are probably not equally important to the two groups.

The basic idea advanced by Lefley's research is the destructive impact that acculturation has on self-esteem and the unfortunate prognosis that the intrusive agents of socialization in American culture will further increase the likelihood that younger members of relatively traditional groups will experience lowered self-concepts. Miller (1981) also viewed a number of these agents of socialization as powerful and insensitive forces shaping American Indian family life. In a study of the effects of one such institution, Metcalf (1976) concluded that religious and federal boarding schools undermined self-esteem as well as the maternal behaviors among Navajo women in adulthood. Metcalf stated (1976:543) that "a disruptive school experience had significant detrimental effects on the women's measured levels of commitment to the maternal role, their attitudes toward their children and family life, and their sense of competence as mothers." This, in turn, negatively affected their children's self-esteem. A vivid illustration of the negative influence boarding schools had on parenting and children's self-esteem is provided by a Menominee/Lithuanian woman, whose father ended up in boarding school and "was not able to be a good parent because he had no experience of parenting" (Katz, 1995:133). She also pointed out that "the elders were not able to protect the generation of Indian who grew up in boarding school" (Katz, 1995:132).

Adolescence. Another modern American stage of the life course, adolescence, is much in evidence among Native Americans. The problems of American Indian adolescents such as drug use, suicide, and difficulties with identity and self-esteem have been well researched and publicized (Berlin, 1987; Blum, Harmon, Harris, Bergeisen, and Resnick, 1992; Dinges, Trimble, and Hollenbeck, 1979; Dodd, Nelson, and Hofland, 1994; May, 1987, 1996). Indeed, Liu and colleagues (1994:336) have summarized what is known about this period of the life course in the following manner: "Native American adolescents have an increased incidence of high-risk behaviors such as pregnancy, childbearing, school dropout, alcohol abuse, substance abuse, and mental health problems such as depression, suicide, anxiety, low self-esteem, alienation, and running away."

Unfortunately, no community, regardless of how remote, is immune from these changes in adolescent behavior. For example, Christopherson (1981) recognized that adolescence had arrived on the largest and, in many ways, most traditional of the reservations. Christopherson (1981:105–106) pointed to "alcohol, glue and gasoline sniffing, venereal disease, and a variety of delinquent behaviors" as evidence of adolescence among the Navajo. However, he did not estimate the prevalence of these behaviors. More recent research (Bachman, Wallace, O'Malley, Johnston, Kurth, and Neighbors, 1991) has documented the extent of the drug problem in a nationwide sample of American adolescents. They found that Native American seniors had the highest prevalence rates for most illicit drugs, alcohol, and cigarettes of the six ethnic/racial groups studied.

On a more positive note, Bachman and colleagues' analysis did show an overall decrease in use of marijuana, alcohol, and cigarettes by Native American seniors from 1976 to 1989. Unfortunately, this downward trend does not apply to adolescent suicide rates. May (1987) has reported that the suicide rates for Indian males vary significantly between tribes. However, the overall suicide rate for 1990 to 1992 reported by the Indian Health Service (1995) for Native American males age 15–24 is almost three times (60.8 per 100,000) that of white males (21.9 per 100,000) in the same age group. Berlin (1987) attributed the high incidence of suicide to chaotic family structures resulting from divorce and disruption and to family disruption from death or alcoholism. He associated suicide rates to the degree of cultural tradition maintained by a tribe (i.e., the more traditional the tribe, the lower the rates of suicide). Berlin gave the existence of a functioning extended family substantial credit for the maintenance of tribal traditions. Levy and Kunitz (1987) add weight to the idea that the family may be the most important factor in self-destruction, reporting that suicides cluster within families more than within particular tribes.

LaFromboise and Bigfoot (1988) surmised that several cultural values and beliefs contribute to the high suicide rate among Native American youth. The idea that death is a part of the circle of life as opposed to a terrible event to be feared, the traditional emphasis on personal autonomy and choice, the idealization of the deceased at giveaways, and some tribes' belief in reincarnation may all fail to act as deterrents to suicide. In addition to these factors, LaFromboise and Bigfoot (1988:147) claimed that:

> Continuous periods of mourning within close-knit extended families due to suicide, homicide, and accidental deaths coupled with the daily hassles of long-term poverty, social and political tension, unavailability of employment and underachievement in education understandably undermine an Indian adolescent's coping efforts.

In addition, according to LaFromboise and Bigfoot (1988), suicide rates among American Indian adolescents may be underreported. Their list of reasons include the use of automobiles as "suicide weapons" or the reporting official's unwillingness or inability to classify the death as a suicide. For instance, the death may be classified as a homicide, when in fact, the adolescent who was killed instigated an incident with the intent of suicide.

Although these extreme behaviors have received much attention, we must not let them skew our perceptions of Native American youth. Berlin

(1987:229) also emphasized that "some tribes and pueblos have suicide rates that are the same as or lower than the present white adolescent suicide rate," and Dodd and colleagues (1994) explained in detail many incidents that are interpreted negatively by non-Indian teachers and counselors, when in fact Indian adolescents are exhibiting positive self-concept and high self-esteem in a culturally prescribed manner.

Berlin (1987) noted that the prevention of suicide has become a top priority in many tribes and summarized several successful intervention programs. The use of tribal elders to help mitigate the loss of parental involvement and early nurturant figures in the lives of Native American adolescents have been especially effective. LaFromboise and Low (1989) have also identified possible interventions in managing the multitude of problems faced by Indian adolescents. They noted that Indian youth expect practical advice from counseling, not the reflective analysis that most conventionally trained counselors are taught to administer. The use of extended family, which they defined liberally as those persons who are influential and supportive in the adolescent's life, can be crucial in designing an effective intervention strategy for Indian youth. In each case, it appears to be the involvement of respected and caring individuals in the adolescent's life that delineates success from failure in the counseling process.

Adulthood and Middle Age.   Adulthood and middle age among Native Americans have received very little attention. Christopherson (1981:106), quoting a study by the Office of Indian Education, characterized gender differences among the Navajo that I believe are relatively common among Native Americans in general. There is a tendency among females to settle down at an early age while "males . . . do not reflect qualities of sociological adulthood until their very late 20s or early 30s. Until then, males typically defer marriage, maintain their peer-group orientations, and have very little job stability" (see also Guillemin, 1975). This is undoubtedly related to the scarcity of employment opportunities on reservations as much as any other factor. When young Indians do settle down, as in American society in general, mate selection is based upon romantic love.

Despite this similarity, there are attitudinal differences between Native American and other youth toward marital practices. Edington and Hays (1978) conducted a comparative study of the difference in family size and marriage age expectation and aspiration of Anglo, Mexican American, and American Indian youth living in rural New Mexico. They found that Native American youth wanted more children and expected to have more children than Anglo or Mexican-American youth. Based on his analysis of 1980 census data, Snipp (1989) concluded that two to three children was the preferred number of offspring among American Indian women.

Edington and Hays (1978) also found that the age at which American Indian youth wanted to marry and expected to marry was higher than the responses from the other two groups. On balance, however, Edington and Hays concluded that Native American youth were less certain of their desires and expectations regarding marriage and procreation because of a higher rate of nonresponse than Anglo or Mexican American youth.

Very little is known about husband-wife interaction among Native Americans. Only one such study (Strodtbeck, 1951) compared ten Navajo, Texan, and Mormon couples on how they interacted during decision making and whose opinion prevailed when asked to characterize families in their community. Strodtbeck hypothesized that Navajo women, because of their economic power and independence gained through the control of property, would win more of the decisions than either Texan or Mormon women. This hypothesis was confirmed by his study. Strodtbeck also discovered that the character of the dyadic interaction was very different among the Navajo couples.

Without commenting directly on this study by Strodtbeck, Witherspoon (1975) corroborates the relative lack of verbal interaction during the decision-making process among Navajos. Because of the emphasis on unity, cooperation, and consensus in Navajo family life, when important decisions need to be made, feelings, attitudes, and decisions are sensed rather than verbally expressed. Serious matters are seldom dealt with at the level of speech, and important decisions are seldom discussed. Decisions are felt and sensed before they reach a verbalized conclusion. According to Witherspoon (1975:98), family members think over the situation until one of their number "has the sense of the group" and then offers a suggestion to the group that either resolves the issue or results in further deliberations. Because the Navajo live and work together closely, over the years they "learn to communicate with each other without the use of language."

This nonverbal approach extends to other tribes as well as other areas of family life. Quoting one of her informants, the first strength of Indian families identified by Miller and Moore (1979:457) was that "relatives 'help without being asked. It's just our way.' " Elders, too, do not feel that they should have to ask for assistance but that family members, tribal officials, and service workers should be able to sense their needs and respond to them (John, 1988a, 1991b).

Guillemin (1975) provided a reasonable explanation for the nonverbal capabilities of American Indians when she characterizes the socialization process of Micmac children. "Micmac children learn by observation and are not subjected in the family to intense verbal instruction. Younger children are expected to imitate their older siblings in the basics of eating, toilet training, and general physical dexterity without individual instruction" (Guillemin, 1975:94–95). Williams (1958) and Underhill (1965) and also documented this approach among the Tohono O'Odham (Papago).

Little is known about gender roles among Native Americans. Coming from cultures that traditionally had rigid gender roles,[6] contemporary Native Americans have modified their gender role behaviors toward the androgenous norms of American society as a whole. However, this point should not be overdrawn. Based on a small sample from Los Angeles, Price (1981) characterized the primary emotional concerns of women as largely expressive and men as instrumental. Price found that women were more concerned with kinfolk, family, marriage, and sexual relations, and men were more concerned with employment, money, success, and material matters. Guillemin (1975) characterized other aspects of gender roles, including same-sex confidants and peer groups.

Elders.   Another body of recent research on the life course has investigated the other end of the life cycle. The nature of the research that has been conducted during the last twenty-five years has changed greatly from anthropological accounts and issues to more practical investigations (John, 1988a), the goal of which is to improve the quality of life of Native American elders. For the most part, this applied, social policy research has investigated the current status, service needs, and service use of Native American elders (Barón, Manson, Ackerson, and Brenneman, 1990; Bell, Kaschau, and Zellman, 1978; Brown, 1989; Edwards, Edwards, and Daines, 1980; Hennessy and John, 1996; John, 1988b, 1991a, 1994, 1995; John and Baldridge, 1996; John, Hennessy, Roy, and Salvini, 1996; Johnson and Taylor, 1991; Joos and Ewart, 1988; Lefkowitz and Underwood, 1991; Kramer, 1991; Kramer, Polisar, and Hyde, 1990; Kunitz and Levy, 1991; Murdock and Schwartz, 1978; Manson, 1989a, 1989b, 1992; National Association of State Units on Aging, 1989; National Indian Council on Aging, 1981, 1983; Red Horse, 1982b). The general findings are that American Indian elders experience a number of disadvantages in old age compared to the general population.

However, there are significant differences between urban and reservation aging American Indians in their current status and need for services, as well as the mix of support they receive from informal and formal sources. Based on a nationwide sample of Indian elders over the age of 55 (John,

---

[6]A particularly misguided interpretation of American Indian gender roles can be found in Gonzales (1994). Indeed, because of the value Native American cultures placed on personal autonomy and taking direction from communion with the spirit world, one could say that personal forms of deviant behavior were institutionalized in native cultures. These types of personal deviance include "contraries," men practicing the berdache, and women warriors, healers, and "chiefs" (Allen, 1986; Garcia, 1994; Roscoe, 1991; Williams, 1986). The type of deviance that could not be tolerated was deviance that threatened group survival (e.g., young hunters giving chase to a herd of buffalo before the signal was given by the hunt leader). The conceptualization of gender roles were rigid but not strictly tied to an individual's biological sex. Regardless of the sex of the role occupant, the role was open to anyone who was willing to practice the role in the prescribed manner. Women warriors were to perform the role set of men, and men who wished to be wives were to perform the role set of women.

1991a) it is possible to characterize urban and reservation differences in current status. Without doubt, the deprivation experienced by aging reservation Indians is substantially greater than among urban Indians. In general, the reservation group is poorer, has greater financial concerns, supports more people on their income, has fewer social contacts, has somewhat lower life satisfaction, and is in poorer health.

As is true of the general population, the greatest service needs for both groups of elders are for nonpersonal (i.e., housework, shopping, transportation) rather than personal (i.e., bathing, dressing, eating) assistance. The top four activities of daily living for which both urban and reservation groups need ongoing assistance are help with housework, transportation, using the telephone, and going shopping, and the foremost unmet need of both groups is for information and referral assistance. However, the levels of need are substantially greater in rural environments. Despite these differences, family is important in providing services for both reservation and urban Indians, although the relative demands on the family network are greater on reservations.

The issue of the existence and extent of the family support network is important during all periods of the life course but is especially important to the well-being of children and frail elders. Among Native Americans, the absence of family support has been linked to child abuse and neglect (Metcalf, 1979; Oakland and Kane, 1973), adolescent pregnancy (Y. Red Horse, 1982), psychological disturbances (Fox, 1960), and problems adapting to urban life (Metcalf, 1979; Miller and Moore, 1979). More recently, elder abuse and neglect within American Indian families has been acknowledged (Brown, 1989; National Association of State Units on Aging, 1989). Although the full extent of elder abuse and neglect is not known, Brown's study (1989) among a random sample of thirty-seven Navajo elders aged 60 years and over found that the most frequent type of abuse was being left alone when elders needed help followed by financial exploitation, and that elder abuse was associated with the suddenness of becoming dependent, having mental problems, and the personal problems of the caregiver. Instances of abuse and neglect contrast sharply with two common forms of intergenerational family caregiving that are important expressions of extended family support.

Among American Indian families in which extended family relationships are present, the grandparent-grandchild relationship is of special importance (Bahr, 1994; Ball, 1970; John, 1988; Lewis, 1981; Ryan, 1981; Tefft, 1968). Indeed, the grandmother is the center of American Indian family life, and she holds the family together. Although Medicine (1981) cautioned that the literature may popularize the role of grandmother at the expense of the broader kin group, many authors (Bahr, 1994; Bradford and Thom, 1992; Crow Dog and Erdoes, 1990; Fisher, 1980; Green, 1992; Shomaker, 1989) have described the grandmother's role as primary caregiver for grandchildren, especially on reservations.

Because of the tendency among American Indians to begin childbearing at a very early age, it is common for a woman to be a grandmother by the time she is 40 and often by the time she is in her mid-thirties. Although motherhood is an important transition in the life course marking the status of becoming a woman, grandmotherhood may be an even more important transition because of the additional responsibilities a woman assumes. Recognizing that not all grandmothers live up to the cultural ideal, Bahr (1994:245) succinctly characterized the ideal Apache grandmother as a woman who has entered "the full strength of her maturity."

Among American Indians, young women who have children, especially teenagers, frequently have little inclination or preparation for motherhood and some irresponsibility is anticipated and tolerated (Bahr, 1994; Metcalf, 1979), as long as it does not endanger the well-being of the child. Generally, the young woman looks to her mother for assistance and training and frequently passes a great deal of responsibility for the care of the child to her mother. On occasion, the grandmother takes over rearing one or more grandchildren because she or other family members feel that the child is not being raised properly or the parent(s) decide that it will benefit the child (Guillemin, 1975; Miller and Moore, 1979; Shomaker, 1989). A child may also go to live with a family member who needs help or if a family member would like to have a child around (Shomaker, 1989; Underhill, 1965). It is also possible for a child to ask to live with grandparents, a request that is honored if not a manifest impossibility. Bahr (1994) concluded that her respondents considered Apache children disadvantaged if they did not have a grandmother able to provide whatever care was needed.

The other important example of intergenerational family caregiving is eldercare. Consistent with tribal values that emphasize familial obligations and interdependence (Red Horse, 1980a), the extended family remains the primary and often sole provider of long-term care for functionally impaired relatives, especially among rural American Indians (John 1988). However, because of the pervasive lack of formal long-term care services, family members often undertake extreme demands in caring for and preventing the institutional placement of an elderly relative (Manson 1989; 1993). As John (1991b:46) has pointed out:

> It is true that American Indian families continue to provide most of the care elders receive, but American Indian families are not immune to the stresses and strains that can compromise their ability to care for American Indian elders. Indeed, there are a variety of threats to the informal support system among American Indians.

John and Huntzinger (1994) outlined the variety of these threats to the informal family support system that most Indian elders currently rely upon.

In addition to disruptive cultural influences from the educational system, missionary efforts, and the mass media, declining fertility, the necessity for young adults to seek employment in distant urban areas, and restrictive program requirements and eligibility guidelines undermine extended family support (John, 1991b). This last problem is especially apparent in programs like Supplemental Security Income that count total household income rather than personal income in the determination of program benefits. In this case, elders are penalized economically for practicing a widely held American Indian cultural value to live in an extended family unit.

In a qualitative study of family caregiving among Pueblo Indians, Hennessy and John (1995) highlight the culturally patterned attitudes toward dependency and the expectation, ready acceptance, and assumption of the role of primary family caregiver to a frail elder, especially by Pueblo women. For these caregivers ($N = 33$), providing care to functionally dependent elders was a significant expression of their identity as American Indians and reflected the importance of interdependence within the extended family and the tribe that continues into infirm old age.

Overall, although some caregivers and their families had worked out an acceptable caregiving arrangement, in many cases it was clear that the family arrangement was fragile or in need of periodic maintenance. In some instances, the caregiving system was in evident danger of exhausting the family's resources to provide care, particularly if the caregiver's or elder's health deteriorated further. Two factors emerged as important elements in establishing a satisfactory caregiving arrangement among Pueblo caregivers, including organizing caregiving into a predictable routine with a known magnitude of demands, and stabilizing family relationships around the caregiving situation through a consensual family process. Hennessy and John (1995) found that mobilizing family support to assist with eldercare appears to be a salient, if not unique, consideration important to the success of caregiving in Pueblo Indian families.

Despite the obvious difficulties and the lack of access to essential long-term care services, Hennessy and John (1996) found a strong cultural mandate to provide eldercare. However, a number of formal services would alleviate some of the strains and burdens experienced by these family caregivers. Caregiver training and support groups, enhanced care coordination or case management, adult day care and respite care, and family counseling or mediation were the supportive services most needed by these caregivers.

This series of studies strongly supports a general conclusion that extended family support networks continue to be extremely important to the well-being of American Indian elders. However, the idea that the mere existence of an extended family is sufficient to meet the needs of elders places a number of them at risk, since the extended family is not a universal feature in the lives of either rural or urban American Indians. In fact, John and

Huntzinger (1994) estimated that the proportion of American Indian elders in both urban and rural environments who are without an adequate family support network ranges from 16 percent to 20 percent. The clear implication of the research on family caregiving is that a comprehensive, responsive, and culturally sensitive community-based aging services system must be created if American Indian elders are to have the same kind of caregiving alternatives that are now available to the general population.

Unfortunately, the lack of formal services and a number of other barriers to service use are a significant problem among American Indian elders. As is true of other minorities (National Indian Council on Aging, 1981; U.S. Department of Health and Human Services, 1979), Native American elders, in general, have very low formal service utilization. Although the family's role as a direct service provider is well documented, scholarship has also suggested that the Native American family network is an important source of indirect assistance as well. That is, the family network is also instrumental in facilitating formal service use by family members. According to Murdock and Schwartz (1978), the availability of and contact with family members is an important factor in both the perception of needs and the use of services. In fact, they claim that "family structure is clearly related to objective indicators of need: the smaller the family unit, the greater its financial and housing needs" (Murdock and Schwartz, 1978:476-477). Murdock and Schwartz (1978:480-481) conclude that "children may assist elderly persons by both creating greater awareness of the needs for and availability of services, and in directly obtaining the required services."

Although Murdock and Schwartz (1978:481) stated their conclusion in a tentative manner, they suggested that "extended families serve to increase the mechanisms for service usage as well as the sources of information concerning services." Or further, that "levels of use as well as awareness . . . appear to be increased by living in a couple or in an extended family setting" (Murdock & Schwartz, 1978:479).[7] In their view, family members are not only the primary caregivers within the support network, but also serve an indispensable mediator role between family members and alien service bureaucracies. Whether as direct provider or intermediary, then, the existence of an extended family network is no less crucial now compared to the not too distant past when they were the sole source of support of Indian family members.

---

[7]Murdock and Schwartz are right to emphasize the important intermediary role of family members in service utilization. However, my research (John, 1986) suggests that this role is more important on reservations than it is in urban environments, primarily because of smaller households and fewer intact marriages among urban Indians. This does not contradict their findings since their study was of reservation Sioux. It does question the generalizability of their findings to urban environments. However, even on reservations, the role of family members as direct service providers is more important than their mediator role.

CHANGE AND ADAPTATION

Among the industrialized nations, the United States remains one of the few without a formal family policy. Moroney succinctly characterized the existing bias evident in social policy in the United States, a bias that is attributable to precisely the prevailing ideology and social interests arising from the concrete social location of most politicians and social planners. According to Moroney (1980:33–34),

> most social policies are oriented to individuals and not to families. Furthermore, when the object of the policy is the family, invariably it defines the family as nuclear. To shift policy development so that the modified extended family is explicitly included would require a major reorientation. . . . If successful, such a reorientation could result in policies that set out to maximize available resources, the natural resources of the family, and the resources of the social welfare system. Such an approach begins with a search for ways to support families by complementing what they are already doing—intervening directly and indirectly, but not interfering.

Without doubt, pressures to modify Native American family life in the direction of the patterns of the cultural mainstream will continue. By and large the greatest influence on Native American families will be the same as it is for Americans as a whole. The capitalist political economy sets the conditions of employment and indirectly shapes the family structure and relationships within it for the ever-increasing number of people who wish to pursue American-style success. Generally, such success can be achieved only at the sacrifice of family life.

The United States asks everyone to make a mutually exclusive choice: Dedicate yourself to your work or your family. Although this statement may continue a controversy within family sociology since it denies the ideological but mythical belief that American culture is family oriented, the sad truth is that family structures in the United States are fragile, temporary, and shrinking in size and importance. Any number of social trends attest to the truth of this statement: high rates of divorce, the institutionalization of cohabitation and singlehood, prenuptial agreements, the dramatic increase in the number of female-headed families, the escalation of women's labor force participation, the economic pressures that encourage dual–wage earner families, the increasing number of people of all ages who live alone, declining fertility, the rise of voluntary childlessness, and the delay of marriage and childbearing. I should make it clear that my intent in listing these trends is not for the purpose of making any invidious comparison with other family practices past or present nor to make any moral judgment on these practices. They are symptomatic and do reveal something about how family life has changed in response to our political economy and culture.

Indeed, each of these trends can be explained as a rational response to the political economy and American culture. Children, from a strictly economically rational viewpoint, are unalloyed economic liabilities for an entire lifetime. Economically rational behavior dictates delaying childbearing, having only one or at most two children, or not having children at all. Working women and dual–wage earner families have become a necessary response to the steady decline in the standard of living in the United States that has occurred since the early 1970s. Concomitant development of a focus on self and immediate gratification (whether these are labelled narcissism or hedonism), so promoted by commodified, prepackaged American mass culture, is consistent with most of these trends. I raise these issues not in order to call for sacrifice or devotion to some presumed duty. I merely wish to recognize these family trends as the most likely response and consequence of living in American society and the fact that the absence of a comprehensive governmental policy fails to adequately mitigate the negative influences that the political economy has on family life.

The impact of the political economy on family life is most clearly evident in the dire financial position of most female-headed families, and the fact that the impoverished in our society are disproportionately children, women, minorities, and elders. Each of these groups is now under renewed attack with the changes that have been introduced to welfare, a range of affirmative action policies, and discussions of how to "save" Medicare (by some form of the reduction of benefits). The lack of an adequate family policy (or even the idea that one is needed) means that structural changes in the American economy can be dealt with through public exhortations that plenty of jobs exist and go unfilled; through cutbacks in public financial, housing, medical, and food support in the face of growing poverty, hunger, homelessness; and deficiencies in medical care in the United States. Likewise, the consequences of decisions made in corporate boardrooms to shut down operations or move them to another state or country are not seen to have large costs that families must ultimately absorb.

Despite the fact that Native American families are not immune to the larger social structural forces in operation in the United States, I believe that Native American families continue to exhibit a unique character attributable to longstanding cultural differences from American culture as a whole. Indeed, Native Americans continue to exhibit a great deal of cultural diversity and divergence from the American cultural mainstream. Culture change has occurred as the result of contact with whites, but not to the degree that some observers would have us believe. The recognition by several researchers that even when Native American family practices have a formal resemblance with Anglo-European practices there is something distinctively

Native American in the way in which that practice is experienced should make academics circumspect in their use of an acculturation paradigm to explain family change among Native Americans. The rebirth of Native American cultural pride and the concomitant invigoration of tribal entities, clearly a direct outgrowth of the Red Power movement of the 1960s, have protected substantial numbers of Native Americans from total acculturation and assimilation.

However, it is true that Native American elders are more exclusively "Indian oriented" than middle or younger generations. Among the middle and younger generations, the best description of their value orientations would be "bicultural," having knowledge of two different cultural worlds and being able to operate in either one. Family practices have also changed. Although extended families remain the cultural ideal among Native Americans, in reality extended families are not universal and within families that exhibit extended family characteristics are prodigal sons and daughters who have moved outside the sphere of routine extended family operations. Nonetheless, it is true that Native American families are based more on interdependence and consanguine ties in comparison to the independent and conjugal emphasis within Anglo society.

The extent to which Native Americans adopt, resist, or adapt in modified form the family practices of the cultural mainstream depends on a number of factors. Certainly, some groups will have an advantage over others in retaining the cultural grounding of their tribal family practices. Among these, tribes that maintain or expand their land base (i.e., their cultural community) will have an advantage over tribes that do not have a community locus. Similarly, the largest groups will fare better than small ones in preserving their cultural heritage and unique family practices. Furthermore, tribes that succeed in building a tribal economy capable of sustaining their cultural community will have an advantage over tribes with weak and dependent economies. In addition, groups that maintain tribal spiritual practices and teach their children the tribal language will fare better than other groups.

However, the forces of change and cultural homogenization at work in American society as a whole will also have an effect on Native Americans. In addition to the American political economy, a number of other factors will pressure Native Americans toward practices of the cultural mainstream. American popular culture, education grounded in Anglo-European intellectual ways of knowledge, institutions or social movements (like Christian churches or the women's movement) that consciously or unwittingly undermine Native American values and practices, racial exogamy, and urbanization present a challenge to Native Americans. How Native Americans respond to these external pressures remains to be seen, but their history of cultural resilience suggests that they will be able to absorb them and adapt their family practices to meet their own cultural needs.

REFERENCES

Aginsky, B. W., and E. G. Aginsky. 1947. "A Resultant of Intercultural Relations." *Social Forces, 26*: 84–87.

Allen, P. G. 1986. *The Sacred Hoop: Recovering the Feminine in American Indian Traditions.* Boston: Beacon Press.

Bahr, K. S. 1994. "The Strengths of Apache Grandmothers: Observations on Commitment, Culture and Caretaking." *Journal of Comparative Family Studies, 25*: 233–248.

Ball, E. 1970. *In the Days of Victorio: Recollections of a Warm Springs Apache.* Tucson: University of Arizona Press.

Barón, A. E., S. M. Manson, L. M. Ackerson, and D. L. Brenneman. 1990. "Depressive Symptomatology in Older American Indians with Chronic Disease: Some Psychometric Considerations," in C. C. Attkisson and J. M. Zich (Eds.), *Depression in Primary Care: Screening and Detection.* New York: Routledge.

Bachman, J. G., J. M. Wallace, Jr., P. M. O'Malley, L. D. Johnston, C. L. Kurth, and H. W. Neighbors. 1991. "Racial/Ethnic Differences in Smoking, Drinking, and Illicit Drug Use Among American High School Seniors, 1976–89." *American Journal of Public Health, 81*(3): 372–377.

Bell, D., P. Kasschau, and G. Zellman. 1978. "Service Delivery to American Indian Elderly," in J. P. Lyon (Ed.), *The Indian Elder, A Forgotten American,* pp. 185–198. Albuquerque, NM: National Tribal Chairmen's Association.

Berlin, I. N. 1987. "Suicide Among American Indian Adolescents: An Overview." *Suicide and Life-Threatening Behavior, 17*(3): 218–232.

Blanchard, E. L., and S. Unger. 1977. "Destruction of American-Indian Families." *Social Casework, 58*(3), 312–314.

———, and R. L. Barsh. 1980. "What is Best for Tribal Children? A Response to Fischler." *Social Work, 25*(5): 350–357.

Blanchard, K. 1975. "Changing Sex Roles and Protestantism Among the Navajo Women in Ramah." *Journal for the Scientific Study of Religion, 14,* 43–50.

Blum, R. W., B. Harmon, L. Harris, L. Bergeisen, and M. D. Resnick. 1992. "American Indian-Alaska Native Youth Health." *Journal of the American Medical Association, 267*(12): 1637–1644.

Bock, P. K. 1964. "Patterns of Illegitimacy on a Canadian Indian Reserve: 1860–1960." *Journal of Marriage and the Family, 26*(2): 142–148.

Boggs, S. T. 1956. "An Interactional Study of Ojibwa Socialization." *American Sociological Review, 21:* 191–198.

Bradford, C. J., and L. Thom. 1992. *Dancing Colors: Paths of Native American Women.* San Francisco: Chronicle Books.

Brendtro, L. K., M. Brokenleg, and S. Van Bockern. 1991. "The Circle of Courage." *Beyond Behavior, 2*: 5–11.

Brieland, D. 1973. "Far from the Reservation: A Book Review." *Social Service Review, 47*(2): 310–311.

Brody, E. M. 1995. "Prospects for Family Caregiving: Response to Change, Continuity and Diversity," in R. A. Kane and J. D. Penrod (Eds.), *Family Caregiving in an Aging Society: Policy Perspectives,* pp. 15–28. Thousand Oaks, CA: Sage.

Brown, A. S. 1989. "A Survey on Elder Abuse at One Native American Tribe." *Journal of Elder Abuse and Neglect, 1*(2): 17–37.

Byler, W. 1977. "Removing Children—Destruction of American-Indian Families." *Civil Rights Digest, 9*(4): 19–27.

Cantor, M. H. 1980. "The Informal Support System: Its Relevance in the Elderly," in E. F. Borgatta and N. G. McCluskey (Eds.), *Aging and Society: Current Research and Policy Perspective,* pp. 131–144. Beverly Hills: Sage.

Christopherson, V. A. 1981. "The Rural Navajo Family," in R. T. Coward and W. M. Smith (Eds.), *The Family in Rural Society,* pp. 105–111. Boulder: Westview Press.

Clayton, R. R. 1979. *The Family, Marriage, and Social Change,* 2nd ed. Lexington, MA: D. C. Heath.

Crow Dog, M., and R. Erdoes, R. 1990. *Lakota Woman.* New York: Harper Collins.

Davis, S. M., and M. B. Harris. 1982. "Sexual Knowledge, Sexual Interests, and Sources of Sexual Information of Rural and Urban Adolescents from Three Cultures." *Adolescence, 17*(66): 471–492.

Dinges, N. G., J. E. Trimble, and A. R. Hollenbeck. 1979. "American Indian Adolescent Socialization: A Review of the Literature." *Journal of Adolescence, 2*: 259–296.

Dobyns, H. F. 1983. *Their Number Become Thinned: Native American Population Dynamics in Eastern North America.* Knoxville: University of Tennessee Press.

Dodd, J. M., J. R. Nelson, and B. H. Hofland. 1994. "Minority Identity and Self-Concept: The American Indian Experience," in T. M. Brinthaupt and R. P. Lipka (Eds.), *Changing the Self: Philosophies, Techniques, and Experiences,* pp. 307–336. Albany, NY: State University of New York Press.

Dorris, M. 1989. *The Broken Cord: A Family's Ongoing Struggle with Fetal Alcohol Syndrome.* New York: Harper & Row.

Downs, J. F. 1964. *Animal Husbandry in Navajo Society and Culture.* Berkeley: University of California Press.

Driver, H. E. 1969. "Larger Kin Groups, Kin Terms," in H. E. Driver (Ed.), *Indians of North America* 2nd ed., pp. 242–267. Chicago: The University of Chicago Press.

Dukepoo, F. C. 1980. *The Elder American Indian.* San Diego: University Center on Aging, San Diego State University.

Edington, E., and L. Hays. 1978. "Difference in Family Size and Marriage Age Expectation and Aspirations of Anglo, Mexican American and Native American Rural Youth in New Mexico." *Adolescence, 13*(51): 393–400.

Edwards, E. D. 1978. "Destruction of American Indian Families." *Social Work, 23*(1): 74.

———, M. E. Edwards, and G. M. Daines. 1980. "American Indian/Alaska Native Elderly." *Journal of Gerontological Social Work, 2*(3): 213–224.

———, and M. Egbert-Edwards. 1989. "The American Indian Child Welfare Act: Achievements and Recommendations," in J. Hudson and B. Galaway (Eds.), *The State as Parent: International Research Perspectives on Interventions with Young Persons,* pp. 37–51. Dordrecht, The Netherlands: Kluwer Academic Publishers.

Eschbach, K. 1993. "Changing Identification Among American Indians and Alaska Natives." *Demography, 30*(4): 635–652.

Eschbach, K. 1995. "Enduring and Vanishing American Indian: American Indian Population Growth and Intermarriage in 1990." *Ethnic and Racial Studies, 18*(1): 89–108.

Fanshel, D. 1972. *Far from Reservation: The Transcultural Adoption of American Indian Children.* Metuchen, NJ: Scarecrow.

Feagin, J. R., and R. Anderson. 1973. "Intertribal Attitudes Among Native American Youth." *Social Science Quarterly, 54*: 117–31.

Fischler, R. S. 1980. "Protecting American Indian Children." *Social Work, 25*(5): 341–349.

Fisher, D. (Ed.). 1980. *The Third Woman: Minority Women Writers of the U.S.* Boston: Houghton Mifflin.

Fox, J. R. 1960, November. Therapeutic Rituals and Social Structure in Cochiti Pueblo." *Human Relations, 13*(4): 291–303.

Garcia, D. W. 1973. "Far from Reservation—Transracial Adoption of American Indian Children." *Social Work, 18*(1): 125.

Garcia, M. 1994. "A Higher Power of Their Understanding: Cheyenne Women and Their Religious Roles," in V. Demos and M. T. Segal (Eds.), *Ethnic Women: A Multiple Status Reality.* Dix Hills, NY: General Hall.

Gonzales, J. L., Jr. 1994. *Racial and Ethnic Families in America.* Dubuque, IA: Kendall/Hunt.

Goodluck, C. T. 1993. "Social Services with Native Americans: Current Status of the Indian Child Welfare Act," in H. P. McAdoo (Ed.), *Family Ethnicity: Strength in Diversity,* pp. 217–226. Newbury Park, CA: Sage.

Green, R. 1992. *Women in American Indian Society*. New York: Chelsea House.

Gregory, R. G., A. C. Abello, and J. Johnson. 1996. "The Individual Economic Well-Being of Native American Men and Women During the 1980s: A Decade of Moving Backwards," in G. D. Sandefur, R. R. Rindfuss, and B. Cohen (Eds.), *Changing Numbers, Changing Needs: American Indian Demography and Public Health*, pp. 133–171. Washington, DC: National Academy Press.

Guillemin, J. 1975. *Urban Renegades: The Cultural Strategy of American Indians*. New York: Columbia University Press.

Harris, D. 1994. "The 1990 Census Count of American Indians: What Do the Numbers Really Mean?" *Social Science Quarterly, 75*: 580–593.

Haynes, T. L. 1977. "Some Factors Related to Contraceptive Behavior Among Wind River Shoshone and Arapaho Females." *Human Organization, 36*(1): 72–76.

Heinrich, A. 1972. "Divorce as an Integrative Social Factor." *Journal of Comparative Family Studies, 3*: 265–272.

Henderson, E. 1979. "Skilled and Unskilled Blue Collar Navajo Workers: Occupational Diversity in an American Indian Tribe." *Social Science Journal, 16*(2): 63–80.

Hennessy, C. H., and R. John. 1995. "The Interpretation of Burden Among Pueblo Indian Caregivers." *Journal of Aging Studies, 9*(3): 215–229.

———. 1996. "American Indian Family Caregivers' Perceptions of Burden and Needed Support Services." *Journal of Applied Gerontology, 15*(3): 275–293.

Indian Health Service. 1995. *Trends in Indian Health*. Rockville, MD: Indian Health Service.

Ishisaka, H. 1978. "American Indians and Foster Care: Cultural Factors and Separation." *Child Welfare, 57*(5): 299–308.

John, R. 1985. *Aging in a Native American Community: Service Needs and Support Networks Among Prairie Band Potawatomi Elders*. Ph.D. dissertation, University of Kansas.

———. 1986. "Social Policy and Planning for Aging American Indians: Provision of Services by Formal and Informal Support Networks," in J. R. Joe (Ed.), *American Indian Policy and Cultural Values: Conflict and Accommodation*, pp. 111–133. Contemporary American Indian Issues Series, No. 6. American Indian Studies Center, University of California, Los Angeles.

———. 1988a. "Native American Families," in C. H. Mindel, R. Habenstein, and R. Wright, Jr. (Eds.), *Ethnic Families in America*,(3rd ed., pp. 325–363. New York: Elsevier.

———. 1988b. "Use of Cluster Analysis in Social Service Planning: A Case Study of Laguna Pueblo Elders." *Journal of Applied Gerontology, 7*(1): 21–35.

———. 1991a. *Defining and Meeting the Needs of Native American Elders: Applied Research on Their Current Status, Social Service Needs, and Support Network Operation*. Final report to the Administration on Aging, grant 90AR0117/01. Vol. 1. *Urban and Rural/Reservation American Indian Elders: A Reanalysis of the 1981 National Indian Council on Aging Nationwide Sample*.

———. 1991b. "Family Support Networks Among Elders in a Native American Community: Contact with Children and Siblings Among the Prairie Band Potawatomi." *Journal of Aging Studies, 5*(1): 45–59.

———. 1994. "Health Research, Service and Policy Priorities of American Indian Elders," in C. Barresi (Ed.), *Health and Minority Elders: An Analysis of Applied Literature 1980–1990*, pp. 136–161. American Association of Retired Persons-Minority Affairs.

———. 1995. *American Indian and Alaska Native Elders: An Assessment of Their Current Status and Provision of Services*. Rockville, MD: Indian Health Service.

John, R., and D. Baldridge. 1996. *The NICOA Report: Health and Long-Term Care for American Indian Elders*. A Report by the National Indian Council on Aging to the National Indian Policy Center. Washington, DC: American Association of Retired Persons.

John, R., P. H. Blanchard, and C. H. Hennessy. "Hidden Lives: Aging and Contemporary American Indian Women," in J. M. Coyle (Ed.), *Women and Aging: A Research Guide*. Westport, CT: Greenwood Press.

John, R., C. H. Hennessy, L. C. Roy, and M. L. Salvini. 1996. "Caring for Cognitively-Impaired American Indian Elders: Difficult Situations, Few Options," in G. Yeo and D. Gallagher-

Thompson (Eds.), *Ethnicity and the Dementias*, pp. 187–203. Washington, DC: Taylor and Francis.

John, R. and P. Huntzinger. 1994. "The Legacy of the Columbian Exchange: A Policy Analysis of American Indian Aging at the Quincentennial." *Southwest Journal on Aging*, 9(2): 23–30.

Johnson, A., and A. Taylor. 1991. *Prevalence of Chronic Diseases: A Summary of Data from the Survey of American Indians and Alaska Natives*. AHCPR pub. no. 91–0031. Rockville, MD: Agency for Health Care Policy and Research.

Joos, S. K, and S. Ewart. 1988. "A Health Survey of Klamath Indian Elders 30 Years After the Loss of Tribal Status." *Public Health Reports*, 103: 166–173.

Katz, J. (Ed.). 1995. *Messengers of the Wind: Native American Women Tell Their Life Stories*. New York: Ballantine.

Kramer, B. J. 1991. "Urban American Indian Aging." *Journal of Cross-Cultural Gerontology*, 6(2): 205–217.

Kramer, B. J., D. Polisar, and J. C. Hyde. 1990. *Study of Urban American Indian Aging*. Final Report to the Administration on Aging, grant 90AR0118.

Kroeber, A. L. 1939. *Cultural and Natural Areas of Native North America*, Vol. 38. Berkeley: University of California Press.

Kunitz, S. J. 1974. "Factors Influencing Recent Navajo and Hopi Population Changes." *Human Organization*, 33(1): 7–16.

Kunitz, S. J., and J. E. Levy. 1991. *Navajo Aging: The Transition from Family to Institutional Support*. Tuscon, AZ: University of Arizona Press.

Kunitz, S. J., and J. E. Levy. 1994. *Drinking Careers: A Twenty-Five-Year Study of Three Navajo Populations*. New Haven: Yale University Press.

Kunitz, S. J., and J. C. Slocumb. 1976. "The Use of Surgery to Avoid Childbearing Among Navajo and Hopi Indians." *Human Biology*, 48(1): 9–21.

Lamphere, L. 1977. *To Run After Them: Cultural and Social Bases of Cooperation in a Navajo Community*. Tuscon, AZ: University of Arizona Press.

LaFromboise, T. D., and D. S. Bigfoot. 1988. "Cultural and Cognitive Considerations in the Prevention of American Indian Adolescent Suicide." *Journal of Adolescence, 11*: 139–153.

LaFromboise, T. D., and K. G. Low. 1989. "American Indian Children and Adolescents," in J. T. Gibbs, L. N. Huang, and Associates (Eds.), *Children of Color: Psychological Interventions with Minority Youth*, pp. 114–147. San Francisco: Jossey-Bass.

Lefkowitz, D. C., and C. Underwood. 1991. *Personal Health Practices: Findings from the Survey of American Indians and Alaska Natives*. AHCPR pub. no. 91–0034. Rockville, MD: Agency for Health Care Policy and Research.

Lefley, H. P. 1974. "Social and Familial Correlates of Self-Esteem Among American Indian Children." *Child Development, 45*(3): 829–833.

———. 1976. "Acculturation, Child-Rearing, and Self-Esteem in Two North American Indian Tribes." *Ethos, 4*(3): 385–401.

Leighton, D., and C. Kluckhohn. 1948. *Children of the People*. Cambridge: Harvard University Press.

Levy, J. E. 1967. "The Older American Indian," in E. G. Youmans (Ed.), *Older Rural Americans: A Sociological Perspective*, pp. 221–238. Lexington: University of Kentucky Press.

Levy, J. E., and S. J. Kunitz. 1987. "A Suicide Prevention Program for Hopi Youth." *Social Science Medicine, 25*(8), 931–940.

Lewis, C. 1970. *Indian Families of the Northwest Coast: The Impact of Change*. Chicago: University of Chicago Press.

Lewis, R. G. 1981. "Patterns of Strengths of American Indian Families," in J. G. Red Horse, A. Shattuck, and F. Hoffman (Eds.), *The American Indian Family: Strengths and Stresses*, pp. 101–111. Isleta, NM: American Indian Social Research and Development Associates.

Liberty, M. 1975. "Population Trends Among Present-Day Omaha Indians." *Plains Anthropologist, 20*(69): 225–230.

Liberty, M., R. Scaglion, and D. V. Hughey. 1976. "Rural and Urban Omaha Indian Fertility." *Human Biology, 48*(1): 59–71.

Liu, L. L. Slap, G. B., S. B. Kinsman, and N. Khalid. 1994. "Pregnancy Among American Indian Adolescents: Reactions and Prenatal Care." *Journal of Adolescent Health, 15*: 336–341.

Manson, S. M. 1989a. "Long-Term Care in American Indian Communities: Issues for Planning and Research." *The Gerontologist, 29*(1): 38–44.

———. 1989b. "Provider Assumptions About Long-Term Care in American Indian Communities." *The Gerontologist, 29*(3): 355–358.

———. 1992. "Long-Term Care of Older American Indians: Challenges in the Development of Institutional Services," in C. M. Barresi and D. E. Stull (Eds.), *Ethnic Elderly and Long-Term Care*, pp. 130–143. New York: Springer.

Manson, S. M., and A. M. Pambrun. 1979. "Social and Psychological Status of the American Indian Elderly: Past Research, Current Advocacy, and Future Inquiry." *White Cloud Journal, 1*(3): 18–25.

May, P. A. 1987. "Suicide and Self-Destruction Among American Indian Youths." *American Indian and Alaska Native Mental Health Research, 1*: 52–59.

———. 1996. "Overview of Alcohol Abuse Epidemiology for American Indian Populations," in G. D. Sandefur, R. R. Rindfuss, and B. Cohen (Eds.), *Changing Numbers, Changing Needs: American Indian Demography and Public Health*, pp. 235–261. Washington, DC: National Academy Press.

McKinlay, J. B., S. L. Crawford, and S. L. Tennestedt. 1995. "The Everyday Impacts of Providing Informal Care to Dependent Elders and Their Consequences for the Care Recipients." *Journal of Aging and Health, 7*(4): 497–528.

Medicine, B. 1981. "American Indian Family: Cultural Change and Adaptive Strategies." *The Journal of Ethnic Studies, 8*(4): 13–23.

Mercier, J. M., and E. A. Powers. 1984, October. "The Family and Friends of Rural Aged as a Natural Support System." *Journal of Community Psychology, 12*: 334–346.

Metcalf, A. 1976. "From Schoolgirl to Mother: The Effects of Education on Navajo Women." *Social Problems, 23*: 535–544.

———. 1979. "Family Reunion: Networks and Treatment in a Native American Community." *Group Psychotherapy, Psychodrama, and Sociometry, 32*: 179–189.

Miller, D. L. 1981. "Alternative Paradigms Available for Research on American Indian Families," in J. G. Red Horse, A. Shattuck, and F. Hoffman (Eds.), *The American Indian Family: Strengths and Stresses*, pp. 79–91. Isleta, NM: American Indian Social Research and Development Associates.

Miller, D. L., and C. D. Moore. 1979. "The Native American Family: The Urban Way," in E. Corfman (Ed.), *Families Today: A Research Sampler on Families and Children*, pp. 441–484. Washington, DC: U.S. Government Printing Office.

Moroney, R. F. 1980. *Families, Social Services and Social Policy: The Issue of Shared Responsibility.* Rockville, MD: U.S. Department of Health and Human Services.

Murdock, S. H., and D. F. Schwartz. 1978. "Family Structure and the Use of Agency Services: An Examination of Patterns Among Elderly Native Americans." *Gerontologist, 18*(5): 475–481.

Nagel, J. 1995. "American Indian Ethnic Renewal: Politics and the Resurgence of Identity." *American Sociological Review, 60*(6): 947–965.

National Association of State Units on Aging. 1989. *American Indians and Elder Abuse: Exploring the Problem.* Report of Albuquerque Meeting Convened by the National Aging Resource Center on Elder Abuse. Washington, DC: Author.

National Center for Health Statistics. 1995. *Report to Congress on Out-of-Wedlock Childbearing.* Hyattsville, MD: National Center for Health Statistics.

National Indian Council on Aging. 1981. *Indian Elderly and Entitlement Programs: An Accessing Demonstration Project.* Albuquerque: National Indian Council on Aging.

———. 1983. *Access, a Demonstration Project: Entitlement Programs for Indian Elders.* Albuquerque: National Indian Council on Aging.

National Tribal Chairmen's Association. 1978. *The Indian Elder: A Forgotten American.* Final report on the First National Indian Conference on Aging, Phoenix, AZ; June 15–17, 1976. Washington, DC: National Tribal Chairmen's Association.

Oakland, L., and R. L. Kane. 1973. "The Working Mother and Child Neglect on the Navajo Reservation." *Pediatrics, 51*(5): 849–853.

Passel, J. S. 1976. "Provisional Evaluation of the 1970 Census Count of American Indians." *Demography, 13*: 397–409.

———. 1996. "The Growing American Indian Population, 1960–1990: Beyond Demography," in G. D. Sandefur, R. R. Rindfuss, and B. Cohen (Eds.), *Changing Numbers, Changing Needs: American Indian Demography and Public Health*, pp. 79–102. Washington, DC: National Academy Press.

Passel, J. S., and P. A. Berman. 1986. "Quality of 1980 Census Data for American Indians." *Social Biology, 33*, 163–182.

Pipestem, F. B. 1981. "Comments on the Indian Child Welfare Act," in J. Red Horse, A. Shattuck, and F. Hoffman, (Eds.), *The American Indian Family: Strengths and Stresses*, pp. 53–69. Isleta, NM: American Indian Social Research and Development Associates.

Porter, F. W., III. 1983. *Nonrecognized American Indian Tribes: An Historical and Legal Perspective.* McNickle Center for the Study of the American Indian paper no. 7. Chicago: Newberry Library.

Powers, E. A., P. M. Keith, and W. J. Goudy. 1981. "Family Networks of the Rural Aged," in R. T. Coward and W. M. Smith (Eds.), *The Family in Rural Society*, pp. 199–217. Boulder, CO: Westview Press.

Price, J. A. 1976. "North American Indian Families," in C. H. Mindel and R. W. Habenstein (Eds.), *Ethnic Families in America: Patterns and Variations*, pp. 248–270. New York: Elsevier.

———. 1981. "North American Indian Families," in C. H. Mindel and R. W. Habenstein (Eds.), *Ethnic Families in America: Patterns and Variations*, 2nd ed., pp. 245–268. New York: Elsevier.

Queen, S. A., and J. B. Adams. 1952. *The Family in Various Cultures.* Chicago: JB Lippincott.

Red Horse, J. G. 1980a. "Family Structure and Value Orientation in American Indians." *Social Casework, 61*(8): 462–467.

———. 1980b. "American-Indian Elders—Unifiers of Indian Families." *Social Casework, 61*(8): 490–493.

———. 1982a. Clinical Strategies for American Indian Families in Crisis." *Urban and Social Change Review, 15*(2): 17–19.

———. 1982b. "American Indian and Alaskan Native Elders: A Policy Critique," in E. P. Stanford and S. A. Lockery (Eds.), *Trends and Status of Minority Aging*, pp. 15–26. San Diego: San Diego State University.

———. 1988. "Cultural Evolution of American Indian Families," in C. Jacobs and D. D. Bowles (Eds.), *Ethnicity and Race: Critical Concepts in Social Work*, pp. 86–102. Silver Spring, MD: National Association of Social Workers.

Red Horse, J. G., R. Lewis, M. Feit, and J. Decker. 1978. "Family Behavior of Urban American Indians." *Social Casework, 59*: 67–72.

Red Horse, Y. 1982. "A Cultural Network Model: Perspectives for Adolescent Services and Para-Professional Training," in S. M. Manson (Ed.), *New Directions in Prevention Among American Indian and Alaska Native Communities.* Portland: Oregon Health Sciences University.

Rindfuss, R., and J. Sweet. 1977. *Postwar Fertility Trends and Differentials in the United States.* New York: Academic Press.

Roscoe, W. 1991. *The Zuni Man-Woman.* Albuquerque, NM: University of New Mexico Press.

Rotenberg, K. J., and F. R. Cranwell. 1989. "Self-Concept in American Indian and White Children." *Journal of Cross Cultural Psychology, 20*(1): 39–53.

Ryan, R. A. 1981. "Strengths of the American Indian Family: State of the Art," in J. Red Horse, A. Shattuck, and F. Hoffman, (Eds.), *The American Indian Family: Strengths and Stresses*, pp. 25–43. Isleta, NM: American Indian Social Research and Development Associates.

Sandefur, G. D., and C. A. Liebler. 1996. "The Demography of American Indian Families," in G. D. Sandefur, R. R. Rindfuss, and B. Cohen (Eds.), *Changing Numbers, Changing Needs:*

American Indian Demography and Public Health, pp. 196–217. Washington, DC: National Academy Press.

Sandefur, G. D. and T. McKinnell. 1986. "American Indian Intermarriage." *Social Science Research,* *15:* 347–371.

Schlegel, A. 1973. "The Adolescent Socialization of the Hopi Girl." *Ethnology, 12*(4): 449–462.

Schweitzer, M. M. 1983. "The Elders: Cultural Dimensions of Aging in Two American Indian Communities," in J. Sokolovsky (Ed.), *Growing Old in Different Societies: Cross-Cultural Perspectives,* pp. 168–178. Belmont, CA: Wadsworth.

Shomaker, D. M. 1989. "Transfer of Children and the Importance of Grandmothers Among the Navajo Indians." *Journal of Cross-Cultural Gerontology, 4:* 1–18.

———. 1990. "Health Care, Cultural Expectations and Frail Elderly Navajo Grandmothers." *Journal of Cross-Cultural Gerontology, 5:* 21–34.

Slaughter, E. L. 1976. *Indian Child Welfare: A Review of the Literature.* Denver: University of Denver Research Institute.

Snipp, C. M. 1989. *American Indians: The First of This Land.* New York: Russell Sage Foundation.

———. 1996. "The Size and Distribution of the American Indian Population: Fertility, Mortality, Migration, and Residence," in G. D. Sandefur, R. R. Rindfuss, and B. Cohen (Eds.), *Changing Numbers, Changing Needs: American Indian Demography and Public Health,* pp. 17–52. Washington, DC: National Academy Press.

Staples, R., and A. Mirande. 1980. "Racial and Cultural Variations Among American Families: A Decennial Review of the Literature on Minority Families." *Journal of Marriage and the Family, 42*(4): 157–73.

Steele, C. H. 1972. *American Indians and Urban Life: A Community Study.* Ph.D. dissertation, University of Kansas.

Strodtbeck, F. L. 1951. "Husband-Wife Interaction Over Revealed Differences." *American Sociological Review, 16:* 468–473.

Tefft, S. K. 1967. "Anomy, Values and Culture Change Among Teen-Age Indians: An Exploratory Study." *Sociology of Education, 40:* 45–57.

———. 1968. "Intergenerational Value Differentials and Family Structure Among the Wind River Shoshone." *American Anthropologist, 70:* 330–333.

Thornton, R. 1987. *American Indian Holocaust and Survival: A Population History Since 1492.* Norman, OK: University of Oklahoma Press.

———. 1996. "Tribal Membership Requirements and the Demography of 'Old' and 'New' Native Americans," in G. D. Sandefur, R. R. Rindfuss, and B. Cohen (Eds.), *Changing Numbers, Changing Needs: American Indian Demography and Public Health,* pp. 103–112. Washington, DC: National Academy Press.

Thornton, R., G. D. Sandefur, and C. M. Snipp. 1991. "American Indian Fertility Patterns: 1910 and 1940 to 1980." *American Indian Quarterly, 15:* 359–367.

Troll, L. 1978. "The Family of Later Life: A Decade Review," in M. M. Seltzer, S. L. Corbett, and R. C. Atchley (Eds.), *Social Problems of the Aging: Readings,* pp. 136–164. Belmont, CA: Wadsworth.

Trosper, R. L. 1996. "American Indian Poverty on Reservations, 1969–1989," in G. D. Sandefur, R. R. Rindfuss, and B. Cohen (Eds.), *Changing Numbers, Changing Needs: American Indian Demography and Public Health,* pp. 172–195. Washington, DC: National Academy Press.

Underhill, R. M. 1942. "Child Training in an Indian Tribe." *Marriage and Family Living, 4:* 80–81.

———. 1965. "The Papago Family," in M. F. Nimkoff (Ed.), *Comparative Family Systems,* pp. 147–162. Boston: Houghton/Mifflin.

Unger, S. 1977. *The Destruction of American Indian Families.* New York: Association on American Indian Affairs.

U.S. Congress. 1986. *Indian Health Care.* Washington, DC: U.S. Government Printing Office.

U.S. Department of Commerce. 1973. *Subject Reports: American Indians.* Washington, DC: U.S. Government Printing Office.

———. 1983. *General Social and Economic Characteristics: 1980.* Washington, DC: U.S. Government Printing Office.

———. 1986. *American Indians, Eskimos, and Aleuts on Identified Reservations and in the Historic Areas of Oklahoma (Excluding Urbanized Areas)*, part 2, sections 1 and 2. Washington, DC: U.S. Government Printing Office.

———. 1992. *General Population Characteristics: United States.* Washington, DC: U.S. Government Printing Office.

———. 1993. *Social and Economic Characteristics: United States.* Washington, DC: U.S. Government Printing Office.

U.S. Department of Health and Human Services. 1979. *Policy Issues Concerning the Elderly Minorities.* Washington, DC: U.S. Government Printing Office.

Wagner, J. K. 1976. "The Role of Intermarriage in the Acculturation of Selected Urban American Indian Women." *Anthropologica, 18*(2): 215–229.

Ward, R. A. 1978, October. "Limitations of the Family as a Supportive Institution in the Lives of the Aged." *Family Coordinator, 27:* 365–373.

Warren, C. W., H. I. Goldberg, L. Oge, D. Pepion, J. S. Friedman, S. Helgerson, and E. M. LaMere. 1990. "Assessing the Reproductive Behavior of On- and Off-Reservation American Indian Females: Characteristics of Two Groups in Montana." *Social Biology, 37*(1–2): 69–83.

Weibel-Orlando, J. 1990. "Grandparenting Styles: Native American Perspectives," in J. Sokolovsky (Ed.), *The Cultural Context of Aging: Worldwide Perspectives*, pp. 109–125. New York: Bergin & Garvey.

Williams, G. C. 1980. "Warriors No More: A Study of the American Indian Elderly," in C. L. Fry (Ed.), *Aging in Culture and Society: Comparative Viewpoints and Strategies*, pp. 101–111. New York: Praeger.

Williams, T. R. 1958. "The Structure of the Socialization Process in Papago Indian Society." *Social Forces, 36:* 251–256.

Williams, W. L. 1986. *The Spirit in the Flesh: Sexual Diversity in American Indian Culture.* Boston: Beacon Press.

Witherspoon, G. 1975. *Navajo Kinship and Marriage.* Chicago: University of Chicago Press.

Yellowbird, M., and C. M. Snipp. 1994. "American Indian Families," in R. L. Taylor (Ed.), *Minority Families in the United States: A Multicultural Perspective*, pp. 179–201. Englewood Cliffs, NJ: Prentice Hall.

17 The Jewish-American Family

Bernard Farber
Bernard Lazerwitz
Charles H. Mindel

This chapter is about Jewish-American families. To be Jewish in America is to be a member of a religious faith, the followers of Judaism, but also importantly, it means to share a sense of "peoplehood," an ethnicity, with a vast number of people sharing a distinct cultural identity. This duality has often presented confusion to many, especially non-Jews, who cannot decide whether Jews are a religious group or a "nationality." On the wider global stage, though the Jewish religion can be traced back to the ancient Israelite Jews, the Jewish religion is practiced by people of diverse racial and ethnic backgrounds, a result of the continual historical process of conversion to Judaism. Thus, Jews throughout the world can be considered descendants of converts as well as direct descendants of ancient Israelite Jews. In the United States, there tends to be less of this ethnic diversity since most American Jews are descendants of *Ashkenazic* Jews— that is, European, especially eastern European, Jews.

Worldwide, Judaism embraces approximately 13 million followers, concentrated mainly in a few key areas throughout the world. Although North American Jews form the largest constituent, the Jewish people are to be found in societies all over the globe. Obviously, Jews in Israel constitute the other major segment. Other groups include Arab and Yemeni Jews as well as Jews of Persian origin. The largest groups of non-Caucasian Jews include Jews from Ethiopia; there are also small Jewish communities such as the *Kaifeng* Jews of China (now mostly assimilated), and Jewish communities in India. Until 1960, a community of cave-dwelling Jews was said to exist in southern Libya. A community in Burma claimed to be Jews, and reports and legends abound about African, Native American, and other tribes claiming Jewish ancestry. A twentieth-century convert community, the *Abayudaya* Jews, lives in Uganda.

Until the Holocaust , the largest concentration of Jews lived in Europe. At present, approximately 46 percent of the world's Jews, or approximately 5.5 million, live in North America, where they now constitute a distinct subgroup among world Jewry (NJPS, 1990).

HISTORICAL BACKGROUND

The settlement of Jews in America is an old one. Jews have been in America since the colonial period, though they began arriving in large numbers only one hundred years ago. The immigration of Jews to America occurred in three major historical waves involving people from three national locations: *Sephardic* Jews, originally from Spain and Portugal; German Jews from the Germanic states; and eastern European Jews, largely from Poland and Russia but also from Rumania, Hungary, and Lithuania. It would be inaccurate to assume no overlap among these three waves of immigration because immigration from Germany took place at the same time as immigration from Poland and Russia. These three waves of immigration are important because they define three distinct cultural patterns that tend to distinguish Jewish communities in America.

A smaller fourth wave from the former Soviet Union emerged in the 1980s and 1990s. Numbering less than 100,000, these refugees from the former Soviet empire have taken up residence largely in New York City. Because of Soviet policies, they are a largely secular group with little knowledge of Jewish religious and cultural traditions. Their impact on American culture is as yet limited, although they along other new immigrants in New York City are making their presence felt. Only the future will tell the extent to which they influence the American Jewish community.

Immigrants from the nearly destroyed Sephardic, German, and eastern European Jewish communities differed for a variety of historical, cultural, and economic reasons. Descendants of migrants from eastern Europe were the last to arrive, constituting by far the largest number of America's Jews— probably more than 90 percent. The Sephardic and German Jews are and have been important not for their numbers but largely because of their social position and influence.

The Sephardic Jews. The earliest Jewish settlement in America occurred in 1654 in what was then New Amsterdam (now New York City), a colony of the Dutch West India Company. The Jews who settled there followed a circuitous route, ultimately traceable to the large medieval Jewish population of Spain and Portugal. However, the Jews were not particularly welcome in New Amsterdam. Peter Stuyvesant, the governor, resisted, arguing that "none of the deceitful race be permitted to infest and trouble this new colony" (Golden and Rywell, 1950:13). However, the Dutch West India Company decided to allow the Portuguese Jews to live in New Netherlands "provided the poor among them shall not become a burden to the Company or the community but be supported by their own nation" (Golden and Rywell, 1950:14). From this beginning there continued a steady flow of immigration of Sephardic Jews, and, increasingly, German Jews, who numbered approximately 15,000 in 1840.

The German Jews. The middle of the nineteenth century, from approximately 1840 to 1880, saw a second wave of Jewish immigration, mostly German Jews. Conditions in Germany—or, to be more accurate, the collection of Germanic states—were quite inhospitable to Jews and non-Jews alike at mid-century. Anti-Jewish medieval laws of oppression were enacted, especially in Bavaria, that among other items provided for heavy, discriminatory taxation; designated areas to live in; restricted occupations; and limited the number of Jewish marriages. These conditions prompted many German Jewish single men to leave for America to seek opportunity. In the later part of the nineteenth century, when these laws were relaxed, immigration of German Jews slowed down to a trickle (Glazer, 1957; Weinryb, 1958).

Many German Jewish immigrants started out as peddlers, an occupation that did not require great skill or large capital investment. They spread out all over America and gave many non-Jews their first glimpse of a Jewish face. Originally starting out with a pack carried on their back, they traversed the countryside. If they were reasonably successful, they would graduate to a horse and wagon. If they were able to accumulate a little money, they might open a dry goods store in one of the many towns and cities in which they traded. These were the origins of what later became the great clothing and department stores in America, such as Altman's, Bloomingdale's, Bamberger's, Goldblatt, Nieman-Marcus, Macy's, The May Company, Maison Blanche, Stix, Baer & Fuller, and others.

The importance and influence of the German Jews is crucially linked to their spectacular financial success. Although certainly not all German Jews became wealthy, the rise of several families, many of whom started out as peddlers, had enormous implications for the status of Jews in America. They became important figures in banking and finance in a period of American history when industrialization was just beginning and there was a need for large amounts of capital to feed the growing industrial base.

The German Jewish influx into America was great enough to overwhelm the Sephardim in numbers. By 1848, there were 50,000 Jews in America; and by 1880, there were an estimated 230,000, largely German Jews (Sklare, 1958).

Eastern European Jews. It was, however, the arrival of the Jews from eastern Europe that has had the greatest impact on Jewish American life. Beginning around 1881 and largely ending by 1930, almost 3 million Jews immigrated to America. These individuals and families, though Jewish like their American counterparts, were in fact of another world. Whereas the Germans came from an "enlightened" modern society in which Jews were more often than not integrated into German culture, the eastern European Jews came from a milieu in which a feeling of cultural homogeneity was strongly entrenched. A set of Jewish values and attitudes prevailed, including religious devotion and observance.

Most of the 5 million Jews of Russia and Poland had been restricted from the time of Catherine the Great to an area established for them known as the "Pale of Settlement." Jews were generally not allowed to settle in the interior of Russia and were limited to this area. Extending from the shores of the Baltic south to the Black Sea, the Pale has been described (except for the Crimea) as a 313,000 sq mi, monotonously flat, sand-arid prison (Manners, 1972:30). Within this area, approximately the size of Texas, 808 *shtetlach* (small towns), each of which was perhaps two-thirds Jewish and 94 percent poor, were the social limit in which Jews lived, survived, and "attained the highest degree of inwardness . . . the golden period in Jewish history in the history of the Jewish soul!" (Manners, 1972:31).

The concentration of Jews in these areas for hundreds of years led to the development of a culture and civilization grounded in biblical and Talmudic teachings that remained unchanged to a remarkable degree until the twentieth century. Those who migrated from this society to America and elsewhere have, on the whole, become prosperous; those millions who remained, including most of the devout, were, for the most part, destroyed.

The mass migration of eastern European Jews began in the 1880s and continued at a high level until the passage of restrictive U.S. immigration laws in 1924. The chief instigating factors that started the massive flow were imperial Russia's governmentally inspired *pogroms* (devastation and destruction) in 1881. Pogroms consisted of ransacking, burning, rape, and assorted violence committed in the towns and villages of Russia. The government, driven by an overwhelming fear of revolution, used pogroms as a form of diversion and weapon against dissenting minorities (Manners, 1972).

Beginning in 1882, new laws, the so-called May laws, were issued by the Czar that severely restricted Jewish rights, such as they were. Thousands were forced to leave their homes, especially those who resided in the interior of Russia. These laws and their extensions left most Jews no choice but to emigrate, mainly to America. Some went to Palestine, others went to other parts of Europe, but 40,000 came to the United States in 1881–1882. Another 62,000 came in 1888, and by 1906 the number was up to 153,000 per year (Manners, 1972:57).

The pogroms and restrictive laws that forced the migration of these Jews were but the final chapter of a long process of disintegration of Jewish communities that had been going on for more than a century. Antagonisms and tensions had been developing within for a long period of time. Of more importance were the effects from the world outside the *shtetl*. Industrialization and the decline of the feudal system of relations came late to eastern Europe, but by the nineteenth century its effects were being felt there as well. By the time of the pogroms in the late nineteenth century and early twentieth century, social change, social disintegration, and demographic expansion had already come to this traditional society.

German Jews Versus Eastern European Jews. The arrival of this mass of people was a mixed blessing to Jews already established in the United States, especially to the German American Jews, who feared for their recently achieved middle class status. However, native-born Jews and Americans in general took a compassionate though largely condescending view toward the new poverty-stricken immigrants (at least until 1924, when the U.S. government, in the throes of a xenophobic isolationist wave, passed a restrictive immigration law).

Relations between the older, established Jews, primarily German American Jews, and the newly arrived eastern European Jews were nevertheless difficult. The German Jews were interested in helping the immigrants in order to "Americanize" them so they would not be a source of embarrassment. They saw the strange dress and speech and the poverty of their fellow Jews as reflecting unfavorably on themselves and believed that the quicker these newcomers became indistinguishable from the rest of America, the better. Americanization was made more difficult by the fact that the eastern European Jewish immigrants clustered together in distinct urban neighborhoods, especially in the American northeast and particularly in New York City.

Though the eastern European Jewish immigrants tended to be less observant and traditional than their counterparts who remained in Europe, the religious institutions established by them in America were traditional Orthodox recreations of the institutions that existed in eastern Europe. The immigrants did not recognize Reform Judaism as it was practiced by native-born, predominantly German Jews; to them, it was unacceptable. "They are Jews," declared Rabbi Dr. Issac Meyer Wise, the leading light of Reform Judaism, "We are Israelites." The Russian Jews said with equal assurance: "We are Jews. They are *goyim* [Gentiles]" (Manners, 1972:76).

One important ingredient in the continuing vigor of Orthodox Judaism in America was the immigration during the Hitler and post–World War II years of numbers of Orthodox Chassidic Jews. The Chassidic groups, organized around a particular charismatic leader *(rebbe,* or *Tzaddik)* are identified by the location in Europe from which they originated. These groups, which stress a communal life and close-knit group cohesion, are generally found in the New York area, often in old neighborhoods. One group, however, the Skverer Chassidim, has established their own town, New Square, in the suburbs of New York City, in which they have attempted to recreate the traditional life of the eastern European Jew. The impact of these groups has been to bring new life into what was a disappearing branch of Judaism. The close ties of the members and the emotionalism of the religion as they practice it are attractive to many young people who have been seeking more emotion in their religious practice. Others who have not become members of Chassidic groups have borrowed much of the emotional content of this movement and put it into their own observance.

It has been estimated that today more than 90 percent of America's Jewish population are, or are descended from, immigrants from eastern Europe. Because their arrival has been relatively recent, family patterns that existed in Europe and were brought to the United States can still be expected to have an impact on present-day Jewish American family lifestyles. In the following paragraphs, family life in the small eastern European town—the *shtetl*—where most Jews lived is described.[1]

The *shtetl* was a poor place, a place of unpaved streets and decrepit wooden buildings. It is said that there was no "Jewish" architecture; instead, the most noticeable features of the dwellings were their age and their shabbiness (Zborowski and Herzog, 1952:61). Occupationally, the Jews were generally tradespeople—dairymen, cobblers, tailors, butchers, fishmongers, peddlers, and shopkeepers.

Social Organization

If the marketplace was the economic center of the *shtetl*, the synagogue was the heart and soul of the community. It was impossible to escape and separate the religious from the secular. Religious values infiltrated all aspects of life; every detail of life was infused with some religious or ritual significance.

Chief among the values of the *shtetl* and Jewish culture was the value of learning. One of the most important obligations of a devout Jew is to study and learn. To obey the commandments of the scriptures, one must know them, and one must study them to know them. Studying and learning the Torah[2] became the most important activity in which a man could involve himself—more important than earning a good living. Every *shtetl* of reasonable size contained schools of various levels, including the *cheder* for boys as young as 3 and 4 years of age. A learned young man was considered the most highly prized future son-in-law. In fact, it was considered prestigious for a father-in-law to support his new son-in-law for the first few years of marriage if the son-in-law was bright, so that he could devote himself to full-time study.

---

[1]Much of this discussion of *shtetl* family structure comes from Landes and Zborowski (1968) and Zborowski and Herzog (1952).

[2]Torah literally refers to the Pentateuch, the five books of Moses, or the written scriptures. However, Torah has come to mean much more, including remaining portions of the Old Testament as well as the whole of the commentaries and interpretations on the Pentateuch, known as the oral law or the Talmud. In addition, the numerous codifications and newer commentaries that appeared during the Middle Ages, such as the works of Maimonides, have also come to be included under this rubric. In essence, Torah means all the religious learning and literature including and surrounding the holy scriptures.

The stratification of the *shtetl* was based in large measure on learning and the tradition of learning in one's family. Shtetl Jews were either *sheyneh yidn* (beautiful Jews) or *prosteh yidn* (common Jews). The position of a person in this status hierarchy was, ideally, dependent on learning, but wealth played an important part in determining the *sheyneh*. A third quality, *yikhus*, a combination of family heritage in learning and wealth, was also an important criterion in determining social position. A person with great *yikhus* was able to claim many ancestors of great worth, particularly in learning and philanthropy. To have *yikhus* was very prestigious.

Life in the *shtetl* was guided by written codes of behavior that derived from the Talmud and other religious sources. These standards ideally had the effect of regulating behavior of all Jewish residents of the *shtetl*, *sheyneh* and *prosteh* alike. It is in these codes of behavior and the folklore, proverbs, and other customs that grew up around the *shtetl* that we find the unique cultural basis for Jewish family life, important aspects of which still have an impact today.

Marriage

Duties and roles for men and women were carefully detailed by traditional writings, and chief among these was the injunction that a man and woman marry. It was said "It is not good for man to be alone." Marriage in the *shtetl* was traditionally arranged by the parents of the young couple, frequently through the use of a matchmaker (*shadchen*). It was assumed that the "parents always want the best for their children" (Zborowski and Herzog, 1952:275), and the children went along with the match.

Because marriage was considered such an important institution—indeed, a commandment (mitzvah)—there was great pressure for marriage and families to remain united. In fact, because divorce reflected badly on one's family and stigmatized the individuals involved, it was a relatively rare occurrence. Marital stability was related to a dominant orientation in Jewish family life, *sholem bayis* (domestic harmony or peace). Only when maintaining a satisfactory family equilibrium became impossible and the *sholem bayis* was broken was divorce considered. The relative infrequency of divorce indicates that adaptations of many kinds occurred with some frequency.

Marital Roles

The injunction that a man should study, learn, and promote the book-learning tradition had important implications for the functioning of the husband in the family. The husband or father was often remote from most domestic concerns. If he was a scholar, much of the economic responsibility for the home was left to the wife. The husband's primary responsibility was in the spiritual and intellectual sphere; only the men were taught to read, speak, and write Hebrew, the sacred language; women who were literate spoke and read Yiddish.[3]

In reality, women often played a dominant role in family life and in the outside world. There was a high degree of interchangeability in family roles, and wives were trained to be ready to assume the economic burdens of supporting the family. Women often had wide latitude and opportunity for movement to conduct business or seek employment, and in time of emergency or need, they were able to partake in any number of "male" activities. It has been argued that as a consequence of their subordinate status, women were less regulated than men, and therefore they were able to partake in all activities that were not expressly forbidden to them. As a result, they quite often had greater freedom than men, who were bound up very tightly in a highly regulated way of life (Landes and Zborowski, 1968:81).

The Eastern European Mother. Basic to the eastern European Jewish family with its wide range of rights and obligation was parental love. Seldom demonstrated verbally or physically after the child was 4 or 5, parental affection, especially from the mother, was felt to be an unbreakable bond. "No matter what you do, no matter what happens your mother will love you always. She may have odd and sometimes irritating ways of showing it, but in a hazardous and unstable world the belief about the mother's love is strong and unshakable" (Zborowski and Herzog, 1952:293). The Jewish mother's love was expressed by and large in two ways: "by constant and solicitous overfeeding and by unremitting solicitude about every aspect of her child's welfare" (Zborowski and Herzog, 1952:293). Both paternal and maternal love contained the notions of suffering and sacrifice for the sake of the children. It was said that "she kills herself" in order to bring up her children and care for her husband as well, who also becomes like a child in the family. Her conduct was understood and tolerated by her children, who nostalgically idealized it when they got older; she was remembered as a "loving despot."

Affection among the *shtetl* Jews, as previously mentioned, was not expressed with kisses and caresses after a child reached 4 or 5 and especially not in public. However, a mother was more likely to be demonstrative to her son and a father more demonstrative to his daughter. Furthermore, though much contact between members of the opposite sex, such as between brother and sister, was restricted by avoidance etiquette, there is virtually no avoidance between mother and son. It has been claimed that "though marital

---

[3]Yiddish, a Middle High German dialect written in Hebrew characters, was the common *mamaloshen* (mother tongue) of most eastern European Jews. Its use can be traced back a thousand years, and though Yiddish varied in form and pronunciation in different parts of western and eastern Europe, it provided a common language for Jews across all national boundaries and was a crucial factor in maintaining the unity of this branch of the Jewish people. The other major Jewish branches are the *Sephardim*, who spoke a dialect of Spanish written in Hebrew characters, and the Oriental Jews, who usually used Arabic.

obligations are fulfilled with the husband, the romance exists with the son" and that "when the son marries, he gives the wife a contract and the mother a divorce" (Landes and Zborowski, 1968:80–88).

The father related to his daughter in a similar way as the mother related to her son, only not with quite the same intensity. With his daughter, he was undemanding and indulgent. A father, however, was a distant figure for the most part, one to whom great respect was owed. He was a particularly remote, authoritarian figure for the boy whose growth into a "Jew" and a *mensch* ("whole person" or adult) was his responsibility.

Family Obligations. The *shtetl* was viewed as an extended family. At the very least, Jews consider themselves to be ultimately related as the "Children of Israel," and often, because of extensive intermarriage within the *shtetl*, they were closer than that. In any case, there were strong obligations and pressure to maintain close ties to kin. Particularly strong was the obligation to take care of elderly parents, although there was great reluctance on the part of the elderly parent, especially the father, to accept aid.

THE MODERN AMERICAN JEWISH FAMILY

Jewish families have lived in the United States since before its founding, and it is nearly 115 years since the start of massive Jewish immigration from eastern Europe. With the passage of time, American Jews have become highly "Americanized." However, each successive historical era has generated or magnified concerns about Jewish family life. The immigrant family was concerned about maintaining its traditional family forms in the face of the demands and expectations of modern industrial society. Since World War I, when 70 percent of the Jewish population lived in the Northeast, dispersion has been seen as another factor adding to the problem of maintaining traditional family life; by 1990, only 50 percent remained in the Northeast. Along with these concerns, Americanization brought with it reasons to control fertility and to encourage women to enter the labor force in large numbers. As a result, levels of fertility have fallen significantly below the number required merely to replace the older generation. Finally, these factors, operating together, have resulted in an explosion in the prevalence of intermarriage between Jews and non-Jews in recent decades.

Family and Traditionalism in Religion

Because European Jewish social structure and characteristics are historically the foundation of the American Jewish family, one is tempted to use the number of generations in America as an index of "Americanization" of the Jewish family. However, Jewish denominational preference incorporates historical change, gives a more accurate characterization of lifestyle trends, and simultaneously describes the value stances around which Jewish families are organized. With each successive generation in America, there is a general tendency in family lines to move from the more traditional Orthodox denomination to the lesser traditionalist denominations (Lazerwitz, 1978; 1995a; Harrison and Lazerwitz, 1979).

As of 1990, Orthodox Jews made up 6 percent of the adult Jewish population (down from 11 percent in 1971). They seek to carry out historic Jewish religious practices, value orientations, and social roles into modern life with as few changes as possible. Orthodox Jews rank higher than Conservative or Reform Jews in Jewish education, maintaining kosher homes, observing ritual behavior, and participating in Jewish communal and primary groups.

According to the 1990 National Jewish Population Study (hereafter NJPS) data, Conservative Jews comprise about 40 percent of American Jewish adults (unchanged from 1971). As a whole, they seek a balance between traditional ways and the demands of modern life and are more inclined than the Orthodox toward social change in Jewish life. For example, Conservatives favor retention of kosher dietary laws and the observance of most Sabbath and holy-day injunctions but permit use of electrical devices and automobiles on the Sabbath.

Those persons who regard themselves as Reform Jews constitute 36 per cent of the adult Jewish population in 1990 (up from 30 percent in 1971). As a group, they have given considerable emphasis to doing what they regard as "modernizing" Judaism. For them, traditional practices depend upon individual desires, and they have abandoned many practices and rituals.

At the furthest extreme from the Orthodox are those Jews who have no specific denominational preference, and many in this group are secular in outlook. This group constitutes 15 percent of the Jewish population as of 1990 (down from 19 percent in 1971) and is, as a whole, marginal to the Jewish community and its religious practices.

These findings emphasize the diversity among American Jews. It is likely that the denominational differences in outlook apply to additional areas of life—family patterns, sex roles, leisure activities, and basic value orientations. For example, divorce is much more prevalent among Jews brought up in homes with a low level of religious observance than among those whose parents were ritually observant. Moreover, "the lowest amount of divorce occurs among those who are most committed to the Judaic religious traditions as it is practiced today" (Brodbar-Nemzer, 1986).

Dispersion, Kinship, and Cohesiveness

Dispersion and Cohesiveness.   The initial concerns of immigrant Jewish families in the United States were the effects of their new environment on the integrity of their family life. W. I. Thomas's analysis of the *Bintel Brief* (bundle of letters) in the Yiddish-language *Daily Forward* (Bressler, 1952) focused upon the immigrant generation. Thomas regarded "the key motif expressed in Jewish family patterns [to be] . . . an effort to preserve the solidarity of the family" (Balswich, 1966:165). As time went on, the threat to family solidarity came not only because of isolation from European roots, but also from the process of Americanization, which fostered mobility—both socially and spatially. Table 17-1 presents data on trends in the distribution of the American Jewish population from 1918 to 1990.

Table 17-1 indicates that there have been important shifts in the Jewish population. Although immigration during the first part of the twentieth century concentrated the bulk of the Jewish population in the Northeast, especially in the Middle Atlantic states, since World War I there has been a steady redistribution of the Jewish population, with major losses in the urban centers in the Middle Atlantic and east north central regions.

Dramatic shifts occurred between 1930 and 1990 in the movement of the population to the South Atlantic and Pacific states—often to Florida and California—and by 1990, almost 40 percent of the Jewish population resided in the South and the West (in contrast to 10 percent in 1918).

Goldstein and Goldstein (1996:178) examined the relationship between denomination and migration for the five years prior to the 1990 NJPS survey. They found that only 10 percent of the Orthodox migrated from their local community in that period as compared with the Conservatives (22 percent) and Reform Jews (24 percent), and 26 percent of Jews without a denominational preference. They also found that the percentages of persons aged 18–44 responding that they would "very likely" move within the next three years were

TABLE 17-1. Distribution of the Jewish Population, Percentage by Regions: 1918, 1930, 1963, 1972, and 1990

Region	1918	1930	1963	1972	1990
NORTHEAST	**69.9**	**68.3**	**65.9**	**62.6**	**50.6**
New England	8.6	8.4	6.7	6.8	7.1
Middle Atlantic	61.3	59.9	59.2	55.8	43.6
NORTH CENTRAL	**20.2**	**19.6**	**13.7**	**12.2**	**11.2**
East North Central	15.7	15.7	11.2	9.8	9.2
West North Central	4.5	3.9	2.5	2.4	2.0
SOUTH	**6.9**	**7.6**	**9.1**	**11.8**	**19.3**
South Atlantic	4.0	4.3	6.7	9.4	16.4
East South Central	1.3	1.4	0.8	0.7	0.7
West South Central	1.6	1.9	1.6	1.9	2.2
WEST	**3.1**	**4.6**	**11.5**	**13.3**	**18.8**
Mountain	0.7	1.0	0.9	1.1	2.6
Pacific	2.4	3.6	10.6	12.2	16.3
TOTAL (%)	100.0	100.0	100.0	100.0	100.0

Sources: Data on distribution of Jewish population from *American Jewish Year Book*, 1919:606; 1931:14; 1973:309; 1991:204–224. Data for 1990 also cited in Goldstein and Goldstein (1996: 38–39).

29 percent for the Orthodox, 34 percent for the Conservative, 37 percent for the Reform, and 44 percent for the nondenominational Jews. Goldstein and Goldstein (1996:206), conclude from their analysis of ritual practices that "those whose behavior conforms more closely to traditional practices are generally much more stable than the less observant" and that "with a shift away from extensive ritual practice among large segments of American Jewry, mobility may well increase further than its present level."

Kinship and Cohesiveness. Numerous studies have shown connections between migration and ties with extended family (e.g., Sklare and Greenblum, 1967:252; Litwak, 1985). However, given the diversity of family lifestyles associated with denomination and ritual observance, one would expect that relationship between migration and extended family would vary depending upon the family and kinship orientation.

Anthropologists have used the term *collaterality* to refer to the fact that people regard some kinds of relatives as genealogically closer than others. For example, there are people who are considered too closely related to marry one another—perhaps a first cousin or an uncle. In traditional Jewish law, however, such marriages are permitted. Differences in collaterality are important because they express different ways of looking at family and kinship.

These collaterality systems, or models, are the Parentela Orders model (with origins in ancient Judaism and classical Greece), the Civil Law model (whose source was the Twelve Tables of the early Roman republic), and the Canon Law model (which appeared in the twelfth-century systemization of church law). In the contemporary world, proposals have been made to apply Genetic relatedness (i.e., shared chromosomes) to inheritance and marriage laws. A fifth model, the Standard American model, is a mirror image of the Parentela Orders model—focusing upon an individual's ancestral line instead of the perpetuation of the family line. Its pattern suggests an emphasis upon one's past family history rather than a concern with the family's destiny (Farber, 1981:45–65).

The Civil Law model emerged to balance family and civil interests at the founding of the Roman republic. The Canon Law model, consistent with church writings, is minimally oriented toward family perpetuation, focusing instead upon subordinating family continuity to church interests.

As described in the Torah and the Mishnah, the Parentela Orders model places primary emphasis upon the continuity of the family line. Jews tend to cluster around the Parentela Orders pattern, with persons raised in Orthodox homes showing a greater inclination toward the Parentela Orders pattern than individuals from the less traditional branches. (Farber, 1979, 1981). What does conformity to the Parentela Orders model imply about family relationships? Regardless of religious affiliation, people who hold a Parentela Orders orientation exhibit certain characteristics in their family and kinship ties. Compared with persons who conform to other kinship-collaterality perspectives, (1) their age at first marriage tends to be high; (2) they and their parents and siblings show a high degree of marital stability; (3) their fertility level tends to be above average for their particular religious group (as does that of their parents and siblings); (4) when they marry someone of another faith, both husband and wife adopt the same religious affiliation; (5) there is a somewhat greater proclivity to live near the husband's rather than the wife's parents, but (6) despite residential distance, there is still often intense involvement with relatives (Farber, 1981). A German study by Luschen (1986) suggests that conformity to the Parentela Orders model is also related to a tendency to name children, instead of spouses, as primary heirs (Luschen, 1986: tables 8 and 9).

Moreover, holding a Parentela Orders view of collaterality is related to ethnic identity. A study of the Kansas City Jewish community found that persons with a Parentela Orders orientation, more often than Jews with other kinship orientations, tend to live in areas with a high Jewish concentration and maintain Jewish communal ties. They are generally nonmigrants; their close friends tend to be Jewish; they are more active than their parents in Jewish matters; and they disapprove of intermarriage (Farber, 1979). Research in a Chicago suburb during the 1960s indicated that among Jewish families familism was more a basis for reluctance to migrate than a result of family stability (Winch, Greer, and Blumberg, 1967).

Fertility and Family Roles

Fertility. Several national fertility studies (Freedman, Whelpton, and Campbell, 1959, 1961; Whelpton, Campbell, and Patterson, 1966) report that American Jews have historically been the most successful of American major ethnic groups in the areas of family planning and birth spacing. Indeed, the first birth-control clinic opened by Margaret Sanger was in Brownsville, then a Jewish immigrant neighborhood in Brooklyn, New York. Estimates are that from about 1920 to 1940, the Jewish birthrate in America fell almost 40 percent (Seligman, 1950:42). Rapid fertility reduction has permitted Jewish parents to support the educational desires of their fewer offspring and thereby give strong support to the rapid socioeconomic mobility that has been the outstanding achievement of American Jews (Lazerwitz, 1971).

Reduction in the Jewish birthrate derives not only from effective use of contraceptives but also from late marriage. Goldstein (1971:24) indicates that "later age of marriage has characterized Jewish women since at least 1920." In 1971, the average age at first marriage for Jewish women was 21.3 years. By 1990, the average marital age for Jewish women in the 25–34 age bracket was 23.1, and about one-third of the women in that age range were as yet unmarried (Goldstein, 1992:165, table 16). However, coupled with later age at marriage for career reasons, first births are sometimes delayed until women are in their thirties.

Sergio Della Pergola (1980) estimates that American Jewish fertility at the start of the 1970s was slightly below the level needed to replace the Jewish population and was still declining. By 1990, fertility of Jewish women was well below the replacement level—1.5 children per woman (for women aged 35–39)—and considerably lower than that for younger women (Goldstein, 1992:169, table 18).

Jewish religious involvement accounts for only insignificant portions of variations in fertility among younger women. There is little difference in fertility of women under 40 for denominational Jews by birth, secular Jews, and Jews by choice. Nevertheless, frequent synagogue attenders who prefer Orthodox or Conservative denominations do have higher fertility rates than others (Goldstein, 1992:169, table 18; Lazerwitz, Winter, Dashefsky and Tabory, 1997:chap. 7).

Family Roles. The trimming down of the size of Jewish families implies profound changes in family roles during the twentieth century. The opening section of this chapter portrayed a traditional ethnic base for the Jewish family in America. The dual roots of the American Jewish family—in religious injunctions and European ethnicity—are both vulnerable to the competition of family norms associated with other religions and with the "Americanization" of family life. Those immersed in observance of religious ritual and traditional religious views find reinforcement of the religious aspects of family life. However, as one generation succeeds another, we would anticipate that ethnic family norms and practices would readily disintegrate.

Gordon (1959:59) asserts that among immigrant Jewish families, "there was a far greater degree of equality between husband and wife than is generally assumed. . . . The mother was the homemaker, but it was she whose personal piety and example within the home was expected to influence her children, while winning their love and veneration." The maternal role was, in part, a carryover from her traditional responsibility through the centuries primarily to run the household but also to contribute to its livelihood as well.

In the immigrant family, the proverbial Jewish mother still saw her maternal role as her primary responsibility, but her daughter in the next generation did so a bit less, and so on. In Phoenix in 1978, only 25 percent of Jewish women under 40 reported that their mothers worked during the time that they themselves were growing up—in contrast to 35 percent for non-Jewish responses. However, for the respondents themselves, differences by religion disappear; regardless of religion, approximately 60 percent were working mothers (Farber, 1981).

Traditionally, the father in the Jewish family provided a link between the family and religious community. This link was important to the family's welfare in that Jewish communities in Europe were organized as corporate bodies until the twentieth century (Elazar and Goldstein, 1972). The father's personal religious dedication was the basis for his role in promoting the piety, morality, and ethical standards of family members. In the secularized American context, his position as linking the family to community has been translated into his occupational dedication and his passing on achievement values to his children (Strodtbeck, 1958; Slater, 1969).

Consistent with the concept of family as a descending line of relationships (as suggested by the Parentela Order model of kinship collaterality), the parent-child relationship in the traditional family is "complementary rather than reciprocal. Parents are donors and should not receive from children. The children can make return by passing benefits to their [own] children" (Mandelbaum, 1958:512). Sklare (1971:87) points out that in the traditional Jewish family a child is never considered to be truly emancipated from his or her parents. He suggests that children are extensions of their parents rather than distinct entities. One of the basic forms of exchange for parent and child is for parents to provide a basis for their children's own success in family and community, whereas children have an obligation to supply *nakhus* (prideful pleasure or gratification) for the parents. In establishing the conditions for *nakhus*, the parents create a lifelong obligation for their children. Findings indicate that high-achievement motivation is related to parental praise and expression of parental pride (Rehberg, Sinclair, and Schafer, 1970).

With "Americanization," there has been a dimming of the focus on the concept of "family" as encompassing a line of descent linking one generation to its past and future. Instead, as the association of less traditional Jewish denominations with kinship models other than the Parentela Orders suggests, there is a growing emphasis upon the independence of the nuclear family unit in one's concept of family. With the decay of the lineal conception of family, the basic glue for molding the structure of roles in the traditional family is disappearing.

Traditionally, in the family's socialization of children, "each year adds new responsibilities in the child's life" (Zborowski and Herzog, 1952:350). With each responsibility, the child is seen as becoming more of a *mensch* (a reliant and moral human being, sensitive to the needs of others). Bit by bit, the growing child assumes the *ol fun Yiddishkeit* (the discipline imposed by the Jewish way of life). The shift in socialization practices accompanying the changing views of family life is suggested by the findings on kinship models and school achievement in Phoenix in 1978. In that study, among Jewish respondents, 88 percent of those holding a Parentela Orders conception of kinship collaterality regarded high grades as important, as compared with 82 percent in the Standard American category, 63 percent in the Civil Law group, and only 56 percent in the Genetic and Canon Law approaches to kinship collaterality (Farber, 1981). Moreover, in an analysis of scholastic achievement of students at a large state university, students (of all religions) who conformed to the Parentela Orders model tended to have the highest cumulative grade point averages (GPAs), and those whose pattern of answers conformed to the Canon Law or Genetic kinship models had the lowest GPAs (Farber, 1977).

Intermarriage

It is only in recent decades that the percentage of intermarriage has affected large segments of the Jewish population in the United States. The 1971 National Jewish Population Study (NJPS) found that fewer than 10 percent of married, Jewish-born adults were then in, or had been in, an intermarriage (Lazerwitz, 1981). However, even at that time, for those who were under 35 years of age, 14 percent of married Jewish-born adults had non-Jewish-born spouses. Among these young adults, 34 percent of the non-Jewish spouses had converted to Judaism. By 1985, it is estimated that the overall intermarriage prevalence had climbed from 7 to 16 percent. By 1990, the percentage of intermarriages was even higher (Lazerwitz, 1995b).

Before 1970, there was a greater tendency for men to intermarry, but from 1970 onward that tendency has disappeared. The data from the National Jewish Population Survey in 1990 indicate that among Jewish-born adults who married between 1970 and 1990, 54 percent married Jewish-born spouses (resulting in 36 percent of the marriages), 7 percent married spouses (more often women) who converted to Judaism, and about 40 percent were in religiously heterogeneous marriages. Only a small percentage of spouses who were not Jewish converted to Judaism. The largest growing segment in the Jewish family consists of those homes in which only one of the parents is Jewish. These data suggest that the process of "Americanization" is having profound effects upon the nature of the Jewish American family. (See Farber and Gordon, 1982, on changing influences on intermarriage.) Some of these effects on family life, reported in the 1990 National Jewish Population Survey, are described in the following section.

As we approach the year 2000, American Jewish families can be readily grouped into three family types: (1) *homogeneous families*, consisting of those families in which both spouses were born into Jewish families; (2) *convert-in families*, consisting of those families in which one spouse was born into a Jewish family and the other spouse is a convert into one of the denominational branches of American Judaism; (3) *religiously heterogeneous families*, consisting of families in which one spouse was born into a Jewish family and the other spouse was born into a non-Jewish family but has not converted to Judaism. (Other combinations are either rare or of little interest in the context of this chapter.)[4]

---

[4]Unless otherwise noted, the data presented in this chapter derive from the 1990 National Jewish Population Study (NJPS, 1990), which was sponsored and financed by the National Council of Jewish Federations. The first survey sample step was random digit dialing 125,813 residences nationwide. The households dialed were screened for Jewish residents. Within eligible households, one adult was subsequently selected as the respondent and informant for that household. Eligibility was validated through a second telephone contact, and the interviewing took place upon the third contact. Of eligible households contacted, 316 refused to participate, 670 refused at the start of the interview and 126 during the interview; a total of 2,506 interviews were completed. A weighting system was applied to the data to permit national population and household estimates of American Jews (Waksberg, 1996).

Socioeconomic and Intermarriage Characteristics. In the 1990 NJPS, socioeconomic and intermarriage data were cross-tabulated with the three family types. The educational and income percentages for the religiously heterogeneous family marriage type indicate consistently less education and income than the homogeneous family and convert-in family types. As other socioeconomic analyses have shown, the lower educational and income attainment is reflected in a greater tendency for divorce and remarriage. Whereas four of every five marriages among the homogeneous and convert-in family types are first marriages, only two-thirds of the religiously heterogeneous respondents are in their first marriage. Hence, the 1990 NJPS findings suggest that the religiously heterogeneous marriages are qualitatively different from those in which both spouses are Jewish, either by birth or conversion.

Denominational Preference. Another aspect of intermarriage is Jewish denominational preference in the three family types. While about one-third (34%) of those in religiously heterogeneous families express no denominational preference (and rank themselves as "Just Jewish"), fewer than 10 percent in the other two family types report "no preference." However, whereas over half (55%) of persons in homogeneous families regard themselves as either Orthodox or Conservative, almost two-thirds (63%) in convert-in families see themselves as Reform (Lazerwitz, 1995b).

Thus, the tendency to identify oneself with a denomination is related to family type. Couples in which both husband and wife had been born Jewish tend to identify with the more traditional denominations—Orthodoxy and Conservatism. Convert-in couples feel more comfortable with Reform positions, which place less emphasis upon tradition. The religiously heterogeneous respondents, however, place least emphasis upon traditional Judaism; although 44 percent consider themselves as Reform, fully 34 percent prefer a more ambiguous standing—"Just Jewish."

The 1990 NJPS also includes findings on synagogue membership among the three family types. A majority of persons in both the homogeneous and convert-in family types report synagogue membership (57% and 77%, respectively). However, only 14 percent of Jewish persons in religiously heterogeneous families belong to a synagogue. Inasmuch as virtually all synagogues are affiliated with the Orthodox, Conservative, or Reform movements, the religiously heterogeneous, existing as they do on the margins of Judaism, would not be expected to maintain synagogue membership.

Additional Variations in Jewish Families (1990 NJPS Study).

1. Jewish-born respondents in both homogeneous marriages (i.e., both spouses born in Jewish families) and convert-in marriages are similar in their domestic ritual activities (such as attending Passover seders, lighting Chanukah candles, and fasting on Yom Kippur) and in having completed six or more years of Jewish education.

2. Whereas respondents in homogeneous marriages identify themselves as "belonging" to more traditional (Conservative and Orthodox) denominations, those in convert-in marriages are concentrated in the Reform category.
3. Most respondents in homogeneous marriages report that *most* or *all* of their closest friends are Jewish and that their neighborhood is *somewhat* or *very* Jewish, but only a quarter of the Jewish-born convert-in respondents do so.
4. There is little difference in extent of involvement with the organized Jewish community between the homogeneous marriage and the convert-in respondents. However, the convert-in respondents outdo the homogeneous marriage respondents in participation in general community voluntary associations and in synagogue membership.
5. The Jewish-born respondents in religiously heterogeneous marriages, for the most part, show little religious involvement with the Jewish community, in close friendship, neighborhood, or organizationally. In general community voluntary associations, they are on a par with homogeneous marriage respondents.

Collectively, the 1990 data on intermarriage show the American Jewish family as undergoing a dramatic change. Historically, the American Jewish family has been rooted in Jewish communal life religiously, ethnically, and organizationally. With the dispersion of American Jews geographically, with "Americanization" over the generations, and with general shifts in American marriage norms, the traditional Jewish family is declining. Among those marrying after the 1960s, it represents a minority of *families* with Jewish members. This trend is accompanied by a tendency to abandon the more traditional (Orthodox and Conservative) denominations and to move toward the Reform denomination or to cease identifying oneself with any Jewish denomination.

The findings of the 1990 NJPS suggest that, in the near future, most families formed by American Jews will likely be combinations of born-Jews and spouses born into non-Jewish families. If the spouse "converts in," the 1990 data indicate that involvement with Judaism will be less "ethnic" than is now the case and mainly in terms of ritual behavior, synagogue membership, and the organized Jewish community. If the marriage remains religiously heterogeneous, the family will tend to be marginal to the traditional Jewish community and religion (and to Christianity as well).

The Intersection of Religio-Ethnic Communities: A Fourth Melting Pot?

For a long time, sociology has referred to three American religio-ethnic communities: Protestant, Catholic, and Jewish. The basic contention has been that each of these communities constitutes a cultural caldron that unifies the diverse national, social class, and ethnic components. This unification occurs through a series of basic beliefs, moral principles, and ritual practices, and the religious community incorporates the ethnic backgrounds into its structure. A vital socializing agency in this process is the family, which in some ways symbolizes the close, unifying force in transmitting religious injunctions and practices to the next generation.

The religiously heterogeneous family by its very nature transcends the boundaries of the three "melting pots." In doing so, it has the task of developing a modus vivendi that enables it to endure effectively. This modus vivendi involves beliefs, norms, and practices that permit a religio-ethnic diversity while simultaneously embodying emotional growth and smooth functioning.

To operate effectively, the religiously heterogeneous family would likely be obliged to (1) take on a point of view that accommodates diversity, probably involving a liberal perspective—often secular—that overpowers the traditional religious backgrounds of the married couple; and (2) isolate itself from traditional religio-ethnic traditions that might divide the couple.

Liberality in political orientations generally embody the overall *Weltanschauung* (worldview) of the people who hold them. NJPS findings on marriage types and the political orientation of Jewish-born adult respondents in the 1990 NJPS indicate that compared with about 40 percent of respondents in the other marriage types, 52 percent of those in the religiously heterogeneous category are inclined to hold a "liberal" political orientation. These percentages support the position that to live a religiously heterogeneous marriage successfully, a liberal outlook on life would accommodate the persistence of religious diversity in the marriage and family.

The liberal accommodation of religious diversity in families where one spouse is Jewish and the other is not is suggested in findings on two religious practices: one Christian (having a Christmas tree in the home) and the other Jewish (having a Seder to celebrate Passover). Among couples in which both spouses had been born into Jewish families, virtually no one has a Christmas tree in the home, while almost everyone celebrates with a Seder at Passover (especially among those identifying with any particular denomination). The religious symbolism of the Christmas tree and Seder is somewhat muffled in some convert-in families, in which 22 percent (33% for convert-in Reform families) have a Christmas tree, 87 percent have a Seder. Finally, for the religiously heterogeneous families, 62 percent report having a Christmas tree and 52 percent also report a Seder. However, data also suggest that a significant minority of the religiously heterogeneous couples have neither Christmas tree nor Seder. Thus, the distinction in symbolism between the Christmas tree and the Seder is erased in perhaps most of the religiously heterogeneous families as part of their liberal orientation.

Jewish-Catholic-Protestant Mixtures. As noted earlier, a second element in sustaining a religiously heterogeneous marriage is to isolate oneself from religious services that bind one to a particular religious community. Table 17-2 presents percentages pertaining to marriage types and frequency of attendance at religious services for Catholics, Protestants, and Jews. In contrast to those in religiously homogeneous and convert-in marriages, persons in all three groups—Protestants, Catholics, and Jews—in religiously hetero-

TABLE 17-2. Percentage of Marriage Types and Frequency of Attendance at Religious Services for Protestants, Catholics, and Jews (GSS[a] and 1990 NJPS)

Frequency of Attendance	Homogeneous Marriage Type	Convert-In Marriage Type	Religiously Heterogeneous Marriage Type
	Protestants (GSS)		
Less than once per month[b]	44	39	76
Once to three times per month	17	17	11
More than three times per month	39	44	13
	Catholics (GSS)		
Less than once per month[a]	32	27	56
Once to three times per month	14	15	15
More than three times per month	54	58	29
	Jews (NJPS '90)		
Less than once per month[a]	41	28	77
Once to three times per month	38	46	19
More than three times per month	21	26	4

[a]GSS data are derived from the General Social Surveys conducted by the National Opinion Research Center from 1985 to 1989.
[b]Except for the Jews, the majority of responses in this category were never or once a year. (Because many Jews attend synagogue only on Rosh Hashana and Yom Kippur, a slim majority of responses were 2–11 times per year.) However, for the religiously heterogeneous marriage type for all three religions, more than two thirds of responses in this category were 0–1 times per year.

geneous marriages attend services infrequently (if at all). Especially among Protestants and Jews, those in religiously heterogeneous marriages rarely attend services regularly. Thus, in its isolation from the institutional ties of church (or synagogue), as well as in its relationship to a liberal orientation in the blurring of traditional religious distinctions, the religiously heterogeneous marriage type emerges as a generic kind of family life.

The Religiously Heterogeneous Family and Its Consequences. Given its dramatic growth among American Jews, the religiously heterogeneous marriage type will likely have a profound effect on the character of the future of the American Jewish family (as well as the American Jewish community).

One area of concern is the consequence of the emergence of the religiously heterogeneous marriage for fertility rates and the socialization of children. As an earlier section of this chapter indicates, kinship structures associated with traditional Judaism place great emphasis upon the endurance of a line of descent from one generation to the next. This emphasis is reinforced in the religious service by the frequent repetition of the phrase "generation upon generation" (*l'dor v'dor*) and in the invocation of the blessing to be repeated daily, "Hear O Israel" (the *Shema*)—namely, that one teach the sacred lore to one's children.

In connection with the emphasis upon the continuity of generations, research by Lazerwitz, Winter, Dashefsky, and Tabory (1997) has shown that

Jews who join synagogues, and particularly those who attend religious services at least once a month, have a fertility rate roughly 50 percent higher than do others. In contrast to religiously homogeneous and convert-in families, persons in religiously heterogeneous families rarely join a synagogue or go to religious services regularly. Hence, one would expect the religiously heterogeneous families to have a lower fertility rate than do families classified as homogeneous or convert-in marriage types.

Furthermore, it is not only likely that religiously heterogeneous families will have low fertility, but also that most of them will *not* raise their children to be Jewish. For example, Lazerwitz, Winter, Dashefsky, and Tabory (1997) also report that only 38 percent of the religiously heterogeneous families were raising their children as Jews. Although about half (52%) of Jewish-born women in heterogeneous marriages were raising their children as Jews, only one-fourth (25%) of Jewish-born men in such marriages were raising their children as Jews. This finding implies that the religiously heterogeneous family form may represent a vehicle for intergenerational transition from the Jewish community. It thereby forecasts serious consequences for the future of the American Jewish family.

CHANGE AND ADAPTATION

The American Jewish family is becoming increasingly diverse. This chapter has focused upon some consequences of this diversity. By and large, the major segment of the American Jewish population consists of people descended from eastern European immigrants who arrived in America in the late nineteenth and early twentieth centuries. Further diversification has been wrought by the more recent inflow from post-USSR Russia, Israel, Africa, and various Middle Eastern countries. But this recent migration adds only a small increment to the diversity of family forms.

In the core population, profound changes have taken place in Jewish family life and, more generally, in American family life since 1960. As noted earlier, sociologists have described American society as consisting of three melting pots—Catholic, Protestant, and Jewish. However, the amount of religious intermarriage taking place in the past few decades seems to represent a departure from that characterization. The growing sector of families of religiously intermarried couples may well constitute a fourth melting pot in American society.

The small size of the American Jewish population (relative to that of Protestants and Catholics) magnifies the effects of intermarriage as a percentage of all marriages taking place. The 1990 NJPS data suggest that in the next generation religiously heterogeneous intermarriages may comprise a majority of marriages among Jews (particularly among Reform Jews.) Given this potentiality, one must regard the families who are religiously intermarried as a distinct form of Jewish family life. Part of this distinctiveness derives from the fact that religiously intermarried couples ordinarily are at the margins of the Jewish community and often raise their children as non-Jews. Hence, the potential prevalence of the families evoke questions about the future character of Jewish families in American society.

Forecasts about the future of the American Jewish families fall into three groups: the pessimists, the ambivalents, and the optimists. Each group has its fervent proponents, and each group establishes its case using different facts and assumptions.

The Pessimists

The pessimists view trends in Jewish family organization as mirroring those of middle class families generally. According to this position, the same forces that are weakening traditional family bonds in the American middle class are destroying the Jewish family. This group sees the steady increase in mobility and migration within the United States, the continued growth of individualism, and the heightening of cosmopolitanism as undermining the basis for strong family ties in American society.

Focusing upon the role of the family in establishing Jewish identity to children, Sklare (1971) regards the very social and economic success of American Jews as contributing to the downfall of the traditional *mishpokheh*, which long has acted as a bedrock of Jewish community institutions. Sklare (1971:89–100) proposes the following:

> The changing significance of the family, and particularly declines in the frequency and intensity of interaction with the kinship group means that identity can no longer be acquired through this traditional institution. . . . However significant the communal network and the [Hebrew day] school system are as building blocks, they are a kind of superstructure resting upon the foundation of the family—for it is the family that has been the prime mechanism for transmitting Jewish identity. This system of identity-formation is currently on the decline. . . . [This decline] is traceable to . . . the high acculturation of many Jewish parents, the diminished interaction with relatives, and the presence of Gentiles in the Jewish kinship network.

As Goldstein and Goldstein (1996) indicate, the identity supports among the Orthodox stand in sharp contrast to those families to which Sklare referred. The Orthodox are characterized generally by strong communal ties and ready accessibility to ritual-based facilities and religious schools. These supports are sufficient to inhibit the disintegration of traditional religious practices and of stable relationships with kith and kin. However, the shrinking of the Orthodox community (as a percentage of the Jewish population) bodes ill for the endurance of the traditional Jewish family.

In general, the pessimists emphasize the continuing decrease in differences between Jewish and non-Jewish family life in the American middle class.

The Ambivalent Position

The ambivalent position suggests that there are upper limits to the ability of disruptive factors to interfere with the integrity of Jewish communities and families. For example, Rabinowitz, Lazerwitz, and Kim (1995:429) have found that the dispersion of Jewish families westward and southward may have reduced the concentration of the Jewish population in the large metropolitan centers of the Northeast, but it also eventually provided an opportunity for a multiplicity of new centers to develop. As communities increase in size, so does primary group participation among their inhabitants (see Blau and Booth, 1984 and Fischer, 1984).

Indeed, the association between the size of the Jewish community and extent of primary-group participation among Jews actually increased in the period from 1971 to 1990. The growth of new urban Jewish centers has made possible the spread of support institutions (such as new Jewish day schools, synagogues, availability of kosher products, and so on), as well as local Jewish singles groups, kin groups made possible by chain migration, and other primary groups. Community size is also associated with larger proportions preferring the Conservative denomination (Rabinowitz, Lazerwitz, and Kim, 1995).

What is considered pessimistic by some observers is regarded as optimistic by others. The marginality of religiously heterogeneous couples to the Jewish community is regarded by some as their perceiving "the traditional ethnic network of kin, neighbors and synagogue as constrictive" (Toll, 1991:185). Only a minority of non-Jews who marry Jews convert to Judaism. Of those married between 1970 and 1990, 78 percent of marriages in which the wife was non-Jewish and 89 percent of marriages in which the husband was non-Jewish remained as religiously heterogeneous marriage (Lazerwitz in Greeley, 1995:461). Yet although the percentage of marriages in which one spouse converts to Judaism is small, the 1990 NJPS data indicate much similarity to marriages in which both spouses were born Jewish in behavior and attitudes associated with household ritual, synagogue attendance, and activity in Jewish organizations. Probably this emphasis in convert-in families will endure into the next generation. Moreover, as the new generation of "born Jews" matures, one can expect a lessening of distinctions between marriages in which both spouses are "born Jews" and convert-in marriages. Possibly a new Americanized Jewish ethnicity may emerge—perhaps a blend between the precepts of a Jewish way of life and middle class cosmopolitanism.

The Optimists

For the optimists, the fact that Judaism and its way of life has survived numerous threats to its integrity gives hope for a resurgence of its traditional family forms. These threats include not only the oppression by its enemies but also the threat of freedom from constraints. At this time, the optimists are concerned with the latter threat—that of freedom to live any kind of existence.

With regard to the threat of freedom, there are various parallels between Americanization and the Hellenization that took place in the aftermath of the Alexandrian conquest of the Middle East in ancient times. Politically, Hellenism gave the Jews equal status with other peoples. This meant giving up Jewish law as a basis for governance and accepting Greek institutions—the establishment of Greek educational institutions and the introduction of Greek customs into the daily life of Jerusalem. Although the people were permitted to live their lives according to "ancestral laws," there was "perhaps also public belittlement of the Jewish religious customs existent since the days of Ezra" (Tcherikover, 1977:168–169). The Jewish Hellenists abandoned the Torah, rejecting its divine origin. Instead, they accepted Greek religious opinion that "several features of the Jewish religion (such as self-seclusion, the prohibition of certain food, etc.) were symptomatic of a late degeneration" of Judaism (Tcherikover, 1977:184). Yet with the eventual revival of Jewish nationalism and upheaval, these Hellenistic tendencies subsided.

The revitalization of ethnic identity associated by Tcherikover with political concerns and dominance pertaining to Hellenization Glazer and Moynihan (1974) regard as relevant in the modern world. They propose that (1) diverse ethnic groups occupy conflicting positions in modern social structures; (2) because of their opposing positions, ethnic groups become rallying points in the identification of interest groups in the society; (3) in becoming rallying points, ethnic groups stress those features that define their uniqueness; and (4) these features thereby tend to survive. One of the features Jews have claimed as unique is their family life—concepts such as *nakhus* (parental pride), *yikhus* (honorable accomplishment of one's ancestral line), peace of the household, *besherte* (one's fated spouse) and so on—hence, the optimist would see the effort to sustain Jewish family norms as related to a need to defend the place of the Jewish people in society.

Jonathan Sarna (1995) chooses as the historical inspiration for his optimism the "Great Awakening" in late nineteenth-century Judaism. The Awakening included (1) a heightened sense of Jewish peoplehood as opposed to Judaism simply as another "faith," (2) a renewed emphasis upon "spiritual and emotional" elements in Judaism, and (3) a focus on establishing a Jewish homeland. Sarna's (1995) position is that we use not the specific content of the Great Awakening, but its "four lessons from history" as guides to reinvent American Judaism today. These lessons are

1. Challenging basic assumptions about past applications of Judaism to life in American society—to be willing to change in a fundamental way so that "continuity may depend upon discontinuity."

2. What worked in revitalizing Judaism in the nineteenth century—"spiritual renewal, Jewish education, Zionism, the unleashing the potential of Jewish women, and so forth"—may not work in contemporary society.

3. The search for novel solutions should be sought not so much from current leadership, but from those who do not have a vested interest in the established way of doing things.

4. The act of attempting to meet the challenges of the American Jewish community itself may result in strengthening community and family by increasing self-awareness and sustaining a hope for the future.

REFERENCES

Balswich, Jack. 1966. "Are American-Jewish Families Closely Knit?" *Jewish Social Studies, 28:* 159–167.

Bell, Inge Powell. 1968. *CORE and the Strategy of Non-Violence.* New York: Random House.

Berman, Louis, 1968. *Jews and Intermarriage: A Study in Personality and Culture.* New York: Thomas Yoseloff.

Blau, Peter, and A. Booth. 1984. *Crosscutting Social Circles.* Orlando, FL: Academic Press.

Boroff, David. 1961. "Jewish Teenage Culture." *The Annals of the American Academy of Political Science, 338:* 79–90.

Brav, Stanley R. 1940. *Jewish Family Solidarity, Myth or Fact?* Vicksburg, MS: Nogales Press.

Bressler, Marvin. 1952. "Selected Family Patterns in W. I. Thomas' Unfinished Study of the Bintl Brief." *American Sociological Review, 17:* 563–571.

Brodbar-Nemzer, Jay Y. 1986. "Divorce and Group Commitment: The Case of the Jews." *Journal of Marriage and the Family, 48:* 329–340.

Bumpass, Larry, and James Sweet. 1972. "Differentials in Marital Instability: 1970." *American Sociological Review, 37:* 754–766.

Cohen, Steven M. 1977. "Socioeconomic Determinants of Intraethnic Marriage and Friendship." *Social Forces, 55:* 997–1010.

———. 1983. *American Modernity and Jewish Identity.* New York: Tavistock.

Cromer, Gerald. 1974. "Intermarriage and Communal Survival in a London Suburb," *Jewish Journal of Sociology, 16:* 155–169.

Della Pergola, Sergio. 1980. "Patterns of American Jewish Fertility." *Demography, 17(3):* 261–273.

Elazar, Daniel J., and Stephen R. Goldstein. 1972. "The Legal Status of the American Jewish Community." *American Jewish Yearbook, 73:* 3–94.

Farber, Bernard. 1973. *Family and Kinship in Modern Society.* Glenview, IL: Scott Foresman.

———. 1977. "Social Context, Kinship Mapping, and Family Norms." *Journal of Marriage and the Family, 39:* 227–240.

Farber, Bernard, and Leonard Gordon. 1979. "Kinship Mapping Among Jews in a Midwestern City." *Social Forces, 57:* 1107–1123.

———. 1981. *Conceptions of Kinship.* New York: Elsevier.

———. 1982. "Accounting for Intermarriage: Assessment of National and Community Studies," *Contemporary Jewry, 6:* 47–75.

Field, Peter B. 1962. "A New Cross Cultural Study of Drunkenness," in David J. Pittman and Charles R. Snyder (Eds.), *Society, Culture and Drinking Patterns,* pp. 48–74. New York: John Wiley.

Fischer, Claude. 1984. *The Urban Experience,* 2nd ed. New York: Harcourt-Brace.

Freedman, Ronald, Pascal Whelpton, and Arthur Campbell. 1959. *Family Planning Sterility, and Population Growth.* New York: McGraw-Hill.

———. 1961. "Socio-Economic Factors in Religious Differentials in Fertility." *American Sociological Review, 26:* 608–614.

Glazer, Nathan 1957. *American Judaism.* Chicago: University of Chicago Press.

Glazer, Nathan, and Daniel P. Moynihan. 1974. "Why Ethnicity?" *Commentary, 58* (October): 33–39.

Glikson, P., and S. Della Pergola (Eds.). 1981. *Papers in Jewish Demography,* pp. 215–238. Jerusalem, Israel: Hebrew University.

Golden, Harry, and Martin Rywell. 1950. *Jews in American History.* Charlotte, NC: Henry Lewis Martin.

Goldstein, Sidney. 1992. "Profile of American Jewry." *American Jewish Year Book, 92:* 77–173.

Goldstein, Sidney and Alice Goldstein (Eds.). 1996. *Jews on the Move: Implications for Jewish Identity.* Albany: State University of New York Press.

Goldstein Sidney. 1971. "American Jewry, 1970." *American Jewish Year Book, 72:* 3–88.

Goldstein, Sidney, and Calvin Goldscheider. 1968. *Jewish Americans: Three Generations in a Jewish Community.* Englewood Cliffs, NJ: Prentice-Hall.

Gordon Albert I. 1959. *Jews in Suburbia.* Boston: Beacon Press.

———. 1967. *The Nature of Conversion.* Boston: Beacon Press.

Herman, Manahem. 1980. "Manifestation of Jewish Messianic Movements and Cults." *Journal of Jewish Communal Service, 56:* 91–93.

Hollingshead, A. B., and F. C. Redlich. 1958. *Social Class and Mental Illness.* New York: John Wiley.

Kardiner, Abram, and Lionel Ovesy. 1951. *The Mark of Oppression.* New York: W. W. Norton.

Landes, Ruth, and Mark Zborowski. 1968. "The Context of Marriage; Family Life as a Field of Emotions," in H. Kent Geiger (Ed.), *Comparative Perspectives on Marriage and the Family,* pp. 77–107. Boston: Little, Brown.

Landis, Judson T. 1960. "Religiousness, Family Relationships, and Family Values in Protestant, Catholic, and Jewish Families." *Marriage and Family Living, 22:* 341–347.

Lazerwitz, Bernard. 1971. "Fertility Trends in Israel and Its Administered Territories." *Jewish Social Studies, 33:* 172–186.

———. 1973. "Religious Identification and Its Ethnic Correlates: A Multivariate Model," *Social Forces, 52:* 204–220.

———. 1978. "An Approach to the Components and Consequences of Jewish Identification." *Contemporary Jewry 4:* 3–8.

———. 1980. "Religiosity and Fertility: How Strong a Connection?" *Contemporary Jewry, 5:* 56–63.

———. 1981. "Jewish-Christian Marriages and Conversions." *Jewish Social Studies, 43:* 31–46.

———. 1985. "A Revised Model of Jewish Identification." Research report, Bar-Ilan University, Ramat-Gan, Israel.

———. 1987. "Trends in National Jewish Identification Indicators. 1971–1985." *Contemporary Jewry, 9:* 87–63.

———. 1995a. "Denominational Retention and Switching Among American Jews." *Journal for the Scientific Study of Religion, 34:* 499–506.

———. 1995b. "Jewish Christian Marriages and Conversions, 1971 and 1990." *Sociology of Religion, 56:* 433–443.

———. 1995c. "The American Jewish Community at the End of the Twentieth Century," in Andrew Greeley (Ed.), *Sociology and Religion,* pp. 452–456. New York: Harper-Collins.

Lazerwitz, Bernard, and Michael Harrison. 1979. "American Jewish Denominations: A Social and Religious Profile." *American Sociological Review, 44:* 656–666.

Lazerwitz, Bernard, J. Alan Winter, and Arnold Dashefsky. (1988). "Localism, Religiosity, Orthodoxy, and Liberalism: The Case of the Jews in the United States." *Social Forces 67* (September): 229–242.

Lazerwitz, Bernard, J. Allan Winter, Arnold Dashefsky, and L. Tabory. 1997. *Jewish Choices: American Jewish Denominationalism.* Albany, NY: State University of New York Press.

Leichter, Hope J. and William E. Mitchell. 1967. *Kinship and Casework.* New York Russell Sage Foundation.

Lenski, Gerhard. 1961. *The Religious Factor.* New York: Doubleday.

Lewin, Kurt. 1948. *Resolving Social Conflicts.* New York: Harper & Row.

Litwak, Eugene. 1985. *Helping the Elderly: The Complementary Roles of Informal Networks and Formal Systems.* New York: Guilford Press.

Liebman, Charles S. 1973. "American Jewry; Identity and Affiliation," in David Sidorsky (Ed.), *The Future of the Jewish Community in America,* pp. 127–152. New York: Basic Books.

Luria, Zella. 1974. "Recent Women College Graduates: A Study of Rising Expectations," *American Journal of Orthopsychiatry, 44:* 109–120.

Luschen, Gunther. 1986. "Zur Kontext und Interaktions—Analyse familial—verwandtschaftlicher Netzwerke." Paper presented at symposium on Change and Continuity of the Family, Bamberg, West Germany.

Luschen, Gunther, et al. 1971. "Family Organization, Interaction, and Ritual." *Journal of Marriage and the Family, 33:* 228–234.

Maller, Alan. 1975. "New Facts About Mixed Marriages." *Reconstructionist, 34:* 26–29.

Mandelbaum, David G. 1958. "Change and Continuity in Jewish Life," in Marshall Sklare (Ed.), *The Jews, Social Patterns of an American Group,* pp. 509–519. New York: Free Press.

Manners, Ande. 1972. *Poor Cousins.* New York: Coward, McCann and Geoghegan.

Massarik, Fred, and Albert Chenkin. 1973. "United States National Jewish Population Study: A First Report," in *American Jewish Year Book, 74,* pp. 264–306. New York: Institute of Human Relations.

Mayer, Egon. 1980. "Processes and Outcomes in Marriages between Jews and Non-Jews." *American Behavioral Scientist, 23:* 487–518.

Merton, Robert K. 1941. "Intermarriage and the Social Structure: Fact and Theory." *Psychiatry, 4:* 361–374.

Mitchell, William E. 1978. *Mishpokhe.* New York: Mouton.

Rabinowitz, Jonathan, Bernard Lazerwitz, and Israel Kim. 1995. "Changes in the Influence of Jewish Community Size on Primary Group, Religious, and Jewish Community Involvement—1971–1990." *Sociology of Religion, 56:* 417–432.

Rehberg, Richard A., Judie Sinclair, and Walter E. Schafer. 1970. "Adolescent Achievement Behavior, Family Authority Structure, and Parental Socialization Practices." *American Journal of Sociology, 75:* 1012–1034.

Rice, B. 1976. "Messiah from Korea." *Psychology Today, 9*(8): 36–47.

Roberts, B. H., and J. K. Meyers. 1954. "Religion, Natural Origin, Immigration, and Mental Illness." *American Journal of Psychiatry, 110:* 759–764.

Rose, Arnold M., and Halger R. Stub. 1955. "Summary of Studies on the Incidence of Mental Disorders," in Arnold M. Rose (Ed.), *Mental Health and Mental Disorders,* pp. 87–116. New York: Norton.

Rosen, Bernard C. 1955. "Conflicting Group Membership: A Study of Parent Peer-Group Cross Pressures." *American Sociological Review, 20:* 155–161.

Rosenthal, Erich. 1963. "Studies of Jewish Intermarriage in the United States." *American Jewish Year Book, 64:* 3–53.

———. 1970. "Divorce and Religious Intermarriage: The Effects of Previous Marital Status Upon Subsequent Marital Behavior." *Journal of Marriage and the Family, 32:* 435–440.

Sarna, Jonathan. 1995. *A Great Awakening: The Transformation that Shaped Twentieth Century Judaism and Its Implications for Today.* New York: Council for Initiatives in Jewish Education.

Schmelz, U. O. 1981. "Jewish Survival: The Demographic Factors." *American Jewish Year Book, 81:* 61–117.

Schmelz, U. O., and Sergio Della Pergola. 1982. "World Jewish Population." *American Jewish Yearbook, 82:* 277–290

Seeley, John R., R. Alexander Sim, and E. W. Loosely. 1956. *Crestwood Heights, A Study of the Culture of Suburban Life.* New York: Basic Books.

Seligman, Ben B. 1950. "The American Jew: Some Demographic Features." *American Jewish Year Book, 51:* 3–52.

Sklare, Marshall (Ed.). 1958. *The Jews, Social Patterns of an American Group.* Glencoe, IL: Free Press.

———. 1971. *America's Jews.* New York: Random House.

Sklare, Marshall, and Joseph Greenblum. 1967. *Jewish Identity on the Suburban Frontier: A Study of Group Survival in the Open Society.* New York: Basic Books.

Slater, Mariam K. 1969. "My Son the Doctor: Aspects of Mobility Among American Jews." *American Sociological Review, 34:* 359–373.

Snyder, Charles R. 1958. *Alcohol and the Jews.* New York: Free Press.

Spero, Moshe. 1977. "Cults: Some Theoretical and Practical Perspectives." *Journal of Jewish Communal Service, 53:* 330–338.

Srole, Leo, Thomas S. Langer, Stanley T. Michael, Marvin K. Opler, and Thomas A. C. Rennie. 1962. *Mental Health in the Metropolis.* New York: McGraw-Hill.

Strodtbeck, Fred. 1958. "Family Interaction, Values and Achievement," in Marshall Sklare (Ed.), *The Jews, Social Patterns of an American Group,* pp. 147–165. Glencoe, IL: Free Press.

Tcherikover, Victor. 1959. *Hellenistic Civilization and the Jews.* Philadelphia: Jewish Publication Society.

Toll, William. 1991. "Intermarriage and the Urban West," in Moses Rischin and John Livingstone (Eds.), *Jews in the American West,* pp. 164–189.

U.S. Bureau of the Census. 1958. "Religion Reported by the Civilian Population of the United States: March 1957," *Current Population Reports.* Series P-20, no. 35. Washington, DC: U.S. Government Printing Office.

Wake, Sandra B., and Michael J. Sporakowski. 1972. "An Intergenerational Comparison of Attitudes Toward Supporting Aged Parents." *Journal of Marriage and the Family, 34:* 42–48.

Waksberg, Joseph. 1996. "The Methodology of the National Jewish Population Survey," in Sydney Goldstein and Alice Goldstein (Eds.), *Jews on the Move: Implications for Jewish Identity,* pp. 333–359, appendix A. Englewood Cliffs, NJ: Prentice-Hall.

Weinryb, Bernard D. 1958. "Jewish Immigration and Accommodation to America," in Marshall Sklare (Ed.), *The Jews, Social Patterns of an American Group,* pp. 5–25. Glencoe, IL: Free Press.

Whelpton, Pascal, Arthur Campbell, and John Patterson, 1966. *Fertility and Family Planning in the United States.* Princeton, NJ: Princeton University Press.

Winch, Robert F., Scott Greer, and Rae L. Blumberg. 1967. "Ethnicity and Extended Familism in an Upper-Middle-Class Suburb." *American Sociological Review, 32:* 265–272.

York, Alan. 1979. "Voluntary Associations and Communal Leadership Among the Jews of the United States." Ph.D. dissertation, Bar Ilan University, Ramat Gan, Israel.

York, Alan, and Bernard Lazerwitz. 1987. "Religious Involvement as the Main Gateway to Voluntary Association Activity." *Contemporary Jewry, 8:* 7–26.

Young, Michael, and Peter Willmot. 1962. *Family and Kinship in East London.* Baltimore: Penguin Books.

Zborowski, Mark. 1969. *People in Pain.* San Francisco: Jossey-Bass.

Zborowski, Mark, and Elizabeth Herzog. 1952. *Life Is with People: The Culture of the Shtetl.* New York: Schocken.

18

The Amish Family

Gertrude Enders Huntington

HISTORICAL BACKGROUND

The Old Order Amish are an example of an ethnoreligious group that has had great success in preserving its traditions and preventing wholesale assimilation. The primarily rural Amish, contrary to popular opinion, are probably a growing population that has managed to resist the onslaught of modern technology and major social change. Their ability to resist change is grounded in their religious commitment, which is expressed in their major social institutions.

The Old Order Amish Mennonites are direct descendants of the Swiss Anabaptists of the sixteenth century. "Anabaptist" is a historical and theological term used to designate a number of different theologies and social groups (Littell, 1964) that represent the left wing of the Reformation (Bainton, 1952). Those Anabaptist groups who survive emerged between 1525 and 1536 and are today represented by the Amish, Mennonites, and Hutterites. These churches are characterized by the maintenance of a disciplined community, pacifism, separation from the world, adult rather than infant baptism, and an emphasis on simple living.

The Amish developed between 1693 and 1697 as a dissenting conservative wing of the Swiss Mennonites. Their leader, Jacob Amman, introduced "shunning" (the avoidance of all normal social intercourse with a member who is under the ban), foot washing as a part of the communion service, communion twice instead of once a year, the excommunication of persons who attend the state church, and greater uniformity of dress and hairstyle. The Amman group, or Amish, continue to this day to abide by rules established by Jacob Amman and interpreted by each local congregation.

Although the Amish family today is an American phenomenon, its roots go back to the early days in Europe. Persecution was severe in Europe; the Amish were forbidden citizenship and thus could not own land. Therefore, they were generally unable to establish permanent, stable communities or to develop a distinctive social structure. Their livelihood, their place of residence, even their lives were subject to the whim of rulers and neighbors. Families often had to live at considerable distance from coreligionists; religious services were held irregularly and unobtrusively in the home of a church member. This mobility, isolation, and limited community interaction placed the emphasis for producing Christians directly on the family.

To this day, the family has remained the smallest and strongest unit of Amish culture, the central social institution. Anabaptist theology, which emphasized adult baptism, also supported the role of the family in child development. Protestant religious leaders such as Martin Luther and Philipp Melanchthon were suspicious of parents' ability to rear their children without the help and intervention of the state (Schwartz, 1973:102–114). In contrast, the Anabaptists never equated childrearing with schooling, nor did they believe that the child or the parent was morally subservient to some outside civil or religious authority. Childrearing was the parents' major responsibility. Menno Simons (about 1496–1561), an early leader in Holland after whom the Mennonites are named, wrote, "For this is the chief and principal care of the saints, that their children may fear God, do right, and be saved" (Simons, 1956:950). He also taught that parents were morally responsible for the condition of their children's souls. "Watch over their souls as long as they are under your care, lest you lose also your own salvation on their account" (Simons, 1956:391).

In addition to urging parents to set an unblamable example for their children and to teach, instruct, admonish, correct, and chastise their children as circumstances require, parents were also to protect their children from worldly influences and from wrong companions. "Keep them away from good-for-nothing children, from whom they hear and learn nothing but lying, cursing, swearing, fighting, and mischief" (Simons, 1956:959). Parents were to direct their children to reading and writing, that they might learn from the Scripture what God teaches. They were to instruct them to spin and to earn their bread by the labor of their hands. One example from the *Martyr's Mirror*[1] of practical instruction for child care was written by Jacob the Chandler shortly before he was burned at the stake (Braght, 1951:798–799):

> Furthermore, I pray you, my dear and much beloved wife, that you do the best with my children, to bring them up in the fear of God, with good instruction and chastening, while they are still young. . . . For instruction must accompany chastisement: for chastisement demands obedience, and if one is to obey he must first be

---

[1] *The Bloody Theater* or *Martyr's Mirror*, was first published in Dutch in 1660 and has periodically been reprinted in German and in English. It is a large book of over 1,500 pages recounting, often in vivid detail, the deaths of over 4,000 men and women who remained steadfast to their faith in spite of branding, burning, stoning, sessions on the rack, the severing of tongues, hands, and feet, live burials, and drowning. No one who recanted is considered a martyr, nor is one a martyr if he survived his torture. The *Martyr's Mirror* helps strengthen members "to make every preparation for steadfastness in our faith" (Preface to 5th English edition, 1950) whether in the face of an inquisition, school officials, or universal conscription.

instructed. This instruction does not consist of hard words, or loud yelling; for this the children learn to imitate; but if one conducts himself properly towards them they have a good example, and learn propriety; for by the children the parents are known. And parents must not provoke their children to anger, lest they be discouraged; but must bring them up with admonition and good instruction.

During their years in Europe, the Amish lived in Switzerland, Alsace-Lorraine, the Palatine, France, Holland, Austria, Germany, and Poland. Lack of religious toleration meant that the Amish in Europe remained renters, and that families had limited choice as to where they could settle, frequently being forced to move to new locations as political situations changed. Although an effort was made to stay near members of the faith—an old Amish hymn *(Ausbund,* 1564: hymn 44) quoted a martyr writing to his son: "Live, only where the believers live"—it was impossible for the Amish to establish discrete communities. In some areas they continued for many years as a religious sect, but they never formed a self-perpetuating subculture. Today there are no people left in Europe who are distinctly Amish (Hostetler, 1955).

There is some disagreement about when the first Amish landed in America. A 1709 letter of William Penn's pertaining to the Palatinate immigrants mentions "diverse Mennonites" (Smith, 1920:214), which could be construed as a reference to the Amish. The Amish immigrated to this continent in two major waves: The first wave, from about 1727 to 1770, settled in Pennsylvania, and the second wave, from 1815 to 1860, went primarily to Ohio and Indiana (Luthy, 1973:14).

The first Amish to arrive in America settled in Pennsylvania; there they formed discrete clusters, separate from the Mennonites as well as from the "English."[2] In contrast to their experience in Europe, the Amish immigrants to America found cheap land and religious toleration. They responded by electing to purchase farms near fellow churchmen, away from the influence of cities. This has continued to be the basis of their settlement pattern. The Ohio Amish community was started in 1808; this community in central Ohio is the largest and in many ways the most conservative of the large Amish communities. In 1839, settlers in Indiana formed what was to become the third largest Amish settlement. More than three-fourths of the Amish live in these three states. Smaller settlements are found in Illinois, Iowa, Wisconsin, Missouri, Delaware, Florida, Kansas, Kentucky, Minnesota, Oklahoma, Maryland, New York, Michigan, Tennessee, Arkansas, Montana, and Nebraska. At one time, there were Amish settlements in Oregon, North Dakota, California, Colorado, North Carolina, Georgia, Texas, New Mexico, Mississippi, Alabama, and Mexico.[3] In 1968, small Old Order Amish communities were established in Honduras and Paraguay.

---

[2]A term used for all non-Mennonites (and sometimes for all non-Amish), even those who are German speaking.

[3]Personal correspondence, December 21, 1973; interview March 10, 1980, David Luthy, Alymer, Ontario.

These communities are still in existence. However, the Honduras community has not remained typically Old Order, and that of Paraguay has only three families and one minister.

In 1972, there were Amish families living in eighty-three settlements over sixteen U.S. states, eight settlements in Ontario, Canada, one in Paraguay, and one in Honduras. These settlements ranged in size from one to as many as sixty-eight congregations (Luthy, 1994). The population had grown to include 227 settlements throughout the United States and Canada by 1992. Table 18-1 gives the 1992 Amish population and the date of the first Amish settlement for each state or province. In some instances the first settlements were not successful, and present Amish population is the result of later immigrations. In other cases regular church districts were not established until a considerable time after the earliest settlement.

TABLE 18-1. Amish Population by State and County: 1992

State/Province	Date of First Amish Settlement[a]	Settlements	Districts[b]	Baptized Members[c] (est.)	Total Membership[a] (est.)
Ohio	1808	33	258	20,382	43,344
Pennsylvania	1720	44	221	17,459	37,128
Indiana	1839	16	166	13,114	27,888
Wisconsin	1908	27	53	4187	8904
Michigan	1895	23	39	3081	6552
Missouri	1856	15	32	2528	5376
New York	1833	15	30	2370	5040
Iowa	1840	7	25	1975	4200
Illinois	1829	3	21	1659	3528
Kentucky	1958	12	21	1659	3528
Ontario	1824	7	17	1343	2856
Minnesota	1890	5	9	711	1512
Delaware	1915	1	8	632	1344
Maryland	1772	2	6	474	1088
Tennessee	1872	3	6	474	1088
Kansas	1883	3	5	395	840
Oklahoma	1892	2	4	316	672
Texas	1982	3	3	237	504
Montana	1903	2	2	158	336
Florida	1925	1	1	79	168
Georgia	1990	1	1	79	168
North Carolina	1985	1	1	79	168
Virginia	1895	1	1	79	168
Total		227	930	73,470	156,400

[a]Information supplied by David Luthy, Alymer, Ontario. Luthy (1994)
[b]Luthy (1994) J. A. Raber (1980)
[c]Kraybill (1994). Data calculated using Hostetler's estimate of 79 baptized members and 168 total Amish individuals per church district (Hostetler, 1980:80–81) cross, using data from Ohio, determined the number of baptized members to be 86 and the total membership per district to be 199 (1967:42). Smaller, less densely settled Amish communities have small church districts.

The Old Order Amish are a tradition-oriented, conservative branch of the Mennonite Church. The term "Old Order" came into usage during the last half of the nineteenth century when more liberal congregations separated from them. The Old Order are also known as "House Amish" because they hold their church services in their homes, or "Horse and Buggy Amish" because they do not own cars. The Old Order Amish are distinguished by prohibitions against owning automobiles, telephones, and high-line electricity. They have strict dress codes and forbid rubber-tired tractors (if tractors are used at all), central heating, and cameras. They speak a German dialect known as Pennsylvania Dutch in their homes, read the German Bible, and do not permit attendance at state schools beyond the eighth grade. In this chapter the discussion will be limited to the Old Order Amish.

THE MODERN OLD ORDER AMISH FAMILY

Demographic Characteristics

Many people think of the Amish as a shrinking remnant whose days are numbered, but they are in actuality a growing church. Because the Amish do not proselytize, their growth depends primarily on biological increment combined with the ability to hold their children in the faith.

Fertility. The Old Order Amish have increased from a population of about 8,200 in 1905 to 92,000 in 1980 to 139,500 in 1992. Church districts have increased from forty-three to 930 districts (Table 18-2). Household size varies from those married pairs who have no children to those having fifteen children or more.

Studies of family size show that for completed families the average number of children born alive is about seven. This greatly exceeds the national average for white rural households. Cross (1967:108) reported the annual natural increase of the Holmes County, Ohio Amish population to be 3 percent, or a potential doubling of the population every twenty-three years. Assuming this growth rate to be representative and constant, it is interesting to compare the potential population growth of the Amish with the observed population growth. Taking the estimated 1920 population to be 13,900, the 1943 potential population would be 27,800 and the 1966 potential population would be 55,600. Hostetler (1980:81) gives the actual estimated total population for 1966 as 49,371. This would represent a loss to the church of possibly about 6000 individuals over a forty-six-year period and an observed increase of about 35,500. These estimates would indicate that the Amish are successful in perpetuating their own subculture.

Recent demographic studies of the Amish (Hostetler, Ericksen, Ericksen, and Huntington, 1977; Ericksen, Ericksen, Hostetler, and

TABLE 18-2. Amish Population Growth, North America: 1900–1992[a]

Year	Population	Number of Districts
1900	32	4,800
1910	57	8,550
1920	83	12,450
1930	110	16,500
1941	154	23,100
1951	202	30,300
1961	269	40,350
1971	367	55,050
1981	569	85,350
1991	898	134,700
1992	930	139,500

[a]These population estimates assume 150 persons per district.
Sources: Raber (1993), Luthy (1992), Kraybill (1994).

Huntington, 1979; Kraybill, 1994) have shown that there has been no reduction in Amish fertility over time; in fact, there may have been a slight increase in fertility. Sterility among Amish women appears to be lower than among the general American population. Ever-married American women in the birth cohort 1922–1926 had a sterility rate of 7.5 percent while the rate for ever-married Amish women in the birth cohort 1919–1928 was 4.4 percent, and 2.6 percent for in the cohort 1928–1938 (Ericksen, Ericksen, Hostetler, and Huntington, 1979: 258). Twinning, which seems to be high, may be related to the longer reproductive history of Amish women and the larger number of children born—both of which factors seem to be related to frequency of twinning (Enders and Stern, 1948; Cross, 1967).

Not only do the Amish continue to maintain a high birthrate with no indication of contraceptive practices, but they are also successful in maintaining their grown children within the religious community. Detailed interviews with Amish women in Pennsylvania indicated that over 90 percent of their grown children remained Old Order Amish. The 61 women interviewed had already produced a total of 385 grown children, of whom 347 were Amish (Hostetler, E. Ericksen, J. Ericksen, and Huntington, 1977:39–40). In Holmes County, Ohio the large Old Order affiliation retains approximately 86 percent of their youth within the church (Kraybill, 1994). An analysis of an Amish genealogy (Fisher, 1957) listing all the descendants of Christian Fisher, who was born in Pennsylvania in 1757, indicated that during the ensuing two hundred years there had been no reduction in Old Order Amish fertility. However, there had been an average loss to the religious community (by individuals leaving the church) of about 22 percent (Ericksen, Ericksen, Hostetler, and Huntington, 1979:272). Given the high birthrate of the Amish, even if they sustained a loss of one-quarter of their children, they would still maintain a substantial growth rate.

The Amish have a high standard of living and good medical care, and they prohibit birth control. Therefore, except for the relatively late age of marriage, their birthrate resembles that of nonindustrialized countries, while their death rate resembles that of industrialized countries. When plotted by age and sex, the Amish population forms a wide-based pyramid, with over half the Amish under 20 years of age. This figure is in contrast to the population pyramid of the American rural farm population, which has a relatively narrow base. Within the typical American farm population, there are a disproportionate number of old people in relation to young people. The demographic structure of the Amish makes it relatively easy for the youthful population to carry the burden of supporting the aged; there are many productive young people to care for the relatively few old people.

Divorce.   The Old Order Amish are strictly monogamous. The individual's first commitment is to God; his or her second is to the spouse. There is no divorce, and under no circumstances may an Amishman remarry while his spouse is living. Except for widows, the head of the household is always a man. The rare unmarried farmer will have a sister or perhaps a married nephew who lives in his household and helps out.

Sexual Transgression.   The Amish are strongly opposed to extramarital coitus, and any transgression must be confessed to the total membership of the church whether or not pregnancy results. The male and female have equal responsibility to confess fornication. However, after a period of punishment, during which the transgressor is under the ban, both repentant individuals are welcomed back into full church membership, and they are completely forgiven. Although pregnancy is not always considered sufficient reason to marry, if the couple decides to get married, an effort is made to have the wedding before the birth of the baby. The degree of community pressure to marry applied to a couple who has fornicated or conceived varies from one settlement to another. If the parents do not marry, the mother may keep the baby, or it may be adopted by an Amish couple.

Mate Selecton.   The Amish are endogamous; marriage must be "in the Lord"—that is, within the church membership. Any Amish person who marries outside the church forfeits membership and becomes non-Amish. Even within the Old Order Amish church there are breeding isolates resulting from preferred marriage patterns. Marriage between members of noncommuning churches is discouraged, and marriages tend to take place within one settlement or between closely related settlements. Although first-cousin marriages are forbidden, second-cousin marriages are common. The total Amish population has such a small genetic base that marriage partners are frequently as closely related as second and third cousins. Parents have considerable influence as to which group of young people within the settlement their children will "go with," for whom their children will work, and which communities they will visit. By this means young people are directed into preferred social groups and thereby into preferred marriages.

The Amish perceive the family as a religious and a social unit. Therefore, it is not surprising that Amish weddings are community affairs that fit into the general cycle of activity. The majority of weddings occur during the winter months after harvest and before spring planting—November and December being the most popular months. In Lancaster County, Pennsylvania, over 90 percent of the weddings occur during these two months. Outside the Lancaster County settlement, there seems to be an extension of the wedding season, with more couples being married in late winter. In Ohio, two-thirds of the weddings occur between October and January. Indiana, the least traditional settlement, has only a few more than half the weddings occurring during these four months. The variation in season of marriage may be related to the trend away from farming. Of the three communities, Indiana has the largest number of family heads engaged in nonfarming occupations. In addition to holding weddings at specific times of the year, almost all Amish weddings are on Thursday, with a few held on Tuesday, and occasionally a second marriage incorporated into a Sunday church service. Thursday is the most convenient day of the week to hold an elaborate, daylong celebration, considering the prohibition against all unnecessary work on Sunday. Thursday gives the host family four days in which to "set up" for the wedding and two days to clean up afterward without infringing on Sunday.

Not only have wedding customs remained traditional, the age of marriage has also been relatively stable among the Amish for the past fifty years. (Huntington, 1956: 897; Ericksen, Ericksen, Hostetler, and Huntington, 1979: 257–258). The median age of first marriage for Amish women aged 45–49 in 1966 was 22.1, and 24.7 for their husbands.

Social Structure.   All Amish communities are rural. Although there is a fairly wide variation in family income, there are no extremes of poverty or affluence. The Amish in America have developed a distinctive social structure consisting of the settlement, the church district, the family, and the affiliation or network of communing church districts.

The settlement consists of all Amish living in a given geographically contiguous area. A single Amish family cannot be considered to form a settlement; even a small group of Amish families is not considered to be a settlement until they organize a church district. There is a minimum size necessary for a settlement to be able to sustain itself. This size is related to the number of church officials in the settlement (there must be at least two) and to the distance from the nearest communing church district, as well as the actual number of families and the size of the families that make up the settlement. Those Amish who are isolated geographically and socially from other Amish for too long a period lose their Amish identity. The Amish realize this, and if a new settlement does not attract other Amish settlers quickly enough, it will disband. History shows that those individuals who remain where there is no organized church become absorbed into the surrounding culture (Umble, 1949).

A church district is composed of a contiguous cluster of Old Order Amish families who worship together. Typically, each church district has a bishop, two ministers, a deacon, and twenty-five to thirty-five nuclear families. The number of families is determined by the density of the Amish in the area and the size of the homes; when the group becomes too large to meet in a home or barn for the worship service, the district divides. The geographical area of a single church district is almost never settled exclusively by Amish. The area is crossed by paved roads, perhaps interrupted by a village, and is interspersed with "English" farms and homes. Although there are geographical boundaries, neither the Amish church district nor the Amish community is territorial; it is a cultural, social, and religious grouping. The community is not necessarily made up of one's neighbors but rather of one's fellow church members, who are bound together by an ideology and a way of life.

The family, rather than the individual, is the unit of the church. When one asks an Amishman how big his church district is, he always answers you by stating how many families belong, never by how many individual members there are. The *Ohio Amish Directory* lists the families in each district, with no indication of which individuals have been baptized into the church; unmarried baptized members are not listed unless they own their own home. Growth of the church is related to number of weddings, not number of baptisms.

Because of the congregational structure and the strict rules of discipline, differences that may seem minor to the outsider often arise within the larger settlements. These differences are the basis of various affiliations. Church districts that are "in fellowship" with one another interpret the *Ordnung* (discipline) similarly and exchange ministers for Sunday services. All those churches whose ministers "help out" one another form a single affiliation. The affiliations are informal, often unknown to non-Amish, and frequently changing. The tendency is to divide into more affiliations rather than to coalesce. This functions to keep the groups small, to limit social interaction, and to protect tradition. In the central Ohio community there are at least seven different Old Order Amish affiliations that are not "in fellowship" with one another. These range along a conservative–liberal continuum from churches whose members will not ride in a private car (except to attend a funeral or go to the hospital) to churches in which young men drive cars until they actually join the church. Affiliations extend beyond settlement boundaries and, combined with kinship ties, help to bind different geographic Amish settlements together.

Kinship Relations

Kinship ties are maintained throughout the life of the individual. Excerpts from newsletters in *The Budget,* a weekly paper that goes to almost every Amish settlement, illustrate the importance of kinship ties both to the families and to the community *(The Budget,* August 7, 1973):

> The children grandchildren and great-grandchildren of Levi L. Slabach of Berlin were together for Sunday dinner at Bish. Roy L. Slabach's. All were present but three grandchildren. This was in honor of Levi's birthday which is August 6.
>   Mother and us sisters were together at Benuel Stoltzfous, Jr. (sis. Mary). Mother Fisher is having quiltings this week and next to finish the quilts grandmother Fisher had started.

Extended families gather to celebrate birthdays and Christmas; brothers and sisters meet to work together, to help one another with church, to sew rags for woven rugs, to put up a milk house. And in the case of illness or any other stress, the extended family, the members of the church district, and other Amish neighbors rally round to help.

Members of the Amish settlement are always identified by kinship groups. Husband and wife names are used together: Joe-Annie to signify Annie, the wife of Joe, or Annie-Joe meaning Joe, the husband of Annie; or the father's name is used, Menno's Annie to identify Annie, the daughter of Menno. Traditionally, the Amish children in Ohio were always given their father's first name as a middle initial to help identify them. In some settlements the initial of the mother's first name or maiden name is used for an identifying middle initial. There are generally so few last names in a given settlement that first names are used more frequently than last; thus, families are identified as "the Raymonds" and "the Aden Js" instead of "the Millers" and "the Detweilers." In the central Ohio Amish settlement twelve names account for 85 percent of the families. There are only 124 different Amish surnames found in a population of about 90,000. Therefore, it is not surprising that nicknames are also widely used to distinguish individuals: "Barefoot Sam" or "Turkey John." Individuals are always identified by their families, by their *Fruendschaft.*

Children in the Amish community schools introduce themselves by giving their father's first name. Young people quickly tell who their father and their mother are so that they can be placed genealogically. The signers of some Amish guest books are asked to indicate their date of birth and, if they are unmarried, to add their father's name. Kinship networks function to tie distant settlements together. Families visit married sons and daughters; brothers and sisters visit one another to "help out" or for a family get-together. Marriages, when outside the settlement, tend to take place between settlements that are closely related by kinship ties. Amish both publish and purchase genealogies, and family reunions are widely attended. *The Budget* has a section in the classified ads, "#23–Reunions," and in the late summer many of the columns from different communities mention reunions.

The kinship network, especially that involving parents of married children and brothers and sisters, plays a crucial role in establishing young Amish families on farms. In a study done in 1976 in Lancaster County, Pennsylvania, 76 percent of the young Amishmen who were farming had obtained their farm from relatives and the same percentage had obtained loans from family members. Seventy-four percent of the renters were renting land owned by relatives, and only 10 percent were renting from non-Amish. The typical pattern is for an Amish couple to marry before obtaining a farm. For a short time the groom continues to work for wages, saving his money so he can rent a farm, and, ideally, within a few years he buys his own farm. Although each nuclear family will eventually achieve economic independence, this is not expected of the newly married family. In spite of a strong community, Amish norms stress dependency on the family, especially on the extended family, for normal economic support. For catastrophic events, such as fire or unanticipated hospital expenses, the community supplements the kinship.

Family

Roles are well defined in the Amish family. The man is the head of the woman (I Cor: 3) as Christ is the head of the Church. Although the wife is to be subject to her husband, her first commitment is to God, and her second is to her husband. Because she has an immortal soul, she is an individual in her own right. She is not a possession of her husband, nor is she merely an extension of her spouse. Husband and wife become one flesh, a single unit separable only by God. She follows her husband, but only in that which is good. At council service before communion she decides, as an individual, if she is ready for communion. Should her husband transgress to the extent that he is placed under the ban, she, too, will shun him, as he will her in a similar situation. For the Amishman, the question of sacrificing his family for his job never comes up. The family comes first. A job is of no intrinsic importance; it is necessary because it supplies the economic basis for the family. The work of the household should provide vocational education for the children and fulfill the biblical standard, "In the sweat of thy face shalt thou eat bread." The wife's relative position is illustrated by her position in church, where she has an equal vote but not an equal voice. Farms are owned in the name of both husband and wife. Important family decisions are made jointly.

Unlike the corporation wife, the Amish wife participates actively in any decision to move to a different locality. And unlike the corporation wife, the Amish farm wife makes an active contribution to the production of the household. She may help with the farm work, produce most of the salad material and vegetables consumed by her family, make more than half the clothing, help with the butchering, preserve much of the meat that they eat, and perhaps make soap, in addition to producing an average of seven children who in turn help with the farm work. Thus she has an essential role in the economic survival of the family and of the Amish community. Although Amish women appear docile and submissive, this does not mean that their contribution is not valued. Nor do they have a low self-esteem. Most Amishwomen are happy in their role and confident about the contribution they make to the family. In response to a formal interview question about how much money she had made last year, an Amish wife would sometimes list one-half of her husband's income from the farm, saying, "We're in it together. We're partners" (Abigail Mueller in Hostetler, Ericksen, Ericksen, and Huntington, 1977:107).

Parents present a united front to their children and to the community. In dealing with their children, Amish parents should be of one mind, discussing any differences privately and prayerfully. Admonitions to parents in sermons and in Amish writings are directed not to fathers as such, or to mothers alone, but to parents. Couples are never to disagree in public. The wife is expected to support her husband in all things, especially in his relationship with other people, whether it be their children, their parents, or friends and neighbors. The husband, in turn, should be considerate of his wife with respect to her physical, emotional, and spiritual well-being. The ideal is to be individuals to one another, making decisions jointly, and to be of one mind to all others.

The major role of Amish adults is childrearing. Parents of growing children have no individual rights, only responsibilities and obligations for the correct nurture of their children. They are to be examples to their children in all things, so that the children may become good Amish and eventually, through the grace of God, achieve life everlasting.

The role of children within the family is more closely related to age than to sex. The older children are to care for and help the younger, while the younger are to obey the older in any reasonable demand. Older children do not physically punish younger children but cajole them into obeying. Although there is a division of labor by sex, children help one another and their parents as they are needed rather than strictly dividing the work by sex.

On the small, labor-intensive farms the children make a major economic contribution. Typically children are not paid for their labor until they are 21, and if they work away from home their wages are returned to their father until they reach that age. In turn, the parents try to set up each child in farming. Austerity must be practiced by the whole family in order to help the next generation become established economically. Children do not have a low status, although they are expected to be obedient and polite to those who are older. They are highly valued as "the only possessions we can take to heaven with us," and also as contributors to the family, both economically and emotionally. Children function as socializing agents for the parents, for as parents strive to be good examples for their children, they become better Amish themselves.

Grandparents, as parents of young married couples, have an important role in the Amish community. They are often instrumental in helping their married children get established on farms. They have a great influence on where their children will settle. They help the young people with advice, labor, materials, and loans. Very often, the parents own the land onto which the young couple moves. The parents support their grown children with frequent visits. In Lancaster County, almost 90 percent of the parents saw all of their grown children at least once a month—in a culture in which car ownership is forbidden. Grandparents act as a buffer between the young couple and "the world." They help with labor and supply information as to where within the community the young couple can get produce they do not yet grow themselves. They teach the young family about community networks and help them interact within the community. And, as the young couple's children become old enough to help with the labor, the supportive role of the grandparents diminishes, but they continue to advise and admonish. At some stage the older couple will retire from farming, passing the farm on to one of the children and, depending on his age, the grandfather may run a small business of his own for a few years.

Social Class and Lifestyle

The Amish are a small, homogeneous group within which social class has no meaning. They are exclusively rural, operating small family farms and, in some instances, working in small nonunion factories or on small carpenter crews. In relation to the outside society, these occupations would probably place them in the rural working class. Although there is considerable range in family income and some families have a higher status than others, there are no class distinctions within the community and lifestyle is as important as income level. No matter what the income, the need to accumulate capital to buy land for the next generation reinforces the simple living patterns prescribed by the *Ordnung*.

Family farming is both the typical and the ideal occupation for a head of household with growing children. In each Amish settlement of any size there are Amishmen who own small businesses that are related to farming and the Amish way of life. Thus there will be a blacksmith, a harness maker, a buggy shop, a shop for adapting tractor-drawn farm equipment to horse-drawn, and specialized carpenters who do cabinetwork and make the Amish coffins. The Amish build and remodel their own homes and barns with the help of Amish construction crews. There are Amishmen who can draw up plans, lay brick, and install plumbing. Because of the increasing cost and scarcity of land, a growing number of Amish are accepting employment in small nonunion factories that have sprung up in Amish areas: aluminum plants, small sawmills, trailer factories, and brickyards. Farming continues to be the preferred occupation. Many types of employment are forbidden as incompatible with their way of life. Nevertheless, a growing number of Amish heads of households are working in nonfarming occupations (Kraybill, 1994).

The Amish lifestyle is distinctive and consciously maintained. In an effort to build a "church without spot or blemish" and to remain a "peculiar people," strict disciplinary codes have been developed and are observed by members and their children. Most of these rules are unwritten, vary slightly from one church district to another, and are only completely known to participants. Most of the rules are taken for granted, but those pertaining to borderline issues, about which there might possibly be some disagreement, are reviewed twice a year by all baptized members of the church district. This allows for slow, orderly change in details of their lifestyle that is necessary for group survival. Only if consensus on the rules *(Ordnung)* is achieved, and if there is a unanimous expression of peace and good will toward every fellow member, is communion celebrated. Most church districts reach this degree of integration twice a year.

The Old Order Amish style of life is characterized by separation from the world, voluntary acceptance of high social obligation, symbolized by adult baptism, the practice of exclusion and shunning of transgressing members, and a nurturing attitude in harmony with nature and maintained on a human scale. The Amish interpret separation from the world quite literally. They have a distinctive dress, somewhat similar to that worn by European peasants of several centuries ago. They speak a distinctive language—an Amish form of Pennsylvania Dutch—that separates them from outsiders. Physically, too, they prefer to have some distance between themselves and non-Amish, between their households and non-Amish households. "Be ye not unequally yoked together with unbelievers; for what fellowship hath righteousness with unrighteousness? and what communion hath light with darkness?" (II Cor. 6: 14). The Amish may not be union members or form partnerships with non-Amish, for both would join the believer with the unbeliever. In spite of this created distance, the Amish are not self-righteous nor judgmental in their relations with outsiders, whom they consider to be so different that the same criterion of conduct does not apply to them as it would to a fellow Amishman. "My kingdom is not of this world; if my kingdom were of this world, then would my servants fight" (John 18:36). Observing this teaching, the Amish may not serve in the military. Formerly, if they were called, they paid fines or served prison sentences; now they perform alternative service as conscientious objectors. All forms of retaliation to hostility are forbidden. An Amishman may not physically defend himself or his family even when attacked. He may not defend himself legally even when his civil rights have been violated. He is taught to follow the New Testament teaching of the Sermon on the Mount and the biblical example of Isaac: After the warring Philistines had stopped up all the wells of his father Abraham, Isaac moved to new lands and dug new wells (Genesis, 26:15–18). The Amish take this advice, and when they cannot remain separate from the world according to their own definition of separate, they move to new locations.

The adult Amishman voluntarily accepts a high degree of social obligation. His willingness to take on this responsibility is symbolized by the rite of baptism. Prior to baptism the future communicant renounces the world, the devil, his own flesh and blood, and acknowledges Christ as the Son of God and the Lord and Savior. He accepts a personal willingness to suffer persecution or death in order to maintain the faith. In addition, he promises to abide by the *Ordnung* and not to depart from the discipline in life or death. Each young man promises to accept the duties of minister should the lot ever fall on him. Applicants are warned not to make these promises if they cannot keep them, for once made, there is no turning back. It is not unusual for young people, during the period of instruction, to drop out. Generally they join a year or two later. No one may be married in the Amish church without first being baptized.

When deemed necessary, the Amish use excommunication and shunning *(Bann und Meidung)* to enforce the discipline and to keep the church pure and separate from the world. The full church membership participates in the decision and in the ceremony, in which the erring one is rebuked before all and purged out as a leaven. An Amishman in good standing may receive no favors from an excommunicated person; he may neither buy from nor sell to him, nor may he eat at the same table with the excommunicated person. The ban applies also between husband and wife, who may neither eat at the same table nor sleep in the same bed. The *Bann und Meidung* is used both to protect the individual and to protect the church. An erring member is shunned in order to help him realize the gravity of his sin and his need to return to the church. It is also used as a necessary step in the process of forgiveness, and thus helps the individual deal with guilt. The *Bann und Meidung* serves to protect the church by removing, both from ceremonial and social participation in the community, those individuals who will not follow the *Ordnung*, thus protecting the true believers from disruptive influence and temptations to modify their lifestyle. In some communities, individuals that leave the Old Order Amish to join other Amish churches are put under a limited ban and are no longer shunned forever. These individuals generally maintain kinship ties.

The Amish have an attitude of nurturance for their land, their children, and their people. The Amish nurturing lifestyle is in harmony with nature and functions to keep "the machine out of the garden." Wendel Berry (1978: 7–8) contrasts the exploiter or individual who considers land a commodity with the nurturer, who considers land a trust.

The standard of the exploiter is efficiency; the standard of the nurturer is care. The exploiter's goal is money, profit; the nurturer's goal is health—his land's health, his own, his family's, his community's. . . . Whereas the exploiter asks of a piece of land only how much and how quickly it can be made to produce, the nurturer asks a question that is much more complex and difficult: What is its carrying capacity? (That is: How much can be taken from it without diminishing it? What can it produce *dependably* for an indefinite time?) The exploiter wishes to earn as much as possible by as little work as possible; the nurturer expects, certainly, to have a decent living from his work, but his characteristic wish is to work *as well* as possible. The competence of the exploiter is in organization; that of the nurturer is in order—a human order, that is, that accommodates itself both to other order and to mystery. The exploiter typically serves an institution or organization; the nurturer serves land, household, community, place. The exploiter thinks in terms of numbers, quantities, "hard facts"; the nurturer in terms of character, condition, quality, kind.

The prohibition against electricity holds the Amish workday to the solar day. The Amish home has neither air conditioning nor central heating, yet by modifying their daily routine they manage to live comfortably with the changing seasons, relatively oblivious of energy crises. They do not exploit their environment but care for it. The pea pods are put back on the garden, not thrown down a garbage disposal. There is a human scale to all of Amish life. Within the settlement distances are not too great, social groups are not too big, farms can be managed by a single family, and Amish schools have one or, at the most, two rooms. People know one another and identify with the physical environment in which they worship, live, and work. After a day visiting in a large city, an Amish farmer commented as we turned off the highway onto an unpaved road in his home county, "I know myself around here." He is the very antithesis of alienation.

By exercising a personal and a community discipline that excludes those who will not follow the dictates of the group and that stresses a voluntary commitment to a nurturing life in harmony with nature and socially separated from the outside culture, the Amish have been able to determine to a remarkable extent the style of their lives.

Family Life Cycle and the Socialization Process

The goal of the Amish family is the achievement of eternal life for each member. On an existential level, the goal is to teach children right from wrong, to be socially responsible as defined by the Amish community, to join the Amish church, and to remain faithful in the *Ordnung* until death.

In Amish society, a person passes through a series of six distinct age categories or stages of socialization as he progresses through life. Different behavior is demanded of him at each stage. The stages are: infancy, preschool children, school children, young people, adulthood, and old folks. (For a more detailed treatment of socialization, see Hostetler and Huntington, 1971). Infancy covers the period from birth until the child walks. Children of this age are generally referred to as "babies." Preschool children are referred to as "little children"; they know how to walk but have not yet started school, which they generally enter at age 6 or 7. Schoolchildren are called "scholars" by the Amish. They are fulfilling the eight years of elementary schooling required by the state. They attend either public schools or Amish schools and are between the ages of 6 and 16. Young people are in the period between school (completed at 14 to 16, depending on the state) and marriage. Adults are traditionally married. An unmarried woman, no matter what her age, is referred to as "an older girl." Old folks have all their children married or independent, and they generally live in a "Dawdy House," the grandfather house on the "home place."

Infancy. Babies are enjoyed by the Amish; they are believed to be gentle, responsive, and secure within the home and the Amish community but vulnerable when out in the world. Babies are not scolded or punished, and there is no such thing as a bad baby, although there may be a difficult baby. A baby may be enjoyed without fear of self-pride, for he is a gift from God and not primarily an extension of the parents. A baby who cries is in need of comfort, not discipline. It is believed that a baby can be spoiled by wrong handling, especially by nervous, tense handling, but the resultant irritability is the fault of the environment, not the baby, who remains blameless. Old Order Amish parents give generous attention to their babies' needs, both physical and social. An Amish baby is born into a family and into a community. He is never spoken of as "a little stranger" but is welcome as a "new woodchopper" or a "little dishwasher." Each baby is greeted happily as a contribution to the security of the family and the church.

Childhood. Amish children are taught to respect authority, and respect is shown by obedience. The Amish do not strive for blind obedience but for obedience based on love and on the belief that those in authority have deep concern for one's welfare and know what is best. Most traditional Amish parents teach obedience by being firm and consistent rather than by violent confrontations or single instances of breaking the child's will. The switch is used freely but not harshly. The prevailing attitude is matter-of-fact rather than moralistic in dealing with their children. Not only are children taught to respect and obey those in authority, but they also learn to care for those younger and less able, to share with others, to do what they are taught is right and avoid what is wrong. to enjoy work, and to fulfill their work responsibilities pleasantly.

The parents create a safe environment for their children. They live separated from the world, maintaining the boundary for their children that protects them from malevolent influence. The parent has the responsibility to punish transgressions but also the power to forgive. Punishment is used primarily to ensure the safety of the child: for physical safety ("stay away from that nervous horse"), for cultural safety ("be respectful to older people"), for legal safety ("don't fish without a fishing license"), for moral safety ("be obedient"). Rewards are used to develop the right attitudes in the child: humility, forgiveness, admission of error, sympathy, responsibility, and appreciation of work. Children are motivated primarily by concern for other people and not by fear of punishment.

Although children are primarily the responsibility of their parents, the community plays an important part in their socialization. Families attend church as a unit every other Sunday. The children sit through the long service, learning to be considerate of others, quiet, and patient. Until they are about 9 years old, the girls sit with the mothers or grandmothers, and the boys with their fathers. After the service, the children share in the community meal, and the youngest may nap on a big bed with other babies. The rest of the time the children play freely and vigorously about the house and yard, safe in the presence of many adults who care for them and guide them. A small child who suddenly feels lost will be quickly returned to a family member. Amish children experience the community as being composed of people like their parents, all of whom know them and direct them. They are comfortable and secure within the encompassing community. In many settlements the community also participates in the socialization of children through the Amish "parochial" school, which supports the teaching of the home.

Throughout childhood, Amish children spend the greatest part of their time interacting with family members. Unlike typical suburban schoolchildren, Amish children are usually in a mixed age group rather than isolated with their peers (Bronfenbrenner, 1970:96–102). Amish children's parents and siblings play a central role in their development. Although the Amish generally consider childhood to end with the graduation of the child from the eighth grade or on the sixteenth birthday, they do not feel that their task as parents is even near completion. The desired end product will not be achieved until much later.

Young People.   The age category known by the Amish as "young people" covers the years between 14 or 16 and marriage; it corresponds roughly to adolescence. This is the most individualistic period in the life of an Amishman or Amishwoman and is considered to be the most dangerous. If an individual is to become Amish, he or she must be kept within the Amish community, physically and emotionally, during the crucial adolescent years. Yet at this time the family's control of the young person is somewhat limited, the community's control is informal, and the lure of the world is strongest.

During adolescence the peer group is of supreme importance, for during these years more of the Amish young person's socialization takes place within this group than within the family or the church. If the young person's peer group remains Amish, he or she has a reference point, a buffer, and a support. Even though as an individual or as a member of this Amish peer group he or she transgresses many rules and crosses most of the boundaries between the Amish community and the world, they will eventually return to the church to become a lifelong Amishman or Amishwoman. However, an Amishman or Amishwoman who makes "English" friends and identifies with an alien peer during this time period, even though if well behaved, will probably leave the Amish church never to return.

A certain degree of adolescent rebellion has become institutionalized among the Amish. The Amish child is raised in a carefully protected environment by relatively authoritarian parents. However, during this stage, Amish young persons will make the two most important commitments of their lives: They will decide if and when to join the church and whom to marry. Both of these commitments must be made as an individual, albeit an individual who has the help of God, the concern of parents and the support of the community. In order to make such important decisions, young persons must establish a degree of independence from their family, and to some extent from their community, in order to develop their own identity. This is done in many ways, most of them carefully institutionalized. The family relaxes some of its tight control over young persons. They go to social gatherings of peers rather than having all of their social life with the family. The young persons are learning what it means to be Amish. They may test some of the boundaries of the Amish community, sampling the world by such means as owning a radio, having a photograph taken, attending a movie, and occasionally wearing clothes that are outside the *Ordnung*. As long as these forays into worldliness remain discreet, they are ignored by the parents and the community, for it is believed that young persons should have some idea of the world they are voluntarily rejecting. One of the reasons courtship is secretive is that it is a means of achieving privacy in a closely knit community and within a large family. Young persons are protected by a degree of institutionalized blindness on the part of adults, who thereby give them freedom— within safe boundaries.

The community indirectly counteracts youthful rebelliousness by providing social activities and vocational training for adolescents. Sunday evening singing is an important social event in most Amish settlements. Young people generally begin attending when they have finished day school and are about 16 years old. The family that "has church" has "singing" for the young people in the evening. Generally brothers and sisters go together to the singing, although they frequently return home in couples. In some of the larger settlements there will be Saturday night singing, or the young man may visit his girlfriend in her home. Weddings, wiener roasts, and work bees will provide occasions for the young people to gather.

Proper vocational training is essential if the young person is to become an Amish Christian. Both the young Amishman and young Amishwoman work for a number of different people during these years, learning various acceptable vocational roles and, through their jobs, gaining a knowledge of other Amish families and other Amish settlements, and sometimes even a glimpse of the world by working for "English" people. The skills the Amish need are best learned by doing, and they have worked out an informal community apprentice system that serves the needs of the individual and the culture.

The relative freedom to test the boundaries of the culture, to make mistakes, to become aware of human weakness, counterbalanced by the individual's growing ability to be economically productive, and perhaps an interest in marriage, all function to make him or her think seriously about joining the church. When the young Amishman or women finally makes this commitment in late teens or early twenties, the parents have fulfilled their moral duty to the child, to the church, and to God. However, although in a theological sense they have completed their task as parents, in practice the parent-child relationship continues. Marriage, which even more than baptism is considered the beginning of adulthood, modifies the parent-child relationship but does not basically change it.

Adulthood. Marriage is the beginning of social adulthood, but full adulthood is attained with parenthood. The adult Amish are responsible for the maintenance of their culture. They produce the children, who are expected to become Amish, raise them in such a way that they want to become Amish, and teach them the skills and attitudes that will enable them to remain Amish. The adult Amish watch over the boundaries of their culture, participating in the selective acculturation that is necessary for their survival as "a visible church of God" in twentieth-century America. Economically they must be sufficiently successful to support a large family and to help their children become economically independent after a few years of marriage. The Old Order Amish community is economically self-sufficient, and church members do not accept social security or welfare. Socially they are also self-sufficient, caring for those who are ill and old within the community. The adult Amishman or woman has no set retirement age. Retirement is voluntary, usually gradual, and related to the individual's health and the needs of his family. It generally takes place some time after the youngest child is married and has started to raise a family.

Old Folks. Old folks normally signify their retirement by moving into the grandfather house adjacent to the main farmhouse. This may occur while the grandfather is still young and vigorous, but he moves to a new occupation, such as running a shoe repair shop, in order to free the land for his child. With retirement or semiretirement, the role of the parents is modified but still continues, for the old people remain physically and emotionally close to their children and grandchildren. The young farmer discusses problems of farm management and sales prices with his father; the young mother asks advice about the children. The old folks still engage in the process of helping their youngest children become established economically.

Also, the old people have an increased obligation to attend funerals and to visit the sick and bereaved. When they are ill, members of the community visit them. As long as health permits, old folks spend a considerable amount of time visiting children, nieces, nephews, and friends in different parts of the settlement and in other settlements. They form an important link in the network of informal communication that ties the larger Amish community together. They are often reliable sources of news as well as of local history and of genealogical relationships. They exert a conservative influence as they fulfill their accepted roles of admonishing the young. As they grow older, and perhaps become senile or bedridden, they are still cared for at home, sometimes by one child, often with the children taking turns having them in their homes. With a large number of children available, this responsibility can be more easily shared.

Typically, dying takes place in the home, the person surrounded by family and friends—not in the lonely, impersonal, mechanical environment of a hospital (*The Budget*, August 2, 1973):

> On June 19th she . . . was admitted and put under oxygen. . . . She seemed to be losing out fast, as she had to labor to breathe even with oxygen. On Fri. we pleaded to go home. So arrangements were made with an ambulance to take her home, she being under oxygen all the while. . . . At daybreak in the mornings for the last 3 mornings were her hardest and on the morning at 4:45 of the 26th of June she easily and peacefully faded away.

When death occurs, neighbors and nonrelatives relieve the family of all work responsibility, leaving the relatives free for meditation and conversation with the guests who come to see their departed friend and to talk to the bereaved family. Funerals, especially of elderly people, are large, and often 500 mourners may be present. After burial in an Amish graveyard, the mourners return to the house of the decreased for a meal. With this meal, normal relationships and responsibilities are restored. The family circle has been broken by death, but the strong belief in eternal life indicates that the break is only temporary.

CHANGE AND ADAPTATION

The rapid social changes since the Depression have broken down the isolation of the Amish. Specific threats to their community structure and family organization have been posed by (1) social security, (2) consolidation of elementary and junior high schools, (3) lengthening of the compulsory-attendance period and consequent required high school attendance, (4) conscription, and (5) scarcity of farmland. Minor, more subtle threats are the availability of motorcycles and cars, the cheapness and small size of transistor radios and phonographs, televisions blaring in every store, the ease of travel, and the use of telephones. These are all dangers inherent in our technologically sophisticated mass culture. Technological competition for land use and invasion of farmland also pose problems. In Lancaster County urban uses are pressing hard on land once available for farming. In Ohio, Amish communities have moved because of the intrusion of power plants and the risk that high power transmission lines may be strung across Amish farms, bringing onto Amish family lands noise pollution, corona discharge, the danger of electrical shock, and intrusive personnel who patrol the lines to spray herbicides and perform other maintenance chores. A specific threat to the Amish young people is variants of the Billy Graham type of religious fundamentalism. Fundamentalist radio programs are one of the means for introducing these dissident ideas into the community; local revival meetings are another. The more liberal branches of the Mennonite church also offer a ladder to those who want to climb into "higher" churches step by step, changing their life-style more than their theology.

Social Security

Although these five specific threats to the Amish culture have been somewhat mitigated during the past few years, in every instance certain Amish bore the brunt of the encroachment by the state and paid fines, spent time in prison, and moved to other localities. The Amish do not believe in life insurance or old-age insurance. They live separate from the state, which they will support with taxes but not with their vote or with their lives. They believe that the Christian brotherhood should care for its own, and they are forbidden by the *Ordnung* to accept any form of survivors' insurance. Because they do not and will not accept Social Security payments from the state, they refuse to pay the Social Security tax to the state. After years of conflict, during which some Amish witnessed the sale of their horses and farms at public auction, the Amish were finally granted an exemption from the self-employment Social Security tax. This was a crucial issue for the Amish because both their family and their church structure, with the strong emphasis on social responsibility, would be weakened by reliance on outside funds.

Elementary Schooling

The Amish in many settlements have responded to school consolidation and to rapid changes in the rural American culture by withdrawing further from the mainstream (see Table 18-3). It is not that they want to be more different from their non-Amish neighbors, it is that they do not want

TABLE 18-3. The Growth of Amish Schools in North America: 1965-1994

| Year | Number of | | | |
	States	Schools	Pupils[b]	Teachers
1965	10	150	5,099	174
1970	14[a]	303	9,789	375
1975	17[a]	399	12,037	491
1980	18	490	14,880	640
1985	18	595	17,373	755
1990	17	722	20,499	976
1994	19	846	23,817	1,155

[a]Includes Honduras.
[b]Schools that did not report their number of pupils were estimated to have twenty pupils, and schools that did not report the number of teachers were estimated to have one teacher. Figures for 1994 are used unadjusted from the Blackboard Bulletin.
Source: Huntington (1994).

to change so rapidly; they want to keep the old ways. Large, modern consolidated schools are not suitable agents of socialization for the Amish child. Many of the Amish children still attend public schools. Some of these are rural schools that were not caught in the net of consolidation, some are relatively small village schools, and some are large, sprawling elementary schools. When their children attend public school, the parents attempt to isolate its influence and to counteract the disruption it may cause. Over half of the Amish children attend community schools designed, built, and staffed by members of their own church. In 1994 there were 846 parochial schools with an enrollent of over 23,000 children. These schools were located in nineteen states and in Canada (Blackboard Bulletin, November, 1993).

In the community schools the Amish children learn the three Rs in an environment in which they are protected from the assumptions of twentieth-century America; in which they can learn discipline, humility, simple living, and cooperation. The Amish schools emphasize shared knowledge rather than individual knowledge, the dignity of tradition rather than the importance of progress. The Amish schools do not teach religion, rather a style of living. The school's task is to cooperate with the parents to preserve the faith taught by the parents, for it is the role of the family, not of the school or even the church, to make Amish Christians of the children. The Amish family constellation will change if the school-age children cannot participate in the ongoing work of the home and farm. When the children are removed from the home for many hours each day, as is the case when they must spend long hours on the bus in addition to the hours spent in class, when the school year interferes with the agricultural season, and when the children are physically and ideologically removed from their community, they cannot be taught the skills and attitudes needed to become Amish.

Compulsory High School Attendance

High school attendance is no longer a problem for the Old Order Amish because the Supreme Court ruling of May 15, 1972 protects the religious freedom of the Amish by permitting Amish children who have graduated from the eighth grade to participate in community-based vocational programs in lieu of attending high school. The students spend half a day a week in school under the direction of a teacher and four and a half days working in a modified apprentice system, generally under the direction of their parents. They learn technological skills in a social context as participants in the economy of the community. While working on a family farm, Amish children of high school age learn not only how to perform a task, such as harrowing, but also when to harrow and how to integrate harrowing into all the other work that is required of the vocation "farmer." They also learn wider community work roles by helping in threshing rings and at barn raisings, getting ready for church, and helping care for neighbors' children. Of great importance to the success of the Amish vocational training is the fact that the vocational expectations of the young people coincide with the vocational opportunities available to them.

Conscription

Since the beginning of World War II, the draft has taken young men outside the Amish community at a most vulnerable stage in their development. The I-W program, which provided an alternative to military service, functioned in such a manner that young Amishmen spent two years outside the community, often alone in a city, perhaps wearing non-Amish clothing while at work. These measures separate the young men from community control and to a limited extent made them non-Amish.

The draft was never incorporated into the Amish lifestyle because it interfered with two of the most important rites of passage among the Amish: baptism and marriage. Baptism signifies total commitment to the believing church community, physically and spiritually separated from the world. If the drafted young man were baptized before his alternative service, he could not live physically separated from the world as he was pledged to do. If he were not baptized before his service, he had not committed himself to the church community and so was more vulnerable to outside influence. Was it best for a young man to marry before, during, or after his alternative service? If he went into the world without a wife, he might form friendships with non-Amish girls, and because marriage must be with a coreligionist, such friendships were dangerous. If he had a wife, she helped protect him from worldly influences, but they started their married life with modern conveniences, electricity, and telephones, which were hard to give up when they returned to an Amish way of life. During I-W or alternative service, both the Amishmen and their wives learned non-Amish work patterns, and many received training they could never use on an Amish farm.

The most traditional Amish refused even alternative service when it required them to live in a city or to wear non-Amish garb. As one Amish father explained, "God did not mean for the Amish to take the way of I-W service. It is better for the Amish to go to prison, though it is hard. God is with them there." It is not clear presently whether the draft will once again disrupt the lives of young men. Certainly the Amish community will continue to be affected by the experiences of those young men who have already spent two years outside the protective boundaries of their culture.

Scarcity of Land

The Amish prohibition against contraception, their positive attitude toward high fertility, and their insistence on labor-intensive, diversified family farming as the ideal means of livelihood, coupled with the belief that all one's grown children should settle near the parents (ideally within two miles), places tremendous pressure on farmland in and near Amish communities—even if there are not competing uses for the land. The rate of growth of the Amish community has been increasing while the limits of farmland available are finite. This is especially true for the Lancaster County Amish. They constitute the oldest Amish community in the country, having settled on land along major transportation routes between the expanding urban centers of Philadelphia and Harrisburg. They must compete with factories, shopping centers, and tourism as well as with one another. The Amish in Lancaster have responded to this problem by paying increasingly high prices for their land, subdividing their farms, establishing new communities in other parts of the state (often on poorer farmland), occasionally moving to other Amish communities outside the state, and, less acceptably, leaving the Old Order to join other branches of the church that do not put such a high premium on farming. Very few of the individual families in any state who leave the Amish church are successfully engaged in labor-intensive, general farming at the time they leave. Some Amish young people never join the church, but in Lancaster it is more typical for young Amish to join the church, marry, start a family, and then leave.

In a detailed analysis of the Lancaster Amish population conducted in 1976 (Hostetler, Ericksen, Ericksen, and Huntington, 1977), it was determined that the rate of leaving was not related to a breakdown of family ties but was more closely related to the economic success of the parents, which, because it was accompanied by austere living patterns, contributes to the likelihood of the younger generation becoming established in labor-intensive, family farming (Ericksen, Ericksen, and Hostetler, 1980). Among the Lancaster Amish, heads of households who are farmers are generally more successful economically than those who have other types of employment (except for a few of the self-employed Amish businessmen). Heads of households who are farmers are considered the most successful by their fellow churchmen, for they are able to practice a style of life consistent with Amish values.

Among a sample of Lancaster Amish it was observed that the likelihood of leaving the Old Order Amish was five times as great for children of non-farmers as for children of farmers. This would indicate that there is a connection between the survival and growth of the Amish subculture and the ability of the parents, and to some extent the community, to get their young adults established in farming. Lack of farmland bodes ill for the community. But as it becomes more expensive to get established on a farm, more family heads look for other types of suitable employment. Near Amish and Mennonite settlements, small factories have been built to take advantage of the cheap (nonunion), skilled, reliable labor supply. The trend from farming to nonfarming occupations may have a profound effect on the Amish culture (Kraybill, 1994). The Amish family and Amish patterns of childrearing are built on the concept of shared parental responsibility, on the expectation that both parents work together caring for the farm and the children, that both parents are almost always in the home and available to support one another and to guide and teach their children. For example, family devotions are led by the father, but it is difficult to have these when the father has to punch a timeclock rather than being able to adjust his farm chores to the sleeping patterns of his growing family. The authority patterns within the family change when the father is absent during most of the day. A sick baby or a fussy three-year-old are minor inconveniences when both parents are available. On an Amish farm the boys spend most of the time, when they are awake and not in school, working with or under the direction of their father. In no other occupation can the father so consistently teach, instruct, admonish, and correct his children.

The social structure of the Amish community is based on the availability of brethren and sisters to gather for work bees, barn raisings, daylong weddings, and daylong funerals. The Amish share labor within the family, between families, and among church members whenever there is extra or special work to be done. This combination of mutual aid and social interaction keeps the community strong and of one mind. This interaction can be relatively easily achieved in a church district in which most of the household heads are farmers; it is almost impossible when most of the men work in factories or on construction crews. The traditional Amish culture is dependent on both parents working in the home—that is, being available to each other and to the children and to the community any hour of the day, on any day of the week. Although the Amish are tied to the American market system, their culture mitigates these ties and functions to isolate the Amishman by circumscribing his economic options in such a way that the Amish family-centered culture can be perpetuated both socially and physically.

Other Areas of Change and Adaptation

The *Ordnung* protects the Amish from the encroachment of technology, from a throwaway mentality, and from the overstimulation of the individual (Toffler, 1970). The *Ordnung* further specifically forbids members to have highline electricity, which means that all electrical conveniences, from clothes dryers to vacuum cleaners to toasters, are unavailable. All musical instruments are forbidden, and radios and television sets can come under this prohibition. Telephones connect one with the outside world and "cause women to waste time," because "you can work and talk when you are both in the same room, but neither of you can work while talking on the telephone." In addition, telephones within the home intrude into the family, disrupting meals, work, and conversation.

Cars, and to a lesser degree motorcycles, are threatening because they enable people to travel too far, too fast, and to go beyond the face-to-face community in which everyone is known and everyone is noticed. Movies are forbidden but offer little threat to the community because there is no interest in them; they are too far from the individual's experience and value system to do more than elicit passing curiosity. In many ways the Amish culture is oral rather than literary, and though they have kept out the medium, and along with it the message (McLuhan, 1962), they are not really threatened by the printed word, by radio, or even by television. Consistent with the oral tradition, the Amish stress shared knowledge and the importance of meaningful social interaction. They are so far outside the mainstream of American culture that they have little shared knowledge with average American citizens and little reason to interact socially with them. The area in which they may be the most vulnerable is that of religious fundamentalism, for here the familiarity with the Bible gives a degree of shared knowledge that may open the way for outside influence.

Although the Amish are relatively immune to changes in their worldview and basic thought patterns, they are more open to change in the area of economics. They know they must survive economically in order to survive culturally, but they also believe that it is better to suffer economic and physical hardship than to lose their unique religious orientation. There is more pressure to accept telephones and electricity than to permit radios and movie attendance. Those aspects of the outside culture that can enhance Amish family life and can reinforce community ties and community economic strength are tempting and will continue to be accepted if they can be incorporated without changing the family roles or the social structure and without permitting encroachment of worldly ideas and worldly ways.

During the two hundred and fifty years the Amish have been in America, they have successfully obtained good farmland that would produce high yields on small acreage when cultivated intensively by a large nuclear family. Farms needed to be small and of high quality in order to be worked by one family and to support a relatively dense farming population so that the characteristic social structure, stressing strong kinship and community ties and isolation from the surrounding culture, could be established and maintained. During these two hundred and fifty years the Amish have successfully resisted the lures of mass consumption and mass communication; they have maintained their emphasis on limited gratification and limited consumption, stressing economy, savings, and cash payments. While the urban villagers of Boston argue that money earned should be spent immediately to make daily life more pleasant, because "life is too short for any other way of behavior" (Gans, 1962:187), the Amish argue that "no one would want such a beautiful home here on this earth if they hoped for heavenly home after this time" (*Family Life*, June 1973:11). Life is too short to risk losing one's soul just for comfort or pleasure. "Only one life, t'will soon be past; Only what's done for Christ will last."

The Amish stress on the individual's total commitment to God, thus his responsibility to live according to the Amish *Ordnung*, has enabled the Amish culture to survive, sometimes at tremendous personal expense to the individual. In the early years of their history, some individuals were martyred, and the total group was strengthened by the payment of the few. In recent times certain individuals have lost their farms and savings; they were in a sense economically martyred, and again the total group profited by the payment of the few. The steadfastness of the Amish as individuals finally resulted in changes in the enforcement of various laws—for example, Social Security, high school attendance, noncertified teachers in Amish schools, and alternative forms to military service. The Amish culture will continue to change as it adjusts to economic, technological, and social changes in the surrounding culture, but as long as the Amish are able to maintain their basic cultural figuration, their unique worldview, and their own social structure, they will persist even though the details of their lives change.

REFERENCES

Ausband, Das Ist: Etliche schone christliche Lieder. 1564. 1st ed.

Bainton, Roland H. 1952. *The Reformation of the Sixteenth Century.* Boston: Beacon Press.

Berry, Wendell. 1978. *The Unsettling of America: Culture and Agriculture.* New York: Avon Books.

Blackboard Bulletin. [A monthly published "in the interests of Amish Parochial schools."] Aylmer, Ontario: Pathway Publishing Corporation.

Bronfenbrenner, Urie. 1970. *Two Worlds of Childhood: U.S. and U.S.S.R.* New York: Russell Sage.

The Budget. ["A Weekly Newspaper Serving the Sugarcreek Area and Amish-Mennonite Communities Throughout the Americas."] Sugarcreek, Ohio.

Braght, Thieleman J. van 1951. *The Bloody Theatre or Martyr's Mirror of the Defenseless Christians Who Baptized Only Upon Confession of Faith, and Who Suffered and Died for the Testimony of Jesus, Their Savior, From the Time of Christ to the Year A.D. 1660.* Scottdale, PA: Mennonite Publishing House.

Cross, Harold E. 1967. "Genetic Studies in an Amish Isolate." Ph.D. dissertation, The Johns Hopkins University.

Enders, Trudy, and Curt Stern. 1948. "The Frequency of Twins, Relative to Age of Mothers, in American Populations." *Genetics 35* (May): 263–272.

Ericksen, Eugene P., Julia Ericksen, and John A. Hostetler. 1980. "The Cultivation of the Soil as a Moral Directive: Population Growth, Family Ties, and the Maintenance of Community Among the Old Order Amish," *Rural Sociology, 44:* 49–68.

Ericksen, Julia, and Gary Klein. 1978. "Women's Roles and Family Production Among the Old Order Amish." Paper presented at the National Council of Family Relation, Philadelphia.

Ericksen, Julia, Eugene P. Ericksen, John A. Hostetler, and Gertrude E. Huntington. 1979. "Fertility Patterns and Trends Among the Old Order Amish." *Population Studies, 33*(2): 255–276.

Family Life. [A monthly "dedicated to the promotion of Christian living among the plain people, with special emphasis on the appreciation of our heritage."] Aylmer, Ontario: Pathway Publishing Corporation.

Fisher, John M. 1957. *Descendants and History of Christian Fisher Family.* Privately published by Amos L. Fisher, Route 1, Ronks, PA.

Gans, Herbert J. 1962. *The Urban Villagers.* New York: Free Press.

Hostetler, John A. 1955. "Old World Extinction and New World Survival of the Amish." *Rural Sociology, 20* (September-December): 212–219.

———. 1980. *Amish Society,* 3rd ed. Baltimore, MD: Johns Hopkins Press.

Hostetler, John A., and Gertrude Enders Huntington. 1971. *Children in Amish Society: Socialization and Community Education.* New York: Holt, Rinehart and Winston.

Hostetler, John A., Eugene Ericksen, Julia Ericksen, and Gertrude Huntington. 1977. "Fertility Patterns in an American Isolate Subculture." Final report. NICHD grant no. HD-08137–01A1.

Huntington, Gertrude Enders. 1956. "Dove at the Window: A Study of an Old Order Amish Community in Ohio." Ph.D. dissertation, Yale University.

Huntington, G. E. 1994. "Persistence and Change in Amish Education," in Donald Kraybill and Marc Olshan (Eds.), *The Amish Struggle with Modernity.* Hanover, NH: University Press of New England.

Kraybill, D. B., and M. A. Olshan (Eds.). 1994. *The Amish Struggle with Modernity.* Hanover, NH: University Press of New England.

Littell, Franklin H. 1964. *The Origins of Sectarian Protestantism.* New York: Macmillan.

Luthy, David. 1973. "The Amish in Europe." *Family Life* (March):10–14.

———. 1974. "Old Order Amish Settlements in 1974." *Family Life* (December): 13–16.

———. (1992). "Amish Settlements Across America: 1991." *Family Life* (April): 19–24.

———. (1994). "Amish Migration Patterns: 1972–1992," in Donald Kraybill and Marc Olshan (Eds.), *The Amish Struggle with Modernity.* Hanover, NH: University Press of New England.

Marx, Leo. 1964. *The Machine in the Garden: Technology and the Pastoral Ideal in America.* New York: Oxford University Press.

McLuhan, Marshall. 1962. *The Gutenberg Galaxy.* Toronto: University of Toronto Press.

Mennonite Encyclopedia. 1955. Scottdale, PA: Mennonite Publishing House. Newton, KS: Mennonite Publication Office. Hillsboro, KS: Mennonite Brethren Publishing House.

Ohio Amish Directory. Millersburg, Ohio.

Raber, J. A. (Ed.). 1970, 1973, 1980. *Der Neue Amerikanische Calendar.* Baltic, OH.

Raber, B. J. (Ed.). 1993. *The New American Almanac.* Gordonville, PA: Gordonville Print Shop.

Schwartz, Hillell. 1973. "Early Anabaptist Ideas About the Nature of Children." *Mennonite Quarterly Review, 47* (April): 102–114.

Simons, Menno. 1956. *The Complete Writings of Menno Simons.* Scottdale, PA: Herald Press.

Smith, C. Henry. 1920. *The Mennonites: A Brief History of Their Origin and Later Development in Both Europe and America.* Berne, IN: Mennonite Book Concern.

Toffler, Alvin. 1970. *Future Shock.* New York: Random House.

Umble, John. 1949. "Factors Explaining the Disintegration of Mennonite Communities." *Proceedings of the Seventh Annual Conference on Mennonite Cultural Problems.* North Newton, KS: Bethel College. Published under the auspices of the Council of Mennonite and Affiliated Colleges.

Recommended Films

The Amish: A People of Preservation. John L. Ruth, producer; Burton Buller, cinematographer; John A. Hostetler, consultant. Available through *Encyclopedia Britannica*, 425 N. Michigan Ave., Chicago, IL 60611, in 28–minute and 53–minute versions.

19

The Mormon Family

Bruce L. Campbell
Eugene E. Campbell

HISTORICAL BACKGROUND

Emergence of the Mormons as a Minority Group

Mormonism has its roots in an atmosphere of supernaturalism, millennialism,[1] and religious revivalism that characterized the "Burned-Over" district of western New York during the first decades of the nineteenth century.[2] From the Pilgrims onward, America, with relative religious freedom and readily available land, has historically nurtured a variety of transplanted European Christian-Utopian societies, and these same elements proved vital in the emergence of Mormonism as an American-born religious movement.[3] Mormons regard this constellation of social, political, spiritual, and geographical elements as proof of a divine plan to provide a fertile milieu for the restoration of the Gospel of Jesus Christ during this period, these "latter days."

The early history of Mormonism can be described as a cycle in which the Mormons created a new settlement, prospered, clashed with their non-Mormon neighbors, and then were forced to move and create a new settlement. Each new location was in turn proclaimed a "new Zion"—a divinely chosen spot for the gathering of the faithful from all the world. This pattern was repeated in New York, Ohio, Missouri, and Illinois before

[1] A belief that Christ would soon establish an earthly kingdom over which He would reign for a thousand years.

[2] Allen and Leonard (1976:11) describe the Burned-Over district of western New York as being intensely affected by a religious awakening "characterized by circuit-riding preachers, fiery tongued evangelists, new-grass roots religious movements, fervent emotionalism, and the manifestations of certain physical excesses that demonstrated to new converts divine acceptance."

[3] Harold Bloom, the Sterling Professor of Humanities at Yale University, proclaims Mormons and Southern Baptists models of what he (Bloom, 1992) theorizes is the "American Religion."

they were driven by mobs out of the United States, across the western prairies, through the Rocky Mountains to the valley of the Great Salt Lake, then in Mexican territory. This cycle played out one last time during the protracted battle with the federal government over the Mormon practice of polygamy.[4]

The epic journey from Nauvoo, Illinois, through more than 1,500 miles of untamed wilderness to the Great Basin was a defining moment in Mormon history. First it solidified their identification with the "House of Israel," which had begun in the Kirkland, Ohio era and continued as the church grew (Shipps, 1994). Calling themselves the "Camp of Israel," the Mormons drew an analogy between their trek through the American West and the tempering march of the "Children of Israel" out of Egypt through the desert and into the "Promised Land." Moreover, this journey helped create among Mormons a sense of being a new chosen people; the descendants of those who made their own sacred trip to a new Zion. The courage, faith, and sacrifice demonstrated by the Mormon pioneers provided a standard for new generations of believers.

Perhaps the ultimate standard of sacrifice was set by those pioneers, about three thousand strong, who pulled handcarts from Iowa to Utah.[5] From 1856 through 1860, immigrants from western and northern Europe crossed the Atlantic in voyages ranging from thirty-eight to sixty-five days in length. Then they traveled by train to Iowa City, then to Salt Lake City by handcart. This proved to be an arduous task in the best of circumstances, but tragedy struck the last two parties in 1856. They left Iowa late in the season only to be overtaken by an early October blizzard on the high plains of west-central Wyoming. Many died before relief reached them from the Saints in Salt Lake City. One woman whose husband died from exposure noted in her diary (Hafen and Hafen, 1960:111–112):

> I will not attempt to describe my feelings at finding myself thus left a widow with three children, under such excruciating circumstances. I cannot do it. But I believe the Recording Angel has inscribe in the archives above, and that my suffering for the Gospel's sake will be sanctified unto me for my good.

While most Mormon pioneers did not meet the same fate as this woman, her continued faith in the face of such hardship provides an example with which present-day Mormons compare their daily hardships.

[4]Social scientists usually use the term *polygamy* to refer to all plural marriage patterns, while *polygyny* is the marriage of one man to plural wives, and *polyandry* is the marriage of several men to one wife. However, the Mormons themselves use the term *polygamy* to describe their marriage practice, and subsequent social scientists also employ the term *polygamy* in their analysis of Mormon plural marriage. We will use the word *polygamy* throughout this chapter even though it is technically incorrect.

[5]These events are described in depth by LeRoy and Ann Hafen in *Handcarts to Zion*, 1960.

In the process of taming their wild, arid land, the teachings of Joseph Smith, the Mormon prophet, were translated by Brigham Young and his followers into religious, social, political, and economic systems, forming the basis of Mormonism as we know it today. For the remaining decades of the nineteenth century, somewhat protected by their geographical isolation from the rest of the United States, the Mormons colonized much of the intermountain West, developing from a "near sect" to a "near nation" (O'Dea, 1957).

Having gradually shed many of the temporal aspects of kingdom building, Mormonism seems to have evolved from an isolated "near nation" into a major world religion (Stark, 1984). Once labeled an outcast sect, there is now speculation that the Church of Jesus Christ of Latter-Day Saints should be considered a mainline religion (Roof and McKinney, 1987; DePillis, 1991; Cornwall, 1991).

Launching an American Religion

Joseph Smith, Jr., the Mormon prophet born in 1805, said he had a series of heavenly visions, beginning in about 1820, near Palmyra, New York. According to the Prophet Joseph, as his followers came to call him, in the first vision God the Father and His Son, Jesus Christ, appeared to him and answered his prayer concerning which church he should join. Jesus instructed him to join none of them because His true church was no longer on the earth.

Other visions revealed the location of the Golden Plates, buried by an ancient American prophet (Mormon by name), on which were written the records and religious experiences of ancient inhabitants of America, including an appearance to His followers in the Americas by the resurrected Jesus Christ. After obtaining the Golden Plates and some spectaclelike instruments to aid in translating them, Joseph Smith with the help of several scribes produced the Book of Mormon, an inspired translation of these plates. Mormons accept this book as an important second witness to the divinity of Jesus Christ, and when it was published in 1830 it became an effective missionary tool in the hands of the young prophet. In what has come to be called the Articles of Faith, Joseph Smith wrote in 1842, "We believe the Bible to be the Word of God as far as it is translated correctly; we also believe the Book of Mormon to be the Word of God." Today the Book of Mormon continues to be an effective missionary tool (*Church News*, 1996) and a peculiar feature of Mormon belief.

Smith also claimed to have received heavenly instructions and authority to reestablish the true, restored Church of Christ, which he organized in 1830 at Fayette, New York. In 1838, the phrase "Latter-Day Saints" was added, reflecting the belief that these were the last days before Jesus would return and establish His Kingdom."[6] Thus Mormonism began with a strong eschatological and millennial emphasis.[7]

While these claims may seem heretical to many, the claim to charismatic authority[8]—revelations through a living prophet and a new scripture—seemed to satisfy the religious needs of those disoriented by the religious diversity that characterized nineteenth-century America. The Prophet also preached a brand of communitarianism that may have been responsive to the economic hopes of his followers.

As Mormonism began to grow, it attracted enemies, and for several decades the Mormons and their foes, including at times the government of the United States, clashed. The Mormon assumption that Jesus would someday establish this earthly kingdom was the basis for their high internal and social cohesion. Mormons believed they were chosen to be instrumental in the imminent establishment of Christ's Kingdom, so they often approached their tasks with fanatical religious zeal. Convinced they were engaged in the work of the Lord, many Mormons were willing to make great personal sacrifices to build the Kingdom of God. When building the kingdom of God, no action is secular: Building a house, building a temple, plowing a field, cooking a meal, raising children, it does not matter, because every act builds the kingdom, every act is sacred.

This spirit of cooperation, sacrifice, and religious fervor was fundamental to their success as community builders, but it was also threatening to their more individualistically oriented neighbors on the sparsely settled American frontier (Hill, 1978). Conflict was inevitable, and in Missouri and Illinois Mormons and non-Mormon differences escalated to armed conflict. Anti-Mormon mobs (sometimes including elements of the state militia) attacked Mormon settlements—burning homes, murdering religious leaders, raping Mormon women, and threatening the population with death and destruction if they did not change or leave. In 1838, Governor Boggs of Missouri issued an "Order of Extermination" demanding that Mormons be exterminated or driven from the state for the public good. Mormons felt that government leaders at the state and national level acquiesced in these crimes.

In June 1844, a series of events led to Joseph Smith's arrest at Nauvoo, Illinois, then the church's headquarters. Subsequently, Joseph and his broth-

---

[6]The official name of the Mormon Church: The Church of Jesus Christ of Latter-day Saints.

[7]Eschatology is the doctrine of the last days in a two-stage view of history. This evil age will be followed by a holy age in which Christ will reign on earth.

[8]Weber (1968) describes charismatic authority as outside and antithetical to traditional authority. He argues that acceptance by one's followers is the only legitimization of charismatic authority. If the leader's personal charisma is rejected, he no longer has any powers. A second issue is the charismatic leader's duty to accept his own personal "gift of grace," or calling. Also, it is the duty of his disciples to follow. They can no more escape their duty to follow than the leader can to lead.

er Hyrum were murdered while incarcerated at nearby Carthage, Illinois. Governor Ford of Illinois tried to prevent this mob action, but Mormons perceived governmental contrivance in the plot to murder their beloved leader.

After the death of Joseph Smith, Mormon leaders concluded that they could not rely on the protections guaranteed by the Constitution and decided to leave the United States to settle somewhere in the Rocky Mountains where they would be free to practice their social and religious beliefs, including polygamy. This was a fateful decision: If they remained in Illinois, either extermination or gradual assimilation seemed their likely end. In the West, however, they were able to develop over several decades unique social institutions, relatively free from outside influence. As a result, they became a peculiar people and an important ethnic group.

In February 1846, after continued mob action and in the brutal cold, the Mormons began their trek west. An advanced pioneer company completed its journey to the valley of the Great Salt Lake on July 24, 1847 and established the initial colony of their Great Basin kingdom in what was then Mexican territory, which was ceded to America in the treaty with Mexico in February, 1848.[9]

Brigham Young and the other leaders were effective colonizers; within ten years, approximately one hundred towns had been established in Utah with outlying colonies in California, Nevada, Idaho, and Wyoming. Missionary work continued in many parts of the world, and a steady stream of converts, mainly from the British Isles and northern Europe, poured into the Great Basin, resulting in expanding colonization. By the time of Brigham Young's death in 1877, approximately 300 colonies had been established, primarily in Utah, Idaho, and Arizona.

There were many differences between the Mormons and the other Americans that might have been ignored if gold had not been discovered in California. Chosen for its isolation and apparent desolation, Salt Lake Valley was paradoxically located on the best route to the gold fields of California. Mormon theocratic political power apparently threatened federal control of the Utah territory and hence the route to California, so for several decades the government attempted to alter Mormon social, economic, and political institutions. The Mormons resisted and a period of conflict ensued. Many have concluded that Federal authorities used the Mormon practice of plural marriage as a means of diminishing Mormon political power.[10] Congress passed

[9]Approximately 38 percent of the Mormons who moved from Nauvoo to Utah from 1846 to 1850 were British-born converts to the church (May, 1983). Perhaps this substantial proportion of foreign-born membership helps account for some of the anti-Mormon sentiment among non-Mormons, including political and national leaders.

[10]No doubt many Christian Americans were appalled by the practice of polygamy. It was widely discussed and deplored in the United States, and some thought it would die a natural death like slavery because it was not economically viable. Perhaps, however, federal authorities focused their attack on Mormon polygamy as they later did on slavery because it presented an easier, more emotional target than political or economic practices.

laws making the practice of polygamy in the territories illegal and disenfranchising Mormons who supported it. The church was even disincorporated as legal institution. In 1858, a federally appointed governor assumed political office in Utah, and later that year an occupying army from the United States entered the territory. The Mormons left their homes rather than submit to the occupation. In June of that year, the Saints returned to their homes. Arrington (1958:194) describes this event as follows.

> A decade and more of achievement and social independence, the face of hostile nature and hostile humanity, had ended in poverty and disappointment. The picture of 30,000 pioneers trudging back to their hard-won homes, farms and orchards, with their skimpy and ragged suits and dresses, driving their pigs and family cows, to the accompaniment of jeers from the "cream of United States Army" would live long in the hearts and minds of the pioneer leaders.

The years of conflict and isolation resulted in a mutual feeling of distrust that still reverberates through the political climate of Utah. But the church capitulated in 1890, ending forty years of legal struggles with the government. Presidential amnesty followed, but it was many years before Mormons were regarded as loyal citizens. Mormons faced a political dilemma. They loved the Constitution and were loyal to the principles of the United States, but they felt that state and federal officials had deprived them of constitutional rights to practice their religion freely. Today many Mormons seem to solve this problem by adopting conservative, sometimes ultraconservative, political ideals that allow them to love and support America while they oppose a strong federal government.

Thus the first defining event of Mormonism is a history of persecution and conflict resulting in an epic journey from the edge of civilization into the wilderness of the American West, where they developed a sense of peoplehood. As Timothy Smith (1978) claims, a migratory experience is a theologizing experience, giving a peoplehood unity to those who participated in it. This sense of peoplehood was rapidly enhanced by their isolation, which developed into an actual web of kinship (Shipps, 1994).

THE MORMON FAMILY—HISTORICAL DEVELOPMENTS

A second defining element of the Mormon subculture is found in their practice of polygamy. It has been asserted that all utopian movements have experimented with the family unit. Though Mormonism was utopian in spirit, as various experiments in communal living testify, it did not begin with a fully developed theoretical or theological blueprint for changing the family. In fact, the Mormon practice of polygamy and the subsequent emphasis on the family as a divine unit did not appear until the movement was well underway.

However, plural marriage was related to further persecution and isolation combined with unique perceptions of the role of the family in salvation and the organization of heaven.

There was nothing especially distinctive about early Mormon families. They tended to be large, closely knit, and hardworking, and they came primarily from towns and cities rather than the frontier, as has often been assumed. A considerable number of the important leaders in the church came from New England, including the Smiths, Brigham Young, Heber C. Kimball, and Wilford Woodruff. Most were of the working class: skilled and unskilled laborers. A few were ministers or doctors.

The duty to gather to Zion and the unpopularity of the church often separated new converts from their families. Many sought to replace such ties within the developing structure of the church. By the middle of the Nauvoo period (1839–1846), the family was welded to the core Mormon theology, involving concepts of (1) the eternal family, (2) celestial marriage, and eventually (3) polygamous marriage. While all are important theologically, it was the practice of plural marriage that had the most dramatic impact on the growing church and its unique family-centered theology. Together they form the basis for the pronatal attitudes of Mormons and their high fertility rates at the end of the twentieth century.

The Eternal Family

Many religions are pro-family, but Mormons preach that the Kingdom of God is composed of eternal family relationships. Eternal life with God is organized around family units. Their high fertility levels and strongly held pronatalist views are deeply rooted in this belief system.

Mormons believe that God is literal Father of spirit beings in the same sense that earthly fathers are the procreators of physical bodies. They teach that there are billions of spirit children of God who are awaiting their chance to come to earth to gain bodies to become more like God. Many Mormons assume that through their faith and works, the spirit children of God earn the right to come to certain earthly homes and that being born into a good Mormon family represents the best placement possible. Thus marrying and having a large family are the quintessence of obedience to God's plan of Eternal Progression.

Celestial Marriage

In the process of becoming a god, a man must enter into a "new and everlasting covenant of marriage" by which he and his wife or wives will be married for all eternity and will have the privilege and duty of procreating spirit children throughout eternity even as God procreated us. Mormons call this "celestial marriage," and only faithful members of the church can gain authorization from priesthood leaders to enter the sacred temples built for solemnizing such ordinances are so married.

The Extended Family

According to Mormon theology, the organizational structure of heaven is the extended family kinship network. Closely tied to this concept is the Mormon practice of extending and unifying one's family through sealing ordinances in the temple for members of the family who did not have the opportunity to embrace the Gospel during their lifetime. Because most of the human race is believed to have lived and died without knowledge of the "true" church, Mormons are taught that it is their obligation to seek out the names of their dead ancestors and to act as proxy for them by going to the temple and experiencing baptism and other sacred ordinances in the name of deceased relatives. This belief has resulted in the building many temples in various parts of the world and the development of one of the greatest and most extensive genealogical library systems in the world. It has also resulted in extended family organizations for the promotion of genealogical research and family cohesion.

The Polygamous Family

The concept of eternal marriage was closely tied to the practice of polygamy. The practice was begun secretly by Joseph Smith and other church leaders as early as 1842 and was based on the notion that because all things were being restored in the "latter days," polygamy, which had been practiced by some Old Testament prophets, was also being reinstituted among only the most faithful (Smith, 1994). Recently, George D. Smith (1994) has made a detailed study of polygamy during the Nauvoo era (1841–1846) in which he describes in detail the origins and extent of polygamy before the trek west began. He presents ample evidence that Joseph Smith married a number of women before he was killed in 1844 and that Brigham Young and other leaders continued and enlarged the practice.

Because plural marriage in Nauvoo was clandestine, the church leaders denied its existence on several occasions when asked about it. As late as 1850, representatives of the church in foreign lands continued to deny the doctrine and implementation of polygamy. However, once the Mormons left Nauvoo for their "Promised Land" in the west, the practice became apparent to the membership of the church. However, it was not until they were established in Utah (1852) that plural marriage was publicly announced and defended (Allen and Leonard, 1976).

Some leaders in Nauvoo, including Emma Smith, the Prophet's legal wife, refused to accept plural marriage as being inspired by God and asserted that Joseph Smith was a "fallen prophet" (Smith, 1994; Newell and Avery,

1984). Opposition to polygamy was one of the reasons for the founding of the Reorganized Church of Jesus Christ of Latter-day Saints in 1860. Claiming the Prophet's mantle by right of blessing and lineage, the Reorganized Church formed around his widow and children, who represented one of the major challenges to the charismatic authority of the Mormon Church (Newell and Avery, 1984).[11]

Polygamy as a Practice: Demographics

Perhaps more than anything else, the Mormon experiment with polygamy is responsible for the special attention paid to them as an interesting and significant ethnic group. For decades, Mormons were perceived as a strange, even exotic quasi-Christian sect located on the fringe of civilized society. In 1872, Fanny Stenhouse published *Exposé of Polygamy in Utah: A Lady's Life Among the Mormons*, and Elizabeth Kane's account of family life in Utah, *Twelve Mormon Homes*, also suggests the interest in polygamous Utah from outside.

Studies indicate that most polygamists married only one extra wife, while a few took four wives (Ivins 1956; Smith and Kunz 1976). Brigham Young probably had at least twenty-seven wives, among sixteen of whom he had fifty-six children. Others had more, but there were so many different arrangements that the term "wife" requires definition before accurate totals can be determined.

Foreign-born men and women were more likely to marry polygamously than American-born Mormons (Smith and Kunz, 1980). There is some evidence that in the heavily Scandinavian sections of Utah there were more women than men, suggesting foreign-born women as a likely source of second and third wives (Mulder, 1975). However, the pool of women eligible to become extra wives was created by allowing younger women to marry older men, but not supporting plural marriage for men until they were more economically established and of course already married. The number of males in the 30–39 age group was significantly smaller than the number of available females in the 20–29 age group (Smith and Kunz, 1976).

However, perhaps nothing illustrates the profound Mormon ambivalence toward polygamy than the estimates of the number of members who lived this doctrine, often referred to during this era as the Principle (Kunz, 1980 p. 61): "Perhaps the most quoted estimate of the incidence of Latter-day Saint polygamy is 2 percent, a figure often defensively cited by apologists who

---

[11]Some members of the Reorganized Church (RLDS) labeled those who followed Brigham Young west as Brighamites, implying that the RLDS were the true inheritors of Joseph's powers as a Prophet of God. This was not the only challenge for the mantle of the Prophet. Sidney Rigdon, an early associate of Joseph Smith, claimed this right as did James Strang. Neither was ultimately successful.

timidly indicate that 'after all, only about 2 percent of the males practiced polygamy.' " The bulk of the scholarly evidence indicated that 8 to 10 percent is a more accurate figure (Smith and Kunz, 1976; Arrington 1958; Anderson 1942). However, during the so-called Reformation that gripped Mormons from 1856 to 1858, the percentage marrying extra wives must have been much higher. Ivins (1956:) notes that "as one of the fruits of the 'Reformation,' plural marriages skyrocketed to a height not before approached and never again to be reached." A letter from Wilford Woodruf to George A. Smith—two prominent church leaders—dated April 1, 1857 illuminates this trend:

> We have had a great reformation this winter; some of the fruits are: all have confessed their sins either great or small, restored their stolen property; all have been baptized from the presidency down; all are trying to pay their tithing and nearly all are trying to get wives until there is hardly a girl 14 years old in Utah, but what is married, or just going to be. President Young has hardly time to eat, drink or sleep in consequence of marrying the people.

It is significant to recognize that Mormons of this era apparently considered plural marriage as a religious duty parallel to baptism, honesty, and paying tithing. They saw it as a sin of omission if a man avoided taking an extra wife. Other estimates of the percentage of Mormons living in polygamy vary in their samples and methods of determining just who was in a plural union. Bean and others (1990) found only 9 percent of women married to polygamous husbands in one age cohort, but in another cohort 27 to 31 percent lived on a polygamous union sometime during their life. Cornwall and others (1993) carefully examined records of the wards in the Salt Lake City area in 1860 and found that three out of five married women living in these wards were in polygamous marriages. Perhaps we will never know the exact percentage of Mormons directly involved in polygamous marriages, but it is clear from the record that substantial numbers were involved and that in some locations it was the dominant form of marriage.[12]

From 1850 to 1890, the "Principle," as Mormons referred to plural marriage, was a core belief and practice of the Mormon religion. Church leaders tended to have several wives and admonished others to follow their example (Quinn, 1973). The following quote from Heber C. Kimball (1858:35), a prominent church official, illustrates the claims made in support of polygamy.

> I would not be afraid to promise a man who is sixty years of age, if he will take the counsel of brother Brigham and his brethren, that he will renew his age. I

---

[12]The difficulty in determining what percentage of Mormons were involved in polygamy demonstrates the importance of understanding how statistics are calculated. The population, sample and definition of categories can cause the statistics to vary enormously.

have noticed that a man who has but one wife, and is inclined to that doctrine, soon begins to wither and dry up, while a man who goes into plurality looks fresh, young and sprightly. Why is this? Because God loves that man, and because he honors His work and word. Some of you may not believe this; but I not only believe it—I know it. For a man of God to be confined to one woman is small business; for it is as much as we do now to keep up under the burdens we have to carry; and I do not know what we should do if we had only one wife apiece.

As pressures from the federal government increased, Mormon leaders continued to defend plural marriage, with many of them (1,500–2,000) eventually going to jail or underground in support of the Principle (Allen and Leonard, 1976; Cannon 1978). Only when it became clear that continuing polygamy would result in the total destruction of Mormonism did President Wilford Woodruff issue the "Manifesto" in 1890, accepted as a revelation, it ended the practice of polygamy. The practice, however, has never been renounced as a doctrine.

The Mormon church now opposes living in plural marriages although for those already married in plural marriages at the time, the manifesto created an ambiguous situation. Some men ended all contact with their plural wives, while others stopped having sexual relations with their extra wives but continued to support them financially. Many men including, President Joseph F. Smith, continued to live with their wives but took no new ones after 1890.

However, certain persons felt that the manifesto was not God's will but an example of political expediency, and they determined to keep the practice alive even though it meant excommunication from the church. Some claimed that church officials came to them in secret and called on them to carry on the practice of polygamy (Quinn, 1985). As a result, on the fringe of the Mormon subculture some men still marry plural wives, but because of the clandestine nature of their operation there is little reliable information on their marriage and family practices (Driggs, 1991). It is estimated that several thousand people are involved in polygamy in Utah and neighboring states today (Kunz 1980).

Plural marriage left its mark on the church. Those who have polygamous ancestors are often proud of this fact and see it as a mark of honor and loyalty. This custom also seems to have increased the family orientation of the subculture and made the Mormon religion more family focused than most. However there remains some bitterness in families that can also be traced to this practice.

During perhaps half its existence, Mormon polygamy was conducted in secret, shielding the participants from the public scrutiny usually required to ensure conformity to community norms or standards (Brodie, 1971; Quinn, 1985; Savage, 1993). Mormons lacked experience with polygamous practices, and while they may have been groping toward some generally accepted norms (Young, 1954; Embry and Bradley, 1985), pressure from the federal government and the brief duration of the custom made the development of a mature system of norms governing plural marriage problematic. As a result, regulations delimiting courtship practices, marital interaction, economic cooperation, household arrangements, division of labor, intimate relationships, and inheritance—to mention only a few issues—were not well developed.

Divorce in Polygamous Society

While it is difficult to determine the exact divorce rate among Mormon polygamists, Campbell and Campbell (1978) claim that over 2,000 divorces were granted to polygamists from 1847 through 1890. Quinn (1973) indicates that less than one in five marriages of the church leaders he studied ended in broken marriages, but approximately one-half of the leaders were divorced or separated from at least one wife. Brigham Young (1858:15) was alarmed enough by the number of divorces occurring to declare:

> It is not right for the brethren to divorce their wives, the way they do. I am determined that if men don't stop divorcing their wives, I shall stop sealing [marrying]. Men shall not abuse the gifts of God and the privileges the way they are doing. Nobody can say I have any interest in the matter, for I charge nothing for the sealings [marriages], but I do charge for the divorcing. I want the brethren to stop divorcing their wives for it is not right.

However, the divorce rate alone does not document the level of anomie in the system. For example, in a general conference in October 1861, Brigham Young is reported to have declared:

> Also there was another way in which a woman could leave a man—if the woman preferred a man higher in authority and he is willing to take her and her husband gives up. There is no bill of divorce required in [this] case it's right in the sight of God.

Such exchanges of mates did occur, although sometimes the woman lived with her legal husband and was sealed to a church leader for eternity only with the expectation that she would achieve exaltation through eternal marriage to a more faithful man than her own mortal husband (Smith, 1984; Young, 1954). The record is replete with unusual marital unions from the inception of plural marriage until its demise. Limits and sanctions for polygamous marriage seemed lacking.

MORMONISM TRANSFORMED

Over the last century, Mormonism has been transformed from a "marginal, utopian, socially despised, and exclusive movement to an increasing prosperous, socially respectable, and politically conservative organization of international scope" (Shepherd and Shepherd, 1984a:138). Yet, at the end of the nineteenth century, their difficulties seemed insurmountable. They were being forced to abandon some of their most characteristic patterns—polygamy and building the earthly Kingdom of God, for example—at a time when their physical isolation was ending. These fundamental changes threatened this unique religious movement. Assimilation or extinction seemed likely. Nevertheless, today Mormonism is thriving. It is probably the most rapidly growing church in America (Stark, 1984), and Mormons are widely lauded for their health habits, strong families, religious devotion, and commitment to the work ethic (Stathis and Lythgoe, 1977). They have become the very model of conservative respectability while maintaining many of their unique beliefs and customs.

To succeed, all religions change to some degree to "accommodate to consumer preferences of a modern society," and Mormonism does not seem to be an exception (Shepherd and Shepherd, 1984). It certainly is not the same church as it was in the nineteenth century. A national survey commissioned by the church showed Mormon leaders that most Americans do not know much about the Bible and are not interested in denominational differences, but they are interested in happiness and family life; church public-relations efforts and missionary themes were altered accordingly (Lythgoe, 1977). Shipps (1978:776) observes:

> A change in emphasis has occurred in Mormonism during the past few decades. Now the family unit rather than the priesthood quorum is the most important organization in the Church, and support for families is the central thrust of today's church program. The local ward [parish] is a community of families; ward activities . . . are planned to engender family solidarity. Home teaching and church welfare programs provide mutual support. Genealogy serves to tie in the family from past time and stress on the eternal marriage covenant takes the family into the distant future. Temple ordinances then sanctify family relations so that the entire Mormon experience can be said to uphold the integrity of the LDS family. Because the missionary message is also built on what the Church can do for families, conversion is often a family affair, and every LDS ward seems filled with new families being "fellowshipped" into Mormonism.

An increased emphasis on the family appears to have been the vehicle though which Mormonism made its transformation during the last one hundred years—not the plural marriage that made it so notorious, but a variation of the modern American family, however. As Shipps has indicated, religion and family life are integrated at many levels in Mormonism: The success of one is tied to the success of the other. However, many other churches have also stressed the family, so whether this family focus of modern Mormonism will make it different enough to preserve the peculiar Mormon identity is not clear.

Given past persecutions and their somewhat marginal status in society, it may not be surprising that Mormons have attempted to adjust to twentieth-century America by overcompensation—not just by being good citizens, but superpatriots. Because their family life must be demonstrably superior, they have adopted middle class norms and enshrined the middle class family. Any research findings of weakness or even averageness are often perceived as an attack on them and their church.

THE MODERN MORMON FAMILY

In 1988, a prominent professor at Brigham Young University in 1988, Heaton, characterized the unique qualities of the modern Mormon family by the four Cs; chastity, conjugality, children, and chauvinism. Data drawn from a large national sample (National Survey of Families and Households) supported these characterizations but also revealed that in many ways Mormons are much like other Americans (Heaton, Goodman, and Holman 1994). According to this survey, Mormons resemble most Americans in marital inter-action, evaluations of fairness, time spent with children, socialization, disci-pline, evaluation of marital roles, disagreement, conflict, and interaction with kin. Perhaps Mormons are unique in (1) the level of family-church interface, and (2) their attitudes about family life. It may be that it is not so much what Mormons do (or don't do) as what they believe that makes them peculiar.

Demographic Characteristics

Fertility, Contraception, and Abortion. Perhaps no area of Mormon family life has received more serious scrutiny by social scientists than Mormon fertility patterns. Mormons are proud of their large families and are willing to have this aspect of their lives studied. Their focus on the eter-nal family has lead them to become leaders in genealogical research, result-ing in one of the most significant genealogical research networks in the world. These records have become a valuable resource for researchers interested in various aspects of Mormon family life including fertility pat-terns (Skolnick et al., 1978; Bean, Mineau, and Anderson, 1983; Anderson and Emigh, 1989).

The ideal is to have large families. Mormons take the injunction to mul-tiply and replenish the earth very literally and seriously. They tend to want and have more children than other Americans, including Roman Catholics (Thorton, 1979; Heaton, Goodman, and Holman 1994; Heaton 1992b). On the other hand, all surveys indicate a declining birthrate among Mormons (Bush, 1976; Hastings et al., 1972; Skolnick et al., 1978; Wise and Condie, 1975; Bowers and Hastings, 1970).

It appears that the forces of urbanization and industrialization as well as the cultural values and customs will continue to influence Mormon fertility rates. However, Thorton (1979) concluded that at least in the United States, if the historical trends were to continue, it would be at least 150 years before Mormon and non-Mormon birth rates would converge. As of now, Mormon birth rates are about 50 percent higher than the national rate (Heaton and Calkins, 1983).

There are excellent reviews of the position of the Mormon church on birth control and family size (Hastings et al., 1972; Bush, 1976) that clearly show church opposition to birth control, voluntary sterilization and abortion. However, Mormons are about as likely to use modern contraceptive methods to control births as the general population (Heaton and Calkins, 1983). Mormons seem to want children early in marriage because about half of them do not use contraceptives until after the birth of their first child (Heaton, 1987). They then use contraception to space rather than limit their families. Family income and higher levels of education are also associated with increased fertility among Mormons as opposed to other groups. Heaton differentiates Mormon positive pronatalism—a desire for more children—with negative pronatalism founded on religious or ethical sanctions against the use of contraceptives (1987).

The Mormon church opposes abortion but is not absolute in its prohibition. The church takes no official position on when life begins during pregnancy (or at birth). The church accepts the necessity of abortion in some instances such as rape, incest, or to protect the life or health of the woman (Corporation of the First Presidency of the Church of Jesus Christ of Latter-Day Saints, 1983. Crapo (1987) presents finding that members of the church hold more conservative views than the official position of the church about abortion and the beginning of life.

Marriage Rates and Characteristics.   Mormons are committed to the notion of eternal marriage or celestial marriage. Such a marriage is essential for advancement in the process of eternal progression, which is a core belief of the faith. Celestial marriages can be performed only in a Mormon temple, sacred buildings designated for the performance of ordinances to assist the most faithful in their pursuit of exaltation through eternal progression (Thomas, 1983; Leon, 1979). Mormons believe one cannot become a god outside of an eternal marriage, and unmarried Mormons are encouraged to marry (Benson, 1988). Part of Mormons folk belief is that the eternal progression of unmarried persons would be capped and they would become "ministering angels" instead of gods (Anderson, 1983).

The Mormons try very hard to produce marriages that will last eternally, and Mauss (1989) notes that since 1965 there has been a tremendous increase in the number of temples built, a streamlining of the ceremony, and even changes in the holy garments worn by Mormons married in the temple. Mauss (1989:46) concludes: "These changes have made temple work more accessible geographically, logistically, and even psychologically to a vastly larger proportion of members than ever before."

It is likely that the beliefs Mormons have about marriage distinguish them from their fellow Americans more than their actual behaviors. A higher percentage of Mormons marry than either Catholics and Protestants (Heaton, 1988). About 97 percent of them eventually marry. Mormon males tend to marry younger than comparable non-Mormon males in Utah, but the difference for females is not significant (Heaton, Goodman, & Holman 1994). In other samples, however, Mormon women marry younger than those they are compared with. The majority of LDS women enter marriage before they are 21 (Heaton, 1992). Mormon remarriage rates are also higher than the national average (Heaton, 1992).

Divorce Rates and Attitudes.   Mormons are opposed to divorce, especially for those who enter into eternal marriage vows in the temple. Once, divorces for temple marriages were practically impossible to obtain, but they are more frequently granted today. However, it is far from an automatic process and members are encourage to do everything they can to work things out and avoid divorce.

Mormon divorce rates in aggregate seem to be about the same as for other Americans—22 percent for ever-married, Mormon males, 23.3 percent for others; 28.1 percent for ever-married Mormon females, and 27.8 percent for others (Heaton, Goodman, and Holman, 1994). In another study, Mormons had lower divorce rates (males, 14.3%; females, 18.8%) than Catholics (males 19.8%; females, 23.1%) and Protestants (males, 26.4%; females 30.9%) (Heaton and Goodman, 1985). Mormons who attend church often have even lower divorce rates (males, 10.2%; females, 15.2%), while those with temple marriages have even lower (males, 5.4%; females, 6.5%) divorce rates (Heaton and Goodman, 1985).

Intermarriage Rates and Assimilation.   Intermarriage is discouraged by Mormons, with low rates of intermarriage (about 5%) in Utah, Mexico, and Central America, but the rate climbs to 20 percent in other areas. In Utah, marriages are usually racially homogamous partly because of the low concentration of minority members in the population.

Assimilation is not the major reason for Mormon opposition to intermarriage, however. Because the non-Mormon spouse would not be eligible to enter the temple to enter into eternal marriage vows, Mormons would oppose such marriages. Mormons would like to convert entire families in to the church, but in some cases only one partner wishes to be baptized a member of the church. In many such circumstances, baptism occurs with the hope that the spouse will soon join also. However, this does not always happen, so some mixed marriages among Mormons are a result of assimilation into the church, not the opposite direction.

Family Roles

Power and Authority and Gender Role Performance. The expected authority pattern in Mormon life is patriarchal. This is an area of high integration between religion and family. Active Mormon males beginning at age 12 play an important role in worship services. In weekly sacrament meetings, the young men of the congregation prepare the sacrament table (Teachers 1–15), break the bread and bless the sacrament (Priests 1–19), and pass the sacrament to the congregation (Deacons 12–13). At age 19, they become elders, ready to serve on missions. Mormon men have been socialized to function in the church using their priesthood and move easily into the priesthood role of father, head of the household. They perform important religious ordinances such as blessing and naming children (christening), baptism, priesthood ordination of sons, some temple ordinances, the blessing of sick family members, and ensuring that family and individual prayers are said. In fact, almost all of the religious ordinances that a minister or priest might perform are performed by the Mormon father, provided he is worthy. Most Mormon men and women value the husband's priesthood. For many Mormon women, her potential mate's priesthood worthiness and performance is an important factor in mate selection. Women, and children will often testify in testimony meeting about the value of their husband/father's priesthood actions in the home (Shepherd and Shepherd, 1984).

Given this dual role as father and patriarch, the Mormon male might be expected to be very powerful in his marriage. In fact, Heaton (1988) claims this is one of the four distinguishing characteristics of the Mormon family—chauvinism. Certainly, it is the ideal. Christopherson (1963) concluded that "the Mormon family has always expressed democracy in its family relations to a very high and pronounced degree," Bahr and Bahr (1977) says Mormon attitudes about family power and division of labor differ from their Protestant and Catholic neighbors, but that their actual behavior is not very different. Others suggest that Mormons may be moving toward a wider acceptance of female participation in the provider role while remaining traditional in the areas of child care, housekeeping and others (Albrecht, Bahr, and Chadwick, 1979). A study comparing gender attitudes among college students (Brinkerhoff and Mackie, 1984) indicated that Mormons scored higher on a *macho* scale than Catholics, mainline Protestants, and those with no religious performance. Mormon scores were comparable to those of fundamentalist Protestants.

Actual performance may differ from attitudes. Bahr (1982) found the gap in role enactment between Mormon men and women much smaller than stated attitudes. A recent study by Thomas (1988) strongly suggests that at least in the area of shared childrearing Mormons married in the temple are likely to share the task, resulting in higher levels of marital satisfaction and adult well-being. He concludes that his findings indicate that temple marriage and home religious observance are important sources of egalitarian role performance in childrearing. Thomas (1988), in fact, believes his data help reconcile the difference in research findings that show Mormons stressing role separation in theory but acting egalitarian in practice. For him, the temple marriage commitments favor love and equality in marriage, not male dominance.

Women and the Work Place. Church officials proclaim the role of mother to be equal to, although different from, the male's priesthood role. Women are urged to make motherhood a career (Benson, 1981), and women who desire other careers are cautioned that it is sinful to place a career above their God-given duty to be a mother. As one might expect, the leadership of the church reacted very negatively to the Women's Liberation Movement, which they regarded as being against children and families and in favor of abortion, sexual freedom, and lesbianism. The movement also presents a challenge to the authority of the exclusive male priesthood in the church. The church opposed the Equal Rights Amendment. Warenski (1978) suggest that on this issue the church to some degree became a captive of the far right wing of the American political spectrum.

In a national survey, Mormon men and Mormon women are more likely than other Americans to disapprove of a women with young children working, even part-time work, and they do not approve of putting children under three in daycare environments (Heaton, Goodman, and Holman, 1994). These patterns are similar to those of other Americans, however, and it should be noted that taken together, a majority of Mormons would approve of part-time employment for the mother even if she has small children.

In the important area of woman's employment outside the home, however, it appears as though Mormon women are being affected by the same social and economic forces as their American sisters. Howard Bahr (1978) reports that the labor force participation of Utah women resembles the national condition. A recent study confirms the implication that Mormon men and Mormon women are employed at about the same rate as the national average (Heaton, Goodman, and Holman 1994).

Mormons seem no happier in marriage than other Americans. They are as likely to express conflict and disagreement in marriage as others. Sex relations and children seem to be two areas of most conflict or disagreement (Heation, Goodman, and Holman, 1994). However, several other studies indicate Mormons are as happy as other Americans in their marriages (Duke and Johnson, 1981, Bahr and Bahr, 1977; Rollins and Cannon, 1974).

Extended Family Relationships and Care of the Elderly. Surprisingly, there is little research on the elderly and extended family relationships. One study of intergenerational contact in Mormon families (Albrecht and Chappell, 1977:74) revealed that the Mormon pattern of intergenerational contact does not differ from the more general societal pattern and that this contact "provides no guarantee that there will be an absence of growing feelings of powerlessness and a lack of sense of meaning and purpose in life." A more recent study supports the general finding that Mormons are not much different from other Americans in their contact with the elderly or over the generations (Heaton, Goodman, and Holman 1994:111), stating: "We might speculate that LDS husbands and wives feel, at the church's urging, that they should assist relatives, but that support has not translated into improved relationships."

Temple work, which involves participating in sacred dramas and rituals as proxy for the dead, is doctrinally important in the Mormon church and is a regular source of activity among the elderly, who have looked forward to the day when they could work in the temple. Some families in the church have also used the importance of genealogy as a foundation for forming family organizations and holding family reunions.

The church has no special program designed to meet the needs of its elderly members; rather, it stresses the religious obligation of the family to provide for its aging members (Featherstone, 1975). If there are no family members ready or willing to care for an elderly church member, the church may provide for them, but this is not a guaranteed retirement program.

Values Transmission

Socialization and Childrearing Behaviors. Mormons are serious about children, but they focus on results rather than methods. They do what they think will produce the desired outcome and are willing to accept religious and secular advice they believe will help. them succeed (Kunz, 1963). Thomas (1983:282) claims that "Mormon parents may be described as affectionate, inclined to establish and enforce rules, and are very concerned about their children's welfare." In a study of 200 Mormon families perceived by local religious leaders as effective families, Dyer and Kunz (1994) found strong supporting evidence for Thomas's assertion. Family goals were clear: having children serve missions, 100 percent; having children married in the temple, 100 percent; having children get a good education, 99 percent; having children active in the church, 100 percent. The clear picture Dyer and Kunz (1994) present is of families committed to instilling Mormon values in their children through love, support of a few general rules of behavior, communication, public and private religious devotion, and setting a good example of a Christlike life. The primary goals have not changed in almost three decades. In 1964, Bacon found Mormons wanted their children to become good Mormons, with serving on a mission and temple marriage as primary goals. When all Mormon parents are considered, however, they are not much different in parenting behaviors than other Americans (Heaton, Goodman, and Holman 1994).

Wilkinson and Tanner (1980) and Thomas (1988) report that temple marriage of the parents is an important element in producing family affection in Mormon homes. Among Mormon youth, there appear to be significant religious factors that reduce their involvement in delinquent acts (Chadwick and Top, 1993). Specifically, youths' private religious behaviors (prayer, reading scriptures, reading church publications) and youths' feelings of integration into the local Ward were associated with decreased levels of delinquent behavior. It is significant to note that even when peer pressure and family factors were considered, religious factors made a significant independent impact on the delinquent behavior of Mormon teens.

Clearly, the family and the ward work together to produce young men willing serve on missions. Preaching the Mormon Gospel and calling others to salvation may be the core demand of Mormonism. As a result, over 45,000 Mormons missionaries are on missions at any one time, with the need to recruit about 25,000 each year to replace those who finish their two-year missions and return home (Shepherd and Shepherd, 1994). To serve on a mission, a young person (usually male, about 19 years old) must be willing to go anywhere in world he or she is assigned, proselytize with enthusiasm and devotion for two years, often learn a new language, and be financially self-supporting. This requires a considerable financial sacrifice for the missionary and his or her family, not to mention postponing educational or occupational plans at this critical juncture. It is also a time when many other American young people begin to have premarital sex, experiment with drugs, and otherwise test the limits of their parents and society.

About one-third of eligible Mormon males serve on missions (*Ensign*, 1984). Returning missionaries report their experiences emphasize important conversion experiences, sacred insights derived from the work, and the high value they place on the experience, one they would not have missed. The effort required to learn a new language, meet and converse with many indifferent or even actively hostile individuals, live 24 hours a day with an assigned companion, live within rather narrow behavioral rules, study the gospel, and keep house is enormous (Shepherd and Shepherd, 1994; Parry, 1994; Wilson, 1994). Many returned missionaries will testify for years after that their mission was the two most significant years of their life and that later success at school, in marriage, and at work were related to the socialization they received as missionaries (Mauss, 1972b).

Dating and Premarital Sex: The Law of Chastity

Although premarital chastity has always been important to Mormons, they seem willing to risk some premarital sex to ensure a more important goal—an eternal, freely chosen, love-based marriage. Given their view of heaven and the pivotal importance of a loving, eternal marriage as the basis of progression toward godhood, it is not surprising that they would create many opportunities for young people to mix socially and develop romantic love relationships. Mormons expect formal dating to be delayed until after the sixteenth birthday, but they sponsor dances, parties, and other special activities that further courtship among the unmarried. The church educational system, especially for college students, was developed at least partially to facilitate mate choices among similarly educated young Mormon adults. Thus, while Mormons value premarital chastity highly, they value the sacred fundamental doctrine of free agency, or free choice, more. Of course, they are also influenced greatly by modern American culture.

In the last three decades, the sexual revolution has presented more sexual opportunities to American youth, Mormons included. The response by the church has been to place increasing emphasis on the "law of chastity" and make their opposition more direct and explicit (Rytting and Rytting, 1982). In general, church leaders increasingly expressed opposition to abortion, pornography, homosexuality, sex education, birth control, and sex in the media (Rytting and Rytting, 1982). Thus the church has responded to the sexual revolution by favoring societal limitations on sexual information and expression as well as encouraging private morality.

On the whole, they seem to have been relatively successful in this attempt. Most studies have documented lower rates of premarital sex among Mormon youth than among other groups (Christensen, 1976, Smith, 1976, Miller and others, 1985; Chadwick 1986). Most of these studies found substantially less than 20 percent of unmarried Mormon youth had experienced intercourse. Not only that, but active Mormons were much less likely to have premarital intercourse than inactive Mormons.

CHANGES AND ADAPTATIONS

In this chapter we have suggested there are three major trends or factors that have impacted Mormonism. The first is the conflict and persecutions experienced by Mormons at the beginning of the church. These together with the trek west were a sacralizing event that increased feelings of peoplehood fighting for survival against a hostile physical and social environment. The second major factor was polygamy. The battle over polygamy increased this sense of peoplehood and cemented the perception of having a uniquely superior family system in Mormon self-awareness. It also probably resulted in a relatively strong perception of high kinship ties among Mormons. They were a chosen people and they were practicing celestial marriage as commanded by God. They also believed they were all literal sons and daughters of God; all members of the same celestial family. Actually they believe we all are children of God, but because of their isolation and outside persecution, they focused more on the fact of their eternal relationship as His children.

The third factor influencing Mormonism is its missionary zeal. From the beginning a central tenet, perhaps the central tenet, of Mormonism is the necessity to spread the news that the Gospel had been restored in these latter days and that all the world should prepare for the immediate Second Coming of Jesus Christ. The world needed to be warned and converted so that the Kingdom of God could be set in place to facilitate His return. The practice of polygamy was part of this same urgency, as was the fanatical cooperative city building that was related to friction with their neighbors. After 150 years, the same issues, missionary work, and level of tension between Mormonism and the larger society are still intimately related to its continued success.

Church membership, which was about 1,100,000 in 1950 (Allen, 1994), grew to an estimated 9,400,000 in 1996, with the majority living outside the United States (Church News, March 2, 1996). This phenomenal growth overwhelms all other issues when we consider the future of Mormonism. Paradoxically, the growth of this American religion is isomorphic to the changing demographic of America itself. The church, like America, is changing from a mostly white group relatively isolated from the world to a racially and ethnically diverse organization. The parallel is even more remarkable in that the major growth of the church is occurring in Latin America, especially Mexico. Like the United States, the church is growing most rapidly from an infusion from Mexico and other South American countries!

There have been changes that facilitated this growth. First, and perhaps most important, was the revelation that accepted men of African descent into the priesthood. In June 1978, President Kimball announced a divine revelation that blacks were to be given the priesthood. It was a electrifying event, remembered in detail by Mormons—where they were, who told them, who they called next, and how they felt—much as other Americans remember Pearl Harbor or the assassination of John Kennedy, and not negatively, but profoundly. There seemed to be two general reactions: disbelief, as in "I didn't think this would happen in my lifetime," and relief or joy, as in, "Thank God! It's about time." There was wide acceptance, and the church seems to have adapted without any problems. Nothing in the record indicates a loss of membership because of this change.

It would appear that like other revelations, particularly the Manifesto that ended polygamy, this revelation came only after the present practice seemed to limit the potential growth of the church. However, in the case of the priesthood revelation, the missionary program seemed to reach out (successfully) to convert others to Mormonism and in the process changed a basic feature of the movement.

The missionary program aggressively sought new members, who in turn presented dilemmas to the church. To some degree, the problem was resolved by the church's changing a significant practice. In changing the world, the world is changing the Mormons, and the church faces significant problems in attempting to blend Mormonism to the needs of a growing, universal church (Allen, 1992; Shipps, 1994; Stark, 1994; Mauss, 1994; Young, 1994; Shepherd and Shepherd, 1994; Knowlton, 1992). For decades, the major issue will be how much the church will be assimilated into the larger American society.

Now that the church has become more universal, it cannot focus solely on the assimilation/cultural tension dance within the United States. Brazil, Mexico, Japan, England, Nigeria, New Zealand, Fiji, Russia, Hungary, and perhaps eventually China will all present special demands on the assimilation/tension equation. It is likely that events in these countries will influence the church and its structure as much or more than events in Utah. Tax laws or changing approaches to welfare, educational reforms or ecological problems in the United States are likely to pale compared to the requirement of an ever expanding church. Church leaders see some of the implications of this potential. One leader said (Copeland, 1988:8):

> Now we are moving into those countries, but we can't move there with all the baggage we produce here! We can't move with a 1947 Utah Church! Could it be that we are not prepared to take the gospel because we are not prepared to take (and they are not prepared to receive) all of the things we have wrapped up with it as extra baggage.

Some Mormon leaders see the church's position as an analog to Christianity as it moved from the confines of Jewish traditions and practices to becoming a world religion in its own right. An important question at that moment was: Did one need to become Jewish before one could become a Christian? In the Mormon case, the question is less theological: Must one become an American/Utahan before becoming a Mormon? Reynolds (1978:18), a Mexican convert, puts it succinctly: "How much of what has through the years evolved as 'LDS doctrine' is merely the expression of the collective neurosis of that culture to which the gospel has been restored?" No longer will Mormons move physically to a Utah Zion and become assimilated into American culture. Mormons instead will necessarily become citizens of the world, influenced and influencing "every nation, kindred and tongue."

REFERENCES

Albrecht, S. L., and B. Chappell. 1977. "Intergenerational Contact and Alienation in Elderly Mormon Families," in P. R. Kunz (Ed.), *The Mormon Family*, pp. 62–77. Provo, UT: Brigham Young University Press.

Albrecht, S. L., H. M. Bahr, and B. A. Chadwick. 1979. "Changing Family and Sex Roles: An Analysis of Age Difference." *Journal of Marriage and the Family, 41:* 41–50.

Assessment, S. L., and T. Heaton. 1984. "Secularization, Higher Education and Religiosity." *Review of Religious Research, 26* (1): 43–58.

Allen, J. B. 1992. "On Becoming a Universal Church: Some Historical Perspectives." *Dialogue: A Journal of Mormon Thought, 25* (1): 13–36.

Allen, J. B., and G. M. Leonard. 1976. *The Story of the Latter-Day Saints.* Salt Lake City, UT: Deseret.

Anderson, D. L., and R. J. Emigh. 1989. "Polygynous Fertility: Sexual Competition versus Progeny." *American Journal of Sociology, 94* (4): 832–855.

Anderson, L. 1983. "Ministering Angles: Single Women in Mormon Society." *Dialogue: A Journal of Mormon Thought, 16* (3): 59–72.

Anderson, Nels. 1942. *Desert Saints: The Mormon Frontier in Utah.* Chicago: University of Chicago Press.

Arrington, L. 1958. *The Great Basin Kingdom: An Economic History of the Latter-Day Saints 1830–1900.* Cambridge, MA: Harvard University Press.

Bacon, M. R. 1964. "Comparative Study of Expressive and Instrumental Concerns of Homemakers in Wastch County." Unpublished paper, Brigham Young University.

Bahr, H. M. 1979. "Mormon Families in Comparative Perspective: Denominational Contrasts in Divorce, Marital Satisfaction and Other Characteristics." Provo, UT: Brigham Young University.

———. 1981. "Religious Intermarriage and Divorce in Utah and the Mountain States," *Journal for the Scientific Study of Religion, 20* (3): 251–261.

———. 198. "Religious Contrasts in Family Roles." *Journal for the Scientific Study of Religion, 21:* 201–217.

Bahr, H. M., and B. A. Chadwick. 1987. "Religion and Family in Middle America and Mormondom: Secularization, Role Stereotypes and Change." Paper quoted in T. B. Heaton, "Four Characteristics of the Mormon Family: Contemporary Research on Chastity, Conjugality, Children and Chauvinism." *Dialogue: A Journal of Mormon Thought, 20* (2): 101–114.

Bahr, S. J., and H. M. Bahr. 1977. "Religion and Family Roles: A Comparison of Catholic, Mormon, and Protestant Families," in P. Kunz (Ed.), *The Mormon Family,* pp. 45–61. Provo, UT: Family Research Center, Brigham Young University.

Bean, L. I., G. P. Mineau, and D. L. Anderson. 1983. "Residence and Religious Effects on Declining Family Size: A Historical Analysis of Utah Population." *Review of Religious Research, 35:* 91–101.

———. 1990. *Fertility Changes on the American Frontier: Adaption and Innovation.* Berkeley, CA: University of California Press.

Benson, E. T. 1988. "To the Single Adult Brethren of the Church." *Ensign* (November): 96–97.

Bowers, D. W., and D. W. Hastings. 1970. "Childspacing and Wife's Employment Status Among 1940–41 University of Utah Graduates." *Social Science Journal, 7:* 125–136.

Brinkerhoff, M. 1978. "Religion and Goal Orientations. Does Denomination Make a Difference?" *Sociological Analysis, 39*(3): 203–218.

Brinkerhoff, M., and M. Mackie. 1984. "Religious Denominations' Impact on Gender Attitudes: Some Methodological Implications." *Review of Religious Research, 25*(3): 365–78.

Brodie, F. 1971. *No Man Knows My History: The Life of Joseph Smith, the Mormon Prophet.* New York: Knopf.

Burgess-Olsen, V. 1975. "Family Structure and Dynamics in Early Utah Mormon Families, 1847–85." Ph. D. dissertation, Northwestern University.

Bush, L. E. 1976. "Birth Control Among Mormons: Introduction to an Insistent Question." *Dialogue: A Journal of Mormon Thought, 10:* 12–44.

Campbell, B. L., and E. E. Campbell. 1978. "Divorce Among Mormon Polygamists: Extent and Explanations." *Utah Historical Quarterly, 46:* 4–23.

Cannon, K. L. 1978. "Beyond the Manifesto: Polygamous Cohabitation Among L.D.S. General Authorities after 1890." *Utah Historical Quarterly, 46*(1): 24–36.

Cannon, K. L., and S. Steed. 1972. "Relationship between Occupational Level, Religious Commitment, Age of Bride at Marriage and Divorce Rate for L.D.S. Marriages," in *Developing a Marriage Relationship,* pp. 285–292. Provo, UT: Brigham Young University Press.

Chadwick, B. A., and B. T. Top. 1993. "Religiosity and Delinquency Among LDS Adolescents." *Journal for the Scientific Study of Religion, 32*(1): 51–67.

Christensen, H. T. 1972. "Stress Points in Mormon Family Culture." *Dialogue: A Journal of Mormon Thought, 7* (Winter): 20–34.

———. 1977. "Some Next Steps in Mormon Family Research," in P. R. Kunz (Ed.) *The Mormon Family,* pp. 1–12. Provo, UT: Family Research Center, Brigham Young University.

———. 1994. "The Persistence of Chastity: Built-in Resistance in Mormon Culture to Secular Trends," in B. Corcoran (Ed.), *Multiply and Replenish,* pp. 67–84. Salt Lake City: Signature Books.

Christensen, H. T., and C. F. Gregg. 1970. "Changing Sex Norms in America and Scandinavia." *Journal of Marriage and the Family, 6* (November): 602

Christopherson, V. A. 1956. "An Investigation of Patriarchal Authority in the Mormon Family." *Marriage and Family Living, 18* (November): 328–333.

———. 1963. "Is the Mormon Family Becoming More Democratic?" In B. Porter (Ed.), *The Latter-Day Saint Family*, pp.317–338. Salt Lake City, UT: Deseret.

Copeland, L. 1988. "From Calcutta to Kaysville: Is Righteousness Color-Coded?" *Dialogue: A Journal of Mormon Thought, 21* (Fall): 89–99.

Cornwall, M. 1987. "The Social Bases of Religion: A Study of Factors Influencing Religious Belief and Commitment." *Review of Religious Research, 29* (1): 22–40.

———. 1991. "Mormonism and the Challenge of the Mainline." *Dialogue: A Journal of Mormon Thought, 24* (4): 68–73.

———. 1994. "Institutional Role of Mormon Women," in M. Cornwall, T. B. Heaton, and L. A. Young (Eds.), *Contemporary Mormonism: Social Science Perspectives.* Chicago: University of Illinois Press.

Cornwall, M., C. Courtright, and L. Van Beck. 1993. "How Common Was the Principle? Women As Plural Wives in 1860." *Dialogue: A Journal of Mormon Thought, 26* (2): 139–153.

Crapo, R. H. 1987. "Grass-Roots Deviance from Official Doctrine: A Study of Latter-Day Saint (Mormon) Folk-Beliefs." *Journal for the Scientific Study of Religion, 26* (4): 465–485.

De Phillis, M. S. 1991. "Mormonism Becomes a Mainline Religion: The Challenges." *Dialogue: A Journal of Mormon Thought, 24* (4): 59–68.

Driggs, K. 1991. "Twentieth-Century Polygamy and Fundamentalist Mormons in Southern Utah." *Dialogue: A Journal of Mormon Thought, 24* (4): 44–58.

Duke, J. T., and B. L. Johnson. 1981. "Causes and Correlates of Marital Adjustments." Paper presented at the Western Social Science Association. San Diego, California.

Durkheim, Emile. 1951. *Suicide.* New York: Free Press.

Dyer, W. G., and P. R. Kunz. 1994. *10 Critical Keys for Highly Effective Mormon Families.* Springville, UT: Cedar Fort.

Ellsworth, S. G. 1951. "History of Mormons Missions in the United States and Canada 1830–1860," Unpublished paper, University of California at Berkeley.

Embry, J., and M. Bradley. 1985. "Mothers and Daughters in Polygamy." *Dialogue: A Journal of Mormon Thought, 18* (3): 99–107.

Esshom, F. 1913. *Pioneers and Prominent Men of Utah.* Salt Lake City: Pioneers Book Publishing Company.

Featherstone, V. J. 1975. "The Savior's Program for Care of the Aged." *Conference Reports,* October.

Foster, L. 1981. *Religion and Sexuality: Three American Communal Experiments of the Nineteenth Century.* New York/Oxford: Oxford University Press.

Goodman, K., and T. Heaton. 1986. "Divorce," in T. Martin, T. Hiton, and S. Bahr (Eds.), *Utah in Demographic Perspective: Regional and National Contrasts.* Provo, UT: Signature Books.

Grover, M. L. 1990. "The Mormon Priesthood Revelation and the Sao Paulo, Brazil Temple." *Dialogue: A Journal of Mormon Thought, 23* (1): 39–53.

Hafen, L. R., and A. W. Hafen. 1960. *Handcarts to Zion.* Glendale, CA: Arthur C. Clark.

Hastings, D., C. H. Reynolds, and R. Canning. 1972. "Mormonism and Birth Planning: The Descrepancy Between Church Authorities' Teachings and Lay Attitudes." *Population Studies, 26:* 19–28.

Heaton, T. B. 1987. "Four Characteristics of the Mormon Family: Contemporary Research on Chastity, Conjugality, Children and Chauvinism." *Dialogue: A Journal of Mormon Thought, 27* (2): 169–183.

———. 1988. "Four C's of the Modern Mormon Family: Chastity, Conjugality, Children, and Chauvinism," in D. Thomas (Ed.), *The Religion and Family Connection,* pp. 106–122. Provo, UT: Religious Studies Center, Brigham Young University.

———. 1992. "Demographics of the Contemporary Mormon Family." *Dialogue: A Journal of Mormon Thought, 25* (3): 19–34.

————. 1994. "Familial, Socioeconomic, and Religious Behavior: A Comparison of LDS and Non-LDS Women." *Dialogue: A Journal of Mormon Thought, 27* (2): 169–183.

Heaton, T. B., and S. Calkins. 1983. "Family Size and Contraceptive Use Among Mormons, 1965–75." *Review of Religious Research, 25* (2): 102–113.

Heaton T. B., and K. L. Goodman. 1985. "Religion and Family Formation." *Review of Religious Research, 26* (4): 343–359.

Heaton, T. B., K. L. Goodman, and T. B. Holman. 1994. "In Search of a Peculiar People: Are Mormon Families Really Different?" in M. Cornwall, T. B. Heaton, and L. A. Young (Eds.), *Contemporary Mormonism: Social Science Perspectives*, pp. 87–117. Chicago: University of Illinois Press.

Hill, M. S. 1978. "The Rise of the Mormon Kingdom of God," in R. Poll (Ed.), *Utah History.* Provo, UT: Brigham Young University Press.

Ivins, S. 1956. "Notes on Mormon Polygamy." *Western Humanities Review, 10:* 224–239.

Johnson, B. L., J. T. Duke, S. Eberely, and D. H. Sartain. 1988. "Wives' Employment Status and Marital Happiness of Religious Couples." *Review of Religious Research, 29* (March): 259–270.

Kane, E. W. 1974. *Twelve Mormon Homes.* Salt Lake City, UT: Tanner Trust Fund.

Kimball, H. C. 1958. "Temples and Endowments." *Journal of Discourses, 5:* 22.

Kimball, S. W. 1976. "Marriage the Proper Way." *The New Era* (February): 4–7.

Knowlton, D. 1992. "Thoughts on Mormonism in Latin America." *Dialogue: A Journal of Mormon Thought, 25* (2): 42–53.

Kunz, P. R. 1963. "Religious Influences on Parental Discipline and Achievement Demands." *Marriage and Family Living, 24* (May): 224–225.

————. 1980. "One Wife or Several: A Comparative Study of Late 19th Century Marriage in Utah," in T. Alexander, and J. Embry (Eds.), *The Mormon People: Their Character and Traditions.* Provo, UT: Brigham Young University Press.

Leon, M. 1979. *The Roots of Modern Mormonism.* Cambridge, MA: Harvard University Press.

Louge, L. M. 1988. *A Sermon in the Desert: Belief and Behavior in Early St. George, Utah.* Urbana, IL: University of Illinois Press.

Lythgo, D. 1977. "Marketing the Mormon Image: An Interview with Wendell Ashton, Jr." *Dialogue: A Journal of Mormon Thought, 10* (3): 15–24.

Martin, T. 1986. "Abortion," in T. Martin, T. Heaton, and S. Bahr (Eds.), *Utah in Demographic Perspective: Regional and National Contrasts.* Provo, UT: Signature Books.

Mauss, A. L. 1969. "Dimensions of Religious Defection." *Review of Religious Research, 10:* 128–135.

————. 1972a. "Moderation in All Things: Political and Social Outlook of Modern Urban Mormons." *Dialogue: A Journal of Mormon Thought, 7:* 57–64.

————. 1972b. "Saints Cities, and Secularism: Religious Attitudes and Behaviors of Modern Urban Mormons." *Dialogue: A Journal of Mormon Thought, 7:* 8–27.

————. 1976. "Shall the Youth of Zion Falter? Mormon Youth and Sex: A Two City Comparison." *Dialogue: A Journal of Mormon Thought, 10:* 82–93.

————. 1983. "The Angel and the Beehive: Our Quest for Peculiarity and Struggle with Secularization." *B.Y.U. Today, 37* (4): 12–15.

————. 1989. "Assimilation and Ambivalence: The Mormon Reaction to Americanization." *Dialogue: A Journal of Mormon Thought, 22* (1): 30–67.

————. 1994a. "Refuge, Retrenchment: The Mormon Quest for Identity," in M. Cornwall, T. B. Heaton, and L. A. Young (Eds.), *Contemporary Mormonism: Social Science Perspectives*, pp. 24–42. Chicago: University of Illinois Press.

————. 1994b. "The Mormon Struggle with Assimilation and Identity: Trends and Developments Since Mid-Century. " *Dialogue: A Journal of Mormon Thought, 27* (1): 131–149.

May, D. L. 1983. "A Demographic Portrait of the Mormons, 1830–1980," in T. G. Alexander and J. L. Embry (Eds.), *After 150 Years: The Latter-Day Saints in Sesquicentennial Perspective*, pp. 39–69. Midvale, UT: Signature Books.

McConkie, F. R. 1978. "All Are Alike Unto God." Address to the Church Educators Symposium, Brigham Young University, 18 August.

Mulder, W. 1957. *Homeward to Zion.* Minneapolis: University of Minnesota Press.

Newell, L. K, and V. T. Avery. 1984. *Mormon Enigma: Emma Hale Smith.* Garden City, NY: Doubleday.

O'Dea, T. 1957. *The Mormons.* Chicago: University of Chicago Press.

———. 1972. "Sources of Strain in Mormon History Reconsidered," in M. S. Hill and J. B. Allen (Eds.), *Mormonism and American Culture,* pp. 147–167. New York: Harper & Row.

Parry, K. 1994. "The Mormon Missionary Companionship," in M. Cornwall, T. B. Heaton, and L. A. Young (Eds.), *Contemporary Mormonism: Social Science Perspectives,* pp. 182–206. Chicago: University of Illinois Press.

Peterson, E. D. 1971. "Attitudes Concerning Birth Control and Abortion as Related to L.D.S. Religiosity of Brigham Young University Students." Unpublished paper, Brigham Young University.

Peterson, E. D. 1977. "Parent-Adolescent Relationships in the Mormon Family," in P. R. Kunz (Ed.), *The Mormon Family,* pp. 108–115. Provo, UT: Brigham Young University.

Quinn, D. M. 1973. "Organizational Development and Social Origins of the Mormon Hierarchy, 1832–1932. A Prosopographical Study." Unpublished paper, University of Utah.

Quinn, M. 1985. "L.D.S. Church Authority and New Plural Marriages, 1890–1904." *Dialogue: A Journal of Mormon Thought, 18* (1): 9–105.

Reynolds, N. B. "Cultural Diversity in the Universal Church," in F. L. Tullis (Ed.), *Mormonism: A Faith for All Cultures,* pp. 7–22. Provo, UT: Brigham Young University Press.

Rollins, B. C., and K. L. Cannon. "Marital Satisfaction over the Family Life Cycle." *Journal of Marriage and the Family, 36* (May): 271–282.

Roof, W. C., and W. McKinney. 1987. *American Mainline Religion: Its Changing Shape and Future.* New Brunswick, NJ: Rutgers University Press.

Rytting, M., and A. Rytting. 1982. "Exhortations for Chastity: A Content Analysis of Church Literature." *Sunstone, 7* (2): 15–21.

Savage, J. H. 1993. "Hannah Grover Hugsted and Post-Manifesto Plural Marriage." *Dialogue: Journal of Mormon Thought, 26* (3): 101–117.

Seggar, J. F., and H. B. Reed. 1970. "Post-Joining Non-Participation: An Exploratory Study of Convert Inactivity." *Review of Religious Research, 11:* 204–209.

Shepherd, G., and G. Shepherd. 1984a. "Mormon Commitment Rhetoric." *Journal for the Scientific Study of Religion, 23* (2): 129–139.

Shepherd, G., and G. Shepherd. 1984b. "Mormonism in Secular Society: Changing Patterns in Official Ecclesiastical Rhetoric." *Review of Religious Research, 26* (1): 28–42.

Shepherd, G., and G. Shepherd. 1994. "Sustaining a Lay Religion in Modern Society: The Mormon Missionary Experience," in M. Cornwall, T.B. Heaton, and L. A. Young (Eds.), *Contemporary Mormonism: Social Science Perspectives,* pp. 161–181. Chicago: University of Illinois Press.

Shipps, J. 1978. "The Mormons: Looking Forward and Outward." *The Christian Century, 16* (August): 761–766.

———. 1985. *Mormonism: The Story of a New Religious Tradition.* Chicago: University of Illinois Press.

———. 1994. "Making Saints: In The Early Days and the Latter Days," in M. Cornwall, T. B. Heaton, and L. A. Young (Eds.), *Contemporary Mormonism: Social Science Perspectives,* pp. 64–83. Chicago: University of Illinois Press.

Skolnick, M., L. Bean, P. May, V. Abon, K. DeNehs, and P. Cartwright. 1978. "Nuptiality and Fertility of Once-Married Couples." *Population Studies, 32* (1): 5–19.

Smith, G. D. 1993. "Nauvoo Roots of Mormon Polygamy, 1841–46: A Preliminary Demographic Report." *Dialogue: A Journal of Mormon Thought, 27* (1): 1–72.

Smith, J. E., and P. R. Kunz. 1976. "Polygyny and Fertility in Nineteenth Century America." *Population Studies, 30:* 30.

Smith, T. L. 1987. "Religion and Ethnicity in America." *American Historical Review, 83* (5): 1155–1185.

Smith, W. 1959. "The Urban Threat to Mormon Norms." *Rural Sociology, 24:* 355–361.

———. 1976. "Mormons' Sex Standards on College Campuses, or Deal Us Out of the Sexual Revolution." *Dialogue: A Journal of Mormon Thought, 10* (2): 76–81.

Stark, R. 1984. "The Rise of a New World Faith." *Review of Religious Research, 26* (1): 19–27.

———. 1994. "Modernization and Mormon Growth: The Secularization Thesis Revisited," in M. Cornwall, T. B. Heaton, and L. A. Young (Eds.), *Contemporary Mormonism: Social Science Perspectives,* pp. 13–23. Chicago: University of Illinois Press.

Stark R., and W. Bainbridge. 1980. "Networks of Faith: Interpersonal Bonds and Recruitment to Cults and Sects." *American Journal of Sociology, 85* (6): 1376–1395.

Stathis, S., and D. Lythgoe. 1977. "Mormonism in the Nineteen Seventies: The Popular Perception." *Dialogue: A Journal of Mormon Thought, 10* (3): 95–113.

Stenhouse, Fanny. 1872. *Exposé of Polygamy in Utah: A Lady's Life Among the Mormons.* New York: American News Company.

Thomas, D. 1983. "Family in the Mormon Experience," in William D'Antonio and J. Aldous (Eds.) *Families and Religion: Conflict and Change in Modern Society.* Beverly Hills, CA: Sage Publications.

———. 1988. "Future Prospects for Religion and Family Studies: The Mormon Case," in D. Thomas (Ed.), *The Religion and Family Connection: Social Science Perspectives,* p. 357. Provo, UT: Religious Studies Center, Brigham Young University.

Thorton, A. 1979. "Religion and Fertility: The Case of Mormonism." *Journal of Marriage and the Family, 40:* 131–142.

Tullis, L. 1983. "The Church Moves Outside the United States: Some Observations from South America," in T. Alexander, and J. Embry (Eds.), *After 150 Years: The Latter-Day Saints in Sesquicentennial Perspective.* Midevale, UT: Signature Books.

Van Wagoner, R. 1985. "Mormon Polyandry in Nauvoo." *Dialogue: A Journal of Mormon Thought, 18* (3): 67–83.

Warenski, M. 1978. *Patriarch and Politics: The Plight of the Mormon Woman.* New York: McGraw-Hill.

Weber, M. 1968. *Max Weber on Charisma and Institution Building.* Chicago: University of Chicago Press.

Widsoe, J. 1952. "Does Temple Marriage Reduce Divorce?" *Improvement Era, 55* (January) 14: 15.

Wilkinson, M., and W. Tanner. 1980. "The Influence of Family Size on Interaction, and Religiosity on Family Affection in a Mormon Sample." *Journal of Marriage and the Family* (May): 297–304.

Wilson, W. A. 1994. "Powers of Heaven and Hell: Mormon Missionary Narratives as Instruments of Socialization and Social Control," in M. Cornwall, T. B. Heaton, and L. A. Young (Eds.), *Contemporary Mormonism: Social Science Perspectives,* pp. 207–217. Urbana, IL: University of Illinois Press.

Wise, J., and S. J. Condie. 1975. "Intergenerational Fertility Throughout Four Generations." *Social Biology, 22:* 144–150.

Woodruff, W. 1857. *Journal History of the Church,* April.

———. 1884. "Discourse." *Millennial Star, 56* (April 1884): 229. Delivered October 8, 1883.

Young, B. 1858. *Journal History,* December 15.

———. 1861. *Conference Reports,* October 8. [Reported by George D. Watt. Also found in the Journal of James Beck.]

———. 1925. *Discourses of Brigham Young, Arranged by J. A. Widsoe.* Salt Lake City, UT: Deseret.

Young, K. 1954. *Isn't One Wife Enough?* New York: Henry Holt.

Young, L. A. 1994. "Confronting Turbulent Environments: Issues in the Organizational Growth and Globalization of Mormonism," in M. Cornwall, T. B. Heaton, and L. A. Young (Eds.), *Contemporary Mormonism: Social Science Perspectives,* pp. 43–63. Chicago: University of Illinois Press.

Index